D0803885

DATE DUE

12/12/06		
DEC 1 4 P.M.		
DISCARD		

HIGHSMITH #45115

SOCIAL INSTITUTIONS AND SOCIAL CHANGE

An Aldine de Gruyter Series of Texts and Monographs

EDITED BY

Michael Useem • James D. Wright

OF HUMAN BONDING

Parent-Child Relations Across the Life Course

Alice S. Rossi and Peter H. Rossi

Aldine de Gruyter
New York

ABOUT THE AUTHORS

Alice S. Rossi holds a Ph.D. from Columbia University and was the recipient of six honorary degrees. She is Harriet Martineau Professor of Sociology at the University of Massachusetts (Amherst). She has been President of both the American Sociological Association and the Eastern Sociological Society; was the 1989 recipient of the Commonwealth Award for Distinguished Scholarship in Sociology; and was elected a Fellow of the American Academy of Arts and Sciences.

Peter H. Rossi is currently the Stuart A. Rice Professor of Sociology and Acting Director, Social and Demographic Research Institute, at the University of Massachusetts (Amherst). He was Director of the National Opinion Research Center at the University of Chicago (1960–1967). He is past-president of the American Sociological Association and was the 1985 recipient of the Commonwealth Award for contributions to sociology. He has served as editor of the *American Journal of Sociology* and *Social Science Research*. He has been elected a Fellow of the American Academy of Arts and Sciences and of the American Association for the Advancement of Science.

Copyright © 1990 Walter de Gruyter, Inc. New York

ALDINE DE GRUYTER
A Division of Walter de Gruyter, Inc.
200 Saw Mill River Road
Hawthorne, New York 10532

Library of Congress Cataloging-in-Publication Data
Rossi, Alice S., 1922–
    Of human bonding : parent-child relations across the life course/
Alice S. Rossi and Peter H. Rossi.
      p.cm.—(Social institutions and social change)
    Includes bibliographical references.
    ISBN 0-202-30360-8.—ISBN 0-202-30361-6 (pbk.)
    1. Parent and child. 2. Intergenerational relations. 3. Kinship.
4. Life cycle, Human. I. Rossi, Peter Henry, 1921–   II. Title.
III. Series.
HQ755.85.R67 1990
306.874—dc20   89-71418
                                          CIP

Manufactured in the United States of America

10 9 8 7 6 5 4 3 2 1

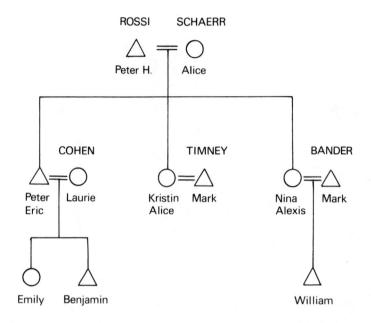

Contents

Preface

This book has had a long gestation period. In some ways its roots go back some 60 years, to childhoods spent in ethnic communities in New York City. In Peter's case, this was a mixed Italian–Irish–Black community in Queens; in Alice's case, a mixed German–Irish community in Brooklyn. Our childhood was spent in households that included several extended family members: for Peter, in addition to two older brothers and his parents, a maternal aunt, her husband, and two daughters shared a small six-room house; for Alice, in addition to her parents and a younger brother, a maternal grandfather, an unmarried uncle, and three aunts shared a tall, narrow, four-story brick townhouse. These households provided us with other adults besides our parents to relate to, and an opportunity to observe numerous kin relationships across gender and generation that did not include ourselves.

We have drawn deeply on our early family experiences in thinking about relations between men and women, old and young family members, over the years. Until 5 years ago, however, our discussions were more personal than professional: reworking and reassessing the past as we traversed our way across the life course. Our professional interests had taken very dissimilar directions for most of the almost-40 years we have lived together: Urban renewal, political power, natural disasters, crime seriousness, and evaluation research had absorbed Peter's interests; ethnicity, family and kinship, sex and gender, social movements, biosocial science, and feminist history had absorbed Alice's interests. Beneath such substantive concerns was a further difference between us: Although we both took our graduate training at Columbia University, Paul Lazarsfeld was Peter's primary mentor, and Robert Merton was Alice's primary mentor. For many years, our mentors' mark was clearly discernible in our work, for Peter relied primarily on large-scale quantitative surveys, and Alice relied far more on scholarly research, as a marginal sideliner attempting to make connections between disparate social and historical phenomena.

We each underwent an important midlife transition in the methodology we relied on in our work, upgrading statistical skills and broadening our grasp of design and measurement. In an interesting and unusual experience, Alice learned new statistical procedures through a summer of work on mood cycles with her son, then an undergraduate mathematics and history major at Oberlin College. Under the tutelage of this son, Peter Eric Rossi, she transformed a study based on daily mood ratings over 40 days, classified by both day of week (social time) and day of menstrual month (body time), from a simple analysis of daily means to a complex multivariate regression analysis that used the Durbin–Watson statistic to estimate the coefficient of autocorrelations and fitted a polynomial curve to the daily mood ratings (A. S. Rossi & P. E. Rossi, 1977).

During those same years of the 1970s, Peter developed a new technique for analyzing and measuring complex judgments, the factorial survey method, which combines dimensions relevant to a topic under study in computer-generated random combinations, each dimension independent of every other that enters a vignette describing a life situation that calls for a judgment or decision of some kind (P. H. Rossi & Nock, 1982). Little did we know that this development would be the source of a collaboration between us a decade later.

We suspect another process has also worked subtle changes in our intellectual styles: a gradual blurring of the differences between us, through years of daily conversation and reading of each other's work. We have had the rare opportunity, as husband and wife working in the same discipline, to blend the perspectives of our original mentors, Lazarsfeld and Merton. This is reflected in our recent work, as Peter infused an overview of very recent research on contemporary homelessness with an historical analysis of homelessness in America in years past (P. H. Rossi, 1989), and Alice moved from social-historical analysis (A. S. Rossi, 1970, 1973) to quantitative survey analysis (A. S. Rossi, 1982).

In the early 1980s, Alice began to think about a study of the parent–child relationship of a new sort. It seemed to her that we knew a great deal about this core family relationship while children were growing up, and then not again until the parents were very old; as Gunhild Hagestad has put it, the alpha (developmental psychology) and omega (social gerontology) of the parent–child relationship had occupied almost exclusive attention in the social sciences. But what happened during the intervening decades from the time the child left home (or completed schooling while remaining in the parental household) at say 22 years of age, and late middle age when the parent was likely to be an elderly widowed mother? Very little was known about these critical decades of the life course. The result of such musings was the development of a research proposal that was funded by the National Institute on Aging in

1984, the primary funding source for the study reported in this volume (RO1 AGO4263).

An important question in the design of the study was how to "place" the parent–child relationship in a larger context of other kin relationships, or even nonkin relationships. Just *how* central or different is obligation, sentiment, and interaction between parents and adult children, compared to the relationship to grandparents, siblings, aunts and uncles, friends, neighbors, or even ex-spouses? Many fruitless hours were spent trying to develop specific questions for each of a great variety of kin and nonkin under various circumstances of crisis or celebration, but as the items proliferated, the operationalization of this contextual placement of the parent–child relationship in the larger kinship framework threatened to occupy more than half of an instrument that had to cover many dimensions of the relationship of respondents to each of their parents, if living, and to each of their adult children.

This impasse was resolved during a memorable cocktail hour conversation when it dawned on us that the factorial survey method could be used to measure normative obligations toward a great number of kin and nonkin under a variety of circumstances, and even to specify the gender and marital status of each vignette person. Hence, we decided to design a self-administered vignette booklet that respondents could fill out at the end of the personal interviews, while interviewers checked over the questionnaire for errors or omissions. The vignette data could therefore contribute to the macrostructural framework of the study, while also providing an individual measure of overall level of kin obligation felt by respondents.

So it came to pass that the proposal called for personal interviews with a random probability sample of adults in the greater Boston area, supplemented by self-administered vignette booklets, and spinoff samples of telephone interviews with a parent or an adult child of the Boston respondents. After 35 years of largely independent, parallel careers, we joined forces with a loose differentiation of responsibility: Peter for the design and analysis of the vignette data and Alice for the design and analysis of the questionnaire data. We say "loose" differentiation advisedly, because all aspects of design, analysis, and writing have been reviewed, criticized, and revised by both of us, although Chapters 4 and 5 heavily represent Peter's work, and the remaining chapters Alice's.

When funding was assured in the spring of 1984, we entered an exciting period of intense collaboration in the design, pretesting, and revision of the major instruments. Those were exhausting, heady days and nights, often with memoranda moving between our two studies several times in the course of a single day. We began to realize that archiving the study called not just for "dates" on planning memoranda but "hours" as well! At one point, exhilarated by the infinitely improved items to measure some construct that came out of this interaction, we regretted that we had postponed such collaboration to so late a stage in our lives. This was quickly followed by the realization that perhaps such collaboration was possible, with so pure a task-orientation and so small an element of ego-defensiveness, only *because* it was taking place in the calmer waters of a marriage that had survived more than 35 years!

Of course, we were not a solitary pair of researchers, and we are indebted to a great number of people who contributed to the study. We are deeply grateful to the National Institute on Aging, for generous funding of the study in its first 3 years of data collection and preliminary analysis, from 1984 through 1986, and for permission to expend the funds remaining, during 1987. We feel very special gratitude to our Program Officer, Kathleen Bond, and to the Director of the Behavioral and Social Research division of NIA, Matilda W. Riley, for their persistent and enthusiastic support of our work. Alice owes yet another debt of gratitude to the Rockefeller Foundation, which provided a research grant to her during a sabbatical year's leave devoted to data analysis and manuscript preparation in 1987–1988.

Alice in particular wishes to express her long-standing gratitude to two women social scientists who played very important roles in her professional and personal life. Bernice Neugarten was a colleague at the University of Chicago in the early 1960s and a friend for all the years since. Bernice's work on the psychology of aging and studies of middle age and old age provided important insights into adult development, and her friendship was a major source of personal support at several crisis points in my life. Matilda Riley has also been an inspirational mentor and valued friend. Matilda's work on the sociology of age and theories concerning age stratification provided a sociological balance to Bernice's psychological perspective; between them they have had profound influence on the development of my own perspective on the life course. Matilda Riley and her husband Jack Riley have also been personal models of a creative husband–wife collaboration over the years of our association; Matilda and Jack are a wonderful example of high productivity and personal congeniality in a dual career marriage that has lasted more than 50 years. We hope our next decade of life and work together will be as happy and productive as theirs has been.

A keenly felt intellectual debt is due to Vern Bengtson, whose longitudinal study of three-generation families provided a fruitful source for the conceptualization of core dimensions of the parent–child relationship, and who provided a critical input to the design of our study in its earliest phase. We acknowledge a similar debt to Glen Elder, whose own work on the life course and intergenerational relations provides a model to all who seek to bridge the gaps between history, sociology, and psychology. Glen Elder, together with Peter Uhlenberg, served as incisive and supportive reviewers of the manuscript prior to publication. We are indebted to them both for their helpful suggestions, and have tried hard to meet the challenge they posed to us by revising, rather extensively, four chapters in the book. We hope they will be pleased by the revised manuscript, though whatever shortcomings remain are entirely our responsibility.

We are also indebted to the Center for Survey Research on the Boston campus of the University of Massachusetts, which carried responsibility for the field phase of data collection, and we wish to give our very special thanks to several members of their staff: Floyd J. Fowler, who developed the sampling plan for the study, to Tom Mangione, for helpful feedback on the pretest instruments, and to Dorothy Cerankowski, who trained and supervised the field staff of interviewers. The Center did a superb job under difficult circumstances: With a rapidly dropping unemployment rate in the Commonwealth, 1984–1985 were years of special difficulty in hiring, training, and retaining competent survey interviewers.

We are also very grateful to the support staff at our own research center, the Social and Demographic Research Institute at the University of Massachusetts, where all data processing and analysis took place. In particular, we are indebted to Eleanor Weber, who served as Data Base Manager, designed the computer program to generate the vignettes used in the study, and provided overall management of data processing; to Marianne Geronimo, who served as Coding Supervisor; and to Debbie Sellers, who served as a Research Assistant for the first 3 years of the project, working with us through the pretest trials, the fielding, data processing, and preliminary analysis of the data. Debbie did a fine job of record-keeping, testing the data via factor analysis, constructing indices, and preparing detailed codebooks. We also acknowledge our gratitude to Bhavani Sitaraman, who served as Research Assistant on the project during its last year of funded support, with primary responsibility for the preliminary analysis of the vignette data.

The ultimate expression of gratitude must go to the hundreds of people who gave of their time and thought as respondents in the several surveys: the core sample of 1393 people in the greater Boston area, who shared so much of their lives as parents or adult children in the personal interviews, and had the time, interest, and patience to also fill out a booklet of 31 vignettes after a long personal interview; and to more than 600 people in all parts of the United States and Canada with whom telephone interviews were conducted, people whose parent or adult child had referred us to them, so that we might analyze the parent–child relationship as it is viewed by both partners to the relationship.

Finally, we acknowledge our gratitude to Trev Leger, Senior Editor, and the staff of Aldine de Gruyter, for their patience and enthusiastic support in the final stages of manuscript review and revision, and book production.

Deepest gratitude of all is to each other, for the countless occasions when help was needed and given unstintingly during the 5 years of collaboration. That help was not painless, for it often involved pointed criticism as well as praise for the work of the other. The collaboration was extremely gratifying, both personally and professionally, and may even set a precedent in work we undertake in the future.

Alice S. Rossi
Peter H. Rossi

Introduction _____ Part I

Problem and Design _____ 1

Introduction

One stormy night in the early days of jet-propelled airplanes, I (A. Rossi) happened to share a flight from Boston to Chicago with an exuberant basketball team celebrating its victory earlier that evening. The plane hit an unusual amount of turbulence, lost altitude rapidly, and oxygen masks dropped before our faces. The incident was over within minutes, as the pilot regained control and climbed back to our assigned altitude. When the cheers of released tension subsided, I leaned across the aisle to another woman passenger and asked if she had heard what I thought I had heard when the oxygen masks first appeared: several deep masculine voices crying out "Mama!" She nodded that she had and we compared notes on what *we* thought about during those frightening moments: We had not uttered a sound, but we both thought of the children we might leave motherless that night.

I have thought of that incident many times in the past 25 years, musing on the fact that the young athletic men and the two older women might have spent the last moments of their lives thinking of either mothers or children. The experience emphasized the deep psychological salience of the parent–child relationship: Under duress, the young adult men cried out for their mothers, and the women experienced panic at the prospect of their children bereft of their care while still very young. The children of the two women were then under 5

3

years of age, while the basketball players were young men in their early 20s. We wondered what the reactions would be of men our age who had young children, or of young women the age of the basketball players. Would 40-year-old men think of their children in a moment of peril as the two women passengers did? Would young 20-year-old women invoke their mothers or their fathers in such perilous moments?

Close encounters with death often bring into consciousness our deepest concerns and attachments, and may be reviewed mentally innumerable times over the years that follow. In our experience, these private musings focused on two intriguing questions: To what extent does the parent–child relationship remain a core attachment across the life course, even as we personally shift from the role of child to that of parent? And second, to what extent does the emotional salience of this relationship vary as a function of the gender of the parent and of the child and does this vary by age?

These two questions are at the heart of the story to be told in this book, for we shall explore the parent–child relationship as it varies by stage of the life course and by gender. In the development of the research designed to pursue these questions, we have built on the work of others, but we have also departed from that work in several important and innovative respects. In this chapter, we discuss the intellectual roots of the research, sketch the theoretical issues we address, and describe their implementation in the design of the study. We also report our sampling decisions, the major constructs and how they were measured, and the organization of the substantive chapters to follow this introduction.

Theoretical Foci of the Study

Research on the relationship between parents and children has been conducted in a variety of social sciences. Child developmental psychologists have focused on children in the first formative decade of life and their attachment to their parents, family sociologists have focused on the transition to parenthood and the parenting of young children and adolescents, and social gerontologists have concentrated on elderly parents and their middle-aged children. Each field has concentrated on particular sectors of the life course as a function of interest in young children, young adults, or elderly adults. Reading across these various studies, varying as they do in substantive foci, does not provide a profile of how the parent–child relationship changes over the decades from the birth of a child to the death of the parent.

The overriding conclusion of sociological research on the parent–child relationship in the past several decades has been to debunk the myth of an isolated nuclear family or the elderly as alienated from their children. Marvin Sussman (Sussman & Burchinal, 1962), Bert Adams (1968a, 1968b), Eugene Litwak (1960a,b, 1969), Reuben Hill (Hill et al., 1970), and Lucy Fischer (1979, 1981, 1983), among others, provided descriptive evidence of high levels of contact and exchange of goods and services between young married children and their parents.

Similarly, in gerontology, many authors have shown high levels of contact and help between elderly parents and their middle-aged children. For example, Lilian Troll and Vern Bengtson (1979), from a review of 25 major surveys, report that most adults have some close kin who live nearby, and they keep in touch even with those who live afar by visits, phone calls, and letters. Ethel Shanas, in a series of studies, consistently reported that nearly 80% of the elderly see a child at least once a week (Shanas, 1980; Shanas et al., 1968). In more recent years, gerontologists have given special attention to the very old, (those over 85 years of age, the fastest growing subgroup in the American population), and estimate that 80% of the care those who need it receive is provided by family members, typically wives and daughters (Brody, 1981; Brody & Lang, 1982; Brody et al., 1983; Troll et al., 1979; U.S. GAO, 1977).

Each of these areas of research has concentrated on particular age groups in the population: developmental psychologists study young children at highly specific ages, e.g., youngsters from 18 to 36 months of age, but although the child's age is of critical significance to child psychologists, the age of their mothers is not, yet it may vary from the mid-20s to early 40s, depending on the women's age at first birth and birth order position of the particular subject child. Gerontologists similarly select samples of very elderly persons, whose children may vary widely in age. Family sociologists have typically followed a family stage typology, where age of oldest or youngest child defines family stage rather than age of the parent. This makes it very difficult to gain an overall perspective on the life course curve in social interaction, affective closeness, or help exchange, not only because there is no representative distribution by age of either parent or child, but because the content of the measures used were tailored to the substantive focus on a particular age group of concern, e.g., youngsters under 12 or oldsters over 85.

Even three-generation studies suffer from this lack of a representative age distribution in any of the three generations studied, with the exception of the national three-generation study of black families (Jackson, 1979; Jackson & Hatchett, 1986; Taylor, 1986). In addition, many three-

generation studies selected only those families in which all three generations resided within 50 miles of one another or within the same city, a
pragmatic fielding decision to facilitate interviewer access (e.g., Hill et
al., 1970; Hagestad, 1982a,b, 1984; Markides et al., 1986). As we shall
see, this is a problem we have resolved by basing our study on a random
probability sample of all adults 19 years of age and older.

The concentration in most parent–child studies on childhood and
adolescence at the beginning of the life course, and old age at its end,
prompted Gunhild Hagestad to characterize this research as the alpha
and omega tendencies in parent–child research, each carried out by
researchers "who were trained in different disciplines and who publish
in quite separate journals" (Hagestad, 1987, p. 407). As a result, there is
great difficulty bridging the gap between research at these two ends of
the life course. For one thing, the constructs relevant to the study of the
parent–child relationship in the tender years before puberty have no
counterparts in the study of the relationship in the last quarter of life.
Dependency, dominance, and reciprocal influence do not translate
readily from their base in child development research to old parents and
middle-aged children, just as frequency of contact or exchange of goods
and services do not translate from their base in gerontology to young
children and their parents. Perhaps the single most salient construct
relevant to all stages of the parent–child relationship is that of attachment or affective closeness.

A further consequence of the alpha–omega concentration has been a
paucity of knowledge concerning the long stretch of time during which
the "child" is an independent adult and the "parent" a vigorous middle-
aged adult or healthy, independent oldster. Because of our greatly
extended years of life, the parent–child relationship may last 50 or more
years and undergo much renegotiation during the long years that intervene between a childhood of dependency on parents and what is only a
"potential" dependency of parents on children in very old age (Riley,
1983). Unless the same measurement instruments are used in an age
heterogeneous sample and applied to the roles of both parents and of
adult children, it is nearly impossible to chart the life curve on any
dimension of the parent–child relationship of substantive interest, nor to
detect the extent to which there is reciprocity or an imbalance in the flow
of affection, comfort, or goods between the generations. If childhood
dependency is followed by adult balanced reciprocity for several decades, then old age dependency on children during terminal illnesses
will seem a far less dramatic reversal than the concepts of the "parentification of the child" or "reversed socialization" suggest (Brim, 1968;
Mortimer & Simmons, 1978).

Another important gap in our knowledge that flows from the alpha–
omega concentration of research attention is the fact that increased

longevity also means adults now spend several decades being *both* parents *and* children. Yet research attention to the middle-aged caregiver of elderly parents has concentrated on the potential overload of such middle-aged children, typically the daughters, caught between caring for an elderly parent while simultaneously caring for their own children, the "superwoman squeeze" as Betty Friedan (1981) calls it (Brody, 1981; Brody & Lang, 1982). Similarly, several authors have written of middle-aged men and women as intergenerational "patrons" giving to both young and old members of their families (Adams, 1968b; Hagestad, 1987; Hill et al., 1970; Kennedy & Stokes, 1982). But with parents surviving well into their 70s and widows into their 80s, the probability is rapidly decreasing that middle-aged daughters are in fact still rearing their own children when they take on caregiving responsibilities for an elderly parent. Such children are not likely to be living at home, but married and rearing their own children. Furthermore, as Hagestad suggests, many middle-aged women caring for terminally ill mothers may in fact receive attention, affection, and advice from their young adult children (Hagestad, 1987).

More importantly, the neglect of the decades when adults are both parents and children represents a lost opportunity to place the parent–child relationship in the context of the larger kinship structure that contains not one but two or three parent–child dyads. This makes middle-aged adults important strategic informants concerning stability and change in a core family relationship, both in historical, intergenerational terms, and in individual developmental terms. Such adults could inform us about their own biographies, tracing the quality of their relationship to their parents in their childhood and youth and their relationship to their own children when the latter were young, as well as their *current* relationship to both surviving parents and young adult children. With such data, we could then explore continuity and change in the parent–child relationship over time and across generational dyads in the same lineages. As we shall see, this is a central focus in the study reported in this book.

All three-generation studies hold the potential for such reliance on the middle generation as strategic informants, but the problem foci of such studies and their analytic methods have not maximized this advantage. The focus, for example, of the three-generation study initiated in the 1970s by Vern Bengtson was on the "generation gap" between the two proximate generations of parents and children (an issue of widespread public concern during the 1970s), and typically contrasted mean scores on similar measures in the older dyad of the G1–G2 generations with the mean scores in the younger G2–G3 dyads (Bengtson et al., 1984), rather than how three-generation lineages vary and why, in the extent to which values were shared across the three generations. For three generations to be included in a lineage sample also imposes a relatively narrow age restriction to each of the three generations: with an average generational replacement of approximately 25 years, the grandparental generation tends to be adults in their 60s, the parental generation in their 40s, and the young adult grandchildren in their early 20s. Without a representative age distribution, an analyst cannot deal with life course development and change. And in the absence of any biographic information, the current values that differentiate the generations cannot be explained in terms of individual or family life history; hence an analyst can only "infer" period effects that impact differentially on the age cohorts represented in the three-generation sample, or explore only what family themes or similar social statuses characterize lineages with shared values as opposed to lineages in which the generations differ in values.

Indeed, we suggest that one common gap across the variety of sociological and gerontological studies we have discussed is the fact that attention is narrowly focused on *contemporary* relations between parents and children, as though they were not influenced in any significant way by past events earlier in the life course of either the parent or the child. Yet this seems to be one of the most fruitful ways of building bridges between life span research on child development and life course research on adult development. A good example can be seen in post-divorce studies. We have learned much in recent years about the impact of divorce on subsequent reliance by divorced adults on friends and kin (Gerstel, 1988), and on the development of boys and girls whose parents divorced (Hetherington & Arasteh, 1988). The time frame in such studies tends to be the narrow one of 1 to 10 years postdivorce, but whether the experience of a family broken by divorce in youth has continuing impact on adults several decades later remains moot, although readily ascertained with life history data on adult subjects or respondents.

On many topics of interest to both life span psychologists and life course sociologists concerned for parent–child relationships, it is almost impossible to establish linkages between the two genres of research, because the child psychologist at most studies child development in the short run, and the sociologist of adult relations does not know the earlier history of the parent–child relationship. At issue, of course, is the general resistance among American social scientists to reliance on retrospective data, a resistance not shared by many European scholars. We were pursuaded, by contrast, that an important opportunity for fuller explanation would be missed had we not built in many measures of the stability and quality of early family life. This is not an either–or decision: our concern was with the extent to which early family experiences contribute to contemporary variance in social interaction, affective closeness, and the exchange of help between parents and adult children, *over and above* current exigencies in the lives of parents and adult children, such as access, health status, degree of family responsibilities, or economic resources.

Several unique characteristics of this study have been mentioned in the course of this discussion. The most important are as follows:

1.   **A representative age distribution of adults**, so that any dimension of parent–child solidarity we investigate can be charted across the full range of the adult life course.

2.   **Measures of parent–child solidarity, whether social interaction, affection, shared values, or exchange of help must be appropriate to adults of any age**, whether a 20-year-old unmarried child or an elderly parent of 90.

3.   **Respondents would be interviewed concerning their past and current roles as both children and as parents** (actual or hypothetical). This also implies that identical measures would be used for parents' characteristics in the family of origin of respondents and for respondents' roles as parents in their families of procreation. This provides an important opportunity to investigate continuity and discontinuity across the generations within a lineage.

4.   **Any social relationship includes a minimum of two partners, and ideally the relationship should be examined with data from *both* partners to that relationship**. This is as true of the parent–child as of the husband–wife relationship, though research in family sociology and gerontology has tended to rely on data obtained from only one partner to the dyad. It seems reasonable to assume the relationship between parents and adult children may be viewed as differently from each other as Jessie Bernard has argued is the case with the marital relationship (Bernard, 1972). If there is both a "his" marriage and a "her" marriage, there is probably also a "parent's" view and a "child's" view of their relationship. This is particularly likely to be the case when parents and adult children are asked to describe their relationship during the years the child was growing up, because the parents will be sensitive to issues of concern to them when they were young adults, whereas adult children will be sensitive to issues of concern to them during the tender years of childhood and the often turbulent years of adolescence.

5.   **The parent–child relationship should be viewed in the context of the larger kindred within which it is embedded**. Several unique features of our design are relevant here: for one, by viewing respondents as both children of older parents and as parents of their own children, we test for and attempt to explain variation in cross-generational transmission of values, marital stability, and affection. Second, we wished to

compare the extent to which obligations to the primary kin of parents and children are more deeply felt than obligations to less closely related kin, such as aunts and uncles, grandparents, grandchildren, cousins, or, indeed, to such nonkin as friends and neighbors. As we shall see, the approach we have taken to study normative obligations among kinpersons relies on the factorial survey method, an innovative technique applied for the first time in this study to kinship issues. Third, we were concerned to demonstrate empirically just how prevalent lineages are that contain four or more generations of direct lineal kin. It is widely believed that four and even five generations are now common, but no existing data set has shown just *how* prevalent this is, or how generational composition varies across the life course.

6. **Gender of parent and adult child will be a significant axis showing differences in social interaction, feelings of obligation, degree of intimacy, and the extent and kind of help exchanged between the generations**. This is a uniform finding across a wide array of studies of course; hence our study should anticipate such a pattern and attempt to explain it. As we shall see below, this involved the use of a measure of personal traits that has been found to differentiate men and women, such as the widely used Masculinity–Femininity scales. In our usage, however, we avoid any assumption of biological maleness being identical with men's social roles or biological femaleness being equivalent to women's social roles, by labeling our constructs Expressivity and Dominance. Our usage of these measures centers on testing the extent to which they "explain" differences in social behavior and affect between men and women, and exploring the effect of intragender variance in such qualities on intergenerational relations. For example, will men high on Expressivity relate to their parents or their children as women do? And do parents relate differently to children high on Expressivity than they do to children low on Expressivity?

As seen in these summary characteristics of the study, age and sex are major variables in the design, as they are to any structural analysis of a family system. Each poses a different set of conceptual issues to a researcher, and it is to these issues that the next section is devoted.

Complexities of Age and Gender as Research Variables

Age and gender are among the simplest and most visible social markers in human interaction, but among the most complex and puzzling variables with which social scientists deal. Even in a casual social encounter we can identify a person's sex and make a reasonably accurate guess as to a person's age, give or take a few years. From birth to death we move in a social world organized around these two major human characteristics. Up to a few decades ago, social scientists used age and sex as research variables in much the same way the public at large did: age merely marked where on the trajectory from birth to death a person was located, and sex was a dichotomy rooted in human nature and elaborated by social expectations. Men were men and women were at least girls.

Age as an Empirical Variable

Over the past 20 years, theoretical and empirical treatment of the variable of "age" has become more sophisticated than treatment of the variable of "gender." No one would argue that "age" is purely a social construction as many do where "gender" is concerned. The conceptual elaboration that has occurred in the theoretical and empirical treatment of "age" has focused on efforts to distinguish between age as a maturational marker and age as an index of cohort characteristics or historical period effects. "Place sensitivity" was the hard-earned insight garnered from cross-cultural studies in the immediate post-World War II era; these studies built on the participation of social scientists in the war effort (as military personnel or researchers for the War Department), which encouraged their awareness of the importance of cultural differences in a shrinking global community. In the past 20 years, "time sensitivity" has become the hard-earned insight of social scientists, as the rapidity of technological, political, and social change encouraged their awareness of the importance of cohort differences and period effects.

Over the past decade, there has been a lively dialogue between life span psychologists and life course sociologists. It has been our observation that life span psychologists now concede the significance of social structure, social situations, ecological settings or niches, and so on, for psychological understanding of individual motivation, personal traits, adult development, and aging. By contrast, life course sociologists have not been nearly so gracious in incorporating biopsychological constructs as such into their formulations. Rather, one reads that many psychological variables on adult development are "epiphenomena" (Dannefer, 1984; Featherman, 1986); that the life course is so thoroughly institutionalized that even such psychological traits as self-esteem, efficacy, initiative, and achievement orientation are themselves institutionalized (Meyer, 1986); that the causal origins of adult development cannot be ascertained by a personological approach (Featherman, 1986). In a paper presented at the 1986 meetings of the American Sociological Association, Randall Collins argued that "emotional energy" was not a biopsychological but a positional sociological variable (Collins, 1986). Ira Reiss, in his presidential address to the National Council on Family Relations, even argued for a purely sociological model to explain sexual initiation and sexual behavior in adolescence (Reiss, 1986).

With life course sociologists emphasizing cohort and period effects, and life span psychologists tracing the influence of social setting on personal traits, "aging" as a maturational phenomenon seems to be left to the biomedical specialties. Perhaps, as Lonnie Sherrod and Bert Brim have suggested, we are in a period of overreacting to earlier deterministic models of adult development and of aging as programmed senescence; by taking an optimistic view of the human organism and our development potential, we are trying to throw the burden of proof on those with more pessimistic, static, and deterministic views (Sherrod & Brim, 1986, p. 575).

Were we further along in the integration of the social sciences, we might not link life course analysis to sociology and life span analysis to psychology. In both disciplines, we might restrict the usage of "life span" literally to time length or span of life, and use the more general "life course" concept in both fields when we chart either biopsychological processes of individual development and aging or institutional patterns that affect the timing, duration, and sequencing of statuses along the life line. We will be using "life course" in this broader sense in this book, and we assume further that by "adult development" no one will infer any fixed, hierarchic, immutable sequence of growth, nor that "aging" necessarily means senescence and decline, though considering human mortality, it does include such changes. It seems pointless to deny the bittersweet character of growing old and sensing the shrinking span of years that lie ahead before one's death. Further, we assume a transactional model of adult development that allows for individual proactive initiative as well as socially constrained and biologically restricted behavior (Lerner, 1984; Sherrod & Brim, 1986).

The implication of this discussion is that the age variable in this study of the parent–child relationship cannot be explored with a narrow angle of vision. To understand observed differences between parents and adult children requires close attention to where on the life course the parent and child are located, and to what these positions imply in terms of cohort and aging correlates of these positions.

Parents are by definition from different birth cohorts than their children, and each generation carries the mark of their cohort. We know that on average parents today have less education than their children, reflecting the trend toward higher educational attainment over the past 50 years. Demographic trends in marriage and fertility rates will also be reflected in any sample of parents and children: The average age difference between parents and children will reflect age at marriage and the timing and number of births in the parental generation. Societal trends in unemployment rates or housing shortages may be reflected in whether young adult children prior to marriage still reside with their parents or live independently. Fortunately, many cohort differences can be built into an analysis by means of empirical "control" variables, e.g., educational attainment, family size, age at marriage or first birth, marital status, and age difference between parent and child.

There are limits to what a researcher can do about historical period effects. Few surveys ask direct questions about past military service, political involvement in protest movements, or whether one's family of origin suffered economic hardship during the Great Depression of the 1930s or inflation during the early 1980s. We are indebted to Glen Elder's creative reconstruction and reanalysis of the Oakland–Berkeley growth studies for tracing the long-term consequences of income loss or stability during the years of the depression (Elder, 1974, 1982; Elder & Liker, 1982; Elder, Liker & Cross, 1984; Elder & Rockwell, 1976, 1978). But these data sets are small in size and did not include the kinds of variables of interest to scholars of intergenerational relations in the 1980s.

What one *can* do with contemporary cross-sectional data sets is to use respondents' age to determine the historic period during which they were at some developmental stage of analytic interest, and to compare, for example, respondents whose adolescence took place during one era vs. another. By this means, we shall test the idea that the parent–child relationship was marked by greater stress when the child's adolescence took place during the more turbulent decade of the 1970s than when the child passed through adolescence in the domestically and politically calmer decade of the 1950s. In a similar way, we can sketch historical change in gender role socialization by parents, by tracing the extent to which traditional domestic skills were taught to daughters and masculine skills to sons over the decades represented by the childhood years of our oldest respondents (the first two decades of the twentieth century) and test whether traditional socialization of this sort will be weaker in the decades just ahead, when our youngest respondents will be rearing their sons and daughters.

Gender as an Empirical Variable

One of the residual puzzles that remained after the airplane incident with which we began this chapter relates to the young men's invocation of their mothers and the women's concern for dependent age children. It was not God, a husband, or a lover, and it was not a father who dominated our thoughts, but mothers and children. But why would men call on their mothers rather than their fathers in their moments of panic? And why didn't the women call on their husbands rather than feel concern for their children in such moments? After all, men are supposed to be the towers of strength, the protectors of the defenseless young and dependent wives, and women are supposed to be weak, submissive, shy, and dependent on men. Yet under stress the ball-players invoked their mothers, and the women empathized with their potentially motherless children. Both instances seemed to link women with strength, not weakness and dependency.

Nothing in this experience matched the functionalist interpretation of gender roles in the early 1960s. Even 25 years later, family sociologists tend to fuse the parent and spouse roles, and hence to compare the wife–mother role set with the husband–father role set. This fusion of parent and spouse roles encourages the association of strength, reserve, and dominance with the family roles of men, and subordination, emotionality, and dependence with the family roles of women, yielding a functionally complementary balance between the expressive wife–mother and the instrumental husband–father. The consequence of this fusion of spouse and parent roles has been much theoretical confusion and underestimation of the strength and abilities of women. Even feminist analysis in the 1970s and early 1980s has shared in this confusion by seeing only weakness and subordination in the family roles of women held "in place" by male dominance or patriarchy.[1]

A counterpart tendency can be found in psychology, in the longstanding acceptance of the notion that men and women differ in some persistent ways rooted in biological sex and reinforced by socialization that could be captured by measures of the personal traits of femininity and masculinity that were assumed to predominate across the whole array of social roles men and women fill. The traits subsumed under femininity were a strange mix: shy, submissive, dependent, clinging, timid, along with affectionate, helpful, empathic, altruistic. But once the wife role is differentiated from the mother role, it seems clear that it is not as mothers but as wives that many women are dependent, timid, and submissive, while as Miles Newton reminded us many years ago (Newton, 1973), and Miriam Johnson more recently (Johnson, 1988), as mothers women have to be and are active, productive, and strong. Even in gerontological research the overriding impression is of the strength shown by women in their spouse roles as they provide major caregiving during the terminal illnesses of their husbands, or serve as major kinkeepers or "ministers of the interior," as Hagestad describes the specialized roles of many older women in dealing with family dynamics (Hagestad, 1987). We shall see a comparable profile in the chapters of this book, as we compare the relations between mothers and daughters with the other three parent–child dyads.

In recent years, feminist scholars have shown particular interest in the mother–daughter relationship, as in Rose Coser's ongoing study of Italian and Jewish immigrant mothers and their daughters. But the problem in restricting analysis to one same-sex dyad is its lack of a comparative framework. How can we tell what is special to the mother–daughter relationship unless we show how it differs from the mother–son relationship or the father–daughter relationship?

A special problem exists in sociological research on gender: the tendency to interpret empirical differences between men and women in purely social terms when the data set includes nothing but the sex of the respondents. A test of a sociological interpretation of sex or gender differences would require us to develop sociological measures of what is *meant* by the social construction of gender, and to demonstrate that with controls for these sociological measures, the original sex difference disappears. To our knowledge, no study has attempted such a demonstration. Here too, we hope to explain some portion of the gender differences in our data by reliance on the measures of Expressivity and Dominance previously referred to.

An implicit component of the perspective we bring to the analysis of the parent–child relationship is a bioevolutionary approach to both parenting and gender (Lancaster et al., 1987; A. S. Rossi, 1977, 1984), and it is well to be as explicit as possible from the outset on this underlying perspective. The fact that no known society lacks institutional rules and norms allocating responsibility for rearing its young is rooted in a unique characteristic of our species: Compared to all other mammalian species, the human infant is born premature. The prematurity of the human neonate is the price our species pays in every generation everywhere both to stand upright and to have an enlarged cortex. The female pelvis could not evolve to a width sufficient to permit the birth of a large-brained human infant as developmentally advanced as a chimpanzee at birth (equivalent to a 9-month-old human baby), without producing a very unwieldy gait. The evolutionary adaptation to bipedalism *and* large brains was birth of highly dependent fragile creatures requiring a long period of care and training before they could sustain themselves on their own. Despite all manner of historical change and cultural diversity, this fundamental fact has made long-term human parenting a universal pattern of our species.

A bioevolutionary approach also sensitizes us to the special significance of gender. Sexual dimorphism is, after all, most apparent in those aspects of species functions involving sex and reproduction, and we take this to mean that gender, particularly in the domain of the family, cannot be viewed in any unidimensional manner purely as a "social construction." It has become a useful linguistic device to differentiate between *sex* and *gender*, reserving "sex" for those aspects of the male and female that are rooted in fundamental differences in reproductive biology and anatomy, and "gender" for all other social and cultural differences between men and women. This is a useful convention, but also a misleading one, because it bypasses the connections between sex and gender, i.e., the extent to which social and psychological differences between men and women, while largely independent of sex dimorphism, are nevertheless linked in some ways to the basic physiological differences in reproductive functioning between males and females. This is nowhere more relevant than in family roles. Thus, there is much greater cross-cultural variation in who is socially defined as a child's father than a child's mother, and far greater social control of women's sexuality than of men's, for the reason that birthing links the newborn definitively to its biological mother but not to its biological father. Paternity, after all, rests only on circumstantial evidence.

That women prefer and actually marry men somewhat older, taller, heavier, and of higher status than themselves has been found across so many cultures that Kingsley Davis suggests hypergamy is one of the few universal human patterns (Davis, 1984; Davis & van den Oever, 1982). It does not follow, however, that this is purely a social psychological pattern of culturally determined engenderment. It is intrinsically connected to the fact of the shorter fertile phase of the female life span than of the male, and to the fact that the female has had to be more selective in choosing a dependable mate because the consequences of pregnancy, birth, and infant care have been largely hers to bear. It is when women do *not* exercise such caution that many women are sexually exploited or deserted by men who fathered their children.[2]

A bioevolutionary perspective does not imply a rejection of powerful socialization pressures and a continuing pattern of social expectations for differentiated gender role behavior. Indeed, social and family influences on gender roles will be documented throughout the chapters to follow. There is ample evidence that men can be taught skills that might come more easily to women; it is, after all, men who predominate in a field such as neurosurgery, despite the general tendency for women to have greater finger dexterity than men. So too, one could argue that some men are just as driven by "raging hormones" as some women are, and perhaps even more so, for example, in the intensity of their sex drives or aggressive impulses and behavior. Socialization involves learning self-control and socially approved behavior that keeps such limbic impulses in check. Indeed, it is often an impoverished weak socialization that underlies socially deviant behavior in adolescent and young adult males.

In addition, some proportion of stereotypically dominant male behavior has more to do with earlier involvement in male peer groups in late childhood and adolescence than it does with innate biological predispositions of the male sex. As Nancy Chodorow (1978) and Miriam Johnson (1988) have argued, male sex identity may *require* such intense absorption into the male peer group to counteract the very intense attachment to the mother in the first years of life, a phase of differentiation that is not necessary to the development of a female sex identity. Note, however, that socialization in a male peer group, clearly a social experience, is in reaction to the intense attachment between mother and child, an intensity that is *not*, in our view, a purely social phenomenon, but one rooted in reproductive biology and the intense bonding that takes place between mother and infant during the first weeks of the neonate's life, an attachment whose intensity comes as a surprise to many first-time mothers. However overlaid with strong social pressures for gender role compliance, we state as our initial assumption that some proportion of the gender differences we have observed in our study is rooted in sex differences in reproductive biology.

However, it is also the case that in the late twentieth century in western societies, there has been considerable social change in gender roles and sexual behavior. More women now share breadwinning with their husbands, and, although to a lesser extent, more men share parenting and home maintenance with their wives.[3] And whatever the edge of a greater predisposition to intense bonding between mothers and infants than between fathers and their infants, by the time the children are late adolescents, most fathers as well as mothers have invested heavily in rearing their children, have worked hard to provide for them and to protect them from harm, and both mothers and fathers face the same process of "letting go" and renegotiating their relationship to young adult children.

Despite the considerable change in gender role attitudes and the increasingly important role women play in the economy over the past decade and more, one persistent gender difference has been highly resistant to social and political change, and it is a difference that is of particular importance to an interpretation of why family research continues to find women more deeply involved in and dependent on family and kin ties than men are: the lower pay and more precarious socioeconomic position of women compared to men. Despite a decade or more of political effort, and a significant shift of women from service and clerical jobs to professional and managerial jobs, American women still earn only two-thirds of what men earn who do comparable work, not over 90% as women do in a country like Sweden (Popenoe, 1988). In addition, precisely because women still tend to marry men who are older and of higher status, the proportion of total family income earned by married women tends to be modest. It is income discrepancy *within* marriage that is most relevant to decision making concerning who carries more and who less responsibility for home and child care.

And when marriages fail, it is divorced women whose standard of living is lowered, whereas their ex-husbands' income tends to improve following divorce (Hoffman & Duncan, 1988; Weitzman, 1985). Widowhood also leaves more women impoverished than it does men: Because women tend to be younger than their husbands and live longer than men do, the drain on accumulated savings associated with terminal illnesses of spouses is far more the experience of women than of men.

The important point to note is that at all points of the life course, women have a greater developmental stake in maintaining close relations with their own parents, their siblings, and their grown children than do men, precisely because the probabilities are much higher that women will *need* the help and emotional support of family members than men. We believe women are also aware that others will have need of *them*, so the developmental stake is not a one-directional dependency but a matter of anticipated interdependence. Medicaid, social security, and local programs for the elderly notwithstanding, when crises hit, significant social and emotional support and caregiving are not things people seek from bureaucratic agencies but from intimate ties with significant others.

There are costs attached to any significant social change, and in the transitional era we are now living through, marriages between men and women who have equal incomes do not automatically translate into greater gender egalitarianism in family roles. Marriages in which women earn as much as their husbands, together with the even smaller minority of marriages in which wives earn more than their husbands, have higher rates of divorce than traditional marriages of higher earning husbands to homemaker or part-time employed wives (Benson-von der Ohe, 1987; Popenoe, 1988). Consequently, whether as young unmarried women, or married women with husbands who cannot pull their weight as providers, or divorced women, or widows, women continue to have a greater probability of needing the financial, emotional, and social support of their kin than do men, and they can anticipate many occasions in life when they will be called on to meet the needs of other family members, e.g., a divorced daughter, a widowed mother, a pregnant sister, or a sick grandchild.

Implicit in the points made above on the conceptual framework within which we shall examine gender differences in the parent–adult child relationship is the influence of three factors that press in a similar direction: First, women have a physiological edge in attachment to infants that is inherent in pregnancy and birthing, which is further intensified by the fact that women do the major job of parenting young children. Second, despite efforts at minimizing differences in rearing boys and girls, gender role socialization further reinforces greater role investment by girls in anticipated mothering than by boys in anticipated fathering. As a consequence, when they reach adulthood, women have acquired greater affiliative and relational attributes than men, as their mothers have before them. Third, persistent socioeconomic differences between men and women means that all the women in a family—mothers, sisters, daughters, grandmothers—will experience many times of need and crisis during which the "latent matrix" of family relations, as Matilda Riley describes them (Riley, 1983), will come into play and women will provide help or be helped in turn.

It was this complex array of factors—embracing biology, socialization, and socioeconomic position—that underlaid our central expectation in approaching this study of parent–child relationships, i.e., that gender of parent and child would be a major source of variation in the emotional quality and content of interaction between the generations, with the greatest intimacy, most frequent interaction, and most extensive pattern of reciprocal help in the same-sex dyad of mothers and daughters; the least intimacy, interaction, and help exchange between fathers and sons; and with opposite-sex dyads falling in between the two same-sex dyads.

Design Implications of Theoretical Foci of the Study

Several design characteristics flowed from the three foci on gender, life course, and relationship perspective. The primary determinant was the life course framework, which pressed for a random probability sample with a representative age distribution of adults, rather than any purposive selection of parent–child dyads at specified points along the life course. This had the further advantage of ensuring the presence of adults who never had any children. Elderly adults in the 1980s represent cohorts with quite high rates of childlessness, and the odds are high that today's young adult cohorts will also have a high childless rate. Indeed, Ronald Rindfuss predicts an eventual 30% childless rate in cohorts now in their early childbearing years (Rindfuss et al., 1988). The salience of the parent–child relationship in late adulthood might be illuminated through a comparison of older adults who had children with those who had none.

A second design implication was to develop spinoff samples consisting of either a parent or an adult child of respondents in our main sample. By using identical measures for the same dimensions of their relationship, we could explore the question of whether parents and children differ, and in what respects, in their views of the relationship between them.

We shall follow the convention adopted by Vern Bengtson in his three-generation study in referring to our three data sources. Respondents in the main personal interview sample of the Boston SMSA will be referred to as G2, the middle generation; parents of these G2 respondents will be referred to as G1, with data obtained either from their G2 children in our main sample, or from the G1 spinoff sample of the parents themselves; and adult children of G2 respondents will be referred to as G3, with data either from their G2 parents in the main sample, or from the G3 spinoff sample of the adult children themselves.

To fulfill our desire to give systematic attention to gender of parent and child, a third design implication was to select parents and adult children for the spinoff samples that assured sufficient cases of the four gender-specified parent–child dyads. In view of the greater longevity of women than men, it was predictable that respondents would have more living mothers than living fathers (835 mothers vs. 599 fathers), and it also seemed possible that women might be more interested in the study than men, with the result that we might gain greater access to the parents or children of women respondents than of men respondents. Despite our efforts, the G1 spinoff sample of 323 parents consists of more mothers than fathers (194 mothers, 129 fathers), while equity was more readily obtained in the G3 spinoff sample of 278 adult children (142 daughters, 136 sons).

A last design implication was reliance on retrospective questions concerning early family life. We were not embarking on a decades-long longitudinal study, but a cross-sectional survey in 1984 and 1985. The use of retrospective measures raises both theoretical and methodological questions. They have been viewed with suspicion in sociology,[4] partly because they are subject to distorted memories and partly because the discipline views human action as purposive and volitional: Sociologists prefer an image of adults creating their futures rather than responding to impulses internalized in the past. To demonstrate the continuing influence of early formative experiences on current behavior restrains the impulse of social scientists to make "quick-fix" policy pronouncements on the basis of their research. On the other hand, if the past does exert influence on current behavior to some significant degree, and we do not allow for such influences in policy formation, our recommendations, if implemented, are likely to show weak effects. Hence it seems the wiser course to include, not to exclude, independent variables that measure potentially relevant earlier determinants of the contemporary human behavior under study.

Family sociologists whose research is focused on late adolescence and early adulthood may also exaggerate the extent of intergenerational dissimilarities between the subjects and their parents, without adequate recognition of the fact that the late adolescent and early adult phase of the life course is unique in many ways. In youth, young adults are still struggling to become independent, to make decisions on their own by distancing themselves from parental influence. Once the transition into adulthood has taken place—with marriage, a young family, and a settled line of work—young adult children can renegotiate their relationship to their parents. A son at 18 may view his parents with some disdain and resent them on the grounds of limiting his freedom to do as he pleases, but come to view them, when he is a young father himself, as reasonable and interesting people after all, with the result that mature children's values and life style become more like that of their parents than was the case when the children were adolescents. This suggests that early family life may have a "sleeper effect," not detectable to a researcher with adolescent subjects in the throes of differentiating themselves from their parents, but visible when our subjects are fully independent adults.

There is undoubtedly a good deal of slippage between what *really* happened in childhood and what adults recall about their childhood, as there is between what parents of middle-aged children recall about the early years of childrearing and what really happened during those years. But if contemporary sentiment is important, so too is recalled sentiment. Even a fantasy can have real consequences that may have as much to do with the quality of the contemporary relationship as any truly valid measure obtained 20 or more years ago in a longitudinally designed study. Note too, that prospective longitudinal studies in recent years tend to be of much shorter duration than would be required for an age-heterogeneous sample if we wished to obtain contemporary data on parent–child relations in the child's youth to relate to a middle-aged child's relationship to elderly parents. Our oldest respondents are over 70 years of age; hence their reports concerning the families they grew up in refer to not one decade ago but five or more decades in the past.

In sum, we were persuaded that our analysis of contemporary relations between parents and adult children would be enriched by the inclusion of biographic measures concerning the early years of the child's life and the parent's childrearing. While longitudinal study designs are better able to establish the direction of causality between variables, they are also extremely expensive, require a commitment to many years of research effort, and run the risk of not having the right variables or the appropriate measures of those variables that future theory calls for.[5]

It should also be noted that the study emphasis on the parent–child *relationship* means retrospective data are more accurately described as *sociographic* than as *biographic*. We wish to characterize the quality of the relationship of our respondents to their parents during childhood and the stability and cohesiveness of the families in which they grew up. The families of orientation were in turn not isolated units but embedded in a wider network of kin, and we have explored which specific kin had emotional salience for our respondents during their childhood and how such early kin salience affects current obligations to a variety of kinpersons. This takes on special significance when it is realized that all individual lives are embedded in these larger kindreds, and, if anything, this will be even more prevalent in the future than it has been in the past, precisely because of the unprecedented longevity humans now enjoy. It is not just individuals who live longer than ever before, but the kindreds they belong to have enlarged to embrace more generations as well.

We have exercised great care in the design of the retrospective questions. We did not ask trivial questions or questions that required very precise answers to be of analytic use. Thus, for example, to get a measure of the socioeconomic status of the family of origin of our main sample respondents, we asked them merely to rate how well off the family was financially, with categories ranging from "very poor" to "very well off," not how much money their fathers earned when they were teenagers. To tap the quality of their relationship to their mothers when they were children, we asked simple direct questions: how easy it was to talk to their mothers, whether their mothers encouraged them to talk about their troubles, whether their mothers made time for them when they needed her, and to what degree their mothers showed a lot of love and affection to them.

Major Features of the Design

Sample Site

As indicated above, the life course framework of the study determined the decision to secure a random probability sample of adults 18 years of age or older, so that respondents would vary normally in age and could be studied as both adult children in relationship to living parents, if they had them, and as parents of children who could also vary in age from infancy to late middle age. The decision also ensured the inclusion of unmarried and childless adults at all points of the life course.

Our choice was to secure a random probability sample from the Boston Standard Metropolitan Statistical Area. This permits us to "locate" our respondents in a historical framework and to compare how the Boston SMSA differs from other SMSAs in the United States, a topic covered below. The choice of the Boston SMSA rather than a national sample was also a decision based on pragmatic grounds. For one, the design called for multiple measures concerning each of a potentially great number of parent–child relationships from each respondent: e.g., a respondent both of whose parents were alive and who had four or five children, and we wished to use the same measures in personal interviews with respondents as we would use in telephone interviews in the spinoff samples of parents or adult children of our respondents. The implication was that we would have to restrict construct measures to relatively few operational items for each of the major dimensions of the parent–child relationship and we would have to format the questions in a manner appropriate to telephone as well as personal interviews. From a review of relevant measures used in previous studies of family relationships (Mangen et al., 1988), we concluded that we would have to design new measures for almost all the major variables in the research design. This suggested the desirability of securing a less-expensive local sample rather than a national sample. Estimates we obtained suggested the field costs of a national sample would be in the vicinity of $300,000, whereas the fielding of the three surveys with the Boston sample as the base survey would cost only $90,000.[6]

Sampling Design and Fielding

A very brief summary of sampling design and fielding results is provided here. A detailed account is given in Appendix A.

The selection of respondents for the G2 main sample was based on an area probability sample of housing units in the Boston SMSA. One adult was selected as respondent per household from a list of oldest to youngest adult household members, following a randomized "Kish" selection table stamped on the interview forms. Interviewing took place between the fall of 1984 and early spring of 1985, with a refusal rate in the G2 main survey of 24%, and in the spinoff samples of G1 parents and G3 adult children of 6% each. The main sample consists of 1393 G2 respondents, while the spinoff samples consist of 323 G1 parents and 278 G3 adult children.

A comparison of G1 parents we interviewed with G1 parents we did *not* interview (based on information gathered from their G2 respondent-children), showed only a few consistent but nonproblematic differences. Respondent G1 parents are on average 2 years younger than nonrespondent G1 parents; somewhat better educated, but with a mean difference of only 1 year of schooling; in slightly better health; seen somewhat less often; and involved in help exchange with their G2 children to a slightly lesser degree. A similar comparison of respondent G3 adult children with nonrespondent G3 children also showed minimal differences, and none was health and age-related as in the case of G1 parents. It was our impression from this profile and comments by interviewers that some G2 respondents took a protective stance in refusing to give us access to their parents, to spare elderly fragile or ill parents undue stress, or to spare them embarrassment because of language difficulties or impaired hearing.

The Boston SMSA and the G2 Main Sample

Contemporary Boston is a lively, energetic city, best known for its many colleges and universities, the site of numerous electronic industries, and a major producer of communications equipment. Known in some circles as the "education capital" of the United States, it is the home of 10 major colleges and universities, numerous museums, art institutes, and the internationally famous Boston Symphony under the baton of Seiji Ozawa.

Boston is also a major attraction to those interested in American history. Situated on the Bay of Massachusetts and crossed by the Charles and Mystic Rivers, Boston has a long history as a port for the shipment of fish, lumber, and manufactured products, particularly textiles, shoes, and paper products, and as an immigration port receiving people from abroad. Even today, there are 30 miles of berthing space with some 250 wharfs along the bay and rivers of the city. From the Boston Common, itself the oldest public park in the United States, pedestrians can roam in many directions, enjoying the city's layers of architectural history, including such historic sites as the Park Street Church where abolitionist William Lloyd Garrison began the American antislavery campaign in 1828, and where the hymn *America* was first sung in 1831; Faneuil Hall, the "cradle of liberty" where colonial protest groups met, and the adjacent colonaded Quincy Market. As every American school child knows, this was also the site of the Boston Tea Party. South of the Common, Back Bay is a well-preserved neighborhood of elegant brownstone rowhouses, many with recognizably nineteenth-century style exteriors, however gutted and renovated their interiors are now that many have been converted to condominiums. Less well known is the fact that Back Bay itself resulted from a colossal mid-nineteenth-century landfill project. In nearby Beacon Hill, lilac-tinted glass in front bay windows of the many Georgian style townhouses still grace the neighborhood and delight tourists.

Ethnic history is also highly visible in Boston City. A touch of Italy still lingers in the North End, home turf for the earliest generations of Italian immigrants, with bakeries and trattorias sharing close proximity to many landmarks of revolutionary Boston, including the Paul Revere house and the old North Church, where lanterns were hung to launch Revere's famous ride from Charleston. The North End has also become familiar to several generations of college sociology majors who were first introduced to its Italian flavor and its street gangs through William Whyte's depiction of the neighborhood in *Street Corner Society* (Whyte, 1943). Even more widely known is the prominence of Boston Yankee and Irish families, who have played so large a role in national, state, and local politics. From the Adams family to the Kennedy clan, from literary figures such as Nathaniel Hawthorne and Ralph Waldo Emerson to Edwin O'Connor's *The Last Hurrah*, Americans have witnessed the political succession from Yankee to Irish politicians; from Adams, Cabot, and Lodge, to Mayor James Curley, President John F. Kennedy, Senator Ted Kennedy, and former House Speaker Tip O'Neill.

Boston, like the Commonwealth of Massachusetts itself, is far more diverse ethnically than racially. Only 3.8% of the state population of 5.7 million is Black and 2.3% is Hispanic. As with other coastal cities in the United States, there has been a recent infusion of Asian immigrants, especially Vietnamese and Chinese, but the state population is largely white Caucasian (91.2% in 1980) from diverse European ethnic backgrounds.

Boston City proper is the twentieth largest city in the United States, with a population estimate for 1984 of 570,719, close in size to cities such as Milwaukee, Wisconsin; Columbus, Ohio; Jacksonville, Florida; and New Orleans, Louisiana. With massive urban renewal, and expanding suburban towns and cities, Boston City declined in population by 12% between the census of 1970 and that in 1980. The result of city size shrinkage along with suburban expansion can be seen in the fact that although Boston City proper is twentieth in size among American cities, the Boston SMSA is the tenth largest one in the country, with a population in 1980 of 2.8 million. This places the Boston SMSA close in population size rank with the SMSAs that included Dallas–Fort Worth, Houston, St. Louis, and Pittsburgh. Unlike the Texas SMSAs, however, which grew over the preceding decade by 25% (Dallas–Fort Worth) and 45% (Houston), the Boston SMSA, like the city at its hub, declined over the decade by close to 5%, making it similar to the population decline of the Pittsburgh SMSA (5.7% decline) and the St. Louis SMSA (2.3% decline).

Table 1.1 summarizes these SMSA figures, and shows, as well, the counterpart figures for the three largest SMSAs in the United States (New York, Chicago, and Los Angeles). Hemmed in by bay and rivers, the population of the city of Boston itself represents a small proportion of the total SMSA population (20%), with a population density of roughly 12,000 people per square mile, a marked contrast to the more recently

Table 1.1.   Population Size, Density, and Rank of Boston City and SMSA vs.
Selected Other U.S. Cities and SMSAS: 1980 [a]

| | Central City | | SMSA | | City Pop. | |
City/SMSA	Pop. Size (in 1000s)	Rank	Pop. Size (in 1000s)	Rank	as % of SMSA	Pop. Density (number of persons per square mile)
Comparable Size SMSAs						
Boston	571	20	2763	10	20%	12,143
Pittsburgh	424	30	2264	13	19%	7,708
St. Louis	453	26	2355	12	19%	7,428
Dallas–Fort Worth	1289	[b]	2975	8	43%	2,262
Houston	1595	5	2905	9	55%	2,868
Largest U.S. SMSAs						
New York	7072	1	9120	1	77%	23,262
Los Angeles	2967	3	7478	2	40%	6,353
Chicago	3005	2	7102	3	42%	13,353

[a] Almanac Atlas and Yearbook (1987).
[b] Dallas ranks seven in city size and Fort Worth ranks thirty-third.

developed, sprawling Texas cities whose population density is less than
a quarter that of Boston (e.g., 2,868 in Houston vs. 12,143 in Boston).
Traffic congestion and pollution pose serious problems for any future
growth of the Boston SMSA, though there is a long way to go before it
approximates the sheer population density of New York City, with its
23,262 persons per square mile.

A more qualitative profile of the Boston SMSA and how the city itself
differs in social composition from the suburban rings surrounding the
city within the SMSA can be inferred from Table 1.2, which shows the
sociodemographic characteristics of the total sample, Boston City proper, and the two inner and outer suburban rings around the city. The
most unique characteristic of the city is perhaps its religious, ethnic, and
racial composition. Catholics are the majority religious affiliation represented in our G2 sample of the Boston SMSA, evenly distributed across
the city and suburban rings. Like the state, the Boston SMSA is largely
white, though the distribution of Blacks and Asians is concentrated in
the city proper: Blacks were 18% of the city residents in our sample, but
less than 1% in the outer suburban rings. The Irish are well distributed
by region, as they now are in terms of socioeconomic status, while those
of Italian background are more prevalent in the city (13%) than in the
outer suburbs (9%). Other more recent migrants to the area are reflected
in the greater concentration of respondents from Middle Eastern, Hispanic, and Oriental backgrounds in the city than in the suburbs.[7]

On other sociodemographic characteristics, the Boston SMSA shares
characteristics with other large SMSAs in the United States: The city
proper has a larger proportion of young adults in their 20s, more single,
separated or divorced adults, those with no religious affiliation, and
those attending school, whereas the outer suburbs show a slight edge in
older, retired adults. Like the New England economy all told, very few
respondents in the G2 sample are unemployed, only 2% overall, with no
significant variation by residential location.

Table 1.2. Social-Demographic Characteristics of G2 Main Sample by Residential Location in Boston SMSA

Characteristic	Total Sample	Boston City	Inner Suburban Ring	Outer Suburban Ring
A. Age				
19–30	22.5	41.3	20.0	15.8
31–40	26.2	22.3	25.3	29.7
41–50	16.3	10.1	16.1	20.0
51–60	14.4	12.6	13.9	16.0
61–70	12.1	7.7	14.2	11.3
71 +	8.6	6.1	10.5	7.2
N	(1351)	(247)	(660)	(444)
B. Marital Status				
Never Married	18.6	37.2	18.4	8.6
Married	62.5	43.7	62.1	73.4
Separated/Divorced	10.8	13.4	10.7	9.5
Widowed	8.1	5.7	8.7	8.6
N	(1354)	(247)	(663)	(444)
C. Gender				
Female	57.8	55.9	58.8	56.5
Male	42.2	44.1	41.2	43.5
N	(1393)	(247)	(663)	(444)
D. Race				
White	93.5	77.4	96.5	98.0
Black	4.3	17.7	1.8	0.7
Asian	1.6	3.3	1.2	1.4
Other	0.5	1.6	0.5	—
N	(1342)	(243)	(659)	(440)
E. Religious Affiliation				
Catholic	53.8	54.9	53.6	53.5
Protestant	26.3	19.1	25.2	31.8
None	8.8	11.0	8.5	7.9
Jewish	6.8	5.3	8.8	4.5
Other	4.5	9.8	3.9	2.3
N	(1348)	(246)	(659)	(442)
F. Ethnicity [a]				
American	36.9	32.9	38.2	37.0
Irish	17.6	17.3	17.0	18.5
British	15.0	7.6	15.2	18.7
Italian	10.8	13.1	11.0	9.2
West European	7.2	4.2	7.3	8.8
Hispanic	4.0	11.4	2.6	1.8
Middle East	3.0	5.1	3.4	1.4
East European	2.7	3.4	2.5	2.5
Oriental	1.5	1.7	1.5	1.2
Other	1.5	3.4	1.2	0.9
N	(1316)	(237)	(646)	(433)

Table 1.2. (continued)

		Location in Boston SMSA		
			Inner	Outer
	Total	Boston	Suburban	Suburban
Characteristic	Sample	City	Ring	Ring
G. Employment Status				
Employed				
Full Time	53.1	53.8	53.8	52.9
Part Time	13.0	9.7	12.9	15.3
Not Employed				
Attending School	5.5	13.4	3.6	3.2
Keeping House	13.4	12.1	13.9	13.5
Retired	12.5	7.7	14.4	12.6
Unemployed	1.8	2.0	1.6	2.0
Other	0.7	1.2	0.8	0.5
N	(1391)	(247)	(661)	(444)

[a] Summarized from a detailed 68-country code based on the question: "To which nationality background or ethnic group do you feel you belong?"

A few of these social characteristics mask differences by gender. Table 1.3 shows the distribution of respondents by gender and residential location on marital and employment status. Separated, divorced, and widowed men show much less variation in residential pattern than do

Table 1.3. Marital and Employment Status of G2 Respondents by Gender and Residential Location in Boston SMSA (G2 Sample)

	Location in Boston SMSA					
	Boston City		Inner Ring		Outer Ring	
Characteristic	Men	Women	Men	Women	Men	Women
A. Marital Status						
Married	46.8	41.3	68.1	57.9	79.3	68.9
Never Married	43.1	32.6	20.9	16.7	8.3	8.9
Sep/Divorced	8.3	17.4	7.4	13.0	9.3	9.6
Widowed	1.8	8.7	3.7	12.3	3.1	12.7
N	(109)	(138)	(273)	(390)	(193)	(251)
B. Employment Status						
Employed						
Full time	63.3	46.4	73.5	38.6	77.7	33.9
Part time	4.6	13.8	4.0	19.0	2.6	25.1
Not Employed						
Attend School	15.6	11.6	3.7	3.6	3.1	3.2
Retired	10.1	5.8	16.2	13.1	15.0	10.8
Keep House	0.9	21.0	0.4	23.4	—	23.9
Unemployed	2.8	1.4	1.1	1.8	1.0	2.8
Other	2.8	—	1.1	0.5	1.0	2.8
	(109)	(138)	(272)	(389)	(193)	(251)

unattached women: Separated and divorced women are more prevalent in the city itself than in the suburban outer ring (17 vs. 10%), whereas widows are more prevalent in the suburbs than they are in the city. City men have a higher unemployment rate than outer ring suburban men (3 vs. 1%), whereas unemployment shows the reverse pattern for women, more unemployment in the suburbs than in the city. Part time employment absorbs fewer suburban than city men, while again, the reverse holds for women, 25% of the suburban women working part time to only 14% among city women.

Constructs and Measurement

Contemporary Parent–Child Relationship Measures

In a sociological tradition that draws on the work of George Homans on the human group (Homans, 1950) and the more recent research of Vern Bengtson on generations in the family (Bengtson & Schrader, 1982), we conceptualize the parent–child relationship in terms of three major dimensions of solidarity: sentiment, interaction, and similarity (Bengtson & Black, 1973). Our major construct of sentiment will be referred to as *Affectional Solidarity*, the feelings associated with the parent–child relationship in terms of affective closeness and intimacy vs. strain and tension. The construct of interaction, or associative behaviors, will be further specified into *Associational Solidarity* (frequency of contact) and *Functional Solidarity* (extent of help given to and received from the parent—or child). Similarity will be referred to as *Consensual Solidarity*, the perception of how alike ego is to the relationship partner on some basic values.

G2 respondents in the main sample provided ratings on these four dimensions of solidarity in terms of the current relationship to each living parent and each adult child. G1 parents provided identical ratings for their relationship to the adult child in our G2 sample, and G3 children did similarly for their relationship to each of their parents.

Table 1.4 provides information on the operationalization of these major constructs. The actual questions cited in the table are from the G2 interview concerning the relationship of respondents to their mothers (or mother substitutes). Identical questions were asked concerning the relationship to their fathers and to sons and daughters, as applicable. Several considerations guided the design of the specific items used to measure the solidarity constructs. Because many respondents would be rating two parents and several children, our measures had to be parsimonious. Thus, for example, to measure Associational Solidarity, interaction measures were limited to face-to-face visiting and telephone con-

Table 1.4. Dimensions of Current Parent-Child Solidarity: Constructs, Variables, and Operational Measures

Construct	Variable	Example of Operational Measure [a]
Associational Solidarity	Interaction Frequency	*Major items* "How often do you *see* your mother [MOTHER SUBSTITUTE] [b] these days?" "How often do you *speak* by *phone* to your mother [MOTHER SUBSTITUTE] these days?" (8 response categories from Never to Daily)
	Contact Satisfaction	*Supplementary items* "If you could do so, would you *like* to be in touch with your mother [MOTHER SUBSTITUTE] *more often, less often,* or *about the same as* now?"
	Contact Obligation	"Do you feel you *should be* in touch with your mother [MOTHER SUBSTITUTE] more often than you are these days?" (Yes, No, DK)
Consensual Solidarity	Value Consensus	"Parents and children are sometimes similar to each other in their views and opinions, and sometimes different from each other. Would you say you and your mother [MOTHER SUBSTITUTE] share *very similar* views, *similar* views, *different* views, or *very different* views, on (1) Religion (2) Politics (3) General outlook on life?"
	Topic Avoidance	"Sometimes parents and grown children *avoid* talking about certain topics when they are together. For example, do you *avoid* talking about *politics* with your mother [MOTHER SUBSTITUTE]?" Question repeated for (2) Money Matters, (3) Sex, (4) Religion, and (5) Personal Problems. (Yes, No, DK)
Affectional Solidarity	Affective Closeness	"The relationship between parents and children often varies from one stage of life to another. Imagine a scale from 1 to 7, where 1 means *very tense and strained,* and 7 means *very close and intimate.* What number between 1 and 7 best describes the relationship between your mother [MOTHER SUBSTITUTE] and yourself when you were . . . (1) about 10 years old, (2) about 16 years old, (3) about 25 years old, (4) Nowadays."

Functional Solidarity

Extent of Help Given/Received

"In the past year or so, have you *given* any of the following kinds of help to your mother [MOTHER SUBSTITUTE]? Just answer Yes or No."

1. Advice on a decision she had to make?
2. Help in connection with a job, such as telling her about a job prospect, or contacts that helped her in her job?
3. Taking care of her pets, plants, or home while she was away?
4. Financial help with money or a loan?
5. Helping out during an illness she had?
6. Fixing or making something for her, like painting a room, repairing an appliance, or sewing something?
7. Comforting her in a personal crisis of some kind that upset her?
8. Giving her a special gift of some kind?
9. Helping her with regular chores, such as shopping, yardwork, or cleaning?

(Identical items asked re *Received* from parent (or child), with "baby sitting" added to Regular Chores (item 9) and "you or someone in your family" added to Illness (item 5) for help given by parent to child.)

Help Reciprocity

Indices constructed separately for mothers and fathers, (or adult children) that count the number of types of Help exchanged reciprocally between child and parent.

---

[a] In the G2 and G3 samples, respondents were asked these questions separately for mother and father. In the G2 sample, respondents answered similar questions concerning each child over 18 years of age whom they reared, while in the G1 sample questions were asked only concerning the son or daughter in the G2 sample.
[b] Early in the interview, it was established who reared the respondent for most of their childhood and adolescence (up to age 16). The Solidarity questions were then couched in terms of the woman (or man) with primary responsibility; e.g., stepmother, grandfather.

31

tact. We bypassed who initiated the contact by merely asking: "How often do you *see* your mother these days?" and "How often do you *speak* by *phone* to your mother these days?" In this way we relied on two rather than four questions for the measures of interaction frequency.

Functional Solidarity was the most important construct in the study design, but here too, parsimony dictated that our measures be concise and easy to administer in both a personal and telephone interview. We opted for a "Yes–No" response format, with a diverse list of nine types of help that included both expressive (e.g., comfort) and instrumental help (e.g., money or a loan), phrased in a way that would apply equally well to a young adult child or an elderly parent. The time frame was left very broad, i.e., "in the past year or so," but no further probes were possible to tap frequency or amount of help on each of the nine types of help. The indices developed from these items therefore provide a crude measure of the *extent* of types of help provided or received. To minimize any tendency to link certain types of help to gender, examples were given to project the item's relevance to both mothers and fathers, or sons and daughters. For example, on household chores, we mentioned shopping and cleaning (which might be linked to women) and yardwork (which might be linked to men).

Retrospective Measures on Early Family Life

A variety of measures was developed to tap stress and solidarity of the families in which G2 respondents grew up, together with several dimensions of the role played by their parents in those early formative years. Three aspects of the parental role were measured: (1) the level of affection shown by each parent, (2) the extent to which each parent exercised disciplinary authority vis-à-vis the child, and (3) the extent to which the parents showed parental investment in childrearing as measured by training the child in a variety of skills.

Affection and authority are the two major dimensions of parental responsibility, often with significant variation by gender of the parent, with mothers higher on affection and fathers higher on authority. In addition, we wished to have some global measure of Family Cohesion not bound into a particular parent or child role, or the specific dyad our G2 respondents belonged to, but rather an overall measure of the family of origin as a social group. We selected three characteristics to measure this global quality of Family Cohesion: open display of affection among family members, cooperative teamwork, and a feeling that the family was interesting and fun to be with. As seen in Table 1.5, items were developed accordingly, with questions eliciting the extent to which each characteristic was felt to be applicable to the families in which respondents grew up.

Stress in the family of origin was also of concern, and a special measure was devised that would provide a summated index of the number of specific troubles that affected one or more members of the family. For this purpose, a special card was designed, listing 15 different types of troubles, so respondents merely had to call out the letters associated with the types of troubles their families of origin had experienced. As seen in Table 1.5, a great variety of difficulties were covered, including serious illness or a death in the family, alcohol or drug problems, trouble with the police or school authorities, a child going with the "wrong crowd," quarreling with relatives, between the parents, or among the children, and physical or sexual abuse.

Our initial goal in devising a measure of Skill Transmission by parents to the child was to tap traditional gender role socialization. Accordingly, we selected four items that dealt with Domestic Skills (cooking, cleaning, laundry, and sewing), traditionally associated with the socialization of daughters; four items dealing with Masculine Skills (use of power machinery, carpentry, fishing or hunting, and one or more sports); and four more diverse types of skills we thought might cohere as an index of Cognitive or Cultural Skills (music or singing, foreign language, reading, and arithmetic or math). A factor analysis showed satisfactory eigenvalues (1.00 or higher) for the four items tapping Domestic Skills, but "one or more sports" dropped out of the Masculine cluster, and the cognitive/cultural items showed significant loadings only on the reading and math items, resulting in a 2-item Cognitive Skill index, a 3-item Masculine Skill index, and a 4-item Domestic Skill index. Preliminary analysis also suggested that a combination of all the items could be construed as a proxy measure for Parental Investment in childrearing. G2 respondents also rated the general financial well being of their families of origin while they were growing up, and rated the happiness of their parents' marriage during their childhood and adolescence.

The last measure shown in Table 1.5 concerns the qualities respondents considered important in rearing children. For this dimension, however, respondents were asked to provide ratings only in their capacity as parents, not as children recalling what their own parents had stressed. Respondents in all three samples were asked these questions. Factor analysis showed three significant clusters on these childrearing qualities, which we have labeled Status, Conformity, and Autonomy.

Interpretive Variables

One large group of variables in the design of the study provides a variety of measures on age and health-related dimensions, on personal traits, and on kinship-related matters. Since the study was formulated in

Table 1.5. Major Variables Characterizing the Family of Origin " of G2 Respondents

Construct/Variable	Operational Definition
Family Cohesion	"Tell me if each of these statements describes your family during most of your childhood and adolescence. Would you say *most of the time, some of the time, or hardly ever?*" 1. The family had lots of fun together. 2. The family worked well together as a team. 3. Family members showed great concern and love for each other. 4. The family did interesting things together on weekends. (Summated score after factor analysis confirmed unidimensionality.)
Family Troubles	"Looking back over the years of growing up, did anyone in the family household(s) you lived in have any of the following problems? (HAND CARD A TO RESPONDENT). Just read out the letters to me of any problems that occurred at any time while you were growing up." A. Someone very sick for a long time. B. A serious drinking problem. C. Someone in trouble with the law or police. D. A serious drug problem. E. Bitter quarrels with relatives. F. An adult or a child died. G. Frequent bouts or a long bout of unemployment. H. The adults quarrelled a great deal. I. The children quarrelled a great deal among themselves. J. One or more adults worked at an extremely exhausting job. K. Someone had a very serious emotional or psychiatric problem. L. Someone got into the "wrong crowd." M. One or more children had serious troubles with school authorities. N. Physical or sexual abuse of a family member. O. One or more children was very rebellious against their parents. P. None of these.
Financial Well-Being	"How well off financially was your family most of the time you were growing up? Would you say *very poor, poor, just so-so, well off, or very well off?*"

Parental Skill Transmission

- D = Domestic Skills
- M = Masculine Skills
- C = Cognitive Skills
- * = Not included in any index

"Now I'd like to ask you about the extent to which your parents [PARENT SUBSTITUTE(S)] made special efforts to see that you learned a variety of skills while you were growing up, by teaching you themselves, or by your taking lessons. For example, how much effort did they make to see that you learned *one or more sports*—would you say *no effort at all, some effort, or a great deal of effort?*"

- *   1. One or more sports
- D   2. Cooking or baking
- *   3. How to sing or play a musical instrument
- M   4. How to use heavy machinery, such as a plow, tractor, or power tools?
- D   5. Cleaning house
- *   6. Speaking a foreign language
- M   7. Hunting or fishing
- D   8. Doing laundry
- C   9. How to read
- M 10. Carpentry or wood working of any kind
- D 11. Sewing or needlework
- C 12. Arithmetic or mathematics

Maternal Affection/Paternal Affection

"Now think of your mother [MOTHER SUBSTITUTE] as you knew her when you were growing up, and tell me how true each statement I read is. Would you say it is *very true, somewhat true, or not true at all* of your mother [MOTHER SUBSTITUTE]?"

1. She was easy to talk to.
2. She showed you a lot of love and affection.
3. She encouraged you to talk about your troubles.
4. She always had time for you when you needed her.

Maternal Authority/Paternal Authority

Same Question as above, with the following items:

1. She was a strict parent.
2. She always punished you when you did something wrong.
3. She gave you regular chores to do.
*4. She set high standards for you to meet.
   (Item not included in index because it did not show significant loading on either Affection or Authority construct.)

35

Table 1.5 (continued)

Construct/Variable	Operational Definition
Parental Marital Happiness	"How would you describe the relationship between your parents [PARENT SUBSTITUTES] when you were growing up? Would you say their marriage was *very happy, happy, just so-so, unhappy,* or *very unhappy?*"
Qualities Important in Rearing Child S = Status C = Conformity A = Autonomy * = Not included in any index	Question asked of Respondents in all three samples in their role as Parents. In G1 sample Question read: "In rearing children, how important was it to you at that time that your children develop each of the following qualities?—*not important, somewhat important,* or *very important* that they be . . . ." C 1. Respectful to adults S 2. Competitive * 3. Imaginative C 4. Obedient to parents S 5. Ambitious A 6. Independent C 7. Neat and clean S 8. Successful A 9. Self-reliant C 10. Well-behaved S 11. Athletic A 12. Open-minded * 13. Religious * 14. Sensitive * 15. Sociable (Asterisked items did not load significantly on any construct in factor analysis of 15 items)

a Comparable questions, appropriately phrased, were asked of G2 respondents concerning their families of procreation for many of the variables shown in this table. Cf. Table 1.8 for a detailed overview of which family or relationship variables were included in the three samples concerning families of origin (Respondent as child) or procreation (Respondent as parent).

a life course framework and we wished to explore several dimensions of the age variable, health, energy level, and subjective feelings about the stage of life respondents were at were important to tap. Table 1.6 shows the variety of measures developed for this purpose: a self-rating of current health on a 10-point scale, what age people feel like (Subjective Age), what age they would like to be (Desired Age), and an assessment of the past 5 years in the context of their life as far as they have lived it (Best/Worst Years of Life). The Bradburn Affect Balance scale was also included in the design; the Negative Affect Index was of particular interest, since Vern Bengtson reported it correlated highly with a standard Depression scale in his three-generation data set (Bengtson, personal communication, 1984).

Of particular interest was a measure of Drive, or energy level of our respondents, which seemed a likely proxy for direct physiological measures of metabolism and physical energy level. Factor analysis showed significant loading on this construct of Drive of self-ratings on a 1 to 6 scale depicting the extent to which respondents reported they were "hard-working," "energetic," and "easily aroused sexually." Because we had special interest in the very elderly in our samples, who may well have experienced considerable change on this dimension in recent years, we supplemented their ratings of themselves "nowadays" with a second rating on themselves "10 years ago." As seen in Chapter 2, this permitted an interesting comparison of perceived recent change in themselves with actual change (by comparing *retrospective* ratings of respondents in an older age group with *current* ratings of respondents now 10 years younger).

The second cluster of variables shown in Table 1.6 is of very special significance: measures of Expressivity and Dominance. As noted earlier in this chapter, researchers rely for the most part only on the sex of subjects as a variable even when they subscribe to the view that all gender differences are socially constructed. We wished to have an additional measure of sex and gender-linked personal traits that might go some distance in "explaining" gender differences as well as variation within gender. In the pretest, we used the Spence–Helmreich Masculinity and Femininity scales (Spence & Helmreich, 1978), but found the items to be so multidimensional they clearly could not meet our analysis purposes.[8] Hence, we selected traits as closely related to the core constructs as possible. (See Table 1.6 for the specific items in each index.) Rather than Femininity, we have labeled this construct Expressivity, and instead of Masculinity, we use Dominance. These will be seen to be very useful and interesting variables in the analysis, enriched by our measures on early family life and characteristics of parents while respondents were very young, which permits an analysis of the determi-

Table 1.6. Interpretive Variables and Their Operational Definitions

Variable	Operational Measure
A. Age and Health Related	
Health Status	"Think of a scale from 1 to 10, where 1 is a person with a *very serious health problem* and 10 is a person in the *very best health*. Where would you place yourself on this scale?" (Same item was asked concerning G2 respondents' spouses, mothers, and fathers.)
Subjective Age	"Many people feel older or younger than they actually are. What age do you *feel like most of the time?*"
Desired Age	"If you could be *any age you wanted to be* right now, what age would that be?"
Best/Worst Years of Life	"How would you describe the last five years? Would you say they were the *very best years, among the very best, much like always, among the worst,* or *the very worst years* of your life?"
Bradburn Affect Balance	"Now I will ask about events that may have happened to you in the past few weeks. For example, in the past few weeks, did you ever feel *pleased about having accomplished something?* Just answer *Yes* or *No* to all the things I will ask you."
	Negative Affect Items:
	1. So restless that you couldn't sit still.
	2. Bored.
	3. Depressed or very unhappy.
	4. Very lonely or remote from other people.
	5. Upset because someone criticized you.
	Positive Affect Items:
	1. Pleased about having accomplished something.
	2. That things were going your way.
	3. Proud because someone complimented you on something you had done.
	4. Particularly excited or interested in something.
	5. On top of the world.
	(In interview, the positive and negative items were alternated.)
Drive	(Self administered rating sheet at end of Vignette Booklet in Main Survey)
Drive Reduction	"As they grow older, some people remain pretty much the same kind of person they were in the past, while other people change as they grow older. On each of the following personal characteristics, circle the number that best describes you (A) Nowadays and (B) as you were 10 years ago. (Numeric scale from 0—Not at all to 6—Very Much)

1. Energetic
2. Easily Aroused Sexually
3. Hard-working

(Summated scale for Current Drive. Drive Reduction computed by substracting Current rating from rating 10 Years ago.)

B. Personal Traits, Gender-Related

Expressivity   Rating scale similar to Drive scale, 0 to 6 (Not at all to Very Much) for items:

1. Affectionate
2. Eager to help others
3. Concerned to please others
4. Able to express your deepest feelings

Dominance   Similar rating of items on scale from 0 to 6 for items:

1. Competitive
2. Like to be in charge of things
3. Ambitious
4. Aggressive

C. Kinship-Related

Kin Embeddedness   Weighted Index based on four items:

1. "What proportion of your friends did you meet through family members?" (Almost all, Some, None)
2. "When you think of the people you can count on in life, are they *mostly friends or mostly relatives?*" (Mostly relatives, mostly friends, both equally, neither)
3. "When you visit people, are you more likely to visit *friends* or to visit *relatives?*" (friends, relatives, both equally, neither, hardly ever visits)
4. "Who visits you more often? *Friends or Relatives?*" (friends, relatives, both equally often, neither, hardly ever has visitors)

(Item 1 scored Almost All = 2, Some = 1, None = 0; Items 2 thru 4 scored Mostly Relatives = 2, Both equally = 1, Neither or Mostly Friends = 0.)

Kin Salience   Index on salience during G2 Respondents' childhood, four relatives from mother's side, and four from father's side of the family: grandmother, grandfather, aunt, uncle. Question read:

"Many people say that other adults—besides their parents—were particularly important to them when they were very young; people they were very close to, or admired in some special way. Tell me whether each of the following people was important to you in any of these ways—*not at all important, somewhat important, or very important to you.*"

nants of Expressivity and Dominance. Furthermore, we were particularly interested in exploring whether gender per se produces differences in affective closeness and help exchange between the generations in a family, or whether it was these gender-linked personal traits that mattered. In other words, would men high on Expressivity report more intimate relations with parents (or children) than men low on Expressivity, and would high Expressivity evoke different responses from others?

The last two indices in Table 1.6 tap kinship-related characteristics of the G2 respondents. The Kin Embeddedness index was designed to measure the extent to which respondents' social life is closely linked to the world of family and kin ties or to friendship circles. Hence the items concern the balance of visiting or being visited between mostly relatives or mostly friends, the extent to which friends were acquired through kinship ties or not (e.g, a friend of a brother becoming ego's friend as well), and the overall assessment of whether it is mostly relatives or mostly friends people can "count on in life." The Kin Salience index does not pertain to the current life circumstances of respondents, but rather the extent to which relatives other than the parents were of special socioemotional importance to respondents in their youth. The battery of items on this variable was interwoven with nonkin as well as kin (e.g., a friend of one's mother, father of a friend, or a teacher), but the Kin Salience index is restricted to aunts, uncles, and grandparents.[9]

Family of Procreation of G2 Respondents

All the measures described thus far concern G2 respondents in their roles as children, either as adult children vis-à-vis still living parents, or to earlier years when they were growing up. In much the same way, G2 respondents were interviewed concerning their roles as parents, again with reference to their current relationship with each of their children and to their past roles as parents if their childrearing is now behind them. The only modification of question format and array of measures obtained was a function of the child's age. For children of G2 respondents currently under the age of 18, information was obtained on a limited range of variables: each child's age, sex, and a rating of the affective closeness of the relationship between the child and the respondent-parent, the other parent, and to each of the child's four grandparents (parents and parents-in-law of the respondents). For each child over the age of 18, G2 respondents rated the relationship on the same solidarity indicators shown above for their relationship to each of their parents: Interaction Frequency, Contact Satisfaction, Contact Obligation, Value Consensus, Topic Avoidance, Affective Closeness, and Extent of Help Given and Received.

Table 1.7 brings together, in one convenient place, all the major variables included in the three samples: Panel A includes all the measures concerning the early family years and Panel B includes the variables bearing on contemporary relationships between parents and children. Asterisks in the body of the table indicate the inclusion of a particular variable in one or more of the three samples: for example, the questions used to measure Family Cohesion, shown in the first row of the table, were asked not only in all three samples, but in the case of G2 and G3 respondents, the same questions were asked concerning both the respondents' families of origin and their families of procreation (if they were married and had at least one child). Hence, G1 parents of our

Table 1.7. Sample Sources of Major Family and Relationship Variables [a]

Variable	G1 Sample	G2 Sample		G3 Sample	
	G1 as Parent	G2 as Child	G2 as Parent	G3 as Child	G3 as Parent
A. Past: Family or Pt–Ch Relationship Variables					
Family Cohesion	*	*	*	*	*
Family Troubles		*	*		
Parental Affection + [b]	*	*		*	
Parental Authority +	*	*		*	
Affective Closeness to Child 10/16/25 +	*	*	*	*	
Parental Marital Happiness		*			*
Skill Transmission to Child		*	*		
Financial Well-Being	*			*	
Qualities Considered Important in Child-Rearing	*		*	*	*
Affective Closeness to Grandparents in Childhood +				*	
B. Current: Family or Pt–Ch Relationship Variables					
Interaction Frequency +	*	*	*	*	
Contact Satisfaction +	*	*	*	*	
Contact Obligation +	*	*	*	*	
Value Consensus +	*	*	*	*	
Topic Avoidance +	*	*	*	*	
Affective Closeness Parent–Child +	*	*	*	*	
Gdpt–Gdchild +	*			*	
Help Received/Given +	*	*	*	*	
Help Reciprocity +		*		*	
Mileage Distance to Parent/Each Child		*	*		

—ᵃ Rated by both partners to the parent–child relationship, within family of origin or family of procreation.
--→ Potential cross-generational transmission from family of origin to family of procreation.
  ᵇ "+" Indicates measures were obtained separately for mothers and fathers when respondents reported as children in G2 and G3 samples. Control for gender of child and parent obtained comparable gender-specific dyads when respondents reported as parents themselves.

main sample respondents were interviewed only concerning their roles as parents, whereas G2 and G3 respondents were asked about their roles as parents and as children.

Solid lines joining two asterisks indicate on which variables we obtained data from both the parent and child. Again using the first row on Family Cohesion as an example, it can be seen that Family Cohesion questions were asked for two different parent–child dyads: G1 parents and G2 adult children comprise the first dyad (in which G1 respondents are describing their family of procreation, G2 respondents their family of origin), and G2 parents and G3 adult children comprise the second dyad (here G2 respondents are describing their family of procreation, and G3 respondents their family of origin). It is clear that these two views of the same relationship are concentrated on variables dealing with the current relationship between parents and children, with fewer pairs of identical measures for past family relationships.

The dashed lines shown in Table 1.7 identify the variables with which we can explore cross-generational transmission, by asking if a characteristic of G2 respondents' families of origin shows any impact on the same characteristic of their families of procreation: for example, are G2 respondents who grew up in highly cohesive families more likely to also have highly cohesive families of procreation? Is Trouble-proneness transmitted from one generation to the next? These examples of cross-generational transmission involve the influence of a parental role in one generation on the parental role in the next generation.

A second analysis path to be pursued concerns the influence of variables in Panel A on variables in Panel B: in this instance, the question concerns the extent to which early family experience continues to exert influence on the quality of the parent–child relations a decade or more later: for example, to what extent, if any, is current affective closeness between parents and children minimal if years earlier, the family had experienced a lot of stress, or parents had shown little affection toward the child? And is there a difference between parents and adult children in the extent to which past family characteristics affect the current parent–child relationship?

Table 1.8 is patterned in much the same way as Table 1.7: It provides a convenient overview of the array of social–demographic and personal–attitudinal variables we can bring to bear in the analysis, together with an indication of their presence or absence in the three samples. As a quick inspection will show, most of the variables were included in the instruments used for all three samples, and on many of them, questions were asked concerning the spouse as well as the respondent: for example, we asked for the religious affiliation of respondents as well as their spouses in all three samples. By contrast, personal earnings were ob-

Table 1.8. Current Social–Demographic and Personal Characteristics of Respondents in the G1, G2, and G3 Samples [a]

	G1 Sample		G2 Sample		G3 Sample	
Characteristic	Self or Mo	Spouse or Fa	Self	Spouse	Self	Spouse
A. Social–Demographic						
Age	**	**	*	*	*	*
Educational Attainment	*	*	*	*	*	*
Employment Status	*	*	*	*	*	*
Ethnicity	*	*	*	*	*	*
Financial Well-Being		*		*		*
Income						
Total Hshold		*		*		*
Personal Earnings			*			
Marital Status	*		*		*	
No. of Children	*		*		*	
Race	*	*	*		*	*
Religious Affiliation	*	*	*	*	*	*
Religious Services Attendance	*	*	*	*	*	*
B. Personal/Attitudinal						
Attitudes on Contemporary Issues						
Abortion	*		*		*	
Contraception	*		*		*	
Religious Instruction	*		*		*	
Women's Rights	*		*		*	
Best/Worst Years	*		*		*	
Current Marital Happiness	*		*		*	
Desired Age	*		*		*	
Dominance	*		*		*	
Drive-Nowadays			*			
10 Years Ago			*			
Expressivity	*		*		*	
Health Rating	**	**	*	*		
Kin Embeddedness			*			
Kin Saliance			*			
No. Friends			*			
Political Orientation	*	*	*	*	*	*
Positive/Negative Affect	*		*		*	
Subjective Age	*		*		*	

[a] (*) Data from this sample re self and, if married, spouse where shown. (**) Questions asked of G2 respondents re Self, Mother and Father; G1 respondents re Self and Spouse.

tained only from G2 respondents, but total household annual income was obtained in all three samples. *The reader might make special note of the two tables—Tables 1.7 and 1.8—as convenient references to lists of available variables in the three samples to consult in the course of reading the chapters to follow.*

Normative Obligations

One major dimension of the study design remains to be described. Although the study was to concentrate on the relationship between parents and adult children, we wished to place this core family relationship in a larger context of less closely related kin to ascertain the extent to which obligations adults feel toward parents and children exceed those toward aunts or grandparents, cousins or siblings. Indeed, we thought it would also be of interest to compare obligations to kin with obligations to such nonkin as friends, neighbors, or former spouses.

To retain our concern for gender on this dimension of the design would require, at a minimum, that all kin types be specified by gender. Just as we distinguished between mothers and fathers, and sons and daughters, so too it would be necessary to specify the gender of siblings or grandparents as well. Further, we thought obligations might vary by whether a particular kinperson was married or not. It could be, for example, that adults feel obliged to help an unmarried sibling to a greater extent than a married sibling who, after all, had a spouse to provide whatever help was needed. Then too, we thought it highly likely that the level of obligation adults feel toward others may depend on the circumstances involved, and how long a need for help was likely to persist. For example, would the degree of felt obligation vary if a relative had surgery and would be laid up for a long time, compared to the same relative who needed help for only a few weeks?

But if we wished to select even two kinds of crises that relatives might face, each specified by short or long duration, and we restricted the types of kin and nonkin just to say six relatives (parent, child, sibling, grandparent, grandchild, cousin) and three nonkin (neighbor, friend, ex-spouse), each specified by gender and marital status, and with one rating scale on obligation level, we would require 144 questions ($2 \times 2 \times 9 \times 2 \times 2$). This was clearly impossible in a design that required a great many other measures on core variables.

It is precisely this kind of problem for which the factorial survey (or vignette) method is ideally suited (Rossi & Nock, 1982). Indeed, it was the realization that this was the method of choice that led to the study becoming a collaborative effort between us, because Peter Rossi was the originator of the method and had considerable experience in using it across a wide range of substantive issues. Kinship obligations seemed a natural application of the method, because there was reason to believe that normative obligations to kin were highly structured by degree of closeness of the relationship, but with variation by further characteristics such as gender, marital status, and the nature of the life circumstances requiring help or celebration. The method would also permit a considerable expansion in the number of kin types we could include in the design. This meant, for example, that we could add such kin types as stepparents and stepchildren, who are quite prevalent in a society with high divorce and remarriage rates. The method would also permit us to specify the connecting link between a respondent and a relative in our array, i.e., whether the relative was related through a mother or a father, such as "your mother's mother" (maternal grandmother) or "your father's brother" (paternal uncle). Because of our prediction concerning the central role women play in the nuclear family and the larger kindred, this specification would permit us to test whether relatives linked to ego through women evoke higher obligations than relatives linked through men.

Full details of the design of the vignettes will be covered in Chapter 4. Here it suffices to indicate the dimensions built into the vignettes, and where and how they were used in the fielding of the study. This technique requires a specification of the major *dimensions* to be explored, each further divided into specific *levels*: e.g., the dimension of life circumstances was specified by seven *levels*, four of them *crisis* situations (a serious personal problem, unemployment, a household fire, and surgery) and three of them *celebrations* (a birthday, moving into a new place, and winning an award of some kind). The major dimensions in the vignette design were, in order of predicted importance: kin or nonkin type, each specified by gender and marital status, life circumstance (type of crisis or celebration), and duration (in the case of crises). A computer program compiles vignettes in which the levels of these five dimensions are randomly combined, and respondents are asked to rate the degree of obligation they would feel to the person under the circumstance described in the vignette. A typical vignette might read:

> Your married brother has undergone major surgery and will be disabled for a very long time. This problem is straining his financial resources.
> How much of an obligation would you feel to offer him some financial help?

A numeric rating scale follows this question, ranging from "0" (No obligation at all) to "10" (Very strong obligation). Two types of obligation ratings were built into the design: an *instrumental* obligation, in the form of financial help, as illustrated above, or an *expressive* obligation, for which the question was "How much of an obligation would you feel to offer him comfort and emotional support?" Our expectation was that respondents would feel more obligation to provide expressive than instrumental help to others in need.

Each G2 respondent was given a booklet containing 31 vignettes, which was self-administered at the end of the personal interview. The interviewer checked a practice vignette (the one shown above), to be sure the respondent understood the task, and checked over the personal interview schedule while the respondent filled out the booklet, a procedure that took an average of 15 minutes. The last page of the vignette booklet contained the personal trait items that were used in the indices on Expressivity, Dominance, and Drive, described above.[10]

The vignette data provided a rich analysis of the macrostructural organization of normative obligations to kin, as well as of the level of obligation felt by individual respondents, as measured by their mean obligation level across the 31 vignettes they rated. Hence, the vignette data are analyzed separately at both the aggregate and individual levels, and the mean rating is used in the analysis of other dimensions of the parent–child relationship described above.

Organization of the Book

The substantive chapters of the book are organized into three major sections. The first section (Part II) focuses on the biopsychological and social structure dimensions of age, our major indicator of phase of the life course. Chapter 2 deals with the biopsychological dimensions of age. We chart the life course profile of the three personal trait indices—Expressivity, Dominance, and Drive—with special attention to the Drive Index as the characteristic most relevant to the aging process. The chapter also includes an analysis of Subjective and Desired Age in relation to actual age, and the overall assessment made by respondents of recent years in their lives, charting how assessments of "the best" or "worst years" of one's life vary by age and other related characteristics such as marital status and the timing of widowhood.

Chapter 3 focuses on macrostructural dimensions of age, in an effort to locate our respondents in historical context, by pinpointing the major historical markers of their lives, and illustrating the impact of historical context for the few instances in which our data permit such a demonstration. A second emphasis of the chapter is to show cohort differences that are reflected in the particular sample of parents and adult children in the study, and the economic resources that differentiate the lives of adult children and their parents at various ages. The last topic in Chapter 3 is the structure of the multigenerational lineages within which our respondents are embedded, and how the composition of these lineages changes over the life course.

Part III of the book consists of two chapters on normative obligations to kin and nonkin: as described above, Chapter 4 focuses on the macrostructural organization of kin norms, and Chapter 5 on the determinants of levels of felt obligation on an individual level of analysis.

The heart of the analysis of the parent–child relationship will be found in Part IV on intergenerational solidarity. In Chapter 6 we show how the various dimensions of solidarity are related, and how similar or different the ratings are when obtained from parents as opposed to adult children. We also describe the analysis model in terms of which we assume the several dimensions of parent–child solidarity are related, a model that dictated the sequence of analysis reported in Chapters 7 through 9.

Chapter 7 focuses on affectional closeness, using ratings of closeness to parents, children, parents-in-law, and children-in-law, and between grandparents (G1) and grandchildren (G3). The biographic roots of current intimacy or strain in the parent–child relationship are traced to early family life, and we test whether family characteristics and experiences during the formative years show persistent effects on current relations. We also report three examples of cross-generational transmission, and one example of intergenerational influence, i.e., the effect of parents' attitudes on adult children's attitudes on contemporary issues and the reciprocal effect of children's attitudes on parental attitudes.

Chapters 8 and 9 focus on social interaction (Chapter 8) and help exchange (Chapter 9) between the generations. Detail is provided on the determinants of interaction frequency (controlling of course for geographic distance between parents and adult children), as of help exchange patterns (controlling for distance and interaction frequency, which together set the opportunity pattern within which help exchange is analyzed.)

Family and kin ties do not end with one's death; many of us inherit a variety of goods of sentimental value from our parents and other relatives, and make provision for doing similarly by writing wills. It seems fitting, therefore, in a book with a life course framework, to end the substantive analysis in Chapter 10 with some detail on inheritance and provision for kin in actual or intended wills reported by our respondents.

Chapter 11 draws together the numerous threads of the findings reported in this volume, with some suggestions for directions future research could appropriately take to amplify and extend our work.

Notes

1. For a full and brilliant exploration of this point, see Miriam Johnson's book, *Strong Mothers, Weak Wives* (1988).

2. This is in fact, a thesis elaborated by Annette Lawson (1988). In a study of extramarital relationships, Lawson argues that contemporary women have moved toward a male script in pre- and extramarital sex behavior, while men are showing a lesser degree of change toward a female script in intimate communication. Hence Lawson speaks of the "masculinization of sex" combined with a "feminization of love" as a particular mark of gender relations in contemporary western societies.

3. For an excellent overview of recent changes in behavior and attitudes of American women and men, see McLaughlin et al. (1988). For an example of current research on shared parenting, see Kimball (1988).

4. This is particularly the case among American social scientists; in France and Germany, researchers are less skeptical and believe a great deal can be learned from biographic data.

5. For a fuller discussion of the limitations of longitudinal studies, see A. S. Rossi (1989).

6. A further budgetary consideration argued for the selection of the Boston SMSA rather than any other metropolitan area: The Center for Survey Research of the Boston campus of the University of Massachusetts had considerable expertise in sampling and fielding of social surveys in the Commonwealth on which we could rely. The distance between Amherst and Boston being only 90 miles also ensured that we could supervise the field operation with ease, and reduce postage costs by relying on intercampus mail service for the several thousand questionnaires and vignette forms that would flow between our research offices and the survey center offices.

7. In our G2 sample of 1393 adults, 311 respondents claim an ethnic identification as Irish, compared to 187 who identify themselves as Italian. These are the two largest ethnic categories represented in the sample, contributing to the large 54% with a Catholic religious affiliation. Only 66 respondents are Black, and 22 identify themselves as belonging to an Oriental racial group. Fewer than 25 respondents define themselves ethnically as Russian, Polish, Swedish, or Canadian.

8. Factor analysis of the pretest data suggested not two clusters of Femininity and Masculinity, but six latent constructs that cut across the two expected constructs. We do not know why this result was obtained, unless our more heterogeneous sample of much older adults is responsible. Most of the subjects Spence and Helmreich used were young high school and college students.

9. These relatives were carefully specified by whether they were related to respondents through their mothers or their fathers, because we wished to see if a particular grandparent was more apt to be cited than another. The expectation, of course, was that links through mothers to other female kin would be of particular emotional salience, such as mother's mother (maternal grandmother) or mother's sister (maternal aunt), reflecting the greater intimacy and involvement of women with other women in the kindred than men have with their kinsmen. These data were useful in an analysis of the obligations respondents feel toward kin other than parents or children, for as Chapter 5 will show, those high on Kin Salience show higher levels of normative obligations toward secondary kin than do those who did not report special emotional significance of kin in their youth. We will also report, in Chapter 7, that respondents have closer ties to maternal grandparents, especially mother's mother, than to paternal grandparents, a pattern much stronger when the parental marriage is not a happy one.

10. In the telephone interviews, the Expressivity and Dominance self-ratings were included in the interview schedule. No vignettes were administered to G1 parents or G3 children, because we thought they would be too difficult to administer by phone.

The Organization of Lives: Age, Aging, and Kinship — Part II

The central theme of this book concerns the relationship between parents and adult children. But an appropriate place to begin our story is with the individual respondents themselves, and what life is like for them in the very varied positions they occupy on the adult life course. Some are unmarried young adults of 20, still living with their parents, others are mature young adults just beginning their own families, and still others are elderly widows in their 80s. It is a sociological truism to say that individual lives are embedded in social networks of kin, neighbors, friends, and co-workers, and we shall see evidence of such embeddedness in the intergenerational relations that are the major focus of the study.

But there is also an interior life that matters, and an outer shell of a biological organism that houses that interior life. Much that occupies our interior dialogue with ourselves concerns our bodies and our feelings. In adolescence most people welcome each sign of physical and psychological maturity and their daydreams center on the lives they hope to lead in the future. When our years are numbered, we are not likely to welcome signs of physical change in our bodies, for they foretell our own mortality, and our interior musings may center on past experiences rather than hopes for the future. Growing up is an exciting adventure oriented to a bright but yet unknown personal future; past midlife, however, aging is a bittersweet experience, perhaps rich with a sense of accomplishment, but also fraught with regrets, sorrows, and nostalgia.

In the introductory chapter, we made the point that one cannot approach the variable of age in cross-sectional studies with any narrow angle of vision, but must be alert to the fact that age can carry many meanings: changes in social status attend passage through life; individuals carry the mark of the families they grew up in and the birth cohort they belong to. A few years difference in year of birth can affect our life chances in terms of military service, GI educational benefits, mortgage rates for homeowners, pension benefits, and even whether and when we marry and the size of the families we rear. One cohort may have a high childless rate because early adulthood took place during the lean

49

hard years of the Depression, as was true for today's elderly, but a later cohort, like today's young adults, may show an equally high childless rate because childbearing and childrearing are viewed less positively today compared to 50 years ago, and the costs in terms of interrupted careers and deferred personal gratification have tipped the balance to a voluntary decision to remain "child free" for many young adults in the 1980s.

Age differences are notoriously complex to interpret, because they may compound maturational with cohort and historical effects. Nevertheless, we shall attempt to make such distinctions, and to seek an understanding of how life is viewed in comparative terms by adults at various stages of the life course. Those topics that seem most strongly to reflect maturational change will be the focus of Chapter 2, and those that depict social structural characteristics will be the focus of Chapter 3. Biopsychological constructs will therefore be the focus of Chapter 2, in an effort to understand how individuals feel about their phase of the life span at the time we interviewed them in 1985. We introduce our personal trait measures of Expressivity and Dominance, and a measure we believe taps aging more directly, an index of Drive. The items in this index—how energetic, hard-working, and easily aroused sexually respondents judged themselves to be—were rated in terms of "today," and, retrospectively, "10 years ago." The discrepancy between the two ratings provides an insight into self-perceptions of change that attends the aging process. Several other measures also provide a window on the subjective experience of aging: One is the discrepancy between chronological age and the subjective age adults "feel" like; another is the discrepancy between actual age and the age adults would "like to be," a discrepancy we use as a measure of Age or life phase Dissatisfaction. The most direct individual assessment from our respondents is their judgment of the past 5 years as among the "best" or "worst" years of their lives.

It is not always possible to make empirical linkages between subjective feeling states and social role compliance. Many of us put in hard days of work when our preference would be to remain in bed. Social obligations and social scripts may preclude disclosure of how we "really" feel; keeping a "stiff upper lip" and trying to be cheerful and pleasant to others when we are feeling deeply depressed are experiences most of us have had. We believe it is important to penetrate some of the subjective phenomenology of aging, precisely because parents and children are at very different phases of the life course. However intimate or interdependent they are in social interaction, there is an average of 28 years separating parents from children. There is obviously an enormous developmental gulf between a 5-year-old child and a 33-year-old parent.

The subjective and social meaning of the age difference between parent and child will undergo dramatic changes as parent and child move across their respective life trajectories. When the child is 33 and the parent is a healthy 61, the gap between them may narrow in subjective terms, and change yet again when the child is 61 and the parent 89. It is not always realized that when we note differences between young adults and late middle-aged adults, or middle-aged adults and elderly persons, we have tapped contrasts that are highly relevant to an understanding of the parent-adult child relationship as well.

This point applies not only to the biopsychological changes involved in adult development, but to more formal structural changes in economic resources or the size and composition of a kindred as well, and it is to these more formal variables that our attention will be directed in Chapter 3. They provide the structural context within which intergenerational relations and interaction take place. Their relevance can be seen in the example of the life course trajectory in personal earnings. One critical cohort difference between today's elderly and young adults is in educational attainment levels. But it takes time in adulthood for education to pay off in terms of earnings. Whether an individual is a high school or a college graduate makes less difference in personal earnings when an individual is in their 20s than when he or she is in their 40s. Earnings go up between the ages of 20 and 45, and they begin to drop after the age of 50, dramatically so among those over the age of 65 at all educational levels. Putting a parent–child relationship against this life course curve in earnings helps to demonstrate the shifting balance in personal economic resources between the two generations: when a child is 25 and a parent 53, the child is at a low point of earnings and the parent at a peak of earnings, but when the child is 40 and the parent is 68, this balance is reversed, for now the child is enjoying peak earnings and the parent is living at a reduced income level. This shift in relative economic resources over the life course is clearly a fundamental structural characteristic with implications for the nature of help exchange between the generations, and hence of importance to describe early in the unfolding story we have to tell.

Much the same point applies to changing kindred size and composition across the life course. The point is frequently made that American families now typically contain four or even five generations, but, strangely enough, this has been an interpretation of the significance of increased longevity, not a conclusion drawn from empirical evidence. It is certainly possible to find five-generation families, or 30-year-old grandmothers, or 70-year-old daughters caring for 95-year-old mothers, but a moment's reflection suggests how infrequent any of these three social phenomena are. How many births take place at 15 years of age in two proximate generations? Very very few. With an average of 28 years separating parents from children, a woman would be 84 when a great-grandchild is born, and such a four-generation family is not likely to last very long before the greatgrandmother dies.

Chapter 3 will place our G2 respondents in this larger context of their lineage and show how prevalent multigenerational lineages are and how they change with life course phase. Although any portrait that relies on the current ages of respondents in a cross-sectional survey is only a still snapshot that does not allow for future cohort changes in longevity, it provides at least some empirical evidence on an important point that does not exist in any other data source, and a useful caveat against the claim of vastly expanded multigenerational families in the United States.

One general issue needs to be confronted before turning to the chapters in this part of the book: the use of the variable of age. Our decision was to rely on chronological age rather than a more sociological definition based on phase of a family life cycle for several reasons. Precisely because we are aware of potential cohort and historical effects, the use of chronological age permits us to make a direct link to the birth cohort or historic era during which respondents of various ages were at critical developmental phases of their lives. This takes on special importance because we have relied quite heavily on retrospective questions concerning the families of origin and of procreation in a representative age sample.

Figure II.1 helps clarify the significance of this point. The figure shows the most common use we shall make of respondents' age, into six decades of the life course, i.e., a division into those in their 20s, 30s, 40s, 50s, 60s, or 71 or older. The oldest group spans a wider age range than any other simply because there were only 118 respondents 71 years or older in our sample. A finer age classification could have been used for young adults, because there are 315 respondents in their 20s and 365 in their 30s. We decided against a finer age distinction, however, because there is so much variation in the timing of life transitions in early adulthood. It seemed preferable to use employment status, marital status, and childedness as controls within the decade-long age categories.

Figure II.1 places the lives of our respondents into an historic context, by charting the years during which respondents in each of the six age groups were growing up and the years during which they were in turn rearing children of their own. These phases of the life course were arbitrarily defined, with the "growing up" years defined as from birth to 16 years of age, and the years "rearing children" similarly defined as from birth to 16 years of age of the children, among parents between 22 and 30 years of age at the birth of children, the age span when most

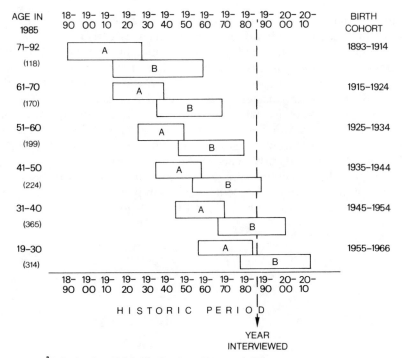

AGE IN 1985	18-90	19-00	19-10	19-20	19-30	19-40	19-50	19-60	19-70	19-80	19-90	20-00	20-10	BIRTH COHORT

71–92 (118)   A   B   1893–1914

61–70 (170)   A   B   1915–1924

51–60 (199)   A   B   1925–1934

41–50 (224)   A   B   1935–1944

31–40 (365)   A   B   1945–1954

19–30 (314)   A   B   1955–1966

HISTORIC PERIOD

YEAR INTERVIEWED

[a]Defined as from birth to 16 years of age: Boxes marked A.

[b]Arbitrarily defined as years from birth to 16 years of age of children among parents between 22 and 30 years of age at birth of children: Boxes marked B.

Figure II.1. Historic era during which G2 respondents were growing up[a] and rearing children[b] by chronological age in 1985.

births occurred. The birth cohorts represented by each of the six age groups are shown in the right-hand column. Thus, for example, our oldest respondents, aged 71 to 92 in 1985, were born between 1893 and 1914. Hence when they reported about the families in which they grew up, they were referring to the years from 1893 to 1930, and when they described their own childrearing, they were referring to a very long stretch of years from 1915 to 1960. A woman 92 when she was interviewed in 1985 was born in 1893, turned 16 in 1909, 22 in 1915, and 30 in 1923. If she had a first birth at 22 and a last birth at 30, she was rearing children from 1915 to 1939, when the youngest child would have turned 16.

The vertical dash line in Figure II.1 marks the year, 1985, when most of our interviews took place. That marker helps emphasize the point that for the majority of our respondents over 40 years of age, data concerning the rearing of their own children refers to past events just as much as data concerning their childhood and adolescence, whereas for those in their 20s, childrearing was either at a very early stage in 1985, or will begin only sometime in the 1990s. A young man who was 20 in 1985 belongs to the 1965 birth cohort, turned 16 in 1981, may marry at 30 in 1995, and have a child who becomes 16 in the year 2013. Hence the potential historic canvas against which we will be depicting the lives of our respondents covers 100 years, from an old woman of say 78 describing what her early family was like in the early years of this century, to a young man of 20 informing us about what qualities he hopes to instill in his teenagers in the early years of the twenty-first century.

But now, let us get acquainted with our variously aged respondents and explore how they describe themselves in personal traits and subjective feelings, and how they assessed their stage of life.

Age and Aging _____ 2

An old widowed fisherman in Maine, in conversation with a visitor:

"There ain't nobody here but me. I try to keep things looking right, same's poor dear left 'em . . . None of 'em thought I was goin' to get along alone, no way, but I wa'nt goin' to have my house turned upsi' down an' all changed about . . . I said I was goin' to make shift, and I have made shift. I'd rather tough it out alone."

"You must miss her very much?" I said at last.

"I do miss her," he answered, and sighed again. "Folks all kep' repeatin' that time would ease me, but I can't find it does. No, I miss her just the same every day."

"How long is it since she died?" I asked.

"Eight year now, come the first of October . . . I can't get over losin' of her no way nor no how . . . There, 't ain't so much matter, I shall be done afore a great while. No, I sha'n't trouble the fish a great sight more."

Sarah Orne Jewett, *The country of the pointed firs*, pp. 121–122

Introduction

The epigram for this chapter captures the mood of many elderly widowed adults, still feeling the loss of their life's partner in an acute way after 8 years, and resigned to the short time remaining to their own lives. Thus, the passage expresses the bittersweet quality of life in its ebbing years, a quality novelists seem better able to portray than the social scientists who study the elderly.

We begin this chapter with the example of a widowed elderly man, not because our emphasis will be confined to the elderly, but because the sense of loneliness and resignation captured by Sarah Jewett is a prescient indicator of our analysis results on age and aging. Any description of a stage of life is implicitly if not explicitly comparative, and our task in this chapter is to provide an overview of the psychological and physiological characteristics that differentiate one age group from others. As will be seen in what follows, the major inflection points along the life course on the biopsychological constructs we have measured occur in late middle age and old age.

We shall examine age differences among the adults in the main G2 sample of Bostonians on a variety of measures that tap their interior life as they viewed themselves when they were interviewed in 1985, how they believe they have changed over the preceding decade, what the balance is of negative and positive moods that characterizes their daily lives, how old they feel and what age they would like to be, and how they assess the past 5 years compared to the whole stretch of their lives as far as they have lived them.

Age Trends in Personal Traits

In the best of all possible worlds, a researcher interested in bio-psychological constructs would use standardized personality tests and direct biomedical measures of health and physical well being. This was not possible in a study designed to measure several dimensions of the relationships between respondents and each of their parents and each of their children. We had to rely on self-ratings by respondents them-selves, on constructs deemed relevant to an analysis focused on gender and age differences.

Two of the three constructs are relevant to gender analysis: Expres-sivity and Dominance, roughly analogous to psychological measures of Femininity and Masculinity. The third construct was Drive, which we considered most likely to indicate the aging process. The data were obtained in the main sample from a self-administered rating sheet ap-pended to the vignette booklets, which asked respondents to circle a number between "0" and "6" that best described themselves (0 indicat-ing Not at All, 3 Somewhat, 6 Very Much).[1] For items that were candi-dates for the Drive Index, we asked respondents to rate themselves as they were "10 years ago" as well as "nowadays," to gauge the extent to which adults are aware of recent changes in themselves.[2]

Factor analysis of the items confirmed the presence of the three latent constructs we wished to measure, except for one candidate for the Drive index, "thinking about the past," which did not show any loading on any latent factor and was therefore discarded.[3] The specific traits includ-ed in each index are as follows:

Expressivity: Affectionate, concerned to please others, able to express your deepest feelings, eager to help others.

Dominance: Competitive, ambitious, aggressive, like to be in charge of
    things.
Drive: Energetic, hard-working, easily aroused sexually.

Figure 2.1 shows the mean scores on the three indices by age, separately for women and for men. The graph readily shows that Dominance and Drive decline sharply by age among women, whereas among
men only Drive is age related. Expressivity shows no significant relationship to age for either men or women, but as with more standard
measures of Femininity and Masculinity, women score markedly higher

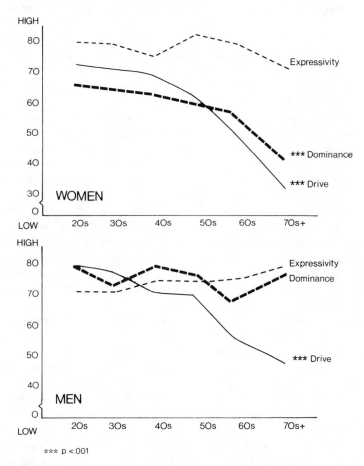

Figure 2.1. Mean scores on Expressivity, Dominance, and Drive, by age and
    gender of G2 adults (G2 sample) (scores converted to 0–100).

on Expressivity than do men, and men higher on Dominance than women.

We have no data that could definitively distinguish between the physiological and the social–psychological components of the three indices. That average scores on Drive decline sharply for both sexes from the middle years on is presumptive evidence that this index reflects some aspects of the aging process. There has been some suggestion in the literature on sex roles and personality in relation to aging, that as they get older women become more assertive and men more tender and nurturant (Gutmann, 1968, 1975; Neugarten, 1973; Neugarten & Gutmann, 1968). Our measure of Dominance does not, however, show any increase with age among women; in fact there is a significant decline in mean Dominance rating among women over 60 years of age; nor does Dominance decline with age among men. It seems likely that the social roles of men require the retention of the qualities measured by the Dominance index in late middle age whereas the social roles of most older women do not.

In addition, there may be a cohort factor in the Dominance–Age relationship among women, such that younger women today have higher Dominance scores not just compared to older women today, but higher scores than older women had in *their* youth, as a consequence of social and political pressures in recent years for younger women to achieve higher levels of education and to aspire to higher prestige jobs. One crude test of such a cohort interpretation was attempted with the use of attitudes toward women's rights, and the analysis showed that Dominance scores were indeed significantly higher among young women who were pro-women's rights than among those opposed to women's rights, whereas attitudes on women's rights was not related to Dominance among men of any age or among older women (data not shown). But this is a weak test at best.

We are in a better position to tease out the physiological component of the Drive index and to compare the results across all three personal trait measures by means of a regression analysis that uses both chronological age and condition of physical health. The self-rating of current Health, one assumes, reflects both disease and normal aging, whereas current age net of health may reflect a combination of other aging factors, plus changes in social status or cohort differences. We also include the Bradburn Affect Scale, which measures the balance between positive and negative moods. The items included in the Bradburn measure of positive moods include feeling "proud of what one has accomplished," "on top of the world," "particularly excited or interested in something," and "things are going my way." These items imply an active engagement in the social world, and hence share some element in common with the items in the Dominance index. A balance tipped to more positive than negative moods may therefore be particularly significant in connection with Dominance ratings, and perhaps to Expressivity as well, though less strongly so.

Table 2.1 provides some confirmation of these expectations: Drive does show equally high coefficients on the predictor variables of age and health status, net of each other, as well as significant effects of gender and Affect Balance. Dominance, by contrast, is not affected by health status, while age is a significant negative predictor along with being male and scoring high on the positive side of the Affect Balance scale. Note that Expressivity is independent of age and health status, reflecting the influence only of gender and a modest contribution of positive moods.

Another vantage point from which to view the trait measures is the *balance* between them over the life course. One can infer this balance from Figure 2.1, but it is more readily grasped in Figure 2.2. Figure 2.2A shows the balance between Drive and Dominance, separately for men and women. The horizontal lines in the figure indicate that the average Drive score is *higher* than the Dominance score; the vertical lines indicate that the average Drive score is *lower* than the Dominance score. Note that there is a switch in midlife: Up to their 40s for men, and their 50s for women, the Drive score is higher than the Dominance score, a gap that is much larger among younger women than younger men, suggesting a kind of "energy to burn" excess that social roles do not fully absorb. By contrast, Dominance scores exceed Drive scores from midlife on, particularly among men, a gap that suggests potential "burn out" or stress related to the fact that for many men, work and family demands require them to continue performing as though they were still young, when in fact their energy levels may be diminishing. This profile is consistent

Table 2.1. Regressions on Drive, Dominance, and Expressivity (G2 Sample)

	Beta Coefficients		
Predictor Variables	Drive	Dominance	Expressivity
Current Age	−.47***	−.30***	−.04
Current Health	.21***	.00	.02
Affect Balance	.13***	.14***	.10*
Female	−.10***	−.24***	.18***
R^2	.35***	.17***	.05***
N	(1052)	(1157)	(1157)

***p < .001
*p < .05

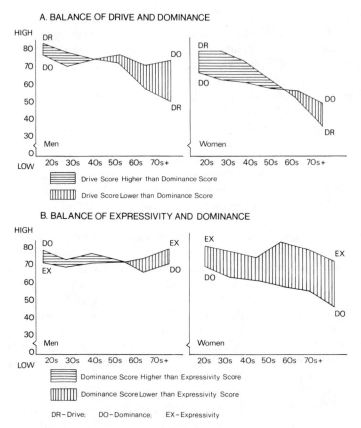

Figure 2.2. Balance of (A) Drive and Dominance, and (B) Expressivity and Dominance, by age and gender of G2 adults (G2 sample).

with the rise in psychosomatic illness and cardiac diseases among men in their late 40s and 50s.

Figure 2.2B shows the balance between average Expressivity and Dominance scores, separately for men and women, which also undergoes change over the life course, though with a reversal only among men: Younger men through their 40s show higher Dominance than Expressivity scores, whereas over 50, the balance tips to higher Expressivity scores, suggesting that some men do indeed show more tender than assertive qualities as they get older. There is no similar reversal among the women, however, only a life-long profile of higher Expressivity than Dominance, with the gap increasing with age as Dominance scores decline. Hence there is no evidence here to confirm the inversion among older women on these personal traits.

These are profiles based on central statistical tendencies. It is also possible to define this balance notion as an individual characteristic, by computing the difference between scores on Dominance and Drive. We shall explore such a computed difference variable at a later point in the analysis. First, however, we turn to the gap between current and retrospective ratings on the items that comprise the Drive index. Our interest in doing so is to determine whether older adults are aware of aging-related changes in themselves.

Current Drive and Perception of Change

It will be recalled that the items in the Drive index were rated in terms of "nowadays" and "10 years ago." Figure 2.3 shows the contrast between the current and retrospective ratings for each of the three items, by age and gender of the respondents. The current ratings, shown by the solid lines, all show a sharp and precipitous decline from the age of 40 on, though the decline occurs somewhat later in the case of men than women. In four of the six figures, adults show an increasing awareness of change in themselves, as indexed by the much higher ratings of themselves as they remember themselves 10 years ago than "nowadays."

The two cases in which this is not so, i.e., where current ratings are in fact *higher* than the retrospective ratings, are interesting because they reflect social and biological changes the youngest respondents have undergone in the transition from adolescence to early adulthood over the preceding decade. Those who were in their 20s when interviewed were only teenagers 10 years earlier. As a consequence, they report much higher ease of sexual arousability today than a decade earlier. As would be expected in view of the earlier age of sexual initiation by males than females, the gap between current and past ratings is particularly sharp for young women in their 20s; no doubt they engaged in much less sexual experimentation as teenagers than did boys their age.

The middle two graphs, on "hard working" self ratings, also show much higher mean ratings today than young people judge themselves to have been as adolescents. Young adults are in effect saying that the transition from being a student to an employed adult involves a marked increase in hard work. Adolescent school days may have seemed to involve hard work at the time, but once adult responsibilities are acquired, nostalgia may color the memory of adolescence in rosier hues.

Clearly there is a keen awareness on the part of older adults that libido and energy level have undergone considerable diminution over the preceding decade of their lives. On the other hand, they seem to have an

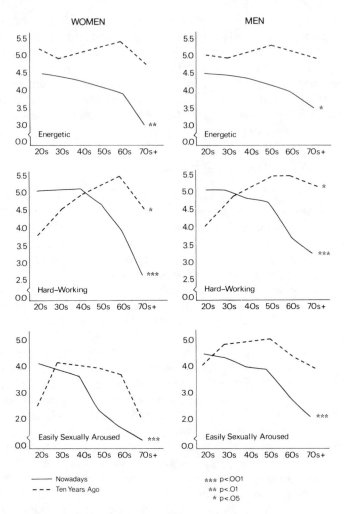

Figure 2.3. Average scores on Drive items "Nowadays" vs. "10 years ago" by age and gender (G2 sample) (0–6 score range).

exaggerated conception of the *extent* to which they have aged. This can be seen more clearly in Figures 2.4 and 2.5, which show the gap (and hence perceptual exaggeration) between the *retrospective* ratings of adults in one age group with the *current* ratings of adults in the age group currently 10 years younger. Thus if 60-year-old men report a mean energy score 10 years ago, when they were 50, of 4.0 on the 6-point scale, 50-year-old adults should report the same mean of 4.0 in rating themselves "nowadays," *if* there was no perceptual exaggeration

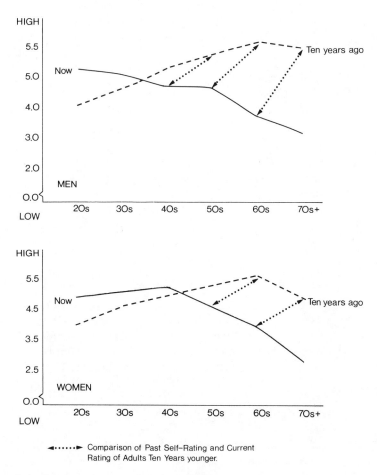

◄······► Comparison of Past Self–Rating and Current
Rating of Adults Ten Years younger.

Figure 2.4. Mean ratings on "Hard-working" nowadays vs 10 years ago, by age and gender (G2 sample) (0–6 score range).

of change in themselves as the 60 year olds look back to when they were 10 years younger.

Figure 2.4 shows the relevant ratings for the item on "hard-working" and Figure 2.5 for the item "easily sexually aroused." The dotted lines between the small arrows facilitate comparisons between the two relevant ratings: retrospective ratings by one age group versus the current ratings by an age group 10 years younger. If these ratings were identical, i.e., if memory matched reality, the dotted lines would be horizontal. To the extent they show a sharp upward angle, there is an exaggerated perception of change with age. Of the 16 dotted lines shown in the two figures, it is only among the very oldest women, on ratings of sexual

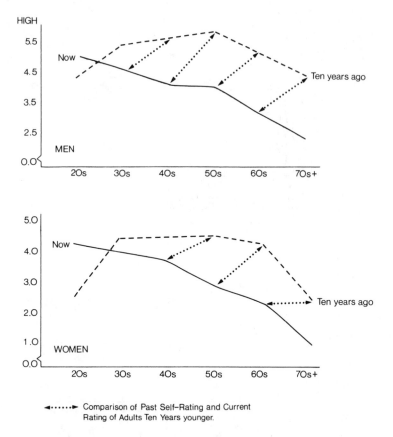

Figure 2.5. Mean ratings on "Easily sexually aroused" nowadays vs 10 years ago, by age and gender (G2 sample) (0–6 score range).

arousability, that actual change may be in accord with individual perception: Women over 70 years of age give retrospective ratings of themselves 10 years earlier with the same mean level as women in their 60s rate themselves today. In all other comparisons, perceived change is greater than it probably was in fact.

Men perceive a great deal more change than women on these aging aspects of themselves. Note, for example, that in the "hard working" ratings, over the life course men's current ratings show a steady decline in average scores from the 30s on, yet the retrospective ratings show a steady *increase* in average scores well into late middle age. That the pattern is more marked for men than for women is yet another indicator of potential personal and physical stress in middle-aged men as they face and undergo the transition into old age. Job demands on men between the ages of 50 and 65 may be as great as they ever were, and any slackening of effort that might attend sheer ebbing of physical energy could carry severe penalties, from loss of the job to reduction in pay to being rejected for promotion. Women between 50 and 65 may be spared much of the stress men experience in this regard, since their parttime work and earnings contribute less to total family income, and housekeeping can be paced to an individual's physical and motivational capacity far more than paid employment.

Figure 2.6 summarizes the life course profile in perceived change in the self, using the Drive index rather than the individual items. The measure shown is the difference between current and retrospective scores on the Drive index for each age group, separately for men and women. Gender differences are minor on the composite index, but the gap in mean ratings between today and 10 years earlier increases steadily across the life course. The balance is tipped toward higher Drive today than in the past only for those in early adulthood, and turns increasingly negative with each older age group over 40 years of age. Standard deviations, shown at the bottom of the figure, suggest a curvilinear relationship with age: least variance, in the sense of a changed and aging self, is found among women in their 30s and men in their 40s, with much greater variance among both the youngest and oldest adults.

One source of increasing variance past the age of 40 is probably the health condition of older adults. Beyond age 40, some adults continue in excellent health for 25 or more years, whereas others begin to cope with chronic disease, e.g., a worsening case of diabetes, a diagnosis of hypertension, a bout with an ulcer, and so on. We did not ask for details about chronic disease, or recent hospitalization, or use of medication, but the life course profile of self-ratings on health by gender are consistent with biomedical knowledge of increasing health problems with age, and of the earlier onset of worsening health conditions among men than women (Brody et al., 1987). Table 2.2 shows the proportion of men and women in each age group who gave "poor" health ratings (defined as the bottom quarter on the scale distribution for the total sample).

The profile of increasing proportions in "poor" health with age differs somewhat between men and women. There is no significant increment in poor health among women until they are in their 60s, whereas an increase in poor health begins much earlier for men, i.e., an increase of 11% between men in their 30s and those in their 40s, another 10% by their 50s, followed by little change in the next two older age groups. The male profile reflects, in part, higher death rates at younger ages than female death rates show, with the result that surviving men are in better health. Among the oldest group, the surviving men in fact report a slightly lower proportion in poor health than do the oldest women.

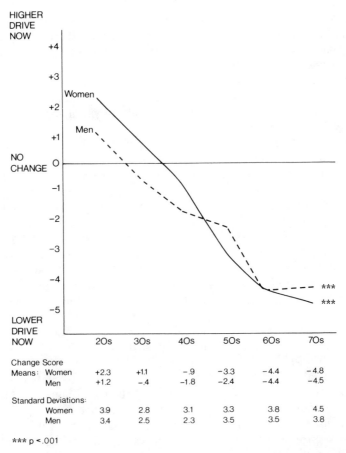

Figure 2.6. Average extent and direction of change in Drive over past 10 years, by age and gender (G2 sample).

Table 2.2. Current Health Condition by Age and Gender of G2 Adults (G2 Sample)

| | Percentage in "Poor" Health [a] | |
Current Age	Men (%)	Women (%)
19–30	12.9	13.0
31–40	16.4	16.7
41–50	27.2	19.9
51–60	36.9	24.2
61–70	35.2	40.2
71–92	52.6	60.4

[a] Poor health = bottom quarter of the distribution on a scale ranging from 1 to 10, i.e., scores between 1 and 6.

Consistent with other data shown earlier, and to be seen again below, the sharpest contrast between men and women in health condition is among adults in their 50s, with 37% of the men reporting poor health compared to only 24% of the women.

Positive and Negative Mood States

The Bradburn Affect Balance scale has been widely used as an easily administered indicator of the subjective psychological state of survey respondents. Preliminary analysis suggested that the separate scales on Positive and Negative Affect were more readily interpreted than the Balance scale, and Vern Bengtson reports the Negative Affect Scale is significantly correlated with an abbreviated Depression scale in his analysis of the California three-generation data set (Bengtson, personal communication, 1985).

A good example of the greater utility of the separate scales than the Balance scale is seen in Figure 2.7: There is a steady decline in the average ratings on both Positive and Negative Affect with age, a pattern that is hidden when the Balance scale is examined (shown numerically at the bottom of the figure). In his original study, Norman Bradburn reported the same pattern on the relationship between the two scales and age of his respondents (Bradburn, 1969). Since Bradburn's data were obtained more than 20 years ago, it is not likely that these age-related patterns reflect any cohort effect. Mean ratings on Positive Affect remain higher than Negative Affect at all points of the life course, but both decline with age.

It is tempting to infer a reduction in general mood volatility with age, a softening of the peaks and valleys as life winds down, fewer challenges lie ahead, and the focus of life centers not on aspirations for the future, but assessment and acceptance of the shape one's life has taken. On the other hand, such an interpretation would be more consistent with a reduction of Positive Affect and an increase in Negative Affect with increasing age, not, as the graph shows, an even sharper reduction in Negative Affect than in Positive Affect.

It is well to examine the items that comprise the two indices before attempting an interpretation of the Affect–age relationship. They are as follows:

Positive Affect

Pleased about having accomplished something.
That things were going your way.

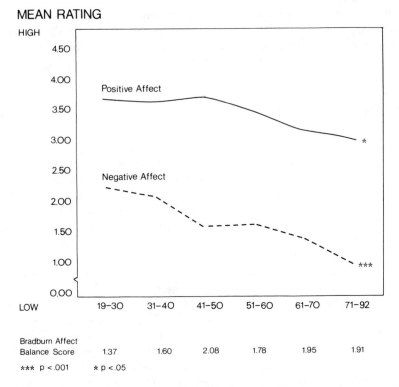

MEAN RATING

Figure 2.7. Mean ratings on Positive and Negative Affect scores by age of G2 adults (G2 sample).

> Proud because someone complimented you on something you had done.
> Particularly excited or interested in something.
> On top of the world.

Negative Affect
> So restless you couldn't sit still.
> Bored.
> Depressed or very unhappy.
> Very lonely or remote from other people.
> Upset because someone criticized you.

A number of the items are purely intrapsychic indicators of mood and satisfaction or dissatisfaction with the self (bored, depressed, restless, on top of the world), but other items focus on social interaction and

activity (being complimented or criticized by someone, lonely and remote from others, accomplishing something, being excited about something). Positive Affect may decline with age if one leads a less active,
socially engaged life. You cannot be complimented or excited unless you
are *doing* something to trigger such responses. By the same token, one
reason for the decline in Negative Affect with age may be an increase in
introspection and life assessment, a solitary and absorbing activity that
has no necessary connection with feeling lonely, bored, or depressed.
With the release from job and family responsibilities in the later years of
life, there is simply less that needs doing on any tight time schedule, but
it does not follow that one becomes restless, bored, or withdrawn. Social
circles may contract, organizational membership lag, with no necessary
implication of depression or disengagement. It may simply be the case
that the narrower circles of family and close friends take on added
subjective meaning when there is time for thoughtful planning of private social events with significant others.

Indeed, many of the people encountered in early and middle age are
not freely chosen, but are functional to one's role as worker or parent.
Chatting with parents of one's children's friends, participating in PTA
meetings, or entertaining business or professional associates may not
involve any intrinsic gratification, and in fact can be a source of irrita-
tion. Hence it may simply be that in late middle and old age one is free to
relate only to those people with whom one genuinely wishes to be.

These suggestions are consistent with our study data on friendship
and Kin Embeddedness. We find no reduction in the number of friends
people at varying ages report: In all age groups, the average is 10 to 12
friends. What we do find is a shift toward greater involvement with kin
rather than friends, and greater preference for friends met through
family connections, with increasing age. Figure 2.8 gives dramatic evidence of the life course trend in Kin Embeddedness.[4] Marital status is
also shown in the figure, because it varies with age and is highly
relevant to the extent of kin embeddedness shown by our Boston respondents.

On a scale from 0 to 100, the group with the *lowest* scores on Kin
Embeddedness is composed of adults in their 30s and 40s who have
never married, who have a score of 30, whereas the group with the
highest average score on Kin Embeddedness is composed of very elderly
widowed adults, with a score of 64. Within each marital status, there is
an increasing trend toward greater kin embeddedness across the life
course. It is particularly interesting to note that the increase in Kin
Embeddedness with age holds strongly even among adults who have
never married. One might have expected such singles to focus increasingly on friendship connections as they get older. They do, in fact, show

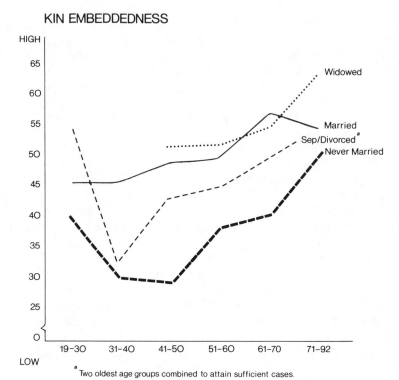

KIN EMBEDDEDNESS

Figure 2.8. Kin Embeddedness by marital status and age (G2 sample) (mean scores converted to 0–100 metric).

less Kin Embeddedness than any other marital status at all stages of life, but with increasing age, they also show the same marked increase in reliance on family and relatives that widowed and divorced persons do. They have no descendants to interact with, but most do have siblings, nieces and nephews, and cousins and their families. We shall see in Chapter 10 that these kin figure importantly in the wills unmarried and childless adults make.

Young adults in their 20s appear to be a special case, particularly if they are separated or divorced. Many young unmarried and married adults retain close ties with parents and other kin familiar to them during the years they were growing up. Marriage itself enlarges the kindred through the acquisition of in-laws. But when marriages break, early family ties become critical sources of emotional and often financial support during the difficult period of postdivorce adjustment (Gerstel, 1988). Later in life, divorced adults are like the never married in showing lower Kin Embeddedness than those who are married or widowed.

When one's remaining years of life are few in number, kin ties may take on ever greater emotional and social significance for those without a marital partner.[5]

Because Kin Embeddedness increases with age, while both Positive and Negative Affect decline with age, it is unlikely that the reasons for the Affect declines have to do with loosened social bonds. This should not be rejected out of hand, of course, but put to an empirical test. This we attempt to do by regressing a variety of potential predictors on the Positive and Negative Affect scores. It also seems quite possible that different factors are involved in elevating positive and negative moods among young adults compared to old adults. Hence we shall run regressions separately for three age groups: adults under 40, those between 41 and 60, and those over 60.

Three sets of factors are used for this analysis. The first concerns *social bonds*, on which we use four variables: being married or not, living alone or not, degree of Kin Embeddedness, and number of friends. The second set of factors relates to *socioeconomic status*, for which we use total family income, and a dummy variable on employment status, with those who are neither employed nor a student coded "1," and employed persons and students coded "0."[6] The third set consists of *age-related* variables: chronological age, self-rating on Health, score on the Drive index, and Age Dissatisfaction.[7] The latter index measures the extent to which adults express a "desired age" younger than their actual age. Very few respondents said they wanted to be older than they are; hence a low score on the Age Dissatisfaction index implies acceptance of one's actual age, while high scores indicate increasingly younger desired age compared to chronological age.

With two dependent variables—Positive and Negative Affect—and three age groups, there are six regression equations shown in Table 2.3. The first thing to note about the results is that very few significant coefficients are found in the social bonds set of factors (only 2 of 24 coefficients are significant). Most of the significant coefficients are in the age-related cluster of factors (13 of the 24 coefficients are significant, 2 verge on significance). The second observation on these results is that, as we suspected, some predictor variables are significant in one age group but not others, or they predict Positive Affect but not Negative Affect. Thus, for example, being married lowers Negative Affect, but only among middle-aged adults, and with no positive increment to Positive Affect. It may be that being single in early adulthood or widowed in old age are socially expected statuses, whereas social expectations are that middle-aged adults will be married. Those middle-aged adults who do not meet this social expectation are, as a result, more likely to be depressed, lonely, and bored.

Table 2.3. Regressions on Positive and Negative Affect Scales Within Age Groups (G2 Sample)

Predictor Variables	A. Positive Affect			B. Negative Affect		
	Under 40	41–60	61–92	Under 40	41–60	61–92
Social Bonds						
Married [a]	−.01	.01	.05	−.07	−.13***	−.06
Live Alone [a]	−.02	.03	.03	.09*	.02	.01
Kin Embeddedness	−.01	−.06	−.10	−.01	−.06	−.05
Number of Friends	.01	.01	.08	−:05	−.09	.05
Socioeconomic Status						
Total Family Income	.13***	.08	.06	−.05	.03	−.16*
Not Employed or Studying [a]	−.11**	−.01	−.01	−.01	−.06	.04
Age Related						
Age Dissatisfaction	−.16***	−.14***	−.16*	.03	.10+	.10+
Health	.13***	.19***	.11	−.11**	−.20***	−.32***
Drive	.09*	.23***	.20**	−.08*	−.03	.11*
Age	−.01	−.03	.08	−.08	−.06	−.20**
Female	.03	.05	.08	−.07+	.02	.05
R^2	.12***	.20***	.14***	.07***	.09***	.15***
N	(569)	(324)	(177)	(569)	(324)	(177)

[a] Dummy variables: Married = 1, all other marital status = 0; Only one adult in household = 1, More than one adult = 0; Not employed and not student = 1, Full or part-time employed = 0.
*** p < .001
** p < .01
* p < .05
+ p < .10

Among young adults under 40 years of age, it is not being unmarried but living alone that elevates Negative moods. Living alone is less prevalent now than in the past, because premarital cohabitation and residential sharing of apartments and houses by several young adults have become quite widespread. Hence, what matters now in elevating negative affect among young adults is not whether they are married or not, but whether they live alone or not.

Socioeconomic status has a bearing on mood states among the youngest and oldest adults, but in quite different ways. High income and being a student or employed person is conducive to elevated Positive Affect among young adults, but the reverse (low income or not being employed or a student) does not increase Negative Affect among young adults. Socioeconomic factors have no significant effects among the middle aged, but for elderly adults low income is a significant predictor of negative affect. Social bonds do not enhance positive affect and their absence does not significantly increase negative affect among the elderly. High income is a stimulus to positive outlooks and moods among the young, but for the elderly, it does not; for them, low income matters, by increasing depression and unhappiness, and perhaps by restricting options for how to pass one's days; low income produces boredom and restlessness among the elderly.

The most powerful set of factors with significant effects on mood states are the age-related variables, and most of them work in a reciprocal way. That is to say, good health increases positive affect, and poor health increases negative affect. The connection between poor health and negative affect is also increasingly strong with each older age group, from a low but significant beta coefficient among the young ($-.11^{**}$), to a standardized coefficient almost three times greater among the old ($-.32^{***}$).

It is particularly interesting to note that Drive has a significant enhancing effect on positive affect for all three age groups, especially in view of the fact that this is independent of self-ratings on Health. Adults whose metabolism facilitates high energy expenditure and hard work, whether on a job, home chores, or leisure time activity, and who report easy libidinal arousability, show enhanced scores on Positive Affect. They have the energy, spark, and bounce to be active, to accomplish things that stimulate praise from others. By contrast, it is only among the youngest adults that low Drive is associated significantly with elevated negative affect. Departing from what is expected of young adults may involve negative self-assessments that spill over into boredom and depression. If you are 20 or 35 you are "supposed" to be energetic and hard-working. Interestingly, we shall see in Chapter 9 that the Drive index shows significant effects in the help exchanged between parents and adult children, with high-Drive parents providing more extensive help to adult children than low-Drive parents, especially to young adult children who report low Drive in themselves, a rather interesting example of family support expanding to assist fragile children who lack the bounce and vigor to make it on their own.

Social expectations and age norms also seem to be involved in the very different way in which Drive relates to Negative affect among young adults compared to old adults. Note that *low* Drive contributes to negative affect among the young ($-.08^{*}$), but among the old, it is *high* Drive that contributes to negative affect ($.11^{*}$). If high drive is socially expected and more prevalent among the young, and low drive among the old, then departures from such age norms could well trigger negative moods. It may be that for many elderly adults, particularly those who are retired and widowed, high Drive is a handicap rather than an asset, because they have physical and sexual capacities that exceed their social opportunities to express them, with the result that they feel lonely, bored, and depressed.

Age Dissatisfaction is another age-related factor that is significantly related to affect level. Wishing to be much younger does not trigger a rise in Negative Affect (though the signs are all positive), but it does depress Positive Affect, we suspect because looking wistfully and long-ingly back to an earlier age can be an escape from present unsatisfying social reality, as suggested in an earlier study of middle-aged married women (A. S. Rossi, 1980).

It is also worth noting that current age per se has a significant effect on Negative Affect only among the old adults. Despite the presence in the equation of other age-related measures, the variance in age among those from 61 to 92 is apparently great enough for current age to have a significant effect on negative moods: the older the person, the *less* negative the affect level. Despite the greater probability of widowhood and ill health among the elderly, those who survive to old age may make an accommodation to retirement, widowhood, and a chronic health problem to such an extent that they can derive pleasure from small daily events and a narrowed but subjectively significant set of friends and kin in a way that holds off boredom and depression, whereas the same set of circumstances would elevate negative affect among younger persons.

Summarizing the Affect profiles by phase of the life course suggests the following: In *early adulthood*, good health, high energy, easy sexual arousability, a job or full-time study combined with high income contrib-ute to feeling on top of the world, as one of the items in the Positive affect scale puts it, while poor health, low drive, and living alone press in the direction of elevated Negative Affect. In the *middle years*, Positive Affect is largely a matter of retaining a youthful bounce and energy, enjoying good health, and accepting the fact of growing older rather than nostalgically looking back and wishing to be young; Negative affect in midlife is triggered by being in poor health and lacking a spouse. In *old age*, the scenario changes yet again: High drive and acceptance of one's age are conducive to Positive Affect, while being in poor health, having a low income, excess energy to burn, and undergoing the early phase of adjustment to old age combine to increase Negative Affect.

The use of marital status as a dummy variable in the regression equations may mask differences worth noting, and clearly, how long one has been undergoing a painful transition from being married to being divorced or widowed may have significant effects on the Positive and Negative Affect scores. Figure 2.9 compares separated and divorced women and men in their Negative and Positive Affect scores as a function of how long it has been since the break with a spouse.

The gender difference that stands out in this figure is the very differ-ent balance between Positive and Negative Affect among those sepa-rated or divorced less than a year. Still undergoing the painful post-

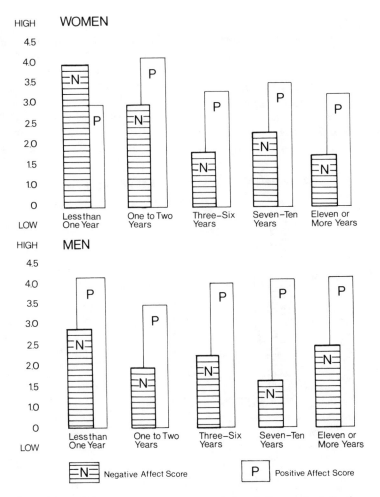

Figure 2.9. Mean Affect scores among separated and divorced adults, by number of years since separation or divorce, and gender (G2 sample).

divorce adjustment, with its complex blend of relief in being free of a stressful emotional relationship and difficulty in coping with being alone and responsible for all aspects of life on one's own, women show a high elevation of Negative Affect over Positive Affect in the first year after a divorce, one of the few circumstances in which we have found higher Negative than Positive scores. It would appear that separation and divorce have a less painful impact on men: Although their Negative Affect score is somewhat elevated in the first year after the break, this is not accompanied by any reduction in Positive Affect. Perhaps men's work roles continue as a source of gratification that sustains Positive

Affect, while it is only in their private lives that being alone in the immediate aftermath of divorce elevates Negative Affect. Looking across the graphs depicting changes in affect profile with the number of years since the breakup, women show a rapid recovery after the first year (as suggested by the increase in Positive Affect between the first and second postdivorce years), while Negative Affect declines slowly.

There were not enough widowed men in our sample to examine how years of widowhood relate to Affect profile, but there were enough widows to compare with divorced women. Figure 2.10 suggests that the

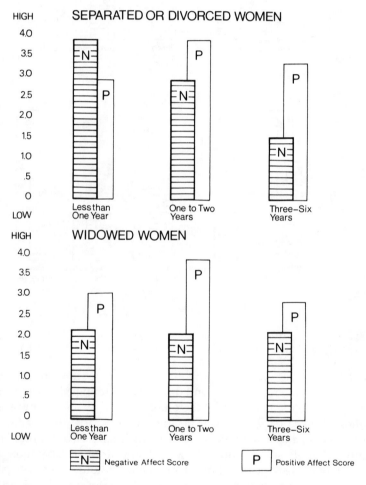

Figure 2.10. Mean Affect scores of separated or divorced women vs widowed women, by number of years since separation or death of spouse (G2 sample).

immediate aftermath of a marital breakup and divorce is more painful for women than the immediate aftermath of the death of a spouse. Coming later in life, often after their husbands were seriously ill for some period of time, older women may be better prepared to cope with early adjustment to widowhood than younger women are to the aftermath of a divorce. Both the widowed older woman and the divorced younger woman undergo significant declines to economic well being, but the younger woman typically carries responsibility for young children as well as herself. On the other hand, Negative Affect declines sharply by the time 3 years have passed since a marital breakup. By contrast, among widows Negative Affect levels remain high over the years following their husbands' deaths, and Positive Affect, after a temporary improvement in the second year of widowhood, declines again among those widowed for more than 3 years. Age-related factors may be implicated here.

Subjective, Desired, and Chronological Age

A frequent experience in youth is daydreaming about adulthood and wishing time would pass more quickly than it does. A year can seem endless to youngsters of 12 or 14, but if they bemoan this fact to their parents, they may well be told to "enjoy being young while you can" and that "life is too short to wish it to pass so quickly." Implicitly the parents are saying that youth is wasted on the young. At the other end of life course, it is rare for an old person to look very far ahead with any quickened sense of pleasure; happiness is more apt to be recalled than anticipated, as the passage from Sarah Jewett's encounter with the widowed old fisherman in Maine suggested. Bernice Neugarten captured the contrasting perspective on the passage of time, in suggesting that up to the meridian of life in middle age, one calculates time in terms of years since birth, whereas from midlife on, one calculates time in terms of years left to live (Neugarten & Datan, 1973). The "life review" that Butler (1963) pointed to as a key characteristic of old age is not only an integrative process paving the way to acceptance of the shape one's life took, but a nostalgic trip back to happier, more exciting times. To be a "senior officer" of a bank is to enjoy a prestigious status. To be "senior citizen" carries no such aura of glamour and success; in our time and culture, it is a euphemism for survivorship.

That youth looks ahead and the elderly look backward in time may simply be a reflection of the human condition, common to all times and places. It is certainly the profile our Boston respondents projected when we asked them how old they "feel most of the time" (Subjective Age) and what age they would "most like to be now" (Desired Age). There is a strong and consistent pattern when Subjective and Desired Age are examined in relation to adults' actual chronological age. The overall profile can be readily seen in Figure 2.11.

The general pattern is for adults to *feel* slightly younger than they actually are, but to *wish* they were younger still, with the gap between actual and Desired age increasing across the life course. Adults in their 20s, wish to be, on average, just a few years younger than they are; 11 years younger if they are in their 40s; 20 years younger when they reach

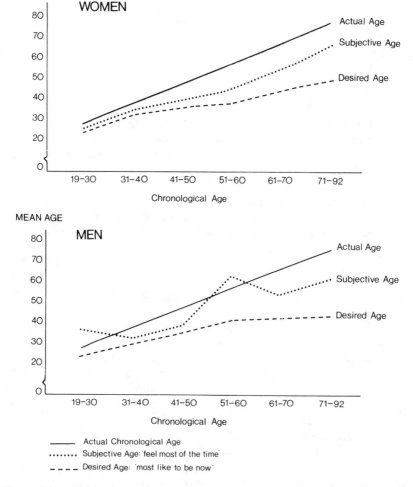

Figure 2.11. Subjective and Desired age by chronological age and gender (G2 sample).

their 60s; and over 30 years younger when they are over 70 years of age. Desired age also goes up with increasing age, of course: those under 40 in 1985 wish to be in their 20s; those over 70 wish they were in their 40s. Only 47 of 1393 respondents expressed a wish to be older than they actually were. Thirty-five of these 47 respondents specified an age less than 10 years older than they were, and almost all were in their early 20s, suggesting some impatience to get on with life, to be finished with professional training or apprenticeship jobs, or to be settled with a family of their own. All were unmarried.

Men show two points of departure from this general profile: Those in their 20s and those in their 50s report feeling older than they actually are. Some of the young adult men may be reflecting a sense of having moved too quickly into adult responsibilities, but the middle-aged men may be reflecting the pressure of excessive demands in relation to their capacity to cope with them. We have seen hints of this earlier, in noting the increase in poor health among middle-aged men compared to middle-aged women, in the gap between average Dominance scores and Drive scores among middle-aged and older men, and we shall see it again when we examine life phase assessment in the context of the total life course of men compared to women.

One marked gender difference is highlighted in these data: Among men and women in their 50s, both have the same average age—55—but the women report feeling 12 years *younger* than they are, whereas the men on average report feeling 4 years *older* than they are. The 55-year-old woman who feels 43 wishes to be 40, only a few years younger than she feels; the 55-year-old man who feels 59 also wishes to be 40, but that is 19 years younger than he feels.

Analysis of Age Dissatisfaction (the difference between Desired and Actual Age) pointed up the significance of both actual age and the gap between Dominance and Drive. Table 2.4 shows two regression equations relevant to this point. The first equation (Panel A of the table) regresses the Dominance to Drive Balance Score on current age, gender, and health, and shows that all three variables are highly significant, to roughly the same extent (as measured by the size of the standardized coefficients). Poor health, being older, and male are equally significant in producing the gap between Dominance and Drive. We then introduced the Dominance to Drive Balance Index into a regression equation on Age Dissatisfaction, again including current age, gender, and health, as well as a new index, Role Overload. The Role Overload index is a weighted index to tap the extent of role obligations in four domains of life, with points given for being married, working full time, added points for each child under 18 years of age, and extra points if respondents were solo parents. Our expectation was that adults with high Role Overload may seek escape from such pressure by wishing they were

Table 2.4. Regressions on (A) Balance of Dominance to
Drive, and (B) Age Dissatisfaction (G2 Sample)

Predictor Variables	Beta Coefficients
A. Regression on Balance of Dominance to Drive	
Current Age	.22***
Female	− .21
Health	− .20
R^2	**.16***
N	(1100)
B. Regression on Age Dissatisfaction	
Current Age	.55***
Balance of Dominance to Drive	.15***
Health	− .01
Role Overload	.01
Female	− .02
R^2	**.37***
N	(1180)

*** $p < .001$

much younger than they were, either to be out from under current
responsibilities or out of a desire for the vigor and bounce of a younger
age. As a consequence, we predicted high Age Dissatisfaction, the
higher the Role Overload score.

The results of this second regression (Panel B of Table 2.4) show only
two significant coefficients: actual age and the Dominance to Drive
Balance score. Whatever contribution gender, health, and Role Overload make is clearly indirect, for none shows any direct net effect on Age
Dissatisfaction. It is the sheer fact of being older and having a gap
between physical capacity (low Drive) and the combination of role
demand and personal trait indexed by the Dominance score that accounts for most of the variance in Age Dissatisfaction, with a highly
significant R^2 of .37.

Assessment of Current Phase of Life

The most global age-related rating respondents made was in response
to a question asking them to rate the past 5 years of their lives: Were
they the very best, among the best, among the worst, or the very worst
years of their lives? Figure 2.12 charts the percentage who assessed the
past 5 years as "among the best" or the "very best" years of their lives,
by age and gender (Panel A) and by age and Health (Panel B). Figure
2.13 charts the same life course profile by marital status.

There is an overall decline with age in the proportion who view the
past 5 years as among the "Best" years of their lives, a pattern that holds

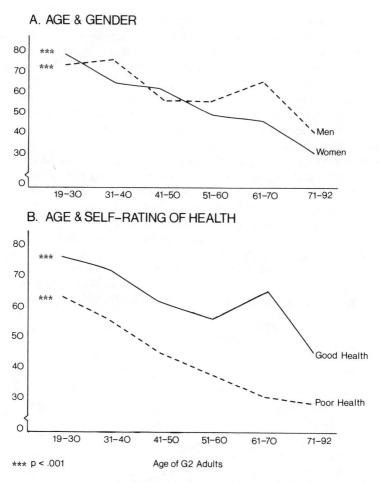

Figure 2.12. Assessment of the past 5 years as "Among the best" years of their lives by (A) age and gender and (B) age and health status (G2 sample) (percentage "Among the best" years).

for men as well as women, and for those in good health as for those in poor health. Note too, that in the later years, men give more positive assessments than do women. Indeed, men in their 60s actually show an upturn in positive assessments, as do adults in good health. Why would men in their 40s and 50s assess their stage of life less positively than men in their 60s? We have already noted that ill health in midlife is greater for men than for women, and we have noted much greater Age Dissatisfaction among middle-aged men. But the upturn in positive assessments among men over 60, which does not characterize the assessments by older women, suggests the need to consider additional factors to explain the pattern among men. Is it that retirement in their 60s is experienced by men as a release from the breadwinner pressure of meeting childrearing expenses in their late middle years, when many children are attending college? Have they accommodated to the decline in Drive that we noted was particularly problematic for men in their 50s?

One clue to the elevated positive assessment by older men compared to older women is seen in the relationship of marital status and age to Life Phase Assessment (Figure 2.13). More elderly men are married, while a large proportion of older women are widowed. Figure 2.13 clearly shows that being married is highly related to generally positive assessments of life phase. At all ages, married adults report the highest proportion with positive assessments and widowed adults the lowest, while separated or divorced adults are more negative about the recent years of their lives than those who never married. The range represented in these data is very dramatic, from 85% of young married adults viewing their recent years as among the best they have known, to under 20% of the widowed adults in their 70s. "Off-time" early widowhood (in an adult's 50s) is associated with fewer positive assessments than widowhood in one's 60s, a pattern consistent with the heightened Nega-

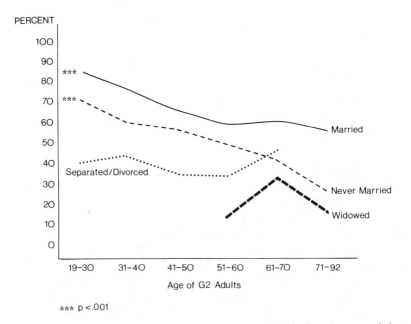

*** p < .001

Figure 2.13. Percentage say the past 5 years "Among the best" years of their lives, by marital status and age (G2 sample).

tive Affect we noted during the first postwidowhood years. Widowhood may be socially "expected" over the age of 65, but it is not expected in one's 50s, with the result shown in the figure, of very low proportions with favorable life phase ratings among widowed adults in their 50s compared to those in their 60s.

We can pinpoint the contrast between late middle age and early old age among men, and thus narrow our interpretation by a specially focused regression analysis for the two age groups of men: those in their 50s vs. those in their 60s. If family pressure is relevant to the stress and low positive assessments made by men in their 50s, then the larger the number of children they have had, the more negative may be their Life Phase Assessment. If retirement triggers some euphoric release from pressure, then retirement as a dummy variable should show a significant positive coefficient on Life Phase Assessment among men in their 60s. Of particular interest is the role of Drive compared to Health, because signs of aging are increasing and health is beginning to worsen among men in their 50s and 60s. It is possible, however, that these two age-related factors will carry different weight in the two age groups of men. Being married should be a significant positive predictor of life phase assessment in both age groups of men.

Table 2.5 shows that neither family demands, as indexed by family size, nor retirement have any effect on Life Phase Assessment. As expected, being married shows a positive coefficient in both equations. The real story hinges on the contrasting role played by Drive and Health between the two age groups of men. It is Drive that is more significantly related to positive assessment for men in their 50s, and Health that

Table 2.5. Regression on "Best/Worst Years" Assessment of Past Five Years: [a] Men in Their 50s vs Men in Their 60s (G2 Sample)

	Beta Coefficients	
Predictor Variables	Men in Their 50s	Men in Their 60s
Married (dummy variable)	.36***	.30**
Drive Index	.25*	.17
Health Status (Hi = Excellent)	.13	.26*
Retired (dummy variable)	.03	− .07
Family Size	− .03	− .02
R^2	.21***	.27***

[a] High = Very best years of life.
*** $p < .001$
** $p < .01$
* $p < .05$

matters more for men in their 60s. As proxies for the early signs of aging, changes in energy, capacity for hard work, and sexual arousability—the items in the Drive index—may tap precisely the two issues most troubling to men in late middle age: their financial ability as providers and their sexual potency.

It will be remembered that men in their 50s also showed a distorted sense of the extent to which they had changed in Drive level compared to 10 years ago. They show all the marks of finding adjustment to the prospect of old age a difficult one. Once old age becomes a reality rather than a prospect, Drive level has no significant impact on Life Phase Assessment, presumably because an accommodation has been made to declining sexual potency and lowered energy levels. In its stead, health condition is a greater preoccupation to men in their 60s: If health continues good, old age is assessed favorably; if health is poor, life phase assessment slips to the "worst" years of their lives.

Conclusion

Looking back over the age-related characteristics we have reviewed, the overwhelming impression that emerges in the comparison of the elderly with young and middle-aged adults is the bittersweet pathos associated with becoming old, the quality Sarah Jewett captured so well in her encounter with the old Maine fisherman: waning energy, declining health, the loss of a sexual spark, the loss of a partner of long standing, and, all too often, a sharp decline in income as well. Is it any wonder, one may ask, that adults over 70 wish they were in their late 40s, and that close to half believe the past 5 years have been among the worst in their lives?

The profile that emerges from our analysis bears little resemblance to the romantic vision of old age often portrayed in the media, and described by many advocates of the elderly, even the social gerontologists among them. Euphemisms like "modern maturity," "prime time," and "senior citizens," and the vision of old age as endless middle age when you can travel, play golf, or attend Elderhostel seminars seem shallow beside the assessment by elderly adults themselves, that old age is more bitter than it is sweet. Nor can sheer survival per se any longer provide very much gratification. Indeed, the elderly today are confronted with many messages suggesting their growing numbers are posing unprecedented and serious problems for the society.

Standing back even further from the fine-grained analysis we have pursued, one wonders what the answers would have been a hundred years ago, had there been a survey researcher to ask people what age they would like to be. It does not surprise us that our Boston respondents show a yearning to be younger than they are, but a hundred years ago, many more adults might have given ages older than they were. When death was a pattern of relative randomness that could strike at any age, rather than confined so largely to old age, sheer survival to 60 might have been a much-to-be-wished-for, but unlikely experience.

Martin Kohli (1985) points out that the importance of the historic change in mortality is not so much the rise in mean age of death, but the drop in variance of age at death. In our time, individuals can realistically draw up "life plans" and feel confident they will live long enough to experience their fruition, in a way young people in the past could not do. On the other hand, there is a downside to this more predictable life course. As death at younger ages becomes infrequent, a societal tendency to deny death may be reinforced. Adjustment to aging and one's imminent demise may be more difficult when a lifetime is spent without concern for one's mortality. For one thing, those on the young side of 60 who *are* coping with impending death have a narrow circle of age-peers with whom to share the experience. When we hear people describe a parent's death as "courageous," it generally means the adult child was spared any sharing of the parent's rage and pain, which has the effect of keeping intact the adult child's own death-denying tendency. Social scientists are not exempt from this denial pattern, which may explain the "upbeat" tone to some of their writings on old age, and the widespread neglect in social science research of physiological indicators of aging during the middle years. We sense that this feeds into the sociologist's inclinations to treat age differences as evidence of cohort and period effects rather than of maturational and aging effects.

Parents and children may share very different perspectives on time, depending on the age difference between them, and the relative positions they hold on the life course. Young adults and their children may share a perspective that looks ahead more than it does to times past. So too young adult children and their middle-aged parents are likely to be either present or future oriented: the parents at the meridian of life carry diverse responsibilities and are likely to be enjoying relatively high and stable incomes; hence they are in a position to give considerable assistance to their young adult children. But when parents are over 75 years of age, and children are in midlife, the time perspectives each holds may be quite different: the children are at the command post, and the parents are on the waning side with declining energy, concern for making income cover present and anticipated expenses, nostalgic for the good times enjoyed in the past. Some elderly parents may derive gratification from close identification with their children and grandchildren; if their descendants are doing well, are healthy, and show promise of living personally meaningful lives, the parents may derive sufficient satisfaction to sustain a positive outlook on what life remains for them.

What is not clear, however, is how much the elderly share their interior lives with their children. Many elderly people have told us that no one wants to hear a real answer when they are asked "how are you?" Even their children want to hear that everything is fine, health problems manageable, and spirits bright and hopeful. The down side of being old may be something shared more with spouse and age peers than with children and grandchildren. And yet, as we saw earlier in this chapter, with increasing age, adults come to feel it is family and kin who matter most to them, on whom they can rely, and with whom they interact most. Consequently, a visit from a 40- or 50-year-old child is likely to carry far more subjective significance to the elderly parent than to the child, but it is not clear how openly the elderly parent shares his or her interior life and subjective feelings.

But this gets us far ahead of our story. In the next chapter, we turn from changes in aging and the interior subjective feelings about age and life phase, to more sociological considerations for how economic resources, timing of family transitions, size, and composition of the lineage change across the life course. The aging process necessarily led to special attention to respondents in middle and old age. On the more sociological factors analyzed in the chapter to follow, we shall see economic and family status transitions and change in lineage composition among young adults as well as those in midlife or old age.[7]

Notes

1. The same ratings were obtained in the G1 parent and G3 child samples, but the items were asked directly by interviewers in the course of the telephone interviews, and did not include the Drive items, only those for the Expressivity and Dominance indices.

2. To preclude any suggestion that we expected change to be reported, the question was introduced with the phrase, "As they grow older, some people remain pretty much the same kind of person they were in the past, while other people change as they grow older."

3. We were surprised to find that the frequency of "thinking about the past" did not show any relationship to age of respondents. We had predicted it would, on the grounds that the elderly are more apt to engage in a "life review" (Butler, 1963) than younger adults, a process that by definition absorbs one's attention in events in the past, but this was not the case for our Boston respondents.

4. See Table 1.7 for the specific four items and the scoring used for this index.

5. Other analysis (not shown here) revealed no significant gender differences in the relationship between age, marital status, and Kin Embeddedness. Divorced men, like divorced women, turn to family in their 20s, and later (in their middle years) show a reduction of Kin Embeddedness compared to married adults. Like widowed women, widowers show an increasing trend toward greater Kin Embeddedness in their old age.

6. The "1" on the dummy variable therefore includes those who are retired, keeping house, or unemployed, hence lacking social ties through either schools or the workplace.

7. Age Dissatisfaction will be examined in its own right in a later section of this chapter, but, because it is relevant to the present analysis, it is introduced at this juncture.

Age, Historic Change, and Kinship _____ 3

"We hear a lot about Yuppies these days. Of course, these same people were the Hippies of the 1960s and the baby-boomers of the 1950s.

I'm from a different generation entirely . . . the one that wore T-shirts but had nothing printed on them . . . And now we are the parents of the DINKS—Double Income, No Kids!

I'm thinking of organizing a new national club: the PODWOGS—Parents of Dinks without Grandchildren!"

Paraphrase of a December 1988 Mark Russell TV Comedy Show.

Introduction

Older adults in 1990 can bear witness to how rapid social and economic change has been over the past 50 years. Indeed, by virtue of the memories of youth that our grandparents shared with us, our sense of a personal connection with the past may go back into the nineteenth century. Some great aunts who worked 12-hour days at simple repetitive tasks in a textile mill have descendants skilled in the use of electronic sewing machines and 4-thread sergers. In the suburban rings around Boston, many adults whose grandfathers unloaded fish or produce in the markets around Faneuil Hall work for leading high-tech firms. The ancestors of many older Bostonians who spent a month crossing the Atlantic have descendants who can visit the "home country" on 3-hour Concorde or 7-hour Pan Am flights.

Our oldest Boston respondents and many of the surviving parents of our younger respondents were themselves born at the turn of the twentieth century. The youngest respondents, now in their 20s, will be the elderly in American society in the third decade of the twenty-first century! It is difficult to imagine, but highly likely that the social and economic changes they will experience over the next 50 years will be as great as the changes their grandparents experienced over the past 50 years.

Scholars of the life course in developed societies have a more complex task than anthropologists who share their interests but study more stable societies undergoing slow rates of social change. At least this was true in the past, for by 1990 there are very few places on earth where contemporary anthropologists can assume the society they observe and that their young informants take for granted is similar to the society experienced by old informants in their youth. Because of improved sanitation and health care, in many parts of Africa today young adults can live out their agrarian grandparents' dream of bearing and rearing eight or more children to adulthood; but sadly, their societies no longer have the resources to support such high fertility (Cain, 1985; LeVine & LeVine, 1985). In our sample of Bostonians, 196 respondents grew up in families with 8 or more children, including some 35 who came from families with 12 or more children! None of our youngest respondents has such fertile aspirations.

Hence, historic change is built into the very structure of family genealogies, and social scientists who study any aspect of adult development must cope with the fact that age differences are a complex blend of historical, cohort, and maturational influences. When we compare the relationship between a 75-year-old mother and her 50-year-old daughter with a 45-year-old mother and her 20-year-old daughter, we are comparing individuals whose earlier years were spent under very different circumstances, including idiosyncratic biographic elements, the mark of the birth cohorts the individuals belong to and of the historic events they experienced at different stages of their lives.

Precisely because parents and children by definition belong to different birth cohorts, it is important to examine respondents' age from the point of view of potential cohort and historical effects. Our interest in early family life and respondents' relationship to their parents when they were children and adolescents adds to this concern for cohort and period effects. Fortunately, current chronological age can be translated into the historic time periods during which respondents were growing up or rearing their own children. This permits us, for example, to test the idea that adolescence was a more turbulent time for parents and adolescent children during the 1970s than it was in the 1950s, by comparing ratings of parent–child intimacy for those who were adolescents in the 1970s with the ratings for those who were adolescents in the 1950s. In a similar translation of current age into birth cohorts, we can chart long-term trends in several aspects of childrearing over the decades when older respondents were rearing children through the decades ahead when younger respondents will be rearing children yet unborn. For example, because of our interest in gender of parent and child, we obtained measures on the extent to which parents taught skills to children along traditional gender lines (e.g., cooking for daughters, carpentry for sons). Younger respondents answered in terms of what they will teach sons and daughters in the future. This permits us to trace the extent to which there has been a retention or relaxation of gender-stereotyped skill transmission by parents to their children from many decades ago to the decades that lie ahead. Following a similar analysis mode, we shall examine the qualities parents wish to encourage in their children, and can demonstrate a long-term social trend away from conformity and toward autonomy in childrearing values.

There are obvious limits to our ability to link historical events to direct impact on the lives of our respondents. We did not ask respondents if they had served in the military during a war, suffered economic hardship during the Great Depression, or participated in the antiwar movement or counterculture life-style in the 1970s. Hence, we must work with a broad brush on a very large canvas. We cannot "explain" the dynamics through which intimacy was reduced between parents and adolescent children in the 1970s, nor why the trend has been toward increasing emphasis on individual autonomy in childrearing. At least we cannot offer such interpretations grounded in empirical variables. We are at best testing for the "fit" between empirical patterns and what we know generally about the social ambience or condition of the economy at one point in history compared to another. But perhaps this is why theories of social change generally lack very great specificity.[1]

We are on better grounds in anticipating the respects in which significant demographic trends over the past five or six decades will be mirrored in the lives of young compared to old adults in our 1985 sample. Trends in educational attainment, age at marriage, family size, and morbidity and mortality rates have been established and are widely known by life course analysts. Less widespread is the application of such demographic knowledge to the probable structure of family lineages or intergenerational relations. There has been, of course, much speculation about potential effects of demographic change, but much of it is not firmly grounded in actual data (Bengtson et al., 1990; Hagestad, 1988; Riley, 1987; Shanas, 1980). We believe it is the lack of articulation between demographic facts and actual data on kinship structure that is responsible for some widely held but false assumptions concerning the prevalence of multigenerational families.

In this chapter, we begin with a detailed description of the age distribution of our G2 respondents, their G1 parents, and their G3 children. This description will show the considerable generational overlap in age in our two samples of parent–child dyads, G1 parents and G2 children, and G2 parents and G3 children. But our primary reason for detailing the age distribution of our three samples is to link these individual lives to their birth cohorts, and to sketch what were the special historical markers of the period in the past 80 years when respondents from different cohorts were children, or young and middle-aged adults.

A second topic in this chapter is a closer look at some major characteristics of the families of origin and of procreation of our G2 respondents. Included are trends in family stability, family troubles, family size, gender-role socialization, and qualities considered important in rearing children. Where our data permit, we test for specific period effects on some aspect of family relations.

The third topic is to place our individual respondents in the larger kindred within which they are socially embedded. Family sociologists have debunked the idea that household composition is any index to kinship structure. The proportion of households that contain only one adult is increasing rapidly in American society, as young adult children reside in apartments of their own and postpone marriage to older ages; as divorce rates remain high and remarriage rates, at least for women, decline; and as the proportion of elderly widows in the population increases. But the increasing prevalence of single-adult households does not necessarily imply increased isolation from meaningful social connections. In fact, we suspect that many adults who live alone in 1990 devote more time to daily conversations by phone with friends and relatives than adults in crowded extended family households spent in conversation with each other in the past. We have already seen, in the previous chapter, that even never married and divorced adults consider kin of increasing emotional and social salience to them as they get older. Which kin are available to adults at different points along the life course will vary of course, as the dynamics of births and deaths unfold. It is the purpose of the last section of this chapter to trace such dynamics as best we can with cross-sectional data, by showing how the depth and composition of the direct-line kindred change over the life course.

One caveat is called for before turning to the substantive analysis of these topics. It is tempting in our day, in an era marked by considerable social change and with cohorts of such varying sizes in our age stratification system, to hold the view that everything about family life and kinship structure is in a state of flux, and that explanations of age differences must necessarily center on historical and cohort influences. That is an exaggeration of the human condition that neglects ongoing processes and kinship structures that vary little from one era to another. No one is older than their parent or grandparent, or younger than a child or grandchild. Historical and demographic trends affect the extent of the age difference between the generations as a function of age at marriage, birth spacing, and family size, but the human reproductive cycle sets the fundamental parameters. Although there are some exceptions because of wide birth spacing, size, and age at marriage in a sibling set, most adults are older than their nieces and nephews and younger than aunts and uncles. Most people begin life with two or more older generations in their families; as they move into adulthood they become a middle generation and with the death of the last surviving parent they become the oldest generation with two or more generations younger than themselves. So too, there is for most people a period of time between adolescence and marriage formation when they live as independent adults; in midlife, the majority is embedded in a complex multigenerational family; and in late life, especially if they are female, they will again become a solo individual without a marital partner. In a fundamental sense, cohort shifts represent only minor fluctuations around a stable ongoing drama of generational succession.

In a similar vein, there may be great variation from one period to another in personal income in constant dollars. But there is also an underlying life course curve to earnings that is important to note, precisely because adult children and parents are at different but constantly changing positions on the life course trajectory. Most adults earn less in their first job than in the job they hold in midlife. Peak earnings may differ by social class, with high school graduates in blue collar jobs earning the most they will ever earn in their late 30s and college graduates in their late 40s and early 50s; and most elderly adults undergo a significant decline in income following retirement, although many middle and upper class elderly have other wealth in property and investments. Here too, we tap a life course phenomenon that may show great stability from one era to another. The source of income may vary with age more than actual income in constant dollars, and that was certainly true in a broad historic sense. Thus, for example, Michael Haines (1985) showed, with nineteenth-century data, the same peak household earnings in midlife that we find with contemporary data, but the source of such earnings differed in the two historic periods: In the late nineteenth century, men's income declined at a relatively early age, and was supplemented by children's earnings as they entered the labor force in their teens, whereas household income today increases from youth to midlife as a consequence of wage increases with seniority or promotion of adult men and the contribution of wives' earnings.

A special section of this chapter will be devoted to life course earnings, both personal and total household income, because this provides important clues to underlying potential economic needs and resources relevant to the intergenerational relations with which subsequent chapters are concerned.

Age and Birth Cohorts of the Generations

Age Distribution

We begin with an examination of the age distribution of our G2 sample of adults, whether and which of their parents are still alive, and what the average ages are of both G1 parents and G3 children of our main sample respondents. The age information for all three generations was obtained from G2 respondents; where parents are concerned, age was obtained only if the parent was still alive. We did not ask any questions that permit us to tell how old deceased parents were when the respondent was born, nor their age when they died. Hence we can draw only inferences from certain of the data on age shown in Table 3.1.

Panel A of Table 3.1 demonstrates the rapidly changing presence of one or both parents across the life course of G2 respondents. Death of a parent is a rare event for adults in their 20s, but increasingly parental mortality is experienced by adult children during the following two decades: the loss of a father is not uncommon for adults in their 30s—a third have lost a father by 40 years of age. By 50 years of age, 70% have lost a father, but two-thirds still have a mother alive. Few G2 adults over 60 years of age report a living parent. Even above the age of 50, there were only 22 respondents with a living father, 85 with a living mother, i.e., only 4% of those over 50 have a father alive and 17% a mother alive.

One striking point shown in the age data is the critical watershed that seems to be represented for G2 adults when they pass their fiftieth birthday: Up to the age of 50, the typical middle-aged adult had children at home; during their 40s, these G3 children were passing through adolescence while many of the G1 parents (the children's grandparents) died. After 50 years of age, two striking changes are apparent: the G3 children are typically young adults, and very few G1 parents remain alive. In the average but still uncommon case of parents over 80, grandchildren are well into adulthood. If the parent's death was preceded by a long period requiring caregiving, few G2 adults had very young children; most of the G3 children were at least adolescents when their parents may have been involved in taking care of the grandparent. Children may therefore lose a grandfather during their adolescence, but a grandmother only when they are themselves young adults. Since in most cases, elderly men who require care during terminal illnesses still have their wives alive to provide it, very few middle generation daughters would be carrying primary responsibility for caregiving to elderly widowed mothers until their own children were young adults and on their own (Hess & Waring, 1978).

It is also of some interest to note that the age difference between G2 adults and living parents *decreases* across the life course, because parents

Table 3.1. Presence and Average Age of G1 Parents, G2 Respondents, and G3 Children, by Age of G2 Adults (G2 sample and Childset Files)[a]

| | Total | Age of G2 Adult | | | | | |
		19–30	31–40	41–50	51–60	61–70	71–92
A. Living Parents (%)							
Both parents alive		81.5	58.2	25.9	5.0	1.2	—
Only Mother Alive		13.1	24.7	41.1	28.6	9.4	.9
Only Father Alive		3.2	8.8	4.0	4.0	1.2	—
Neither Parent Alive		2.2	8.3	29.0	62.4	88.2	99.1
B. Average Ages[b]							
G1 Parents							
Fathers	62.5	55.8	65.2	71.9	83.8	—	—
	(594)	(263)	(242)	(67)	(18)	(4)	(0)
Mothers	63.4	53.7	63.5	71.5	80.4	86.7	—
	(818)	(291)	(296)	(146)	(66)	(18)	(1)
G2 Adults	45.1	26.1	35.4	45.1	55.5	65.5	77.9
	(1393)	(314)	(365)	(224)	(199)	(170)	(118)
G3 All Children	23.1	4.3	9.3	17.9	25.7	34.4	46.7
	(2737)	(152)	(579)	(588)	(634)	(449)	(246)
Oldest Child		4.7	10.8	20.2	29.3	38.2	49.2
Youngest Child		2.8	6.7	14.2	22.0	30.7	42.5

[a] Childset file consists of all children of G2 respondents, duplicating parent characteristics accordingly.
[b] Dashed line box marks the largest pool for G1–G2 parent–adult child dyads and dotted line box the largest pool for G2–G3 parent–adult child dyads.

markedly older at the birth of children are less likely to survive when their children enter the middle years. Note, for example, that there is 28 years separating G2 adults in their 20s and their mothers, but only 21 years for G2 adults in their 60s and their few remaining mothers, despite the fact that most older adults in this sample married at older ages than younger adults, which in turn reflects the tendency for American Catholics to have married at older ages than non-Catholics until more recent times. Even with our restriction to still living parents, 42% of the G2 adults had fathers more than 30 years older than themselves, and 34% had mothers more than 30 years their senior. Since these are the surviving parents, even larger proportions with wide age differences between the generations would have been apparent had we obtained information on the age of *all* respondents' parents when they were born.

This is already an early warning that samples of a general population do not include very many cases of five-generation families that gerontologists often discuss, e.g., when children are born to mothers 15 years of age in several successive generations. Teenage pregnancies and births, much discussed in recent years, are not widespread, but a very minor part of the American fertility pattern (Vinovskis, 1981). Thirty-year-old grandparents and 45-year-old greatgrandparents are very rare phenomena in the national population, and a small proportion even among the Black urban communities in which they have been studied (Bengtson et al., 1990; Burton, 1985).

The age distribution also hints at the following fact: When we analyze G2 respondents in terms of their current relationship to their parents, we will for the most part be dealing with adult children well *under* 50 years of age, and when we analyze G2 respondents in their roles as parents of adult children, most cases will be of G2 adults *over* 50 years of age. The bulk of the G1–G2 dyads of parents and adult children is shown in the upper left portion of the table, marked off by dashed lines, and the bulk of the G2–G3 dyads of parents and adult children is shown in the lower right portion of the table, marked off by dotted lines. Note too, that the ages of the two generations are symmetrical: G2 respondents in their 20s have an average age of 26 with parents in their mid-50s. G2 respondents in their 50s have children with an average age of 26. A fair inference from these data is that very few adults still have a parent alive when they themselves become a grandparent, which means even four-generation families are not very prevalent, as we will see in more detail later in this chapter.

A second inference is that any three-generation study that requires the youngest generation to be an adult over 20 years of age would be difficult to obtain from even a sample as large as ours: Respondents under 50 tend to have adolescent or younger children, and few respondents over 50 have living parents. Of the 278 G3 children and 334 G1 parents we interviewed, only 79 cases were from the same lineage, not a large enough number for any statistical analysis of three-generation lineages. Hence, for the most part, our analysis is confined to two dyads, in which one group of G2 respondents is adult children, and the second, largely separate group of G2 respondents is the parents of adult children.

Age differences between generations look much sharper when we deal with statistical averages rather than the full age distribution of the generations. To say the average G1 parent is 63, the G2 respondent 45, and the G3 child 23 projects a misleading image. What the means obscure is the high degree of generational overlap in age within the two parent–child dyads that will concern us in subsequent chapters. The age distributions of parents and adult children in the G1–G2 dyads and the G2–G3 dyads are shown in Figure 3.1, in which the generational overlap on age is shown by the cross-hatched portion of each pair of bar figures. Note that the base Ns of G2 respondents in this figure are restricted to those whose parent or whose child was also interviewed. In some G1–

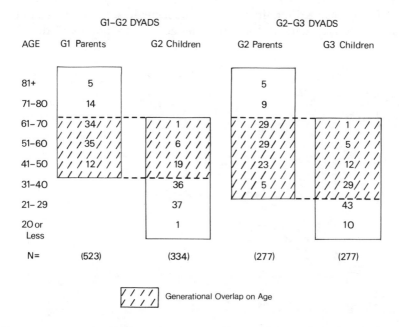

Figure 3.1. Age distribution of parents and adult children in G1–G2 dyads and G2–G3 dyads (G1 and G3 samples) (in percent).

G2 dyads the "children" are indeed young adults in their 20s, but in other G1–G2 dyads the "children" are in their 40s and 50s, with the parents ranging in age from their early 40s to their late 80s.

Birth Cohorts and Historical Context

Figure 3.2 provides yet another perspective on the age distribution of the three generations: the numeric distribution of age of G1 parents (separately for mothers and fathers), G2 respondents, and G3 children. Below the 5-year age groupings in this distribution, we show the birth cohorts to which each belongs. Inspection of the overlap among the four age distributions quickly makes the point that there are in fact some G1 parents who are younger than G2 respondents, and even a small group of G1 parents who are younger than G3 adult children. The figure also indicates the range of each distribution in terms of when, in historic time, the three samples were born: G1 parents who are still alive were born between 1890 and 1954, G2 respondents between 1890 and 1969, and G3 children of our main sample respondents between 1925 and 1985.

Defining phase of life in cohort terms facilitates the identification of major historical markers that characterize various phases of develop-

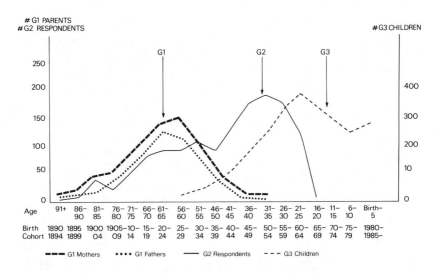

Figure 3.2. Case distribution of G1 Parents, G2 respondents, and all G3 children by age/birth cohort.

ment of our respondents. Since we will be using the six-decade-long age classification of the G2 respondents throughout the analysis, we will note the predominant historical events or period characteristics for three developmental phases in each of the six age groups of G2 respondents. In Table 3.2, therefore, we link the historic years during which each age group was in Adolescence (taken here to be 15–20 years of age), Early Adulthood (defined as 21–35 years of age), and Middle Adulthood (36–55 years of age). A profile of each of the six age groups follows.

19–30. G2 adults in their 20s were born between 1955 and 1966 (the oldest among them were part of the end of the high post-World War II fertility boom), and they spent their adolescent years during the troubling times of the 1970s and early 1980s, during which the antiwar movement, feminism, and civil rights movements peaked and then ebbed. Many men and women in their early 20s are still students in colleges and graduate schools, others are working adults still residing with their parents, and, as a group, they show signs of late marriage and low fertility.

31–40. G2 adults in their 30s are the baby-boomers born in the decade after World War II (1945 through 1954); some no doubt were in military service in Vietnam during their early 20s or were active in political opposition to or support of that war. They entered the labor force during years of inflation and rising unemployment, due in part to their own very large numbers. A tightened job market has meant postponement of marriage for many, generally low fertility, increased employment of married women in the early childrearing years, and high divorce rates. Many are the DINKS (Double Income, No Kids) that Mark Russell referred to in a December 1988 comedy routine paraphrased in the epigram to this chapter.

41–50. G2 adults who were in their 40s when interviewed in 1985 are members of the baby-bust cohorts of the later years of the depression or wartime babies, some born while their fathers were serving in the military (1935–1944 cohorts). They were also the advance first wave of suburban adolescents now so familiar in shopping malls, because many of their parents were modern pioneers in settling the expanding suburban developments in the 1950s. In our sample of Bostonians, many moved from inner city neighborhoods or inner ring older suburbs such as Brookline and Belmont to the outer suburban ring. The adolescence of our 41 to 50 age group was spent in the relatively quiet years of the 1950s and early 1960s, when colleges and universities were expanding rapidly, and an affluent economy quickly absorbed them. Now, in their middle years, many may be curbing expenditures in anticipation or the reality of the higher costs of educating their children (their youngest child is on

Table 3.2. Historical Markers by Developmental Phase of Major Age Groups (G2 Sample)

Age of G2 Adults	Birth Cohort	Adolescence (15–20)	Early Adulthood (21–35)	Middle Adulthood (36–55)
19–30 (314)	1955–1966 Post-WW II Affluence	1970–1986 Vietnam War Civil unrest Feminism	Late 1970s–1990s Late marriage, low fertility Tightening job market Inflation/unemployment	1990s–2020s
31–40 (365)	1945–1954 Post-WW II Suburban expansion Affluence Baby-Boomers	1960–1974 Vietnam War Civil Rights Feminism	Late 1960s–1980s Inflation Low Fertility	1980s–2010s Massachusetts economic boom
41–50 (224)	1935–1944 Depression WW II	1950–1964 Korean War Affluence Early marriage	Late 1950s–1970s Expanding higher education/economy High marriage rate High fertility	1970s–1990s Inflation Economic cutbacks, then boom in state
51–60 (199)	1925–1934 Boom and bust economy	1940–1954 WW II draftees Postwar expansion	Late 1940s–1960s Veterans' benefits (school/homes) High fertility	1960s–1980s Parents of youth protest movements
61–70 (170)	1915–1924 WW II Postwar affluence	1930–1944 Depression WW II	Late 1930s–1950s Veteran's benefits Wartime boom High fertility	1950s–1970s Easy promotions Consumerism
71–92 (118)	1893–1914 Economic expansion High immigration	1908–1934 WW I	Late 1910s–1940s Depression Low marriage and fertility rates WW II	1930s–1960s Affluence Secure retirement ahead

average 14, oldest child 20 years of age, as shown in Table 3.1). A large proportion has already seen their fathers through terminal illnesses and their mothers through adjustment to widowhood.

51–60.   Those in their 50s in 1985 were born in the boom and bust era of the late 1920s and early 1930s. The older among them are highly likely to have been drafted into the military in late adolescence during World War II, returning to enjoy GI benefits and an affluent, expanding economy that ensured stability and promotions as they married and moved to the suburbs to rear their baby-boom children in the 1950s and 1960s. Compared to the dark days of their youth, their lives were far brighter in the postwar era, as they indulged in what Cleveland Amory once called their "cave and clan" withdrawal from public life into home and family enmeshment.[2]

61–70.   G2 adults in their 60s are familiar to sociologists from Glen Elder's Great Depression study (1974): Born right after the first world war or during the early 1920s, they were old enough to understand the "hard times" many of their parents experienced in the depression years, and to have served in World War II. Like their juniors now in their 50s, this cohort also benefitted from the GI Bill to secure more education than they would otherwise have had, as they did from special mortgage rates for veterans. For most of their adult lives, it was relatively easy to find and retain niches in an expanding economy, and, at an older age, to enjoy the assured, if reduced, income that goes with contemporary retirement under Social Security and private pension plans.

71–92.   The oldest age group, respondents between 71 and 92 when interviewed, suffered the most severe impact of the hard times of the depression years. Those in their 70s were late adolescents when the Depression began; many did not marry, one in four never had children, and many probably had illegal abortions when it seemed too difficult to provide economic support for any additional children. Some experienced greater economic success in their middle years than in early adulthood, particularly if they engaged in war-related work and were able to make a financially successful transition to the peacetime economy. For those who were living in New England at the time, there may well have been occupational dislocation, as textile, paper, and shoe manufacturing declined as regional industries and new plastic and light communications and electronic industries replaced the old style manufactories. If not immigrants themselves, many of the current elderly in the Boston sample were the children of immigrants, whose parents had none of the protective buffers of pensions and health insurance that ease the circumstances of today's elderly.

It is clear from even these brief profiles of the six age groups by which we define the life course that our variously aged respondents were children and young and middle-aged adults under widely varying social and temporal conditions. Our task now is to establish what links we can between our survey data and these cohort and historical influences. That task is made somewhat easier when we concentrate on some common developmental stage of the life course, because when we do so, the age differences among respondents are translated into six broad birth cohorts so that differences can be viewed in terms of what we know about the demographic trends or historical events taking place at some point in twentieth-century history. It is from this perspective that we turn next to an analysis of how the early families in which our respondents grew up differ by the historic period in which they were children or adolescents.

Figure 3.3 provides an orientation to the underlying mode of analysis on which we are embarking. The figure is a schematic device for describ-

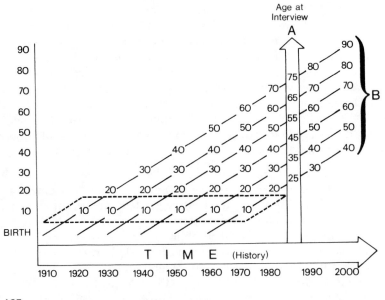

ᵃFor simplification, birth year for mid-point of the age group is shown.

Figure 3.3. Cross-sectional vs. cohort analysis of age.ᵃ (A) Cross-sectional analysis: vertical bar, using age differences at point of interview, e.g., current relations between parents and children in 1985. (B) Cohort analysis: diagonal lines represent aging of individuals moving horizontally with historical time. Analysis of a developmental phase, e.g., years growing up (shown in dashed line portion of the figure), permits analysis of cohort or historical change.

ing the difference in analysis mode between cross-sectional survey analysis of age differences in contemporary behavior and a cohort analysis that seeks to explore the impact of historical events and trends. The vertical bar "A" shows the midpoint in age of respondents for each age group in the sample when they were interviewed in 1985. The diagonal lines grouped as "B" in the figure sketches the ages respondents were at specified points in historic time. This represents the translation of the variable of current age into the developmental profile of each of the six birth cohorts. The dashed line-enclosed portion at the bottom of the figure represents the childhood and adolescence of respondents from the six birth cohorts. In an analysis of several aspects of early family life, then, we will be dealing with the span of years from 1910 through the 1970s. This 70-year period is the historical canvas on which we shall attempt to sketch cohort differences or historical era impact on respondents whose youth was spent in different time periods.

We shall also try to chart secular trends across an even broader time span, in an analysis of the qualities parents wish to instill in children or the skills they taught their children. Here the historic canvas will enlarge to include future decades, because our youngest respondents reported on children they do not yet have. Assuming childrearing spans the years from roughly 25 to 45 years of age, the reader can imaginatively extend a boxed-in portion of Figure 3.3 that indicates what the time frame would be from the 1930s when our oldest respondents were rearing children to the beginning of the twenty-first century when our youngest respondents will be rearing young adolescents.

Early Family Life, Historical Context, and Social Change

Early Family Stability and Causes of Disruption

The overwhelming majority (86%) of our G2 respondents grew up in households headed by both their natural parents, as shown in Table 3.3. Only five respondents reported they had been adopted, 7% that they were reared by one parent alone (6.3% by mother alone, 0.6% by father alone). Four percent were reared by one parent and a stepparent (evenly divided between stepmothers and stepfathers) and another 4% by someone other than the natural parent.[3]

Table 3.3 shows the composition of respondents' families of origin by their current age and the decades during which each age group was under 16 years of age. There are very small differences in family composition over the eight decades during which the various cohorts of respondents were dependent minors. There is a *rise* in the proportion of those who were reared by solo mothers, and a *decline* in the proportion reared by single fathers or fathers and stepmothers, reflecting the trend

Table 3.3. Composition of Family of Origin Household, by Age of G2
         Respondents. (in Percent) (G2 Sample)

Family Composition	Age of G2 Respondents					
	19–30	31–40	41–50	51–60	61–70	71–92
Natural Parents	87.6	87.4	86.2	83.4	80.6	85.6
Adoptive Parents	1.0	—	0.4	—	0.6	—
Mother Alone	7.3	6.3	5.8	6.5	6.5	4.2
Mother and						
Stepfather	1.6	2.2	1.8	0.5	1.8	—
Father Alone	0.3	0.5	0.4	1.0	0.6	1.7
Father and						
Stepmother	0.6	1.1	—	1.5	2.9	5.1
Other	1.6	2.5	5.4	7.0	7.1	3.4
N	(314)	(365)	(264)	(199)	(170)	(118)
Years from birth to						
16 years of age	1955–82	1945–70	1935–60	1925–50	1915–40	1893–1930

over the past half-century in the primary cause of family disruption, as
shown below.

There has also been a decline in the proportion reared by adults *other*
than one or both natural parents. Closer inspection of the 56 cases
involved shows that one or both grandparents (18 cases) was the predominant pattern. Other situations involved a parent together with a
grandparent or sibling (10 cases), aunts and uncles (11 cases), foster
homes or institutions (11 cases), an older sibling (5 cases), or "many
different relatives." Only one of the 56 cases involved a man alone:
Typically, the people carrying childrearing responsibility are a married
couple (e.g., grandparents, married aunts, older married sisters—29
cases), or a woman alone (grandmother, aunt, or sister—14 cases).[4]

The major social change these data reflect is the change in the *causes* of
a marital break over the past half-century during which *divorce* has
replaced *death* as the major reason for family disruption while children
are young (Uhlenberg, 1980). Three-quarters of the respondents over 60
years of age who were not reared by both parents for most of their youth
had experienced the death of one or both parents, compared to 18%
among those now in their 20s. Only one in four of the older respondents
whose families were disrupted had experienced a parental divorce compared to four of five of the youngest respondents (data not shown in
tabular form).

Not only has death declined as a cause of family disruption, but the
sex ratio of parents who died while their children were very young has
also shifted over time. More of the older respondents lost a mother than
lost a father, whereas the reverse situation applies to younger respon-

dents. The sharp decline in maternal mortality now spares almost all children the death of a mother, while occupational hazards, military casualties, and terminal illnesses in midlife, all more frequent among men generally and more probable in light of the age differences between spouses, still rob a significant minority of children of their fathers.[5]

Troubles in the Family of Origin

The G2 respondents reported a variety of family troubles during the years they were growing up. Table 3.4 shows the percentage in each age group reporting each of 15 "troubles" in their families of origin. The most common problems, affecting one in four or five of the families, concern life and death issues: someone ill for a long time, or the death of a child or adult.[6]

Most of the other family troubles reflect, we suggest, the tenor of the historic period during which respondents were growing up. Note, for example, that the incidence of prolonged unemployment is higher for those now in their 50s and 60s, who were adolescents during the depression years of the 1930s, than for those in their 30s and 40s, who were adolescents during the high employment decades of the 1950s and 1960s. These same two age groups also rated their families' financial status to have been "poor" while they were young adolescents to a lesser extent (16%) than those in their 50s (26%) (data not shown in tabular form). There is an upturn in the proportion citing unemployment among the very youngest respondents in the Family Troubles battery (10%), some of whose fathers and older siblings may have lost jobs during the 1970s and early 1980s before the recent economic boom in the Massachusetts economy.

What is of far greater interest is the finding that the highest incidence of family troubles likely to have involved adolescent members of the family are reported by the youngest respondents: drug usage, trouble with the police or school authorities, someone in the "wrong crowd," a child rebellious against his or her parents. Perhaps as a reflection of these difficulties, family friction is also most frequently reported by the younger respondents: quarrels among the children, between adults in the family, and with relatives. These are all difficulties that seem to reflect the tumultuous years of the late 1960s and 1970s, when tension was often present in families in whom adolescent children were attracted to counterculture values, involved in challenges to authority, or showed explicit rebellion against their parents' demands and values. These were the years when our youngest respondents were adolescents. By contrast, middle-aged respondents now in their 40s and 50s were adolescents during the socially and politically quieter times of the 1950s,

Table 3.4. Incidence of Family Troubles in Families of Origin of G2 Adults
(G2 Sample)

Problem [a]	Age of Respondent					
	19–30	31–40	41–50	51–60	61–70	71–92
Health/Emotional						
Sickness	24.9	22.7	22.4	27.4	23.9	25.2
Death	21.6	20.1	23.7	24.7	21.5	25.2
Drinking Problem	23.9	20.4	18.7	19.4	11.0	8.7
Emotional Problem	15.6	11.6	9.6	7.0	7.4	3.5
Drug Problem	8.3	3.4	0.5	—	—	0.9
Physical/sexual						
Abuse	3.7	6.8	3.2	2.7	0.6	—
Family Friction						
Rebellious Child	26.9	22.9	10.0	8.6	3.7	2.6
Adults' Quarrels	18.6	19.5	12.5	12.9	4.3	4.3
Quarrels with						
Relatives	17.9	19.5	9.1	10.8	1.2	2.6
Children's						
Quarrels	15.3	13.3	5.9	5.4	2.5	4.3
External to Family						
Exhausting Job	28.2	24.1	18.7	15.6	14.1	11.3
Wrong Crowd	15.0	11.9	5.5	4.8	3.1	0.9
In Trouble with						
Police	13.2	8.2	3.2	3.2	3.1	0.9
In Trouble with						
School						
Authorities	10.0	6.5	3.2	4.8	2.5	—
Unemployment	10.3	5.9	6.4	10.2	11.0	6.1
N	(314)	(365)	(224)	(199)	(170)	(118)

[a] Percentage who report that someone in the household they grew up in had this problem. Percentages
exceed 100% since more than one problem could be identified.

and show a much lower incidence of such family troubles as rebellious
children, trouble with authorities, internal family friction, or drug or
alcohol abuse.

It is possible, of course, that the negative relationship with age is a
reflection of a tendency for older adults to underreport difficulties in the
past because they look back through a rosier lens to those early years
when their now deceased parents were young adults and they were
children and adolescents. This is precisely a point at which we can test
empirically whether the differences shown by age in 1985 reflect period
effects. We can do so by comparing the results shown in Table 3.4 on
troubles in the family of origin, with results concerning troubles in the

family of procreation. If the influence of the larger political and cultural climate of the society is being reflected in our data, then the respondents who should report the highest incidence of troubles of this social deviance variety should be middle-aged respondents in their 50s and 60s who had adolescent children in the 1960s and 1970s. By contrast, our very oldest respondents, whose children were adolescents prior to 1960, should report very low incidence levels on the social deviant types of family troubles.

This specific test for period effects is shown in Table 3.5, which brings together the reported incidence level for four types of family troubles most likely to reflect the impact of the more turbulent 1960s and 1970s on family life: One or more children were rebellious, got in with the "wrong crowd," or caused trouble with the police, or with school authorities. To

Table 3.5. Incidence of Selected Family Troubles in Family of Origin and Family of Procreation, by Age of G2 Adults (G2 Sample) [a]

	Age of G2 Adult					
	19–30	*31–40*	*41–50*	*51–60*	*61–70*	*71–92*
Report a Rebellious Child (%)						
Family of Origin	26.9	22.9	10.0	8.6	3.7	2.6
		A	B	C		
Family of Procreation	1.3	5.8	16.1	19.8	12.3	1.1
Report Someone in "Wrong Crowd" (%)						
Family of Origin	15.0	11.9	5.5	4.8	3.1	0.9
		A	B	C		
Family of Procreation	5.1	4.5	12.8	17.4	12.2	—
Report Trouble with the Police (%)						
Family of Origin	13.2	8.2	3.2	3.2	3.1	0.9
		A	B	C		
Family of Procreation	3.8	2.7	5.6	14.5	7.9	—
Report Trouble with School Authorities (%)						
Family of Origin	10.0	6.5	3.2	4.8	2.5	—
		A	B	C		
Family of Procreation	1.3	2.2	8.3	11.0	7.2	—
Report Family Member Sick for a Long Time (%)						
Family of Origin	24.9	22.7	22.4	27.4	23.9	25.2
		A	B	C		
Family of Procreation	9.0	13.8	15.6	26.2	12.2	19.8

[a] Pairs marked A were families with adolescents in the 1970s, B in the 1960s, and C in the 1950s.

provide a contrast to what we take to be historically bound indicators, we add one other type of trouble—sickness—that could be found in any time period.

The diagonal lines in Table 3.5 link pairs of age groups that identify families in which adolescent children were present in different historical periods: for example, the lines marked "A" involve respondents now in their 20s reporting on their families of origin, paired with respondents in their 50s who had adolescent children in the same time period—the 1960s. The "B" diagonal line identifies families with adolescents in the 1970s. By contrast the "C" pairs refer to families with adolescent children in the quieter decade of the 1950s. Hence, our prediction was that the highest incidence level of rebellious, deviant, and antiauthority behavior should be shown in the A and B pairs, while pair C should show very low incidence levels.

Inspection of the results strongly supports the prediction: The two youngest age groups, those in their 20s and 30s, report two to three times higher levels of rebellious behavior in their families of origin than any of the four older age groups. That a maturational effect interpretation is not appropriate can be seen by comparing the profile on the families of procreation: When respondents report *as parents*, it is those in their 40s through their 60s who show the elevated incidence levels of rebellious behavior on the part of their children. The very oldest respondents report hardly any trouble of this kind in their families of procreation, because their children were adolescents in a quieter time. The only "maturational" factor suggested by these data concern the families of procreation now being formed by our youngest respondents, whose children are all still under 10 years of age, close to home, and hence still relatively immune from societal influences.

Note that the incidence level for "sickness" in the family while children were growing up remains stable across the age groups where families of origin are concerned, with roughly one in four respondents reporting prolonged illness of a family member in all six age groups. The incidence of illness in the families of procreation reflects the youth and healthiness of both children and parents in the early phase of family formation and childrearing: Since respondents were asked to respond to this question in terms of the years they were "rearing children," the sickness incidence level is very low for respondents under 40 years of age, peaks among adults in their 50s, and then falls off, no doubt because the children are themselves adults and have left home.[7]

One other analysis step further illustrates the impact of turbulent social times upon family life. G2 respondents were asked to rate, retrospectively, the degree of closeness or strain in their relationship to their parents at three specified ages: when they were about 10 years of age (preadolescent parent–child affect), at 16 years of age (adolescence-induced stress in the parent–child relationship), and at 25 years of age (when most children have settled into adult roles and live on their own). The general profile of parent–child intimacy shows the predictable slump in closeness when children are engaged in adolescent individuation from their families. We tested whether this general pattern is affected by the time period when children in the family were adolescents, with the prediction that parent–child relationships should show lower intimacy ratings when the social–political atmosphere of the society was turbulent than during times of relative social calm. Hence, we compare an age group in which adolescence took place between 1966 and 1975 (the birth cohorts from 1950 to 1959, identified with solid lines marked "B" in Figure 3.4), and an age group whose adolescence was

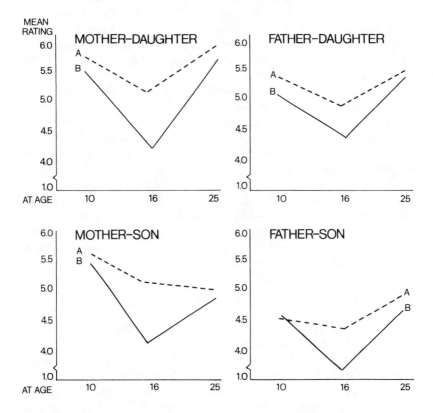

A Birth cohort 1925–1939, whose adolescence was during 1941–1955 (Aged 46–60 in 1985).
B Birth cohort 1950–1959, whose adolescence was during 1966–1975 (Aged 26–35 in 1985).

Figure 3.4.   Affective closeness of G2 adults and their parents: cohorts whose adolescence was in 1941–1955 vs. 1966–1975 (G2 sample). (Mean rating on 1–7 closeness scale.)

spent in the quieter years of 1941–1955 (the birth cohorts from 1925 to 1939, identified with the dashed lines marked "A" in Figure 3.4). Both selected cohorts show the adolescent dip in affective closeness, but a comparison of the A and B groups shows a far more marked dip in average rating of Affective Closeness for those who were adolescents in the 1960s and early 1970s than in the 1940s and 1950s.

Note, too, that there is little difference between the two cohort groups (A and B) at 10 years of age or 25 years of age, suggesting there were no disturbed family relations that preselected for strained relations in adolescence, nor any aftermath of troubled relations in early adulthood as a consequence of adolescent strain. There are dynamics *internal* to the families of origin that produce strain in the parent–child relationship that persists when children are independent adults, as we shall see in a later chapter, but the *external* events that impacted on adolescents in recent decades do not have persistent effects on the parent–child relationship. Parents forgive, and rebellious adolescents often become conventional adults. As one parent of a 33-year-old son commented, "My Hippie son is now a Yuppie."

In the examples we have covered thus far, the focus was on the impact of particular historical events associated with particular recent points in American history—the great depression, the postwar affluent 1950s, and the turbulent late 1960s and 1970s. Long-term secular trends in the society can also be analyzed by translating current age of respondents into birth cohorts at particular stages of the life course. The combined use of respondents' ages, the childrearing phase of the life course, and data concerning both the family of origin and the family of procreation will permit us to chart changes over historic time in two dimensions of family life: the qualities parents seek to instill in their children and the extent to which sons and daughters were taught gender-stereotyped skills. It is to these two topics that we turn next.

Child Qualities Parents Consider Important

Family sociologists have had longstanding interest in childrearing practices and in parental values underlying those practices. By parental values most sociologists mean the standards parents use to evaluate the behavior of their children. As early as the Middletown studies by Robert and Helen Lynd (1929), a general distinction among parental values has been drawn between *independence* and *obedience*. Sometimes the labels vary, but the constructs remain pretty much the same. Thus, Gerhard Lenski (1961) distinguishes between "intellectual autonomy" and "intellectual heteronomy," which he links to a counterpart contrast in parental preferences for "thinking for oneself" vs. "obedience." The long tradition of research by Melvin Kohn in this area has also drawn the

distinction between "self-direction" and "conformity to external authority" (Kohn, 1959, 1969; Kohn et al., 1983).[8]

In more recent years, sociologists have become interested in parental
values for clues to unraveling the processes of social change. A leading
example of this focus is the work of Duane Alwin, using data from a
variety of attitude and opinion polls, including the long series of Detroit
area surveys (Alwin, 1984, 1988, 1989). Questions on the qualities parents consider important in rearing their children have been asked in
many surveys from the 1950s to the present time. Alwin draws the
distinction between "obedience" and "autonomy" as central values that
have been undergoing change over the past several decades, as parents
show less emphasis on obedience in their children and more concern for
their acquiring independence and autonomy.

We also included items on parental values in the Boston surveys, a
battery of 15 qualities we asked respondents to rate in terms of how
important each quality was (or would be, in the case of young respondents who have not yet had children) in rearing their children. A factor
analysis of the 15 items showed three latent constructs that could be
measured by 11 of the 15 items (see Table 1.5 and relevant text in
Chapter 1 for details). Two constructs in particular bear a close resemblance to Alwin's distinction between obedience and autonomy, though
we have labeled them Conformity and Autonomy; the third construct in
our data is Status. As a reminder of the content of the three indices, the
qualities associated with each are as follows:

Autonomy: Independent, Self-Reliant, and Open-minded
Conformity: Respectful to adults, Obedient to parents, Neat and clean,
and Well-behaved
Status: Competitive, Ambitious, Successful, and Athletic

Our analysis of these parental values focused on two issues. The first
was whether there was in fact a polarity between valuing autonomy and
conformity. Much of the literature assumes this to be the case, by merely
showing a decline in the one value over time and an increase in the
other. Thus, for example, Theodore Caplow and his associates (1982), in
their return to Middletown, report a decline in "strict obedience" as one
of three emphases in childrearing between Lynd's 1924 study and their
repeat study in 1978 (from 45 to 17%) and an increase in "independence" (from 25 to 76%). We question whether it is not possible for
many parents to urge obedience in the context of family and home,
while encouraging independence on the part of children away from
home, at school, or later, at work.

Second, because the parental value items were included in all three
surveys, we can see the extent to which correlations among the three
constructs are similar or different in the three samples, and, more

importantly, whether by using the age of the respondents as an index to the period during which they were rearing children, we can capture the same kind of trend shown in previous studies. Having data from all three generations also means we can test the extent to which the values stressed by parents in one generation are stressed by parents in the following generation.

We report below, the highlights of the analysis conducted in pursuit of these two issues.

Consistent with earlier surveys, Conformity was more heavily stressed by older G2 respondents, whereas larger proportions of young respondents stressed Autonomy rather than Conformity or Status. Of greater interest is how the three values relate to each other *among* young vs older respondents. To explore this, Table 3.6 shows four small correlation matrices on the three values, first among older cohorts (Panel A), then among younger cohorts (Panel B). Two sources of data are shown in each of the cohorts: among the older cohorts, data are shown from G1 parents (in A1) and from older G2 respondents (aged 51–92) in their roles as parents (in A2); among the younger cohorts, the correlations are shown with data from younger G2 respondents (under 40 years of age) as parents (in B1) and from G3 adult children in their actual or hypothetical roles as parents (in B2). By limiting the G2 respondents to older and younger age groups, we effectively match them to the ages of G1 parents and G3 adult children, as shown by the mean age in the paired groups in each of the panels in the table.

The average G1 parent and older G2 parent, both now in their 60s, were rearing their children about 40 years ago, during and immediately after World War II. As can be seen in the matrices in Panel A, there are significant and positive correlation coefficients among the three parental values: Self-reliance and independence were not considered at odds with conformist behavior or striving for status. Perhaps the rugged entrepreneur is the image that embraces the values covered across the three indices. It also strikes us that many older parents may have drawn clear distinctions between appropriate behavior at home and at work, with respect toward the elderly and being squeaky-clean and respectful at home, but being competitive and ambitious in school, office, or factory.

It is only among the younger respondents that Autonomy is at odds with parental stress on Conformity and Status, with a significantly negative coefficient between Autonomy and Conformity among the G3 adult children we interviewed. This may bring a smile of recognition to those who grew up in an era when overt gestures of respect were owed to parents and older relatives, when one dressed up in one's "Sunday best" every week, and mothers devoted hours to starching and ironing

Table 3.6. Correlations Within Cohorts and Between Generations on Qualities Considered Important in Rearing Children: Autonomy, Status, and Conformity (G1, G2, and G3 Samples)

A. Within Older Cohorts

(1) G1 as Parents (mean age = 63)	Autonomy	Status	Conformity		(2) Older G2 as Parents (mean age = 64)	Autonomy	Status	Conformity
Autonomy	—	.31***	.17**		Autonomy	—	.31***	.17***
Status		—	.33***		Status		—	.33***
Conformity			—		Conformity			—
		(N = 320)					(N = 462)	

B. Within Younger Cohorts

(1) Younger G2 as Parents (mean age = 32)	Autonomy	Status	Conformity		(2) G3 as Parents (mean age = 31)	Autonomy	Status	Conformity
Autonomy	—	.14*	-.08		Autonomy	—	.03	-.10*
Status		—	.32***		Status		—	.24***
Conformity			—		Conformity			—
		(N = 650)					(N = 277)	

C. Between Generations

(1) G1–G2 generations			(2) G2–G3 generations	
Autonomy	.11*	(316)	Autonomy	-.03	(277)
Status	.16**	(310)	Status	.13*	(272)
Conformity	.17***	(321)	Conformity	.22***	(277)

*** p < .001
** p < .01
* p < .05

countless cotton blouses, dresses, and pinafores. Our parents emphasized hard work, making something of yourself, *and* respect for authority. By contrast, one senses far greater variation among young parents
today, some emphasizing the older values of getting ahead and showing
respect, while others encourage independence, tolerance, and self-
reliance. What seems to be associated with these latter indicators of
autonomy is less investment in parenting responsibilities, and a more
casual approach to home maintenance, dress, and demeanor in public.

Panel C of Table 3.6 indicates two further points. First, there *is* some
cross-generational transmission of parental values, with significant if
not very large correlation coefficients between the value stress of G2
respondents and their G1 parents, as well as between G2 respondents
and their G3 children. Second, there is much less transmission of Autonomy as a parental value from one generation of parents to the next than
there is of Conformity, suggesting a wider spectrum of influences encouraging independence as a parental value than is true for Conformity.
Parental values are not discrete and distinct from other societal values
that are undergoing change over time; nor is family structure a closed
system immune from the variety of currents in the society at large.

One very general trend in western societies is away from institutional
control over a wide array of life domains to increasing preference for
individualism, the rights of the individual over the claims of a collec-
tivity. This is beautifully demonstrated, using European Value Studies
data (from surveys conducted over the past 16 years in a dozen countries
affiliated with the European Economic Community), in the work of Ron
Lesthaeghe and Jon Surkyn (Lesthaeghe, 1980, 1983; Lesthaeghe &
Surkyn, 1988). They argue, for example, that secularization involves a
declining adherence to organized or institutionalized religion, such that
Western religious institutions have undergone a change from an overarching system that sought to control all aspects of life to a subsystem
alongside other subsystems. The loosening of religious institutional
controls translates into more latitude in individual morality and greater
tolerance of individual discretion and choice. Lesthaeghe's theory seems
to apply very well to Catholic Americans, who have gradually rejected
church control over many private aspects of life (e.g., premarital sex and
divorce, use of contraceptives, and preference for small families) while
retaining core religious beliefs (e.g., in salvation and damnation, God,
the soul and life after death) (Lesthaeghe & Surkyn, 1988).

We turn now to gender role socialization, using data concerning the
skills parents taught to their sons and daughters.

Parental Skill Transmission and Gender–Role Socialization

A persistent finding in contemporary research on gender roles in the
family and the economy is that women continue to carry the brunt of

home maintenance and childcare responsibilities, whether or not they are employed, and whether or not they subscribe to a traditional or a feminist conception of gender equality (e.g., McLaughlin et al., 1988). Gender-differentiated occupational choice and salaries, together with age differences between husbands and wives, indicate a gender imbalance in home duties; the partner with the higher salary may be spared more home duties because his or her work and time is more "valuable" to family support.

But there is another source for such gender imbalance: who has the greater competence to perform with ease and efficiency the numerous tasks associated with family and home. It is from this perspective that earlier gender role socialization takes on special significance. Because gender was an important axis in the design of our study, we included measures of the skills parents teach their children that have tended to be strongly gender linked. As described in Chapter 1 (Table 1.5 and related text), the skill areas we measured were Domestic, Masculine, and Cognitive Skills.[9]

Table 3.7 shows the frequencies with which G2 men and women report their parents made a "very great effort" to ensure they learned each of these skills (Panel A) and the counterpart frequencies indicating the extent to which they themselves, as parents, have invested (or would invest in future) in training their own children (Panel B). Separate

Table 3.7. Parental Skill Transmission to Children in the Family of Origin and Family of Procreation of G2 Respondents, by Gender [a] (G2 Sample) [b]

Skill Area	A. Family of Origin		B. Family of Procreation	
	Women	*Men*	*Daughters*	*Sons*
Domestic Skills				
*Clean	51.1	19.9	42.4	19.3
*Cook	36.8	8.7	44.8	12.3
*Laundry	34.0	8.9	34.7	15.2
*Sew	31.4	3.0	29.2	3.5
Masculine Skills				
Sports	15.4	21.6	21.8	38.7
*Carpentry	5.3	18.9	5.7	20.4
*Hunt/Fish	4.5	14.5	4.5	12.9
*Use of Power Machinery	3.4	12.3	3.0	15.2
Cultural/Cognitive Skills				
*Read	57.2	48.6	83.4	82.7
*Math/Arithmetic	33.5	36.4	69.5	69.8
Music/Sing	27.6	22.2	26.1	20.4
Foreign Language	18.0	13.0	27.1	24.3

[a] Gender of G2 respondent in case of family of origin; separate questions were asked of G2 respondents concerning actual or hypothetical training of daughters and of sons.
[b] Percentage of parents who expended "Very Great Effort" to teach child.
*Items included in indices on these constructs.

questions were asked for daughters and for sons. Note that for both family types, there is a very strong distinction drawn between sons and daughters: Daughters are from two to ten times as likely to be taught Domestic Skills as sons, and sons are from two to five times as likely to be taught Masculine Skills as daughters. (The asterisks indicate which of these specific skills were included in the skill indices as a consequence of factor analysis of all the items.) This sharp contrast by gender predicts the competencies men and women will bring to their own marriages, thus contributing to the retention of gender-differentiated tasks in home maintenance.

No sharp differences emerge between families of origin and procreation, in part because there are both old and young respondents reporting on both family types. Testing for social trends in gender-linked skills is best done by estimating the decades during which childrearing was or will be taking place. By this means we can test whether there has been any lessening of the strong gender-linkage implied by the data in Table 3.7.

Figures 3.5 (on Domestic Skills) and 3.6 (on Masculine Skills) chart the average scores on the two skill measures in a way that highlights the gender linkage over time. In both figures, the average scores for training daughters are indicated by solid lines and those for sons by dashed lines. The "P" symbol refers to data concerning the family of procreation and the "O" symbol to the family of origin. The trends range from the early decades of the century (1900s through 1930s) when our oldest respondents were children to the 1980s and 1990s when our youngest respondents are or will be rearing children. Note that by using data concerning both types of families, we have overlapping data for the two middle time periods (1930s–1950s and 1960s–1970s); for example, middle-aged G2 respondents were growing up in the 1930s–1950s, and older G2 respondents in their 60s and 70s were rearing children in that same time period. Inspection of both figures shows the scores of the overlapping groups to be not markedly different from each other, although respondents tend to claim they emphasized more skill training of their own children than they report receiving from their own parents in the past, a bit of self-aggrandizement perhaps.

The more general and important finding highlighted by Figures 3.5 and 3.6 is that gender role differentiation in parental skill transmission to children is "alive and well": In whatever period childrearing was taking place, from the 1920s or anticipated for the 1990s, the average scores on the skill indices show significantly higher emphasis on Domestic Skills for daughters than for sons, and, reciprocally, higher scores on Masculine Skills for sons than for daughters.

Second, over the decades there has been a general increase in parental teaching of Masculine Skills to *both* sons and daughters (see Figure 3.6),

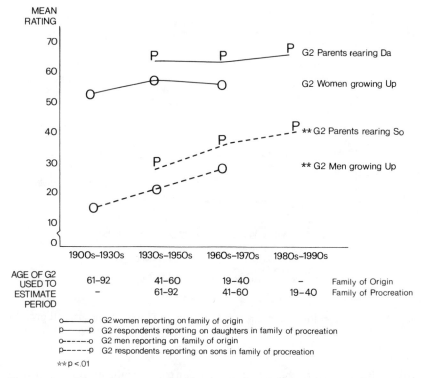

Figure 3.5. Domestic skill training of children in families of origin and procreation of G2 adults: 1900s–1990s (G2 sample). (Scores converted to 0–100 metric.)

but in Domestic Skill transmission there is an increased emphasis in more recent years *only for sons*. Since there are no changes shown in the average Domestic skill score for daughters, *what is narrowing the gender gap in socialization is an increased emphasis by parents on the domestic competencies of sons, not a decreased emphasis on the training of daughters.* A variety of factors may have contributed to this trend. Some parents in recent years may have been aware that many young men will remain unmarried until their late 20s, and will need to be competent in caring for their own domestic needs for the span of time between leaving home and acquiring a wife. Still other parents, especially mothers, may be aware that their future daughters-in-law may expect more domestic competence and sharing of responsibility from their husbands than past generations of brides expected of their spouses. Then too, smaller family size in recent cohorts means more families with sons only, in which case sons may be taught more domestic skills in the absence of any daughters, a pattern that would provide some assistance from sons in home maintenance for employed mothers.

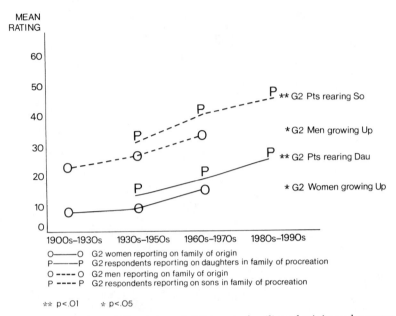

MEAN
RATING

Figure 3.6. Masculine skill training of children in families of origin and procreation of G2 adults: 1900s–1990s (G2 sample). (Scores converted to 0–100 metric.)

We shall return to these data on gender role socialization in Chapter 7 in an analysis of what parental characteristics are associated with traditional vs. countertraditional skill training of children.

Family and Social Status Characteristics by Age

Sampling methodology in survey research encourages a primary focus on individuals, because we draw a sample of households and randomly select one household member as a respondent. Although this satisfies our concern for the representativeness of a sample of individuals, it neglects the social embeddedness of respondents in larger social structures beyond the residential household. But in the dailiness of real lives, most individuals are members of social networks of varying degrees of density and social interaction. High points of a calendar year are typically occasions for the gathering together of such social intimates— friends and relatives—that provide a measure of the degree to which individuals are socially embedded. Clinicians report the most severe episodes of depression and suicidal impulses at precisely these high points of the year: to be alone at Christmas, New Year's Eve, Memorial Day weekend is to become acutely aware of deviation from the cultural mode or past experience with the coming together of kith and kin. To live at a distance from family members on a memorable personal occasion such as a birthday, and not to receive some recognition of that occasion by a card, a letter, or a phone call if not a visit, may stimulate an especially keen sense of isolation and depression. An elderly woman acquaintance of ours actually kept a personal "score card," a running record of the number of greetings she received each year on the occasion of her birthday, a practice we learned about the year she sadly reported that there had been a great decline in recognition, as indexed by the fact that she received only six birthday cards compared to 20 a few years before. It did not faze her that fewer cards came from friends because many were by then deceased; what mattered to her was the fact that she did not hear from several cousins and a sibling who had acknowledged her birthday for many consecutive years in the past.

Judging from the reports we received from our G2 respondents, reaching out to others on celebratory occasions is a very pervasive social pattern, much as Ted Caplow reports for Middletown (Caplow, 1982). When we asked respondents to estimate the number of Holiday and Birthday greetings they sent each year—by card, letter, or phone call— they reported an average of 47 holiday greetings and 25 birthday greetings (see Table 3.8). Only 46 respondents said they sent no birthday greetings, 80 no holiday greetings to anyone, while at the other extreme, 49 reported sending more than 100 birthday greetings, and over 200 sent more than 100 holiday greetings. When asked what the balance was in terms of greetings to friends or to family members, it was clear that birthday greetings are restricted to family more than holiday greetings are: 54% reported birthday greetings were largely or all to family members, compared to only 30% in the case of holiday greetings.

A birthday has many social meanings, for the individual, his or her parents, the extended family, the circle of friends, and often of co-workers as well. The birth of a first child marks a critical transition point in the lives of the parents, and may mark the acquisition of new kinship roles for others by their becoming an aunt, a grandfather, or a great-grandmother. Within a few years, the birthday becomes a highpoint in the child's life as well, an occasion for receiving gifts and cards and holding a birthday party. Vivian Paley, a remarkable kindergarten teacher at the Laboratory School of the University of Chicago, describes the pervasive use of birthdays by kindergarten youngsters as a social device for inclusion or exclusion from the children's network of friends: An argument over the use of a toy or refusal to accept an assigned role in a game quickly leads to charges "I won't invite YOU to my birthday party next year" (Paley, 1984). Paley suggests that potential birthday invitation lists undergo contraction and expansion several times a week for each of the 20 5-year olds in her class.

On a more structural level, the timing of births and the number of births determine the range and size of the kindred, and the timing of

Table 3.8.   Number of Birthday and Holiday Greetings *a* Sent Per Year and to
          Whom (G2 Sample) (in percent)

		Birthday Greetings	Holiday Greetings
A.	**Number of Greetings Sent**		
	10 or Less	33	20
	11–20	31	16
	21–30	19	19
	31–60	13	23
	61 of More	4	22
	N	(1375)	(1373)
	Mean number of Greetings	25	47
B.	**To Whom Greetings Sent**		
	All or more to Friends	11.8	28.2
	Equally, Friends and Family	34.6	41.7
	All or more to Family	53.6	30.1
	N	(1331)	(1298)

a Questions read: *Birthday Greetings:* "Approximately how many birthday greetings—cards, letters, or phone calls—do you [IF MARRIED: and your (husband) (wife)] give to people in the course of a year? Just give your best estimate." *Holiday Greetings:* "Approximately how many holiday greetings—cards, letters, or phone calls at Christmas, Easter, Yom Kippur—do you [IF MARRIED: and your (husband)(wife)] give people in the course of a year? Just give your best estimate."

deaths determines the depth of a kindred or lineage. The more siblings one's parents had, the larger the number of aunts, uncles, and first cousins one will have; the more children one has, the more children-in-law and the more grandchildren one is likely to have. And the longer people live, all else being equal, the more living generations there will be in a lineage.

It is from this broader concern for the structure and composition of the lineage that we inspect the marital status and family size of our respondents across the life course. Individual choice is of course involved, but so too is the social ambience and state of the economy in early adulthood when marriages are contracted and fertility decisions are made. Early adulthood in the 1930s was associated with postponement of marriage, restriction of family size, and reliance on illegal abortions; early adulthood in the 1950s was associated with early marriage and increased family size. In the 1980s, gender role debate, inflationary prices of housing, and high levels of consumption have been associated with postponement of marriage, more voluntary childlessness, small size families, high divorce rates, and more than in the past, lower remarriage rates, especially among divorced women (Parke, 1988; Sweet & Bumpass, 1987).

All these trends are manifested in the marital status and family size of respondents at different stages of the life course in 1985. Table 3.9 provides a profile of the six age groups in marital status, age at first marriage, cohabitation and marital expectations among those not married, and family size in both family of origin and family of procreation. Because the timing of marriage and marital status vary between men and women, gender is a control in the four marital status variables.

Marriage Formation

As shown in Panel B of Table 3.9, age at first marriage was older by 3 years for those over 70 years of age (28 for men, 25 for women) compared to adults in midlife (24 for men, 22 for women). Since there has already been significant mortality in the birth cohorts represented by our oldest respondents, there may be an underestimate of the drop in age at first marriage over the past several decades. The final story is not yet in of course on the age at marriage among the youngest respondents in the sample: Only the early-to-marry individuals are represented in the mean age at marriage.

The life course profile of marital status is very different for men than for women. Men marry later and more remain married in old age than is the case for women; the most marked gender contrast is among the elderly over 70 years of age, among whom 78% of the men are married to only 23% of the women. Widowhood increases with each age group above 50 for both sexes, but at very different rates: 20% of the women in their 50s are widows to only 4% of men, whereas among those over 70, 56% of women but only 20% of men are widowed. These figures are roughly comparable to national data on age, gender, and widowhood (Sweet & Bumpass, 1987; Uhlenberg, 1980).[10]

Our Boston sample includes more never married elderly adults than is generally found in national data, especially among women. Although we have 10% among women in their 60s who report never having been married, Keith reports only 5% among women 65–74; to our 14% among women over 71, Keith reports only 6% among elderly women over 75 years of age (Keith, 1986). This is partially due to the large majority of Catholics in our Boston sample, among whom remaining single has been more prevalent than among non-Catholics.[11]

The very different life course probabilities of being without a marital partner for women compared to men can be seen more readily in graphic than numeric form. Figure 3.7 shows the proportion who are without a life partner (never married, divorced and widowed) by gender and age. Above the age of 30, the percentage of "solo" men remains a flat plateau of only one in five. For women, it is only from 30 to 50 that two of three women have a husband; once they pass their fiftieth birthday, there is a steady climb in the proportion of women alone. The chances are very high indeed that from midlife on, women will need the

Table 3.9. Marriage and Family Size Characteristics of G2 Adults, by Age and Gender (G2 Sample)

Variable	Age of G2 Adults					
	19–30	31–40	41–50	51–60	61–70	71–92
A. Marital Status (in Percent)						
Women						
Never Married	45.9	10.2	11.0	1.7	10.1	14.3
Married	47.6	69.9	66.2	68.7	55.6	23.4
Separated/Divorced	6.4	18.5	20.6	9.5	10.1	6.5
Widowed	0.0	1.5	2.2	20.0	24.2	55.8
N	(170)	(206)	(136)	(115)	(99)	(77)
Men						
Never Married	60.4	14.5	3.4	4.8	9.9	2.4
Married	33.3	76.7	76.1	79.8	80.3	78.0
Separated/Divorced	6.3	8.8	17.1	12.0	4.2	0.0
Widowed	0.0	0.0	3.4	3.6	5.6	19.5
N	(144)	(159)	(88)	(84)	(71)	(41)
B. Age at First Marriage						
Women						
Mean Age	22.2	22.4	22.4	23.0	23.7	25.2
N	(91)	(185)	(121)	(113)	(87)	(66)
Men						
Mean Age	23.4	24.3	24.3	24.6	26.6	27.5
N	(57)	(136)	(85)	(79)	(62)	(38)

C. Cohabitation

Percentage not married but living with someone						
Women	28.4	11.3	15.6	8.6	6.8	5.3
N	(88)	(62)	(45)	(35)	(44)	(57)
Men	34.4	37.8	23.8	17.6	21.4	22.2
N	(96)	(37)	(21)	(17)	(14)	(9)

D. Marital Expectations

Percentage not married but expect to marry in future						
Women	88.5	55.3	45.9	13.8	11.6	7.5
N	(78)	(38)	(37)	(29)	(43)	(53)
Men	92.0	78.1	64.7	33.3	7.7	0.0
N	(87)	(32)	(17)	(12)	(13)	(8)

E. Family Size

Number of Children—Family of Origin (mean)	4.7	4.2	4.2	4.9	5.2	5.1
SD	(2.7)	(2.5)	(3.0)	(2.7)	(3.1)	(3.1)
Number of Children—Family of Procreation (mean)	1.7	2.3	3.2	3.8	3.3	2.9
SD	(.9)	(1.2)	(1.6)	(2.2)	(2.0)	(1.8)
Percentage No Children	—	31.5%	15.6%	9.5%	17.2%	24.6%

121

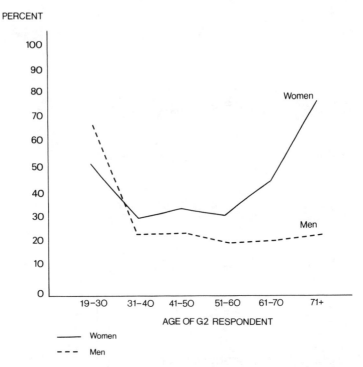

Figure 3.7. Percentage "single" (never married, separated/divorced, or widowed) by gender and age (G2 sample).

skills to support themselves, the capacity to deal alone with all kinds of domestic crises (e.g., blown fuses, tax return preparation, and stopped up drains), and the support of friends and family to maintain psychological equanimity and social stability.[12]

But Figure 3.7 provides only a partial view of the gender difference in solo status. Not being married does not mean being unattached, because there has been an increasing reliance on cohabitation, and this is reported by a significant proportion of men of all ages, whereas for women it is largely a pattern of early adulthood. A full third of the unmarried men in their 20s report living with someone, and this is true for more than one in five elderly men as well. By contrast, unmarried women living with someone declines rapidly from 28% among women in their 20s to only 5% among the oldest women.

That future marriage looms large in the expectations of adults is suggested by the very high proportion who are not now married but say they expect to do so in the future. Here too, however, there is a sharp difference between men and women: To the age of 60, a much larger proportion of men say they expect to marry than of women. Among those in their 40s, for example, two in three men still expect to marry

(65%), but fewer than half the women (46%). For both sexes, marital expectations drop rapidly after 50, though more so for women than men (from 46 to 14% for women in their 40s vs. 50s; for men the comparable percentages are 65 to 33%). The gender difference in marital expectations is consistent with actual remarriage rates among older Americans (Sweet & Bumpass, 1987; Treas & VanHilst, 1976).

That the age of 50 seems to be a watershed in marital expectations may be cohort bound: those in their 50s in 1985 show the very lowest proportion of "never married" adults, reflecting the very high marriage rate of this cohort (2% of the women, 5% of the men in their 50s had never married). But 20% of the women in their 50s are widowed and 10% are divorced, whereas just the reverse is found among women in their 40s: 2% widowed and 21% divorced. It may be that divorced middle-aged women are more likely to anticipate remarriage than are widowed women in midlife.

Family Size

Several features of American fertility trends are reflected in the data shown on family size in Panel E of Table 3.9. Note the very high proportion of the elderly who have never had children (25%). Today's elderly were young adults in their childbearing years during the 1930s and early 1940s. Their high childless rate reflects higher infertility in their cohort, the impact of depression hard times on family formation, and World War II casualties, which made widows of some young wives. This same period effect is shown in the smaller average number of children today's elderly had (2.9) compared to the two next-youngest age groups. The highest average family size is shown among those now in their 50s, parents of the baby-boom generation (3.8), with a steady decline in average family size among those in early adulthood, who either have lower family size expectations or are still moving through the childbearing years, but who are likely to have very few children.

Overall family size is larger for families of origin than for families of procreation, even when one matches age groups of children and parents: for example, respondents in their 20s and 30s report having grown up in families of 4.7 and 4.2 children, respectively, whereas respondents in their 50s and 60s, from the same birth cohorts as the parents of our youngest respondents, report having had only 3.8 and 3.3 children, respectively. Even when the overall fertility rate is very low, *most* children grow up in large families. This is a statistical artifact of the shift in the unit involved from "families" to "children": even if only 10% of all *families* have four or more children, 30% or more of the *children* will grow up with three or more siblings.

It will be recalled that a slight majority of our Boston sample report a Roman Catholic religious affiliation. That this is so in part reflects the higher fertility rate of Catholics than non-Catholics in the early decades of this century. The long-term trend in fertility and the difference between Catholics and non-Catholics can be seen graphically in Figure 3.8, which shows the average number of children in the family of origin and of procreation. Among our oldest respondents, born between 1893 and 1914 (the top two lines grouped as "A"), Catholics report an average family of origin size of 6.1 children (including themselves), whereas non-Catholics in the oldest cohort report growing up in much smaller families (4.2). Across the time span represented by the five younger birth cohorts, the family size of Catholics shows a steady decline and a smaller difference from non-Catholics. The overall family size difference between Catholics and non-Catholics declined from 1.9 children to half that difference, 0.8, among the youngest cohort.

In their own families of procreation, the religious affiliation differences have all but disappeared. Both Catholics and non-Catholics show the baby-boom peak of fertility, and both Catholics and non-Catholics in,

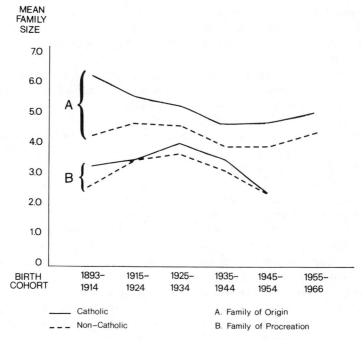

Figure 3.8. Average family size in family of origin (A) and family of procreation (B) by birth cohort and religious affiliation (G2 sample).

their 30s in 1985 (birth cohort of 1945–1954) report an average family size of 2.3 children.

Religious Intermarriage

It is highly likely that religious intermarriage contributes to the blurring of family size between Catholics and non-Catholics. Because we obtained the religious affiliation of respondents, and their spouses, mothers, and fathers, we can chart the trend over time toward more religious intermarriage. For this analysis, we defined "any" difference in religious affiliation as "different": that is, if a father was reported as having "no" religious affiliation and a mother as "Catholic," the parental pair was classified as having a different religious affiliation. Hence an "intermarriage" in this analysis is an inclusive one that embraces both Catholic–Protestant marriages and Catholic–Agnostic or Catholic–Jewish marriages (though, in view of the distribution of religious affiliation in the Boston SMSA, Catholic–Protestant is the predominant type).

To chart historical trends in intermarriage, we calculated the most probable decades during which marriages were contracted by respondents and their parents on the basis of their reported ages in 1985, i.e., the years during which they were in their 20s and early 30s. Accordingly, in Table 3.10, respondents are divided into three age groups, and we indicate the most probable historical decades during which the marriages were contracted, together with the percentage of intermarriages among G1 parents and married G2 respondents. The time span is therefore from the 1900s–1920s, when parents of respondents now over 60 were marrying (shown in the upper left cell of the table), to the 1970s–1980s, when respondents now under 40 years of age were marrying (shown in the lower right cell of the table). As the percentages indicate, the incidence of intermarriage increased from 8% among the marriages contracted in the first two decades of the century, to 31% among the marriages contracted in the past two decades. The diagonal lines shown in the table link together marriages in the two generations that were most likely to have taken place in the same historical period. In both pairs, the level of intermarriage is either close to or intermediary between the extremes of 8 and 31% in the furthest distant and most recent marriages.[13]

Economic Resources

Whether and when to marry, and whether and how many children to have, are individual decisions made within the parameters set by sexual

Table 3.10.   Historical Trends in Religious Intermarriage ^{a} (G2 Sample) ^{b}

		Age of G2 Respondents		
		61 or Older	41–60	19–40
A.	**Decades in which G1 Parents'**			
	Marriages took place	1900s–1920s	1920s–1940s	1950s–1960s
	Parents have Different Religious			
	Affiliation	8.0%	11.1%	14.0%
	N =	(276)	(416)	(663)
	Respondents and Spouses have			
	Different Religious Affiliation	13.5%	19.5%	31.1%
	N =	(251)	(389)	(466)
B.	**Decades in which G2 Adults'**			
	Marriages took place	1920s–1940s	1950s–1960s	1970s–1980s

^{a} Percentage of spouses who have *different* religious affiliation.
^{b} Arrows link G1 parents' marriages and G2 respondents' marriages that took place during same historical period. Marriages classified as "different" in religious affiliation of spouses include a spouse with "no" religious affiliation while the partner has a specified religious affiliation, i.e., a "Protestant and No Affiliation" and "Protestant and Catholic" are both classified as intermarriages.

maturity and fecundity, and subject to the social climate, economic conditions, and cultural ethos of particular historical times. Personal earnings are similarly affected by individual choice as well as societal factors. Individual choice of educational goals and occupation contribute significantly to an adult's earnings, but so too do labor market conditions in a city, region, or industry. In addition, and independent of personal choice and market conditions, there is a life course curve to personal earnings.

Personal earnings, however, have no necessary fit with family needs in a society with no family allowance system and no obligation on the part of employers to pay an employee with five children more than an employee with only one. Nor do many young married couples calculate the consequences of several closely timed births for the financial strain that may be felt when two or more children attend college at the same time. Valerie Oppenheimer suggests two critical points along the life course when the lack of articulation between family needs and income produces a "life cycle squeeze," as she puts it (Oppenheimer, 1974, 1982): early in the childbearing years (typically in the parents' 20s), and when children are late adolescents still attending school (typically in the parents' 40s and early 50s). Whether earnings are adequate to meet family needs depends on the nature of one's job and the timing of family formation. To marry and bear two children early in one's 20s is an invitation to financial stress that is not present when children are born in one's mid-30s. We were persuaded that economic resources represent a basic underpinning of social interaction and help exchange between the generations represented by parents and children, and therefore explored the extent to which personal and family earnings vary by stage of the life course.

It must be recognized, of course, that cross-sectional data on earnings have limitations. The relevant variables we have for such an analysis of life course variation in earnings are educational attainment, personal income, and the total income received by all adult family members; the time unit is annual income for the preceding year (1984). We do not have job and salary histories, and cannot describe the considerable volatility of earnings over a lifetime of employment, with bouts of unemployment, shifts in jobs, periods of temporary lay-offs, and so forth. We did make every attempt to get estimates of *total* income, not just wages and salaries, but income from all sources: social security, pensions, alimony or child support payments, food stamps, unemployment compensation, welfare payments, interest and dividends, rent, or armed forces' or veterans' allotments.[14]

Table 3.11 provides a detailed profile of the educational attainment, personal income, and total family income of men and women in the six age groups in the sample. Average educational attainment clearly reflects the historic trend toward more schooling: Adults over 70 have on average close to a high school completion rate, whereas young adults have a few additional years of education beyond high school graduation.

Most adults complete formal education in late adolescence or early adulthood; relatively few older adults today have added significantly to total years of schooling beyond the age of 30, though many may have attended adult education or job-related refresher courses. Hence, a long time has intervened for respondents over 50 since they sat in classrooms. In the intervening years, they have acquired job histories and experienced fluctuations in their earnings. Educational attainment is an important credential for occupational choice and placement, but it is a modest predictor of adult income, precisely because a diverse job history of experience, some luck, and regional variation in labor markets intervene between school completion and current income level. In our data, educational attainment shows a significant but modest correlation of .34 with current personal income. Two implications flow from this modest correlation: One is that educational attainment is heavily cohort determined and influenced by historic period during adolescence, and the second is that personal earnings, by contrast, may change dramatically over the life course in response to changes in the biographies of individuals, motivation to succeed, and the segment of the economy within which they work.

Table 3.11. Mean Educational Attainment, Personal and Total Family
Income by Gender, Age, and Marital Status (G2 Sample)

Variables	Age of G2 Adults					
	19–30	*31–40*	*41–50*	*51–60*	*61–70*	*71–92*
A. Educational Attainment (Years of Schooling)						
Men	14.7	14.9	14.7	13.8	12.6	11.7
Women	14.2	14.3	13.0	12.5	12.3	11.9
B. Personal Income (in 1000s)						
Men	18.0	27.5	34.9	31.9	21.4	15.0
Women	11.0	13.1	11.9	10.0	9.0	7.9
C. Total Family Income (in 1000s)						
Men	28.3	34.3	40.8	37.5	27.0	17.6
Women	24.6	31.5	30.3	27.1	19.5	10.8
D. Personal Income by Marital Status (in 1000s)						
Never Married	14.5	19.7	22.4	[21.3] [a]	12.9	14.2
Married	14.2	19.2	21.1	19.5	15.0	12.9
Separated/Divorced	11.2	19.6	19.5	22.8	12.5	[5.6]
Widowed	—	[20.9]	[23.3]	13.2	12.8	4.5
E. Total Family Income by Marital Status (in 1000s)						
Never Married	25.8	21.1	24.3	22.5	13.9	13.6
Married	28.6	36.2	37.1	35.3	26.1	17.7
Separated/Divorced	15.9	24.3	29.0	26.3	13.2	[6.0]
Widowed	—	[36.7]	[27.9]	15.2	17.8	9.3
F. Personal Income by Gender & Marital Status (in 1000s)						
Married						
Men	19.7	29.2	37.2	33.8	23.1	15.6
Women	10.9	10.9	9.1	7.9	6.8	8.0
Solo [b]						
Men	17.1	22.0	27.8	24.8	14.8	[13.1]
Women	11.0	18.3	17.4	14.6	12.1	7.9
G. Family Income by Gender & Marital Status (in 1000s)						
Married						
Men	28.3	37.0	41.8	39.9	29.2	18.8
Women	28.7	35.4	33.6	31.3	22.9	15.8
Solo						
Men	28.3	25.1	37.4	27.3	18.1	[13.4]
Women	20.8	22.2	23.5	17.4	14.5	9.3

[a] Fewer than 10 cases.
[b] "Solo" includes all never married, separated, divorced, and widowed adults.

To more readily show the life course profile of earnings, Figures 3.9 and 3.10 show the same results in graphic form that appear in Table 3.11. Together the two figures highlight the significant effects of gender and marital status on personal and total family income.

The overall profile of both personal and family income shows a strong curvilinear pattern by stage of the life course, income rising in the early adult years to a peak in the decade of adults' 40s, followed by a steady decline in income after the age of 50. Today's elderly have been cushioned by social security and pension benefits compared to earlier cohorts of American elderly, but they live at much reduced income levels when compared to younger adults today. Indeed, the elderly show lower

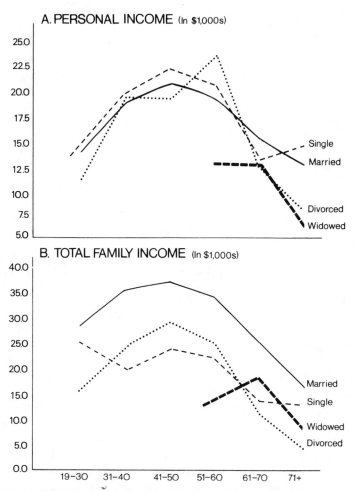

Figure 3.9. Life course trajectory on (A) personal income (in 1000s) and (B) total family income (in 1000s) by marital status (G2 sample).

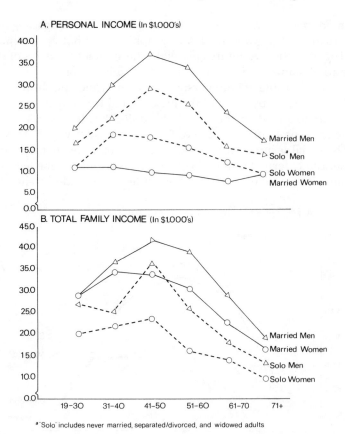

Figure 3.10. Life course trajectory on (A) personal income (in 1000s) and (B) total family income (in 1000s) by gender and marital status (G2 sample).

personal earnings and total family income than young people in their 20s who are just beginning their occupational careers. Of course, it must be realized that most young people depend largely on the income they earn each month, whereas elderly retired adults may have other wealth in the form of property, savings certificates and annuities, and insurance policies. But this is not liquid wealth to meet daily and monthly needs; most elderly fortunate enough to have such holdings think of them as reserves against potential medical and funeral expenses, with the residual after estate taxes are paid viewed as inheritance, typically for spouses and children. From the perspective of how income may relate to social interaction, travel, visits with kin, and help extended to or needed from adult children in the here and now, the level of personal monthly income remains highly salient when comparing young with old respondents.

Figure 3.9 shows that personal earnings peak among respondents in their 40s for both single and married adults. Among divorced adults, the income crest is extended into their 50s. We have no ready explanation for why this is so, but whatever income edge the divorced enjoy in their 50s does not hold in old age, where both personal earnings and total family income show averages below those of elderly single or married individuals. Note, too, that in the oldest age group (over 70 years of age), adults who never married do much better in personal income than do divorced adults. It seems likely that elderly single men and women long ago accepted remaining unmarried, made provisions for old age, and now enjoy retirement benefits that flow from steady uninterrupted employment and savings. By contrast, divorced elderly adults, particularly women, are on average in very poor financial shape, with incomes as low on average as the widowed elderly.

A comparison of Panel A on Personal Income with Panel B on Total Family Income in Figure 3.9 underlines the considerable economic advantage of marriage, implying as it does, nowadays, dual career households, particularly among younger adults in their 20s through their 40s. Marriage is economically advantageous to women at all ages. That single adults in their 20s report higher total family income than single adults in their 30s should be interpreted with caution. The primary reason for this result is that many single adults in their 20s are still residing with their parents, whereas very few single adults in their 30s do so. This means that many younger singles included the incomes of their parents in reporting total family income.

Figure 3.10 provides dramatic evidence of the decided contrast in the economic circumstances of women compared to men, particularly among those who are not married.[15] As seen in Panel A in Figure 3.10, married men at all phases of the life course enjoy the highest personal income, followed by unattached men. Unattached women are next in the income hierarchy, earning more than married women largely because the latter hold part-time jobs or are penalized with an income loss as a consequence of unstable attachment to the labor force. But unattached women earn markedly lower wages than unattached men, reflecting not differences in educational attainment, but in the sharp segregation by gender in the occupational world, and the lower wages earned by women in similar or comparable occupations to those held by men.

Marriage markedly improves the income level of women: From the lowest income group in terms of personal income, shown in Panel A of Figure 3.10, married women move up to the second highest group in terms of family income, shown in Panel B of the same figure.

These data are hardly newsworthy to sociologists and economists, but they do provide an important basis for thinking about intergenerational relations. As noted earlier, adult children with living parents are largely in their 20s through their 40s, while parents of adult children are largely in their 50s through their 70s and 80s. This means most adult children are located on the left-hand side of the graphs, where we see *rising* income levels with age, whereas most parents are located on the right-hand side of the graphs, where income levels are *declining* rapidly with increasing age.

These economic resource differentials between the early versus the later decades of the life course predict a very changing dynamic in help exchange between the generations. Young adult children in their 20s have low incomes or are still in training for professional careers, while their parents are either at the peak-earning phase of their lives, or just over the peak. Now project the scenario of parent–child relations ahead in time to the decade of the 30s and 40s in the children's lives: They are enjoying rising income levels as they gain job experience, promotions, and salary increases, often added to by spouses' wage increases as well. But now their parents are well past their earnings peak, being retired elderly in their 60s and 70s.[16]

If we reexamine Panel B of Figure 3.9 with the parent–child relationship in mind, we can note several other important features of life course variance in income levels as affected by changes in marital status. Think of married parents in their 50s relative to adult children in their 20s and 30s who are not married; there is a marked difference in their income levels, with parents having far more resources than their young single or divorced children. In terms of total income, married adults in their 50s show an average income of $35,300, compared to $15,900 among young divorced adults in their 20s, or $21,100 among young unmarried adults in their 30s. As we shall see in later chapters, this is precisely the combination in which, on both normative and behavioral grounds, there is very high obligation and commitment by parents toward children: Concern for the welfare of unattached daughters heads their list, and from the generational differences in income noted above, we can understand the parents' concern as well as their ability to do something to help.

But now, consider the impact of the death of a spouse in one's 50s, and note the marked difference in income levels of married vs. widowed adults in late middle age ($35,300 vs. $15,200); widowed middle-aged parents are likely to have lower personal earnings than their young unmarried or divorced children. Early widowhood is followed by a sharp decline in economic resources, and hence a marked shift in the relative economic circumstances of the two generations. Assuming resources flow more readily from those who "have" to those who "have-not," the scenario has shifted from married well-to-do parents in their

50s able to help young adult children, to low income widows in their 50s with incomes lower than those of young unmarried children. In view of the considerable difference in income between men and women in early adulthood, one might predict that widowed mothers turn to sons for financial aid and advice, and to their daughters for personal caregiving and comfort. An important implication of this analysis is that economic resources may structure gender-differentiated roles in intergenerational relations as they do the relations within the conjugal family.

An important question concerning the life course trajectory of earnings remains to be addressed: Is the pattern we have observed merely the profile of those occupying different positions on the life course in the 1980s, or is this pattern more persistent, such that one could predict a similar curvilinear profile a few decades from now? Older adults today have had less education than middle aged adults, to say nothing of the much greater proportion of young adults with advanced degrees.

We explored this question in a variety of ways. For one, by examining the life course pattern of earnings *within* three levels of educational attainment. Second, on the possibility that there was some particularity about the Boston SMSA we were unaware of, we explored the relationship between income, age, and education with data from a national NORC General Social Survey for the same year as the Boston sample. And third, we repeated the NORC analysis with comparable information from a General Social Survey conducted 10 years earlier, in 1974.

None of these three lines of inquiry changed the basic pattern we have already seen. Figure 3.11 shows the results for the Boston sample when both personal income and total family income are examined within the three educational attainment groups of high school graduates or less, some post-high school, and college graduates or more. Table 3.12 provides similar data but with an additional control for gender of respondent. Inspection of the graphs in Figure 3.11 shows that each of the three educational attainment groups shows the same curvilinear profile, a steady rise during the first two decades of adulthood, cresting in middle age, and then declining steadily until, in old age, income levels are lower than they were in early adulthood. The income of college graduates retains a high peak through their 50s, while the income of noncollege graduates falls after a crest in their 40s. Hence, even if future cohorts of the elderly have a much larger proportion of college graduates than today's elderly, the same life course curve of income will probably be found that we see in these cross-sectional data with the 1985 sample reporting on 1984 income.

It is also of interest to note, in the graph on Personal Income in Panel A of Figure 3.11, that educational contributions to income take time to develop. There are much smaller differences in average income levels by

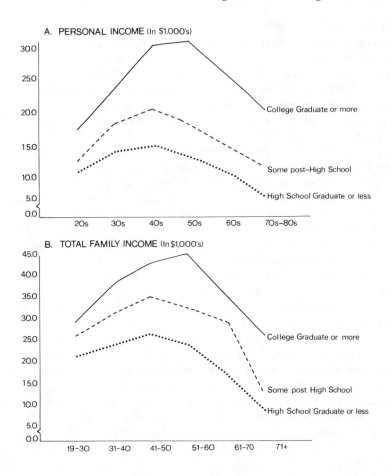

Figure 3.11. Life course trajectory in (A) personal income (in 1000s) and (B) total family income (in 1000s) by educational attainment (G2 sample).

education early in adulthood, when many young adults headed for advanced degrees are either still in school or serving various kinds of professional apprenticeships, while others get their footing on a professional ladder at salaries that differ little from those earned by high school graduates. One thinks of many health care and human service workers with college degrees whose beginning salaries are often in the $12,000 to $15,000 range, lower than the wages earned by most high school dropout truck drivers. College education pays off in the long run, not the short run, as the widening income gap between the three educational attainment groups suggests for the years between early adulthood and middle age.

Table 3.12. Personal and Total Family Annual Income (in 1000s) by Gender, Educational Attainment, and Age (G2 Sample)

		Age of G2 Adults						
Gender	Educational Attainment	19–30	31–40	41–50	51–60	61–70	71–92	Total
A. Personal Income								
Men	HS or Less	17.4	20.7	28.1	24.8	17.4	10.5	20.0
	Some Post-HS	14.0	26.9	30.4	[32.8] [a]	25.7	[16.6]	23.2
	College Grad. +	21.3	31.8	43.8	41.5	30.9	[25.6]	31.8
Women	HS or Less	7.5	9.1	9.5	7.6	7.1	5.6	7.8
	Some Post HS	11.4	11.1	12.5	11.3	8.3	9.0	10.9
	College Grad. +	13.7	17.4	16.9	17.1	19.8	17.3	16.3
B. Total Family Income								
Men	HS or Less	25.7	26.2	32.4	28.5	22.3	12.4	24.9
	Some Post-HS	26.8	34.8	37.4	[40.6]	32.5	17.8	31.9
	College Grad. +	31.1	38.5	49.8	49.0	37.5	31.0	39.3
Women	HS or Less	20.8	23.8	25.4	22.4	13.9	8.0	19.7
	Some Post-HS	26.8	30.3	35.2	29.2	28.0	10.3	28.6
	College Grad. +	27.0	38.2	36.8	41.6	32.7	24.1	34.1
C. Correlation Coefficients								
between Personal Income and Education within Age Groups		.25	.30	.40	.42	.38	.50	

[a] Fewer than 10 cases.

Another way of expressing this point is to examine the correlation coefficients between educational attainment and personal earnings *within* age groups, as shown in Panel C of Table 3.12. The correlation is only .25 among those in their 20s, gradually increasing to .42 by the time adults are in their 50s. After a slight dip during their 60s, the correlation among the elderly reaches a high of .50. It seems likely that the correlation dips for the 61–69 age group because they vary widely in the timing of retirement and hence of income. That education seems to pay off the best after retirement may reflect the lifelong higher earnings of college graduates, who were able to make investments and increase savings during their working lives, to supplement their income following retirement.

The comparison of personal and family income of respondents in the Greater Boston area with national data for the same year, as well as with national data for 10 years earlier, confirms the essential contours of the analysis reported above. Figure 3.12 shows only one illustrative set of graphs from this analysis: the personal income and total family income of men college graduates in the three data sources.[17] No attempt was made to transform the 1974 income data into constant dollars, since our concern is not with level of income, but the life course trajectory of income. The pattern is striking in the similarity of life course curves: Both across time, and between local and national samples, the life course trajectory in earnings is the same. Hence, the pattern established in the earlier analysis of the Boston data may be taken to be robust and not particular to the Boston SMSA or the income distribution by age in 1984.

Demographic and economic factors may of course alter the life course curve in earnings in the future. There may be changes in the national and international economic picture we can perceive only dimly in looking ahead. There are, however, some demographic factors that we have quite solid empirical reasons to consider relevant to changes in the future. A major one is the relative supply of young vs. older workers. The labor market in recent years has been affected not only by aggregate demand factors, but by a swollen, larger than usual supply of workers, as baby-boomers grew to adulthood and attempted to penetrate an economy in which the cohorts ahead of them were much smaller in size. Richard Easterlin (1987) suggests that precisely because the oncoming cohorts of young adults who will enter the labor market in the early 1990s are from the Baby-Bust birth cohorts of the 1970s, they will find it easier to be absorbed into the economy and at higher pay, which in turn may influence their personal decisions concerning the timing of marriage and the formation of families. Easterlin predicts that young adults

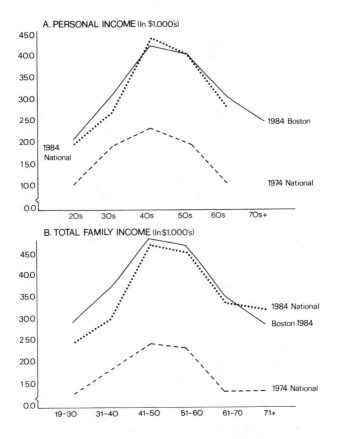

Figure 3.12. Life course trajectory on (A) personal income and (B) total family income of men college graduates: Boston 1984 income, national income, 1974 and 1984 (G2 sample; NORC General Social Surveys 1975, 1985) (Annual income in 1000s).

a decade from now will marry at younger ages and have larger families than the young adults currently in their 20s and 30s.

We do not concur with Easterlin's predictions, for they do not take into account the changes that have occurred in the status and aspirations of women, nor much longer term historic trends. Kingsley Davis provides what we take to be a more fundamental thesis, in arguing that the historic period from the post-Civil War through the 1950s was an historic deviation from the pattern that has held for all of human history (Davis, 1984). In all past societies, women shared in production along with men. The 1880–1960 era, which Davis calls the "breadwinner era," was the historic exception, during which the majority of women played little role in the productive economy. Hence, shared breadwinning by husband and wife, late marriage, and low fertility seem the more likely scenario for the future.

But from the point of view of the general and persistent tendency for income to rise gradually in early adulthood, to crest in the middle years, and to then undergo a decline, the economic resources underlying intergenerational relations that we have examined may be as relevant in the future as they are for an understanding of today's parents and their adult children.

There now remains one last topic we wish to discuss in view of the findings on the life course curve of income: This concerns the impact the timing of births in the early phase of the life course may have for the economic and social reality confronting parents and adult children at much later points in their lives. Discussions in the media, in demography, and in sociology concerning the timing of births have concentrated on the implications of birth timing only for the early phase of the life course. Thus, for example, Daniels and Weingarten (1982) compare couples whose first births took place in the early 20s of the mother with couples whose first births took place when the mother was in her 30s, considering the impact of early vs. late births on career development and adjustment to parenthood. Others have pointed out that postponement of births permits women to become established in careers in their 20s, with the result that short-term withdrawal surrounding one or two births will have less negative impact on women's careers and earnings than early births before a career "record" has been established. Demographers have long pointed out that the longer a first birth is postponed, the smaller the eventual family size in a population. But social scientists have not traced the longer term implications of early vs. late timing of births. We wish now to do so, within the framework of our findings on variation in economic resources over the life course.

Imagine two scenarios: one in which a child is born when the mother is 20 and the father is 22 and the second in which the mother is 35 and the father is 40. Let us further assume that the early vs. late timing of births persists across the generations, such that the children of our two types in turn time their births in a similar way. If we extrapolate the relative ages of members of each of three generations in these two scenarios, the profiles might be as shown at the top of p. 139.

In the early birth scenario, life may be very difficult for the couple in early adulthood, when the expenses of birthing and the costs of child-rearing are high and the parents have not yet reached an adequate earnings level. On the positive side, however, when the children are of college age, early birth couples will be at their peak earning ability, and

Early Births When Mother is 20, Father is 22							
Father	22	32	42	52	62	72	82	92
Mother	20	30	40	50	60	70	80	90
Child	0	10	20	30	40	50	60	70
Grandchild			0	10	20	30	40	50

Late Births When Mother is 35, Father is 40						
Father	40	50	60	70	80	90
Mother	35	45	55	65	75	85
Child	0	10	20	30	40	50
Grandchild					5	15

hence able to support those children desiring advanced education. When the early birth couples reach their 70s and experience declining health, much reduced income, and widowhood, their children will be mature adults at *their* earnings peak, and the grandchildren will no longer be dependent, but young adults on their own.

The life course profile is very different in the second scenario: Late births may facilitate the launching of careers and increase the probability that married women will have jobs to return to after their pregnancies. Late-birth couples will also experience the early stages of parenthood in the context of a more mature marital partnership with a better prognosis for marital stability, and they will have greater ability to cover childrearing costs without financial strain. On the other hand, the profile of intergenerational relations as the dynamics of aging take hold looks quite different for late-birth couples. When they are in their late 60s and 70s, their children will be only in their 20s and 30s, some years away from their peak income, while the parents have already undergone a reduction in income level, with many living on modest retirement incomes. If their late-birth children in turn have late births, this middle generation will face a complex intergenerational situation: in their 40s, they will have heavy job responsibilities of their own, still have young children entering puberty and adolescence, while their parents, typically widowed mothers, are very elderly and in need of personal support and care.

Thus, elevated stress may occur in early adulthood for early birth couples, and in late adulthood for late-birth couples.[18] It is not our intention to argue in favor of one or the other of the birth-timing scenarios, but to point to the complex positive and negative factors that flow from the timing of births when viewed in the overarching context of the total life course. Personal decisions about the timing of births are grounded in more proximate factors, not concern for intergenerational relations several decades down the pike. Our discussion serves the purpose only of emphasizing the long-term consequences that flow from the timing of births for intergenerational relations, and the relative economic resources and needs that underlie the relations between parents and adult children as a consequence of the combined effect of birth timing and the life curve in income.

Lineage Depth and Composition

From our general reading in gerontology and demography, we anticipated that a probability sample of 1400 adults would contain several hundred cases of respondents who had *both* a living parent and an adult child. Our expectations in 1985 were based on claims such as 50% of people over 65 are members of four-generation families (Shanas, 1980); or that grandparents' ties to adult grandchildren, perhaps even greatgrandchildren, may extend for more than 20 years (Barranti, 1985; Hagestad & Burton, 1985). The claims of great depth to American families have been pervasive in the social science literature. Examples are given of successive generations of teenage births, such that a woman became a grandparent at 30 and her mother a greatgrandmother at 45 (Burton, 1985).

These expectations, we realize with the benefit of hindsight, had several sources. For one, they were extrapolations from awareness of the lengthening of the life span for an increasing proportion of the American population. Others derive from clinical observations in the human services field of numerous cases of elderly women themselves providing care for even older widowed mothers. Others consisted of reports that 20% of women who died over 80 years of age were great-greatgrandmothers, implying a five-generation family (Hagestad, 1988). But to our knowledge, neither the census nor any national sample has included direct questions on whether and how many living kin adults had in *both* the ascendant and descendant generations of their family line, even such direct line kin as greatgrandparents, grandparents, parents, children, grandchildren, and greatgrandchildren.

It was therefore to test these claims that we asked our Boston respondents how many direct line kin were still alive in each of three generations ascendant from them, and how many direct line kin they had in each of three generations descendant from them, a depth of seven generations, including respondents' own generation. It is to these data that we now turn.

Table 3.13 provides a first perspective on the prevalence of direct-line kin in the total sample. It is readily seen that very few Bostonians report having even one living greatgrandparent (1.3%) or greatgrandchild

Table 3.13. Number and Type of Direct-Line Living Kin in Six Generations (G2 Sample).

Kin Type	Number of Living Kin							Total N
	None	1	2	3	4	5–8	9+	
Greatgrandparents								
%	98.7	1.1	.1	—	.1	—	—	
N	(1316)	(15)	(2)	—	(1)			(1334)
Grandparents								
%	77.7	13.9	5.5	2.1	.9			
N	(1039)	(186)	(73)	(28)	(12)			(1338)
Parents								
%	35.6	25.7	38.7					
N	(495)	(358)	(538)					(1391)
Children								
%	32.8	13.7	22.1	15.4	8.8	6.3	.9	
N	(456)	(191)	(307)	(214)	(122)	(88)	(15)	(1392)
Grandchildren								
%	74.9	4.0	5.0	3.2	2.7	6.9	3.5	
N	(1042)	(55)	(70)	(44)	(37)	(97)	(47)	(1392)
Greatgrandchildren								
%	96.2	.9	.8	.6	.4	.4	.8	
N	(1339)	(12)	(11)	(9)	(6)	(6)	(9)	(1392)

(3.8%). In fact, only one in four reports that at least one grandparent is alive, and the same proportion (one in four) reports having at least one grandchild. One in three does not even have one living parent, and one in three has no children.

The dynamics of generational succession, of births and deaths, are obscured by the marginal profile provided in Table 3.13. We have already seen, earlier in this chapter, that 1 in 10 of our oldest respondents did not marry, and one in four had no children. Childlessness, Robert Parke reminded us, is the surest route to a short, slim lineage (Parke, 1988). Many of our youngest respondents are unmarried, or have not yet begun to bear children. To assess the depth of family lineages requires that we examine family lines at various stages of the life course. To gain a more meaningful profile of multigenerational lineages, Table 3.14 shows the distribution of living kin in seven generational positions, from greatgrandparents through greatgrandchildren, the seventh generation represented by the prevalence of spouses in ego's generation.

Note that the percentages shown in Table 3.14 are based on the total number of adults in each age group. Our concern is with the prevalence of ascendant and descendant kin across the life course. Hence, for example, the 28% of adults in their 20s who have at least one child is not based on the proportion married in this age group, but the total number of respondents in their 20s.

Looking across the rows of Table 3.14 provides a picture of the constant process of change in the composition of lineages across the life course. An even more dramatic presentation of the same data can be seen in Figure 3.13. Rarely does a sociologist see such steep inclines and declines across age groups in any social phenomenon we study, to compare with these data on lineage composition. The truly remarkable demographic change over the twentieth century is the impact of increased longevity on the number of years when the majority of the population may still have at least one living parent. As seen in the row on parents, there is no significant drop in the proportion with at least one living parent until respondents pass their fiftieth birthday: 71% of those in their 40s but only 37% of those in their 50s have at least one parent alive.

But grandparents show a comparable significant decline between ego's 20s and 30s; from 62% for adults in their 20s, there is a drop to only 28% among adults in their 30s with at least one living grandparent. Greatgrandparents are hardly a presence even among our youngest respondents, where only 5% of those in their 20s report having one living greatgrandparent. There is no support in these data for the view that the relationship between greatgrandparents and greatgrand-

Table 3.14. Prevalence of Ascendant and Descendant Direct-Line Kin by Generational Position and Life Course Phase (G2 Sample)

Generation	Specific Kin	Age of G2 Adults						
		19–30	31–40	41–50	51–60	61–70	71–92	Total
Up 3	1+ Greatgrandparents	5.4	—	.9	—	—	—	1.3
Up 2	1+ Grandparents	61.5	27.3	6.9	—	4.6	1.7	22.3
Up 1	1+ Parents	97.8	91.8	71.0	37.7	11.8	0.9	64.4
Same	Spouse	41.1	72.9	70.1	73.4	65.9	42.4	61.9
Down 1	1+ Children	28.0	68.2	83.9	90.5	82.8	74.6	67.2
Down 2	1+ Grandchildren	.3	1.4	16.1	50.8	71.0	71.2	25.1
Down 3	1+ Greatgrandchildren	—	0.3	—	2.0	7.1	28.8	3.8
N		(314)	(364)	(224)	(199)	(169)	(118)	(1391)
Number of generations with 20% or more		4	4	3	4	3	4	5
Number of Generations with 50% or more		2	3	3	3	3	2	3

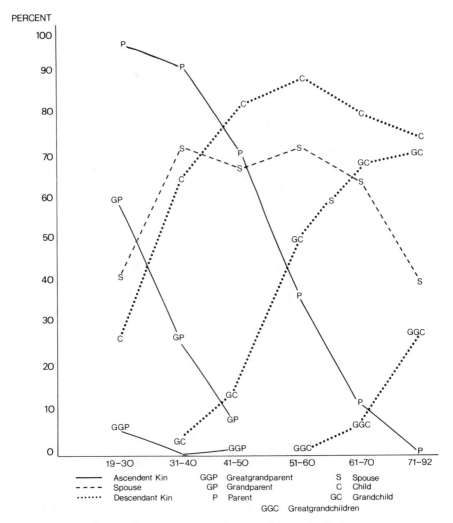

Figure 3.13. Prevalence of ascendant and descendant direct-line kin by phase of the life course. (Percentage who have at least *one* of each Kin Type.)

children persists into early adulthood of the greatgrandchildren. The sharp drop in proportion with a living grandparent between one's 20s and 30s also discounts the notion that grandparents may provide financial assistance to college-age grandchildren should their parents not be able to do so, particularly in view of the fact that the surviving grandparent is most apt to be a widowed maternal grandmother who, as shown in the earlier section on economic resources, is likely to have undergone a significant decline in income with the death of her husband.

If, instead of noting the points of sharp increases or decreases across the life course, we instead focus on the balance between the incidence of ascendant kin to descendant kin, several other striking points in the data shown in Table 3.13 become apparent. Some recent essays suggest that the average age at which adults become grandparents is 45 (Bengtson et al., 1990). We very much doubt this: An average age difference between the older 45-year-old parent and a child is 28 years, which would mean the child would have to produce the grandchild at 17 years of age. This is a rare event, as suggested in our data by the fact that among adults in their 40s, only 16% report having a grandchild. Grandparenthood becomes a major pattern only for adults in their 50s.

Deaths often accompany births: As adults move from their 20s to their 30s, many will experience the death of a grandparent within a few years of the birth of their own children. Similarly, as they pass from their 40s to their 50s, there is a sharp drop in the prevalence of any living parent (from 71 to 38%), accompanied by a sharp rise in the birth of grandchildren (from 16 to 51%). The third transition takes place between one's 60s and 70s: Here the loss is of a spouse, while the gain is the birth of greatgrandchildren (from 7% among adults in their 60s to 29% among those over 70 years of age).

Overall, there is a bittersweet shift in the balance of births and deaths over time, to more and more painful losses compared to pleasurable gains. Grandparents may be close and beloved figures in childhood, but the pain of their death during one's early adult years is surely less than the pleasure associated with the birth of one's own children. In midlife, the birth of grandchildren may temper the loss of a last remaining parent. In old age, however, the pleasure associated with the birth of greatgrandchildren cannot compensate for the painful loss of a spouse and the onset of widowhood. Indeed, many elderly men and women know little about their greatgrandchildren beyond the knowledge that they exist.

What criteria ought one adopt to define the generational composition of a lineage in describing a population of lineages? Do we say Americans live in multigenerational lineages of five generations if only 5% of any age group report having a greatgrandparent? If 7% of adults in their 60s report having at least one greatgrandchild, do we define this phase of life as a five-generation lineage? If the criterion is that *half* of the adults at a particular stage of life should have at least one kinperson in each of the generational tiers, then the depth of the lineages is at most *three* generations. Even if we take a more modest criterion as a cutoff, say 20%

reporting at least one kinperson in each generational tier, then the lineage depth is at most *four* generations (see bottom two rows of Table 3.14).

But whether the criterion is 20 or 50%, these figures do not inform us of the prevalence of multigenerational lineages at an *individual* level, only at the aggregate level of a total age group. Using a minimal criterion of having *at least one* kinperson in a direct line generational tier, Table 3.15 shows the percentage distribution by phase of the life course of the *number* of generations in individual lineages. By this more exacting criterion, the *modal* lineage depth is only *three* generations at all stages of the life course. For adults up to the age of 60, approximately one in four has lineages of only *two* generations, while only one in five has lineages of *four* generations. *Five*-generation lineages, about which we hear so much speculation, are practically nonexistent; less than 1% of the G2 adults in the Boston sample have five-generation lineages of living direct line kin, and their existence in any number at all is limited to the early adult phase of life.

Indeed, more prevalent than five-generation lineages are respondents who have *no* ascendant *or* descendant kin: 6% of the total sample, with a range from 2% among those in their 20s to a high of 19% among the very oldest respondents. Almost one in five of these elderly G2 adults has no direct-line kin either older or younger than themselves.[19] These are adults for whom there is no generational succession through gains of young descendants, but only loss, first of grandparents, then of parents, with no spouses, children, or grandchildren to compensate for the losses. We know relatively little about childless, especially unmarried childless adults in old age, though what little research exists suggests they were more prevalent in New England historically, as a consequence of higher educational opportunities for women coupled with a low sex ratio in the region and the positive valuation of remaining single among Irish Catholic women (Susan Ferguson, personal communication, June 1989; Simon, 1987).[20] Barbara Simon's study of elderly never married women in New York suggests a rich friendship network, and especially close relations with parents and siblings (Simon, 1987). On the other hand, several of our childless elderly friends in their 60s who have lost both parents and an only sibling now bemoan their lack of any close blood ties.[21]

Another common assumption concerning the impact of increased longevity for lineage depth and composition is the notion of "skipped" generations, that is, a missing link in a generational kin line, as represented by having no living children but at least one grandchild, or a grandparent but no living parent. Inspection of our data on lineage composition from this point of view yielded only 24 cases out of 1327

Table 3.15. Lineage Depth of G2 Adults by Phase of the Life Course (G2 Sample) (in Percent)

Number of Generations in Lineage	Age of G2 Adult						
	19-30	31-40	41-50	51-60	61-70	71-92	Total
A. Number of Generations							
One	2.0	2.3	6.0	6.5	13.5	18.6	6.2
Two	24.4	25.4	28.4	24.3	15.3	11.5	23.1
Three	53.9	54.3	47.7	49.2	56.4	40.7	51.5
Four	18.0	17.7	17.4	20.0	14.1	29.7	18.7
Five	1.7	0.3	0.5	—	—	—	0.6
Six+	—	—	—	—	—	—	—
N	(295)	(350)	(218)	(185)	(163)	(113)	(1327)
B. Composition of Modal Type Lineage	⌈Grandparent Parent Ego⌋	⌈Parent Ego Children⌋		⌈Ego Children Grandchildren⌋			

(2%) with a generational skip of any kind in their family lineages. Most of the cases involved the death of a parent while the grandparent was still alive, or the death of a child after the birth of grandchildren. The latter situation was most frequent among the very elderly, 5.3% of whom have at least one grandchild but no living children. Such cases may have involved the death of a son during military service.[22]

It is important that national data be obtained to follow up on our Boston findings that there is, to date, no evidence of any great lineage depth to contemporary American families. They may exist in small numbers in black urban families that are poorly represented in a New England sample. They may also increase in the future, but we suspect only to a limited degree, for the reason that young people are postponing first births, hence increasing the age difference between generations, and many intend to remain childless. We are on surer grounds in anticipating a narrow range to American families, on the assumption of a continuing decline in fertility. Thus, although it is fairly certain that the collateral shape of the American lineage will be on the "skinny" side, it is *not* clear at all that the shape will approximate the "beanpole" Vern Bengtson and his associates have recently predicted, which assumes great depth (Bengtson et al., 1990).

Even if four-generation lineages were to become more prevalent in the future, it is unclear what the social and psychological implications are. Clearly a four-generation family would have three parent–child pairs, but what would that mean for any particular parent–child dyad in the lineage, or for alternate generation pairs such as the grandparent–grandchild or greatgrandparent–greatgrandchild dyads? Children and adolescents would have an opportunity to observe their parents in interaction with grandparents, or their grandparents in interaction with greatgrandparents, and perhaps acquire a more informed sense of what the parent–child relationship is like at the later stages of the life course. But the cultural and age differences, and sheer question of geographic accessibility, might be so great as to make the more distant ascendant or descendant kin little more than a genealogical presence, not a significant partner in social interaction, sentiment, or exchange. Here too, the recent literature on grandparenthood speaks more to the alternate generations' relationship while the grandchild is literally a youngster, but tells us little at all about these relationships after the grandchild reaches maturity (Bengtson & Robertson, 1985; Cherlin & Furstenberg, 1986).

Conclusion

In this chapter we have described the major characteristics of the historical eras during which respondents of various ages spent their childhood, adolescence, and early adulthood. We have discussed such relevant cohort characteristics as differential marriage and fertility rates and educational attainment, and explored the secular trend toward religious intermarriage among our married respondents, from the low incidence among parents of older respondents to more recent marriages of young respondents which show close to 31% of intermarriage. We have also sketched the long-term trend away from a childrearing value focus on Conformity to an increasing emphasis on Autonomy among our young prospective parents. We have shown considerable stability in gender role socialization by parents, with, if anything, greater change toward the training of sons in domestic skills than any departure from the teaching of domestic skills to daughters, with important consequences in view of young married couples following the groove of competencies in who does what in domestic maintenance. We have shown that adolescence was associated with a more prevalent slump in parent–child intimacy for those whose adolescence took place during the era of personal and political ferment in the 1970s than for those who were adolescents during the calmer years of the 1950s.

We have demonstrated the marked curvilinear profile of personal earnings across the life course, with peak income in adults' 40s, independent of educational attainment level, a pattern also found in national surveys for 1984 as well as a decade earlier in 1974. By exploring differences in income levels by gender and marital status across the life course, we have discussed underlying economic resource differences that carry important implications for the kin types with the greatest potential need for assistance from parents or adult children, among whom unmarried and divorced children, and old widowed mothers predominate. We also mentioned the implications for relations between the generations that flow from a pattern of early vs. late timing of births, which takes on special significance in view of income variation, health problems, and the extent of family responsibilities in the second half of life.

Finally, we dispelled the notion that any great number of contemporary American families are embedded in multigenerational lineages of great depth. Our data show a modal profile of only three generations in each of the six decades of the life course, with less than 1% of the sample reporting a lineage of five generations. The major impact of the considerable demographic change that has occurred over the past five decades is the fact that parents and children can expect to share 50 or more years of "cobiographies," with many more years when both generations are adults than there are of years when the children are being reared.

In the next section of the book, we shift from historical, cohort, and maturational factors that impinge on the parent–child relationship and create differences in the biographies that lie behind this relationship at various points in the life course, to quite a different issue—the topic of normative obligations—and we will show how obligations toward parents and children differ from obligations felt to numerous other kin varying in degrees of relatedness to ego, as well as to nonkin.

Notes

1.   This is less true in western Europe than in the United States, because there has been heightened and shared interest among European social scientists to collaborate in repeat surveys over the past two decades on a wide array of attitudinal and value domains (Inglehart, 1977; Lesthaeghe, 1983; Lesthaeghe & Surkyn, 1988). These data, from the European Values Studies of more than a dozen countries, have permitted a cohort analysis of value change over the past two decades in European societies that has no counterpart in American social science. The General Social Surveys conducted by the National Opinion Research Center are the closest approximation to the European studies, but no overarching theory of value change has determined the items in the NORC surveys; periodic repeat items merely cover an array of discrete attitudinal domains.

2.   Simons (1980) links both the baby-boom phenomenon and the renascence in traditional religious participation in western Europe in the immediate decades following World War II to renewed trust in basic institutions after that trust had been undermined by the economic and political turmoil between the two world wars. That same renewed confidence characterized American society between 1945 and the mid-1960s, following the shattering experience of the depression and the war. Hence Simons' argument may apply just as well to the United States as to west European countries, in that both the sharp rise in fertility and the renascence in religious fundamentalism took place in the postwar years on both sides of the Atlantic.

3.   Note that these percentages refer to the people who reared the respondents for "most" of their youth under the age of 16. If a parent died or parents divorced before the respondents were 7 years of age, and the custodial parent remarried shortly afterward, the respondent was classified as having been reared by a natural parent and a stepparent. If a respondent reached the age of 11 or 12 before a death or divorce broke the family, he or she was classified as having been reared by the natural parents. In dubious cases, i.e., where roughly half the first 16 years of life was spent in an intact family and half with a single parent, stepparent, or other relative, coding was done in terms of the most recent family situation during puberty and adolescence. All the questions asked in the interview concerning the family of origin were then couched in terms of the parent, relative, or stepparent who was in charge of rearing the child for most of their youth.

4.   In the remaining 11 cases, gender of the adult was unclear.

5.   Of the 64 parental deaths G2 respondents reported before they reached the age of 16, sex of the deceased parent varied by age of the respondent: among those over 50 years of age in 1985, 50% involved a mother's death, 37% a father's death, and 13% both parents. Among those under 50 years in 1985, by contrast, just the reverse pattern is found: 31% reported a mother's death, 65% a father's death, and only 4% both parents.

6.   The proportion reporting a death struck us as unusually high, particularly among the youngest respondents (22%). It may be that adults were thinking of a grandparent's death rather than the death of a parent or a sibling, especially under circumstances that involved a grandparent living with the family during terminal illnesses. There may also be a tendency for the oldest respondents to underreport the death of siblings in infancy and early childhood.

7.   It is also possible that some women in their 50s were thinking of serious illnesses of their husbands, some of whom will have died by the time the women are in their 60s.

8.   There has been an interesting shift in Kohn's research over the years, from concern for the relationship between social class and parental values (Kohn, 1959) to recent concern for the interaction between work and personality in the context of social stratification (Kohn et al., 1983), though with less attention to the family and more to the nature of work per se as it influences personality processes and characteristics.

9.   We retain the label "Masculine" Skills, not out of any acceptance of social appropriateness, but merely for lack of a better alternate term.

10.   Sweet and Bumpass report the following percentage of widowed elderly by age and gender: among those 65–69, 34% of the women and 7% of men are widowed; among those 75–79, 60% of the women and 18% of the men; and among those over 85 years of age, 82% of the women and 43% of the men are widowed (Sweet & Bumpass, 1987, p. 298).

11.   We believe singlehood has a more positive aura in Catholic communities than non-Catholic communities, in part because having children who become nuns and priests has been highly valued. "My son, the priest," has been as valued in Catholic ethnic communities as "my son, the doctor" has been in Jewish communities. Hence, celibacy among the religious may have contributed a positive impact on remaining single among those who did not choose a religious life of service. But this is only a speculation and personal observation on our part.

12.   There has been only limited research on never-married elderly men and women. From what evidence exists, the general finding is that family relations are very important to the never married elderly, especially single women, who have more intensive relations than their married peers with their parents, and, later in life, when parents are deceased, with extended kin such as nieces and nephews (Allen & Pickett, 1987; Johnson & Catalano, 1981). It will be recalled from Chapter 2 that our data also suggested an increasing significance of family over friends among never-married adults as they got older. We shall see further evidence of their family-embeddedness in later chapters.

13.   We will report, in Chapter 7, that in addition to the historical trend toward more intermarriage, there is also some cross-generational transmission within families, for children whose parents intermarried are significantly more likely to intermarry themselves.

14.   Respondents were provided with a card showing an income distribution and asked to identify by letter the income grouping most appropriate to their circumstances. They were reminded verbally and on the bottom of the card that they were to include income from all sources, with a specific list of all such sources, as itemized in the text.

15.   This is similar to the finding reported by Mindel (1979) that older married women are less likely to be poor than both unmarried and widowed older women.

16.   In the Boston sample, 5% of the men in their 50s are retired, increasing to 59% among those in their 60s, and 86% among those over 70 years of age.

17.   In data not shown here, the same effect of marital status and gender on income at various phases of the life course was shown in both the 1974 and 1984 national data. One critical difference between a sample from the Boston SMSA and a national sample is the far greater educational attainment of Commonwealth residents in the Boston area compared to adults in the nation at large. Our G2 sample showed 44% were high school graduates or less, compared to 78% of the 1985 NORC national survey; a full 33% of our respondents held at least a college degree, which was the case for only 18% in the national sample.

18.   Note too that if a late birth pattern persists across two generations, there is an enormous difference in the age of grandchildren and their grandparents. Most of the late birth couples will not live long enough to experience the birth of their grandchildren,

whereas the early-birth couples will still be vigorous adults in their 50s when their grandchildren are growing up.

19. As noted earlier in this section, our sample, half of whom are Catholic, has more never-married elderly women than national samples. Hence, there may also be a slight excess in our sample of elderly respondents with no ascendant or descendant kin.

20. The historical pattern summarized here comes from research on older single women by a graduate student in sociology at the University of Massachusetts, Susan Ferguson.

21. Beckman and Houser (1986), in a study of childlessness among elderly women, report no differences between childless and childed elderly women whose husbands were still alive, but a significantly lower level of psychological well-being among childless widows compared to widows with at least one child.

22. A small number of these elderly respondents also reported that although they had no living parent, they do have a living grandparent. Such a grandparent would have to be close to or over 100 years of age. A check of the original questionnaires of the two respondents involved confirmed that there had not been any coding or data-processing error, e.g., a 72-year-old woman had a 105-year-old grandmother, while her mother was deceased.

Normative Obligations to Kin ———— Part III

The Structure of Kinship Norms _____ 4

" . . . attachment behavior is both intimate and profound . . . and it is to attachment behavior and the primary bond . . . that we can trace both the 'axiom of amity' and the fact that kinship is inescapably binding."

Derek Freeman (1974, p. 115)

Introduction

A kinship system is a network of social relationships whose basic skeletal framework consists of lines of descent. In the abstract, every human being is kin to every other: we need only trace our lineages back far enough to find some common ancestor. In practice, however, in common with most modern societies, Americans have a nearsighted view of kinship, focused primarily on a few generations up and down the lineage, and a few degrees of collateral relatedness. Those we recognize as kin are distinguished from other people by the presence of consanguineal blood ties, as in the parental bond; by sharing a common ancestor one or more generations in the past, as in the relation to cousins; or by the presence of an affinal tie through marriage, as in the relationship to a sister-in-law or son-in-law. Near kin are distinguished from distant kin by the number of links in a lineage that connect the persons involved. Ordinarily we recognize only short distances in the kinship linkage: Beyond three or four links, distant kin fade quickly into nonkin.

A kinship system can be viewed both as a culturally defined normative structure and as a network of concrete social relationships. These two aspects of kinship are clearly related, although separate. The normative structure defines which kinds of persons are kin, but marriage, fertility, and mortality determine whether an individual has any, a few, or all of the kin so defined. Kin norms are culturally defined rights and

155

duties that specify the ways in which any pair of kin-related persons is expected to behave toward each other, ranging from prescribed terms of address through rights of access, to obligations to exchange and provide support. A concrete kin relationship may be affected by those norms, but may also be conditioned by the geographic distance among the kin-persons involved, their respective resources, and the idiosyncratic history of their relationship. Kinship norms may affect concrete behavior toward kin, but hardly can be expected fully to determine it.

This chapter is concerned with the normative structure of kinship, not with the actual kinship structure of our respondents. Here our focus is on the levels and strengths of obligations evoked by different kin in a variety of circumstances, whether or not respondents have ever had an actual person occupying a particular kin position. Our goal is to uncover the general principles underlying the American kinship system as revealed in obligations acknowledged to specific kin. This larger canvas of kinship obligation norms provides an important context within which to locate the parent–adult child relationship with which the study is primarily concerned.

No empirical research is needed to demonstrate the existence of norms governing kin relationships. We experience these norms in our own daily lives and in our beliefs about what is appropriate behavior toward various kin, and we observe other people expressing similar rules for themselves and for others.

Our ideas concerning what is appropriate behavior toward kin of all sorts cover a wide variety of circumstances. We also experience how other persons believe they should act toward their kin, and may observe the similarities between our own and others' felt obligations. From introspection and observation of what others believe and how they act, we develop some fairly specific ideas about what is proper and appropriate in relationships among kin. These beliefs and observations reflect kinship norms, a phenomenon that is both internal to oneself, and observable in the social behavior and expressed beliefs of others.

The culturally defined rules that govern relationships among kin are rich in detail, covering a wide range of behavior, and varying in the degree of obligation involved. The behavior covered in these rules may be as trivial as a prescribed kiss or handshake on first encounter, or as major as providing shelter or significant financial aid. Among the more important rules are those specifying which kin should have valid claims on each other in extending help in crisis circumstances, or in celebrating important life events, occasions that we will study.

Indeed most social science commentary on our kinship system and its norms has not been based on systematically collected empirical data, most likely because those systems are so easily accessible to direct experience (Schneider, 1980). A systematic survey is not needed to establish that the parent–child relationship is either the strongest kinship bond or yields first place only to the bonds between spouses. Nevertheless, there are ample reasons for systematic research on kinship, among the most important of which is the fact that the general principles underlying kinship norms are not directly observable and that there is obviously incomplete consensus on those norms.

We may all readily agree that kin relationships are strongly affected by social norms, without being able to specify what the structure is that underlies them. By "structure," we mean the latent organization of the norms according to general principles. For example, we may agree that there is less normative obligation to help a first cousin than a sibling, without being able to express this felt difference in terms of the degree of relatedness to a first cousin compared to a sibling. Indeed, many Americans may be totally unaware of any systematic structure underlying norms they themselves adhere to in relating to various kinds of kin, although they may be quite aware of what should be the content and style of relationships to a wide variety of specific kin.

It is also problematic how much consensus there is in American society on kin norms. Whether most Americans subscribe to the same kinship norms to the same degree is unknown. The extent of general normative consensus may be obscure because we usually think about and act on such norms in highly specific terms, for example, by following the maxim to "Honor thy father and mother," or to be polite to older relatives. Often we are more aware of special characteristics of particular kin, for example, a very funny uncle compared to a stiff and formal uncle, rather than how uncles differ from aunts, or uncles from brothers. The statements made by social scientists about the strength of obligations between parents and their children reflect a perceived lack of firm consensus among contemporary Americans (Hagestad, 1987), with some asserting that families set up their "own norms" (Aries, 1978; Riley, 1983) and others claiming normlessness (Hess and Waring, 1978). It should be stressed, however, that these statements are not based on systematic study of the matter.

This chapter differs from previous social science accounts of kinship by being based on systematically collected data on the strength and nature of the obligations our respondents acknowledge owing to their kin. We shall describe how numerous kin types vary in the level and intensity of obligation they evoke, as well as how much consensus is shown in these kin norms. Most important, we will infer the kinship system that structures these obligations.

The Empirical Study of Normative Structures[1]

The data and analysis presented in this chapter represent a first attempt to use sample survey methods to derive an empirically based outline of the normative structure of kinship obligations. To do so, we used the factorial survey approach (P. H. Rossi & Nock, 1982), a method that is specially suited to the task. Further details on the methods used are given in the next section of this chapter.

Social norms are a chief concern of sociologists and the family is a primary context for the acquisition and application of norms. Yet very little concrete empirical research has been conducted on social norms, let alone on norms governing kinship. Indeed, there is some evidence for a decline in such interests: A *Handbook of Sociology* (Faris, 1964) published in the early 1960s contained a lengthy chapter on "Values, Norms and Sanctions" (Blake & Davis, 1964), but a volume with the same name published in 1988 (Smelser, 1988) has no chapter devoted to that topic and only four entries under "norms" in its index.

There are reasons for this neglect. We believe that the empirical study of normative structures has been hampered by a lack of understanding of how to recognize normative structures in the kind of data typically collected by social researchers. In part, these difficulties arise because the concepts "norms" and "normative structure" have not been given appropriately operationalized forms. In part, the difficulties are caused by the fact that, when seen through conventional perspectives, data that indicate norms and normative structures appear to be defective in some ways. These two points are elaborated below.

Norms and Normative Structures

In the social science literature definitions of the concepts of norms and normative structures vary somewhat from author to author. Despite variation among definitions, there are certain key elements that are common to most. First, most sociologists recognize that norms consist of widely acknowledged rules specifying what a society or social group considers appropriate and inappropriate behavior in specified circumstances (Blake & Davis, 1964). Norms may be formulated as prescriptive statements, proscriptive rules, or statements that establish the relative or absolute values of social objects. They may be embodied in the legal codes or simply function as rules of etiquette.

Second, there is agreement that norms are statements of obligatory actions or evaluative rules. Norms as rules stating how persons in particular positions are obligated to behave or to think under specified circumstances distinguish them from attitudes, opinions, and personal preferences. Thus, the norms dealing with the obligations of parents to provide support to their young children apply to *all* parents, not just *some* parents. In contrast, individuals can hold different views about the obligations of parents to support adult children over 30 years of age, an issue on which there appears to be no firm normative consensus. Similarly adults are free to choose their friends, recognizing those choices as expressions of personal preferences that may or may not hold for other members of the society. Which of your neighbors you really should like is simply a matter of personal preference; whether your 10-year-old son should live in your home is not a matter of personal preference but a strongly sanctioned, widely held normative expectation that is also incorporated into the legal codes.

Norms as evaluative rules are statements about how social objects are to be evaluated, ordering them into hierarchies of preferment. Familiar sets of evaluative norms provide rank orders for occupations, the seriousness of crimes, and, to some extent, preferences among foods.

The third common thread that runs through the definitions of norms is that they are widely, if not universally, acknowledged rules, recognized as binding to some degree by most members of a society. Hence the definitions imply high consensus, at least about the content of the norms and possibly also on the degree of obligation implied. That is, the concept of norm implies that members of a society know the norms and agree on the strength of the obligation accompanying them.

Neither of these common threads implies that members of a society must completely internalize all the norms or even agree with all of them. Some large degree of consensus about the content of at least the central norms of a society *is* implied, but how much consensus there need be over the extent to which the norms are binding on individuals or over which are the central norms of a society both allows some latitude.

Like all rules, norms must necessarily be stated in general terms, in the sense of applying to classes of circumstances, defined fairly generally. Hence there are many ways in which disagreement may arise over whether a norm is applicable to some specific circumstance. Thus, although all Americans may believe that parents should support their minor children, some might make exceptions in the cases of parents who have divorced and remarried, or in cases involving severely mentally retarded children. The ambiguity concerning specific applications of general rules is both an opening through which the empirical order of actual behavior may vary from the normative order and an indicator that social change may be under way.

This loose fit between actual behavior and the normative order can be seen most clearly in the workings of legal norms. Much of the work of our legal system lies precisely in making determinations about how the

legal norms apply to specific instances of behavior. The general principles may be embodied in the statutes, but the prosecutors, attorneys,
and judges in the courts have to fit specific instances of behavior into the
meaning of those principles.

Hence, by the very nature of norms, we can expect a greater degree of
consensus in a society when norms are stated in general terms and a
lesser degree of consensus over how norms apply in specific behavioral
contexts.

These characteristics of norms and of normative order need to be
properly incorporated into whatever measurement model is used to
study them. There are several key issues that need to be addressed.
First, how best to conceptualize consensus, allowing for inevitable measurement error? Second, how to uncover basic structure in the welter of
specific applications of norms? And, finally, how to collect such data
efficiently from respondents within the usual constraints of time and
resources? The next section addresses these issues.

The Problem of Consensus

The measurement practices that have dominated the fields of sociology and social psychology seem designed to avoid finding empirical
evidence for norms, beliefs about which there is some large degree of
popular consensus. Indeed, when we find measures on which individual subjects agree, we tend to discard them because they will reveal little
about differences among individuals. For example, when we find items
in the pretest of a survey questionnaire with highly skewed marginals,
we often throw them out because they can tell us little about interindividual variation. We prefer items with maximum variance and hence
with corresponding minimum agreement among subjects, a strategy
that makes good sense in measuring interindividual variation in the
amount of cognitive achievement, but may not make good sense for
sociologists who are trying to understand the overall normative patterning of human behavior. Indeed, it is often precisely those measurement
instruments that we conventionally reject as useless that are most indicative of norms. Thus, few social scientists would ask respondents
whether they approve of murder because we would expect almost
everybody not to. From the perspective of conventional survey analysis,
very high agreement among respondents leaves little room for analysis:
No variation means there is nothing to "explain."

The same faulty interpretations occur for data sets that have findings
that are relatively invariant over method, population, and time. Thus,
studies of crime seriousness (U.S. Department of Justice, 1984; P. H.

Rossi et al., 1974, 1985) and occupational prestige (Hodge, Siegel, & Rossi, 1964; Reiss & Hatt, 1961; Treiman, 1977; Goldthorpe & Hope, 1980) are puzzling to many because these measures are relatively unchanging over time, and are quite insensitive to changes in measurement method. In addition, although these data sets show an appreciable amount of interindividual variance, that variation appears to be related only weakly to characteristics of the individuals studied. Efforts to find correlates of interrespondent variation around these steady means have yielded only weak findings, a sign that much of the variation consists of "errors" of measurement. An approach to their empirical study should explicitly allow for measurement error.

In addition, there is a problem in how to reconcile the generality of norms with the multitudinous situations to which each applies. When stated at the level of general principles, norms necessarily are very silent on their application to specific circumstances. The maxim, "Honor thy father and mother," may serve as a general guide to how a child should act toward parents, but it is silent on many issues, including the context and the meaning of honor. An understanding of the role of norms in affecting concrete interkin relationships requires understanding how such general rules are interpreted in specific settings with specific kin. Since there are so many specific applications to kin, the issue becomes how properly to "sample" from among the many possible settings to which the general norm may be applicable to gain an appreciation of how general norms are translated into specific guides to behavior.

This last consideration suggests that the best measurement approach to studying norms is through specific applications, inferring the general structure through the patterning of reactions to specific instances. By asking about many specific kin, we may be able to draw out the general principles lying behind why we honor some kinship relations more than others. Through observing the different circumstances that evoke kin obligations we may be able to understand the boundaries that separate what kin owe to each other from the ordinary obligations that unrelated persons have to one another.

Obligations between kinpersons can be studied either as actions owed to ego or as actions owed to alter, e.g., "What do you owe to your father?" versus "What does your child owe to you?" (addressed to fathers). In a tightly integrated society, we would expect that each mode is the mirror image of the other. In our society, reputedly rife with "conflicting expectations," there is likely some difference between them. We chose to study the obligations our respondents owed to their kin more out of concern to limit the burden placed on our respondents than out of any conviction that one mode is preferable on theoretical grounds. Indeed, as we will discuss in the next and in the last chapter, we propose that future researches investigate the variance across modes.

Finally, the measurement approach to the study of norms necessarily has to be efficient. To accommodate measurement error, to study specific applications, and to allow for the uncovering of normative structures using conventional approaches ordinarily implies a research effort of considerable size and complexity. It was precisely with the aims of such efficiency criteria that the factorial survey approach was developed. We turn now to an exposition of that approach through a description of its application to the study of the normative structure of kinship obligations.

Key Features of the Factorial Survey Approach

The essence of the method used to obtain empirical measures of the strengths of kinship obligations was to present each respondent with a set of vignettes, each containing a short description of a specific kinperson in common situations that might evoke a sense of obligation to make some appropriate gesture toward that kinperson. The set of vignettes given to each respondent covered a range of kinpersons and a range of situations, designed to be a "sample"[2] of circumstances that could evoke felt obligations toward the kin in question.

The factorial survey was given as a supplement to the kinship main interview. When the main interview was completed, all of the respondents were asked to write their responses to a series of vignettes bound in a booklet, each vignette describing a possible situation in which a particular kinperson was involved. One of two types of situations was described: (1) "Crisis Events," in which the situation described was one of need following a traumatic event in the life of that kinperson and that called for financial help or comfort; and (2) "Celebratory Events," in which the situations were occasions that called for a sign of recognition or appreciation. Each vignette was followed by a question asking how strongly obligated the respondent would feel to make a specified gesture to the kinperson in question. The gestures included offering financial aid, or comfort and psychological support, in the case of "crisis events," and visiting or appropriate gifts in the case of celebratory occasions. In all, 32 unique vignettes were printed in each respondent's booklet.

Respondents were asked to read each vignette and to mark on a scale numbered 0 to 10 that accompanied each vignette how strongly they would feel obligated to provide the gesture in question. These "obligation" ratings constitute the raw observations on which the analyses presented in this chapter are based.

Illustrative vignettes of "crisis events" and "celebratory events" are shown in Table 4.1. Although each respondent was given only 32 vignettes to rate, there were 1628 unique vignettes in the total set of all possible vignettes, each unique vignette being an unduplicated combination of a kinperson, a situation in which the kinperson was involved, and an action to be taken by the respondent. The set of vignettes given to each respondent was a separately and independently drawn[3] probability-based sample of all possible vignettes. Although it is possible that the sampling procedure produced several identical sets, such an outcome is highly unlikely. The booklet given to the respondent was printed by computer and contained that respondent's unbiased sample of the total set of unique vignettes. Combining respondents' sets yielded a data set in which ratings existed on each and every vignette.[4]

The purpose of this procedure was to be able to obtain a rich and diversified set of measures on felt obligations of different sorts toward a large number of kin in a large number of obligation-evoking situations. It is useful to regard the full set of more than 1600 unique vignettes as defining a "vignette space"—in this case, also a "kinship obligation space"—that is, in turn, demarcated by the dimensions along which the vignettes are differentiated. The dimensions that define the vignette space are shown in Table 4.2.

The first dimension is that of kin: The kin[5] involved consisted of 74

Table 4.1. Vignette Examples [a]

A. Illustrative Crisis Event Vignette

Your *unmarried sister* has *undergone major surgery and will be bedridden for a few weeks. This problem is straining her financial resources.*

How much of an obligation would you feel to *offer her some financial help?*

No Obligation At All			Mild Obligation			Strong Obligation			Very Strong Obligation	
0	1	2	3	4	5	6	7	8	9	10

B. Illustrative Celebratory Event Vignette

Your *widowed father* is *going to have a birthday.*

How much of an obligation would you feel to *give him something appropriate to the occasion?*

No Obligation At All			Mild Obligation			Strong Obligation			Very Strong Obligation	
0	1	2	3	4	5	6	7	8	9	10

[a] The segments of the vignette texts in italics represent portions of the text that are rotated randomly and separately for the composition of each vignette used. Thus, the first rotated segment in each vignette contains a kin designation that is chosen randomly from a list of kin designations each time a vignette is written.

Table 4.2.   Dimensions Defining the Kinship Vignette Space

A.   Kin Dimension—74 levels

74 kinship designations specifying a specific kin relationship, systematically crossed with gender and current marital status, e.g., "widowed mother," "married female cousin on your mother's side." Note: This amounts to three dimensions rolled into one: kin, gender, and marital status.

B.   "Crisis" Dimension—8 levels

1. "Undergone major surgery" followed by being "disabled for a long time."
2. "Undergone major surgery" followed by being "bedridden for a few weeks."
3. "Serious personal troubles . . . to last for a long time."
4. "Serious personal troubles . . . to last for a few weeks."
5. "Lost almost everything in a household fire . . . no insurance."
6. "Lost almost everything in a household fire . . . a few weeks for the insurance company to settle."
7. "Run out of unemployment benefits with no job in sight."
8. "Used up all unemployment benefits but expects to be called back to work in a few weeks."

C.   "Celebratory Event" Dimension—3 Levels

1. "Won an award after years of effort."
2. "Going to have a birthday."
3. "Just moved into a new place."

D.   "Crisis" Ratings

1. Comfort Obligation: To offer "comfort and emotional support."
2. Money Obligation: To offer "some financial help."

E.   "Celebratory Event" Ratings

1. Gift Obligation: To give "something appropriate to the occasion."
2. Visit Obligation: To "visit."

---

relationships, so structured to distinguish in almost[6] every case between the two genders and between a "married" state and an "unmarried" or "widowed" state.[7] Using the respondent as the reference point, the kin designated ranged from four grandparents, each described as a grandmother or grandfather, whether in the maternal or paternal line and whether married or widowed, through the parental generation (e.g., mother, father, uncle, or aunt), through the respondent's generation (siblings and cousins) to children and grandchildren. Each kin type was further specified by gender and marital status. Children and grandchildren were implicitly described as adults, the other kin being explicitly defined as such. To provide a contrast with the level of felt obligations toward nonkin, we also included "friends" and "good neighbors" and "former spouses" as designated categories.

It is unfortunate that an extremely important kin category, spouses, could not be accommodated within the framework of this factorial survey and consequently had to be omitted from the list of kin types. It simply did not make sense to ask how much respondents felt obligated to provide financial help, comfort and emotional support, visit, or give gifts to spouses. The marital bond so clearly involves such obligations at so high a level that including spouses among the kin in the vignettes would seem foolish to the respondents. It appeared impossible to treat obligations to spouses in the same way as obligations to other kin. Hence spouses as kinpersons were omitted.

Because the main study focused on parent–adult child relationships, the vignette study design was designed to have one-third of the vignettes describe parent–child relationships. Correspondingly, kin some distance removed from the respondent (e.g., cousins) were sampled with lower probabilities.

The situations evoking the obligations covered "crisis events" and "celebratory events," respectively. The eight crisis events, shown in Table 4.2, were chosen to describe situations that would ordinarily represent personal setbacks, each having both negative economic and personal implications.[8] Each event was accompanied by one of two ratings tasks.

The "celebratory events" were chosen to represent familiar situations calling for congratulations, rejoicing, or celebration, as shown in Table 4.2. To measure the obligation evoked by such events, we asked respondents to rate how strongly they would feel any obligation to acknowledge those situations, as shown in Table 4.1.

Since the main questionnaire administered to the respondents concentrated on helping relationships between parents and their adult children, the set of vignettes in each respondent's booklet consisted of a majority of crises. Each respondent received a set of 32 vignettes, composed of the following mix:

  1 "Practice" vignette that was identical for all respondents.[9]
 26 Traumatic event vignettes.[10]
  5 Celebratory event vignettes.

Response to the Vignette Booklet

Although filling out the vignette booklet did not require a high level of literacy and virtually no writing skills, some respondents were unable to undertake the task because their skills were not up to it. Others apparently felt they had contributed their share to our research by answering the questions posed in the interview and refused to undertake the booklet task. Usable booklets were filled out by 84.4% of the respondents.

As usual, respondents who completed the task were different from those who did not. Vignette booklet completion rates were highest among the better educated and among younger respondents, as shown in Table 4.3. Over 90% of the college graduates filled out vignette booklets, compared to two of three among those who did not finish high school. Over 90% of all respondents under 30 but only 70% of those over 70 filled out booklets. Although older persons had lower educational attainment, both age and education worked independently, so that lowest completion rates were among the respondents who were over 70 and had not completed high school, as shown in Table 4.3.

Panel B of Table 4.3 uses regression analysis to summarize the results shown in Panel A. The dependent variable in Panel B is the number of vignettes each respondent rated, ranging from 0, for those who did not undertake the booklet task at all, to 32, for those who provided a rating for each and every vignette in the booklet. In addition to age and education (both in years), we also used the self-reported health status of the respondents as predictor variables, reasoning that respondents in poor health might have found that their energy levels would not sustain the booklet task.[11]

The findings of Table 4.3 indicate that persons with low levels of formal literacy training avoided undertaking the vignette booklet task, and, when they undertook to do so, were less likely to complete the task. Although respondents could not know in advance how demand-

Table 4.3.   Correlates of Vignette Booklet Completion

A. Vignette Booklet Completion Rates by Respondent Age and Education						
Respondent Education	*19–30*	*31–40*	*41–50*	*51–60*	*61–70*	*71 +*
Less than HS Grad	70.0	64.3	69.2	78.9	75.6	65.0
N	[20]	[28]	[38]	[38]	[41]	[40]
HS Grad	90.8	91.4	72.9	71.5	82.4	67.6
N	[76]	[81]	[81]	[81]	[68]	[37]
Some college	89.2	91.8	91.8	75.0	78.1	66.7
N	[83]	[97]	[24]	[24]	[32]	[21]
College Grad	92.5	93.7	92.4	87.3	92.6	90.0
N	[133]	[159]	[55]	[55]	[27]	[20]

B. Regression of Completion on Age, Education, and Self-Reported Health	
Independent Variables	*Beta*
Education (years)	.168***
Age (years)	− .131***
Reported health	.014
R^2	.062***
N	[1380]

*** $p < .001$

ing of their literacy skills the task might be, it was obvious that the ability to read printed materials and follow written instructions were involved. It is not altogether clear why older respondents also rejected filling out the booklets. The best explanation we can give is that many of the analyses of the kinship study data, presented throughout this volume, contain evidence that older persons feel less obligation to others in general, including perhaps the interviewers used in the field. (See in particular, the analysis of the age-related vignette results presented in Chapter 5.)

Overall Obligation Strength

In reacting to each of the vignettes, respondents recorded how strongly they would feel an obligation to the kinperson designated in the vignettes,[12] were that person in the circumstances described. The strength of that felt obligation was recorded by appropriately marking a scale ranging from 0 signifying "no obligation at all" to 10, representing "very strong obligation." (See Tables 4.1 and 4.2 for the exact wording of the rating scale.)

In Table 4.4 the distributions of ratings are shown separately for each kind of obligation. Overall, respondents believed that they would have felt strongly obligated in response to most of the kin involved. Average ratings ranged from 6.2 to 6.9 with medians ranging higher; still all central tendency measures registered in the "strong" to "very strong" segments of the rating scale. The Boston Metropolitan area version of American kinship norms appears to be strong and vigorous.

As indicated, one-third of the kin in the vignettes were either parents or children, to whom the strongest obligations can be expected to be shown; hence an uneven distribution of ratings is to be expected. The most popular rating was 10, the highest level of felt obligation that could be registered, with 24–30% of the ratings falling into that category. Respondents also favored the rating of 7, marked on the scale as "strong obligation," with weaker preference manifested for 5, the middle of the scale.

A total of 36,731 vignettes were returned from the field operation. Of this large number, 823 (2.2%) were returned without a rating or without an interpretable rating, a proportion that compares quite favorably with previous vignette studies.[13] When we consider that the vignettes were administered after a lengthy interview, this proportion of unrated vignettes appears to be very small. No marked differences in "no rating" rates appeared among rating dimensions. Reports from interviewers who conducted the field work were that most of the respondents enjoyed rating the vignettes.

Table 4.4. Distributions of Vignette Obligation Ratings

	Kind of Obligation Evoked			
Obligation Strength Score	Money (%)	Comfort (%)	Gift (%)	Visit (%)
0 No Obligation at all	6.2	3.9	6.2	7.2
1	3.4	2.1	1.7	3.5
2	4.5	3.1	3.0	3.7
3 Mild Obligation	9.5	8.0	9.0	9.3
4	6.2	5.4	6.1	6.5
5	10.2	8.5	9.5	10.4
6	7.4	7.4	7.5	7.0
7 Strong Obligation	13.7	14.2	14.2	14.1
8	8.5	9.5	8.5	7.5
9	6.7	8.2	7.2	7.0
10 Very Strong	23.8	29.6	27.0	23.8
Rated Vignettes 100% =	[15222]	[15357]	[2918]	[2899]
Not rated	2.1%	2.3%	2.0%	2.4%
Total Vignettes (Rated + Unrated) N	[15557]	[15717]	[2977]	[2968]
Mean Rating	6.2	6.9	6.5	6.2
Median Rating	6.7	7.3	7.0	6.7

Total Respondents   = 1189
Total Rated Vignettes = 36731

Mean differences across rating dimensions are small, with the highest average level of felt obligation being shown for the obligation to give comfort and emotional support (6.9) and the lowest for giving gifts (6.2). It appears that obligations that are easier to fulfill in the sense of requiring lesser commitments of time and resources are more easily evoked: "Offering comfort and emotional support" or "sending a gift" are both less demanding responses than "visiting" or "offering financial aid."

The Generality of Kinship Obligations

A major feature of the kinship obligation vignettes was that they permitted differentiating among four types of obligation, ranging in the degree of commitment asked of the respondent. This feature was built into the design because we expected the structure of obligations to vary by the kind of obligation involved.[14] To some extent those expectations were fulfilled as the differences among the averages in Table 4.4 indicate. The obligation to offer financial aid was not as easily evoked as the obligation to offer comfort and emotional support.

As a further and more specific check on whether the rating tasks were seen as distinct by the respondent, the vignette booklets each had a built in replication feature. In each vignette booklet, three "crisis" vignettes were randomly selected, duplicated, and given to the respondent to rate with different rating tasks, rotating between the "financial aid" and "comfort" ratings. For example, if the first appearance of the chosen vignette in a booklet asked for a financial aid rating, then the second appearance asked for a "giving comfort" rating.

The findings of the replication "exercise" are shown in Table 4.5, where the regression of the comfort obligation rating on the financial aid obligation is shown. Note that the correlation across replicated pairs of vignettes was .79. This means that offering comfort and offering financial aid to a given kin tend overall to go hand in hand, respondents stating that the relatives to whom they feel strongly obligated to give comfort and emotional support are also highly likely to be the same kin to whom they feel strongly obligated to offer financial help. However, respondents do discriminate between the two kinds of obligations, as the intercept term indicates: On average, respondents feel a much stronger obligation, 2 points higher, to give comfort and emotional support than to offer financial aid. Although vignettes that produce strong obligations to offer financial help also induce a strong obligation to offer comfort and emotional support, it appears that the obligation to provide financial help is the weaker of the two.[15]

We can use these data to examine the structure of kinship norms by shifting our unit of analysis from respondents to kin types. In this structural analysis, each of the kin included in our vignettes is characterized by the averages of the ratings received by each. These averages are measures of the strengths of the obligations owed to a particular kinperson, and are characteristics of the kin in question.[16] That is, the

Table 4.5. Regression of Comfort Rating on Financial Aid Rating for Replicated Vignettes [a]

(Dependent variable is Comfort Obligation)

Independent Variable	b [a]
Financial Obligation	.73
Intercept	2.0
R^2 =	**.62** [r = .79]
N =	[3567 replicated vignette pairs]

[a] Unstandardized regression coefficient

average rating received by vignettes referring to fathers can be regarded as a characteristic of fathers as a kin category.

The first issue we will address is the generality of kinship obligations. Does each type of obligation define a different structure for kinship? Is there a different order of obligations to provide financial aid in crises as compared to the order that is defined by the obligation to give gifts on celebratory occasions? Or, do the obligations owed to kin form a single system?

Table 4.6 provides considerable evidence that the normative order of kinship obligations is a highly general one, as shown in the high correlations in the upper left-hand triangle of Table 4.6. These six correlation coefficients were calculated by correlating the kin ratings received by each of the 74 kin types on one obligation type with ratings received on another. These correlation coefficients measure the extent to which the average ratings given to kin on one dimension covary with the average ratings received on the other obligation in question. For example, the .93 correlation shown between the gift obligation and the visit obligation average ratings means that those two average ratings are very closely related: Kin that induce a strong sense of obligation to visit are also kin that evoke a strong sense of obligation to give gifts, and, correspondingly, kin to whom little or no obligation to visit is acknowledged tend also to be the kin to whom little or no obligation to send gifts is felt.

All of the six correlation coefficients shown in the upper left triangle of Table 4.6 are unusually high, .92 or above. For all practical purposes, an obligation of one sort owed to a kinperson is matched by a comparable level on each of the other obligation types.[17] No matter which kind of obligation is involved, the orderings of kin by the obligation strengths are very much the same. We will take advantage of this generality of obligations to kin in many of the analyses to follow by presenting

Table 4.6. Correlations among Means and Standard Deviations of Rating Dimensions

	Obligation Means			Standard Deviations			
	Visit	Money	Comfort	Gift	Visit	Money	Comfort
Gift	.93	.92	.93	.23	.05	−.05	−.61
Visit		.92	.96	.14	−.02	−.09	−.70
Money			.94	.10	.02	−.08	−.62
Comfort				.11	.02	−.08	−.69
Gift SD					.28	.33	.36
Visit SD						.31	.28
Money SD							.50

findings based on one or two of the obligation types, on the grounds that using all four would be to present largely redundant information.

These very high correlations should not be interpreted to mean that the different types of ratings are identical: In each regression pair, there are significant intercept terms, as suggested by the differences in the means shown in Table 4.3. That is, for example, mothers are more strongly obligating than cousins on each of the rating tasks, but obligations to give comfort and emotional support to mothers and cousins are higher than the obligations to offer financial aid.

There are important implications of these findings in understanding the structure of kinship norms. The extremely high correlations[18] among kin obligation ratings indicate that kinship obligations are general. Thus, the kin to whom you may be strongly obligated in any one respect are the same kin to whom you are obligated in other respects.

Although averages are general measures of how ratings cluster, there is usually variation around each average that represents the extent to which individual ratings depart from those overall measures. A conventional measure of such individual rating variation is the standard deviation. Across all the ratings, the standard deviation was 3.1, indicating that about two-thirds of the ratings fell within a band defined by 3.1 points on either side of the average. For example, two-thirds of the financial aid obligation ratings fell between 3.1 and 9.5, centering around the average rating of 6.2. This wide range cannot be interpreted as indicating serious amounts of disagreement among individuals because some of the variation can be accounted for by the fact that some kin are more obligating than others. About a third of the overall standard deviation can be accounted for by the variation in scores given to specific kin, the average standard deviation of ratings around each of the kin terms being 2.0.

A standard deviation can be computed for each of the 74 kin terms used in the study, measuring the extent to which individual respondents differed from each other in their ratings of the kin in question. Although the absolute sizes of the standard deviations are affected by the dimensions used in the vignettes, their relative sizes can be used to indicate the kin about whom there is more or less consensus: A kin type with a larger standard deviation is one to which respondents varied more widely in their ratings[19] and hence a kin type over which there is less consensus.

The lower right-hand triangle in Table 4.6 contains the correlations *among* the standard deviations. All of the coefficients are positive and quite small, especially in comparison to those displayed in the upper left-hand triangle. There appears to be only a slight tendency for consensus over one kind of obligation to be matched by a similar degree of consensus over another type of obligation.

The upper right-hand rectangle of Table 4.6 contains the correlations between standard deviations and the means, measuring the extent to which consensus is related to levels of obligation. There is no overall patterning of these correlations. The correlations that involve visiting and financial aid obligations are very small, meaning that consensus over these obligations does not cluster in any uniform way. The obligation to give gifts, however, shows a different pattern: Although these correlations are small they are all positive, indicating that there is a slight tendency for consensus to be lower over the more obligating kin. A strong and opposite pattern is shown for the obligation to give comfort and emotional support. These correlations are high and negative, -.61 or less, indicating that consensus is lowest for kin for whom there is the least obligation. This finding hints that there is agreement over the "core" kin and disagreement over where the periphery should be drawn. (We will return to this topic in Chapter 5.)

Genealogical Mapping of Kin Obligations

The generality of kinship obligation discussed in the last section decidedly does not apply when we consider the specific kin involved. It was not surprising that the most important element in kinship obligations is the kind of relative in question. This section explores the ways in which different kin evoke varying strengths of kinship obligations, drawing from the findings some of the general principles that define the normative structure of our kinship system.

We begin with a very familiar classification of kin, the broad categories of relatives who represent the most commonly encountered people in the intimate world of family: parents, siblings, grandparents, aunts, uncles, and cousins, persons we are endowed with at birth or acquire in early childhood, and the children, nieces and nephews, and grandchildren we acquire in adulthood. To these "consanguineal" kin we add primary affinal kin of parents-in-law and children-in-law. To provide an anchor outside the world of family against which to gauge kin obligations, we add the nonkin of close friends and good neighbors. Yet another "anchor" is provided by relationships increasingly present as a consequence of a high divorce rate—stepparents, stepchildren, and ex-spouses.

Table 4.7 shows the overall profile of normative obligations in these various kin and nonkin types of relationships for all four ratings of degree of obligation: the obligation to provide "social and emotional

Table 4.7. Mean Obligation Ratings by Type of Crisis or Celebration and Type of Relationship (G2 Sample)

	"Crises"				"Celebrations"				Range within Kintype
	Comfort		Money		Gift		Visit		
Relationship	Mean	Rank	Mean	Rank	Mean	Rank	Mean	Rank	
Own Parents	8.71	(1)	8.32	(1.5)	8.11	(2)	8.13	(1)	.39
Own Children	8.68	(2)	8.32	(1.5)	8.36	(1)	7.86	(2)	.82
Siblings	7.60	(3)	6.90	(4)	6.94	(4)	6.50	(5)	1.10
Grandchildren	7.22	(4)	6.47	(6)	6.40	(8)	6.81	(4)	.82
Children-in-law	7.12	(5)	7.11	(3)	7.19	(3)	6.10	(7)	1.09
Parents-in-law	7.04	(6)	6.58	(5)	6.37	(9)	6.82	(3)	.67
Grandparents	7.01	(7)	6.30	(7)	6.67	(6)	6.43	(6)	.71
Stepchildren	6.93	(8)	6.10	(8)	6.88	(5)	5.91	(8)	1.02
Friends	6.37	(9)	4.86	(10)	5.55	(12)	5.67	(10)	1.51
Stepparents	6.05	(10)	5.43	(9)	5.94	(11)	5.77	(9)	.62
Nieces/Nephews	5.57	(11)	4.81	(11)	6.57	(7)	4.91	(11)	1.76
Neighbors	5.05	(12)	3.28	(13)	4.32	(13)	4.17	(13)	1.77
Aunts/Uncles	4.77	(13)	4.03	(12)	6.05	(10)	4.33	(12)	2.02
Cousins	4.09	(14)	3.25	(14)	3.56	(14)	2.75	(14)	1.34
Ex-spouses	3.45	(15)	2.84	(15)	2.19	(15)	2.11	(15)	1.34
Grand Mean	6.86		6.23		6.53		6.19		
Range across Type of Relationship	5.26		5.48		6.17		6.02		

comfort" and "financial aid" in four types of "crises" and the obligation to send an appropriate "gift" or to "pay a visit" in three types of "celebratory" occasions.

Table 4.7 emphasizes the considerable stability of the obligatory response to the critical and celebratory stimuli. As shown earlier (and repeated in the grand means at the bottom of Table 4.7), there is only minor variation in the overall level of obligation, with the obligation to provide comfort evoking the highest general level of felt obligation, and visiting the lowest level of obligation, but with only a modest degree of difference across the rating types.

The major determinant of obligation levels is the type of relationship referred to in the vignette. The specific kin and nonkin types in Table 4.7 are shown in the rank ordering of obligations to offer social–emotional comfort under crisis circumstances. (Rank order position is shown for each of the four ratings in parentheses to the right and below each mean rating.)

An inspection of the rank order positions across the four ratings shows only minor variation, typically only a difference of one or two positions in the ranking hierarchy. Parents and children head the list on all four ratings. There is some variation by rating task in which specific kinpersons follow the primary kin in rank order positions: siblings and grandchildren in the case of providing comfort in crises, children-in-law and siblings in the case of providing financial aid or a gift, and grandchildren and parents-in-law in paying a visit to mark a special occasion.

More distant kin—parents' siblings and siblings' children, along with cousins—evoke roughly the same level of obligation as do friends and neighbors, with ex-kin in the form of divorced spouses at the bottom of the hierarchy. Hence, the rank order across types of obligatory responses shows little variation at the top and bottom of the hierarchy, with the greatest differences in rank order position among secondary and distant kin.

On the other hand, it is at the bottom of the hierarchy that one also finds the greatest variation by type of obligations, as indexed here by the range in mean scores among the four rating scales. There are clearly very high and uniform obligations to parents and children. Regardless of situational circumstance or the nature of the obligation, the felt obligation is very high (rank positions one or two) and there is little variation across ratings (a range of only .39 points). As one moves out toward more peripheral kin and to nonkin, there is more variation by the nature of the situational stimulus: a range of 2.02, for example, in the case of aunts and uncles, and 1.77 in the case of neighbors.[20] That the key determinant of obligation level is the type of relationship involved is summarily illustrated by the far greater range produced *across* kintype (shown in the bottom row of Table 4.7) than the range involved *within* kintype (shown in the last column of the table). The relationship range also shows that crises evoke less variation in obligation level than do celebratory occasions.

Figure 4.1 confines attention to financial aid obligations and provides another perspective on the ranking of obligations to various kin and nonkin. Each circle on this "wheel of obligation" represents at least one

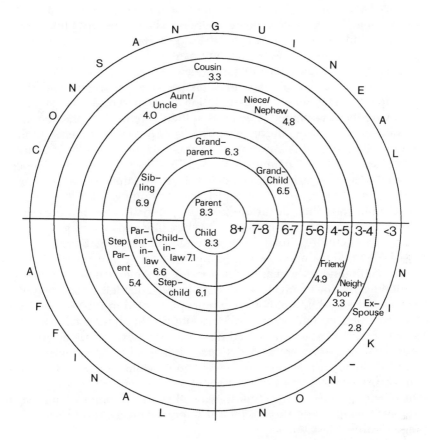

Figure 4.1. Layering of normative obligations: mean ratings of financial aid obligations by degree and type of relationship (G2 Sample).

full point on the 0–10 rating scale, with the highest obligations at the hub of the wheel and the lowest at the periphery. Further, the upper half of the circled wheel shows the consanguineal kin; affinal kin are in the lower left quadrant and nonkin are in the lower right quadrant.

Obligations radiate out in an interesting manner from the peak of obligations to parents and children. All the kinpersons located in the two circles surrounding the hub of the obligation wheel are connected to ego through only one of three figures: a child, a parent, or a spouse. A child is the connecting link to children-in-law and to grandchildren, a parent is the connecting link to siblings and grandparents, and the spouse is the connecting link to stepchildren and to parents-in-law. Once children marry, there is little differentiation between offering financial aid to a daughter or to a son-in-law; to help one is to help the other, since financial aid tends to go into a common shared household account. Indeed, since men carry the larger degree of family financial responsibility, one of the ways many parents can help their daughters financially is via assistance to sons-in-law.

That obligations to children-in-law take precedence over obligations to grandparents may reflect the assumption on the part of adults that one's own parents carry higher obligations to their parents than one does as a grandchild vis-à-vis grandparents. This is also a realistic demographic assumption, since it is a very rare circumstance to have a living grandparent but no living parent; as we saw in Chapter 3, such "skipped generations" are practically nonexistent in the family lineages of our respondents. By contrast, the direct and continuing concern for one's children beyond their departure from the parental home and the establishment of their own families can often be expressed only by gestures of help toward children-in-law. The patterning of kin obligations is clearly sensitive to who stands as connecting links between ego and alter.

The centrality of the marital relationship in American kinship is also underlined by the relatively high levels of obligation felt toward parents-in-law and stepchildren, both of whom are located in the same second band of obligation in Figure 4.1. Many of our respondents have not yet married, and very few have had direct personal experience as either a stepchild or a stepparent. Yet stepchildren evoke the same level of obligation (6.1) as a grandparent (6.3) or grandchild (6.5), and do so, we suggest, because a spouse is as salient as a parent in the structure of kinship obligations. In a similar way, the central bond of marriage involves sharing obligations with one's spouse toward spouse's parents (ego's parents-in-law).

Note, too, that the same ranking appears for the three types of parents as for the three types of children: Biological parents and children evoke the highest obligation (8.3 and 8.3), followed by parents-in-law and children-in-law (6.6 and 7.1), and the lowest level of obligation by stepparents or stepchildren (4.4 and 6.1). This suggests that affinal kin acquired through remarriage evoke less obligation than affinal kin acquired through first marriages.

Friends follow these affinal kin in the next outer circle of the obligation wheel, sharing a position with aunts and uncles and nieces and nephews, while neighbors are on a par with cousins in evoking obligations to provide financial help, all with mean ratings well below the mid-point on the rating scale. Ex-spouses stand alone in the outermost circle, with the lowest obligation rating of all types (2.8). Had the vignette design included other "ex" types of kin (e.g., a divorced daughter's former husband), we suspect the obligation wheel would have had to have yet another peripheral circle, with obligations toward ex-kin showing much the same distancing pattern as shown for the close versus distant consanguineal and affinal kinpersons in the design. It seems likely that ex-spouses of an aunt or distant cousin would evoke no obligation at all.

Returning now to Table 4.7: Another way of examining these numerical data is to note the ranking of the four types of obligations *within* kin types. "Comfort" is a more plentiful resource, something that can be demonstrated by a few minutes' phone call, a note expressing concern, or several lengthy intimate conversations lasting many hours. It is also a flexible resource, and compared to hard cash, a less limited resource one could provide to several people simultaneously. But it is also the case that offering social–emotional support to someone presumes some degree of intimacy in the relationship, since intimacy would seem to be intrinsic to meaningful conversations concerning surgery, emotional problems, or the worry caused by financial drain brought on by a household fire or a period of unemployment. This may be why "Gifts" take priority over "Comfort" as the gesture with the highest mean rating in obligations to more distant kin such as parents' siblings, siblings' children, and children-in-law. A gift sent by mail can be a neutral gesture that bypasses the intimate interaction called for in providing social–emotional comfort to or visiting someone coping with a personal crisis.

On the other hand, gifts, like direct financial aid, dip into a possibly more restricted supply of income and savings, and may therefore compete with the more imperative demands posed by the needs for shelter, food, and clothing for oneself and one's dependents. In a similar way, visiting to express obligation to others is limited by the distance to be traveled and by more imperious demands on one's time for hours devoted to employment, family care, and home maintenance. This suggests that money and visits move in narrower circles of exchange than do giving comfort or gifts.

The implied social protocol would then mean that money is least apt to be in first place in evoking the highest mean ratings where nonkin are concerned. Close friends are almost by definition freely chosen intimates in one's present life, but the relationship does not carry as much responsibility to provide financial assistance as even secondary blood kin. Living close to each other, neighbors are predisposed to some level of intimacy through sharing or being aware of each other's daily comings and goings, social interactions that involve knowledge of the crises and celebrations that occur in each other's families, but again, this does not extend to any great obligation to provide financial assistance to neighbors. Consistent with these comments is the sharp contrast between comfort ratings and money ratings where friends and neighbors are concerned: for friends a drop from 6.37 for comfort to 4.86 for money, and for neighbors, from 4.05 to 3.28, differences of 1.51 and 1.77, compared to only .39 in the case of parents or .71 in the case of grandparents.

We are so intimately embedded in our own kinship system, and take its rules so for granted, that it is difficult to sense the principles conveyed by the empirical patterning shown in these ratings. To note as we have in Figure 4.1 that parents-in-law evoke quite high levels of obligation is not surprising, because we take for granted the primacy of the marital relationship and respect the primary bonds of our husbands or wives to their parents. Obligations would look quite different in a unilateral kinship system. In a matrilineal system, for example, a man would not be a member of his wife's matrilineage but of his mother's, and his children would owe more obligation to his wife's family than to himself or his parents (the children's paternal grandparents). So too, we take it for granted that we owe more obligation to our father than to our aunt, but in a matrilineal system, obligations might well be greater to a maternal aunt than to a father.

What *is* surprising is how close to the hub of normative obligations to primary kin are those affinal kin linked to us as a result of remarriage following death or divorce. We had predicted, in particular, that stepparents would evoke less obligation than good neighbors, and stepchildren less than close friends. We were wrong on both counts. The cruel and wicked stepmother who figured in childhood fairy tales notwithstanding, stepparents evoke financial aid obligations to a greater extent than an aunt or a niece. And although stepchildren clearly evoke less obligation than biological children, as noted above, they nonetheless show mean ratings of obligation on a par with a sibling, a grandparent, or grandchild. It seems quite likely that the "parent" and "child" *positions* in family structure implied in these affinal relations are taken as more salient than their tenuous status as affinals. Being in the position of parent, or the position of child, takes priority over the fact that they are figures who move into a kindred (and may move out of the kindred as well, at some future time) as a consequence of divorce or death and subsequent remarriage.

Range and Depth

There is a second way to reorder the various kin and nonkin relationships that will help to highlight another implicit principle in the structure of normative obligations. This involves classifying the various relationships in terms of the two basic dimensions anthropologists consider in analyses of kinship systems: the *depth* and *range* of a kindred. Starting with some individual, or ego, as reference point, the *depth* dimension is defined in terms of the number of generations "up" or "down" from ego of each specific kin and nonkin in the vignette design. Thus, friends and siblings are defined as members of the *same* generation as ego; parents, aunts and uncles, parents-in-law, and stepparents are one generation up from ego; and grandparents are two generations up from ego; children, nieces and nephews, children-in-law, and stepchildren are one generation down from ego, and grandchildren two generations down from ego, for a total depth of five generations being represented in the vignettes.

The *range* of a kindred can be defined in a variety of ways. In complex kinship systems where fine social and genealogical distinctions are drawn, collateral range can be very finely defined, allowing for a specification of "cousinship" in terms of degrees of collateral distance from ego, to differentiate among kinpersons about which the American kinship system rarely distinguishes. The conventional modes for measuring range or collateral distance rely primarily on counting the number of connecting consanguineal links between ego and a kinperson, tracing up the generational ladder to a common ancestor of ego and his or her kinperson, and down the generational ladder to the person in question. In the case in which ego is an ancestor the links are counted down the generational lineage. By this system one can differentiate among cousins in terms of collateral distance from ego: for example, a first cousin on one's mother's side is three links distant from ego, with the links connecting mother, mother's mother (the common shared ancestor), and mother's sister intervening between ego and a maternal first cousin. First cousins share a common grandparent, second cousins a common greatgrandparent, and so on. Technically, a daughter of a first cousin is a "first cousin once removed," although in common American usage this figure tends erroneously to be called a second cousin, a practice illustrating the tendency to push away a kin figure to a lesser degree of relationship than in fact exists.

As a first empirical venture into the study of kinship norms using a factorial survey method, and in view of our desire to provide only a comparative framework for highlighting how obligations to parents and children differ from obligations to other relatively close kin, it did not seem pertinent to elaborate cousinship in any refined manner. Indeed, we did not specify "cousin" in any way except to indicate if this person was male or female, and on the mother's or father's side of the family. We can assume, therefore, that most of our respondents had in mind kin most likely to have figured in their personal lives, namely, children of their parents' siblings, ego's first cousins, or at least those of the first cousins who are relatively close in age to respondents, with whom they may have played on family and holiday occasions as they were growing up.

Our measurement of the range involved in kin relations is a simple one, consisting of the number of connecting links between ego and alter. Since a parent and a child have a direct relationship with no intermediary figure between them, we classify both as *primary kin*. *Secondary kin* are those who have one connecting link between them: among consanguineal kin, grandparents and siblings (connected through parents) and grandchildren (connected through children). Parents' siblings are more distant kin, with two connecting links (parent and grandparent), as are siblings' children, with the two connecting links of parent and sibling. Even first cousins are more distantly related to ego than an aunt or a niece, since, as we described above, there are three connecting links to a first cousin (parent, grandparent, and parent's sibling).

For our purposes, however, we have combined cousins with parents' siblings and siblings' children as *distant kin*, all involving two or more links. But we might note that our respondents in fact showed sensitivity to the distinction between third- and fourth-order relationships, giving cousins lower financial aid obligation ratings (3.25) than parent's siblings (4.03) or siblings' children (4.81). Indeed, if all the kin types in the design are classified in terms of the number of connecting links, it can be seen that there is great variation in the obligation ratings (financial aid) by the number of connecting links and very little variation among kin related by the same number of connecting links, even when these include affinal kin of different generations from ego:

No Link (primary kin)—8.3 (parents), 8.3 (children)
One Link (secondary kin)—6.1 (stepchildren), 6.3 (grandparent), 6.5 (grandchildren), 6.9 (sibling), 6.6 (parent-in-law), 7.1 (child-in-law)
Two Links (distant third-order kin)—4.0 (aunts/uncles), 4.8 (nieces/nephews)
Three Links (distant fourth-order kin)—3.2 (cousins)

If means are computed for each category in this four-part classification by number of connecting links, then there is a steady linear progression from 8.3 for primary kin, followed by 6.5 (one link), 4.4 (two links), and 3.2 (three links).

Table 4.8 is a reordering of the data shown in Table 4.7 and Figure 4.1, but in a manner that permits easier inspection of the effect of range and depth as the two primary dimensions of kinship structure on normative obligations. (Note that a distinction is drawn in the case of empty cells in this table between those that are logically empty—identified by an "x," and those that are possible but simply not built into the vignette

Table 4.8. Mean Ratings on Financial Aid Obligations by Range and Depth of Relationship (G2 Sample)

Depth	Range					
	Consanguineal Kin			Affinal Kin		
	Primary	Secondary	Distant	In-laws	Step	Nonkin
Two genera- tions UP	x [a]	6.30 (gdpts)	— [b]	—	—	—
One genera- tion UP	8.32 (pts)	x	4.03 (aunt/ uncle)	6.58 (pts-in- law)	5.43 (step- pts)	—
Ego's genera- tion	—	6.90 (sibs)	3.25 (cousins)	—	—	4.86 3.28 2.84 (fds) (ngbr) (exSp)
One genera- tion DOWN	8.32 (ch)	x	4.81 (nieces/ nephews)	7.11 (ch-in- law)	6.10 (step- ch)	—
Two genera- tions DOWN	x	6.47 (gdch)	—	—	—	—
Grand Mean by Range	8.32	6.56	4.03	6.85	5.77	3.66
Connecting Link	—	(Parent or Child)	(Sib of Parent or Ego)	(Child or Spouse)	(Parent or Spouse)	

[a] "x" denotes logically empty cell.
[b] "—" denotes omission in vignette design.

design—identified by an "—"). The rating used in this table is the obligation to provide financial aid.

With the data organized in this manner, it becomes very clear that holding degree of relationship constant (i.e., by comparing mean ratings within a column of this table), there is a general tendency to express higher obligations to descendant than to ascendant generations: Higher obligations are felt toward children-in-law than to parents-in-law, to stepchildren than to stepparents, to nieces and nephews than to aunts and uncles, and to grandchildren than to grandparents.

Since respondents may feel that the young have greater need for financial assistance from their older kin than older kin need from their younger kin, one may question whether the pattern shown in Table 4.8 is a function of the specific rating involved, i.e., financial aid in crisis circumstances. To test this, we reorder the data in a comparable way for the comfort ratings, shown in Table 4.9. An inspection quickly confirms that the pattern of greater obligation to descendants than ascendants is

Table 4.9. Mean Ratings on Comfort Obligations by Range and Depth of Relationship (G2 sample)

| | Range | | | | | | | |
| | Consanguineal Kin | | | Affinal Kin | | Nonkin | | |
Depth	Primary	Secondary	Distant	In-laws	Step			
Two generations UP	x [a]	7.01 (gdpts)	— [b]	—	—	—		
One generation UP	8.71 (pts)	x	4.77 (aunt/uncle)	7.04 (pts-in-law)	6.05 (step pts)	—		
Ego's generation	—	7.60 (sibs)	4.09 (cousins)	—	—	6.37 (fds)	5.05 (ngbr)	3.45 (exsp)
One generation DOWN	8.68 (ch)	x	5.57 (niece/nephew)	7.12 (ch-in-law)	6.93 (step ch)	—		
Two generations DOWN	x	7.22 (gdch)	—	—	—	—		

[a] "x" denotes logically empty cell.
[b] "—" denotes omission in vignette design.

not specific to financial assistance but holds for providing social–emotional comfort as well. That the pattern of greater obligations to descendants than ascendants is somewhat stronger in the case of financial aid than comfort can be seen by computing mean ratings for the two generational positions for which there are four kin counterparts: one generation up vs. one generation down from ego. These means are as follows:

	Money	Comfort
One generation UP	6.09	6.64
One generation DOWN	6.59	7.07
Difference between means	.50	.43

On both rating scales, obligations are higher toward descendants than toward ascendants in the kindred, but this holds to a slightly greater extent (.50) for money assistance than for providing comfort (.43).[21]

From the various ways in which the vignette data have been analyzed to this point, there is clearly a robust and consistent underlying structure to normative obligations to kin. Types of situational stimuli or types of obligatory responses show only minor differences, compared to the inherent structure determined by the degree to which respondents are related to the kinperson in the vignette. Obligations radiate out in lessening degrees from the high obligation to primary kin, with greater obligations toward descendants in all categories of kin than to ascendants. Secondary affinal kin, acquired through marriage or remarriage, generally evoke greater obligations than distant consanguineal kin.

Friendship involves considerable obligation to provide social–emotional comfort, on a par with secondary blood kin, but when times are hard and money is short, friends do not stimulate as high an obligation to provide financial aid as do blood and affinal kin. We have also seen the importance of the connecting links between ego and alter in the kindred in structuring obligations.

A Regression Interpretation of Depth and Range

The preceding section identified a number of ways in which obligations to kin vary by the depth and range of the kin tie involved. Obligations to kin vary in apparently lawful ways according to these structural features of kinship. The issue we now address is how much of the variation in obligation to kin is explained by these structural features. To accomplish this aim, multiple regression models are used.

Each of the 74 kin types used in the vignette design was coded according to the structural position of the kinperson in question vis-à-vis the respondent as ego. Each kin term was coded either 1 or 0 according to whether the term refers to a primary, first-order, second-order, or third-order kin, terms that represent the kinship range, or number of links, between ego and the kinperson in question. Nonkin were also binary coded as neighbors and friends (treated together) or as ex-kin. Binary codes were also used to distinguish the depth of the kin relationship, ascendant kin and descendant kin being coded according to the generational distance and direction from ego. Finally affinal kin, stepkin, and female kin are specified.

Table 4.10 shows the equations that resulted from regressing each of the four types of obligation on the set of binary variables. The most striking findings are that the handful of coded structural features of kinship accounted for almost all of the variation in the strengths of obligations to the kin in question. The R^2 values for the four kinds of obligation in Table 4.10 range from .89 to .94, which are considerably higher than ordinarily found in social science research. These findings further indicate that there is a very robust normative structure to American kinship: Obligations to kin vary in a lawful and regular way according to the position of the kinperson in question vis-à-vis ego.

Note that the regression coefficients in Table 4.10 are always relative to an omitted category and hence are not identical to the means shown

Table 4.10. Kin Mean Variance Explained by Kinship Depth and Range (N = 74 Kin Specific Averages)

Independent Variables [a]	Dependent Obligation			
	Money	Comfort	Visit	Gift
Constant	2.84***	3.45***	2.11***	2.19***
Kinship Range [b]				
Primary Kin	5.11***	4.85***	5.67***	5.42***
First Order	3.56***	3.62***	4.18***	4.44***
Second Order	1.21***	1.34***	2.30***	2.37***
Third Order	0.31	0.50	0.74	1.24**
Friends and				
Neighbors	1.13**	2.13***	2.65***	2.61***
Affinal Kin	− 1.48**	− 1.53***	− 1.40***	1.43***
Step Kin	− 2.57***	− 2.26***	− 2.16***	− 1.82***
Kinship Depth [c]				
Down One	0.54***	0.51***	0.11	0.99***
Down Two	− 0.02	0.02	0.35	0.48*
Female Kin	0.21*	0.27**	0.31	0.26*
R^2	**.94**	**.94**	**.89**	**.91**
R^2 for Range				
Measures Alone	.80	.79	.79	.76

[a] All independent variables are dummies, coded 1 and 0.
[b] Omitted category is ex-kin.
[c] Omitted categories include same generation, one up, and two up. More than one category had to be omitted because of multicollinearity problems.
*** $p < .001$
** $p < .01$
* $p < .05$

in earlier sections. Thus, the money obligation coefficient for primary kin, 5.1, is to be interpreted as showing that primary kin are on the average 5.1 points higher on that obligation rating than ex-spouses, the omitted category.

The strongest structural dimension of kinship is clearly range, the number of links separating ego from the kin in question, as indicated by the bottom row of Table 4.10. With *only* the range measures included, the resulting R^2 values range from .76 to .80: Hence, between 84 and 89% of the *explained variance*[22] is generated by the number of links between ego and the kinperson.

Although the differences in constant terms from equation to equation mirror (as they should) the differences in the means from obligation to obligation, the regression coefficients for the kinship ranges tell much the same story as was told in previous sections of this chapter. Primary kinship relationships are the most obligating, with obligations declining rapidly as the number of links between ego and the kinperson increase.

Affinal kin are more obligating than step kin, but both are less so than consanguineal kin. Finally, kinship relationships that go down the generational ladder are more obligating than those involving the same or ascendant generations. The differences among the generations also account for a large portion, around 10%, of the variance in obligations.[23]

Note also that female kin are slightly more obligating than male kin, a generalization that does not hold for visiting, but does hold for the other obligation types. We will have more to say about these kin gender differences in a later portion of this chapter.

If one accepts the argument that it is at the point where friends and neighbors are more obligating than kin that the kindred boundaries appear, the findings of Table 4.10 can be used to identify those boundaries. Following that argument, it is certainly the case that kin who are three links removed (fourth-order kin) are not part of the kindred with respect to any of the obligations studied. But there are differences in boundaries that are defined by some of the obligation types. Friends and neighbors come right after second-order kin, as far as gift giving and visiting on celebratory occasions are concerned. In crises, friends are less obligating than third-order kin where financial help is involved, but come after first-order kin where offering comfort and emotional support is involved. Kindred boundaries vary according to what is implied as appropriate kinship behavior and according to whether the evocative event is a crisis or a celebration.

Structural and Situational Variations in Normative Obligations

When stated in the most general terms, norms appear to be absolute rules. But, in their application to specific circumstances, recognized exceptions abound. Minor predicaments may not elicit as much help from kin as major ones. The situations of kin may vary: Married kin who are surrounded by primary relationships may be less obligating than those who live alone. Personal characteristics of the kin may affect how specific persons are regarded by their relatives: When it comes to financial help, prodigal children may be treated differently than prudent ones. Helping a relative who lives across the continent requires more resources than helping one who lives next door. Someone who is poor is not expected to offer financial help to his wealthy relatives.

These variations in the individual circumstances of both ego and the kinperson modify kin obligations in recognizable ways. They may also be the vehicle for changes in normative structures. When structural

changes on the societal level produce widespread changes in the circumstances of classes of individuals, then we may expect to see corresponding shifts in both the level of obligations owed to kin and in the amount
of variation about those levels.

In this section, we explore some of these variations in the strength of
kinship obligation that go beyond range and depth. As we will see, none
of these variations can rival range and depth to any great degree as
explanations of kin obligation strength. These will be shown to be minor
themes, elaborating on the basic structural framework of kinship as
described above.

Situational Variation in Kin Obligations

To evoke obligations to kin, the vignettes described either a crisis
occurring to a kinperson or an occasion that would call for some celebration. To give specific content to the crises and celebratory occasions,
each crisis vignette contained one of eight crises and each celebratory
vignette contained one of three different celebratory events. (The specific wording of these events were given in Table 4.2.) The average
obligation ratings [24] received by each of the specific events are shown in
Table 4.11.

The situations were chosen because we thought they represented
fairly typical events of their class. We entertained no a priori expectation
about which situations would evoke the stronger and which the weaker
obligation. Indeed, it seemed to us likely that there would be at most
small differences among the rating averages for those specific crisis or
celebratory events.

As it turned out, the ratings given were responsive to the situations
depicted in the vignettes, as shown in Table 4.11: The differences among
the means in each column are statistically significant. However, it is also
clear that substantively these are relatively small differences, especially
in comparison to differences by range and depth.

Turning first to the ratings given to crisis situations, obligations to
provide comfort and emotional support are evoked more strongly by
surgery and household fires and least strongly by unemployment. A
slightly different pattern is shown by money obligations: Household
fires as crises are the source of stronger obligations, with unemployment
as the source of the weakest. Differences between crises of long and
short duration are very weak and inconsistent. There is some hint in
these findings that crises that are completely out of the control of the
individual affected are reacted to with the strongest sense of obligation:
Household fires and surgery are more obligating than personal troubles

Table 4.11.   Situational Variation in Kin Obligations

A. *Variations in Crises Events* [a]

	Mean Ratings for	
Crisis Situation [b]	Comfort	Money
Surgery—long-lasting effects	7.1	6.3
Surgery—short-term effects	7.1	6.4
Personal Troubles—long duration	6.8	5.9
Personal Troubles—short term	7.0	6.2
Household Fire—no insurance	7.0	6.6
Household Fire—short-term	7.1	6.5
Unemployment—long-term	6.6	5.8
Unemployment—short-term	6.3	5.9

B. *Variations in Celebratory Events* [a]

	Mean Ratings for	
Celebratory Occasion [b]	Gift	Visit
Received an award	6.8	6.5
Birthday	6.7	5.9
Moved to a new place	6.1	6.2

[a] All differences among means are statistically significant at beyond the .0001 level.
[b] See Figure 4.2 for fuller description of these events, as used in the vignettes.

or unemployment, the latter possibly being viewed as the outcome of bad judgment as much as bad luck.

The bottom panel of Table 4.11 shows the mean ratings received by each of the three celebratory occasions. Receiving an award is the most obligating for gestures involving both gift giving and visiting. Having a birthday is least obligating for visiting, and moving to a new place least obligating for sending a gift. With only three celebratory occasions, even tentative conceptions about the kinds of occasions that evoke gestures of acknowledgment are necessarily very shaky.

Although Table 4.11 contains evidence that the crises that evoke kin obligations affect the strength of the obligation in question, the variations involved are minor. Crises and celebratory occasions are obligating to much the same degree whatever their content, constituting further evidence about the generality of obligations to kin.

Gender and Marital Status of Kin

In producing the vignettes, the gender and marital status of each kin type described was randomly varied. Parents and grandparents were described as either widowed or currently living with their spouses. Other kin along with friends, neighbors, and ex-spouses were described as either married or unmarried.[25] In many cases, the kin term used directly implied gender, as in uncle or aunt. Where the kin term was gender neutral, as in cousins, friends, and neighbors, we modified the kin term with an explicit reference to gender, as in "female cousin." Of course, since the gender of an ex-spouse depended on the gender of the respondent, no gender modifier was used for this category.

Our a priori expectations were that female kin generally would evoke stronger obligations than male kin, but also that marital status would interact with gender to produce stronger obligations to kin who were especially vulnerable because they lacked a marital partner. The generally more obligating status of female kin has already been shown in Table 4.10 where significant coefficients were reported for three of the four[26] obligation types, indicating that the strength of obligations to female kin was overall slightly higher (.21 to .31) than to males. But the generally higher obligations to female relatives is only part of the full story, as we will see in this section.

To simplify the analysis, we will be concerned only with the two crisis event obligation types, since the celebratory event obligations carry largely redundant information. Table 4.12 provides the full details of the two crisis obligation ratings with the vignette kin classified simultaneously by gender and marital status within each of the broader kin and nonkin categories. The data in this table permit us to detect the number and the specific relationships involved that show significant differences by gender or by marital status. The results shown in Table 4.13 simplify the greater detail shown in Table 4.12.

Table 4.13 permits 72 possible comparisons by gender and 70 by marital status. We chose a cutoff of at least a difference of .30 points to classify either gender or marital status differences as substantively significant.[27] Thirty-nine percent of the gender comparisons involved higher obligation ratings toward a woman than toward a man in the identical kin type and marital status, compared to only 4% that involved higher obligations to a man than to a woman. (Note that this also means approximately 60% of the comparisons did *not* show significant differences by gender of the vignette kin.) Where gender differences do exist—the 28 instances of substantively significant gender differences—they overwhelmingly involve higher obligations to women than to men (25 of the 28 gender differences, or 89%).

Gender differences were only slightly more apt to show on the financial aid than on the comfort ratings (16 vs. 12). It is interesting to note that the three cases in which higher financial aid obligations were expressed to men than to women were to a married stepfather, a son-in-law, and a married son's son; in other words, all are married men. Since loyalty and affection are generally deeper in relations with parents than stepparents, by helping a married stepfather one is effectively helping one's own mother. By the same attention to the connecting link, to give more financial aid to a son-in-law is to extend help to a daughter as well. A basic reason why we believe adults show some favoritism or greater obligation to sons-in-law than to daughters-in-law has to do with the particularly close relations between mothers and daughters. A son's wife is closer by far to her own mother than to her in-laws, and, from the perspective of parents-in-law, therefore, they are more apt to bring their sons-in-law into relative intimacy, reflecting the close bond to a daughter, than they are to bring daughters-in-law into their lives. We believe it is the greater affective closeness of the mother–daughter relationship than any other parent–child dyad that ripples out into more distant kin relations, and provides the asymmetrical tilt to the maternal side in the American kinship system. The implication is, once more, that one must pay close attention to the connecting links between kinpersons in interpreting variance in affection or obligations toward secondary and distant kin.

We are on shakier interpretive grounds concerning the third kin type that showed significantly greater obligations to a male than a female: a married son's son versus a married son's daughter. In part, the same centrality of the mother–daughter relation may be involved, since a grandchild of this type—a son's daughter—would be in closer relations to *her* mother, ego's daughter-in-law. By contrast, a son's son, particularly when he is an adult married man, is the carrier of the patronym, and, by that token alone, of considerable concern to his paternal grandparent (our respondent in this account).

In the 25 instances in which it is the woman who invoked higher obligations than the man, the reverse pattern is shown: In 17 of the 25 instances (68%) it was an unmarried or widowed woman who figured in the vignette, e.g., a widowed mother, widowed mother-in-law, unmarried sister, or an unmarried sister's daughter. This is an interesting pattern from many points of view. In another area of analysis, we find a comparable concern for the unmarried members of a family. Often the burden for elderly parents rests on the shoulders of the unmarried daughter, the child assumed to be free of any family responsibilities of her own, unlike her married siblings. Parents also make greater provision in their wills for unmarried than married children, especially daughters. The other side of this is that unmarried adults themselves invest more heavily in kin relations: An unmarried aunt, for example, may look upon her nieces and nephews as quasichildren of her own, just as she may be the favorite aunt in the lives of her siblings' children.

Table 4.12. Mean Obligation Ratings by Gender and Marital Status of Kinperson and Type of Obligation

	Type of Obligation			
	Financial Aid		Social–Emotional Comfort	
Type of Relationship	Alone [a]	Partner	Alone	Partner
Parents				
Mother	8.72	8.16	8.90	8.74
Father	8.13	8.27	8.55	8.63
Mother-in-law	6.96	6.71	7.67	6.81
Father-in-law	6.66	5.97	6.91	6.79
Stepmother	5.96	4.88	6.08	5.91
Stepfather	5.22	5.69	6.91	6.79
Children				
Daughter	8.51	8.19	8.74	8.73
Son	8.34	8.26	8.62	8.62
Daughter-in-law	x [b]	6.74	x	7.20
Son-in-law	x	7.48	x	7.04
Stepdaughter	6.49	—[c]	7.08	—
Stepson	5.72	—	6.78	—
Grandparents				
Maternal Grdmother	6.48	6.49	7.22	7.28
Maternal Grdfather	6.60	6.20	7.09	6.68
Paternal Grdmother	6.55	6.10	6.98	7.09
Paternal Grdfather	5.97	6.01	6.76	6.94
Grandchildren				
Daughter's Daughter	6.72	6.63	7.35	7.20
Daughter's Son	6.74	6.34	7.19	6.91
Son's Daughter	6.61	6.03	7.21	7.56
Son's Son	6.32	6.42	7.11	7.26

	Type of Obligation			
	Financial Aid		Social–Emotional Comfort	
Type of Relationship	Alone [a]	Partner	Alone	Partner
Siblings				
Sister	7.19	6.92	7.77	7.67
Brother	6.69	6.78	7.45	7.49
Aunts and Uncles				
Mother's Sister	4.05	4.11	4.70	5.37
Mother's Brother	4.21	4.25	4.41	5.29
Father's Sister	4.28	3.97	4.77	4.85
Father's Brother	4.05	3.36	4.69	4.10
Nieces and Nephews				
Sister's Daughter	5.31	4.93	5.97	5.76
Sister's Son	4.87	4.83	5.59	5.29
Brother's Daughter	4.86	4.56	5.93	5.34
Brother's Son	4.78	4.34	5.42	5.29
Cousins				
Woman, Mother's Side	3.51	3.66	3.76	4.20
Man, Mother's Side	2.80	3.35	3.97	4.31
Woman, Father's Side	3.58	3.22	4.34	4.15
Man, Father's Side	3.09	2.79	3.81	4.15
Friends				
Woman	4.80	5.06	6.80	6.48
Man	4.74	4.83	6.12	6.10
Neighbors				
Woman	3.29	3.58	5.62	5.37
Man	3.29	2.97	4.51	4.70
Ex-spouses	3.38	2.30	3.84	3.05

[a] "Alone" indicates widowed in the case of parents and grandparents, unmarried in case of children and grandchildren; "partner" in all cases means person is married and living with spouse.

[b] x, logically empty cell.

[c] —, vignette design did not include married stepchildren.

Table 4.13. Significant [a] Gender and Marital Status Differences Among Kin and Nonkin in Financial Aid and Comfort Obligations

Type of Difference Comparisons	Financial Aid	Comfort	Significant Differences (%)	Percentage of Total
Gender Differences				
Male more than Female	3 [b]	0	10.7	4.2
Female more than male	13 [c]	12 [d]	89.3	34.7
	(16)	(12)	(28)	(72)
Marital Status Differences				
Married more than Alone	3	5	26.6	11.4
Alone more than Married	15	7	73.3	30.5
	(18)	(12)	(30)	(70)

[a] Differences in excess of .30 between men and women, or unmarried/widowed and married within each kintype.
[b] Married stepfather, son-in-law, married son's son.
[c] Widowed mother, widowed stepmother, widowed mother-in-law, unmarried stepdaughter, widowed father's mother, unmarried sister, unmarried sister's daughter, unmarried woman cousin on both sides of family, married mother-in-law, married father's sister, married woman cousin on both sides of family.
[d] Widowed mother, widowed mother-in-law, unmarried stepdaughter, unmarried sister, unmarried sister's daughter, unmarried brother's daughter, unmarried woman cousin, married mother's mother, married father's sister, married sister's daughter, married woman friend, married woman neighbor.

Then too, it is culturally assumed that men can fend for themselves in life, and have less need for either financial help or emotional comfort than do unattached women. There is, of course, some reality in such an assumption, so long as women are in occupations that pay less well than the occupations in which men predominate, and so long as women earn less than men even in the same occupation. Hence, the variation in the patterning of normative obligations seems to mirror a commonly held image of the family in sociology, that it acts as a "latent matrix" of relationships, stimulated to action when a crisis hits the life of a family member to absorb and help cushion the hurt, or to expand when a celebration is an occasion for the expression of family pride (Riley, 1983).

The marital status differences shown in Table 4.12 illustrate this implicit assumption that it is more important to help individuals within a kindred who have no life partners than it is to help married adults in the kindred. Where significant differences are found by marital status of the vignette person, almost three-quarters of the 30 instances (73.3%) involve higher obligations to widowed or unmarried persons than married persons of the same kintype.

There is clearly an interaction here between gender and marital status: The key figure associated with an extra edge of obligation in our respondents is a woman alone; an unmarried aunt, a widowed mother, or an unmarried woman cousin on either side of the family. In keeping with the earlier finding that there is much less variance where children and parents are concerned, we see here that marital status and gender differences become sharper further out in the web of the kinship system. Where significant differences appear that involve parents and children, it tends to be marital status or marital status in conjunction with gender that is the more important stimulus to heightened obligation, not gender per se.

Gender of Respondent

But what of the influence of gender, not of the kinperson but of the respondents? To what extent, and in which specific kin relationships, do women express significantly more obligation to kin, and are there particular relationships where men express higher obligations than women?

This analytic issue appears to move the discussion from the macrostructural level to that of individual differences. However, we are discussing the *gender role* structuring of norms rather than individual differences between men and women, an approach that is consistent with the structural theme that runs through this chapter.

Table 4.14 permits a first approximation to answering these questions. In this table we ignore the gender of the vignette kin so that we can look specifically at the effect of the gender of the respondent. As shown by the column reporting the differences in mean ratings of men versus women, and summarized at the bottom of the table, there are at most modest differences by the respondent's sex. Using the same criterion of at least .30 mean differences, 4 of the 15 gender comparisons on financial aid ratings are significant, and 9 of the 15 in the case of comfort ratings.

This gender contrast is of course in part a reflection of social expectations concerning women's roles compared to men's—i.e., men provide, women nurture—but those expectations are not remote from an individual. They have been internalized, and serve as components of an adult's self-image, and they continue to manifest themselves in the actual social behavior of men and women, nowhere more so than in their family roles. Combining the financial aid and comfort ratings, 13 of the 30 gender comparisons show significant differences (43%), and of these 13 instances, 77% involve women respondents showing higher obligations than men.

Note that two of the three instances in which men show greater obligations than women involve ex-spouses. It seems reasonable to find

Table 4.14.   Gender and Normative Obligations: Financial Aid and Comfort
Mean Ratings by Type of Relationship and Gender of Respondent
(G2 Sample)

Type of Relationship	Financial Aid		Mean Difference Women Minus Men	Comfort		Mean Difference Women Minus Men
	Men	Women		Men	Women	
Parents						
Own parents	8.32	8.32	.00	8.70	8.71	.01
Parents-in-law	6.38	6.43	.05	7.26	6.89	− .37
Stepparents	5.49	5.39	− .10	6.02	6.08	.06
Children						
Own Children	8.35	8.29	− .06	8.62	8.73	.11
Children-in-law	7.02	7.17	.15	6.71	7.47	.76
Stepchildren	5.84	6.31	.47	6.64	7.11	.47
Grandparents	6.24	6.28	.04	6.76	7.16	.40
Grandchildren	6.26	6.63	.37	6.99	7.40	.41
Siblings	7.01	6.80	− .21	7.49	7.67	.18
Aunts/Uncles	3.94	4.09	.15	4.52	4.97	.45
Nieces/Nephews	4.09	4.92	.83	5.24	5.83	.59
Cousins	3.19	3.00	− .19	4.04	4.12	.08
Friends	4.92	4.80	− .12	6.05	6.57	.52
Neighbors	3.16	3.36	.20	4.93	5.12	.19
Ex-spouses	3.19	2.58	− .61	4.11	2.94	− 1.17
Number of kintypes with .30 or more difference by gender	4 of 15			9 of 15		
Women Higher than Men	3			7		
Men Higher than Women	1			2		

that men feel more financial obligations to their former wives than
women to their former husbands, since this accords with conventional
practice in legal settlements following divorce, but there is an even
greater difference on the Comfort ratings, with men reporting a mean of
4.11 to women's 2.94. Of course, only a minority of the men respondents have themselves experienced a divorce, and they may merely be
projecting a highly honorable side of themselves as they think they
would behave to former wives. By contrast, women respondents may

find any prospect of divorce more threatening; they may also assume it is men who break up marriages, not women, and hence imagine circumstances in which anger and hurt preclude providing comfort to a former husband. The same cultural assumption of who was responsible for a marital breakup, even in a no-fault divorce era like our own, may stimulate guilt in men that in turn motivates them to report higher obligations to provide comfort to former wives.

The single other instance in which men report higher obligations than women is to parents-in-law, where men exceed women by .37 points on the comfort rating. We defer any detailed discussion of this until a later point, but suggest this reflects the reality experienced in American families: Once again, it is likely that women's closer ties to their parents than men's has the effect after marriage of involving men in closer and more frequent relations with their parents-in-law than women experience with their husbands' parents.

But what now, of the 10 relationships in which women express greater obligations than men? Three kintypes account for six of these instances: Women show higher comfort and financial obligations than men to stepchildren, grandchildren, and nieces and nephews. The remaining instances involve gender differences in comfort ratings but not financial aid ratings; children-in-law, grandparents, aunts and uncles, and friends. Gender role constraints may play a role in restricting the expression of nurturant concern in providing comfort by men except to very closely related and familiar family members—parents, children, siblings—and, in particular, to kin older than themselves such as grandparents, aunts, and uncles. Sexual taboos, or the fear of having the expression of intimate concern misunderstood, may similarly restrain men from providing comfort to friends, while such concern is consistent with social expectations for how women will relate when friends face painful events.

A second thread in these gender differences may be the general linkage of nurturance with the young. Indeed, women do exceed men to some degree in feeling obliged to comfort descendants such as children-in-law, grandchildren, siblings' children, and even, for most, the purely hypothetical stepchildren.

Table 4.15 shows this gender contrast in a more generalized sense, comparing kin varying by whether they are located in an ascendant or descendant generation. The differences between means, shown in the bottom line of each half of the table, measure the extent to which obligations are greater toward descendants than ascendants, by the gender of respondents. The general pattern is for women to show a stronger tipping toward higher obligations toward descendants than do men. Neither men nor women show any significant distinctions be-

Table 4.15. Mean Ratings on Financial Aid and Comfort Obligations by Range and Depth of Relationship and by Gender of Respondent (G2 Sample)

	Range of Relationship									
	Primary		Secondary		Distant		In-Laws		Step	
Depth	Men	Women	Men	Women	Men	Women	Men	Women	Men	Women
A. Comfort Obligation Rating by Respondent Gender										
Two UP	x[a]		6.76	7.16		—[b]	—	—	—	—
One UP	8.70	8.71	7.49	7.67	4.52	4.97	7.26	6.89	6.02	6.08
Ego	x		x		4.04	4.12				
One DOWN	8.62	8.73	6.99	7.40	5.24	5.83	6.71	7.47	6.64	7.11
Two DOWN	x									
Descendant minus Ascendant	-.08	-.02	.23	.24	.72	.86	-.55	.58	.62	1.03
B. Financial Aid Obligation Rating by Respondent Gender										
Two UP	x		6.24	6.28		—	—	—	—	—
One UP	8.32	8.32	7.01	6.80	3.94	4.09	6.38	6.43	5.49	5.39
Ego	x		x		3.19	3.00				
One DOWN	8.35	8.29	6.26	6.63	4.09	4.92	7.02	7.17	5.84	6.31
Two DOWN	x									
Descendant minus Ascendant	.03	-.03	.02	.38	.15	.83	.64	.74	.35	.92

[a] "x" denotes logically empty cell.
[b] "—" denotes omission in vignette design.

tween parents and children, but in seven of the eight gender comparisons in which other types of relationships are concerned, the descendant tipping is stronger among women than men: this holds, for example, in the greater obligation to children-in-law than parents-in-law, nieces and nephews compared to aunts and uncles, and stepchildren compared to stepparents. There is even one strong reversal shown in Table 4.15: Men show significantly greater obligation to parents-in-law than to children-in-law, while women show the reverse, stronger obligation to children-in-law than to parents-in-law. Once again, the differential attachment to parents between men and women is mirrored in their differential relations to in-laws.

In Chapter 5 we will again take up gender differences in obligations to kin and explore in greater depth the qualities in gender socialization that lead to higher obligations expressed by women to kin.

Women as Connecting Links in the Kindred

Earlier in the analysis, we noted the importance of who stands as the connecting link between ego and a specified kinperson, i.e., that those kin related to ego through a parent, child, or spouse stimulate higher obligations than those related through a sibling, or a parent's sibling. This helped to explain why affinal kin such as parents-in-law or children-in-law had obligation ratings as high as they did, exceeding many blood ties. Here we are seeing the relevance of gender as an additional characteristic of connecting links: Women in their roles as mothers, wives, or daughters serve as particularly salient connecting links to other members of the kindred. As wives, women bring men into close relations with their own kin to a greater extent than husbands bring wives into close relations with their families. And the analogous pattern holds for women in their daughter roles, facilitating the integration of their husbands into their parents' lives to a greater extent than they experience vis-à-vis their husbands' families.

It is also the case that as mothers, women bring their children into closer touch with grandparents, aunts, and uncles on the maternal side of the family than men do to the paternal side. Family sociologists have often noted that as affective gatekeepers and as kinkeepers in managing the social life of families, women play a more critical role than do men. Here we are finding that this applies to the domain of normative obligations as well.

Our study has limited coverage on social interaction or affective closeness among kin outside the parent–child relationship. But we can illustrate the similarity of pattern between normative obligation and affective significance of at least grandparents, aunts, and uncles. This is made possible by a retrospective question asked of respondents, on the extent to which a variety of relatives, friends of parents, or teachers were particularly important to them while they were growing up. The question carefully specified each grandparent or parent's sibling, so the connecting links are known. Hence we can compare the frequency with which respondents cited grandparents of each sex and each side of the family, as well as which side of the family an aunt or uncle was located.

Table 4.16 brings these data together with the two measures of normative obligations we have been discussing, and helps to reinforce the judgment that comfort ratings mirror the structure of affective closeness to a greater extent than money ratings do. (Chapter 5 will later demonstrate, on an individual level, that an index of the number of kinpersons defined as significant in the early years of growing up—Kin Salience, as the index is labeled—is an important early determinant of overall level of normative obligations held by respondents.)

These data show that the gender of the kinperson as well as the gender of the connecting links are relevant to both social–emotional salience of grandparents, aunts, and uncles and to normative obligation levels. Grandmothers and aunts were more often cited as "very important" to respondents when they were growing up than grandfathers and uncles. But of special interest here, this is particularly the case if the connecting link is the mother of respondents: Hence it is the maternal aunt (ego's mother's sister) and maternal grandmother (ego's mother's mother) who stand out as the most significant figures in the lives of our respondents, indirectly reflecting the special closeness of mother–daughter and sister–sister bonds.

The "low man" on the totem pole on all three measures shown in Table 4.16 for both grandparents and parents' siblings is literally a

Table 4.16. Normative Obligations and Childhood Salience of Grandparents and Parents' Siblings by Gender of Kinperson and of Connecting Links

Relative	Normative Obligations		Percentage "Very Important" While Growing Up
	Money	*Comfort*	
Grandparents			
Mother's Mother	6.48	7.25	42.6
Mother's Father	6.40	6.88	35.7
Father's Mother	6.32	7.04	31.7
Father's Father	5.99	6.85	25.2
Aunts and Uncles			
Mother's Sister	4.08	5.04	34.5
Mother's Brother	4.23	4.85	27.5
Father's Sister	4.12	4.81	26.1
Father's Brother	3.70	4.39	22.1

"man," in particular a male relative related to ego through another man: Father's father and father's brother are least apt to be cited as "very important" in the earlier lives of respondents, and these same figures evoked the lowest obligation ratings in the vignette study.

Some Effects of Structural Ambiguity

The normative structure of kinship obligations also reflects some of the ambiguities in our kinship system that have emerged as a consequence of social change in longevity and in marriage patterns. These ambiguities show up with particular force with respect to grandparents and to affinal kin acquired through remarriage. The remarkable changes in mortality over the past half century have meant that grandparents are kin positions that are more likely to be occupied. Recent historical changes in marriage and divorce patterns have also meant that stepkin are more frequently in everyone's kindred. These structural changes in the size and composition of the concrete kindreds of Americans have their reflections in the normative structure of kinship obligations, as we will see below.

Grandparents.   Family sociology and life course analysis have shown a resurgence of interest in the role of grandparents (Bengtson, 1985; Bengtson & Robertson, 1985; Cherlin & Furstenberg, 1986; Eisenberg, 1988; Hagestad, 1985). Typically, sociologists emphasize three features of the grandparent role and relationship with grandchildren. First, with increased longevity, there are more grandparents alive through the adolescence and early adult years of their grandchildren, and, hence, they may be more significant kin figures in the lives of young people at more mature ages than in the past. Second, with rapid changes in women's roles, healthier conditions in old age, and numerous changes in life-styles and values, there is much more ambiguity in the roles of grandparents than in earlier periods of our history. Many grandparents today are healthier and more youthful in pursuit of independent interests of their own than many parents were 50 years ago. And, third, with the sharp rise in the divorce rate, particularly in marriages involving children, there is special strain imposed on the grandparent–grandchild relationship brought on by the older generation often being cut off from regular or easy contact with their sons' children as a result of custody typically being vested in the hands of mothers. Hence grandparents are assured steadier, less risky relations if they invest in their daughters' children than in their sons' children.

Yet a fourth historical development may be relevant to changes in the grandparent role. With far greater financial security than previous cohorts of the elderly experienced, it is possible for elderly adults more frequently to avoid dependence on their children; they can act out the American preference for independence and, by that fact alone, reduce the temptation to "intrude" on their children's management of their own lives and the rearing of the grandchildren. By the same token, however, the elderly may vary more today in the degree of investment they make in being grandparents, and this may be reflected in more variation in obligation levels to grandchildren or to grandparents than to other kinpersons.

These new complications impacting on the grandparent–grandchild relationship have several contradictory implications. Being healthier and more financially secure, the elderly may find it easier to be with young children. They also may be able to help their grandchildren financially to a greater extent than grandparents could only a few decades ago. At the same time, the very characteristics of good health and financial security may predispose the elderly to more active and involved lives outside of family relations, through travel, migration to a retirement community in a warmer climate, or volunteer work, choices that may reduce invest-ment in and obligation to grandchildren.

These counter pressures contribute to the view that these alternate generations have more ambiguity in relating to each other today than in the past.

Remarriage and its aftermath. Furthermore, the same divorce rate that complicates the roles of grandparents has the effect of making step-parents and stepchildren a more prevalent feature of contemporary family life and household composition. These two trends raised the question of whether our data would show greater ambiguity, as indexed by higher standard deviations around the means in the obligation rat-ings, toward grandparents and grandchildren than toward primary kin or other consanguineal secondary kin, e.g., siblings. Similarly, one might predict more variance in the obligation ratings toward stepparents and stepchildren, kin types becoming perhaps common enough to counter some of the negative stereotypes encountered in childhood literature and films. We have already seen that stepparents and step-children are by no means low in the level of obligations they evoked in the vignettes; their position as substitutes for blood ties in the position of parents or of children seemed pertinent, by the same principle of the significance of connecting links to ego that held for all other types of kin.

Table 4.17 shows the mean standard deviations of the financial aid ratings across the range and depth classification of kin and nonkin. The standard deviations are lowest for the primary kin, parents and children (2.35 and 2.20, respectively). Taking as a high standard deviation one in excess of 2.70[28] around their means is found in the predicted kin catego-

Table 4.17. Variation in Normative Obligations: Mean Standard Deviation of Financial Aid Ratings by Range and Depth of Relationship (G2 Sample)

| | Range | | | | | | | |
| | Consanguineal Kin | | | Affinal Kin | | Nonkin | | |
Depth	Primary	Secondary	Distant	In-laws	Step		Nonkin	
Two generations UP	x [a]	2.84 (gdpts)	—[b]	—	—		—	
One generation UP	2.35 (pts)	x	2.57 (aunts/uncles)	2.79 (pts-in-law)	2.86 (step-pts)		—	
Ego's generation	x	2.63 (sibs)	2.49 (cousins)	—	—	2.68 (fds)	2.47 (neighbor)	2.63 (ex-spouse)
One generation DOWN	2.20 (ch)	x	2.68 (nieces/nephews)	2.48 (ch-in-law)	2.74 (step-ch)		—	
Two generations DOWN	x	2.70 (gdch)	—	—	—		—	
Grand Mean SD by Range	2.28	2.72	2.58	2.63	2.80			

[a] "x," logically empty cell.
[b] "—," omission in vignette design.

ries: grandparents (2.84), grandchildren (2.70), stepparents (2.86), and stepchildren (2.74). High variance is also noted in a category we did not predict, parents-in-law (2.79). It strikes us as significant that so mixed and ambiguous a category as "neighbors" shows less variation (2.47) than the secondary kin types.[29]

Without historical data on how kinship obligations were structured in the past, we cannot be sure that the lack of consensus over step-kin, affinal kin, and grandparents is a consequence of the historical changes in the size and composition of the kindred. Nonetheless, the findings are in line with our expectations that structural changes in concrete kindreds can lead first to ambiguity concerning the kin involved and, in the long run, to changes in normative structures.

The Socialization of Kinship Norms

The beautiful symmetry that has emerged from the detailed analysis covered above forces the question of what produces it? Why do adult men and women, of all ages, show largely the same hierarchy of obligations along the lines we have shown? No one learns genealogy in school, and parents do not self-consciously teach their youngsters the rules of kinship or exactly how Aunt Sally is related to them compared to Aunt Sue.[30]

Nor is simple opportunity to observe others in various kin roles a sufficient explanation. Many people never had an aunt or an uncle, and others never knew a grandparent of any type because they died before their birth or lived in another country. But we predict the same normative hierarchy will be found whether or not our respondents had any aunts, knew a grandparent, or have yet become an aunt or a parent themselves.

Kinship always refers to some linked dyad; an aunt to a niece, a parent to a child, a grandchild to a grandparent. This is true by definition, whether or not specific pairs are in frequent social interaction with each other. The telephone lines in the United States buzz with conversations between aunts and nieces, grandfathers and grandsons, who rarely see each other apart from ceremonial occasions and brief vacations. Does this pairing become part of how we are socialized in advance to what it means to be an uncle, or a grandfather, i.e., by being oneself a nephew or a grandson? A moment's thought puts this in doubt when we think of instances integral to our own life experience: Most of us have to become parents to really understand what it means to be a parent; having been someone's child all one's life was clearly not sufficient to prepare one for the experience of parenthood. This may, of course, be overstating the case, since it could be that although observing one's own parent does not prepare us to fill completely the role of parent, we learn enough of the nature of the parent–child relationship to acquire a generalized sense of its powerful emotional and normative significance. As a result, all other kin relations may be gauged by the degree to which they differ in intensity from the parent–child relation known from early infancy on.

A child can also observe many other parent–child relationships within the family; a grandparent with the child's mother, an aunt with the child's niece, and so on.

Children *are* taught to make distinctions among the adults whom they encounter in life. When parents warn a child not to be too friendly with strange adults they meet in the neighborhood, while they encourage, indeed sometimes force, a child to "kiss your uncle" or "your cousin" whom the child has never seen before, a fundamental distinction is being laid down in the child's mind between kin and nonkin, with the "kiss" serving as an index to the presumed intimacy of kin whom the child can trust, versus the parental warning to stay away from strangers as an index to the possible harm and distrustful reserve that is proper to adults outside the family. Admonitions to "go play with your cousin," "give your aunt a kiss," "show respect to your Nana," "take care of your little brother," or "never call an older relative by their first name" abound in the family experiences of the young.

The use of kin labels reinforces these experiences: Full terms of respect with no first names are used in addressing grandparents, which is not the case for grandchildren. To sense the strangeness of reversing the generational direction in such usage, try saying "granddaughter" as a term of address to a grandchild, compared to the familiar use by a child (or adults, for that matter) of "grandpa" or "granddad". Little differentiation is made in our kinship system where parents' siblings are concerned except their gender: Aunt Sue and Aunt Sally are both addressed in the same way, varying only in first name, with nothing to indicate that Aunt Sue is the child's mother's sister while Aunt Sally is the wife of the child's father's brother.

Everyday language makes frequent use of kin terms, typically carrying associations that reinforce important and subtle similarities between kinpersons and the matter at hand: "God the Father," a powerful symbol of eternal authority; "Mother Earth," a powerful symbol of deep-rooted ties and our link to the natural world; "Big Brother," an often ambivalent metaphor alternating between connotations of affectionate protective care and of intrusive monitoring and "snitching" to a powerful authority—the parent or the state; "Uncle Sam," the beloved and benevolent mother's brother ready to treat you but not scold you.

Age-peer loyalty between pairs of individuals or large group entities is often invoked and reinforced with calls of brotherhood or sisterhood, or in their latinized garb, fraternities and sororities.

Associated with such childhood exposure are frequent lessons that reinforce the general concepts that deference and respect should flow upward to older persons, while responsibility and nurturance flow down the generations from the older to the younger. One's pals and confidantes are age peers, like siblings, and often invoked as such: "she's like a sister to me," "we're even closer than brothers." On occasion in some families an uncle can be a pal to a nephew, perhaps the only older male relative known to a small boy with whom comradeship and affection can rule uncontaminated by the discipline and authority that goes with fathering. A young anthropologist on our research staff many years ago reported from interviews with young black girls in Chicago that two of her informants, neither of whom had sisters of their own, had acquired "blood sisters" through the same ritual—pricking their fingers and rubbing them together to exchange their blood.

In enumerable ways children have impressed on them some fundamental rules of behavior and an implicit set of norms: to distinguish between kin and nonkin, between young and old, between fathers and uncles, aunts and mothers. High social valuation of kin ties and family loyalty get reinforced by religious invocations of the "parent–child" metaphors, and by the school's emphasis on fraternal and sororal relations.

Perhaps, like language itself, it will never be possible to fully unravel exactly how children acquire an understanding of the rules of kinship. They acquire "examples" of kin types, as they accumulate vocabulary, somehow cognitively able to make synaptic leaps that suddenly produce grammatically correct whole phrases and sentences, without learning until fifth grade what the rules of grammar are that they have followed for years. In a similar process, we may intuit from hundreds of discrete instances that we owe more to parents than aunts, more to nieces than cousins, and so on. In this respect, the normative structure of kinship is not different from other kinds of structures, such as occupational prestige and the seriousness of crime, knowledge that is acquired without ever being formally taught.

Theoretical speculation about the kinship norms socialization process does not end here. We must deal with the fact that the structure of kin norms our data show is consistent with predictions a sociobiologist might make. In particular, "inclusive fitness" theorists would argue that the pattern shown by the degrees of connectedness between our respondents and the several kin alters is in general accord with the extent to which these various kinpersons share similar genetic material. They would even argue that the underlying reason for the tipping toward closer ties to maternal kin inheres in the fact that paternity is only circumstantial, whole biological maternity is assured. On that ground alone, they have argued that the reason why a mother's brother (but not a father's brother) in many kinship systems carries obligations for his sister's children stems from the fact that a man can be more assured of sharing genetically with his sister's children than with the children borne by his wife.

Whether inclusive fitness theory is relevant to an interpretation of our data remains moot. There may, in fact, be physical and social cues to the degree of shared genes within family lines that provide intermediary roles more familiar to sociologists: Similarity of stature, eye, hair, and skin color, and to some degree intelligence and various specialized aptitudes may be subliminally sensed if not consciously identified by people belonging to the same lineage. In-marrying affines from very different ethnic backgrounds may provide diversity, at the same time they reinforce the sense of similarity among those sharing the more common ethnic background. A colleague recently returned to the Norwegian village in which she grew up and which she left as an adolescent. Although two decades had passed since her last visit, she claimed she could identify dozens of young children and adolescents she encountered on the street in terms of what families they belonged to because of their physical and social similarity to their parents, a process of identification facilitated by the fact that the children were the age of her village friends at the time she left Norway. If that holds in a quite ethnically homogeneous society such as Norway, the sense and salience of physical similarity between genetically related individuals may be even easier and more significant to a sense of lineage membership in a very heterogeneous society such as our own. This possibility relates to the symmetry we have seen in that the greater the collateral distance from ego, the more in-marrying affines dilute the proportion of shared genes.

But much new research would be necessary to explore the extent to which physical similarity and difference between members of a kindred are in fact related to any of the indicators of interaction frequency or normative obligation with which this study is concerned. With our present data, the best we can do is suggest the general directions such future research may take. In addition, the next chapter contains findings concerning how various influences stemming from childhood family experiences and experiences in adulthood affect the strength of individuals' attachment to the norms of kinship obligation. This analysis will suggest what are some of the variations in socialization experiences that pave the way to individual variation in the strength of kin obligations.

Summary

The major points we have established in this analysis are as follows:

1. *Normative obligations to kin are highly structured, and are only modestly affected by variation in situational stimuli.* The most important dimension in this structure is the degree of relatedness between ego and the kinperson in question. The mean obligation ratings were more responsive to the number of connecting links between respondents and kinpersons than they were to the type of relative within a link category. Most of the variance in mean obligation ratings was accounted for by the number of links between ego and the kinperson. Figure 4.2 summarizes the highly systematic nature of this structure. Here we disregard gender of respondent and kin and restrict attention just to the consanguineal kin in the design. Five generations in the direct line through Ego are shown, with

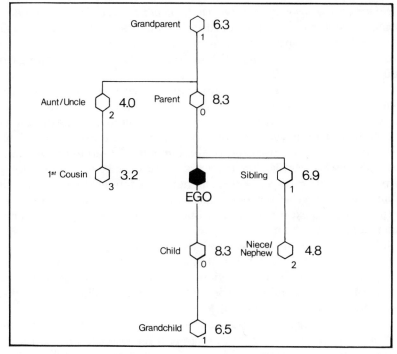

⬡ Gender Unspecified

Note: Large numerals indicate Mean Ratings; small numbers below symbol refer to the Number of Connecting Links between Ego and Alter.

Figure 4.2. Mean rating on financial aid obligations by number of connecting links between ego and kinperson: selected consanguineal kin only.

the collateral blood kin related to ego through parents and parents' siblings. The mean financial aid rating is used here, shown in large penned figures next to the symbol for alter. To the right, just below each gender symbol, are the number of connecting links between ego and the kin, with the specific kin involved shown in the margins.

There is a beautiful symmetry to the normative pattern: Mean ratings decline as one moves up or down the direct generational line from ego, with roughly the same level of obligation in each up or down position relative to ego, just as they do on the collateral dimension through the sibling relationship. The means are extremely close to each other if they share the same number of connecting links to ego, regardless of the position on the generational depth or collateral range (seen by comparing the pairs showing the same number of connecting links, the two 0s, 1s, and 2s).

2. *The primary relations of respondents to parents or to children are relatively impervious to distinctions that matter in other kin relationships.* Gender or marital status of parent or child makes little difference in the obligation levels of respondents; nor do the age and gender of respondents show any consistent or significant variation in the mean ratings of obligation to these primary kin.

3. *Higher obligations are expressed toward descendants than toward ascendants in the kindred of respondents.* This is especially the case for women respondents, not merely on financial aid, which one might expect to be directed more to the young than to the old, but also for social–emotional comfort as well. The crises and celebratory events used in the vignettes were all ones that called for responses indicating concern and caring. This suggests that sheer adult experience in family roles and family affairs, which increases by definition with age, may be what is reflected in this pattern of expressing greater obligation to younger people than to older people in the family.

4. *Affinal kin, acquired through marriage or remarriage, evoke lower obligations than consanguineal kin in comparable positions, but the nature of the position is important.* Thus, obligations to stepparents, who fill the *position* of parents, and stepchildren, who fill the *position* of children, are higher than to more distant blood kin.

5. *Gender of the kinpersons matters where secondary and distant kin and nonkin are concerned: Women kin evoke more obligation than men, especially if they are unmarried or widowed.* The few cases of kintypes in which males showed higher obligation levels than females all involved married men (e.g., married stepfather, son-in-law, son's married son.)

6. *Gender of respondent did not matter for close primary kin, but, at the secondary and distant kin level, women showed higher obligation levels than did men.*

7. *There is slightly greater variation, as measured by standard deviations*

around the mean ratings, for grandparents, stepparents, and stepchildren than other kin and nonkin, and the least variance in obligations to children and parents.

8. *The obligation to provide financial aid moves in a more restricted network than the obligation to provide comfort,* the difference in mean ratings between level of comfort obligation and money obligation increasing toward the periphery of the kinship structure, and is particularly large in the case of friends and neighbors.

9. *Who occupies the position of a connecting link between ego and alter is an important additional predictor of normative obligation levels.* Kin related through a parent, child, or spouse take priority over kin related through siblings. Most importantly, significant increments to obligation level are obtained if the connecting link is a woman. It has long been noted that the American kinship system has an asymmetrical tilt to the maternal side of a family. This holds for social interaction, subjective feelings of closeness, and salience of kin who were important in youth. Here we are finding that the same profile obtains for normative obligations, and determines *who* within a specific category of kin will evoke the most obligation: among grandparents, it is mother's mother (maternal grandmother), and among parents' siblings, it is the mother's sister (maternal aunt).

We believe this pattern is rooted in the specially close bond between mothers and daughters, a closeness that begins in childhood and continues throughout life (as we shall see in Chapters 6 and 7). Mothers serve as affective and normative gatekeepers to their own mothers, sisters, and other kinpersons, particularly same-sex kin. When gender of both respondent and the kinperson is considered jointly, the female–female bond predominates in being associated with elevated obligation levels.

We believe it is also the close mother–daughter relationship that explains one unusual finding: Both men and women respondents report higher obligations to sons-in-law than to daughters-in-law, although, in the case of parents-in-law, this reverses to the more usual pattern of higher obligations to the females in the kin position, i.e., mothers-in-law more than fathers-in-law. The explanation, in our judgment, is that daughters-in-law are more closely tied to their *own* mothers, while sons-in-law are brought closer to their parents-in-law as a consequence of daughters' closer bonds with their own parents. Once again, the normative material shows patterns familiar to family sociologists and anthropologists who have explored kinship patterns in England and the United States.

This chapter has been focused primarily on the structure of kinship norms. Although we have seen that structure clearly and boldly outlined by the data, there still remains the issue of variability in the interpretation of how that structure applies to individual respondents.

There is considerable variability around each of the means that served as the center of attention in this chapter and it is this variability to which we turn in the next chapter.

Notes

1.   Many of the central ideas in this section have been stated in fuller form in P. H. Rossi and Berk (1985).

2.   Because the universe of all possible applications is unknown (and possibly unknowable), a serious issue is whether or not the applications selected as sample points properly represent the entire domain. We believe we have drawn a reasonable sample of kintypes, but whether we have fairly sampled occasions and types of obligations is an arguable matter.

3.   The sample was created by a computer program that randomly selected one level from each of the dimensions listed in Table 4.2 and fitted together the selected levels to form a coherent text. Each respondent's booklet was prepared by selecting an independent sample. The sections of the illustrative vignettes in italics are those portions that varied from vignette to vignette according to which levels were selected, the remaining text being identical in each and every vignette.

4.   The design called for a minimum of 50 rated vignettes for each and every one of 74 different kin.

5.   Several categories were not actually kin—neighbor, friend—and one included ex-kin—divorced spouse. The kin set also did not include affinals in any systematic way. Thus, the set includes spouse's mother and father and child's spouse but no other affinals, e.g., brother-in-law and sister-in-law. We have entirely too many cousins in the set (although their weights are low and hence cousins do not appear in the vignettes very frequently). Proverbial accurate 20/20 hindsight suggests that the next kinship obligation study expand the kin type set to include more affinals and perhaps ex-kin, and spouses.

6.   The gender of "divorced spouse" was fixed by the gender of the respondent and hence was not specified.

7.   Ascendant generations (parents and grandparents) were designated as either "living with (mother, grandmother, etc.) or as "widowed."

8.   Unfortunately, we had no guides that we could rely on for our choices of such situations. The best we can say about these choices is that they are situations with which almost everyone would have either personal or vicarious experience and that are rarely regarded as positive events.

9.   The interviewer was instructed to oversee the rating of this vignette to ensure that the respondent understood the task involved, to answer any questions concerning the task, and to correct any errors in understanding that the respondent might have had. The remaining vignettes were rated by the respondent as a self-administered task. In most of the analyses presented in this and the next chapter, the practice vignettes are not included: For analysis purposes, the respondent vignette set consists of 31 rated randomly selected vignettes.

10.   In addition, six of the traumatic events consisted of three pairs of replicated trauma vignettes, with the rating tasks within a pair varied, e.g., if the first vignette to be in a replicated pair was a "comfort" rating, its replicate was to be rated as a "financial aid" task (and vice versa). The purpose of these replications was to measure the extent to which the strength of kinship obligations was affected by the content of the obligation involved.

11.   In several exploratory analyses (not reported here) we also searched for other individual characteristics related to completion of the vignette booklets, all to no avail.

12. The instructions given in the booklet were as follows: "Inside this booklet are descriptions of events that could happen to anyone. We want you to imagine that each of the events actually happened to the person indicated. For example, some of the events are shown as happening to your grandfather or others to sisters, your children or your cousins. Although most people have some of the relatives we want you to think about, few people have every one, or the relative in question may no longer be alive. If we ask you about some kind of relative that you never or no longer have, just try to imagine that you actually have such a relative."

13. Typical "refusal rates" range between 5 and 10%, with the larger rates being registered in studies in which difficult tasks and/or complicated vignettes were given to respondents.

14. In a pretest of the factorial survey, we asked respondents to rate each vignette twice, using much the same rating scales shown in Figure 5.2. The pretest results indicated that respondents were not discriminating within the pairs of tasks presented, leading to correlations between rating task pairs well over .8. Because of the close juxtaposition of the rating scales, we were unable to judge whether these high correlations represented contamination between rating pairs or a substantive finding. As a consequence, we designed the current study calling for only one rating task per vignette, using the replications discussed in the text, to test whether the different kinds of obligation were truly distinct.

15. The correlation shown in Table 4.5 is high enough to lead one to suspect that it might also be reflecting a high degree of reliability in the ratings. Fortunately, additional evidence on whether the correlation in Table 4.5 represents a measure of reliability or represents two distinct but correlated dimensions is afforded by a methodological study conducted by Sarah Saunders and Deborah Sellers, using kinship obligation vignettes. Students in an undergraduate methods class at the University of Massachusetts were given the same rating task attached to pairs of identical vignettes. The duplicated vignettes were placed far apart in the booklet—tenth and twenty-fifth positions, respectively. The correlation between these exactly duplicated vignettes was .96, indicating a very high level of reliability.

16. Although each vignette contains information on events experienced by the designated kinperson, the average ratings are unaffected by this information since over all the vignettes pertaining to a kin type, these events are randomly allocated. Hence vignettes pertaining to parents have, on the average, the same distribution of events attached to them as the vignettes referring to children or cousins or any of the other kinpersons designated.

17. Note that these coefficients are considerably higher than the correlations across replicated vignettes. In the latter case, individual differences in rating tendencies plus random error lead to a lower correlation. These individual differences are obliterated when averages are computed.

18. Looked at from the factor analytic viewpoint, the correlations in the upper left triangle of Table 4.6 indicate that only one underlying factor can be discerned in the patterning of correlations.

19. Individual variation around the average ratings can also be used for other purposes. Some of the variation is due to the remaining content of the vignettes, since some events are more obligating than others. In addition, respondents vary in the way in which each interpreted the scale of obligation strength presented to them: One respondent's marking of 8 may represent the same strength of obligation as another's rating of 6.

20. The same scatter in the strengths of obligations to distant kin is shown in Table 4.5. The standard deviations around the means increase the lower are the strengths of the obligations involved.

21. Chapter 9 will report a similar pattern in actual help exchange between the generations: Money tends to flow down from parent to adult child whereas personal caregiving flows from adult child to parent.

22. Computed by expressing the R^2 with only the range measures included as a percentage of the corresponding R^2 for all measures.

23. It is difficult to calculate the independent effects of generational depth because such positions are correlated by definition with range. For example, there can be no primary kin of the same generation, and there are no primary kin in distant generations.

24. Since the specific events were assigned to the vignettes randomly, these means are composed of ratings given to approximately identical mixes of vignettes. That is, about the same mixture of kin was assigned to each. Hence, each of the means is net of the effects of other characteristics assigned to the vignettes.

25. These designations were used also to imply adult persons, an important dimension for children, grandchildren, and other members of descendant generations.

26. The exception, visiting on celebratory occasions, showed a positive but insignificant coefficient, .31. Since this was the largest coefficient for gender, it indicates that there was much more variability in gender effects on the visiting obligation than for any of the others.

27. Any difference in means greater than about .10 is statistically significant at the .05 level. Statistical significance is easily achieved in these data by quite trivial substantive differences, mainly because of the very large numbers of ratings that go into each of the means. Had we chosen a smaller cutoff point, many more of the kin gender comparisons would have been shown to favor stronger obligations to female kin, as shown in the regression analysis of Table 4.10.

28. The standard error of the standard deviations for the financial aid ratings is .036. Hence, the difference between the lowest standard deviation and 2.7 is 13 standard errors.

29. Multiple regression analyses of the standard deviations around the kin means, as presented in Chapter 5, bear out these analyses. On each of the obligation ratings, significantly higher standard deviations occur for step and affinal kin than for any other kin types. In addition, the standard deviation for grandparents is also significant on two of the obligation ratings, comfort and financial aid.

30. At least not in the northeast; southern culture and literature seem full of references to differences between individuals that reflect one or another side of a family, reflecting perhaps the greater historical primacy of blood ties and the more turbulent nature of southern marriages.

Variation in
Obligations to Kin ———————— 5

Jeanne Pejeau, 60-year-old Maryland woman:
"My daughters and my friends keep telling me to put my mother in a home. They tell me I'm killing myself for her. I don't do it to be a martyr and have someone pat me on the back. I do it because she was a darn good mother. I feel an obligation to her."

Wall Street Journal (January 27, 1989, p. A4)

Introduction

This chapter provides an analysis of differences among our respondents in the strength of their obligations to kin. Chapter 4 provided a *structural* analysis, with kin as units of analysis and showed how *average* obligation ratings given to each of the types of kin were affected by the range and depth of the relationships involved. This chapter is concerned with differences among respondents in how strongly obligated they feel toward kin of different types.

There is an obvious connection between this and the previous chapter. The averages of obligation ratings received by kin represent the central tendencies found within our sample of respondents; averaging stripped out the differences that exist among individual respondents. Although each respondent contributed to those averages, it is likely that no particular respondent gave ratings that corresponded exactly to them. Rather, the obligation ratings given by any individual departed from those averages to some extent. Central tendencies as represented by averages are simply that—values around which individual ratings tend to cluster.

Now we shift attention from the average ratings given to various kin to respondent variation around those means. If we regard the averages as normative measures, the respondent measures we will analyze represent the degree to which each respondent adheres to the normative structure of obligations to kin.

We will first examine the extent to which respondent variation is related to kinship structure, by analyzing the extent to which kin of various types differ in the amount of variation around their means, an analysis that continues the structural theme of Chapter 4, but with concern for how structured are the standard deviations around the means.

Next we will examine differences among individual respondents in their ratings. The units of analysis will be individual respondents and their ratings, measuring individual differences in how strongly the normative obligations are acknowledged. In Chapter 4 our attention was on kin norms and we asked questions such as whether our norms required a stronger obligation to mothers than to fathers; by contrast, in this chapter we explore why some respondents acknowledge stronger obligations to parents than others do.

Structural Determinants of Obligation Strength

We begin with structural effects on ratings variation using the standard deviations of the average ratings used in Chapter 4 as indexes of such variation. This approach examines individual variation around the means as a strategy to identify those parts of the kinship structure over which there is more or less agreement concerning the obligating strengths of particular types of kin. By this procedure, the types of kin with the largest standard deviations are relatives about whom kin norms are least well socially defined.

The standard deviations of the ratings[1] received by kin at various degrees of relatedness are shown in Table 5.1. As seen on the bottom line of the table, the overall standard deviation of the ratings is 3.1, indicating that the ratings ranged widely over the 11-point scale used.[2] In large part this reflects the sharply different ratings given to each of the various kin. The body of the table shows the standard deviations for kin at various degrees of genealogical distance from ego (the respondent). A smaller standard deviation indicates smaller amounts of dispersion of the ratings around the mean, and hence high normative consensus. The findings clearly show that there is the highest consensus over obligations owed to primary kin—parents and children—and lowest consensus on the obligations owed to neighbors, friends, and ex-spouses. In addition, consensus declines (i.e., the standard deviations tend to increase) as the links between ego and the kinperson in question increase. A minor exception to the general pattern is shown for kin three links (cousin) removed who evoke slightly more consensus than kintypes two links away (nieces and nephews). Kinship norms are most clearly and consistently defined, the closer the kinship relationship.

Table 5.1. Standard Deviations of Ratings by Degree of Relatedness

Degree of Relatedness	Standard Deviation	N [a]
Primary Kin		
Parents	2.3	[5617]
Children	2.1	[5647]
Secondary Kin (One Connecting Link)		
Grandparents	2.8	[2800]
Siblings	2.6	[2811]
Grandchildren	2.6	[2847]
Tertiary Kin (Two Connecting Links)		
Aunts and Uncles	2.7	[2807]
Nieces and Nephews	2.8	[2855]
Three Connecting Links		
Cousins	2.7	[2732]
Nonkin		
Friends and Neighbors	2.9	[2848]
Ex-spouses	2.9	[683]
All Vignettes	3.1	[36036]

[a] These Ns are the numbers of ratings that were used in the calculation of the standard deviations.

Typically, about two-thirds of the points in a distribution lie within the range between one standard deviation above and one below the average. This means that the difference in standard deviations of .5 between the ratings of parents and those of grandparents translates into a 1 point greater range for the ratings of grandparents compared to parents. Using the criterion of a difference of less than .5 or more as a measure of greater consensus, the major feature of Table 5.1 is that there is markedly more consensus concerning primary kin (parents and children) than for any of the kin or nonkin categories. There are differences among nonprimary kin, but these differences are not very large. Even ex-spouses do not generate markedly less consensus compared to any of the nonprimary kintypes shown.

Consensus among respondents is affected by the kind of obligation asked about in the vignettes as well as structural aspects of kinship as shown in Table 5.2. A separate multiple regression analysis was done for each type of obligation. The standard deviations around the averages of each of the 74 kin types constitute the dependent variables in each of the multiple regression equations.

Each of the columns of Table 5.2 contains the unstandardized regression coefficients that resulted when the standard deviations of a particular kind of obligation was used as the dependent variable with kinship relations as the independent variables. Thus, the coefficient, .40, at the top of the left-hand column is to be interpreted as the increment in the

Table 5.2. Kin Structure Determinants of Obligation Dissensus (*N* = 74 Kin Types) (Unstandardized b Coefficients)

Kinship Structural Features	Obligation Type [a]			
	Giving Gifts	Giving Comfort	Financial Aid	Making Visits
Range [b]				
One Link	.40**	.51***	.22	.47***
Two Links	.40**	.75***	.26	.35***
Three Links	.18	.72***	.03	.33**
Depth [c]				
Up Generations	−.07	.01	.06	.13
Down Generations	−.27	.00	.03	.09
Nonkin				
Friends and Neighbors	.23	.70***	.29	.42***
Ex-spouses	.22	.91***	−.06	.57***
Stepkin	.05	.18*	.13	.05
Affinal Kin	.14	.12	−.03	.02
Intercept	2.48***	2.01**	2.54***	2.16***
R^2	**.24***	**.70***	**.16**	**.57***

[a] Dependent variables are standard deviations of kintype ratings.
[b] Dummy variables for each kintype. Omitted category is "primary kin."
[c] Dummy variables for each generational depth distance. Omitted category is "same generation."
*** $p < .001$
** $p < .01$
* $p < .05$

standard deviation of the obligation "to give gifts" rating received by one link removed kin, as contrasted to primary kin. Thus, positive coefficients indicate less consensus over the kin in question, compared to the omitted category, primary kin. A negative coefficient indicates more consensus over the kintype in question.

The R^2 at the bottom of each column indicates the proportion of the total variation in consensus (standard deviations) among kintypes that can be accounted for by the structural features of kinship. A large R^2 means that consensus in the type of obligation is highly structured by the dimensions of kinship used in the equation. A small coefficient means that consensus is less well structured by genealogical distance.

There are several important findings in Table 5.2. First, the kinship structural effects vary according to the kind of obligation: At the one extreme, there are no significant structural effects on dissensus concerning obligations to give financial aid, the R^2 of .16 being statistically insignificant. That is, respondents tend to agree to the same degree about all the kintypes distinguished.

At the other extreme, the standard deviations for the "providing comfort" ratings are highly related to kinship structure as shown by the R^2 of .70. Obligations to visit resemble comfort ratings while gift giving obligations are similar to financial aid obligations. We interpret these strong differences to mean that our respondents are less of one mind about their obligations to give comfort and make visits to kin and that this dissensus centers around the obligations owed to kin at greater distances in the respondents' lineages. In contrast, disagreements about obligations to give gifts or offer financial aid do not center on particular types of kin.

The coefficients in each of the columns indicate the kinds of kin over which disagreements center. We have taken primary kin as the standard against which to judge the amount of dissensus, since, as shown in Table 5.1, greatest consensus exists on obligations to parents and children. As a consequence, all of the significant coefficients for kinship range are positive in Table 5.2, indicating that disagreement is greater concerning all nonprimary kin.

Overall, disagreements center on how much obligations are owed to kin who are one or more links removed and to nonkin. Our respondents show the least consensus on the appropriateness of giving comfort to ex-spouses: the coefficient of .91 indicates that the standard deviation for comfort ratings to ex-spouses was .91 larger than the comfort ratings for parents and children. Consistently, there is greater disagreement over what is owed to kin who are once removed, such as siblings and grandparents, or to kin separated from ego by two links, such as uncles, aunts, nephews, and nieces. Three links distant kin—mainly cousins—do not consistently generate great disagreement. Apparently, the respondents do not disagree about giving gifts to their cousins (the obligation level in this case is low), but there is disagreement about whether cousins should be paid a visit to celebrate some occasion or offered comfort when a cousin is under stressful conditions.

Disagreements apparently do not vary with the generational position of kin, the coefficients for older and younger generations being insignificantly different from coefficients for contemporaries. Nor do affinal kin or stepkin differ from consanguineal kin, with the exception of a significant coefficient for giving comfort to stepkin.

The findings of Table 5.2 suggest that our respondents are somewhat uncertain about where in the kinship structure some of their obligations should tail off. In contrast, there is less disagreement about when one is obligated to give financial aid or to send gifts and that amount of consensus holds for all kintypes. As we saw in Chapter 4, primary kin are owed this kind of aid, but everyone apparently agrees that there is not much obligation to offer financial aid to more distant kin or to significant nonkin. The obligation to give gifts on ceremonial occasions is almost as well structured, except that there are disagreements about whether visits are owed to kin one or two links distant. In contrast, there is greater variation about to whom comfort should be offered in times of distress or to whom visits should be paid when good fortune strikes. Everyone fairly well agrees that such obligations are owed to primary kin, but there is greater disagreement about the other kintypes.

These findings suggest that there are some structural determinants of disagreement among respondents. In the remainder of this chapter, we will consider the question of how these disagreements vary according to individual respondent characteristics.

Accounting for Respondent Ratings

It will be recalled that each respondent was given a set of 32 vignettes and asked to mark on an 11-point scale how strong an obligation she or he would feel to the person described in the vignette under the circumstances indicated.[3] More than 36,000 individual vignettes were rated by close to 1200 respondents. By design, the total set of vignettes rated by the respondents was composed of repeatedly and independently drawn random samples of all the possible 1628 unique vignettes that could be assembled. This means that each of the kin was rated by many respondents but none was rated by all respondents.[4] This design feature allows us to consider a very wide range of kin types, as the analysis so far has shown, without imposing too great a burden on any one respondent.

As was shown in Tables 5.1 and 5.2, there are considerable amounts of variation in the ratings given to the vignettes. Even for primary kin, toward whom obligations are the most consistently acknowledged, the associated standard deviation was about 2.0, indicating that approximately two-thirds of the respondents' ratings ranged within 2 scale points of the average given to such kin. A range of this magnitude is quite consistent with the existence of strongly structured kinship obligation norms. Respondents may all agree that obligations to parents are stronger than obligations to cousins, but differ on how obligating mothers and cousins are. *Indeed, the message of Chapter 4 is that the obligation ordering of kin is highly structured. The message of this chapter is that there is variation in the extent to which that structure is seen as obligating by individuals.*

The fact that obligations to kin are so well structured has another important implication for analysis, namely that the variation from respondent to respondent in acknowledged strength of kin obligations will neither be very great nor strongly patterned. In view of the fact that degree of relatedness dominates kinship obligation, one cannot expect that the variation around that structure will be very strongly related to individual characteristics. Another way of stating this point is that there is little room for significant numbers of respondents to conform to alternative and radically different structures of obligations to kin. There is certainly room for idiosyncrasies from individual to individual, and modest variations among subgroups of respondents, but hardly room for alternative definitions of kinship obligations that order kin differently from the strong patterns shown in Chapter 4.

Although almost all respondents tend to order their obligations toward kin along the lines shown in Chapter 4, there are considerable individual differences in how strongly each respondent acknowledges those obligations, with some respondents consistently giving higher ratings to all kin than other respondents. Our respondents all acknowledge the existence of norms of obligations. For some those obligations are quite strong and for others they are quite weak.

The design of the packets of vignettes given to respondents permits measures of the strengths of obligations felt by individual respondents. Although each respondent received an independently constructed set of vignettes, each respondent's set was an unbiased sample of all the possible vignettes. Hence, *the average of the 32 ratings given by a respondent is an indicator of the extent to which that respondent feels obligated generally toward kin.* Although there is some sampling variation from one respondent's vignette packet to another's, the sampling variations are not very large. Most of differences among respondents in the averages of the ratings given for the most part represent individual differences in the strengths with which kinship is obligating to individuals. For convenience, we will call these averages, *The Unadjusted Obligation Index.* Table 5.3 shows how the 1187 respondents who filled out the vignette booklets are distributed. Scores on the Unadjusted Obligation Index ranged over the entire scale, with three respondents with average scores of 0 apparently denying any obligation to any kin, and a somewhat larger group of 21 respondents claiming that they owed the highest level of obligation (average scores of 10) to all the kin they rated. Apart from these extremes, half of the respondents had scores that lay between 5.0 and 8.0, fairly evenly bracketing the overall average of 6.5.

In Table 5.3, the labels used to provide anchor points along the rating scale are placed alongside the score values over which they were placed in the vignette booklets. Using these labels, it is clear that the majority of the respondents had Unadjusted Obligation Index scores that clustered around "strong," hardly a surprising result given that about a third of the vignettes concerned primary kin—parents and children—the most obligating of the kin types in the design.

The Adjusted Obligation Indexes

Although each respondent's sample of vignettes was drawn randomly and hence are "on the average" identical, sampling variation meant that

Table 5.3.   Distribution of Respondent Unadjusted [a]
Obligation Index Scores

	Overall Obligation Scores	%
No Obligation	0–.9	0.5
	1–1.9	0.8
	2–2.9	1.3
Mild	3–3.9	5.3
	4–4.9	9.0
	5–5.9	18.4
Strong	6–6.9	23.6
	7–7.9	19.8
	8–8.9	15.5
Very strong	9–10.0	5.7
Average		6.51
N		[1187]

[a] To be distinguished from the "adjusted" indexes, which are adjusted to take into account interrespondent vignette packet variability.

they were also different one from the other. These sampling-generated differences are, of course, reflected in the Unadjusted Obligation Index: Some respondents by chance may have a greater than average number of vignettes depicting children and others may have had a larger proportion of secondary kin in their samples, the former having higher average Index scores because their vignette packet contained a larger proportion of highly obligating kin. This sampling variation is particularly important when we want to consider the strength of respondents' obligations to some subsample of vignettes, for example, those involving obligations to secondary kin.

To remove the effects of such sampling variation, a set of "adjusted" strength indexes was computed that takes into account the particular mix of kintypes in each respondent's vignette sample. These "adjusted" indexes were computed by subtracting from each rating given by a respondent the average rating given to that kin type being rated. Hence, the adjusted indexes are *relative* measures, indicating how much each respondent expresses in his/her ratings a stronger (plus) or weaker (minus) sense of obligation to kin than is average for the kin vignettes rated.

Seven adjusted obligation indexes[5] were computed, as follows:

1. *Total Obligation Index*: Computed for all of the vignettes included in a respondent's vignette packet.
2. *Primary Obligation Index*: Computed for vignettes that pertain to primary kin (parents and children).

3. *Parental Obligation Index*: Computed for vignettes involving parents.
4. *Children Obligation Index*: Computed for vignettes involving children.
5. *Secondary Obligation Index*: Computed for vignettes involving kin one link removed from respondent (siblings, grandparents, grandchildren, stepparents, stepchildren, children-in-law).
6. *Distant Obligation Index*: Computed for vignettes involving kin two or more links removed (uncles and aunts, nieces and nephews, cousins, parents-in-law).
7. *Nonkin Obligation Index*: Computed for nonkin vignettes (neighbors, friends, and ex-spouses).

The distributions of scores on these adjusted indexes are shown in Table 5.4. Note that a minus (−) score indicates that a respondent gave lower ratings generally to the vignettes in question than was the case for the entire sample. Correspondingly, a positive score (+) indicates a tendency to acknowledge higher levels of obligations than the average respondent. Adjusted index scores were computed only for respondents who had rated at least one relevant vignette, which accounts for the differences in the numbers of respondents involved.

The numerical values of the adjusted indexes have a direct meaning. A respondent whose Total Obligation Index is 1.5 gave obligation ratings that were 1.5 score points higher than the average ratings given to the kintypes included in that person's vignette packet; a Total Obliga-

Table 5.4. Distributions of Adjusted [a] Obligation Scores (in Percent)

Index Score	Adjusted [a] Kin Obligation Indexes						
	Total	Primary	Child	Parent	Secondary	Distant	Nonkin
-3.0 or less	4.7	5.9	5.5	7.7	8.0	7.9	9.2
-2--2.9	6.4	6.3	7.2	6.1	8.6	10.5	9.6
-1--1.9	14.9	10.4	12.0	9.3	11.4	16.3	14.9
0- -.9	22.0	16.4	15.5	13.3	18.0	17.0	16.4
0- .9	23.0	24.5	19.0	22.1	19.5	18.1	16.8
1- 1.9	18.7	36.4	40.7	41.6	17.9	12.6	13.7
2- 2.9	9.3	0.0	0.0	0.0	12.0	9.9	9.7
3- 3.9	1.1	0.0	0.0	0.0	4.6	9.9	9.7
Average	− .011	− .009	.001	− .015	.009	− .054	.012
N	[1189]	[1187]	[1173]	[1169]	[1137]	[1181]	[1108]
SD	1.66	1.70	1.76	1.89	1.99	2.10	2.26

[a] Scores are adjusted by subtracting the average score from the respondents' scores given to the kintype in each vignette. Hence, a positive score means that the respondents gave higher than average scores and a negative score means that the respondents gave lower scores.

tion score of − .5 indicates ratings that were on the average .5 lower than the overall average for the vignettes rated.

The averages for the adjusted index scores all hover around zero and indeed are different from zero only as a result of rounding errors. The standard deviations reflect the extent to which respondents differ from each other in the strengths of obligations they acknowledge to the kin in question. As shown earlier, the larger the standard deviations, the less consensus among respondents on obligations to a kintype. The standard deviations on the adjusted obligation indexes show the greatest consensus in obligations to children (SD = 1.76) and the least consensus in obligations to nonkin (SD = 2.15).

Life Course Trends in Normative Obligations

We first examine trends over the life course in the strengths of normative obligation toward various kin and nonkin through the changes in obligation levels associated with age. Age differences in the strengths of kinship obligations can certainly be expected for a variety of reasons. However, the expected patterns of such differences differ. On some grounds, we can expect that older people will have stronger kin obligations; on other grounds, we can expect the strength of kin obligations to decline with age. Still other considerations envisage an age-related curve, with kin obligations highest for the young and the old and least for the middle-aged.

These conflicting expectations have several sources: First, some gerontologists have regarded old age as a period of disengagement, a viewpoint that has come under severe attack from other scholars. According to the disengagement view, as people approach old age they begin a process of disengaging from social relationships in general, and, by implication, experience some decline in the strength of felt obligations toward kin. To some extent, mortality patterns dictate some degree of disengagement, especially in actual concrete relations to kin. As we have seen in Chapter 3, with reference to direct-line lineages, with increasing age the composition of a person's kindred changes; death drops grandparents, parents, aunts, and uncles from the kin roster, and with age, children, nieces and nephews, and grandchildren are added. Beyond the age of 60, siblings become subject to the toll of mortality as well as friends who become harder to replace as the pool of contemporaries shrinks. The changes in one's kindred accompanying aging may well affect the degree to which kinship generally evokes obligations. If the expectation is that obligation declines to those portions of the kindred where one has no actual kin, then we would expect that older persons would be *lower* in obligations to persons in their grandparental and parental generations and higher in obligations to children, grand-children, and the children of their siblings. In contrast, younger persons who have yet to become parents should manifest higher obligations to their parents and lower obligation to their children (nonexisting).

A second *set* of interpretations arises from the fact that age groups form historical cohorts that also mark their members' participation in unique historical events. Awareness of the impact of rapid social change in a century marked by several wars and a deep economic depression, along with several unexpected changes in the fertility rate, has alerted social scientists to cohort and period characteristics that differentiate age groups that have lived through very different historical times, attained different levels of education, or carry with them different ethnic charac-teristics as a result of peaks and valleys in immigration or fertility rates that varied by socioeconomic level and ethnicity.

A clear cohort difference is marked by the effects of the great expan-sion of public education in this century. Today's elderly went through their school-going years in periods when lower levels of educational attainment were expected; consequently, the elderly have on average lower levels of education than their children, and the children lower than their grandchildren. So too, the proportions of Black and Hispanic are much smaller among today's elderly than will be the case 30 or 40 years from now. The adult population of the Boston Metropolitan area is currently dominated by the descendants of the Irish and Italian immi-grants who arrived half a century ago. The adult population 50 years hence may be composed of greater proportions who are Black, Hispanic, or Oriental, reflecting the results of contemporary immigration, migra-tion internal to our nation, and the differential fertility patterns of the several groups in question.

If we held to the view that age differences in a population were largely reflections of historical and cohort effects, what would one predict in using age as a life course marker? Compared to their parents' life choices 25 years ago, young people in recent years have postponed marriage, moved away from their families of origin to live on their own or to cohabit with a lover, and once married show an increasing rise in voluntary childlessness and very small families if they do have children. One could predict, on the basis of these characteristics of the young, a lower level of obligation toward kin on their part than among middle-aged or older adults.

But except for a steady rise in educational attainment, the three generations represented in a sample of adults in the 1980s are demo-graphically quite different from each other: the grandparental genera-tion passed their youth in the depression years, which meant marital postponement, holding back on fertility, and some frustration of high hopes they may have had for their adult lives. In this sense the grandparental generation is more like the grandchild generation, while the aberrant generation is the late middle-aged generation who participated in the 1950s suburban expansion, married early, and produced the baby boom. Today's elderly also include many who were first- and second-generation Americans, cut off from their older kin who remained behind in European cities and villages. Family and kin relations were highly valued by today's elderly, while many have considered that today's youth wish to minimize family ties and maximize their independence of social ties as they settle into adulthood.

The net result of growing up in such different worlds is a prediction that today's elderly would subscribe more intensely to obligations to kin than today's young people. In our data set, this would mean higher obligation ratings among older than among younger respondents, i.e., a positive correlation between age and obligation level.

A life course perspective that allows for the interplay of maturational aspects of aging, historical and cohort factors, and the existential press of current commitments suggests a very different prediction: a peak of high obligations among middle-aged adults who have good health, still have numerous elderly living kin and children just moving away from home and establishing families of their own.

Another version of the life course perspective might stress the shifting balances of exchange that accompany life course changes. Young persons with their period of dependence on parents only a few years behind them might feel that they owe much to their parents without having had many opportunities to reciprocate. As children pass into adulthood, the "debt" accumulated in their years of dependency is reduced by "payment" in many forms. Passing into old age may mean passing from a debtor to a creditor stage: An elderly person has fulfilled his obligations, but is still owed the obligations of his younger kin, especially children. These considerations apply with particular force to obligations to primary kin, leading to an expected decline in the strength of obligations to primary kin in old age.

Against these expectations, our data, as shown in Table 5.5, on life course trends in normative obligations must come as a surprise. *On each of the several obligation indexes, older persons show less strong obligations toward kin than younger persons.* Not all the trends of age-related declines in obligations to kin are significant, but all of the trends are in the same direction: Statistically significant declines are shown for the Total Obligation Index, the measure of overall obligations, Primary Obligation Index, Children Obligation Index, Secondary Obligation Index, and Nonkin Obligation Index. The life course trends for obligations to parents and to distant kin also show declines with age, although not significantly so.

Table 5.5. Mean Scores on Adjusted Obligation Indexes by Age of Respondents

	Age of Respondent						
Obligation Index	19–30	31–40	41–50	51–60	61–70	71+	Difference: Young − Old [a]
Adjusted Total	.22	.11	.04	−.14	−.33	−.63	.86**
Primary Kin	.17	.11	−.00	−.02	−.38	−.49	.66**
Parents	.20	.07	−.02	.05	−.29	−.34	.56
Children	.17	.16	.12	−.03	−.42	−.73	.90**
Secondary	.27	.16	.08	−.01	−.21	−.93	1.33**
Distant Kin	.14	−.05	.10	−.32	−.23	−.32	.46
Nonkin	.46	.34	−.01	−.34	−.84	−.61	1.07**
N	[266]	[315]	[188]	[155]	[137]	[75]	

[a] Difference in mean scores, youngest age group minus oldest. Double asterisks mark significant differences among age groups: ** $p < .01$.

None of the expectations outlined earlier is borne out. Although obligation strength declines with age, the decline sets in so early in the life course that the postulated disengagement processes cannot be the source. The particular historical interpretation that predicted higher levels of obligation with increasing age is flatly contradicted: The oldest respondents are uniformly the lowest in obligation strength. Finally, although the trends in obligation to primary kin are consistent with the interpretation stressing the balance of obligations owed and fulfilled, the fact that obligations to all kin and to nonkin also decline with age suggests that this theory is also inadequate.

The last column of Table 5.5 contains the difference between the youngest and the oldest age groups, showing that the age declines are greatest for the Secondary Obligation and the Nonkin Obligation Indexes, each registering more than one point difference between the two age groups at the extremes.

The downward trend is not a pattern of uniform decay in the strength of obligations to kin. The very highest level of kin obligations is among the youngest age group, 19–30. The drop in strength shown by those in the 30–39 age group is sharp. During the middle years obligation strength declines more slowly with small differences with age. Above the age of 50, the downward trend appears to accelerate with large drops in obligation until the oldest age group, those over 70 years of age.

The age-related trends are also quite robust, remaining visible when almost any other variable is introduced as a control, as will be shown in later multivariate tables. Men and women, higher and lower socioeconomic levels, and members of major ethnic groups all show the same pattern of decline with increasing age. The general shape of the trends is the same for all of the kintypes, affecting close kin as well as more distant relatives and nonkin. In addition, the same trends are shown for all of the kinds of obligation studied: The strength of kinship obligations declines with age for both obligations to provide comfort and to provide financial aid.

There are several implications of the robust nature of the strong age-related declines. An important inference is that the life course profile is not purely a kinship phenomenon, because it affects both kin and nonkin in comparable ways.[6] The influences of mortality and fertility produce more dramatic changes over the life course in the composition of lineages than in adults' friendship circles. Older respondents do not report smaller friendship circles than younger people do, and, to the best of our knowledge, friendships are no less intense and no less valued in old age than in youth.

If we had only the data on obligations to nonkin, one would be tempted to argue that the pattern of steep decline from early to middle adulthood can be explained by the fact that with full maturity, adults move into a phase of life with peak family responsibilities, for children as they come along, and for older relatives as their need for some degree of personal caregiving increases, leaving little time for generous gestures of aid to friends. Were this the case, however, one would expect higher obligations to kin in the middle years, not the beginning of a decline in the level of felt obligations. The steep decline in obligations that occurs in the older years may also be explained by the older persons' reduced abilities to maintain the patterns of reciprocity that maintain friendship. But, of course, we do not have only obligations to kin in our data: The nonkin patterns match those for kin, a finding that simply contradicts the explanation that has just been advanced.

One other interpretive possibility is also discounted by the similarity of the profiles shown for kin and nonkin. This has to do with the time frame within which one applies ideas of reciprocity to social relations. In the realm of family life, one could argue that obligations build up during the years of childhood and adolescent dependency, the phase of the life course when parents give a great deal more to children than children can give to their parents. During adulthood, parents and children negotiate their relationship anew, with more give and take between them. This is, in fact, the profile we will see in the help exchange pattern between the generations in Chapter 9. As parents enter old age, the reciprocity begins to wane, and for some elderly parents who live long lives with chronic health problems, the roles are reversed as their children provide personal caregiving and parents cannot reciprocate in any way. Some psychologists have referred to this process as the "parentification of the child."

With a whole lifetime as the time frame, the imbalance at the end of life can be viewed as reciprocation for the reverse imbalance when the children were dependents. Indeed, it was this expectation that made us regret that we had not built into the design of the normative obligations, measures of what respondents felt was *owed to them* by various other kin, rather than just what they *owe to others*. This life course perspective on reciprocity would predict that with increasing age, adults might show an increase in the obligations they feel other people have toward them, to match the decline in the obligations they feel they owe to others.

But this theory would not necessarily predict the same profile where friendships are concerned. Most friends are age contemporaries and the patterns of reciprocity should be in balance throughout the life course. It may be that friends who are both old owe each other less, but do friends who are both young owe each other more?

The age-related patterns in Table 5.5 also appear to be insensitive to the composition of respondents' actual lineages. Obligations to parents *and* to children both decline with age despite the fact that with increasing age, parents tend to drop out of the roster of living kin and children do not. Indeed, it is also the case that obligations to children decline more precipitously than those to parents, despite the fact that in the oldest age groups it is rare to have any living parents.

A further complication is presented by the fact that the age-related declines in obligations to kin are stronger for women than for men, as shown in Table 5.6[7] for the Total Obligation Index. Men are most different from women in their younger years and tend to converge in old age. That is, the gender difference starts out initially quite large (almost .4 among the youngest group) and diminishes to .075 for the over 70 year olds.

Although a plausible explanatory theory had not been propounded by us (much less shown to be supported by evidence) for the age-related declines shown in Table 5.5, findings consistent with them will be shown in Chapter 9 in the patterns of help given and received between parents and their adult children.

Table 5.6. Mean Scores on Total Obligation Index by Gender and Age

| | Age of Respondent | | | | | | Difference: |
Gender	19–30	31–40	41–50	51–60	61–70	71+	Young − Old [a]
Men	.00	.00	−.28	.02	−.30	−.67	.68**
Women	.40	.20	−.22	−.24	−.35	−.60	1.01**

[a] Difference in mean scores, youngest age group minus oldest. Double asterisks mark significant differences among age groups: ** p < .01.

Educational Attainment and Obligations to Kin

Almost as strong as age differences are those related to educational attainment. Although we may be accustomed to thinking of less educated and poorer persons as being more embedded in kinship relations of all kinds and more dependent on kin for help and sociability, in fact the better educated have uniformly higher kin obligation scores. In Table 5.7, the index scores for each of the five educational attainment groups are shown. For each of the indexes, average scores are negative for those who did not go to college, indicating lower obligation levels than for the entire sample, and are positive for those who attended a college or university for any period of time. Indeed, those respondents who had some postgraduate training had the highest obligation score on six of the seven indexes. Furthermore, these educational differences are the greatest for obligations to primary kin, and, among primary kin, obligations to parents.

What accounts for the strong educational attainment differences shown in Table 5.7? There are several lines of explanation. First, this trend is consistent with the age differences discussed earlier. Over the past six decades educational attainment levels of each succeeding generation have risen dramatically with the consequence that younger respondents tend to be more highly educated than older respondents. Indeed, when the Total Obligation scores are examined within age and educational attainment levels, as in Panel A of Table 5.8, both educational and age effects are diminished. Nevertheless, with some exceptions, within each age group, the better educated have positive and higher scores than the less well educated and, within each educational attainment group, younger persons tend to have higher scores than the older.

Table 5.7. Educational Level Differences in Kin Obligations

Obligation Index	Up to 11th Grade	High School Grad	Some High Ed	BA, BS	Grad Trng	Difference: High − Low [a]
	Educational Attainment					
Total	−.52	−.23	.10	.18	.37	.95**
Primary	−.62	−.19	.11	.14	.41	1.03**
Parents	−.76	−.20	.16	.25	.44	1.20**
Children	−.45	−.15	.10	.04	.42	.87**
Secondary	−.63	−.15	.15	.20	.37	1.00**
Distant	−.22	−.29	.04	.09	.21	.44**
Nonkin	−.43	−.45	.31	.34	.30	.73**
N [b]	[137]	[348]	[276]	[242]	[183]	

[a] Difference in mean scores, highest educational attainment group minus lowest. Double asterisks mark significant differences among age groups: **$p < .01$.

[b] These are Ns for the Total Index. Ns for the other indexes are slightly lower, as shown in Table 5.4.

Table 5.8. Total Obligation Index by Age and Educational Attainment

A. Total Obligation Scores by Age and Educational Attainment

| Educational | Age of Respondent | | | | Difference: |
Attainment	19–30	31–40	41–50	51+	Young − Old
Less than 12th					
Grade	− .06	.67	− .64	− .81	.75*
High School					
Graduate	− .02	− .34	.16	− .42	.40*
Some College	.21	.05	− .06	.21	.00
College Graduate	.25	.28	− .06	.05	.20
Graduate Training	.74	.34	.58	− .00	.74*
Difference: High ed					
− Low ed	.80*	− .33*	1.22	.81**	

B. Regression of Total Obligation Index on Age and Education

Independent Variable	b
Education	.01*
Age	.04***
Intercept	.19
R^2	.02***
N	[1046]

*** $p < .001$
** $p < .01$
* $p < .05$

Panel B of Table 5.8 measures the simultaneous effects of age and education using multiple regression. The results of a regression equation in which the Total Obligation Rating is the dependent variable show that both education and age independently affect the index scores, although age appears to be more strongly related than education to the ratings (respective b coefficients are .04 and .01).

A second line of interpretation recognizes that educational attainment, especially beyond high school levels, usually represents a past strong parental investment. Going beyond high school ordinarily means that one's parents have paid at least part of the tuition and provided material and psychological support over a period of years (Espenshade, 1984). Going to professional school may entail an even stronger financial investment by parents. The fact that parents have supported a child's going to college and beyond to graduate or professional school may produce a strong sense of obligation to primary kin in adulthood. Certainly the pattern of the highest level of obligation to parents shown in Table 5.7 among those who went beyond the bachelor's degree is consistent with this interpretation. Of course, the fact that this highest educational attainment group is also high in obligation to all other kin indicates that reciprocity for past parental investment cannot be the only explanation for the educational attainment patterns shown in Table 5.7.

A third line of interpretation takes into account how educational attainment affects a person's ability to handle the cognitive aspects of the vignette rating tasks. The demands of the vignette rating task include understanding and interpreting written English as well as understanding what is the normative obligations to kin of different kinds. To handle the task of rating each of the vignettes requires somewhat more than minimal literacy. Although most persons at the lowest educational attainment levels no doubt have such skills, those who do not are *likely* to be concentrated at that level.[8] In addition, at the higher educational attainment levels, literacy skills acquired in formal education are more likely to be maintained at a high level into adulthood and old age.

Although our schools, colleges and universities do not directly teach students the norms of our society, there are many opportunities to observe the norms in action in literature or in exposure to plays, movies, and even television. The mark of education is broadened contact with the world of ideas and to a range of human behavior. Hence, we can expect that with greater exposure to formal education there is also greater exposure to the normative structure of our society in many domains of life, including subtle distinctions concerning obligations to many different kinds of relatives.

It would follow from this last interpretation of educational effects that the more highly educated respondents are more responsive to the content of the vignettes than the less well educated. Accordingly, we should find that the characteristics of the vignettes explain more of the responses of better educated respondents and less for the less well educated. This expectation is borne out in the findings presented in Table 5.9.

In Table 5.9 the unit of analysis is the single vignette. The dependent variable is the rating given to each vignette. The table divides vignettes into those rated by persons who did not graduate from high school, high school graduates, and respondents who attended at least some years beyond high school. Each vignette is characterized by the structural positions of the kin depicted in that vignette. Note that these characteristics—range, depth, gender, and affinity—are the same as those used in Chapter 4.

The main interest in Table 5.9 lies in the amount of variation from vignette to vignette that is explained by the kin structural variables. Since R^2 measures the amount of variation explained, our expectation was that the highest R^2 would be found for the best educated group, and the lowest R^2 for the least well-educated group. Such turns out to be the case: The R^2 for persons who did not graduate high school is only .22,

Table 5.9. The Effects of Educational Attainment on the Structure of Kinship Ratings

Kinship Structural Features [a]	Educational Attainment		
	Some High School or Less	High School Grad	Some College or More
Kinship Range			
Primary	4.52***	4.96***	5.44***
Secondary	3.45***	3.54***	4.00***
Distant	1.32***	1.21***	1.83***
Friends/Neighbors	1.41***	1.47***	2.10***
Kinship Depth			
One generation down	.38**	.36***	.23***
Other kin measures			
Female Kin	.27**	.22***	.25***
Stepkin	−1.63***	−.90***	−.94***
Affinal kin	−.44*	−.11	−.04
Intercept	2.87***	3.14***	3.05***
R^2	.22***	.30***	.33***
N	[3,981]	[19,012]	[13,044]

[a] All variables are dummies.
*** p < .001
** p < .01
* p < .05

whereas the value for those with some college is .33.[9] In other words, the better educated respondents were considerably more sensitive to the content of the vignettes and were more consistent in their responses. In part this is because they could handle the rating task better and in part because they knew more about the kinship normative structure.

It should also be noted that the regression coefficients for the kinship range dummies are almost all lowest for the least educated group and highest for the best educated. This tendency is in line with the interpretation offered above. Because "errors" tend to be in the direction of the mean ratings, the greater error making of the poorly educated groups would tend to lower the regression coefficients (and also lower their ratings). Running counter to this interpretation are the higher regression coefficients for the gender, depth, and affinity measures for the least educated group. However, because the range measures dominate these equations, the least educated group tends to have lower average ratings overall.

Although some of the educational group differences are due to the greater ability of the better educated in handling the vignette rating task, this line of interpretation cannot be the only explanation of such differences. The results shown in Table 5.9 are also consistent with substantive kin obligation differences along educational attainment lines. In sum, although there is some evidence that the relative difficulty of the rating task lowered ratings among the least well educated, there is also evidence that the latter also simply had lower levels of felt obligations toward their kin. On both the low age and educational attainment sides, what may be reflected in these lowered ratings is scarcity of resources at the command of such respondents. Such resources would include income, access to transportation, and facility in sociability. On the upper educational side, an especially attractive interpretation is that the best educated feel more obligated to their parents, perhaps for parent investment in their education. In any event, educational attainment is such a strong influence on the obligation ratings that we will use it as a control in most of the analyses to follow.

The Biographical Origins of the Strength of Kinship Obligations

The strength of a respondent's obligations to kin has its roots in early childhood experiences. In Table 5.10, we present a variety of respondent's childhood family measures. All of these measures show how strongly a respondent's current obligations to kin are affected by the kind of experiences they had in the families in which they spent their childhood.

Those who grew up in intact homes show higher levels of obligations to kin than those whose families of orientation were broken by death, divorce, or separation, as shown in Panel A of Table 5.10. Growing up with both parents is apparently congenial to the development of a stronger sense of obligation to all kin, except those on the distant fringes of a person's kindred.

Stronger impacts on adult kin obligation are made by childhood family experiences of a qualitative sort that differentiate among intact families. In Panel B it can be seen that the more affectionate parents were reported to have been, the more strongly respondents acknowledge obligations to kin. The score differences between having parents regarded as least affectionate and those regarded as most affectionate are quite large, almost .7 points for the overall Total Obligation Index, and 1.2 for obligations to distant kin. Interestingly enough, the degree of parental affection strengthens obligation to *all* kin, with stronger effects on obligations to more distant kin. Among primary kin, the reported degree of parental affection elevates the sense of obligation to children more than to the parents who were the source of that affection.

Degrees of childhood family cohesion are also related to the strength of obligations to kin, as shown in Panel C. Index score differences between those who had the least and the most cohesive childhood

Table 5.10. Childhood Experiences *a* and Obligations to Kin (Mean Index Scores)

Childhood Measure	Total Obligation	Primary Kin	Secondary Kin	Distant Kin	N
		Obligation Index			
A. Childhood Family					
Intact	.05***b*	.10*	.08*	−.04	[1024]
Broken	−.37	−.70	−.37	−.12	[165]
B. Parental Affection					
Low	−.30***	−.20**	−.22***	−.64***	[195]
	−.16	−.04	−.22	−.22	[257]
	.11	.19	.19	−.07	[308]
High	.37	.25	.43	.55	[288]
C. Family Cohesion					
Low	−.45***	−.49**	−.43**	−.77***	[162]
	−.13	−.12	−.11	−.19	[248]
	.11	.12	.14	.02	[416]
High	.22	.23	.30	.30	[340]
D. Kin Salience in Childhood					
Low	−.18**	−.13*	−.16**	−.29***	[385]
	−.09	−.08	−.09	−.22	[391]
High	.25	.18	.33	.35	[395]

a See Tables 1.6 and 1.7 for operational definitions of measures used in this table.
b Asterisks in first entry in column indicate significance of column differences.
*** $p < .001$
** $p < .01$
* $p < .05$

families are about the same order as in the case of parental affection, and the childhood experience of a cohesive family strengthens obligations to *all* kin, not just parents and children.

The final measure considered in Panel D concerns the extent to which kin (grandparents, aunts, and uncles) were important to respondents in childhood. Those who grew up in circumstances in which such kin were important feel stronger obligations to their kin many years, even decades later, as mature adults.

A more complicated set of relationships to kin obligations is presented by measures of the extent to which respondents grew up in families that were beset by problems. These measures are not shown in Table 5.10 because their relationships to the kin obligation indexes are too complicated to be shown in tabular form. A check list of 15 problems that might have occurred in their childhood families, ranging in seriousness from bickering among children to encounters with the criminal courts, was administered to the respondents. The Family Troubles Index[10] counts the number of such troubles experienced by each of the respondents. In addition, the troubles were grouped by similarity in content to form subindexes. Taken one at a time, none of the subindexes formed from the checklist showed consistent and significant relationships to the strengths of most of the obligation indexes. However, two of the indexes—Emotional Troubles and the overall Family Troubles Index—*when considered jointly*, both showed strong and consistent effects, although in opposite directions. The more emotional troubles (alcoholism, mental illness, child or sexual abuse) experienced by someone in their families, the lower the felt obligation toward kin in general. It should be noted that most of the emotional troubles are ones that occurred to the adults, largely parents, in their families. Hence, it is mainly the emotional troubles of parents that depresses kinship obligations. In contrast, the more troubles of all *other* sorts respondents report for their childhood families, the stronger kin obligations are felt. In other words, some troubles apparently reinforce the bonds of kinship, while others undermine them.[11]

Several other measures of childhood family experiences did not affect obligations toward kin. Although higher parental affection increased obligations toward kin, parental authority did not. Nor did family size matter; whether respondents were only children or had many siblings had no effect on their adult obligations to kin. It appears that it is the warmth and closeness of childhood relations to parents, siblings, and kin that encourage the development of strong normative obligations to all kin in adulthood. Harmonious family relations no doubt reflect happy parental marriages and an absence of emotional problems as well.

Of course, the measures shown in Table 5.10 and the childhood family trouble measures are related to each other and also to the age and educational attainment of the respondent. To assess the independent contributions of each to the strength of adult kin obligations, multiple regressions were run using the separate kin type obligation indexes as dependent variables, and the biographical factors as independent variables, with results as shown in Table 5.11. Age, sex, and education have been included as well in these equations because they were shown earlier to be related robustly to obligations to kin.

Despite the fact that age, sex,[12] and educational attainment are almost always significantly related to the strength of each type of kinship obligation, each of the childhood experience measures has an important and independent effect as well. The R^2 values for the five equations range from .05 to .08 and are all significant, representing a modest increment for the childhood factors over and above the effects of age, sex, and education.

Only the effects of Family Troubles extend to all types of kin obligations: The more troubles a respondent experienced in childhood (net of emotional problems) the higher the level of obligation to all kin, no

Table 5.11. Regressions of Obligation Indexes on Biographical Factors (Unstandardized b Coefficients)

Predictor Variables	Obligation Indexes				
	Total	*Primary*	*Secondary*	*Distant*	*Nonkin*
Age	− .01***	− .01**	− .01**	− .01	− .02***
Female	.25*	.11	.30*	.33*	.23
Education	.12***	.11***	.12***	.10*	.13**
Broken Home	− .23	− .61***	− .25	.12	.14
Kin Salience	.13*	.07	.14	.22**	.08
Parental					
Affection	.20**	.08	.21**	.33***	.10
Family Troubles	.20**	.21**	.29**	.20*	.03*
Family Cohesion	.13*	.21**	.15	.12	− .01
Emotional					
Troubles	− .10	− .10	− .15	− .11	.04*
Intercept	− 2.53***	− 2.25***	− 2.74***	− 3.09***	− 1.31
R^2	.09***	.08***	.08***	.07***	.06***

*** p < .001
** p < .01
* p < .05

matter how distantly related, as well as to nonkin. Many of the specific troubles included in the Family Troubles Index concern family quarrels involving "relatives," among adults in the family, and among the children. These are not necessarily entirely negative in their meaning but may be indicative of great involvement and intense family relations. Conflict, as several social theorists have reminded us, can be functionally supportive of group solidarity. Other specific troubles included in the index refer to troubles that children may have had in school or with the police, events that may trigger family solidarity and support, a closing of ranks against the outside world. Experiences that on the surface may appear to be indicative of a fractured, troubled family may in fact indicate a concerned and involved family, a haven against a hostile outside world. Such an interpretation is consistent with the findings; so long as the parental marriage holds together and parents do not have emotional problems, children may acquire a deep sense of rootedness in their family and acquire strong obligations not just to parents but also to the close kin who saw their families through some hard times together.

The remaining childhood factors are important for obligations to some parts of the kindred, but not to others. Not unexpectedly, having experienced a broken home affects only obligations to primary kin,[13] lowering the average strength of obligations by .6 score units. It is likely that a broken home experience lowers the sense of obligation to one or the other parent, perhaps depending on to whom primary custody was given. In the case of childhood families broken by divorce or separation, the fact that one parent, typically the father, left the family also projects the notion to a child that men have lower commitments to their children, a powerful lesson that may have the long-term effect of lowering the child's sense of obligation to parents and to children. Note that the effects of having experienced a broken home in childhood on obligations to nonprimary kin, shown in Table 5.10, are all considerably diminished when the other childhood family measures are introduced.

The influence of Kin Salience is significant only in the Total Obligation Index and the Distant Kin Obligation Index. Indeed, because much of this index is based on respondent recall of how important tertiary (aunts, uncles) and secondary (grandparents) kin were in the respondent's childhood, this last finding is quite understandable. The process involved may reflect primarily parental attachment to such kin that was sufficiently strong to bring such relatives into close contact with the family during our respondents' childhood. The ripple out effect of having grown up in a family that valued such contact and closeness with distant kin as well as the contact itself may leave its residue in adulthood in an overall generally higher level of obligation to all kin.

The effect of parental affection, in contrast, is much more general, affecting secondary and distant kin, not merely primary kin. That is, the more affectionate one's parents were, the more obligating secondary and more distant kin are. At first glance, it may appear surprising that the degree of parental affection does not elevate obligations to primary kin even though parents are, of course, primary kin. But there are many other supports for the strength of the bonds to parents that go beyond simply reciprocating the affection the latter demonstrated in childhood: Being responsive to obligations to parents and children is not contingent but absolute. Perhaps the consequence of having attentive, openly affectionate parents is to develop a similar open and affectionate concern for and obligation to the parents of one's parents and to their siblings, which is to say grandparents, uncles, and aunts and those who have descended from them.

The measure of childhood Family Cohesion is shown to be exclusively related to obligations to primary kin. The more cohesive the respondent's childhood family was, the stronger are felt obligations to parents and children.

Families that experience troubles of all sorts seemingly produce offspring with stronger obligations to all kin. The Family Troubles Index is positively and significantly associated with all the kin indexes. It even affects obligations to nonkin. Respondents who grew up in families that experienced adversity ended up as adults with a stronger sense of responsibility for kin, extending beyond primary kin to the more distant ranges of their kindreds and to neighbors and friends as well.

The two family troubles indexes are shown still to have their effects when other childhood measures are present. The effect of these early experiences may have been to turn the child to the nonkin peer world, paving the way to the development of an adult who feels weak obligations to kin and hence stronger commitment to the people they can *choose* to relate to who are outside the network of kin.

Each of the troubles indexes has only minor and insignificant effects on kin obligations when considered alone. Their joint effects, however, are quite strong and persist throughout the analyses presented in this chapter. The joint effects suggest that adversities that have their roots in events beyond the control of parents—physical illnesses, unemployment, the behavior of children—lead to stronger kin bonding. In contrast, troubles that have their roots in the behavior of parents (or other adults) lead persons who experience such adversities in their childhood to become adults with lower levels of kin obligations generally.

A useful way to summarize the findings of Table 5.11 is to focus on the kinds of kin involved. Overall obligations to kin (as shown in the Total Obligation Index) are affected by the childhood salience of kin and by parental affection. Persons who grew up in cohesive families with affectionate parents who did not experience emotional problems but had more than their share of other problems with which to deal and in which nonprimary kin played important roles are also more obligated to kin in general.

The strength of obligations to primary kin appear to be affected mainly by how close childhood family members were to each other and the extent of their nonemotional troubles. Accordingly, respondents who grew up in broken homes are less obligated to their primary kin as adults. Alcoholic, disturbed, or abusive parents lead to weak primary kin ties. Cohesive intact families ruled by affectionate parents are the childhood origins of respondents with high levels of felt obligations to their parents and to their children.

Obligations to distant kin are mainly affected by whether or not such kin played important roles in the respondents' childhoods and by the degree of affection shown by parents.

In the last column, we can see that obligations to nonkin (friends, neighbors, and ex-spouses) are not affected significantly by any of the measures characterizing the childhood families of respondents, except the absence of emotional problems in family members and the presence of other problems.

Actual Kin and Kin Obligations

Respondents were asked to rate each vignette whether or not they themselves ever had a relative of the type described in the vignette. Everybody has had four grandparents but not everyone had an aunt and many younger respondents have not yet had a child, and grandparenthood is an experience younger respondents may have only several decades from now.

The composition of actual lineages undergoes constant change as a consequence of the complex marriage, fertility, and mortality patterns in preceding and following generations, a process of compositional change that takes place continuously across the life course. Kin relationships in youth may socialize young people for the reciprocal kin relationships that lie ahead of them. A niece learns how to be an aunt from interacting with an aunt, just as a child acquires intimate knowledge of what being a parent or grandparent entails.

It is for these reasons that, as shown in Chapter 4, the normative structure of kinship is tied not to concrete relationships but to categorical kin, abstract types that may or may not exist in the concrete. Hence, our expectation is that the strength of obligations to kin is relatively independent of concrete kin and their characteristics. That is, we believe that our respondents are capable of responding to the norms of kin obligations regardless of the size or composition of their lineages at any point in time and hence we expect to find little impact of the presence of actual kin on felt obligations toward the kinpersons in question.

To test these expectations we have a number of measures of respondents' lineage compositions. These include whether parents are still alive, the number of secondary kin (siblings, grandparents, and grandchildren), whether the respondent has ever been divorced, and how many children the respondents have had. Each of these items reflects the presence or absence of some kinpersons in the respondents' concrete kindreds.

A related issue involves the quality of relationships to living kin. Unfortunately, we have only a few measures of the quality of concrete kin relationships. We can examine whether respondents who had someone in their kindred who corresponds to one or another of the kintypes in the vignettes rated those vignettes differently from those who did not, but we cannot tell whether a beloved cousin, for example, elevated obligations to cousins in general or a disliked cousin had the opposite effect. We do know whether respondents had an uncle, aunt, or grandparent they especially loved or admired, but we did not ask the respondents whether they particularly *disliked* any aunts or grandparents.

The major qualitative appraisals of kin relationships available in our data have already been discussed. In the last section, we learned that having had parents who were reported as affectionate generally increased ratings to all kin. In a later chapter, we will learn that affectionate parents are likely to have children who return that affection to their parents and transmit it to their children. So it appears that warmth in specific kin relationships can strengthen obligations to those kin.

The effects of the few available measures of the presence of particular kintypes in the respondents' living kindred are shown in Table 5.12 along with respondents' gender, age, and education. The latter are used in this table primarily as controls.

The findings of Table 5.12 do not sustain the idea that the living presence of particular kintypes affected the strengths of kin obligations in any uniform way. Neither the number of secondary kin nor the presence of living parents[14] affected any of the measures of kin obligation. Of course, having no or few kin currently in any category may not be very important: Everyone has *had* parents and grandparents and many of those who have no children at the point of being interviewed will have children in the future. If our view of the generality of the kinship normative structure is correct, these are the kin types about which the norms should be strong and robust whether or not there are such concrete relatives among a person's living kin.

Having been divorced affects kin obligations negatively, significantly so for the Total Obligation Index, the Primary Index, and the Distant Kin Index. Note that having been divorced does not significantly depress obligations to Nonkin, among whom ex-spouses are classified. Here again experience with a particular relationship does not affect obliga-

Table 5.12. Regression of Kin Obligation Ratings on Presence of Actual Kin (Unstandardized b-Coefficients)

	Kin Obligation Indexes				
Predictor Variables	Total Obligation	Primary Kin	Secondary Kin	Distant Kin	Nonkin
Age	−.01*	−.01	−.01*	−.01	−.02*
Female	.23*	.11	.28*	.30*	.22
Education	.12***	.13***	.13**	.07	.10*
Number of Secondary Kin [a]	−.09	−.10	−.07	−.12	−.09
Ever Divorced	−.34**	−.33**	−.17	−.47**	−.25
Ever had Children	.39**	.56***	.53*	.13	−.04
Number of Parents Alive	−.00	.09	.02	−.15	.02
Intercept	−1.01	−1.48*	−1.41	−.06	−.21
R^2	.05***	.05***	.04***	.03***	.06***

[a] Respondents divided into quartiles on the combined number of living grandparents, grandchildren, and siblings.
*** p < .001
** p < .01
* p < .05

tions. Most of our respondents have never been divorced and hence have never experienced having an ex-spouse.[15]

Having been divorced may not lower or elevate obligations to nonkin, but that state does lower the strength of Total kin obligations, and also obligations to primary and distant kin. The dissolution of a marriage apparently has reverberations throughout a kin group.

The depressing effect of divorce on obligations to primary kin bears some comment. Marriage is an event involving kin even if they are not present at the ceremony. Through marriage each partner acquires a set of affinal kin, "in-laws," who form a pool of affinal kin with whom strong ties may be formed along with reciprocal help patterns. As we saw in the previous chapter, affinals may not be as highly obligating as the consanguineals in the same line (e.g., mothers-in-law are not owed as much as mothers, but they are owed more than aunts and uncles). Because kinship is a reciprocal relationship, a mother-in-law may develop a strong tie to a child-in-law.

A divorce has an impact not only on one's relations to in-laws but also on the relations between one's affinal and consanguineal kin. Primary ties to parents may be affected by divorce through the resulting decreased contact between one's parents and one's children.

The impact of divorce on relationships to children may also be strong. Divorced men who usually do not assume child custody may feel their ties to children weaken, especially if the custodial spouse remarries. As a consequence, divorce is not only usually a painful experience in and of itself, but also may weaken ties to parents and children, as Table 5.12 suggests.

There are also wider kinship implications. Friendships and reciprocal help patterns established with affinal kin may be terminated. Perhaps the impact of divorce on relationships to former affinal kin explains why the coefficient is negative and significant for distant relatives, a category that includes affinals.

Having at least one child[16] elevates obligations to all kin, although significantly only to primary and secondary kin. In contrast, having children depresses obligations to nonkin, although not significantly. The interpretation for these effects is quite similar, although opposite in implication, to those advanced above for the changes accompanying divorce. Having a child is a lineage event that has repercussions beyond the immediate parents. A child is also a grandchild, a niece, or nephew and so on. A child also unites two lineages with two sets of grandparents, uncles, and aunts, etc. In addition, the obligations owed to one's child may also be ones that are viewed as being owed to oneself. If one's parent does not take on grandparental obligations to a child, the bond to the parent may be thereby diminished. Hence, it is understandable that having children moves one closer to a lineage and elevates obligations to all kin.

Whether one has living parents, or few or many secondary kin, are matters beyond the control of the respondents. These aspects of one's kindred are affected primarily by the fertility decisions and mortality experiences of others. In contrast, having children is at least in part voluntary, as is marriage and divorce. These considerations lead us to suggest that the effects of divorce and having children on obligations to kin reflect in part more general views about kinship. Certainly those who are concerned to maintain a lineage would have children (if they could) and are likely to have stronger bonds to kin in the first place. Getting divorced may also express lesser attachment to kin; people who cared greatly about affecting their lineage may be less likely to actively seek divorce.[17]

The general point of the interpretations of the findings presented in this section is that the presence or absence of concrete kin in a lineage is not very important in and of itself for obligations to kin. What is significant are the implications of divorce and having children, partially voluntary acts, on the lineages involved and the strengths of kin attachment that such actions may reflect.

Ethnic Differences in Obligations to Kin

The Boston metropolitan area has an ethnically diverse population. About one in four respondents (27%) claimed an English nationality background, almost as many (23%) were Irish in origin, and more than 1 in 10 (13%) had Italian backgrounds.[18] The remainder were distributed widely across Europe and the countries bordering the Mediterranean (14%). There were few Jews (7%) in our sample and fewer Blacks (4%).

During the eras that our respondents' ancestors came to the United States, there may have been considerable differences in family structures and in kinship obligations among the various ethnic groups they represented. But most of our respondents were born in the United States; many are generations removed from their ethnic roots in Europe and the Mediterranean basin. In addition, many have descended from several nationality backgrounds. Hence, whatever the strong ethnic differences may have been historically, they are probably present in very diluted forms in our respondents.

This "diluted" effect of ethnic backgrounds is suggested by the data in Table 5.13 on their effects on kin obligations, with sex, age, and educational attainment serving as controls. Each ethnic group was coded as a dummy variable, and each is shown in contrast to the ethnic British (the omitted dummy).

Table 5.13. Regression of Kin Obligation on Ethnicity, Age, Gender, and Education (Unstandardized b Coefficients)

Predictor Variables	Total	Primary	Secondary	Distant	Nonkin
			Kin Obligation Index		
Education	.07***	.07***	.06**	.05*	.05*
Sex	.26**	.16	.32**	.30*	.22
Age	−.01***	−.01**	−.01**	−.01	−.03**
Ethnic Origins [a]					
Irish	.47***	.37**	.50**	.74***	.08
Jews	.53*	.40	.41	.66**	.35
Blacks	.18	−.43	−.10	1.37*	−.15
Asians	.46	.34	−.15	1.28*	−.12
Portuguese	.15	−.11	−.18	.91*	−.02
Mediterranean	.54	.38	.80*	.79	−.02
East Europe	.35	.31	.21	.54	.24
Others [b]	−.35	−.44	−.64	.04	−.30
German	.07	−.19	.06	.51	−.08
West Europe	.20	.17	.17	.30	−.12
Italians	.26	.26	.22	.40	−.10
Intercept	−.78*	−.84*	−.66	−1.10***	.29
R^2	.06***	.06***	.05***	.04***	.05***

[a] Dummy variables for the nationality respondent felt "closest to" used, except for Jews and Blacks. Jews were classified on the basis of an item on religious preference and Blacks were those who answered accordingly on an item on race. Omitted dummy is British.

[b] "Others" consist of those who identified themselves as "Yankees," or as nationalities too rare to warrant separate classification.

*** $p < .001$
** $p < .01$
* $p < .05$

Respondents with Irish backgrounds present the strongest contrast to the British, being significantly higher in overall obligation strength as well as in obligations to primary, secondary, and distant kin, ranging from .5 to .7 points higher in kin obligation strength. Jews are very similar to the Irish, in expressing higher obligation strengths to all kintypes, although because of the small sample size, statistical significance is reached only in Total Obligation Index and Distant Kin indices.

Blacks, Asians, and Portuguese show patterns similar to each other, with very much stronger obligations to distant kin. These ethnic groups apparently draw the line on high obligations much further out in the kindred. Mediterranean respondents (mostly Greece, Asia Minor, and North Africa) are higher in obligations to secondary kin, indicating that their boundaries of obligation are drawn further out than the British but not as far as Blacks, Asians, and the Portuguese. It should be noted that the small sample sizes of these ethnic groups means that only very large differences will reach statistical significance. Were the sample sizes larger, some of the other coefficients might have been significant.

The remainder of the ethnic groups in the table—East and West Europeans, Germans, and Italians—show patterns that are not significantly different from the British.

Although ethnic differences do exist, as Table 5.13 demonstrates, their overall influences on kinship obligations are not very great, as the low R^2 values in the table, ranging from .04 to .06, show. (These coefficients also reflect the influences of age, sex, and education.)

Whereas nationality (or ethnic) origins have slight effects on kinship obligations, race and religious affiliations do not. Catholics and Protestants are quite heterogeneous in their kin obligations as the analysis of ethnicity implies. To be sure, most Irish are Catholics, but so are most Italians, Portuguese, as well as many Germans. Blacks are largely Protestant, but so are most of those who claim England or Scotland as their national origins. Although Blacks, predominantly Protestant, show a distinctive kinship obligation pattern, Protestant whites are so heterogeneous that direct religious comparisons are inconclusive.

Current Influences on Kinship Obligations

Up to this point we have considered either long standing influences on our respondents, such as ethnicity or gender, or experiences rooted in their families of origin. In this section we consider influences that are more proximate in time, arising out of the current life circumstances of the respondents and those that act over a long period of time. Although some of these potential influences have been considered earlier, we reintroduce them because they are also relevant in this context.

Two of the factors we consider here are indicators of "broken" or truncated lineage continuity in the adult lives of the respondent. Those who have ever been divorced have gone through the experience of breaking close ties to a spouse and as a consequence with a set of affinal kin with whom they were related through their spouses. Childless persons have truncated lineages: Without children they have no direct links down the generational ladder. Of course, some of those who are currently childless will have children in the future. However, for those beyond the age of 35 or so, being childless is likely to be a permanent condition. It is not just the absence of children and the gaps down the generations in their lineages that condition implies; it is also that the childless condition, especially among middle-aged and older adults, may also imply that direct descendants are not very important. For these persons, kin ties all told may not be very salient and hence not obligating.

As we suggested earlier, divorce may act for adults in much the same way as broken homes for children. A divorce ordinarily lessens ties to relatives acquired through marriage. Not being the custodial parent may also lower ties to children, an outcome more likely to be experienced by divorced men than women.

Although not all kinship obligations involve the expenditure of significant amounts of resources, those who have many resources may find it easier to acknowledge obligations. We use current family income as a measure of such resources. Certainly income should play a role in financial obligation with persons in affluent conditions perhaps finding it easier to acknowledge obligations to provide financial help.

Obligations to kin may simply be a specific instance of the variety of role obligations to which we are all subject. In our roles as citizens, we have obligations to perform such citizenship duties as filing honest tax returns, serving on juries, or in the military. Less stringent obligations involve contributing to charity and performing volunteer work for our churches and charitable organizations. Respondents who acknowledge strong obligations in a variety of roles may also be persons who feel obligated to kin. Here we are positing a generalized willingness to perform all sorts of "duties" that are implied in all the various social roles we play. To tap a generalized sense of duty, we computed a Civic Duties Index using items that asked how important various civic obligations were—voting, volunteer work, contributing to charity, serving jury duty, and reporting witnessed serious crime to the police. Respondents with high scores on the Civic Duties Index acknowledge high levels of obligations to others.

The final factor we will consider is the respondents' scores on the Expressivity Index, measuring self-assessments of being generally "open" to others, able to express emotions, to care what others think, to regard oneself as affectionate, and to be helpful to others. We expected respondents' scores on the Expressivity Index to be related in a positive way to their willingness to acknowledge obligations to kin, reasoning that this generalized predisposition would affect kinship ties much as it affected other social relationships.

Table 5.14 considers the joint effects, using multiple regression, of all of the factors outlined above on each of the kin obligation indexes. As in previous analyses, we also include education, age, and sex as controls.

The most salient features of Table 5.14 are the important roles played by the Civic Duties and the Expressivity Indexes. The more important respondents saw their civic duties to be and the more expressive they were, the higher their scores on each of the kin obligation indexes. More than half of the effects shown in that table are the results of these indexes.

The effects of divorce and having children are also important, as they were in previous analyses. Having ever been divorced significantly

Table 5.14. Current Influences of Kinship Obligations (Unstandardized b Coefficients)

Predictor Variables	Kin Obligation Indexes				
	Total	Primary	Secondary	Distant	Nonkin
Age	−.01***	−.01**	−.03***	−.01	−.02***
Female	.06	−.02	.11	.10	.08
Education	.09**	.11**	.08*	.06	.09*
Civic Duties	.27***	.17***	.30***	.30***	.30***
Expressivity	.47***	.40***	.52***	.49***	.33***
Income (1000s)	.00	.01*	.01*	−.00	−.00
Ever Divorced	−.41***	−.40***	−.26*	−.50***	−.27
Ever had Children	.32*	.49***	.44**	.07	−.10
Intercept	−3.50***	−3.19***	−3.95***	−3.26***	−2.43***
R^2	**.19***	**.13***	**.16***	**.12***	**.10***

*** p < .001
** p < .01
* p < .05

decreases all of the indexes of obligation except to nonkin, whereas having had children has the opposite effect: Those who have had children feel more obligated not only to primary kin but to secondary kin as well.

The effect of family income is the weakest of the current factors though in the predicted direction. The higher the family income, the stronger the obligation to primary and secondary kin.

It is also important to note that in these equations, females are not significantly different from males. This is largely attributable to the inclusion of the Expressivity Index in the equations. As discussed in Chapter 2, women score much higher on the Expressivity Index than men. What the results of Table 5.14 suggest is that it is not gender per se that explains why women feel stronger obligations to kin than men, but the gender-related, personal trait of Expressivity. Men as well as women who are high in Expressivity show strong obligations both to kin and nonkin.[19]

An Overall Interpretation of Obligations to Kin

The several strands of analysis that we have pursued in this chapter are brought together in the multiple regressions shown in Table 5.15, in which we consider the simultaneous effects of influences stemming from the respondents' childhood families, ethnic backgrounds, and current characteristics.

Table 5.15. Biographic, Ethnic, and Current Determinants of Kin Obligations (Unstandardized b Coefficients)

Predictor Variables	Kin Obligation Index				
	Total	Primary	Secondary	Distant	Nonkin
Age	−.02***	−.01***	−.02***	−.01	−.02***
Female	.06	−.02	.12	.10	.08
Education	.08**	.09**	.08*	.07	.09*
Family of Origin					
Parental Affection	.07	−.01	.09	.17*	−.02
Broken Home	−.18	−.53***	−.20	.08	.17
Kin Salience	.07	.02	.08	.17*	.03
Family Cohesion	.15**	.19**	.18**	.19**	−.03
Troubles Extent	.17*	.19**	.26**	.18*	.01
Emotional Troubles	−.20*	−.18*	−.27**	−.22*	−.03
Ethnicity					
Jews	.25	.22	.14	.23	.21
Irish	.22	.20	.29*	.33*	.04
Blacks	−.15***	−.61*	−.40	.78**	−.25
Current Measures					
Expressivity	.43***	.36***	.48***	.43***	.32***
Civic Duties	.23***	.15***	.27***	.25***	.24***
Income (1000s)	.00	.00	.01*	−.00	−.00
Ever Divorced	−.36**	−.35**	−.22	−.45*	−.28
Ever Had Children	.31*	.51***	.43**	.00	−.09
Intercept	−3.71***	−3.29***	−4.31***	−4.03***	−2.13**
R^2	**.21***	**.18***	**.19***	**.15***	**.10***

*** $p < .001$
** $p < .01$
* $p < .05$

There are several important features of Table 5.15. First, the effects of each of the sources of kin obligation strengths tend to persist when considered jointly, although sometimes lowered in strength. For example, influences stemming from childhood family factors persist when ethnicity and current life conditions are also considered. Some, such as Parental Affection, are diminished in their effects, whereas others are enhanced: The effect of the Emotional Troubles Index is greater in Table 5.15 than it was in Table 5.11 in which the predictor variables included childhood measures. The consequence is that the effects of each of the classes of influences we have considered in this chapter are largely additive. The R^2 values of the equations in Table 5.15 are considerably larger than those for any of the previous tables of this chapter. Indeed, the R^2 of .21 for the equation for the Total Obligation Index is quite large and the equations for the other kin obligation indexes are of the same magnitude. Although the R^2 for the Nonkin Obligation equation is a magnitude smaller (.10), it represents a respectable amount of explained variance.

It is apparent that some of the patterns shown in Table 5.15 are signs of developmental processes. For example, childhood parental affection contributes to higher levels of expressivity in adulthood. So too daughters are more apt than sons to be socialized to become expressive adults. Hence, when we take into account the respondents' adult levels of Expressivity, the effects of Parental Affection is diminished in Table 5.15, and is significantly related only to obligations to distant kin.

Second, age and education effects persist, although in diminished strength. Obligations to kin decline with increasing age, with respondents over 70 averaging .75 lower in kin obligation ratings than respondents in their 20s. Each additional 4 years of formal education leads to an average elevation of .33 score points in kin obligation scores, corresponding to the average difference between college and high school graduates.

Third, current characteristics have the strongest effect on kin obligations. Adding current influences to the equation for the Total Obligation Index about doubles the R^2 for that equation and tends to lower the coefficients for variables from other classes of influence. In short, the effects of ethnicity and childhood family factors work partially through the effects of current characteristics. This includes the effects of gender and Parental Affection in childhood, as noted above, that are diminished by introducing Expressivity. Similar declines are shown for the higher kin obligations of Irish respondents compared to the earlier analysis where ethnicity was considered by itself. Apparently Irish and Jewish respondents are higher in kin obligations because the Irish and the Jews tend to be higher in Expressivity and in their devotion to civic duty.

Interestingly, the effects of being black are also enhanced by adding current characteristics: In Table 5.15, Blacks are significantly lower in overall obligations to kin generally, lower in obligations to primary kin and significantly higher in obligations to distant kin, the first two not being apparent in earlier tables. In the analysis presented earlier, Blacks were significantly different (and higher) only on obligations to distant kin. Apparently the higher Expressivity and lower incomes of Blacks concealed the Table 5.15 differences in earlier analyses.

Finally, some of the influences shown in Table 5.15 operate to affect all kintypes, while others are specific to the degree of lineage distance involved. Those that influence all kin obligations include age, educational attainment, childhood Family Cohesion, experienced childhood Family Troubles, Expressivity, and devotion to Civic Duties.

Each of the kin-specific obligation indexes has a distinctive pattern of determinants:

Primary Kin. Obligations to primary kin are weakened by growing up in a broken home, being troubled by the emotional problems of parents, being ethnically Black, and experiencing a broken marriage. The positive influences that strengthen obligations to primary kin include strong childhood Family Cohesion, experiencing childhood family adversities (that did not involve parental emotional problems), having had children, and being high on Expressivity and Civic Duties.

Secondary Kin. Obligations to secondary kin show much the same pattern as those owed to primary kin, except that some of the influences are no longer significant. Experiencing a childhood broken home or an adult broken marriage weakens secondary kin obligations but not significantly so. Some influences turn significantly positive: The higher the respondents' current family income, the stronger are obligations to secondary kin. In addition, being Irish leads to significantly higher obligations.

Distant Kin. Obligations to distant kin have a very understandable pattern. Those who experienced salient childhood relations to distant kin (especially aunts and uncles) are higher in their obligations to such kin. Among ethnic groups, the Irish and Blacks both show significantly elevated levels of obligation to their distant relatives. Income, childhood broken homes or adult broken marriages have no significant effects.

Nonkin. Obligations to nonkin are affected significantly only by Expressivity and devotion to Civic Duty. Dutiful, high expressive persons feel most obligated to friends, neighbors, and ex-spouses.

The findings of this chapter indicate that virtually all of our respondents feel some degree of obligation to kin as prescribed in our kinship norms. However, some feel strong obligations to kin and in others there are weaker ties to the kindred. Although we cannot explain all of the differences from respondent to respondent, it is also apparent that their childhood families can set down strong or weak patterns, the former by cohesive families presided over by affectionate parents. As adults, the strength of obligations is influenced positively by being better educated, having a strong sense of duty in a variety of roles, and by being an outgoing expressive person.

Notes

1. These standard deviations also reflect the differences among vignettes in other attributes of the vignettes that are not shown in Table 5.1. That is, the standard deviations

also reflect differences among vignettes according to gender, marital status, the kind of obligation involved, and the occasion depicted in the vignette. Hence, the standard deviations are not to be interpreted in absolute terms, but only in relation to the vignette characteristics used in the analysis. For example, the actual standard deviation for mothers is smaller than the standard deviation for primary kin because the latter also reflects differences between mothers, fathers, daughters, and sons, as well as differences in marital status, and other items of information in the vignettes.

2. See Table 4.2 for the full distribution of ratings given.

3. See the first part of Chapter 4 and Figure 4.1 for details on the vignette design.

4. For example, 2824 vignettes concerning mothers appear in the total vignette set, indicating that most respondents rated at least one vignette concerning mothers. In contrast, there are only 683 vignettes containing ex-spouses, indicating that about two of three respondents did not receive vignettes containing ex-spouses. In Chapter 5 we explain that the reason for this imbalance was our desire to focus upon primary kin. Accordingly we sampled more heavily from among primary kin and only lightly from among ex-spouses.

5. Six additional adjusted indexes were computed but will not be used in this chapter because the analysis of each yielded no important findings that differed substantially from those presented in the text. These additional indexes include ones based on the sex of the kinperson being rated, the marital status of kin, and whether the rating involved giving comfort or providing financial aid.

6. In the Nonkin Obligation Index, friends, neighbors, and ex-spouses are combined. However, this index is dominated by friends and neighbors, constituting 80% of the nonkin vignettes. In addition, separate tabulations (not reported here) separately for friends and for neighbors show the same age-related declines shown for the combined nonkin.

7. The pattern shown in Table 5.6 is shown in all of the other obligation indexes as well.

8. In Chapter 4, we showed that about a third of the least well educated declined to fill out the vignette booklets, compared to less than 1 in 10 of the best educated group. This finding is consistent with the interpretation offered in the text.

9. Note that these R^2 values are notably lower than the comparable coefficients shown in Chapter 4. In the previous chapter we were dealing with the effects of kin structural features on the average ratings received by each of 74 kin types. Here we are concerned with individual vignette ratings and hence not only the averages but the dispersions of ratings around those averages.

10. See Table 1.6 for a more detailed description of the construction of the Family Troubles Index.

11. In Chapter 9, we will see that the Family Troubles Index also has positive effects on the extent of help respondents have recently given to their parents and to their adult children. When there were health problems in the family of origin (e.g., prolonged illness or a death in the family) respondents report more varied help given to their parents. When there were problems more likely to involve children in families of procreation (social deviance involving trouble in school or with the police) respondents report more varied help to their children over the past year.

12. Note that although female respondents feel themselves to be more obligated generally to kin, gender differences are significant only for secondary and distant kin. Men and women do not differ significantly in their obligations to primary kin (parents and children) but only with regard to the outer circles of their kindred.

13. Unfortunately, because of the design used, there are not enough separate ratings of obligations to mother and to father available in the respondent vignette packages to support an analysis of the separate effects on obligations to mothers and to fathers.

14.   Without age as a control, respondents who had living parents expressed higher obligations to primary kin. However, when age is held constant, as in Table 5.12, the effect of living parents disappears.

15.   The low proportion ever divorced (10%) may also affect the statistical significance of the coefficient for Nonkin. With a larger number of divorced persons in the sample, this coefficient may well have been significant.

16.   Although having any children is important in obligations to kin, the number of children is not. There are no significant differences in kin obligations among respondents according to the number of children they had.

17.   Among men, having experienced a divorce lowers the sense of obligation toward children, whereas among women divorce leads to a reduction in obligation toward parents. (Data not shown.)

18.   Because their ancestors had extensively married across nationality background lines, we used as a measure of ethnicity an item asking to which nationality the respondents felt closest. We made exceptions for Blacks and Jews, classifying them as such regardless of the nationality they felt closest to. Even so, we could not classify 16% of the respondents either because they provided no answers or because their answers could not be coded. The analysis in this section is based on the 1172 respondents who provided interpretable answers.

19.   Several other current characteristics of respondents were explored to ascertain if they predisposed to higher or lower kin obligation strengths. Initially we considered the health status of respondents to be a resource on a par with income, reasoning that respondents in ill health might find it more difficult to acknowledge such obligations. This supposition proved not to be the case. We also considered the measure of Family Troubles as experienced by respondents in their current families of procreation, and the Bradburn Affect Balance Scale. Neither of these measures showed any relationship to any of the kin obligation indexes.

Dimensions of
Parent–Child Solidarity _ Part IV

"The problem with real intimacy, Walter had long ago learned, is that you cannot just shut it off. Real people have a way of banging against the doors you've closed . . . It was funny—for most of his life he had kept his eyes focused straight ahead . . . he had assumed that by looking only forward, he could eventually lose the sadness and dissatisfactions of his childhood. But the further we went, the more Walter realized that, like it or not, he was inextricably bound with the people who had mattered to him and who mattered to him now, the people whose loves defined him, whose deaths would devastate him."

David Leavitt, *Equal Affections* (1989, pp. 240–241)

Solidarity Overview and Analysis Model _____ 6

"The idea of kin is so deeply and powerfully rooted within us that it is the most common metaphor for describing closeness."

Lillian B. Rubin, *Just Friends*, (1985, p. 6)

Introduction

This section of the book is organized in terms of the major dimensions of solidarity that characterize the contemporary relationship between parents and adult children. In common with all social relationships, the parent–child relationship can be analyzed in terms of social interaction, sentiment, values, and norms. The preceding two chapters on normative obligations have shown that obligations toward the primary kin of parents and children are stronger than to any other members of a kindred or nonkin such as friends and neighbors. Cultural imagery reflects this centrality of the parent–child relationship, for no other human bond is invoked more frequently to suggest deep commitment and stability: mother earth, God the Father, the fatherland, Mother Russia, and so forth. The chapters in Part IV will give special attention to each of the dimensions of solidarity in the study design. This chapter will provide an overview of the dimensions of solidarity, and provide the analysis model for their interrelationships. The chapters to follow are in accord with the rationale provided by the model. Chapter 7 will analyze Affectional and Consensual Solidarity, as indexed by our measures of Affective Closeness and Value Consensus; Chapter 8 will analyze Associational Solidarity, as measured by frequency of visiting and telephone contact; and Chapter 9 will analyze our major dimension of Associational Solidarity, the help exchanged between the generations.

Our concern, however, is not merely to analyze the *current* dimensions of the parent–child relationship, but to explore the biographic roots of these patterns through an analysis of the early formative years when the child was growing up, and to test the extent to which early family life shows significant continuing effects on one or another of the dimensions of current parent–child solidarity. No other human relationship has as long a history as that between a parent and a child, going back as it does not merely to the birth of the child, but to the qualities the parents brought to their marriage, and to their hopes and dreams about the children yet unborn. And no other adult figures are as important to the qualities children will bring to their adulthood as parents are, from shared genes to personality characteristics, status attainment, basic values, and, perhaps, the parenting styles the children bring to the rearing of their own children. As a society, we have never defined parenting skills as a legitimate area for formal training in our schools, which leaves young parents dependent on the models they observed in their own parents, supplemented by reliance on soon well-worn copies of Dr. Spock or books by other childrearing experts, and the advice of their pediatricians.

Two memorable lines in John Milton's *Paradise Regained* read: "Childhood shows the man, as morning shows the day." Psychologists resonate to such a poetic message more than family sociologists, for the typical study in sociology and gerontology pays little heed to the life histories and past experiences of those whose family relationships are under investigation. By contrast, our assumption in designing the study was that an important source of variation in contemporary family relationships lies precisely in experiences in the formative years of childhood and adolescence.

The influence of past family life can be manifested in two primary ways. First, by the persistent influence of some characteristic of the early family on current relationships: for example, having been reared by relatively cold and distant parents may so reduce the intimacy of the relationship between parent and child that no subsequent events later in life can activate an increase in warmth and closeness between the generations. In a family such as this, the quality of the emotional tie in childhood and adolescence, or the degree of affection shown by the parents in childhood may show persistent effects in keeping social interaction and sentiment to a restrained minimum between parents and children once the children have grown.

The second type of continuing effect of early family life is that of cross-generational transmission, in which a parent's characteristic or pattern is replicated in the adult child who shows the same characteristic or pattern. Examples here would include G2 marital happiness being correlated with the marital happiness of G1 parents years ago, or G2 respondents' families of procreation showing a similar profile on family cohesion as did their families of orientation. In both examples, G1 parents would appear to have been models for behavior and sentiment shown in the next generation's marital and parental roles.

Both types of early family influence assume a one-directional model of influence, from the older to the younger generation. A quite different pattern is that of intergenerational influence, in which children are affecting parents as well as parents affecting children. Theoretical models of adult and family development now lay claim to such interaction effects between parents and children, but evidence for this in mature adult relationships is sparse. We will deal with this type of interactive influence in an analysis of attitudes toward several contemporary social–political issues in Chapter 7. But, for the most part, our attention will be on persistent effects and cross-generational transmission.

This chapter will be devoted to an overview of the variables at our disposal for the analysis of current parent–child relationships. Several questions guide this presentation: the first is to establish the extent to which our six major solidarity measures are influenced by sheer geographic distance separating parents from adult children. Obviously, associational solidarity is strongly determined by proximity of households—a mother in Boston cannot drop in for a daily chat with a daughter in Albany—but it is not clear to what extent proximity also affects other dimensions of the relationship, such as affective closeness or the extent to which parents and children share similar or different values. We wish to establish the extent to which this is the case, for it alerts us to a basic opportunity factor that may make for independence of the solidarity measures.

Second, we shall analyze the extent to which parents and adult children give similar or dissimilar ratings on the several dimensions of their relationship, by correlating parents' ratings on each dimension with the ratings given by their children on the same dimension. One assumes there will be high agreement on a factual matter such as frequency of visiting, and less agreement on more subjective matters such as degree of intimacy or judgments of the extent to which values are similar or dissimilar. We take advantage of having two parent–child dyads available—G1–G2 and G2–G3 dyads—for replication purposes, i.e., to check for consistency between the dyadic profiles.

Third, we explore how the dimensions of solidarity "hang together" or not, by correlating each dimension of solidarity with all other dimensions, and comparing the results when they concern relations with mothers with those concerning fathers, as well as when they involve ratings given by parents vs. ratings given by children.

To flesh out this largely statistical introduction to the solidarity measures, we will conclude the chapter by describing two outlier cases in our sample. Both involve a woman respondent in her 50s, who telephoned us when she received a letter alerting her to a pending interviewer's visit. Fortuitously, these two women represented polar extremes that emerged from our later statistical analysis, one with totally fractured relations with her children and a sad history of early family life when she was a girl, and the other with a highly cohesive family of her own, and close ties to her mother and siblings over the whole course of her life. We engaged in informal interviews in the course of these telephone conversations, and subsequently analyzed their personal interview protocols in great detail. We will draw on both data sources in sketching the profile of their lives and the place of children in them.

Geographic Distance and Current Solidarity Measures

We being with the correlations between the mileage distance separating parents and adult children in both dyads—G1–G2 and G2–G3—and each of the six variables that measure the four major dimensions of solidarity between the generations. Frequency of visiting each other is obviously strongly determined by geographic distance, and beyond 50 miles or so, the cost of long distance telephone calls may also restrict the frequency of phone contact. Some of the help items we used in the indices of functional solidarity require physical access, e.g., helping with domestic chores, whereas other types of help are less dependent on proximity, e.g., providing job leads, money, or a loan that can be handled by phone or a letter and a check. Subjective feelings and values have no necessary relationship to proximity. One can feel very close to a parent a thousand miles away, or hold very different values from those held by a child who lives down the block.

Table 6.1 shows the Pearson correlation coefficients between geographic distance and each of the solidarity indices for both dyads of parents and adult children. (Cases of parents and children living together were excluded from the mileage code.) Essentially the same pattern is shown for both dyads. Distance shows a negative effect on all six measures, as indexed by the fact that all 24 coefficients show negative signs. But there is great variation across the measures in the extent of the impact distance makes. Its greatest effect, predictably, is on visiting frequency. Less affected by distance, but still highly significant, are the negative correlations between mileage distance and frequency of telephone contact. Note that the correlation coefficients are much larger in phone contact between mothers and adult children than they are between fathers and adult children. This comes about not because mothers are in less frequent phone contact than fathers with children living great distances from the Boston area, but because women engage in a great

Table 6.1. Intergenerational Solidarity Measures ^{a} and Geographic distance ^{b} Between Parents and Adult Children: Pearson Correlation Coefficients (G2 Sample and Childset File on G2 Sample)

Solidarity Construct	Index	G1 Parents and G2 Adult Children		G2 Parents and G3 Adult Children	
		G1 Mother	G1 Father	G2 Mother	G2 Father
Associational Solidarity	Frequency of Visiting	−.79***	−.72***	−.71***	−.75***
	Frequency of Phoning	−.34***	−.19***	−.31***	−.21***
Functional Solidarity	Help: Child to Parent	−.29***	−.26***	−.19***	−.25***
	Help: Parent to Child	−.19***	−.12***	−.04	−.21***
Affective Solidarity	Affective Closeness	−.04	−.01	−.04	−.15***
Consensual Solidarity	Value Consensus	−.03	−.01	−.02	−.09
Average N^c		(761)	(553)	(737)	(448)

^{a} G1 Parent–G2 Child: Ratings by Main Sample respondents in their roles as adult children. G2 Parent–G3 Child: Ratings by Main Sample respondents in their roles as parents.

^{b} Excluding adult children living with their parents. Range of mileage code is from 1 = Less than 2 miles to 8 = More than 1500 miles.

^{c} Base Ns vary somewhat across the six measures.

*** p < .001

deal more phoning with nearby adult children than fathers do, a point we explore in more detail in Chapter 8.

Help exchange between the generations is modestly affected by geographic distance, though more so for the help children give to their parents than for the help parents give to children. As we shall see in Chapter 9, this is primarily due to the differences in the kinds of help that flow between the generations: The help children give is more dependent on proximity than the help given by parents. Domestic help or care during an illness require physical proximity, whereas advice, money, or a loan, for which parents are more likely to be the donors, can be handled by mail or a phone call.

Affective Closeness and Value Consensus show no significant relationship with geographic distance: Whereas all eight correlation coefficients are negative, they hover near zero for all but one, the closeness between G2 fathers and G3 children, but the correlation coefficient is so low ($-.15$) as to suggest little substantive significance.

These results imply two things relevant to subsequent analysis. First, we need not be concerned for geographic distance as a control variable in the analysis of Affective Closeness and Value Consensus, but must do so in all analysis of social interaction and help exchange; and second, we can assume that the differential impact of distance on the solidarity measures in turn reduces the correlations between the solidarity measures themselves, particularly those that relate affect and values to interaction and help exchange.

One other correlate of geographic distance is worth noting: The tendency for better educated individuals to move in a larger labor market than less educated adults means our better educated respondents live at greater geographic distance from their parents than our less well-educated respondents. We find a correlation of .29, significant at the .001 level, between the educational attainment level of G2 respondents and the geographic distance between them and their G1 parents.[1] A correlation coefficient of the same magnitude (.26) holds between geographic distance and the degree of discrepancy in educational attainment between G2 parents and adult children.

Parents' and Children's Ratings on Solidarity Measures

All the major variables in the study were measured in the same ways in all three surveys, the only difference being that G2 respondents were interviewed personally in their homes, whereas G1 parents and G3 children were interviewed by telephone. Indeed, it is the ability to analyze the parent–child relationship from *both* partners' perspectives that is a unique feature of the study. This gives very special significance to the data presented in Table 6.2: the correlation coefficients between parents' and adult children's ratings on all the major indicators of intergenerational solidarity. The table shows the correlations for both the G1–G2 and G2–G3 dyads, with G2 cases therefore limited to those whose parents (or children) were interviewed. Correlations are shown separately for mothers and fathers in both dyads: G2 respondents were asked separate questions about mothers and fathers in the main survey; for the G2–G3 dyads, gender of respondents (parents in this dyad) provides the analogous correlations.

The most important point to note about the correlations in Table 6.2 is the fact that all the coefficient signs are positive, and only 2 of the 46 coefficients do not reach statistical significance.[2] As a general pattern, then, parents and children do not take opposite views of the relationship between them; on average, they tend to agree.

There is of course great variation across the dimensions of solidarity in the *extent* to which parents and adult children agree. The dimensions of solidarity are listed in the table in the order of the magnitude of the correlation coefficients. The highest agreement, as one would expect, concerns associational solidarity: Parents and adult children are overwhelmingly in agreement when reporting how often they see each other (e.g., .89 in reports of G2 children and their G1 mothers), and slightly less concerning frequency of phone contact (e.g., .62 between G2 children and their mothers).

The next highest set of correlations concerns the reported extent of help exchanged between the generations: The eight correlation coefficients show a range from .26 to .55. There is some tendency for parents and adult children to agree more closely on the help that parents give children than on the help children give to parents; in particular, fathers and children show the least agreement in the help G2 men report receiving from their adult children (.26).[3]

The third dimension of solidarity is Value Consensus: Overall, the measures show moderately high correlations between parents' and children's judgment of the extent to which their values are similar or different. Like the help indices, there is a difference by gender of the parent in the size of the coefficients: Correlations are higher for the two mother–child dyads (.34 and .38) than for the two father–child dyads (.29 and .20). We believe this reflects the tendency for children to discuss intimate matters with their mothers more than with their fathers; in the course of such conversations mothers and adult children learn more of each other's views. Issues bearing on sex, choice of a mate, clothes, and life-style may be more frequently discussed during mother–child conversations than in father–child conversations. This interpretation is consistent with the profile shown on the three items that comprise the Value Consensus index: The coefficients are higher in the mother–child

Table 6.2. Pearson Correlation Coefficients Between Parents' and Children's Ratings on Major Intergenerational Solidarity Measures: G1–G2 Dyads and G2–G3 Dyads (G1, G2, and G3 Samples)

Solidarity Construct	Index	G1–G2 Dyad		G2–G3 Dyad	
		Mother–Child	Father–Child	Mother–Child	Father–Child
Associational Solidarity	Frequency of Visiting	.89***	.90***	.86***	.85***
	Frequency of Phoning	.62***	.60***	.39***	.47***
Functional Solidarity	Help: Parent to Child	.55***	.55***	.37***	.43***
	Help: Child to Parent	.51***	.37***	.42***	.26**
Consensual Solidarity	Total Extent Value Consensus	.43***	.32***	.49***	.16+
	Specific Items				
	Religious Views	.39***	.22**	.53***	.20*
	Political Views	.26**	.40***	.25**	.34***
	General Outlook on Life	.27***	.21*	.25***	.11
Affective Solidarity	Affective Closeness				
	Current	.31***	.37***	.16*	.23**
	When Child is 25	.34***	.31***	—a	—
	When Child is 16	.30***	.35***	—	—
	When Child is 10	.07	.22**	—	—

a Not included in G2 survey.
*** p < .001
** p < .01
* p < .05
+ p < .10

dyads than father–child dyads on *religious* views and *general outlook* on life, whereas they are higher in the father–child dyads on *political* views. The image is of fathers discussing the news of the day, and mothers discussing family affairs and personal values.

The correlations between parents and children on Affective Closeness are of moderate statistical significance: Current ratings, and the measures we shall analyze in some detail in Chapter 7, range from .16 to .37. Least agreement is found for the very earliest retrospective ratings, when the child was about 10 years of age. As we shall see, memories of early family life held by adult children often have different salient features than those held by parents. Consistent with findings from other studies, parents tend to report greater intimacy in the relationship with children than the children themselves do (Bengtson & Schrader, 1982; Mangen et al., 1987). On the other hand, children do not show ratings that are opposite to those reported by their parents, as indicated by the absence of any negative correlations among the affective closeness measures.

A major inference from the relative sizes of the correlation coefficients shown in Table 6.2 is that, although clearly significant statistically for the most part, there remains a good deal of room for very different perceptions on the part of children and their parents concerning their relationship to each other. It also suggests that the impact on children of the years they lived in close proximity to their parents may be quite different from the impact on the parents who reared them. A first approximation to these differences can be seen in how the solidarity measures correlate with each other when adult children provide the information compared to how they hang together when parents provide the information. It is to this issue that we now turn.

The base for this inspection of the solidarity measures is provided by correlation matrices of all six solidarity measures, separately for children and for parents, and for the two G1–G2 and G2–G3 dyads. With six variables, the set of matrices consists of 15 correlation coefficients for four dyads (G1Mo–G2Ch, G1Fa–G2Ch, G2Mo–G3Ch, G2Fa–G3Ch), each with data from the parent and from the child, for a total of 120 correlation coefficients ($15 \times 4 \times 2$). Full details are given in Table 6.3 for the G1–G2 dyads and in Table 6.4 for the G2–G3 dyads. In each table, the upper panel (A) provides the matrix using variables drawn from interviews with the parents and the lower panel B from interviews with the adult children. Within each panel the correlations concerning the mother–child relationship appear to the right of the diagonal, and those concerning the father to the left of the diagonal.

We shall not discuss in detail all the correlations shown in the two tables. Rather, we will extract from the matrices certain relevant correla-

Table 6.3. Correlation Coefficients Between Intergenerational Solidarity Measures for G1–G2 Dyads, From G1 Parents' Perspective and G2 Children's Perspective (G1 and G2 Samples)

| | | | G1 Mothers (to right of diagonal) | | | |
| | | | | | Extent Help | |
	Close	Values	Visit	Phone	Parent to Child	Child to Parent
A. G1 Parents' Perspective						
Affective Closeness	—	.30***	.11	.21***	.12	.25***
Value Consensus	.19*	—	.05	.00	.01	−.03
Frequency Visit	.20*	−.01	—	.33***	.37***	.50***
Frequency Phone	.26***	−.00	.31***	—	.26***	.31***
Help Extent Parent to Child	.18*	.13	.34***	.42***	—	.59***
Help Extent Child to Parent	.30***	.15	.32***	.44***	.57***	—
			G1 Fathers (to left of diagonal)			

(Average *Ns*: Father = 127; Mother = 190)

	Close	Values	Visit	Phone	Parent to Child	Child to Parent
B. G2 Children's Perspective						
Affective Closeness	—	.43***	.24***	.30***	.37***	.30***
Value Consensus	.43***	—	.12*	.08	.21***	.07
Frequency Visit	.37***	.21**	—	.33***	.39***	.42***
Frequency Phone	.37***	.22**	.47***	—	.37***	.36***
Help Extent Parent to Child	.37***	.15*	.43***	.46***	—	.55***
Help Extent Child to Parent	.31***	.05	.42***	.39***	.51***	—
			G1 Fathers (to left of diagonal)			

(Average *Ns*: Father = 217; Mother = 306)

*** $p < .001$
** $p < .01$
* $p < .05$

Table 6.4. Correlation Coefficients Between Intergenerational Solidarity Measures for G2–G3 Dyads, From G2 Parents' Perspective and G3 Children's Perspective (Childset File on G2 Sample and G3 Sample)

| | | | *G2 Mothers (to right of diagonal)* | | | |
| | | | | | *Extent Help* | |
	Close	*Values*	*Visit*	*Phone*	*Parent to Child*	*Child to Parent*
A. G2 Parents' Perspective						
Affective Closeness	—	.32***	.17***	.30***	.11**	.22***
Value Consensus	.21***	—	.03	.16***	.07	.08
Frequency Visit	.33***	.12*	—	.16***	.32***	.41***
Frequency Phone	.37***	.20***	.24***	—	.12**	.13**
Help Extent Parent to Child	.25***	.15***	.43***	.35***	—	.56***
Help Extent Child to Parent	.31***	.14**	.48***	.34***	.62***	—
			G2 Fathers (to left of diagonal)			

(Average *N*s: Father = 607; Mother = 931)

	Close	*Values*	*Visit*	*Phone*	*Parent to Child*	*Child to Parent*
B. G3 Children's Perspective						
Affective Closeness	—	.33***	.10	.16**	.16**	.09
Value Consensus	.35***	—	.08	.16**	.20***	.13*
Frequency Visit	.14*	.16**	—	.17**	.45***	.44***
Frequency Phone	.25***	.30***	.20***	—	.18***	.20***
Help Extent Parent to Child	.22***	.26***	.39***	.29***	—	.58***
Help Extent Child to Parent	.14*	.12	.38***	.21***	.64***	—
			G2 Fathers (to left of diagonal)			

(Average *N*s: Father = 218; Mother = 249)

*** p < .001
** p < .01
* p < .05

261

tions for discussion, and we will compute absolute means for selected sets of correlations to summarize several striking differences in how the measures of solidarity hang together from a parent's perspective compared to a child's, or how they differ by the gender of the parent.

Help Reciprocity

To begin with, all four matrices show the same two variables to be most highly correlated, i.e., the correlations between the extent of help given by parents to children and its reciprocal, the extent of help given by children to their parents. Whether from the child's perspective or the parent's, whether from mothers or fathers, and whether the data refer to G1–G2 or G2–G3 dyads, a high degree of reciprocity in help pattern is implied by these high correlations, which range from .51 to .64. As we shall see in the chapter on help exchange, the balance in such intergenerational exchanges may vary as a function of age, need, resources, and dyad gender composition, but the overall pattern is for a considerable degree of reciprocity in the help exchanged between parents and adult children. *Those who give more also get more from their significant others.*

Contact Frequency ..nd Help Patterns

A second general point can be extracted from the correlations between type of contact (visiting vs. phoning) and level of help exchanged. There are 16 correlations between the two help measures and visiting frequency and another 16 between the help measures and phoning frequency. In 13 of the 16 comparisons (help × visit vs. help × phone), the correlations are higher between help level and visiting than between help level and phone contact. If we compute absolute means between help and visiting, and help and phone frequency, across the two tables, the results are as follows:

	Correlation Coefficients between	
	Frequency of Visiting and Extent of Help	Frequency of Phoning and Extent of Help
Mother–Child		
Mother's Perspective	.40	.20
Child's Perspective	.42	.28
Father–Child		
Father's Perspective	.39	.39
Child's Perspective	.40	.33

Parents and adult children show the same results: The level of help exchanged between mothers and children is much more affected by type of contact (i.e., actual visiting being more important than phone contact), than is the case for fathers, as suggested by the fact that the correlations are just as high between help level and phone contact as between help and visiting in the father–child dyads. The help pattern between mothers and children involves more hands-on types of help that require physical proximity, while fathers and adult children can discuss many issues of mutual concern either by phone or during a visit, e.g., advice on a mortgage, requests or offers of money, job or customer/ client prospects.

Value Consensus and Affective Closeness

A third interesting pattern that can be extracted from the correlation matrices is the relationship between Value Consensus and Affective Closeness. These two dimensions of solidarity are more highly correlated from the adult child's perspective than from the parent's perspective. The relevant correlation coefficients for the two types of dyads are as follows:

	Correlations between Value Consensus and Affective Closeness	
	Parent's Perspective	*Child's Perspective*
G1–G2 dyad		
Mother	.30	.43
Father	.19	.43
G2–G3 dyad		
Mother	.32	.33
Father	.21	.35

The judgment of value accord or dissensus between adult children and their parents plays more of a role for the adult children than it does for parents in how close the relationship is considered to be. Parents may feel there is great intimacy to their relationship with children, regardless of how similar or different their views are on religion, politics, and general outlook on life, whereas children's ratings on the closeness of the relationship are more conditioned by their perception of value similarity between themselves and their parents.

Contact Frequency and Value Consensus

A fourth point that can be extracted from the matrices concerns the relationship between Value Consensus and frequency of social interaction: Here the general pattern is a lack of any significant connection between the two dimensions of solidarity. From the parents' perspective, the absolute mean across four matrices between frequency of visiting and Value Consensus is an insignificant .05, and between phoning and value consensus a similar low absolute mean of .14. From the children's perspective the absolute means are somewhat higher but still quite small, .14 for the visiting-values correlations, and .19 for the phoning-values correlations.

These results suggest two interesting points. For one, some degree of interaction is socially expected, and occurs whether or not parents and adult children are in agreement on life-style, politics, or religious matters. This may be why many of us find short visits with our adult children (or our parents) go more smoothly than prolonged visits, because the novelty and desire to catch up with each other, to enjoy a familiar meal, or to observe developmental change in a grandchild can fill a happy afternoon visit, whereas a week's visit may involve either more opportunity to get into controversial matters on which the two generations disagree or to regress to familial styles of interaction that open up old sources of contention.

A second interesting implication of this pattern is the possibility that parents and adult children engage in a lot of "topic avoidance," self-consciously steering clear of topics on which they know they disagree. This aspect of intergenerational interaction was brought to our attention by Gunhild Hagestad (personal communication, 1984), who observed its operation during in-depth interviews with middle-aged women and their mothers. Hagestad suggested that harmonious relations are maintained by carefully avoiding discussions on topics the parent and child know would cause discord between them. In other words, topic avoidance served the function of protecting the relationship from conflict.

We were sufficiently intrigued by Hagestad's ideas to make an effort to measure the construct of topic avoidance in the interviews. We explicitly asked respondents if they avoided discussions with their parents (or children) on money matters, sex, personal problems, politics, and religion. We were not completely successful in this effort, because so many respondents claimed they did not *avoid* such topics; they just never came up in conversations with their adult children or parents. This pattern made it ambiguous what a response of "no" really means: No, because they never discuss such topics? Or no, because they do not avoid them? The best we could do was to construct an index that counted the number of topics respondents explicitly said they *did* avoid. We found that the Topic Avoidance index shows a negative correlation of $-.44$ with Value Consensus between respondents and their fathers and $-.37$ in the case of mothers: Those who feel their own values and those of their parents are similar are less apt to avoid topics when interacting with parents than do those whose views differ from their parents' views. This tends to support Hagestad's impression that topic avoidance serves to maintain harmonious relations between the generations.

On the other hand, the point needs a further qualification, for there is also a high negative correlation between Topic Avoidance and Affective Closeness ($-.32$ in mother–child relations, $-.25$ in relations with fathers): Those with strained relations with their parents do more topic avoidance than those with warm and intimate relations. This suggests that topics may be avoided to prevent friction from further stressing strained relations between the generations, whereas intimate relationships may be better able to absorb occasional disagreements without threatening the relationship. *Rather than protecting existing harmony, topic avoidance may prevent further worsening of weak and stressed relationships.*

Shared Values, Affective Closeness, and Help Exchange

A general finding here that holds for both parents and children is the lack of any overall significant relationship between the help exchanged between the generations and whether or not parents and adult children hold similar or different values. The absolute mean across eight relevant correlations is only .09 when parents provided the data and .15 when adult children provided the data. Only slightly higher absolute means are found for correlations between Affective Closeness and help patterns, .22 from the parents' perspective and .24 from the adult children's. In this case, however, there is a wide range of specific correlations, from .09 to .37. We shall explore the issues involved in more detail in the chapter on help exchange, but an important implication is that many parents and adult children rise to the needs of their significant others quite independently of their subjective feelings toward each other. Long-standing patterns of interdependency and internalized norms of obligation may provide the motivational base for providing assistance to parents or adult children, quite apart from subjective sentiment.

Throughout this discussion of the ways in which the dimensions of solidarity relate to each other, as indexed by the correlation matrices we summarized, our interpretations have implied a causal "ordering" among the solidarity measures. This, in turn, reflects some assumptions about the roots of solidarity in the history of the parent–child relationship extending back in time to the years the children were growing up. The finding that the solidarity measures all show positive signs in the correlation coefficients among them suggests some common latent construct underlies the discrete measures, but the variance in the size of the coefficients suggests a different set of determinants may be involved for each of the solidarity measures. It is to make explicit our assumptions of the causal ordering among such measures, and their differential relationship to early family experiences that we now turn.

Causal Ordering Among Solidarity Measures

When a number of individuals with no prior knowledge of each other are brought together to form a group of some sort—as sailors are when they are assigned to a new ship or subjects are for an experimental social psychologist's study of group formation and interaction—it is reasonable to assume that the sheer passage of time and shared activities as a team provide the route for the development of group norms and subjective feelings toward each other. In other words, social interaction subserving some work or research goal determines the sentiment between individual group members and the esprit or morale of the group itself.

But a model that claims behavior determines sentiment makes no sense when applied to the relationship between parents and their adult children. What parents and their adult children do *for* each other is a complex matter that includes numerous factors: sheer accessibility to each other, the needs of the recipients of help, and the resources and competing demands on the donors of that help may be important, proximate determinants. An adult child whose father undergoes surgery or a mother whose daughter is giving birth will both drop their usual activities and commitments to provide what help they can to the father or child. Faced with a personal crisis or an important celebration, we turn to our most significant others to share grief and pain, or pleasure in accomplishment, and, on such occasions, parents and children are highly likely to be among the first people we contact. Apart from such out-of-the-ordinary events, however, the frequency of social interaction and the level of help exchanged between parents and adult children are highly likely to be affected by more long-standing characteristics of the relationship that go back in time to when they shared their daily lives in the same household. Whether a parent and adult child, or an adult brother and sister enjoy an intimate relationship or a tense and strained one will have its source in the quality of the family relationships established in childhood. Hence, our model assumes the Affective Closeness of contemporary parent–adult child relationships is the dimension of solidarity *most* deeply rooted in early family life, which in turn sets the stage for the frequency of social interaction and help exchange.

Whether parents and adult children share similar values may be partially determined by early family life as well, but of far greater importance will be the direction the child's life has taken as a function of educational attainment, social–economic status, the sector of the job world they occupy, and exposure to historic events during vulnerable periods in their development. As Lesthaeghe and Surkyn have shown with data from the European Values Studies (1988), changes in basic social values take place early in life and become cohort characteristics that persist over time. In an era of social political turmoil, adolescent children will depart from the ways of their parents, challenge the values parents hold to some degree, and consciously select a life-style that may differ markedly from that of their parents, as many adults whose children passed through late adolescence during the 1970s can testify. This suggests that the determinants of Value Consensus will include the extent to which parent and child differ in educational attainment, religiosity, and political orientation, and perhaps age as well. Most of these factors have their roots in the child's adolescence and early adulthood rather than childhood, as in the case of Affective Closeness. Consequently we place Value Consensus in an intermediary position in the causal pathway among our measures of parent–child solidarity.

Normative obligations toward parents and children are also rooted in early life experience, as we have seen in Chapter 5: Higher obligations toward parents and children are felt by those who grew up in cohesive intact families, and higher obligations to less closely related kin such as aunts or grandparents are shown by those who had close relationships with relatives they loved and admired during their childhood (i.e., high Kin Salience).

Hence, our model of the relationships among the dimensions of solidarity assigns a causal priority to sentiment and norms as rooted in the earliest family experiences; together they affect value consensus, which is more responsive to adolescent experiences. Last in the time sequence is frequency of social interaction and exchange of help between the generations. Associational solidarity is necessarily also a function of opportunity and the press of current life circumstances and needs, but we assume a cumulative snowball influence of earlier patterns as well. The model is summarized in Figure 6.1.

We have added to the model portrayed in Figure 6.1 two variables that did not figure in our discussion, but which will be important parts of the analysis in chapters to follow: Skill Transmission and Expressivity. It will be recalled that Expressivity was an important predictor of individual variance in normative obligations, absorbing most of the effect otherwise linked to gender. This personal trait will also be seen to contribute in interesting ways to the help exchange between the generations. But such personal traits themselves have origins in early experience, and as part of our looking back in time to the quality of relationships in the family of origin of our respondents, we shall explore the family characteristics that predispose a child—son *or* daughter—to acquire the per-

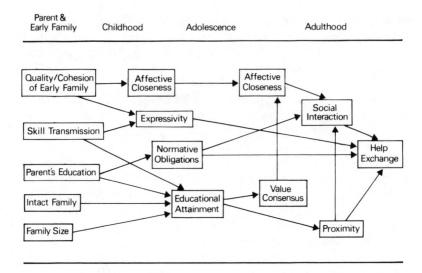

Figure 6.1. Causal model of pathways from early family life to dimensions of current parent–child solidarity.

sonal qualities of Expressivity, i.e., an open, helpful orientation to others, and an ability to express deep feelings. Skill transmission, or parental investment in teaching children a variety of skills, played a complex role in the cultivation of expressivity in the child, and is therefore included in the figure here.

The time order we have imposed on the dimensions of solidarity structures the organization of the three chapters to follow. An unfolding of the story we have to tell begins with current Affective Closeness of the parent–child relationship, tracing it back to the family of origin. We supplement this analysis with other adult characteristics of our G2 respondents, which also have roots in the family of origin, such as the personal trait of Expressivity, cited above, educational attainment, and religious intermarriage. Chapter 7 will show that early family variables have demonstrable persistent effects on the quality of the relationship between parents and adult children years later, and we will also provide several examples of cross-generational transmission from the family of origin to the families of procreation in this chapter.

The above discussion has dealt exclusively with empirical variables in the study design and how they relate to each other in a statistical sense, paving the way for a highly quantitative analysis in the three chapters to follow. But we can bring some of these variables to life by sharing our encounters with two very different respondents, women who represent two polar outliers in the statistical portrait of current parent–child relationships, just as they do in the very different kinds of families in which they grew up.

Case Profiles of Fractured and Highly Solidary Parent–Child Relations

Our encounter with these two "outlier" cases took place in the course of a single morning on a blustering November day in 1984, when we received telephone calls from the two women. We shall refer to the first caller by the pseudonym of Sally Smith, and the second caller by the pseudonym of Mary O'Connor. The women telephoned in response to our letter alerting them to the fact that an interviewer from the Boston Center for Survey Research would be ringing their doorbell one day soon. The letter suggested we would be happy to answer any questions they had about the study in advance of the interview, by phoning us collect in Amherst.

The reasons the women gave for phoning us were themselves indicative of their very different personalities and very different relationships with their own children. Both were women in their late 50s, living in the northern suburbs of Boston, but age, gender, and residential area were perhaps the only things the two women had in common. Sally Smith called to ask if we "really" wanted to interview her, in view of the fact that she had not seen either of her two children in more than a decade. Mary O'Connor called to assure us of her interest in the study, but to warn us that she would have no free time over the next 2 weeks because she was very busy preparing for a daughter's wedding. This was to be the "fourth" daughter's wedding she helped to organize, with "two more to go." It took very little encouragement to get either woman into an interesting and revealing conversation, in the course of which one could readily understand their very different initial inquiries. A sketch of what emerged in these conversations follows, supplemented by information from the personal interviews that were eventually obtained from each of the women.

Mary O'Connor is a woman of 57, happily married to an accountant in a state agency, and the mother of seven children: six daughters and one son. She was born in Somerville, Massachusetts where her widowed mother still lives, and now resides in a suburb she was attracted to because two of her sisters live there. Two of her married daughters live within a mile of her home, and she herself manages a household that includes her unmarried son and three daughters, one of whom would be married in 2 weeks. Her life is very much centered in family and parish activities, a counterpart to her husband's absorption in work, family, and Democratic Party politics.

A week after her daughter's wedding, Mrs. O'Connor was an eager and interested respondent in an interview that lasted over 2 hours, a consequence of her sociable nature and the fact that the interview schedule called for a detailed series of questions concerning each of her seven children. Several months later, Mrs. O'Connor's oldest 35-year-old daughter was also interviewed. The image that emerged from the two interviews with mother and daughter was of a highly cohesive family and kinship network, with much visiting and help exchanged between the generations, the roots of which go back to what the daughter recalled as a happy childhood with an affectionate, well-organized mother at its center. Mary O'Connor recalled a childhood of her own that sounded very similar, though her parents were much less well educated than she and her husband are, and there were persistent financial difficulties and stress caused by her father's alcoholism and periodic unemployment.

Mrs. O'Connor and her sisters are currently trying to persuade their mother to move out of her apartment in a rundown neighborhood of Somerville to an apartment closer to them in the suburbs. The elderly mother resists such a move because it would take her away from the church, neighborhood, and shops familiar to her for more than 60 years. There was a hint in Mrs. O'Connor's comments that her mother much preferred to have her several children visit her in the old neighborhood, taking pride in the eyes of her neighbors from the frequency of her children's visits.

A totally different picture emerged from the telephone conversation and interview with Sally Smith. Mrs. Smith is 59 years old, a very lonely and hypochondriac woman. To our initial astonishment, she informed us that the two children, one son and one daughter, whom she had not seen in more than a decade, lived in the Boston area. In between detailed descriptions of her various physical ailments, Mrs. Smith complained that neither child would visit her while she was in the hospital a few years earlier, despite the appeals of a social worker who traced them down and informed them of the serious nature of their mother's medical condition. A few probes led to the disclosure that the children had been removed from the family when they were 8 and 10 years of age by a social agency, because of severe physical abuse inflicted on them by their father. With some hesitation and appeals for sympathy, Mrs. Smith went on to explain that she had married a man very like her own father, who had beaten and abused her when she was a young girl. She left her family at the age of 17, and despite their residence in the same city, she did not see her father until his funeral 20 years later. Asked to provide us with addresses and telephone numbers for possible interviews with one of her children, Mrs. Smith demurred on the grounds that she had "lost" their addresses, and was quite sure they would not want to be interviewed anyway.

What was striking about these two women's accounts of their family life was not only the stark contrast they revealed between the currently stressed and fractured ties between the generations in the case of Sally Smith and the happy centering of social and emotional life in the intergenerational matrix of the O'Connor family, but the long-standing nature of this contrast, extending back in time not only to their early years of marriage and childrearing, but to the still earlier years when they themselves were growing up. There seemed to be a continuity of pattern that extended across at least three generations in the two lineages. Were our knowledge of these two women limited to a portrait of their lives and relations with their adult children in 1985, we would be hard-pressed to explain the marked contrast between them. It was only when depth was added to the current profiles by their descriptions of their early family life that the quality of their relations with their children today became meaningful.

We were both shaken and enthused by the fortuitous circumstance of encountering two such different women in the course of a single morning in the early field phase of the study: shaken by the pathos of the life story of Sally Smith, but enthused by the realization that our survey contained measures of both the present and past family experiences of our Boston respondents such that the central qualities and experiences of women such as Sally Smith and Mary O'Connor would be captured by our quantitative measures, and we could hopefully interpret the differences in current parent–child relations with variables on their early family life. A comparison of the notes on the telephone conversations with the responses on their questionnaires when they came in from the field contributed to our confidence in the instruments. On methodological grounds, a researcher hopes for a good deal of variance on the measures one devises, but in human terms, we hoped our measures would be skewed in the direction of more Mary O'Connors than Sally Smiths.

The circumstances impacting on human lives are of course far too complex to expect any exact replication of patterns in families of procreation that held in the same individuals' families of origin. Spouses are not typically replicas of parents; often they provide decided contrasts. Mary O'Connor mentioned as an aside that having grown up with an alcoholic father, she dropped any date who was even a moderate drinker long before the relationship took on any emotional overtone that suggested a possible marriage. Many who grew up in families hit hard by the depression of the 1930s reared their own children under more prosperous economic conditions, and their marriages and their children were accordingly spared the kind of stresses experienced by their parents in the earlier period. So too, many healthy, well-adjusted adults spent their childhood in pathological families. Indeed, precisely because they were separated from their families as quite young children, one hopes that Sally Smith's son and daughter have broken the pattern of child abuse so apparent in the grandparental and parental generations and that they are rearing children of their own in safe and happy homes.

Time and budgetary considerations precluded any expansion of our study design to conduct more qualitative interviews even with a subsample of our respondents, as we were tempted to do after the telephone encounters with Mary O'Connor and Sally Smith. We can only do our best to penetrate the quantitative data in such a way that we do not completely mask the private lives behind the numbers and graphs with which we had to be satisfied. It is to that task that the following chapters are devoted.

Notes

1.   There is a warning implicit in these findings: studies of multigenerational relations that require members of two or more generations from the same family to reside in the same community (often done to facilitate field work and lower research costs) are effectively biased against the inclusion of socially mobile generations in a lineage. Well-educated children in one generation will have moved a greater distance from their hometowns than their less-educated siblings have.

2.   In another analysis (data not shown) that compared sibling pairs from the same families with random pairs of children unrelated to each other, only one correlation of a set of 40 even verged on significance in the random pairs, whereas all correlations involving siblings were statistically significant. This suggests that however varied the relationship between parents and one child may be from their relationship to another child, these differences are within some parameter of similar parental styles of relating to children: Interfamily variance exceeds by far intrafamily variance in the relationships we have studied.

3.   We will explore this in more detail in a later chapter, but might mention here one reason for this pattern: Men seem more reluctant than women to report receiving advice, comfort, or money from their children, whereas children report giving these types of help to their fathers almost as often as they do to their mothers.

Affectional Ties: Past and Present _____ 7

"Life can only be understood backwards, but must be lived forward."
                                                    Kierkegaard

Introduction

To be the parents of adolescent children is to know despair and anxiety at first hand. What have we done wrong, parents of adolescents often ask themselves, to produce these young monsters, and how will we survive their adolescent years? Many parents wonder if they caused their own parents as much grief when they were adolescents. It is difficult for a parent of adolescent children to imagine that there are smooth waters ahead, or that their relationship will be transformed yet again when the children become responsible young adults.

Of course the extent of the difficulties experienced by parents of adolescent children, as by the adolescents themselves, reflects not only developmental change in the child, a process that occurs in all times and places, but the pace of social and political change in the larger society that has special impact on the young. We saw examples of this in Chapter 3, in the much sharper drop in the subjective closeness of adolescents and their parents when the child's adolescence took place during the turbulent 1970s rather than in the calmer political era of the 1950s. One or the other of our own children experimented with vegetarianism, Afro-hair styles, pot, sex, and radical politics during the 1970s. Although we shared their political views in campaigning against the Vietnam War, it was with an understanding that we would *not* march next to them in downtown Baltimore, because it would embarrass them in the eyes of their friends. In their view at the time, children were in opposition to, not in sympathy with, their parents' politics. Then,

273

too, those were the years of children's "rights," a time when our own children objected when we introduced them as "our children" to people who came to the house; their preference was to stick strictly to "our son and our daughters," not "our children." At the time, they were 10, 13, and 14.

We shall set the stage for the analysis to follow in this chapter by first charting the developmental profile of Affective Closeness between parents and their children across the life course. This will provide immediate comfort to any reader whose children are adolescents, because our data show a great increase in emotional closeness between the generations once the children are in their 20s. It will also illustrate the difference in perspective between a parent's and a child's view of the relationship.

In charting this developmental overview we will rely on mean scores on the Affective Closeness measure of Affectional Solidarity. The focus of the chapter, however, will be an exploration of *variation* in these ratings of parent–child closeness. That variation, following the model outlined in the preceding chapter (see Figure 6.1), is a function of what transpired during the early formative years when the children were growing up, together with experiences during the intervening years as the children completed schooling and became established in independent lives on their own. We posited that these early family characteristics interact with current social and personal characteristics of the parent and child and together increase the amount of variation we can explain in current Affective Closeness.

The organization of the chapter will be as follows. First, we present the life course overview of the emotional closeness between parents and children referred to above. Second, we will turn back in time to the families of origin in which our G2 respondents grew up. Because all our data were obtained in a single cross-sectional survey, the retrospective variables concerning the parents and the quality of early family life must be ordered in some meaningful way. Hence, we will propose a causal model that specifies a sequence of analyses that can explain variation in the degree to which the early family was a cohesive social unit or one fragmented by tension. In this same section on early family life, we will also analyze several other variables that will be brought into the analysis of contemporary relations between the generations in this chapter and those to follow. This will include a regression analysis of the personal traits of Expressivity and Dominance, the determinants of educational attainment of G2 men and women, and the characteristics of the relationship between parents and children that predispose to consensus or dissensus in life values.

The third and major topic of the chapter is the role of early family life variables in an interpretation of current Affective Closeness, to test whether past family variables have direct persistent effects on contemporary relationships over and above current circumstances and characteristics of the parents and the children. In addition to *persistence effects*, in which the past has direct influence on current profiles, we will also explore *cross-generational transmission*, in which the children in adulthood show characteristics *as parents* similar to those they reported concerning their own parents in the past. Among the factors we analyze in this regard are the level of cohesion in G2 respondents' families of procreation, the extent to which they have married someone of a different religious affiliation, and the transmission of traditional and countertraditional skills to their children.

The fourth section of the chapter concerns *intergenerational influence*. In both persistence effects of early family life and cross-generational transmission, the direction of effect is from the older parental generation to the younger child generation. But most parents and adult children are in frequent contact with each other; just as the quality of their relationship may change over time, and what they do with and for each other may be renegotiated in response to changes in needs and resources of the two generations, so too parents and children may influence the attitudes each holds on current issues of the day. We asked a variety of attitude questions on several such issues, including views toward abortion, contraceptive availability for teenagers, and women's rights. Respondents in each of the three samples were asked these attitude questions, which permits us to test whether the attitudes held by a parent or a child show any significant relationship to the other's views on an issue, net of a wide array of predisposing characteristics generally found to be predictive of liberal vs. conservative views on such issues.

The last topic in the chapter addresses the quality of the parental marriage and how this affects the parent–child relationship as well as the relationship between alternate generations. Analysis of normative obligations in Chapters 4 and 5 emphasized the significance of connecting links between ego and some specified kin person, e.g., that kin related to respondents through their mothers are more obligating to ego than kin related to them through their fathers. In this chapter we explore the emotional intimacy between parents and children under conditions of happy or unhappy parental marriages. We believe the reason mothers are so salient as connecting links is rooted in mother–child attachment; consequently we expected marital conflict or unhappiness would reduce the intimacy between children and their fathers, but not the intimacy of children with their mothers. We further extend this reasoning to the grandparent–grandchild relationship. Again, if mothers are critical emotional gatekeepers for their children, then their unhappiness in marriage should lead to lower levels of intimacy between children and their fathers' parents (paternal grandparents) but show no effect on their relations with their mothers' parents (maternal grandparents).

We turn now to the first task of the chapter: an examination of how the Affective Closeness of the relationship between parents and children changes over the life course.

Life Course Trajectory on Affective Closeness

The youngest of our G2 respondents is 19 years of age, but the emotional bond between parents and children begins at birth, not late adolescence. A full life course trajectory on intimacy should ideally chart this relationship from infancy through the childhood years and into adulthood. Since we were concerned for this fuller view, we asked G2 respondents to rate how close their relationship was to their mothers and fathers at three points in the past: when they were about 10 years of age, when they were 16, and when they were 25 (if they were older than 25 when they were interviewed). The reason for selecting these three time points was to provide "before" and "after" adolescence markers, to gauge the extent of the impact of the adolescent years on the relationship.

We can do better than simply relying on such retrospective ratings, however, because we also asked respondents to rate the intimacy of their relationship to *each* of their children, regardless of the child's age. Many respondents had young infants, others had school-age children, and others had only adult children. Hence, our first evidence of the life course trajectory in Affective Closeness comes from the childset file of data collected in the G2 interviews. Figure 7.1 therefore uses the chronological age of all the children of G2 respondents, divided into seven age groups, from infants through 7 years of age at the young end, to adult children over 40 years of age. (Case Ns did not permit any finer age distinction among the youngest and oldest age groups.) The trajectory is shown separately for each of the four parent–child dyads. Note that the "raters" in this figure are G2 women as mothers (for the Mother–Daughter and Mother–Son dyad) and G2 men as fathers (for the Father–Daughter and Father–Son dyad).

In all four dyads, there is a steady downward slope in average intimacy ratings from infancy to adolescence, though women report an earlier leveling out in their relationship to sons between 8 and 12 years of age, perhaps because prepubescent boys, in noisy play and fractious relations with peers and siblings, have already disturbed the domestic

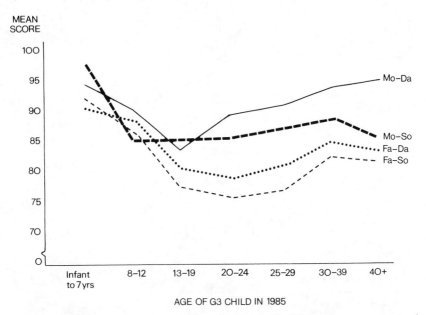

Figure 7.1. Affective closeness of G2 parents and G3 children by current age of G3 children and gender of parents and children (childset file, G2 sample). (Scores converted to 0–100 metric.)

setting and their interaction with their mothers. But up to the adolescent years, there are minor and insignificant differences in average intimacy scores across the four dyads, whereas from adolescence on, there is a growing gap between women's and men's ratings of intimacy with their adult children. By the time the adult children enter early middle age, the mother–daughter relationship stands out sharply as the dyad with the highest average score in Affective Closeness. By contrast, men as fathers do not report any quick recovery from the adolescent slump in intimacy. In fact, the low point in intimacy in their relationship to both sons and daughters is in the child's early 20s.

We must remember, however, that these are all contemporary ratings by parents in 1985. Their adult children in their 20s were adolescents in the 1970s, but the young adolescents shown in Figure 7.1 are adolescents in the 1980s, a much calmer sociopolitical era in the nation's history than the 1970s. In other words, there may be cohort effects entangled with life course developmental effects in the ratings given by G2 parents of adolescent and adult children in their 20s in 1985. This possibility is given some support when we examine the life course trajectory in intimacy with ratings provided by G2 respondents, not as parents, but as children.

In Figure 7.2, therefore, we show the average intimacy ratings that were given retrospectively for the ages of 10 and 16, followed by the

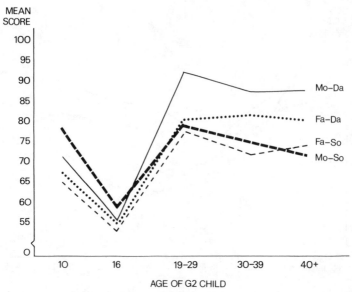

MEAN
SCORE

ᵃ Retrospective ratings for ages 10 and 16; actual current age of child in 1985 for 19 and older.

Figure 7.2. Affective closeness of G2 children and their G1 parents by age of the
child ᵃ and gender of parent and child (G2 sample). (Scores converted to 0–
100 metric.)

ratings in relationship to the actual ages of respondents in 1985. Since a
very large majority of our respondents are young adults in their 20s and
30s (reflecting the large size of their birth cohorts), the adolescent ratings
refer largely to the late 1960s and 1970s, and, accordingly, a decided
slump in the closeness they report to their parents, after which there is a
dramatic increase in the Affective Closeness ratings given by adult
children in their 20s. G2 sons and daughters show a slight decline in
their intimacy ratings for both parents with increasing age, but all four
dyads show much higher average scores as adult children than they
gave to their relationship with parents looking back to their adolescent
years.

One further point of interest can be seen by comparing the rank order
of the parent–child dyads in intimacy level in Figures 7.1 and 7.2: When
parents were the raters, as in Figure 7.1, mothers report higher average
intimacy levels toward both adult sons and daughters than fathers do,
whereas when the adult children were the raters, as in Figure 7.2,
daughters report higher average intimacy levels in their relationship
with both mothers and fathers than sons do. Whether a mother or a
daughter provided the rating, both show the highest intimacy is the
mother–daughter relationship. This suggests some tendency for women

to avow greater intimacy in all their relationships than men do; some men may even veer away from high ratings to avoid any hint of effeminacy.

On the other hand, men's behavior in family roles may involve an avoidance of high levels of intimacy, not just in their marital relationship, as Francesca Cancian reports (Cancian, 1987), but in their parental relationships as well. On the items in our Topic Avoidance index, men reported avoiding discussions of sex and personal problems with their children to a much greater extent than did women, and adult children themselves reported such avoidance with fathers more than with mothers (data not shown).

We did not ask G2 respondents to provide retrospective ratings of closeness for each of their children, although the children themselves, in the G3 spinoff sample, did so. But both G1 parents and G2 respondents as children provided the retrospective ratings for the earlier years. Hence, for the G1–G2 dyad, we can make a direct comparison of the ratings provided by parents and by children across the life course, using the retrospective ratings for the ages of 10 and 16, and actual current age of the children for the adult years. Figure 7.3 provides a graphic overview of the differences in perspectives of parents and children when they rate the intimacy of their relationship. Each parent–child dyad is shown separately in Panels A through D, with the ratings given by the parents shown by the solid lines and those by the adult child shown by the dashed lines. It is clear in all four panels that parents rate their relationship higher on the Affective Closeness scale than adult children do, with the difference far greater in the retrospective ratings than in the current ratings.

All adult children report a sharp adolescent slump in intimacy, as do parents with the single exception of G1 fathers' ratings of their relationship to their sons. G2 fathers *did* show a downward slope in intimacy during their G3 sons' adolescence, even though these sons were adolescents during the mid-1980s (in Figure 7.1); hence, it is puzzling why G1 fathers did not also do so. That this is not a statistical artifact is suggested by another finding consistent with this result. We asked respondents to rate not only their own relationship to each child, but that of their spouses, and we found a confirming result: G1 women report no drop in average intimacy scores for their husbands' relationship to their sons during adolescence. It is conceivable that men *assume* a greater camaraderie exists with sexually mature sons than with younger sons, and women may share that assumption about the father–son relationship, but our data do not suggest that sons themselves hold that view.

We believe one reason for the discrepant ratings of intimacy during the earlier years between parents and adult children is the very different

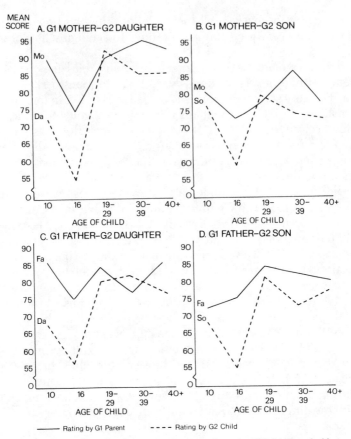

^a Retrospective ratings for ages 10 and 16; actual age in 1985 for 19 and older.

Figure 7.3. G1 parent vs. G2 child rating of affective closeness by age of G2 child[a] (G1 and G2 samples). (Scores converted to 0–100 metric.)

anchor points a parent and child have for assessing their relationship in emotional terms. The anchor point for parents may be the very early years of the child's life, when they as parents held 24-hour supervisory responsibility for the infant and young child's welfare, intimate knowledge through monitoring all the child's body functions, and keen interest in every development milestone the child passed. From that anchor point, each developmental stage represents a departure from total, intimate knowledge of the child, and it becomes the parent's responsibility to encourage those steps of independence and separation for the child's own good.

By contrast, the anchor point or standard of judgment for adult children may be the years of conscious self-awareness in puberty and adolescence when they were first "trying their wings" in independent forays into the larger world around them. Once they achieve that independence in their 20s, and have learned themselves what parenting entails, the adult child may experience a resurgence of warmth and sympathy toward their parents and negotiate a relationship on a rather different basis as mature adults. These quite different life stage anchor points lurk behind the discomfort many adults feel when their parents talk about them as babies, much less show pictures of them in the nude as infants. Two of our children tore up such nude baby pictures of themselves, even as they paraded about the house nude and enjoyed skinnydipping in the pool.

The data presented thus far are restricted to central tendency average scores. We will be in a better position to interpret them when we turn to variation in Affective Closeness ratings in the earlier years, by drawing on variables characterizing the parents and the family as a social unit during those early years. Hence, it is to early family life that we next turn.

Early Family Life

Analysis Model

Our first task in approaching the data on the families of origin of our G2 respondents was to specify a reasonable model of how the various characteristics of the family relate to each other in a causal sense. A family unit can be specified in terms of individual traits of its members as well as a more global measure of the family as a social group. Anticipating the analysis of the persistence effects of early family life, we developed the global measure of Family Cohesion. It will be recalled that the items in this index refer to open displays of affection among family members, working together well as a team, doing interesting things together, and finding home a fun place to be. We considered affection, teamwork, and pleasure in being together to be major characteristics of family structure that describe highly "cohesive" social units, while their absence would be indicative of a fragmented and friction-prone family group. We also reasoned that in giving these general ratings of their families of origin, respondents would have in mind their families as they experienced them in late childhood and early adolescence. Hence, we defined Family Cohesion as our endpoint variable in the causal sequence. The measure also impressed us as a good global rating for the analysis of cross-generational transmission.

The early predictors of Family Cohesion, we suggest, are a variety of other characteristics, including the qualities the parents brought to their marriage, and events that transpire during the early years of marriage. We therefore consider the earliest predictors of Family Cohesion to be the qualities the parents brought to their marriage. For most adults, schooling is completed prior to marriage, and therefore educational attainment is viewed as a stable, early characteristic that in time partly determines the socioeconomic status of the family.

We also assumed that parents bring personal capacities to their marriages that are relevant to the successful development of a cohesive family unit. High among such relevant capacities are the abilities to show affection and to run households smoothly. It was for this reason that we developed indices of parental Affection and Authority, separately for mothers and fathers, because men and women typically differ on these qualities, and our study was to focus explicitly on gender of parent and of child. Few adults can by sheer volition change themselves from reserved and self-centered creatures into affectionate, outgoing parents, or from organized, work-compulsive men and women into overly permissive parents and sloppy householders, or vice versa. Hence, we assume the personal qualities measured by the indices on Maternal and Paternal Affection, and Maternal and Paternal Authority, are rooted in persistent, personal traits of the adults that are in place at the time they married. We view these qualities of the parents as important determinants of the quality of the relationship they establish with their children, and therefore expect the level of parental affection to be strongly related to the children's ratings of how close they were to each of their parents when they were 10 and 16 years of age.

There is another assumption underlying our use of the parental Affection indices as personal traits adults bring to their marriage. The indices are confined to the parental role, not general personality measures. It seems highly likely, however, that adults high in parental affection are also emotionally accessible, openly expressive individuals as wives or husbands, friends or neighbors. Some support for this assumption is found in the correlations between the parental affection indices and the personal trait measure on Expressivity. Most of the analysis to follow is based on our largest possible case base that permits separate analyses of the four parent–child dyads: the G1–G2 dyads and the G2–G3 dyads, with data from the G2 respondents in both instances. We obtained Expressivity ratings from the G2 respondents, which can be used as a child characteristic in the G1–G2 dyad and a parent characteristic in the G2–G3 dyad. G1 parents also provided such self-ratings on Expressivity, but the measure is available only for the small spinoff sample of parents. There are too few cases when spinoff samples are divided into four parent–child dyads to sustain the multivariate analyses we wish to conduct. But the correlation coefficient between G2 ratings on Maternal Affection and the G1 mothers' own ratings on Expressivity was a highly significant .42, thus lending some support to the assumption that the parental affection measures tap general personal traits, not merely role-specific traits.

Figure 7.4 provides a graphic overview of the causal pathways between the characteristics we assume G1 parents brought to their marriage and the final outcome variable of Family Cohesion. The " − " and " + " signs at the arrowheads indicate the direction of effect we assume, e.g., a positive effect of educational attainment on financial well-being of the family, or the negative effect of family size on financial well-being. The model includes other important characteristics of the family of origin that intervene between the parents' marriage and the assessment of Family Cohesion: the size of the family, typically set down in the first decade or so of marriage; the financial well-being of the family; the Family Troubles index; a rating of marital happiness of the parents during the years G2 respondents were growing up; whether the family remained Intact or not (used as a dummy variable at several points in the analysis below); and the Affective Closeness of the parent–child relationship during childhood and adolescence.

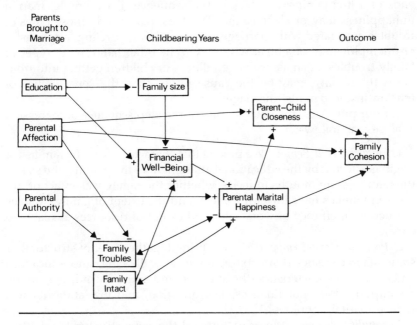

Figure 7.4. Model of causal pathways to cohesiveness of family of origin.

We assume that in rating the financial well-being of their families, most respondents had in mind the late years of childhood and adolescence, when family income level affects whether the child can have or do many of the things youngsters demand of their parents. As we also know, income rises during the early years of marriage and childrearing; by the time most respondents reached their teens, their parents were likely to have reached a crest on the earnings curve that is typical of midlife, as shown in Chapter 3. By that point, the educational attainment of the parents will be highly significant in its effect on the size of a breadwinner's paycheck. Since children are born early in a marriage, we further assume that both income potential measured by educational attainment and family size influence the financial well-being of the family unit as it was reported by G2 adult children. Hence, for example, one pathway is from low educated parents who have larger families and are, as a result, less well off financially, which in turn reduces marital happiness. Low marital happiness will affect all family relationships; hence, we posit the pathway from marital happiness of the parents to the Affective Closeness of parent–child relations and the level of cohesion of the total family unit.

There are less certain grounds for positing any causal sequence among several variables shown in Figure 7.4, as shown by arrowheads at both ends of a line joining variables in the sequence. For example, marital unhappiness may produce Family Troubles, particularly those types of troubles associated with marriage such as adult quarreling, alcoholism, or unemployment of a breadwinner. On the other hand, other types of family troubles, such as prolonged illness or children getting into trouble with the law, may be the cause rather than the consequence of tension in the parents' marriage.

For our purposes, the data permit a three-step sequence of regression analyses, as follows:

1. *Financial Well-Being*: We predict this characteristic of the families of origin is affected by the educational attainment of the parents, the size of the family (more mouths to feed), whether the family was intact or not (broken families have lower incomes), and the extent of family troubles (reduction of efficacy of work roles and extent of resources available to cope).

2. *Parents' Marital Happiness*: We bring together a set of structural or status characteristics (family size, financial well-being, and education) and affective characteristics (the affection and authority indices), on the assumption that poor finances, low affection, and low authority will reduce marital happiness.

3. *Family Cohesion*: We bring forward the same structural and affec-

Table 7.1. Regression on Financial Well-Being of
Families of Origin of G2 Adults (G2 Sample)

Predictor Variable	Beta Coefficient
Father's Education	.26***
Mother's Education	.10***
Intact Family (dummy variable)	.14***
Family Size	− .08**
Extent of Family Troubles	− .07**
R^2	**.17***
N	(1056)

*** p < .001
** p < .01

tive characteristics as in the marital happiness equation, together with
the marital happiness rating itself and the Family Troubles index.

We report the results of this analysis in Tables 7.1 through Table 7.3.
Note that all the data are from G2 respondents concerning their families
of origin in Tables 7.1 and 7.3, but in Table 7.2 on parents' marital
happiness, we also show a replication of the analysis using data from G3
respondents concerning their G2 parents' marriage.

Financial Well-Being of Family of Origin

The results shown in Table 7.1 confirm our prediction, with all five
variables significantly affecting the financial well-being of G2 respondents' families of origin. Higher educational attainment of the parents
and the retention of an intact family increase the financial well-being of
the family, whereas family size and extensive family troubles depress
the financial well-being of the family. Sheer size of the family is of
obvious relevance, since the larger the number of children, the further
family income had to be stretched. The greater the number of troubles
the family had, the less well off financially the family was: illness,
emotional instability, unemployment, exhausting jobs, or a death in the
family are the particular items in the Family Troubles index that impact
on the financial well-being of the family (data not shown).

Marital Happiness of Parents

In the regression analysis of parents' marital happiness during their
years of rearing our G2 respondents, we bring forward the educational
attainment of the parents, family size, and financial well-being, now

joined by four affective measures that tap the internal roles and personal qualities of the parents as measured by the Affection and Authority indices. The results are shown in Table 7.2. Panel A shows the results for the G1 parents' and Panel B for the G2 parents' marital happiness. The same profile is shown in both panels: Educational attainment has no direct effect, presumably absorbed by financial well-being. Both Maternal and Paternal Affection are the most significant predictors of marital happiness in the eyes of the two generations of adult children. An affectionate nature is clearly not role specific, but suffuses all family relationships. Note too that Paternal Affection is the stronger of the two affection measures, implying that affectionate men set the emotional tone in the marriage, to which children are sensitive in rating how happy their parents were in their marriage while the children were growing up. Of course, it is also possible that women may be more openly affectionate toward their children than to their husbands, whereas men capable of open expressions of affection will do so toward both children and wives. Not all men, but probably all children, welcome such open displays of love and affection.[1]

Maternal Authority also contributes to parental happiness in marriage, whereas Paternal Authority does not, at least not in the eyes of the

Table 7.2. Regressions on Parents' Marital Happiness While Children were Growing Up: G2 Children re G1 Marital Happiness, and G3 Children re G2 Marital Happiness (Beta Coefficients) (G2 and G3 Samples)

Predictor Variables	A G2 Children re G1 Parents' Marriage	B G3 Children re G2 Parents' Marriage
Structural Characteristics		
Financial Well-Being	.17*	.12*
Mother's Education	.02	−.07
Father's Education	.01	−.04
Family Size	.01	−.03
Affective Characteristics		
Maternal Affection	.19***	.16*
Paternal Affection	.41***	.40***
Maternal Authority	.07**	.08*
Paternal Authority	.01	.05
R^2	.33***	.25***
N	(1056)	(236)

*** p < .001
** p < .01
* p < .05

children. From the perspective of both G2 and G3 adult children, loving fathers, and firm, well-organized mothers are associated with their perception of the marital happiness of their parents. Mothers who impose rules, get children to share routine chores, and apply sanctions when children misbehave may contribute to an orderly, calm household, with more positive consequences for marital happiness than when fathers impose discipline, assign chores, and are strict with the children.

Cohesion of Family of Origin

The third step in the regression sequence is shown in Table 7.3. The combined effect of the structural and affective predictor variables is a highly significant R^2 of .52, one of the highest in the entire study. Happily married parents, both of whom are very affectionate to the children and presumably to each other, being an intact family with both parents present, reporting few or no family troubles, the presence of mothers who exercise authority in childrearing and home maintenance, and having a large family all contribute significant, independent effects on the level of cohesion of these families of origin. Large sized families may press on the financial resources of a household, but they enhance rather than reduce the cohesiveness of the family.

Table 7.3. Regression on Cohesion of Families of Origin of G2 Adults (G2 Sample)

Predictor Variables	Beta Coefficients
Structural/Status Characteristics of Family of Origin	
Intact Family (Dummy Variable)	.14***
Size of Family of Origin	.05*
Financial Well-Being	.01
Mother's Education	.01
Father's Education	− .00
Affective Characteristics of Family of Origin	
Marital Happiness of Parents	.33***
Maternal Affection	.23***
Paternal Affection	.26***
Maternal Authority	.09***
Paternal Authority	− .03
Extent of Family Troubles	− .15***
R^2	**.52***
N	(1073)

*** $p < .001$
* $p < .05$

Parents' vs. Children's Perspective on Family Cohesion

What we have seen thus far about determinants of Family Cohesion is based on reports from adults looking back to their childhood and adolescent years. During those years, children do not carry responsibility for financial well-being, neither do they decide what routines will be followed in domestic maintenance, nor determine the emotional tone of the household. Children are "acted on" by the adults who guide their development and determine the social–emotional climate of a household. Hence, it is an open question whether the same determinants of Family Cohesion would be found when parents themselves report on the early years of their own childrearing. An adult's family of procreation is primarily an adult world, rooted in a marriage and the work of maintaining a home and rearing children. This may seem odd to a young parent coping with the abrupt change in household routine that attends the birth of a first child. But for the long haul, parents make efforts to live, work, and socialize as adults, quite apart from their childrearing responsibilities. They are the primary actors setting the tone of a family; and in judging how cohesive the family was as a social unit, they may be far less influenced by qualities of their own parenting than by the quality of the marriage, the ease and comfort of their standard of living, and the extent to which they are coping with problems produced by family members, whether that concerns children, a spouse, or themselves.

By contrast, the memories of early family life that children consider most salient from their perspective will be those attributes that impinge most directly on them as the dependent members of the family group, sensitive and responsive to the demands placed on them by parents, by the accessibility of their parents when they need them, and the affection shown toward them by their parents.

Evidence of the difference made by whose perspective and ratings are being used in judging the cohesiveness of the early family can be seen in Table 7.4, where we explicitly compare the profile of determinants of Family Cohesion with data from parents with that from adult children. As we did in the analysis of parental marital happiness, we replicate the identical regression analysis for two parent–child dyads, shown in Panel A (G1 Parent and G2 Child) and Panel B (G2 Parent and G3 Child). Within each panel, the first equation (1) shows the results with data from the adult children and the second equation (2) shows the results with data from the parents. Note that this restricts the case base of all equations, because we omit G2 respondents whose parent (or child) was *not* included in the spinoff samples.

The results fulfill an analyst's dream of consistency in research find-

Table 7.4. Regressions on Family Cohesion:[a] "G2 Child vs. G1 Parent Rating of Cohesion and G3 Child vs. G2 Parent Rating of Cohesion (Beta Coefficients) (G1, G2, and G3 Samples)

Predictor Variables	A. G1 Parent–G2 Child		B. G2 Parent–G3 Child	
	G2 Child Rating (1)	G1 Parent Rating (2)	G3 Child Rating (1)	G2 Parent Rating (2)
Structural Characteristics of Family				
Intact (dummy)	.09*	−.01	−.01	−.03
Financial Well-Being	.02	−.11*	.03	−.11*
Family Size	.04	.05	−.02	.02
Mother's Education	−.09*	.03	.08	.11
Father's Education	.09*	−.02	−.07	−.04
Affective Characteristics of Family				
Marital Happiness of Parents	.35***	.35***	.43***	.20***
Maternal Affection	.28***	−.08	.24***	−.06
Paternal Affection	.21***	.02	.12*	.11
Maternal Authority	.10**	.03	.10*	.10
Paternal Authority	−.12*	−.05	−.11*	−.08
Family Troubles	−.09*	−.17*	−.01	−.29***
R^2	.60***	.13***	.40***	.19***
N	(292)	(292)	(236)	(236)

[a] The Family Cohesion rated is family of origin from point of view of G2 and G3 adults as children and family of procreation from point of view of G1 and G2 adults as parents.

*** $p < .001$

** $p < .01$

* $p < .05$

ings: The same profile of significant determinants is found for both the G1–G2 and the G2–G3 dyads. From the perspective of both G2 and G3 adult children (equations A1 and B1), the qualities of parents *as parents* are strong predictors of Family Cohesion. If the parents were happily married, if both parents were highly affectionate toward the child, and if mothers were high and fathers low on authority, adult children rate their families of origin to have been highly cohesive.

Family cohesion is explained on quite different grounds from the parents' perspective as they look back to their childrearing years; again, the profile holds for both dyads (equations A2 and B2). The affective and authoritative aspects of the parental role fall away, and, in their stead, it is the quality of the marital relationship and the absence of serious family troubles that loom as the most significant predictors. Somewhat surprisingly, Financial Well-being shows a modest effect, but in a direction the opposite of expectation: It is being *less* well-off financially that is associated with high Family Cohesion. We have previously shown that educational attainment of the parents increases financial well-being, which in turn contributes to marital happiness. In Table 7.4, however, all three variables are in the equations (education, financial well-being, and marital happiness), so the importance of the direction of effect must be viewed in terms of "net" effects, independent of other related variables. The results suggest that net of education and marital happiness, some part of very poor financial circumstances may involve greater cooperation among family members in maintaining a home, and creating good times at minimal cost by relying on their own resources for leisure time activities. Together, these characteristics may turn a family inward to each other, and by that means contribute a small increment to the cohesiveness of the family as a social group.

Affective Closeness to Parents from Childhood to Early Adulthood

Now that we have seen how the several dimensions of early family life relate to each other, we can return to the issue of gender differences in the Affective Closeness of parents and children during the critical developmental passage from childhood to early adulthood. The rationale for the inclusion of retrospective ratings on Affective Closeness at 10, 16, and 25 years of age (for those over 25) was to enclose the more turbulent years of adolescence with the calmer developmental periods of childhood and early adulthood. The analysis goal was to test the extent to which parent and family characteristics contribute to an explanation of variance in emotional closeness of parents and young children and adolescents, and eventually to test whether the current relations between the generations bear the mark of earlier formative experiences, in particular whether any adolescent "slump" in intimacy shows a continuing impact on the quality of the parent–child relationship years later.

Several ideas determined the formulation of this step in our analysis of early family life:

1. Parental affection should be a relatively stable characteristic of the relationship with children. In other words, if affectionate parents establish strong and positive attachments with children during early childhood, this is an emotional "headstart" that will persist despite developmental crises during adolescence and the transition to adulthood.

2. Family troubles may reach their peak precisely during the children's adolescent years. Even the calmest family and the best marriage can be severely tested when children become adolescents. Because male adolescents are more prone to engage in socially deviant behavior during adolescence than female adolescents, we expect the Family Troubles index to show a greater effect in lowering the Affective Closeness of sons to their parents than of daughters.

3. Adolescence may be a particularly trying time for well-educated parents, precisely because they have encouraged the development of independence and autonomy in their children. To the extent they have succeeded in inculcating such qualities in their children, adolescence may involve more risk-taking and testing of the limits of parental tolerance and patience in families headed by well-educated parents than in families headed by less well-educated parents. By contrast, to the extent less well-educated parents have succeeded in instilling social conformity in their children, adolescence may involve less risk-taking and more compliance to social norms on the part of the children. Consequently, we predict parents' educational attainment level would be negatively related to intimacy in the parent–child relationship, particularly during adolescence.

4. Closely related to point (3) above, we reasoned that having a number of children could provide a buffer against overly disturbed relations with adolescent children, both because parents will have had more experience with seeing children through the adolescent years, and because having many children lowers the intensity of response to the behavior of any particular child.

5. Last, the age difference between children and their parents was a likely source of variation in the quality of the relationship between parents and children, perhaps of particular relevance during the adolescent years. Earlier research by one of the authors (A. S. Rossi, 1980) concerned the impact of maternal age on intimacy in the mother's relationship to early adolescent children. That study relied on mothers' ratings of intimacy with children between 12 and 15 years of age. In the present dataset, we expected closer relations between mothers and

daughters, and fathers and sons, the smaller the age difference between them, on the grounds of greater ease in sharing of activities and interests and less sharp value differences. But we were not sure how cross-gender parent–child relations might be impacted by the age difference variable, if at all.

Table 7.5 shows the results of this analysis. Panel A provides the equations for the Affective Closeness of mothers and daughters (equation 1) and mothers and sons (equation 2), and Panel B provides the equations on Affective Closeness between fathers and daughters (1) and fathers and sons (2). Within each of the four parent–child dyads the proximate columns provide the equations for the three points on the life course trajectory: at 10, 16, and 25 years of age.

Parental Affection is a highly significant predictor of Affective Closeness in all four dyads, most strongly so in childhood, and with declining but still significant effects by the time the child is an adult of 25, i.e., with each older age, in all four dyads, the coefficient on Maternal and Paternal Affection declines in size but not statistical significance. The declining weight of parental affection is no doubt developmentally related to the emergence of other salient family and parent characteristics as the child grows in maturity. Thus, for example, several predictor variables are *only* statistically significant in explaining variance in Affective Closeness during adolescence: This is true for Family Troubles, parental Authority, family size, and the age difference between parent and child. All four parent–child dyads show the most significant coefficients on Family Troubles during the child's adolescence. Many adolescent children are the *source* of elevated Family Troubles, and our data suggest this involves daughters as well as sons. Note, however, that the largest beta coefficient is found in the father–son dyad while the son was an adolescent, perhaps reflecting the more significant role fathers play in evaluating and disciplining adolescent sons. However, not all the predictor variables are significant in all four dyads, and it is worth noting the specific pattern among several of them.

Take, for example, parental Authority; the signs are negative in all 12 equations, but reach particular significance only in the relationship of daughters to both mothers and fathers. The higher the authority exercised by both mothers and fathers, the less close the G2 daughters report they were to both parents when they were 16 years of age. We suspect parental concern for newly sexually mature daughters may stimulate an increase in rules and restrictions on the daughter at this age, whereas adolescent sons are typically permitted greater latitude. It may also be that adolescent daughters are charged with greater responsibility for domestic chores, with the result that more adolescent daughters than sons chafed at their duties at home and parental supervision of their social life.

As predicted, family size shows a consistently positive effect on parent–child Affective Closeness, but this is a statistically significant effect only in mother–child relationships, not father–child relationships. In the everyday life of a family, mothers tend to spend more time with children than fathers do; consequently, as the children mature, they may also share more activities with their mothers, often aiding her in discharging household duties. Women from large sibsets are particularly prone to report intimate relations with their mothers, perhaps because the older among them served in a special way as sib caregivers to ease their mothers' household duties.

Our core idea concerning the effect of parental education is also borne out by the results: Educational attainment of the parents shows a consistent pattern of negative coefficients on Affective Closeness between the generations, especially during adolescence. Children of less well-educated parents report greater Affective Closeness than children of well-educated parents. As suggested above, adolescence would be a far stormier period in a family that encouraged independence and autonomy in the child, because the adolescent will be attracted to experimentation and risk taking, testing the limits of parental tolerance even while the parents have encouraged precisely the qualities that predispose the child in this direction. It may also be the case that well-educated parents know the importance of "letting go" to encourage the adolescent's growth, and hence withdraw to some degree from intense and intimate relations despite the tension and anxiety such a "hands-off" stance involves.

The cohesiveness of the family of origin shows a consistently positive contribution to intimacy in the parent–child relationship, though only significantly so in early adulthood. We consider this finding important for two reasons: For one, our treatment of this global rating of the family as an "outcome" variable in earlier analysis is consistent with its increasing significance as time passes and childrearing is finished. By contrast, many factors that depress Family Cohesion have yet to develop when children are only 10 years of age. Second, the results suggest that cohesion of the family of origin may have a "sleeper effect," activated when children become adults on their own and can evaluate the kind of family they grew up in from a new angle of vision: If children experienced a cooperative, happy family, as adults the generations are drawn closer together; if early family life was strained, relations between the generations are less close a decade or more later, or remain at the level they were during the stressed adolescent years.

An interesting reversal shows up in the effect of age differences

Table 7.5. Regression on Affective Closeness of G2 Children and Their G1 Parents at 10, 16 and 25 Years of Age by Gender of Parent and Child (G2 Sample)

A. CLOSENESS TO G1 MOTHERS

Predictor Variables	(1) G2 Daughters (Mo–Da)			(2) G2 Sons (Mo–So)		
	At 10	At 16	At 25	At 10	At 16	At 25
Characteristics of Mother						
Maternal Affection	.59***	.52***	.38***	.46***	.42***	.38***
Maternal Authority	-.07	-.08+	-.07	-.04	-.05	-.01
Mother's Education	-.03	-.17***	-.12**	-.11*	-.16***	-.03
Age Difference: Mother–Child	.02	-.01	-.01	-.02	-.01	-.11*
Characteristics of Family						
Extent of Troubles	-.06	-.12**	-.02	-.03	-.15**	-.11
Family Cohesion	.08	.06	.28**	.12+	.06	.17**
Family Size	.07	.12*	.06	.01	.10+	.13**
R^2	.43***	.42***	.34***	.29***	.30***	.27***
N	(286)	(286)	(272)	(240)	(240)	(227)

B. CLOSENESS TO G1 FATHERS

Predictor Variables	(1) G2 Daughters (Fa–Da)			(2) G2 Sons (Fa–So)		
	At 10	At 16	At 25	At 10	At 16	At 25
Characteristics of Father						
Paternal Affection	.59***	.58***	.45***	.55***	.60***	.41***
Paternal Authority	−.04	−.11**	−.02	−.03	−.01	−.01
Father's Education	−.03	−.10**	−.10**	−.07	−.15***	−.04
Age Difference: Father–Child	.08*	.11**	.01	−.08+	−.16*	−.01
Characteristics of Family						
Extent of Troubles	−.08	−.12***	−.07	−.10*	−.17***	−.02
Family Cohesion	.08	.08	.15**	.09	.12*	.18**
Family Size	.05	.05	.03	−.01	.02	.03
R^2	.44***	.48***	.33***	.41***	.43***	.30***
N	(286)	(286)	(272)	(240)	(240)	(227)

*** p < .001
** p < .01
* p < .05
+ p < .10

between parents and children. As predicted, this takes on special significance only during the adolescence of the child, but has an opposite effect on the father–son relationship than on the father–daughter relationship. The closer in age fathers and sons are, the higher the Affective Closeness rating of their relationship, perhaps because a son can enjoy active sports and other masculine activities with a younger father more readily than with an older father.

The situation is very different in the case of daughters, who were closer to their fathers the *greater* the age difference between them. A father who was 22 when a daughter was born will only be 38 when the daughter celebrates her sixteenth birthday, whereas a father who was 38 when she was born, will be 54 when she turns 16.[2] In a society with many June–December sexual pairs, a sexually mature daughter of 16 may find it much more comfortable to relate in an intimate way with a 54-year-old father than a 38-year-old father. That this finding is not unique to a daughter's perspective is suggested by our finding the same positive effect of age difference between fathers and daughters when the intimacy ratings were given by G2 respondents as fathers of G3 daughters.[3]

A final note on the results reported in Table 7.5: A considerable amount of variance in Affective Closeness between parents and children is explained by the characteristics of the parents and the family, with the highest R^2 values shown for the adolescent years, followed by a significant drop in the amount of explained variance by 25 years of age, an indication that as children move into adulthood, a new set of factors become relevant influences on the intimacy of the relationship to parents. We will explore what these influences are in a later section of the chapter.

One of the more important experiences that intervene between 16 and 25 years of age is finishing school and becoming established in some line of work. We know from sociological research that many aspects of a family provide either a headstart or a handicap to the eventual educational attainment of children (Blau & Duncan, 1967; Sewell & Hauser, 1975). As part of our effort to explore the impact of early family life, we turn now to an analysis of the determinants of educational attainment of G2 respondents.

Family Influence on Educational Attainment of Children

Educational aspirations are laid down during the years spent in junior and senior high school, when children are residing with their parents and exploring alternate goals for their lives. College attendance decisions are made while adolescents are still strongly influenced by parental values and aspirations for the child. Using many of our measures on the family of origin, we explore their contribution to individual variance in educational attainment among our G2 respondents.

Toward this end, we regress a variety of structural and affective characteristics of G2 adults' early family circumstances on their educational attainment. Many of the family variables now familiar from analysis reported above have been significant variables in sociological studies of status attainment: the educational level of the parents, the financial well-being of the family during the years children were growing up, whether the family was Catholic, whether the parental marriage was intact or broken by separation, divorce, or the death of a parent, and the size of the family.

The family size variable has been the focus of recent research by Judith Blake (1987, 1989), who attempted to explain why status attainment research has long found that the larger the family, the lower the educational attainment of children, net of the obvious controls for the socioeconomic status of the family and school achievement by the children. Blake's central thesis was that parental investment is diluted as family size increases: Since there are limitations on the time parents can devote to their children, the more children they have, the less the amount of time the parent will spend in interaction with each child.[4]

The family variables included in the regression equations are ratings of the extent to which G2 respondents' parents set high standards for them, emphasized Cognitive Skills by teaching and monitoring their reading and arithmetic performance, and taught them Domestic Skills; the retrospective rating of Affective Closeness in the parent–child relationship when the G2 respondents were 16-year-old adolescents; and the parental Affection and Authority indices.[5]

To control for the cohort effect in educational attainment, age of the G2 respondents is included in the equation as well, because our purpose is to assess how much variance in educational attainment is explained by the affective quality of family life and parental skill transmission, net of cohort and social status characteristics of the families of origin. Since the determinants of educational attainment may vary between sons and daughters, the analysis was done separately for G2 men and women.

Table 7.6 shows the results of this regression analysis. As expected from the tradition of status attainment research, family size is a highly significant predictor of educational attainment, net of parents' education or religious affiliation. The educational attainment of the same-sex parent is more influential than that of the opposite-sex parent: The educational attainment of fathers contributes more than that of mothers to

Table 7.6. Regression of Educational Attainment of G2 Respondents
           on Structural and Affective Characteristics of Family of Origin
           by Gender of G2 Adults (Beta Coefficients) (G2 Sample)

Family of Origin Predictor Variables	G2 Women	G2 Men
Status Characteristics		
Mother's Education	.26***	.10
Father's Education	.21***	.23***
Family Size	−.16***	−.18***
Family Intact [a]	.13***	.10**
Mother Catholic [a]	−.04	−.12***
Financial Well-Being	−.03	−.02
Affective Characteristics		
Parents Set High Standards	.18***	.15***
Parents Emphasized Cognitive Skills	.06+	.15***
Parents Emphasized Domestic Skills	−.06	.01
Affective Closeness to Parents at 16 Years of Age	.07*	−.03
Parental Affection	−.07*	−.04
Parental Authority	−.07*	−.18***
Current age (control)	−.13***	.06
R^2	.42***	.37***
N	(594)	(454)

[a] Dummy variables: Intact = 1, Broken = 0; Catholic = 1, Noncatholic = 0.
*** $p < .001$
** $p < .01$
* $p < .05$
+ $p < .10$

sons' educational attainment, and mothers are more significant than
fathers for daughters' educational attainment.

Growing up in an intact family also contributes to children's educational attainment. That this family characteristic is significant, while
financial well-being is not, suggests there are other aspects of growing
up with both natural parents that are relevant here: Building on the
concept of parental investment, this argues that two parents can simply
provide each child with more attention, adult modeling, and interaction
than one parent can, an extension of Blake's diluted parental investment
thesis. A Catholic religious affiliation among G1 mothers shows a strong
negative coefficient on sons' educational attainment, but no significant
effect in the case of daughters. This suggests that Catholic mothers may
have focused their maternal investment in their sons on intimacy and
religious values, which may "hold" sons close to the family at the
expense of social mobility through education.[6]

Several of the affective characteristics of early family life are highly
significant predictors of educational attainment. Parents who set high
standards for their children and who emphasized cognitive skills con-

tribute to higher educational attainment by their children. This pattern is consistent with previous status attainment research. More interesting, and less predictable, is the finding that Affective Closeness during adolescence, and parental Affection and Authority show six *negative* coefficients in the two equations, four of them significantly so. G2 adults who acquired a high level of education come from families in which parents were *not* highly affectionate toward them, and neither punished children for wrongdoing nor involved children in regular household chores. (Indeed, low Parental Authority is second only to father's education as a predictor of sons' educational attainment!) Allowing children to have considerable freedom of choice in how they manage their own time implies an encouragement of self-reliance and responsibility, as does less closeness in the relationship between parents and adolescents, particularly daughters. This cluster of characteristics suggests such children had parental permission to explore a larger social world and to acquire values and goals that differed from the parents', thus starting them off on an autonomous path in life, for which higher educational attainment provides an important first step.

Lastly, these combined status and affective predictor variables explain somewhat more variance in educational attainment of women than of men (R^2 of .42 vs. .37), the reverse of most status attainment results, which typically explain more of the variance in educational attainment of men than of women. The reason for this may lie in the inclusion of measures on the quality of family relations and parental styles (of greater relevance to daughters' aspirations), whereas status attainment research has concentrated on cognitive and social status variables (of greater relevance to sons' aspirations).

Standing back from this analysis suggests a built-in tension between what families do that encourages warmth, concern for others, close intergenerational relations in the sphere of family and kinship, and what families do to produce competence, independence, and social mobility of children. That is to say, occupational success and social mobility may be attained at the expense of embeddedness in family life and intimate ties between the generations. Parental authority may impose adherence to routines, encourage social conformity, and provide children with the skills needed to run smooth households of their own in later years, but the same parental authority seems to reduce the educational and occupational success of the next generation. An interesting implication of this pattern is that intimacy with parents in youth and adolescence may pave the way for harmonious relations with elderly parents at a later stage of the life course, whereas children with less close ties to parents in their youth continue with more attenuated relations later in life. With a strong secular trend toward low fertility and higher educational attainment, the stage is set for weaker intergenerational bonds but more successful, autonomous adult children.[7]

Determinants of Value Consensus Between Parents and Adult Children

Like educational attainment itself, whether parents and adult children share similar or dissimilar values is more likely to be influenced by experiences the children have in late adolescence and early adulthood than by any qualities of the early family before they entered their teen years. Moving out of their parents' home, developing new friends through job and neighborhood connections and social organizations, and questioning the values they took for granted as children are all conducive to a growing gap between the life values and views held by adult children and those held by their parents.

It was this line of reasoning that led us to suggest, in the analysis model of causal pathways among the intergenerational solidarity measures in our design (Chapter 6), that contemporary Affective Closeness between the generations would be more influenced by the emotional atmosphere and parental qualities in the early family, whereas contemporary Value Consensus[8] between the generations would reflect experiences and judgments at a later stage of development. This independent late line of development could produce value similarity or dissensus, which in turn may impact on the subjective closeness between the generations. In terms of the dimensions of solidarity, we argue that Value Consensus may affect Affective Closeness, but emotional closeness does not determine the sharing of similar values.

It should also be noted that our line of reasoning went against the expectations and research findings of other researchers. Some of that literature suggests that the subjective ties between parents and children are relatively impervious to discrepancies between them of values, politics, or life-style (e.g., Bengtson & Cutler, 1976; Bengtson & Troll, 1978; Troll & Bengtson, 1979). In this view, parents and their adult children may disagree on many issues, with no threat to the warmth or intensity of their ties to each other.

What has not been clear is the extent to which such findings are age related, because the majority of such studies have been based on high school and college samples of young people and their parents. Many critical life experiences that could produce value differences between parents and children have not yet occurred by late adolescence. We felt the time was ripe, with data from a much wider range in age of adult children, to return to this issue, and to entertain a quite different model of the probable causal sequence between subjective affect and value consensus.

At the core of our thinking about value differences between parents and children is the concept of "difference" itself. We argued that it is when children break from the religious heritage they were reared in, and the generations differ in religious values and behavior, that the generations would recognize the value differences between them. So too, we argued that the extent to which children attain levels of education higher than their parents will lead to differences in values and life-styles between the generations. Closely related to the educational difference concept is that the socioeconomic status differences, such that children who are very well-off financially compared to their parents will acquire different tastes, a different life-style all told, from that possible and perhaps desired by their parents. It may also be that both the age of the child and the age difference between children and their parents will press in the direction of value dissensus, age per se because the child will have had more years of living and working in a different social world than the one they shared with their parents, and age difference because age-related and cohort-related perspectives may differ more sharply when parents are significantly older than their children, i.e., all else being equal, the views of a 30-year-old adult are more apt to be like those of a 50-year-old parent than a 65-year-old parent.

We translated these ideas into specific empirical difference scores for an analysis of the extent to which G2 respondents report sharing similar or dissimilar life views or values from those held by their parents. The measures used are as follows:

Religious affiliation difference: A dummy variable on which 1 = any religious affiliation difference between parent and child and 0 = identical religious affiliation.

Educational difference: Number of years of schooling of parent subtracted from number of years attained by the child.

Financial status difference: The Financial Well-being measure for adult child currently and for the family of origin when the child was growing up is a 5-category code from "very poorly off" to "very well off" financially. The difference score subtracted the code value for the family of origin from the code value for the current financial well-being of the adult child.

Age difference: The number of years older G1 parents are than their G2 children. Since the analysis was done separately for mothers and fathers, the age difference measures differ by gender of parent and child.

Two additional measures were included in the regression analysis of Value Consensus. The first is a Social Deviance subscore of the Family Troubles index, which includes the items most likely to involve adolescent children, and hence an early marker of potential emergent value differences between parent and child; the items are problems with drugs or alcohol, trouble with the police and the schools, or going with the "wrong crowd." We considered such social deviance would involve sons more often than daughters and, hence, if the index contributes to the variance in current Value Consensus it should show significant coefficients at least in the father–son dyad.

Unfortunately we have only a crude proxy measure for likely areas of disagreement between parents and daughters. We believe such disagreement is more apt to focus on sexual issues in relations with daughters than in the case of sons; hence, we created a dummy variable on a measure of the adult child's attitudes concerning contraceptive access for teenagers, with 1 = very liberal views and 0 = moderate to conservative views. The expectation was that very liberal daughters on this issue might be at odds with their older, more conservative parents, particularly with their mothers, because this area of life is more often discussed in the mother–daughter dyad than in other dyads.

Table 7.7 provides the results of the regression analysis of Value Consensus between G2 adult children and their G1 parents, with separate equations for each of the four parent–child dyads. It is readily apparent that almost all the measures show negative effects on Value Consensus: 22 of the 28 standardized beta coefficients are negative, implying that value consensus is reduced, the greater the difference between parents and children on our measures. Religious affiliation difference heads the list of significant predictors. This is, of course, partly due to the fact that one of the three items in the Value Consensus index is "views on religion." On the other hand, the dummy variable on religious difference correlates only − .22 with the general Value Consensus index, so there is room for an independent effect as well. Judging from the relevant size of the standardized coefficient, religious differences may be the source of more value dissensus between mothers and adult children than between fathers and adult children. For both daughters and sons, the coefficient on religious difference is larger in relation to mothers than to fathers (− .28 in the Mo-Da relationship and − .14 in the Fa-Da relationship, with only slightly less difference in the case of sons (− .29 in the Mo-So, and − .19 in the Fa-So equations).

Socioeconomic status differences between the generations are only crudely measured by the discrepancy between family of origin well-being and current financial well-being of adult children, but the discrepancy measure nonetheless shows a significant negative coefficient in

Table 7.7. Regression on Current Value Consensus of G2 Adults and Their G1 Parents by Gender of Parent and Child (Beta Coefficients) (G2 Sample)

Predictor Variable	G1–G2 Dyad			
	Mother–Daughter	Mother–Son	Father–Daughter	Father–Son
Value and Status Differences between Parent and Child [a]				
Religious Affiliation Difference	−.28***	−.29***	−.14***	−.19***
Financial Status Difference	−.01	−.13**	.03	−.11*
Educational Attainment Difference	−.01	−.06	−.08	−.06
Age Difference	−.04	−.04	.05	.10
Extent of Social Deviance during Child's Adolescence	−.04	−.08	−.06	−.14***
Adult Child Holds Liberal Views re Sex	−.10*	−.02	−.06	.01
Age of Child	−.18***	.06	−.17***	.03
R^2	.12***	.10***	.06**	.09***
N	(394)	(302)	(271)	(238)

[a] See text for definition of variables in these equations.

*** p < .001
** p < .01
* p < .05

both equations involving sons: The larger the economic status difference, the less sons share similar values with their parents. This suggests
that socially mobile sons depart more sharply from the values and life-
styles of their parents than socially mobile daughters do. Since total
household income is more strongly affected by men's earnings than by
women's, a daughter's financial well-being is very likely to reflect her
husband's earnings. Consequently, more married daughters than sons
may continue to share values with their parents despite socioeconomic
status differences between the two households.[9]

Social deviance in adolescence depresses Value Consensus only between fathers and sons, as predicted, although the signs are all negative
in the other three dyads as well. At least some proportion of adult men
with a history of adolescent deviance of various sorts continue to consider their basic values to be quite different from that of their fathers. We
shall see evidence later in this chapter that Value Consensus has a
greater impact on the current level of Affective Closeness between
fathers and their children, sons in particular, than is the case for
mother–adult child relations.

The counterpart for women to adolescent social deviance among men
is holding liberal views on sexual matters: Daughters who hold very
liberal views on teenager access to contraception tend to hold values
different from their mothers in other areas as well. One reason why the
coefficient is significant only in the mother–daughter relationship is that
mothers and daughters talk about such matters more than fathers and
daughters do. As mentioned above, the least topic avoidance on "sexual
matters" is between mothers and daughters, and the most is between
fathers and daughters. Indeed, fathers and daughters may simply not
know if they hold similar or different views in this sphere of life, while
mothers and daughters know if they disagree or not.

Lastly, age of the adult child has a significant effect only in the
relationship of parents and their daughters: The younger the daughter,
the greater the likelihood that she and her parents share similar values.
Though not statistically significant, the signs reverse for sons: The older
the son, the greater the sharing of similar values. Young adult daughters
remain in closer touch with parents prior to and following marriage,
whereas sons remain at a greater emotional and social distance from
their parents as adolescents and young unmarried men, returning to the
"fold" of family life only when they are married and become fathers
themselves. Recall that emotional intimacy remains low in the father–
son relationship from adolescence through the sons' 20s (Figure 7.1),
whereas the parent–daughter relationship shows a quick recovery from
the adolescent slump in intimacy.

All told, the regression analysis did not explain very much of the variance between parents and adult children on Value Consensus, as indicated by the low, but significant R^2 values in the four equations. What we lack, of course, are any direct measures of experiences outside the family that G2 respondents have undergone that may have changed their values away from those of their parents or from those they held at a younger age before embarking on an adult life on their own. We shall retain some of the specific difference measures concerning the parent and child, as well as the Value Consensus scores when we analyze variation in current Affective Closeness of the parent–child relationship.

Determinants of Dominance and Expressivity

The personal traits of Dominance and Expressivity were introduced in Chapter 2, where we noted that Dominance is strongly related to chronological age but Expressivity is not. Because these personal trait indices will play an important role in subsequent analysis of the contemporary relations between parents and adult children and provide an interpretive handle for explaining some of the gender differences in these relationships, we explored the question of their determinants in early family life. These personal qualities may be to some degree rooted in the genetic make-up of males and females, but they are also highly likely to result from particular socialization experiences in childhood and adolescence. It is also likely that experiences in early adulthood either dampen or enhance the tendency for adults to be high or low in Expressivity and Dominance. This may be particularly the case when adult experiences are counter to traditional conceptions of appropriate male or female behavior.

A very explicit prediction with which we approached the analysis of the determinants of Dominance and Expressivity follows from this idea. Traditional training of daughters may yield low self-ratings on Dominance, but those women who went on to high educational attainment and well-paying jobs may move to much higher Dominance ratings as a consequence of such job success. Further, sons may grow up with only modest Expressivity tendencies, but the adult experience of parenthood may encourage the flowering of tender, nurturant qualities in the men. As some research on the transition to parenthood suggests, becoming a parent involves putting the needs of the young over one's own desires (LaRossa & LaRossa, 1981; Shapiro, 1978). Women do not need the experience of motherhood to develop nurturant concern for others as men may need the experience of fatherhood. Hence, the explicit prediction that flows from this expectation was that having children will show a significant coefficient in an equation on Expressivity for men, but not for women.

To analyze the special contribution of early family variables as well as the adult experiences that may reinforce or activate the personal traits of Dominance and Expressivity, we do a two-step regression analysis, first of early family variables alone, and then with the addition of several salient adult characteristics. The latter include educational attainment, level of personal earnings, age, and number of children. On early family life, we use parental educational attainment, parental Affection, and parents' marital happiness, together with three Skill Transmission indices. Our initial assumption was that parental training in Masculine and Cognitive Skills would be conducive to elevated Dominance in the children (especially sons), and parental training in Domestic Skills would be conducive to elevated Expressivity in the children (especially daughters).

Because the personal traits are strongly gender related, analysis is done separately for men and women. This means we can hope to explain only a modest amount of variance in both personal traits, and we assume quite different profiles of determinants will be significant for women than for men, because Dominance in women and Expressivity in men are countertraditional characteristics.

Tables 7.8 and 7.9 provide the regression results on Dominance and on Expressivity, respectively. In each table, Panel A shows the equations for men (G2 respondents) and Panel B for women. Within each panel, equation (1) is restricted to early family variables, whereas equation (2) supplements the early family variables with the salient adult characteristics of the G2 respondents.

Significant effects are found in all the equations for some of the early family variables, and most retain their significance when relevant adult characteristics of the child are added to the equations (2). Second, parental Affection is a significant contributor to Expressivity in both sons and daughters in all four equations in Table 7.9. Third, at least one and often two parental skill measures contribute to both personal traits among both men and women. Fourth, both measures, but Dominance more strongly so, show negative coefficients on age. That age remains highly significant in an equation with controls on a cohort-related characteristic such as parental education and a life course phase-related variable like income emphasizes the developmental decline of Dominance as an aspect of aging.

Of greater interest than these general tendencies across the two tables are gender differences in the particular combination of variables that significantly predict Dominance and Expressivity in men and women. On Dominance, the emotional tone of early family life is more significant

Table 7.8. Regressions on Dominance by Family of Origin Characteristics Only vs. Combined Family of Origin and Adult Characteristics of G2 Respondents by Gender (G2 Sample) (Standardized Beta Coefficients)

	A. Men		B. Women	
Predictor Variables	Family of Origin Only (1)	Addition of Adult Characteristics (2)	Family of Origin Only (1)	Addition of Adult Characteristics (2)
Family of Origin				
Parent Characteristics				
Mother's Education	.15**	.12+	.06	.01
Father's Education	-.17**	-.18**	.02	-.02
Maternal Affection	.03	.05	.07	.09*
Paternal Affection	-.03	-.01	-.05	.01
Marital Happiness	.01	.00	-.13***	-.12***
Skill Transmission				
Cognitive Skills	.07	.04	.20***	.12**
Domestic Skills	.12*	.13**	.09+	.09*
Masculine Skills	.10*	.09*	.04	.00
Characteristics of G2 Adult Child				
Current Age	—	-.14**	—	-.27***
Own Earnings	—	.17***	—	.16***
Number of Children	—	.06	—	.03
Education	—	-.02	—	.05
R^2	.06**	.10***	.08***	.16***
N	(445)	(445)	(565)	(565)

*** p < .001
** p < .01
* p < .05
+ p < .10

Table 7.9. Regressions on Expressivity by Family of Origin Variables Only vs. Family of Origin and Adult Characteristics of G2 Respondents by Gender (G2 Sample) (Standardized Beta Coefficients)

	A. Men		B. Women	
Predictor Variables	Family of Origin Only (1)	Addition of Adult Characteristics (2)	Family of Origin Only (1)	Addition of Adult Characteristics (2)
Family of Origin				
Parent Characteristics				
Mother's Education	.05	.06	.07	.05
Father's Education	-.12+	-.12+	-.13**	-.14**
Maternal Affection	.19***	.18***	.07	.07
Paternal Affection	.11*	.12**	.12**	.15***
Marital Happiness	-.05	-.06	.09	.08
Skill Transmission				
Cognitive Skills	.00	.00	.13**	.10*
Domestic Skills	.18***	.18***	.14***	.14***
Masculine Skills	-.07	-.08+	-.01	-.00
Characteristics of G2 Adult Child				
Current Age	—	.02	—	-.12**
Own Earnings	—	-.08	—	-.04
Number of Children	—	.14***	—	.07
Education	—	.04	—	.05
R^2	.10***	.11***	.08***	.20***
N	(445)	(445)	(565)	(565)

*** $p < .001$
** $p < .01$
* $p < .05$
+ $p < .10$

for women than for men. Neither marital happiness of the parents nor parental affection has any effect on Dominance level of men, who respond rather to status characteristics of the parents and the training they received at home. High scores on Domestic *and* Masculine Skills predispose sons toward Dominance as adults; by contrast, it is Cognitive and Domestic Skills that predispose daughters to high Dominance.

The significance of the skill measures in this context may lie not in their substantive content but rather as proxies for parental investment of time and energy in childrearing. Indeed, from much preliminary analysis using the skill measures, we became persuaded that a summation score across the three separate skill measures was a good proxy for a general measure of parental investment in childrearing. In the present instance, it is of very special interest that the Domestic Skill index shows significant coefficients in all eight equations in the two tables. We believe now, with the benefit of hindsight, that the Domestic Skill index is a proxy for time spent with mothers (who do most of such training), in the course of which children are influenced by maternal thinking and the expressivity that is a mark of women's family roles. Learning Domestic Skills is not simply a matter of learning how to cook or sew, but acquiring the capacity for and interest in being helpful to others. Fingers may be busy with an iron, broom, or pot, while mothers and children talk of other matters entirely, and one assumes in the process mothers project some of their qualities as caring, nurturant adults providing services for others. Few activities a young child typically engages in focus on doing things for other people; most are centered on the self rather than other family members. Domestic involvement with their mothers in home maintenance may therefore be of particular significance in the development of expressive qualities in sons, whose activities are more likely to involve competitive play than in the case of daughters. By contrast, masculine skills are more likely to be taught by fathers than mothers, and the effect is an increment to the Dominance scores of sons, accompanied by a depression of the sons' Expressivity scores.

The most striking finding in the equation on Dominance in women is the significant negative coefficient on the parents' marital happiness: The array of significant predictors of Dominance in women projects an image of women who had mothers who showed them a good deal of affection (.09* on Maternal Affection) and encouraged them to do well in school (.12** on Cognitive Skills), but were themselves unhappily married (−.12***). The lesson such daughters may have drawn was to feel good about themselves as women but not to center all their life expectations on marriage, which might turn out poorly as their mothers' did. If the daughters did, in fact, do well in school and were later drawn to significant employment at relatively high pay, the women show an increment in Dominance ratings (i.e., own earnings shows a coefficient of .16***).[10]

Three findings in the equations on Expressivity are of particular interest. One is the importance of having had highly affectionate, emotionally accessible parents, especially the parent of the opposite sex. The second is the negative coefficients on fathers' education: Both sons and daughters are more apt to be high on Expressivity if their fathers were less well-educated. It seems likely that better educated fathers invest more heavily in their jobs than in family life, whereas less well-educated fathers invest more heavily in their homes and families. In families including well-educated fathers, then, children are more apt to be influenced by their more accessible mothers than would be the case in families with less well-educated fathers.

The third finding concerns the effect of parenthood. As predicted, having children has a significant effect on the Expressivity levels of men but not of women, supporting our idea that for many American men, it is through becoming fathers that they become tender and concerned for others' welfare. For women, becoming a mother only activates and utilizes the traits most women bring to adulthood, while for men, fatherhood provides a unique opportunity to acquire them. The softening effect of adult fathering experiences, combined with the softening effect of the aging process among older, less driven men, provides the basis for the increased closeness of the relationship between middle-aged men and their fathers that we noted in the previous section of this chapter.

Only a small amount of variance is explained in any of the equations shown in Tables 7.8 and 7.9, even when adult characteristics are added to early family variables, with R^2 values ranging only from .10 to .20. When gender is entered as a predictor variable rather than conducting separate regression analyses for the four dyads, the R^2 values increase markedly, to .42 for Dominance and .50 for Expressivity. Clearly there are many aspects of these gender-linked personal traits that remain unexplained. On the other hand, the measures of Expressivity and Dominance will contribute significantly to the interpretation of gender differences and intragender variance in the analysis of social interaction and help exchange reported in Chapters 8 and 9; hence it was important to learn what we could about their determinants in early family life and adult experiences.

Effects of Early Family Life

Having explored in some detail the internal structure of the families of origin of our G2 respondents and traced the extent to which the personal traits of Dominance and Expressivity are rooted in those early years of development, we are prepared now to test whether early family variables have *persistent effects* on the current relationship between parents and adult children, and the extent to which there are traceable *cross-generational effects* from parents to children when the children in turn become parents. In this chapter we restrict attention to persistent effects of the past for current Affective Closeness, and will demonstrate similar effects on social interaction and help exchange in the two chapters to follow.

Persistent Effects of Early Family Life on Current Affective Closeness

The Adult Child's Perspective. We begin the analysis with data from G2 respondents as adult children, bringing together in a sequence of regression equations the major variables on early parental and family of origin characteristics, current Value Consensus, and a number of current characteristics of both the G1 parent and the G2 adult child. A three-step sequence of regression analyses was conducted, first on the effect of early family variables alone on current Affective Closeness, second with only current characteristics of the parent and the child and the extent to which they share similar or dissimilar values, and third with the combined set of past and current characteristics. The specific variables included in each set of predictor variables are as follows:

1. *Early Family Life*: Affective Closeness between parent and child when the child was 16 years of age, parental Affection and Authority, Family Cohesion, and Extent of Family Troubles.

2. *Current Characteristics of Parent and of Child*: The parent's age and rating of Health, the child's ratings on Expressivity and Dominance, and a dummy variable on whether the child has at least one child or not (and hence produced a grandchild for the parent).[11]

3. *Current Value Consensus between Parent and Adult Child*: The primary variable here is current Value Consensus, supplemented by the three difference measures reported in the previous section: the extent to which the generations differ in age, religious affiliation, and educational attainment.

Table 7.10 shows the results of the three-step regression analysis, separately for each of the four parent–child dyads. The dyads are shown in Panels A through D. Within each panel, equation (1) shows the results when only early family variables are regressed on current Affective Closeness, equation (2) when only current characteristics are regressed on current intimacy ratings, and equation (3) when both past and current variables are in the equations. We will summarize the results of the 12 equations in the table in terms of the sequence of equations within each panel, noting similarities and differences among the four parent-child dyads as we do so.

Table 7.10. Regressions on Current Affective Closeness of G2 Adult Children and their Parents by Gender of Parent and Child (G2 Sample) (Beta Coefficients)

Predictor Variables [a]	A. Mother–Daughter			B. Mother–Son		
	Only Early Family Variables (1)	Only Current Variables (2)	Both Early and Current (3)	Only Early Family Variables (1)	Only Current Variables (2)	Both Early and Current (3)
Early Family						
Close at 16	.09	—	.05	.23***	—	.21***
Maternal Affection	.24***	—	.20***	.16*	—	.14*
Maternal Authority	.01	—	.02	-.02	—	-.01
Family Cohesion	.26***	—	.22***	.14*	—	.08
Family Troubles	.04	—	.06	.02	—	.02
Current Value Consensus	—	.38***	.24***	—	.33***	.22***
Current Parent Characteristics						
Mother's Health	—	.14***	.11**	—	.04	.01
Mother's Age	—	-.01	.01	—	.03	.03
Current Child Characteristics						
Child's Expressivity	—	.05	.01	—	.12*	.05
Child's Dominance	—	-.01	-.02	—	-.06	-.05
Child has Child(ren)	—	.07	.07	—	.01	.05
R^2	.23***	.17***	.29***	.16***	.13***	.22***
N	(250)			(218)		

	C. Father–Daughter			D. Father–Son		
Early Family						
Close at 16	.16*	—	.13[+]	.22***	—	.17***
Paternal Affection	.26***	—	.21***	.17***	—	.16*
Paternal Authority	.03	—	.01	−.06	—	−.04
Family Cohesion	.21***	—	.18**	.18**	—	.10
Family Troubles	−.01	—	−.03	−.01	—	−.09
Current Value Consensus	—	.38***	.22***	—	.52***	.41***
Current Parent Characteristics						
Father's Health	—	.20***	.15***	—	−.01	−.05
Father's Age	—	.07	.08	—	.07	.12
Current Child Characteristics						
Child's Expressivity	—	.08	.01	—	.03	.05
Child's Dominance	—	.02	.07	—	.03	.05
Child has Child(ren)	—	.01	.03	—	.16[+]	.18*
R^2	.28***	.20***	.34***	.22***	.28***	.37***
N	(250)			(218)		

[a] Three difference measures were also in the equations, but showed no significant contribution: age difference, educational difference, and religious difference between parent and child. Value Consensus measure absorbs all the effects of these specific difference measures.

*** p < .001

** p < .01

* p < .05

[+] p < .10

313

Equations (1) on the effect of early family variables for current Affective Closeness shows a consistent pattern of significant effects, centered largely on three variables: Parental Affection, Family Cohesion, and Affective Closeness of the child to the parent during adolescence. There is greater current intimacy between parents and adult children if, earlier, the parents were affectionate and accessible, the family cohesive, and the relationship close when the child was an adolescent. This profile holds for the mother–son, father–daughter, and father–son relationship. The exception, the mother–daughter relationship, departs only in adolescent closeness showing no significant persistent effect on current intimacy in this relationship. Whatever strain mothers and daughters experience during adolescence is lost once the daughter reaches maturity. By contrast, adolescent stress between sons and their parents shows a persistent dampening effect on the current relationship between the generations.

Whether parents were affectionate or not shows a similar strong impact on how close adult children feel toward their parents today. This is particularly the case for daughters and their parents. In fact, Paternal Affection in the earlier years has the largest beta coefficient in the father–daughter closeness equation (Panel C, equation (1): .26***). By contrast, Parental Authority, which we reported earlier to have a depressant effect on parent–child closeness in adolescence, has no effect once the child is an adult. Parental affection can be shown as readily in youth as in maturity, whereas parental authority is largely at an end when children become adults; hence, it loses all salience as an influence on current affection.

The global measure of Family Cohesion contributes some of the same positive afterglow that Parental Affection does, with particularly strong effects on the relationship between daughters and their mothers (.26***), and much less so for mothers and sons (.14*) or fathers and sons (.18**).

Equations (2) shift the focus of attention to current characteristics, holding aside the early family variables. These equations show very strong effects of Value Consensus on current Affective Closeness in all four parent–child dyads. None of the specific difference measures (on age, education, or religion) had any independent effects on the subjective closeness of the relationship, although 9 of the 12 coefficients on these three measures have negative signs, suggesting some slight reduction in closeness when parents and children differ significantly in age, religious affiliation, or educational attainment. (As noted in the footnote to the table, these variables are not shown, to simplify presentation.) Even in the father–daughter relationship, age difference shows no effect on current intimacy, which holds special interest because we showed earlier that during adolescence, daughters' closeness to their fathers increases with an increasing gap between them in age. In 1985, most daughters have men of their own in their lives; hence, the father–daughter dyad may no longer need the protective distancing we imputed to the age difference variable when daughters were adolescents living at home.

One striking finding concerns the effect of the parents' health on the closeness adult children feel toward their parents. This is a highly significant predictor of Affective Closeness, but only in the relationship of daughters to their mothers and fathers, not that of sons. Daughters feel less close to parents in poor health than to parents in good health: Note the significant coefficient of .14*** on parent's health in the mother–daughter relationship, but only .04 in the mother–son relationship, with a similar contrast in the father–daughter (.20***) vs. father–son ($-.01$) relationship. It is typically adult daughters who provide personal caregiving if parents are in poor health, and they probably anticipate having to do so in future even if their parents' current health problems are not yet serious enough to require such personal caregiving. It is tempting to infer that some women may begin an emotional withdrawal from their parents when they notice signs of declining health, in part because poor health alters the interaction and help reciprocity between daughters and their parents, in part as a self-protective defense against the pain of the eventual death of the parents. Poor health, whether characteristic of ego or a significant other, often triggers rehearsals in advance of the loss of an important person in one's life, which may involve some emotional distancing from the significant other.

Two findings in equations (2) in Table 7.10 are unique to sons' relationship to their parents, one where mothers are concerned and the other where fathers are concerned. Sons high in Expressivity report being significantly closer to their mothers than sons low in Expressivity. In part this reflects the childhood closer ties to their mothers that was hinted at in the significance of Domestic Skill training for the sons' acquisition of expressive qualities, and, in part, Expressivity implies a capacity to express deep feelings and to engage in intimate talk, suggesting a greater ease of interaction and a feeling of subjective closeness between a high Expressive son and his mother.

The second finding unique to sons is the contribution of having a family of his own: Sons with one or more children report being closer to their fathers than sons who have not yet become fathers. It is of interest to note that having children shows a significant effect net of the sons' Expressivity, because we earlier noted that being a father was itself related to men's level of Expressivity. The finding in Table 7.10 therefore suggests that whatever the background of strain in the father–son relationship, and however much there is disagreement between them in values and life-style, the transition to shared roles as fathers opens a new channel for communication, shared concern, and affection between fathers and sons.

If we compare the amount of variance in Affective Closeness that is explained by the two types of predictor variables in equations (1) vs. (2)—early family vs. current characteristics—the early family life variables explain more variance in emotional closeness than the current characteristics do. For example, in Panels A and C, the R^2 values are .23 and .28 in equations (1) on early family variables and .17 and .20 in equations (2) on current characteristics. Only in the father–son relationship are current characteristics more significant (.28) than early family variables (.22).

Equations (3) provide a test of the persistent, direct effects of early family variables on the subjective quality of the relationship between parents and adult children. The results indicate that almost all the early family variables that showed significant effects in equations (1) continue to show direct effects on the current level of Affective Closeness. The pattern is most sharp in the relationship between daughters and their parents: Adult daughters who had highly affectionate parents when they were children, whose early family was a cohesive one, who as adults hold values similar to their parents, and who have parents in good health report strong subjective ties of closeness to their mothers and fathers.

Comparing the R^2 values in equations (2) with those in equations (3) emphasizes the importance of having retrospective measures over those restricted to the present: In all four dyads, there is a significant increase when past measures are added to current measures, e.g., from .17 to .29 in the mother–daughter dyad, or from .20 to .34 in the father–daughter dyad.

Yet another inference from the findings in Table 7.10 is the tendency for early family variables to explain less variance in current closeness of men to their parents than of women. Having affectionate parents in youth counts for less for sons than it does for daughters, and Family Cohesion in youth loses any direct effect in equations (3) for sons. Once again, the father–son relationship shows an overall unique profile, with the most significant predictor of intimacy being the extent to which the men share similar values (.41***), followed by the son's having a child of his own (.18*), or having been close to his father during adolescence (.17*).

Finally, the R^2 values are larger in equations on relations to fathers than in those concerning mothers, suggesting again that adult children's relationship with their fathers is subject to more contingent qualifications than is the case for relations with mothers.

The Parent's Perspective.   We shift now to an analysis of current Affective Closeness between parents and adult children as viewed by the G1 parents, rather than, as above, by the G2 adult children. This permits us to inquire whether parents are affected by the same significant factors in their Affective Closeness ratings as the children are. Do parents consider the role they played in rearing the child relevant to the closeness between them in 1985? Does the past matter to parents' current judgments, as it did to the children's judgments of intimacy?

To approximate a regression analysis identical to that shown above, with data from the much smaller G1 spinoff sample, we must drop gender of child as a dimension of the parent–child dyads and instead use child's gender as a variable in mother–child and father–child equations.

All the variables used in the parent equations except one are drawn from the data obtained from the G1 parents themselves, and all the variables in the G2 child equations come from the G2 interviews with children whose parents were interviewed. The single exception is the measure of Family Troubles, which was not included in the spinoff sample surveys because they were conducted by telephone whereas the measure relied on a printed card shown to respondents in the G2 personal interviews. In the interest of keeping the equations as close as possible to those shown in Table 7.10, we opted to use the Family Troubles index in both sets of equations.

The format of the analysis results is similar to that used earlier: a three-equation sequence of only early family variables, only current variables, and a combination of both early and current variables. They appear in Panels A, B, and C in Table 7.11 on Mother–Child and Table 7.12 on Father–Child Affective Closeness. Within each panel, the equations are shown with all the ratings done by the parent (1) and by the child (2).

Inspection of the results in these equations supports the prediction that assessment of intimacy in the parent–child relationship differs by which partner—parent or child—provides the perspective. From the point of view of women as mothers, none of the early family variables contributes anything to their current ratings of Affective Closeness to children, whereas their children are affected by the level of affection shown to them by their mothers in youth and to the level of cohesion of their early family. In the case of fathers, however, both generations agree that the pattern of intimacy that held in adolescence continues to

Table 7.11. Regressions on Current Affective Closeness Between G1 Mothers and G2 Adult Children: Mothers' vs. Children's Perspectives (G1 and G2 Samples) (Beta Coefficients)

Predictor Variables	A Only Early Family Variables Rated by		B Only Current Variables Rated by		C Both Early and Current Variables Rated by	
	G1 Mother (1)	G2 Child (2)	G1 Mother (1)	G2 Child (2)	G1 Mother (1)	G2 Child (2)
Early Family						
Close at 16	.06	.01	—	—	.05	-.05
Maternal Affection	.11	.22**	—	—	.03	.29***
Maternal Authority	.09	-.01	—	—	.03	.03
Family Cohesion	.01	.26***	—	—	.01	.11
Family Troubles	-.01	-.02	—	—	-.02	-.04
Current Differences between Parent and Child						
Value Consensus	—	—	.31***	.52***	.29***	.37***
Age Difference	—	—	.02	-.01	.01	-.04
Educational Difference	—	—	-.01	-.05	-.03	-.05
Religious Difference	—	—	.05	.13*	.05	.12+
Current Characteristics of Parent or Child						
Mother's Health	—	—	-.03	.13*	-.02	.12+
Mother's Age	—	—	.03	.01	.01	-.01
Expressivity [a]	—	—	.19*	.01	.16*	.12
Dominance [a]	—	—	-.11+	-.09	-.12+	-.09
Child's Gender (Da = 1)	—	—	.17*	.21*	.18*	.28***
Child Has Child(ren)	—	—	.00	-.05	-.00	.02
R^2	.03	.18***	.16*	.32***	.16**	.40***
N	(167)					

[a] Expressivity and Dominance Self-Ratings by G1 parents in parents' equations and by G2 adult children in child equations.

*** $p < .001$ ** $p < .01$ * $p < .05$ + $p < .10$

318

Table 7.12. Regressions on Current Affective Closeness Between G1 Fathers and G2 Adult Children: Fathers' vs. Children's Perspectives (G1 and G2 Samples) (Beta Coefficients)

Predictor Variables	A Only Early Family Variables Rated by		B Only Current Variables Rated by		C Both Early and Current Variables Rated by	
	G1 Father (1)	G2 Child (2)	G1 Father (1)	G2 Child (2)	G1 Father (1)	G2 Child (2)
Early Family						
Close at 16	.31***	.24**	—	—	.28*	.28**
Paternal Affection	.09	.09	—	—	.05	.08
Paternal Authority	.05	.01	—	—	.06	.02
Family Cohesion	.06	.28***	—	—	.05	.15*
Family Troubles	.03	−.03	—	—	.03	−.01
Current Differences between Parent and Child						
Value Consensus			.18*	.33***	.13[+]	.29***
Age Difference			.00	−.15	.02	−.05
Educational Difference			.09	−.03	−.07	−.02
Religious Difference			−.06	−.08	−.05	−.07
Current Characteristics of Parent or Child						
Father's Health			.06	.21*	.05	.15*
Father's Age			−.07	.15	−.18*	.09
Expressivity [a]			.25***	.18*	.05	.14*
Dominance [a]			−.01	.16*	−.05	.14
Child's Gender			−.03	.13	−.03	.11
Child Has Child(ren)			.14[+]	.15*	.17*	.15*
R^2	.14**	.27***	.14*	.26***	.21*	.40***
N	(109)					

[a] Expressivity and Dominance Self-Ratings by G1 parents in parents' equations and by G2 adult children in child equations.

*** p < .001   ** p < .01   * p < .05   + p < .10

have a bearing on how fathers and their children rate their current relationship. As seen in equations A1 and A2 in Table 7.12, closeness at 16 years of age is a significant predictor of closeness today between men and their children, from the perspective of both fathers and adult children. By contrast, the quality of the relationship during adolescence has no effect on the current relationship between mothers and their adult children from either generation's perspective. It seems a fair inference that both partners to the mother–child relationship have a more unconditional quality to the bond between them, whereas the father–child relationship is more contingent on events of the past.

Early Family Cohesion shows a similar contrast by generational perspective: no impact on current closeness from the perspective of parents, but, in three of the four equations, a significant effect is shown from the perspective of the child.

Equations B on the effect of current characteristics on Affective Closeness show that parents and adult children are in accord in the effect of Value Consensus: Both parents and adult children who perceive similarity in their own and alter's values report greater Affective Closeness than those who perceive dissensus between them. Fathers also show more closeness to sons who have themselves become fathers, in much the way we reported above from the perspective of the sons. Having a child adds no increment to the closeness between mothers and adult children, from either generation's perspective. As seen by the significant coefficient on gender, mothers and daughters agree that their relationship is closer than dyads including fathers or sons.

It is also clear from these results that the depression of intimacy attending any poor health in the parent that we noted in the earlier analysis from the daughter's perspective is not shared by the parents. Parents in good health do not report any difference in closeness to their children than parents in poor health.

Expressivity has modest and uniformly positive effects on Affective Closeness between the generations: In all eight equations in which the measure appears, the signs are significantly positive in five of the eight. Dominance, by contrast, tends, if anything, to reduce intimacy in the parent–child relationship, with negative signs to the coefficients in six of the eight equations. Dominance may make for success in the outside world, but it reduces harmony and affection in the inner circles of family relations.[12]

Overall, parents tell us that early family life has little bearing on the quality of their current relations with children, though this is more strongly the case for women as mothers than for men as fathers. By contrast, children show a vital emotional link between their earlier relationship to their parents and their feelings of strain or intimacy in their current relationship. As a consequence, when equations contain both past and current variables, the R^2 values are very much larger in the equations based on data from adult children than they are in equations based on data from parents, i.e., in Table 7.11 on mother–child closeness, from .16 with data from mothers to .40 with data from their children, and in Table 7.12 on father–child closeness, from .20 with data from fathers to .40 with data from their children.

Less hampered by the burden of past events, parents have less contingent affect for their children than children have for their parents. If there is any rosy lens through which the past is viewed, it is more apt to be on the eyes of parents than of children. Furthermore, we must remember that a child's view and knowledge of the family are only that dimension of family life that involves children, whereas a parent's view and knowledge of earlier stages of the family during childrearing embrace the equally important dimension of the marital relationship and the time spent as adults while children are bedded down or away from home.

Although it anticipates analysis that will be reported in Chapters 8 and 9, we can put our findings to this point in a larger framework, by means of the correlation coefficients shown in Table 7.13. Here we show the correlations between past Family Cohesion and all the measures of current solidarity in the study design, with ratings from G1 parents (equations 1) and from G2 children (equations 2). All 24 correlation

Table 7.13. Correlation Coefficients Between Past Family Cohesion [a] and Indices of Current Intergenerational Solidarity by Parents' vs. Children's Perspective (G1 and G2 Samples)

| | A G1 Mother–G2 Child Rated by | | B G1 Father–G2 Child Rated by | |
| | Parent | Child | Parent | Child |
Solidarity Measures	(1)	(2)	(1)	(2)
Affective Closeness	.07	.36***	.18*	.40***
Value Consensus	.10	.34***	.19*	.28***
Frequency of Visiting	.16*	.26***	.11	.21**
Frequency of Phoning	.12	.24***	.16	.18*
Help Extent: Parent to Child	.06	.25***	.22**	.32***
Help Extent: Child to Parent	.01	.19**	.18*	.15*
Absolute Mean across Solidarity Measures	.09	.27***	.17*	.26***

[a] Family of procreation of G1 parent and family of origin of G2 adult child.
*** $p < .001$
** $p < .01$
* $p < .05$

coefficients are positive, indicating a general tendency for high cohesiveness of the family in the past to have a significant positive effect on not just current Affective Closeness, but social interaction and help exchange as well. But once again, the impact is uniform and strongly significant for children, but of only modest significance from the point of view of the parents, e.g., absolute means across the solidarity measures of .27*** for G2 children vs. .09 for G1 mothers. Also consistent with findings reported above on Affective Closeness, men show a somewhat stronger effect of the past than do women, as suggested by the individual correlations in equation B1 in the fathers' ratings compared to those in equation A1 in the mothers' ratings, and in the absolute means across the solidarity measures shown in the last row of the table (.09 for mothers and .17* for fathers).[13]

Cross-Generational Transmission

We have selected three issues for an analysis of cross-generational transmission from the family of origin to the family of procreation. The first concerns the impact of the parental marriage on the child's marriage, as indexed by religious intermarriage and marital happiness in the two generations; the second concerns the transmission of Family Cohesion as a characteristic of the family of origin, together with other early family variables, to the family of procreation; and the third concerns cross-generational transmission of gender-role socialization in the skills parents taught to their children.

Cross-Generational Influences on the Marital Relationship. Over the course of the twentieth century, there has been an increasing trend toward religious intermarriages, as the spheres of life controlled by religious institutions have declined. This has been particularly true for Catholic-Americans in more recent decades, during which the church has lost authority over private decisions concerning contraception and family size (D'Antonio, 1985). In Chapter 3, we illustrated the secular trend toward intermarriage from the turn of the century when the parents of our oldest respondents married (among whom 8% showed a different religious affiliation than their spouses) to more recent decades, when our youngest respondents had married (among whom 31% reported a different religious affiliation than their spouses).[14]

The trend toward a greater frequency of religious intermarriage reflects not only larger societal and institutional change, but cross-generational influences within the family as well. With each marital cohort showing higher intermarriage rates, a larger proportion of the children born to each subsequent marital cohort grew up with parents who do not share a common religious heritage. It is a reasonable prediction that parents who have intermarried themselves would impose fewer restrictions on their children's friendships with peers from different religious backgrounds, and would feel less opposition should a child in turn form a marriage with a spouse from a different religious background.

Table 7.14 permits us to see the independent effect of parental intermarriage on the tendency for children to similarly intermarry. Since marriages occur for the most part in early adulthood, a control for the age of the respondent in effect controls for the secular trend toward intermarriage. The table shows the proportion of married G2 respondents who have a different religious affiliation than their spouses as a function of the secular trend and the profile of intermarriage shown by their G1 parents. The table clearly shows that both the model provided by their parents' marriage and the secular trend toward intermarriage have an effect on the level of intermarriage reported by the respondents: only 15% of our older respondents intermarried if their parents shared the same religious affiliation, compared to a high 53% among our youngest respondents whose parents had intermarried. In a Boston sample, half of whom report a Catholic religious affiliation, the predominant type is a Catholic–Protestant marriage.[15]

A second example of cross-generational transmission relevant to the marital bond concerns the quality of the marriage, i.e., a rating of marital happiness. G2 respondents rated the marital happiness of their parents when they were growing up as well as their own marital happiness at the time they were interviewed, and those G3 adult children who were married also rated their own current marital happiness. These ratings permit us to test the extent to which marital happiness in one generation has an effect on marital happiness in the next generation. Table 7.15

Table 7.14. Cross-Generational Transmission and Secular Trend Impact on Religious Intermarriage (G2 Sample) (Percentage of G2 Respondents and Spouses who have Different Religious Affiliation)

| | | Age of G2 Adults | | |
G1 Parents' Religious Affiliation	Total	41 or Older	40 or Younger	Significance of Age
Same	19.9%	15.2%	26.9%	***
	(959)	(567)	(390)	
Different	43.8%	33.9%	53.0%	***
	(128)	(62)	(60)	
Significance of Parental Intermarriage Pattern	***	***		

*** p < .001

Table 7.15. Marital Happiness in Proximate Generations (G2 and G3
Samples) (Pearson Correlation Coefficients)

G1 Parents' Marital Happiness in the past and G2 adult Children's Current Marital Happiness (both ratings by G2 respondents)	.27*** (190)
G2 Parents' Current Marital Happiness (rated by G2 respondents) and G3 married Children's Marital Happiness (rated by G3 respondents)	.23*** (112)

*** $p < .001$

therefore shows the relevant correlation coefficients between marital
happiness in the two proximate generations for the G1–G2 parent–child
dyads and the G2–G3 parent–child dyads.

The magnitudes of the correlations are roughly the same for the two
parent–child pairs. There might be some reservations concerning marital
happiness ratings in the first pair, G1–G2, on the grounds that the same
person rated their own and their parents' marital happiness and there
might, as a consequence, be some projection of one's own state of
happiness or unhappiness in marriage to the assessment of one's parents' marital happiness. But this seems quite unlikely, in view of the fact
that in the second dyad, the ratings were done independently: G3 adult
children rated their own marital happiness, and their G2 parents similarly rated their own marriage. With so many likely sources for differences in the quality of two marriages in two proximate generations—as a
function of personal tastes and values, of socioeconomic status, and
personality matching or mismatching between spouses—it is striking
that such cross-generational effects are present in so subtle and personal
a sphere as marital happiness.

Family Cohesion in Proximate Generations. The most persuasive evidence of cross-generational transmission is found in our analysis of G2
respondents' own families of procreation, as they are affected by a wide
array of early family and current personal characteristics. For this test we
rely on the global rating of Family Cohesion by G2 respondents who
were married and had children. We test whether Family Cohesion of the
family of origin contributes to the cohesion of the family of procreation,
net of other early family variables such as parental Affection and Authority, extent of Family Troubles, and parental investment in childrearing. The latter variable—parental investment in childrearing—is a
summed score across the three skill areas discussed earlier (Domestic,
Masculine, and Cognitive Skills).

The results of the regression analysis with predictor variables restricted to characteristics of the family of origin are shown in Panel A of
Table 7.16. The results show significant effects of all early family vari-

Table 7.16. Regressions on Cohesion of G2 Adults' Families of Procreation, of Characteristics of the Family of Origin, Family of Procreation, and G2 Personal Characteristics (G2 Sample)

Predictor Variables	A Family of Origin Only	B Family of Origin and Personal Characteristics	C Family of Origin, Personal, and Family of Procreation Characteristics
Family of Origin Characteristics			
Family Cohesion	.11**	.10*	.09*
Parental Affection	.08*	.05	.01
Parental Authority	.07*	.09**	.06
Parental Investment in Childrearing	.08*	.05	.06
Extent of Family Troubles	− .01	− .04	− .04
G2 Personal Characteristics			
Early Marriage [a]	—	− .09**	− .07*
Education	—	.06[+]	.12***
Expressivity	—	.21***	.18***
Dominance	—	− .04	− .10*
Family of Procreation Characteristics			
Extent of Family Troubles	—	—	− .23***
Parental Emphasis in Childrearing			
Autonomy	—	—	.08**
Status	—	—	.10**
Conformity	—	—	.05
Parental Investment in Childrearing	—	—	.05
R^2	**.16***	**.20***	**.28***
N	(755)	(755)	(755)

[a] Dummy variable: Married under 20 years of age = 1; Married 20 or older = 0.
*** $p < .001$
** $p < .01$
* $p < .05$
+ $p < .10$

ables except the Family Troubles index, yielding a significant R^2 of .16***.

Since we have already found that parental Affection and skill transmission are themselves determinants of Expressivity, it is to be expected that the addition of current personal characteristics of G2 respondents will reduce the effect of some of the early family variables; in other words that they have *indirect* effects on the cohesiveness of the families of procreation, working through the intermediary of the personal trait of Expressivity. Panel B of Table 7.16 shows this to be the case: Expressivity is a highly significant predictor of Family Cohesion, replacing Parental Affection and investment in childrearing. Parental Authority in the family of origin continues to show positive and significant effects on the cohesiveness of the family in the next generation, perhaps for the same reason we earlier found maternal authority contributed to family cohesion in the family of origin: Shared work chores and discipline of children for misbehavior contribute to smoothly run households and more socially cohesive families. Note, too, that early marriages, when spouses were less than 20 years of age, depress the cohesiveness of the families that result from such marriages. This is the more impressive when one realizes that the finding applies only to the marriages that have survived, since early marriages have a high divorce rate.

Panel C shows the regression results when the widest array of predictor variables enter the equation; not only family of origin and personal characteristics, but other characteristics of the family of procreation: family troubles, parental investment in childrearing, and three measures of the qualities parents sought to instill in their children. Note that cohesiveness of the family of origin shows a continuing direct effect on the cohesiveness of the family of procreation, despite the presence in the equations of many other predictor variables. Other early family variables that were significant in the equations in Panels A and B remain positive but below statistical significance in the final equation C.

Family Troubles in the family of procreation is a major depressant of family cohesion, as is an early marriage and high Dominance as a characteristic of at least one of the parents. As suggested earlier, Dominance may facilitate financial success in extrafamilial roles, but depress harmony at home. Parental emphasis on Autonomy and Status in childrearing shows significant contributions to Family Cohesion, perhaps because it indicates parental commitment to a major function of families, to rear children with sufficient maturity and skills to support themselves comfortably.

Lastly, the array of variables shows an additive effect on the amount of variance in Family Cohesion that they explain, as indicated by the steady increase in the size of the R^2 values, from .16 in equation A to .20 in equation B and .28 in the final equation C.

The Transmission of Traditional and Countertraditional Gender Role Socialization.   Our third example of cross-generational transmission concerns the skills parents report having taught their children. Apart from a few courses in cooking, sewing, and carpentry, schools provide little training in the hands-on skills that home maintenance and childrearing require, presumably on the assumption that parents teach such skills to their children. Family sociologists have given little attention to the teaching function of the parental role, in preference for research on the values underlying childrearing practices, or the qualities parents seek to instill in their children. This is a strange omission in view of the fact that so much attention has been paid in recent years to the division of domestic and childcare responsibilities between husbands and wives, particularly in dual-earner families. It was partly to rectify this omission that we included in the study design questions on the extent to which respondents had been taught a variety of skills by their parents, and identical questions concerning their own role as parents in teaching the same skills to their own children. (The youngest respondents, who did not yet have children, were asked hypothetical questions.) A major reason for including such items was to chart the extent to which sons and daughters were taught different skills, and whether, by using age of respondent, we could detect any social trend toward less traditional gender-differentiated training. In Chapter 3, we reported such a trend only where sons were concerned, with an increase over the past several decades in parental emphasis on teaching Domestic Skills to sons, but there was little change in teaching daughters either Domestic or Masculine Skills.

Two questions guide our analysis of the Domestic and Masculine Skill training of children. The basic question, relevant to this chapter's focus on cross-generational transmission, concerns the extent to which adult children follow in their own parents' footsteps in the teaching of domestic and masculine skills. We will give this analysis a special twist, however, by first posing the question of what determines whether parents follow the traditional groove by teaching Domestic Skills to daughters and Masculine Skills to sons, or whether they show a countertraditional profile by teaching Masculine Skills to daughters and Domestic Skills to sons. An understanding of what it takes to produce countertraditional competencies is clearly relevant to the goal of increasing the interchangeability of men and women in home chores and childcare.

We begin the analysis with this second question, because we wish to impose a harsh test on the cross-generational transmission issue. We did not ask G1 parents the skill training questions; hence our data concerning skill training in both the family of origin and family of procreation were obtained from the same respondents, the G2 adults in our main sample. As a test of cross-generational transmission, then, we want to demonstrate that the past training respondents report they received from their parents contributes to the training they gave their own children, over and above the characteristics of the respondents that they acquired by the time they became parents. Furthermore, we want to determine what differentiates adults who provided traditional training to their children from those who provided countertraditional training.

We begin the analysis with this last question, and do so by regressing a variety of status and attitudinal variables on the traditional and countertraditional training G2 respondents reported they gave (or will give) their children. The status variables are age, educational attainment, family size, and Catholic religious affiliation (as a dummy variable). Parental skill transmission is not likely to be pocketed off as a isolated domain unaffected by larger beliefs. On the expectation that religious and political attitudes may be of special significance in training children in nonconventional ways—e.g., teaching a son to sew or a daughter to use a power tool—we include, among the predictor variables, religiosity (as measured by frequency of church attendance), general political orientation (a self-rating on which high scores mean very conservative, low scores, very liberal or radical), and an index on women's rights (high scores indicating strong opposition, low scores strong support for an enlarged role for women in public life).

Table 7.17 reports the results of the regression analysis of Domestic and Masculine skill training G2 respondents report they have given to their G3 children (or will give, in the case of very young respondents). Panel A shows the equations for Traditional training: equation 1 (in the upper right quadrant), Domestic Skill training of daughters, and equation 2, Masculine Skill training of sons. Panel B shows the equations for Countertraditional training: equation 1 (lower left quadrant), Masculine Skill training of daughters, and equation 2, Domestic Skill training of sons. Within each quadrant, equations are shown separately for G2 mothers and G2 fathers.

Several striking results are shown in these data. Since childrearing takes place in early adulthood, age of respondents is itself an index of historic time. The younger the parent (and hence the more recent the childrearing), the greater is the countertraditional training of both sons and daughters, and the traditional training of sons in Masculine skills. Net of all other characteristics in the equation, age of respondent shows no effect on the traditional training of daughters in Domestic skills, which is consistent with the pattern reported in Chapter 3. Educational attainment shows a very special profile: The more education parents had, the less they emphasized traditional skill transmission to both sons and daughters (three of the four equations in Panel A show significant effects of education), but education has no effect on the encouragement of countertraditional training of sons and daughters, as shown in the four equations in Panel B. Since formal schooling, particularly at the college level, provides no training in the hands-on skills required to maintain a household and care for children, an increase in educational attainment among future cohorts of young people may be associated with lower levels of competence in home maintenance than earlier cohorts had. This augurs well for a consumer society's dependence on paid services, fast foods, and ready-to-wear clothing, but not for a competent self-sufficiency of future householders and parents.

Family size shows a consistent negative sign in both the traditional and countertraditional equations: the larger the family, the lower the scores on Domestic and Masculine Skill training of sons and daughters. One might have predicated the reverse, on the assumption that large sized families reflect more traditional values on the part of parents, and hence at least on the traditional pattern of skill transmission, that daughters in large families would be particularly likely to be taught a variety of domestic skills. This is clearly not the case, we believe for the same reason that family size has been shown to be negatively related to status attainment of children. Parental investment provides the same interpretive clue in skill transmission as it does on status attainment: The more children in a family, the less time and parental attention is available for any one child, and therefore the less training parents provide in any skill area. Single births, our species characteristic, precludes almost all parental teaching of children as a group, because parents know that children must be taught skills appropriate to their age. A child of three can learn to put his toys into a large box but cannot handle a vacuum cleaner or make a bed. Hence, the larger the family, the more the parent must teach each child, at their appropriate age, the skills they need to be effective aides in the home. Many parents feel less patience and interest in reading stories about the "little blue engine" to a third child than to a first born, and, as the family grows, domestic chores increase and there is also less time for the individual attention that teaching a child new skills requires.

Aware that half our sample were Catholics, we have consistently tested for the relevance of religious affiliation in the analysis we conducted for this study, but it was rarely a significant variable. Gender role socialization provides a unique exception. As Table 7.17 shows, Catholic mothers are far less inclined to provide countertraditional training to their sons and daughters than non-Catholic mothers. In analysis not reported in this volume, we also found that Catholic parents gave significantly greater emphasis in rearing their children to social Conformity, and less to Autonomy in the qualities they tried to instill in their children. The combination of these two findings suggested the interesting thesis that Catholic-Americans have shown great change over the past several decades in aspects of life that relate to sex, contraception, and marriage, but have retained more of their ethnic and religious

Table 7.17. Regressions on Domestic and Masculine Skill Training of G3 Sons and Daughters by G2 Parents (G2 Sample) (Beta Coefficients)

Predictor Variables	Training of G3 Daughter		Training of G3 Son	
	G2 Mother Says	G2 Father Says	G2 Mother Says	G2 Father Says
	(1) Domestic Skills to G3 Daughter		(2) Masculine Skills to G3 Son	
A. TRADITIONAL				
G2 Status Characteristics				
Age	−.05	−.01	−.20***	−.20***
Education	−.16***	−.23***	−.06	−.12**
Family Size	−.07 +	−.11*	−.15***	−.06
Catholic (dummy variable)	.01	.05	.02	.05
G2 Personal Characteristics and Attitudes				
Dominance	.04	.08	.08*	.10*
Expressivity	.21***	.15***	.09*	.04
Religiosity	.06	.09*	.06	.04
Political Orientation (Hi=Conservative)	.16***	.07	.14***	.15***
Anti-Women's Rights	−.00	−.03	−.03	−.02
R^2	.12***	.12***	.13***	.09***
N	(640)	(487)	(640)	(487)

B. COUNTER-TRADITIONAL

	(1) Masculine Skills to G3 Daughter		(2) Domestic Skills to G3 Son	
G2 Status Characteristics				
Age	-.22***	-.26***	-.27***	-.28***
Education	.05	-.03	.01	-.01
Family Size	-.19***	-.09 $^+$	-.06	-.12**
Catholic (dummy variable)	-.09**	-.05	-.10**	-.00
G2 Personal Characteristics and Attitudes				
Dominance	.08 $^+$	.05	.11**	-.09*
Expressivity	.03	.04	.12***	.17***
Religiosity	.03	.06	.10**	.10*
Political Orientation	-.10**	-.06	-.01	-.09*
Anti-Women's Rights	-.05	-.13***	-.07	-.18***
R^2	.16***	.11***	.17***	.17***
N	(640)	(487)	(640)	(487)

*** p < .001
** p < .01
* p < .05
+ p < .10

331

heritage in childrearing, reflecting, perhaps, the continuing salience of ethnic neighborhoods, parishes, and parochial schools that provide the larger social context within which their children grow up, even as the parents themselves depart from traditional Catholic views on contraception, sex before marriage, and divorce.

The most interesting finding shown in Table 7.17 is the significance of the parents' political orientation for the skill transmission to children: A conservative political position is significantly linked to traditional skill transmission, and a very liberal political position to countertraditional training. Men are particularly inclined to countertraditional training of sons and daughters if they hold a very liberal position on women's rights: Note the highly significant coefficients on this index in the equations in Panel B based on G2 men's reports of their training of daughters in Masculine skills ($-.13^{***}$) and sons in Domestic Skills ($-.18^{***}$), a finding of special significance in view of the fact that this is independent of the men's general political orientation or educational attainment.

G2 respondents who scored high on Expressivity show a tendency to high levels of skill transmission (all eight equations show positive signs on Expressivity). The beta coefficients are statistically significant only where the teaching of Domestic Skills is concerned, and this holds for all four equations—the traditional training of daughters in Domestic Skills, and the countertraditional training of sons in Domestic Skills—and applies to high Expressive fathers as much as to high Expressive mothers. Note that this does not necessarily mean men themselves teach domestic skills to their children, because the question asked how much effort the respondent made to see that their children learned each of the skills, which implies either direct teaching by the respondent or support for the efforts of a spouse to teach skills to the child.

Dominance as a personal trait of the parent shows several modest but interesting effects on skill transmission. Both mothers and fathers who are high in Dominance report a high emphasis on teaching Masculine Skills to their sons, but high-Dominant mothers and fathers part ways where countertraditional training of sons in Domestic Skills is concerned. The fathers with high Dominance scores give *less* emphasis to such training, whereas mothers high in Dominance give *more* emphasis to teaching domestic skills to their sons. We suspect highly dominant fathers are men deeply invested in their work, because it is the job world where competitiveness and a preference for "taking charge" take place. Such men are not likely to value the cultivation of "feminine" skills of a domestic variety in their sons. Consistent with this interpretation is the finding that high Dominant fathers emphasized Status qualities in rearing their children (competitive, ambitious, successful) to a significantly greater degree than men low in Dominance (data not shown). By contrast, most women in our sample, as in the large society, are not in high-paying and prestigious jobs; hence, those who are high in Dominance have no outlet for their ambition and pleasure in taking charge except on the homefront, and, as a result, they may pour their energies and ambition into training their sons in a variety of skills, both traditional and countertraditional.

We are ready, now, to put our second question to the data on skill transmission: Is there any carryover from the training G2 respondents received from their own parents to their roles as parents themselves in teaching their children a variety of skills? To answer this under a harsh test, we replicated the same equations reported and discussed above, but added the measures on Domestic and Masculine Skills learned in their family of origin. Hence, for the past training to have an "effect" on their own roles as parents, the family of origin measure must have a significant coefficient, net of all the characteristics of G2 respondents that they acquired since they were youngsters.

Table 7.18 provides the data relevant to this harsh test. We do not show the entire array of predictor variables in the actual regression equations involved, since our purpose here is a highly focused one. Instead, we show the standardized beta coefficients on past training, and the overall R^2 values, one brought forward from the previous table and the second from the equation with the addition of the early family measure on skill training.

Inspection of Table 7.18 shows highly significant beta coefficients for the early training in the family of origin in all eight equations, and a marked increase in the total amount of variance explained, as seen by comparing the R^2 values in the first column (equation 1, without the family of origin measure) with those in the last column (equation 2, with the family of origin measure added). The level of training and the area of training in the family of origin are clearly providing a headstart for the next generation's goals in rearing their own children: Those who were taught skills in turn teach them to the next generation.

We were somewhat surprised to note the particularly strong transmission of countertraditional skills suggested by the size of the beta coefficients and R^2 values in Table 7.18 compared to those on the transmission of traditional skills. Thinking about these results suggested a final twist of analysis in pursuit of an interesting idea. The thesis we sought to test builds on the concept of a "forerunner" generation, that minority in one generation that is ahead of their times in holding a view or behaving in a way not yet widely approved but one that receives increasing social approval years later (Bengtson & Black, 1973). Assuming that counter-traditional training by parents of our respondents identifies them as such "forerunners," our thesis is that G2 respondents who received

Table 7.18. Regression Analysis to Test for Cross-Generational Transmission
    of Skill Training: The Contribution of Training in Family of Origin of G2
    Respondents to Their Skill Training of G3 Children (G2 Sample)

Dependent Variable in Regression on Family of Procreation [a]	Equation 1 [b]	Equation 2 [c]	
	R^2 without Family of Origin Variable	Beta Coefficient on G2 Training in Family of Origin	R^2 of Equation Including Family of Origin Training
A. Traditional Training by G2 Parents			
Domestic Skill Training of G3 Daughter			
G2 Mother	.12***	.29***	.20***
G2 Father	.12***	.20***	.16***
Masculine Skill Training of G3 Son			
G2 Mother	.13***	.20***	.16***
G2 Father	.09***	.43***	.27***
B. Countertraditional Training by G2 Parents			
Domestic Skill Training of G3 Son			
G2 Mother	.17***	.24***	.22***
G2 Father	.17***	.45***	.35***
Masculine Skill Training of G3 Daughter			
G2 Mother	.16***	.33***	.27***
G2 Father	.11***	.33***	.21***

[a] All equations included the same predictor variables as shown in Table 7.16: Age, Education, Catholic, Family Size, Dominance, Expressivity, Religosity, Political Orientation, and Anti-Women's Rights.
[b] These are R^2 values reported in Table 7.16, with predictor variables restricted to G2 characteristics.
[c] Equation 2 is identical to equation 1 except for the addition of the relevant skill training G2 respondents received in their families of origin.
*** $p < .001$

such training would be more likely to transmit such skills to their
children than those whose parents taught them traditional skills. In
other words, children of the forerunner generation can draw not only on
the pattern set down by their parents, but also wider social support for
departing from gender-differentiated training of children. By contrast,
children of the traditional generation may be less likely to follow their
parents in their own child training emphasis, because there is less
widespread support in the larger society for perpetuating gender-
differentiated training of children.

Table 7.19. Traditional vs. Forerunner Skill Transmission from Family of Origin to Family of Procreation (G2 Sample) (Pearson Correlation Coefficients)

Gender of G2 Respondent	Traditional vs. Forerunner Skill Transmission	Correlation Coefficient
Women	Traditional: Domestic Skills learned in family of origin and taught to G3 Daughters	.26***
	Forerunner: Masculine Skills learned in family of origin and taught to G3 daughters	.38***
Men	Traditional: Masculine Skills learned in family of origin and taught to G3 sons	.46***
	Forerunner: Domestic Skills learned in family of origin and taught to G3 sons	.54***

*** p < .001

The specific test for this thesis is a simple one: The correlation coefficients between training in one generation and its transmission to the next should be *higher* for the forerunner pattern than for the traditional pattern. Table 7.19 confirms the thesis in both relevant comparisons. Women who were taught Masculine Skills by their forerunner parents are more apt to teach Masculine Skills to their daughters than women who were taught Domestic Skills by their traditional parents and in turn taught them to their daughters (correlations of .38 vs. .26). The same contrast is shown for men (.54 in the cross-generational transmission of countertraditional skills and .46 for the traditional skill transmission).

While these results are interesting, the more basic point in our gender role socialization analysis is the fact, shown in Chapter 2, that there has been little departure from the traditional training of daughters in domestic skills and sons in masculine skills. Unless young adults acquire such competencies prior to marriage, while living on their own rather than in their parents' household, they are likely to perpetuate a gender-differentiated division of labor with their spouses, and through teaching and modeling they will transmit the same pattern to the sons and daughters they rear.

Intergenerational Influences on Attitudes

In both persistence effects and cross-generational transmission, the direction of influence is from parent to child, a one-directional model of influence from parent to child that has been a truism in developmental psychology with a very long history, steeped partially in Freudian theories and partially in empirical research in child psychology. In our analysis of persistence effects and cross-generational transmission, we have taken a long step across time, from parental influences exerted while G2 respondents were children to their roles as adults. Depending on their age, the time span could be less than decade since they were teenagers (i.e., respondents in their 20s) or as many as five decades (i.e., respondents in their 60s).

In even posing the question of persistent effects, we were running counter to more recent theories that have emphasized the influence of age peers, friends, and co-workers, and the general political tone of a particular historical era, rather than deep rooted early family influences. This emphasis on nonfamilial sources of influence was part of the increasing emphasis on adult socialization among social scientists, a new idea in the 1960s (Brim & Wheeler, 1966), which paved the way for the prevalent view in the 1980s that the keynote of adult life is not "constancy" but "change" (Brim & Kagan, 1980).

During the 1970s it also became clear to social scientists that even young children had effects on their parents, as studies accumulated that showed the impact of physically handicapped or mentally retarded children on the parents' marital satisfaction and family interaction (e.g., Howard, 1978; Korn et al., 1978; Lewis & Rosenblum, 1974). So too, studies of older youth suggested there were changes in the attitudes of their parents as a function of influence by their children. Thus, Gunhild Hagestad, in a study of 119 mothers of college-age children, reports that three-quarters of the mothers recalled attempts by their children to influence them, and about two-thirds of these reported they had changed their own views in response to influence from their children (Hagestad, 1977, 1984). Richard Lerner and Graham Spanier brought much of this literature together in a review volume on child influences on the family (Lerner & Spanier, 1978). By 1990, life span psychologists widely share a dynamic interactional view of child and family development.

Much of this literature, however, has been confined to children during their years of dependency on parents, or at most a few years past college graduation. Hence, the intergenerational relationship under study has tended to be middle-aged parents and their late adolescent or very young adult children. Life span psychologists focused on special cases of younger children (disabled, mentally retarded, child victims of abuse or incest), whereas sociologists have studied older youth: radical college students (Flacks, 1967; Keniston, 1968), or late adolescents, as in Hagestad's study referred to above, or the youngest (18–22 years of age) of three generations, as in Reuben Hills' multigenerational study (Hill et al., 1970).

Interesting as many of these studies of children's influence on parents are, they also have serious limitations. One is the age restriction to adolescent and very young adult children. Parental influence may be underestimated during adolescence, because at this stage of development children are struggling for independence and autonomy. This suggests that parental influence may have a "sleeper effect" not detectable unless the "children" are fully mature adults. We believe our findings on persistence effects and cross-generational transmission demonstrate this point: It is when children have married and are rearing children of their own that early family life influences may be demonstrated.

A second shortcoming of research on child influences on parents is reliance on verbal reports of influence from only one partner to the parent–child relationship. In Hagestad's study, it was mothers who reported their daughters tried and sometimes succeeded in influencing them. In Keniston's study, many of the college-age radical youth cited instances of confrontation on political issues between themselves and their parents that the youth claimed led to their parents modifying their views. In another study, Angres (1975) did in-depth interviews with mothers of former radical college students, during which the mothers reported they had changed their attitudes toward cohabitation of unmarried youth as a result of the impact their own children's attitudes and behavior had had on them.

It is quite another matter to analyze intergenerational influence with measures that are independently obtained from each partner to the parent–child relationship, especially if the available data are drawn from an age representative sample with its wide age range among the parents and the adult children. We are in the fortunate position of being able to analyze intergenerational influence under precisely these circumstances, by drawing on data from the three samples of G1, G2, and G3 respondents, and by using several indices of attitudes on contemporary issues. The attitude indices, described below, concern abortion, teenager access to contraception, and women's rights. We therefore have measures of respondents' views on these three issues from G1 parents and their G2 children, and from G3 children and their G2 parents. Our analysis tests the extent to which a parent's attitude on an issue contributes some direct statistical effect on the attitude of the adult child, net of a wide range of measures predictive of the child's attitude. An identical mode of analysis is done for the reverse direction, the influence of the child on the parent's attitude.

From preliminary analysis, we know that views on the three attitude domains are a function of religiosity, general political orientation, family

size, educational attainment, gender, and age (though not all six variables are significant in all three attitude domains). Hence, to demonstrate that a parent's attitude was highly likely to have had an effect on
the child's attitude, the regression coefficient on the parent's attitude
must be statistically significant in an equation on the child's attitude that
includes the six predictor variables obtained from the child that we had
previously established to be significant. An identical test can be conducted for the influence of the child's attitude on the parent's, using the
six variables that are predictive of the parent's attitudes. A further
advantage of this analysis mode is that we can conduct identical analyses for mothers and fathers, and thus establish whether mothers are
both more influential over and more influenced by their children than
fathers are, as we have reason to expect.[16]

Attitude Measures and Preliminary Analysis Results

As reported in Chapter 1, the study design included eight attitude
items that we expected would tap one underlying construct of Moral-
Sexual Conservatism. Factor analysis dispelled that expectation, however, because it showed four latent factors rather than one. In the analysis
to follow, we shall rely on three of the four indices, each measured by two
items, as follows:

Antiabortion Index:
  An amendment to the Constitution should be passed to prohibit
  abortions.
  A woman should have the right to a legal abortion no matter what her
  reasons are.

Teenager Contraceptive Restriction Index:
  Parental consent should be necessary before family planning clinics
  give contraceptives to teenage girls.
  Drugstores should not sell contraceptives to teenage boys.

Anti-Women's Rights Index:
  More women should be encouraged to seek the nomination for the
  Presidency of the United States.
  An Equal Rights Amendment to the Constitution should be passed to
  ensure equality for women.

Several things should be noted concerning the indices. For one, a conservative position on the Contraception index does not mean respondents oppose the use of birth control by adults, only that they draw the
line where ease of access to contraceptives by young adolescents is

concerned. Second, the women's rights index is restricted to the public, political sphere, not the private realm of family. Third, liberal responses on the indices have the lower numeric value; conservative responses have the higher numeric value.

Preliminary analysis established a core set of significant predictor variables of the positions G2 respondents took on the three attitude domains. A conservative political orientation, high church attendance, being older, and low levels of educational attainment are associated with conservative positions on all three attitude indices. Family size was relevant to attitudes on contraceptive access for teenagers, with those who have had large families more restrictive than those with small families. Gender was of particular relevance to attitudes toward women's rights, with women more liberal than men on the issue. Many of these variables are positively related to each other, but the results reported above come from a regression analysis; hence, any variable reported as significant had an independent contribution to the explanation of variance on the attitude indices, net of all others.

Regression Tests of Intergenerational Influence

The results of the regression test of intergenerational influence are shown in Tables 7.20, 7.21, and 7.22. Table 7.20 presents the results for mother–adult child influence, Table 7.21 for father–adult child influence, and Table 7.22 brings together just the coefficients on the parent's attitude in child equations and children's attitude in the parent equations for ease of inspecting the contrast between mothers and fathers.

Table 7.20 shows six regression equations: column 1 shows the equations in which the adult child's attitude is the dependent variable, and column 2 shows the mother's attitude as the dependent variable. Within each column the three attitude domains are shown in Panels A, B, and C. Thus, for example, the first equation in the upper left of Table 7.20 predicts G3 adult children's attitudes toward abortion as a function of a variety of the children's characteristics, together with the scores of their G2 mothers on the abortion index. It can be readily seen that the beta coefficient on the mother's attitude (.27***) is highly significant as a predictor of the child's attitude on the abortion issue, net of all the other child characteristics included in the equation. As in the preliminary analysis, frequent church attendance, a conservative position in general political orientation, and low educational attainment are all conducive to a conservative position on abortion.

Inspection of the first predictor variable entry in each of the six equations in Table 7.20 shows significant beta coefficients for the moth-

Table 7.20. Regression Analysis of the Influence of G2 Mothers and G3 Adult Children on Each Other's Attitudes on Selected Contemporary Issues [a] (Merged G2–G3 Samples) (Beta Coefficients)

Predictor Variables	G3 Child's Attitude (1)	Predictor Variables	G2 Mother's Attitude (2)
A. Antiabortion Index			
Mother's Attitude	.27***	Child's Attitude	.31***
Child's Church Attendance	.31***	Mother's Church Attendance	.18***
Child's Family Size	.06	Mother's Family Size	.10
Child's Political Orientation	.17**	Mother's Political Orientation	.11
Child's Education	−.14*	Mother's Education	−.24***
Child's Age	−.11	Mother's Age	.23***
Child's Gender (1 = Female)	−.13	Child's Gender	.11
R^2	.33***	R^2	.39***
B. Teenager Contraceptive Restriction Index			
Mother's Attitude	.20**	Child's Attitude	.20***
Child's Church Attendance	.26***	Mother's Church Attendance	.14*
Child's Family Size	.20*	Mother's Family Size	.22***
Child's Political Orientation	.09	Mother's Political Orientation	.11
Child's Education	−.09	Mother's Education	−.13*
Child's Age	.02	Mother's Age	.27***
Child's Gender	−.03	Child's gender	−.13*
R^2	.27***	R^2	.34***
C. Anti-Women's Rights Index			
Mother's Attitude	.15*	Child's Attitude	.18*
Child's Church Attendance	.01	Mother's Church Attendance	.04
Child's Family Size	−.07	Mother's Family Size	.06
Child's Political Orientation	.40***	Mother's Political Orientation	.20**
Child's Education	−.01	Mother's Education	−.16*
Child's Age	−.04	Mother's Age	.02
Child's Gender	−.16**	Child's Gender	.01
R^2	.22***	R^2	.13**
N	(156)	N	(156)

[a] High score = Conservative and low score = liberal on all three attitude indices, and general political orientation.
*** $p < .001$
** $p < .01$
* $p < .05$

er's or child's attitude score when regressed on their respective child's or mother's attitude score. If mothers are conservative on abortion, adult children tend to be conservative; if mothers are liberal, their adult children tend also to be liberal, net of all other variables in the equations. Clearly, for the three attitude domains investigated, there is significant, reciprocal, intergenerational influence between mothers and adult children. It is even the case in one equation—mother's attitude toward abortion—that the adult child's attitude toward abortion is the *most* significant predictor of mother's attitude, as indexed by the large standardized beta coefficient (.31) compared to any other predictor variable on mother's attitude, e.g., −.24 on her educational attainment, or .23 on her age.[17]

The profile is very different in the analysis of influence between fathers and adult children. As seen in Table 7.21, in only one of the six equations is the father's attitude a significant predictor of the child's attitude, and it is on women's rights that this is the case. Adult children are more conservative (or more liberal) on this issue if their fathers are conservative (or liberal), net of other characteristics of the child. A similar result was found in the G1–G2 analysis not shown in the text, and, on this issue, G2 adult children also showed significant effects on the attitudes of G1 fathers toward women's rights.

Table 7.22 brings together all the beta coefficients from the 12 equations in Tables 7.20 and 7.21. In all 6 mother–child equations, there is evidence of reciprocal intergenerational influence between mothers and adult children, but in only 1 of the 6 father–child equations is there any evidence of influence between fathers and adult children.

Why should there be more influence between mothers and adult children than between fathers and their adult children? We explored several possible interpretations. One possibility is that there is greater social distance in the relationship of men to their children than of women, particularly when the topics involved, such as abortion and contraception, are of a sensitive, personal nature. To test this we constructed a new measure of the extent to which adult children held more liberal views than their mothers and fathers on the three attitude indices (by subtracting the child's attitude score from the parent's attitude score), and regressed a new set of predictor variables on this attitude difference measure: frequency of social interaction and the rating of Affective Closeness, and measures of the extent to which parent and child differed in age, education, and church attendance. The results (not reported in tabular form in this book) showed that the three difference measures, frequency of phone contact, and closeness of the mother–child relationship related significantly to the extent to which children

Table 7.21. Regression Analysis of the Influence of G2 Fathers and G3 Adult Children on Each Other's Attitudes on Selected Contemporary Issues (Merged G2 and G3 Samples) (Beta Coefficients)

Predictor Variables	G3 Child's Attitude (1)	Predictor Variables	G2 Father's Attitude (2)
A. Antiabortion Index			
Father's Attitude	.09	Child's Attitude	.12
Child's Church Attendance	.20*	Father's Church Attendance	.31***
Child's Family Size	.29*	Father's Family Size	.15 +
Child's Political Orientation	.20**	Father's Political Orientation	.14
Child's Education	− .12	Father's Education	− .19*
Child's Age	− .25*	Father's Age	− .11
Child's Gender	− .15 +	Child's Gender	− .01
R^2	**.24***	R^2	**.25***
B. Teenager Contraceptive Restriction Index			
Father's Attitude	.08	Father's Attitude	.06
Child's Church Attendance	.08	Father's Church Attendance	.29***
Child's Family Size	.03	Father's Family Size	− .05
Child's Political Orientation	.31***	Father's Political Orientation	.19*
Child's Education	− .21*	Father's Education	− .13
Child's Age	.18	Father's Age	.19*
Child's Gender	− .12	Child's gender	.09
R^2	**.23***	R^2	**.23***
C. Anti-Women's Rights Index			
Father's Attitude	.20*	Child's Attitude	.14
Child's Church Attendance	.03	Father's Church Attendance	.09
Child's Family Size	.08	Father's Family Size	− .02
Child's Political Orientation	.26**	Father's Political Orientation	.17 +
Child's Education	− .14	Father's Education	− .08
Child's Age	− .01	Father's Age	− .04
Child's Gender	− .06	Child's Gender	.22*
R^2	**.14***	R^2	**.10**
N	(117)	N	(117)

*** $p < .001$
** $p < .01$
* $p < .05$
+ $p < .10$

Table 7.22. Beta Coefficients on Parents' and Adult Children's Influence on Each Other's Attitudes on Selected Contemporary Issues (Merged G2 and G3 Samples)

	Attitude Domain		
Direction of Influence	*Abortion*	*Contraception*	*Women's rights*
G2 Mother → G3 Child	.27***	.20**	.15*
G3 Child → G2 Mother	.31***	.20***	.18*
G2 Father → G3 Child	.09	.08	.20*
G3 Child → G2 Father	.12	.06	.14

*** p < .001
** p < .01
* p < .05
+ p < .10

held more liberal views than their mothers: The greater the difference between mothers and children in age, education, and church attendance, the more liberal the child was than the mother on the abortion and contraception indices. On the other hand, the more frequent their telephone contact and the closer the relationship, the *less* liberal the child was compared to the mother.

None of the difference, affective, or interaction variables showed significant effects on the extent to which children were more liberal than their fathers. We interpret these results as an indication of the greater openness to each other's views in the case of mothers and adult children, since the more often they talk together and the closer the relationship, the less the difference in their views on sexual and moral issues. On the other hand, status differences as a function of age and education are associated with departure by the children from their mothers' views. That none of these measures shows significant effects on attitude differences between men and their adult children implies an avoidance of the topics of a moral and sexual nature, and perhaps some resistance on the part of men to the kind of interaction that would make them vulnerable to influence from adult children. This is consistent with the more superordinate position of men as husbands and fathers: As the "weaker" family members, mothers would be more amenable to influence by children than men. The results are also consistent with our finding on the items in the Topic Avoidance index: Men report much more avoidance of personal problems and sexual issues in conversation with their children than women do. We take this to mean that no matter how frequently men are in contact with their children, topics bearing on sexuality are not apt to be discussed.

It should not be concluded from this analysis that fathers have little or no influence on their children's views and values. It is quite possible that the attitude domains we have explored were not diverse enough to demonstrate paternal influence. We did find that fathers' attitudes on women's rights had an affect on their children's views. It may be therefore that future research will find more intergenerational influence between fathers and adult children if the attitude domains include less intimate ones than abortion and contraception, e.g., race relations, party politics, environmental safety, or nuclear waste disposal. On the other hand, the abortion and contraception items and indices were *not* posed in intimate personal terms, but as broad social, political, and public policy issues that one assumes were topics of conversation and perhaps debate in many homes in Massachusetts, yet we found more impressive evidence of intergenerational influence between mothers and adult children than fathers and their children. Two-way interaction and influence between the generations should clearly be on the future agenda of family sociologists.

The Impact of Marital Happiness or Discord on Intergenerational Relations

In this last section of the chapter, we return to the central theme on the affectional ties between the generations. In earlier sections, the emphasis was on Affective Closeness of the parent–child relationship, as it varied across the life course, by gender, and as a consequence of the earlier history of the relationship in the family of origin. Here we pose a rather different question, concerning the impact of marital happiness or discord of parents on the Affective Closeness of the parents and their children, as viewed by the parent and the child. We also extend this analysis to explore the impact of marital discord in the intermediate generation of parents on the relationship between grandparents and grandchildren.

In Chapter 4 we reported the special significance of women as connecting links, with higher obligations to those kin connected to ego through women than to kin related through men. Analogously, in this section, we explore the parallel expectation that under conditions of marital stress, children are more apt to retain close relations with their mothers than with their fathers, and, by extension, closer relations with their maternal grandparents than with their paternal grandparents.

The problem as we have defined it differs from much of the literature on marriage, divorce, and grandparenthood. Widespread marital instability and high divorce rates have stimulated a good deal of research in the past decade into the determinants and consequences of divorce (Cherlin, 1981; Gerstel, 1988; Schoen et al., 1985; Thornton & Rodgers, 1987). Particular attention has been given to adult and child adjustment following divorce (e.g., Gerstel, 1988; Leslie & Grady, 1985); remarriage (Cherlin, 1981; Furstenberg, 1981; Spanier & Thompson, 1984), and the plight of divorced women rearing children as solo parents (Garfinkel & McLanahan, 1986; McLanahan et al., 1981). More recently, with a growing interest in grandparenthood, scholars have begun to analyze the impact of divorce on the relations between grandparents and their grandchildren (Bengtson & Robertson, 1985; Cherlin & Furstenberg, 1986; Johnson, 1983, 1985, 1988). Because child custody is overwhelmingly held by women, many paternal grandparents are cut off from easy or frequent contact with their sons' children, whereas maternal grandparents often have increased contact with their grandchildren as they assist their daughters in various ways following divorce.

But divorce is rarely precipitous; it is a final act and point of transition after a process of deterioration in a marital relationship that may have lasted many years. This raises the possibility that there is a process of change, of attenuation of contact and affective closeness in the parent–child and grandparent–grandchild relationship *prior* to divorce, as a consequence of marital discord in the parental marriage. To the extent this is the case, then divorce per se may not represent a totally new realignment of sentiment and contact between family members that has been assumed.

Furthermore, parents typically stand as gatekeepers and affective monitors between their children and the larger kindred. Hence, marital discord in the parental generation may product strain not only between the marital couple and their children (in particular between fathers and children) but in their relationship with parents-in-laws, and the children's relationship with their paternal grandparents as well. Thus, it seems unlikely that a young boy would develop a warm and intimate relationship with his paternal grandmother if his mother was in acute conflict with or actively disliked her mother-in-law.

The analysis reported below consists of three related topics: First we shall establish the extent to which marital happiness or discord of parents relates to the Affective Closeness of children to the parents. Second, we compare the impact of marital happiness or discord of married G2 respondents on their relations to their parents with the impact on their relations with their parents-in-law. Third, we test the extent to which Affective Closeness of the grandparent–grandchild relationship is affected by the middle generation's marital happiness. Finally, we explore the extent to which the relationship between grandparents and grandchildren is affected by the quality of the relationship in the two parent–child relationships that intervene between G1 and G3, the G1–G2 and G2–G3 dyads. Throughout, special attention is focused on gender of parent and child, to test whether, as expected, women's ties to children and parents are more stable in retaining intimacy between the generations than are men's ties when the marital relationship is tense and strained.

The Impact of Marital Discord on Affective Closeness to Children

G2 respondents rated the happiness of their marital relationship at the time they were interviewed in 1985. We show the effect of marital happiness on the Affective Closeness of the relationship between G2 parents and their G3 adult children, using three measures of such closeness: that provided by the respondent parents themselves, their perception of the closeness of their spouses to the children, and, from the G3 spinoff sample, the ratings provided by G3 children themselves. Table 7.23 brings these various perspectives together. To provide an additional dimension to the range shown by marital happiness level of the G2 parents, we have added the parents who have actually separated or divorced to the table. Panels A through D show the three sets of ratings for each of the four parent-child dyads.

We begin with an inspection of Panel A on the mother–daughter dyad. The first row of the table shows the mean Affective Closeness rating between G2 mothers and their daughters as a function of the ratings the mothers gave of their marital happiness (if married) or their status as separated or divorced women. As a glance across this row shows, neither the quality of the marital relationship nor an actual separation or divorce shows any effect on the Affective Closeness of G2 mothers to their daughters; they are uniformly high under all conditions. G3 daughters themselves (shown in the third row of Panel A) confirm their mothers' ratings: they feel just as close to their mothers if their parents' marriage is only low or moderate on happiness as they do if their mothers gave the top rating of marital happiness.[18]

G2 fathers did not share the assessment of their wives when they rated their wives' relationship to the daughters: Men perceive much less closeness to the mother–daughter relationship if the parental marriage is strained or if the parents have separated or divorced than if the marriage is very happy.

A very different profile is shown for the G2–G3 father–daughter relationship (Panel C). As indicated by the asterisks in the right-hand

Table 7.23. Affective Closeness of G2 Parents and G3 Adult Children by Marital Happiness of Parents:[a] Ratings by G2 Parent, G2 Spouse, and G3 Child (Childset File of G2 Sample and G3 Sample) (Mean Ratings on 0–100 Scale)

G2–G3 Dyad	Rater of Closeness	Parents Sep/Div	Marital Happiness of G2 Parents		
			Low	Moderate	High
A. Mother–Daughter	G2 Mother	85.8 (92)	86.8 (57)	90.2 (157)	91.9 (268)
	G2 Father[b]	75.3 (43)	78.5 (37)	86.8 (157)	91.9*** (266)
	G3 Daughter	—[c]	85.2[d] (48)		88.5 (50)
B. Mother–Son	G2 Mother	84.2 (117)	85.2 (53)	88.5 (200)	90.2 (273)
	G2 Father	75.9 (42)	91.9 (33)	88.5 (145)	90.2 (236)
	G3 Son	—	80.2 (44)		83.5 (52)
C. Father–Daughter	G2 Father	78.1 (50)	76.8 (40)	83.5 (164)	88.5*** (273)
	G2 Mother[e]	52.6 (75)	70.8 (57)	85.2 (195)	90.2** (268)
	G3 Daughter	—	72.4 (45)		86.8** (48)
D. Father–Son	G2 Father	77.6 (51)	86.8 (37)	81.8 (149)	86.8 (239)
	G2 Mother[e]	49.3 (86)	71.5 (51)	85.2 (200)	88.5*** (268)
	G3 Son	—	72.8 (43)		83.5* (54)

[a] Current Marital Happiness rated by G2 parents.
[b] G2 men's rating of closeness between their wives and their children.
[c] Too few cases of divorced parents in G3 spinoff sample.
[d] Low and moderate combined to provide sufficient case Ns.
[e] G2 women's rating of closeness between their husbands and their children.
*** p < .001   ** p < .01   * p < .05

margin, marital discord or happiness is significantly related to Affective Closeness between fathers and daughters no matter who does the closeness rating: Men themselves report being less close to their daughters if their marriages are stressed, and both mothers and daughters concur with this. Furthermore, although divorced men rated their relationship to their daughters at about the same level of closeness as married men in unhappy marriages (78.1 vs. 76.8), from the perspective of divorced women looking at the relationship between their ex-husbands and their daughters, this is clearly not the case: From the 78.1 closeness rating divorced men gave their relationship to daughters, the rating drops to only 52.6 when divorced women rate this relationship.

In men's eyes, marital discord does not affect their relation to sons, though being divorced does (See Panel D). But sons do not agree with their fathers, reporting lower closeness ratings under the condition of marital stress than marital happiness. As in the case of the father–daughter relationship, divorced women perceive a decidedly low Affective Closeness level between their ex-husbands and their sons. In fact, this circumstance is associated with the lowest rating 49.3 of all those shown in Table 7.23.

The remaining dyad—mother–son in Panel B—shows no significant impact of the quality of the parents' marriage for closeness between mothers and sons from anyone's perspective: the mother herself, the father, or the son himself. The only contrast is found in the fathers' ratings of closeness: Divorced men report less closeness between their ex-wives and their sons (75.9) than even unhappily married fathers do (91.9).

Across all the results reported in the table, the general finding is a far greater vulnerability of men's relationship with their adult children than of women's relationships: Marital happiness ratings show a significant relation to Affective Closeness between fathers and children in five of the six comparisons, whereas this is the case in only one of the six comparisons where the mother–child relationship is concerned. This suggests that marital tension may often involve a coalition between mothers and the children, while fathers recede to the sidelines of family affection. After divorce, ex-spouses clearly disagree, particularly where the father's relationship to children is concerned: Divorced men report almost as close a relationship with their children as married men, but divorced women disagree, reporting much lower closeness between their former spouses and their sons and daughters than even unhappily married women do. All told, the data suggest a more robust stability in the affectional ties between women and their children than between men and their children.

The Impact of Marital Discord on Closeness to Parents and Parents-in-Law

One's spouse is an important connecting link to parents-in-law, contributing to the formation of sentiment toward in-laws. In our data, the correlation between Affective Closeness to one's own parent and the parent-in-law of the same sex hovers near zero, whereas the perception of spouses' closeness to their parents correlates about .75 with ego's closeness to parents-in-law. It is a fair assumption that as the quality of a marital relationship undergoes change, so too may the relationship to parents-in-law, approximating a kind of "cooling out" process prior to any potential break in the marriage.

Both men and women report higher average scores on Affective Closeness to their own parents than to their parents-in-law, with a much greater difference in average scores for women's relations to parents versus parents-in-law than for men's. As Table 7.24 shows, both men and women agree on this contrast, when reporting their perception of their spouses' closeness to parents and parents-in-law.

In view of the total lack of any significant correlation between affect toward parents and parents-in-law, it seems unlikely that disturbed marital relations will have any effect on relations with parents, though they may depress the Affective Closeness of relations with parents-in-law. In fact, we half expected to find an increase in closeness to parents as a function of marital discord, particularly for daughters and their parents, because parents and daughters are often drawn into more frequent contact and extensive helping patterns in times of trouble in the lives of either generation.

The latter expectation was not confirmed in our data. As seen in Figure 7.5, marital happiness or discord of G2 daughters and sons shows no effect on Affective Closeness of their relationship with parents. By contrast, there is a consistent and significant impact of marital discord on the relations with parents-in-law, a pattern that holds for all four parent–child dyads.

There is also a suggestion that marital discord has more impact on men's relations with their in-laws than on women's, which would be consistent with the greater likelihood that unhappy married women share their personal troubles with their parents, especially their mothers, than men are apt to do with their parents. This would mean that long before any divorce takes place to terminate unhappy marriages, a woman's parents may withdraw from or become alienated from their sons-in-law to a greater extent than do a man's parents from his wife, their daughter-in-law. Daughters-in-law are of course critical connecting

Table 7.24. Current Affective Closeness of G2 Adults to G1 Parents and Parents-in-Law by Gender: (A) G2 Respondents' Closeness and (B) Perception of Spouses' Closeness (G2 Sample) (Mean Rating on 0–100 Scale)

Gender of G1 and G2		Closeness to Own Parents (1)		Closeness to Parents-in-Law (2)		Difference in Mean Rating: Parent Minus Parent-in-Law
A.	**G2 Respondents**					
	G2 Women	Mother	85.2	Mother-in-law	68.5	+16.7
		Father	78.5	Father-in-law	66.8	+11.7
	G2 Men	Mother	78.5	Mother-in-law	71.8	+6.7
		Father	75.2	Father-in-law	73.5	+1.7
B.	**G2 Perception of Spouses' Closeness**					
	G2 Men re Wives	Mother	83.5	Mother-in-law	70.1	+13.4
		Father	81.8	Father-in-law	68.5	+13.3
	G2 Women re Husbands	Mother	78.5	Mother-in-law	73.5	+5.0
		Father	75.2	Father-in-law	70.1	+5.1

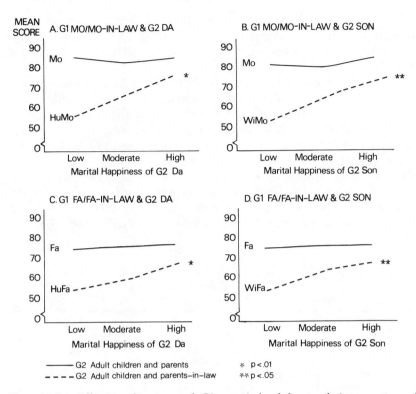

Figure 7.5. Affective closeness of G2 married adults to their parents and parents-in-law, by marital happiness of G2 adults and gender composition of all dyads. (All ratings by G2 respondents) (Mean score on 0–100 scale)

links to the grandchildren, which may impose a restraint on paternal grandparents "taking sides" that is not necessary for maternal grandparents. Should the marriage break, it is likely that the daughter and her children will remain accessible to the maternal grandparents, something not nearly as assured for paternal grandparents should their sons divorce.

Parental Marital Discord and Grandparent–Grandchild Affective Closeness

We can now extend the analysis to the impact of marital discord in the middle generation on the affective closeness between the alternate generations of grandparents and grandchildren. In view of the finding that men's relations with adult children are more strongly impacted by marital discord than women's relations, we predict that marital discord of parents will reduce the intimacy of children with their paternal grandparents but not their maternal grandparents.

We can test these predictions with three sets of data. The first, shown in Table 7.25, shows the average Affective Closeness rating on the relationship of G3 children to all four G1 grandparents as a function of G2 marital discord or happiness. These are all ratings provided by G2 respondents and hence one may suspect some projection on the part of the reporting parents. We counter this by a second dip into the data in the form of G3 children's own ratings of closeness to their four grandparents as a function of how happy they rate their parents' marriage to have been. The third analysis tack is to assess the relative contribution of affective closeness in the two parent–child dyads that intervene between

Table 7.25. G2 Parents' Rating of Affective Closeness Between G1 Grandparents and G3 Grandchildren by Marital Happiness of G2 Parents (Childset File on G2 Sample) (Mean Rating on 0–100 Scale)

| | | Marital Happiness of G2 Parents | |
Relation of G1 to G3	Low	Moderate	High
A. G2 Women re G3 Daughters' Relationship to			
Maternal Grandmother	78.5	85.2	85.2
Maternal Grandfather	81.8	75.2	81.8
Paternal Grandmother	76.8	73.5	81.8
Paternal Grandfather	51.8	70.1	76.8**
B. G2 Women re G3 Sons' Relationship to			
Maternal Grandmother	76.8	78.5	86.8*
Maternal Grandfather	68.5	68.5	81.8***
Paternal Grandmother	61.8	73.5	81.8***
Paternal Grandfather	43.4	68.5	81.8***
C. G2 Men re Daughters' Relationship to			
Maternal Grandmother	78.5	76.8	83.5
Maternal Grandfather	62.1	76.8	88.5***
Paternal Grandmother	63.5	78.5	80.2*
Paternal Grandfather	65.1	75.2	78.5*
D. G2 Men re Sons' Relationship to			
Maternal Grandmother	81.8	85.2	85.2
Maternal Grandfather	61.8	78.5	86.8***
Paternal Grandmother	86.8	81.5	78.5
Paternal Grandfather	75.2	81.8	78.5

*** p < .001
** p < .01
* p < .05

grandparents and grandchildren for the closeness between the alternate generations.

Table 7.25 provides the data for the first question: how the quality of the marital relationship of G2 married couples relates to the Affective Closeness of their G3 children to the G1 grandparents. Gender of the G2 parent is shown in the separate panels (G2 women in Panels A and B and G2 men in Panels C and D.) From the perspective of G2 women, five of the eight G1–G3 relationships show a significant lessening of Affective Closeness between grandparents and grandchildren if their marriage is an unhappy one. Four of the five significant effects of marital happiness of the parents involve the sons, and only one the daughter. The only relationship women see affected by their own marital unhappiness where a daughter is concerned is the daughter's relationship to her paternal grandfather (G2 women's fathers-in-law). In contrast, women perceive an impact of marital discord on all their sons' relationships (Panel B), most strongly so with paternal grandparents (especially the grandfather), and modestly so where the maternal grandmother is concerned (G2 women's own mother). With her own cross-sex relationship impaired, women may perceive other cross-sex relationships to be significantly less intimate than same-sex relationships, particularly female same-sex relations.

From the perspective of G2 men (Panels C and D), only three of the eight relationships are less close under the condition of marital discord than of happiness, two of them involving the child's maternal grandfather (men's fathers-in-law), and one the paternal grandmother (men's mothers). *The only grandparent–grandchild type that shows no significant effect of parents' marital discord is the maternal grandmother–granddaughter relationship.*

Parents in the middle generation may well be projecting their own marital tension and some ambivalence toward parents-in-law in the ratings they gave to the closeness between their parents or parents-in-law and their children. But such projections can have real effects, if parents serve as emotional and social gatekeepers for their children's access to and feelings toward their grandparents. We saw previously that under marital tension, men as fathers seem to move to the periphery of family affection. In these data, grandfathers seem to move to the same periphery more often than grandmothers, and sons are perceived to be more impacted by their parents' marital discord than are daughters in their relations with grandparents.

Fortunately, we can shift now to data provided by the grandchildren themselves, from the G3 spinoff sample in which G3 children rated how intimate they were to each of their grandparents, both during the years they were growing up (when most grandparents were still alive) and currently (but with a reduced number of grandparents still alive). In view of the much smaller sample size of G3 than G2 respondents, we resort to a correlational analysis, i.e., the Pearson correlation coefficients between the ratings on marital happiness of parents while G3 children were growing up and their Affective Closeness to each of their grandparents. Table 7.26 shows the correlations: Panel A shows the retrospective ratings of closeness to grandparents while the G3 respondents were growing up and Panel B shows current ratings in 1985.

Turning first to relations with grandparents during childhood (Panel A), the findings indicate that marital discord in the middle generation had no impact on the relationship of grandsons and granddaughters to their maternal grandparents while G3 children were youngsters, but discord in the parental marriage reduced the closeness of G3 grandchildren to their paternal grandparents in three of the four ratings shown. The only exception is the G3 grandsons' relationship with their

Table 7.26. Pearson Correlation Coefficients Between Marital Happiness of G2 Parents While Rearing Children and Past and Present Affective Closeness of G3 Children to Their Grandparents [a] (G3 Sample)

	G3 Grandchildren	
G1 Grandparent	Grandsons	Granddaughters
A. Past Marital Happiness of G2 Parents and Closeness to Grandparents in Childhood		
Maternal Grandmother	− .05	.07
	(84)	(98)
Maternal Grandfather	− .06	.02
	(74)	(70)
Paternal Grandmother	.33***	.29***
	(82)	(88)
Paternal Grandfather	.04	.38***
	(63)	(57)
B. Past Marital Happiness of G2 Parents and Current Closeness to Grandparents		
Maternal Grandmother	.11	− .02
	(35)	(50)
Maternal Grandfather	.46**	.32*
	(19)	(21)
Paternal Grandmother	.46**	.31*
	(31)	(26)
Paternal Grandfather	.25 +	.43*
	(21)	(17)

[a] All ratings by G3 adult children.
*** p < .001
** p < .01
* p < .05
+ p < .10

paternal grandfathers. Perhaps paternal grandfathers are particularly eager to retain a close connection with sons' sons who share their patrinym.

Panel B, on current relations with grandparents, suggests that the earlier pattern in youth has continued to affect the relationship with surviving grandparents. This is most clearly the case for grandsons' relations with paternal grandmothers, and for granddaughters' relations with both paternal grandparents. The unexpected pattern to emerge in the current closeness ratings is that past marital tension of the parents now extends to maternal grandfathers, suggesting some lag effect of childhood parental marital discord on this relationship. This one unexpected finding aside, what stands out sharply is the fact that neither in youth nor in current relations with grandparents, does parental marital happiness or discord have any bearing on a G3 grandchild's relationship with the maternal grandmother. She was the most salient grandparent in youth, as noted in Chapter 4, and she seems to stand above the fray of discord in the intermediary generation in the affections of her grandsons and granddaughters from youth on.

There are a few discrepancies between what G2 parents report in rating the closeness of their children to grandparents as a function of their own marital quality and what the G3 children themselves report, but a common theme across the two data sets is the more precarious nature of men's family relations, whether in the role of son, father, or grandfather. Overall, our analysis suggests that *marital discord weakens the ties between men and their children, especially sons, and between children and their paternal grandparents, and this process takes place well in advance of any parental divorce.*

Our last analysis step concerns the extent to which the Affective Closeness of the intervening parent–child dyads between G1 grandparents and G3 grandchildren shows a significant impact on the intimacy between the alternate generations. For this purpose, we use data from the childset file on the G2 sample, to utilize the Affective Closeness ratings of all the children of G2 respondents and the children's grandparents. We follow a multivariate mode of analysis this time, by regressing the Affective Closeness ratings of the two intervening parent–child dyads—G1 parent–G2 child and G2 parent–G3 child—on the Affective Closeness between G1 grandparents and G3 grandchildren. Two additional predictor variables are used as well: the global ratings of Family Cohesion in both the family of origin and family of procreation. Geographic distance and age of grandchild are entered in the equation as controls, on the assumption that proximity may have some relevance to G1–G3 closeness and that the alternate generations are closer while grandchildren are very young. Note that we are now using Affective

Closeness ratings for *all* the children of G2 respondents, their young-sters under 18 years of age as well as mature adult children.

Regressions were therefore computed with these predictor variables on the current Affective Closeness of G3 children to all four grandparent types. To avoid any distortion that might be introduced by ratings given by G2 respondents for the relation of their children to their parents-in-law, we limit the analysis to G2 parents' ratings of just their own parents. Hence the two equations on maternal grandparents are based on reports by G2 women respondents, whereas the two equations on paternal grandparents are based on reports by G2 men respondents.

Table 7.27 shows the results of the regression analysis. As an inspec-tion of the top two rows in these equations shows, the Affective Close-ness of the intervening parent–child dyads has significant, independent effects on the closeness between grandparents and grandchildren in all four equations. Second, the degree to which the two families were cohesive also contributes to the closeness of G3 grandchildren to their grandparents. There is, however, a difference by gender of the middle generation in *which* family has the more significant effect: for G2 women (reporting on their own parents' relationship to their children), the cohesion of the family they grew up in is the more important for the G1–G3 relationship. For G2 men, by contrast (reporting on their own par-ents' relationship to their children), it is the cohesion of their families of procreation that is the more significant of the two family cohesion measures. This is consistent with earlier findings: Under conditions of marital tension or divorce, women turn to their parents more than men do to theirs, with much less disturbance in the relationship of women and their children than in the relationship of men and their children. Marital tension lowers family cohesion, as we reported earlier in this chapter. Hence the cohesion of men's families of procreation is relevant to their children's relationship with paternal grandparents, while the cohesiveness of women's families of origin is more salient to their children's relationship with maternal grandparents.

Note that the one exception to this general pattern is the impact of the family of procreation on the relationship between maternal grandfathers and grandchildren. This coefficient is not only significant but negative in sign $(-.12^{**})$. That is to say, low levels of cohesion in G2 women's family of procreation triggers closer relations between their fathers (ma-ternal grandfathers) and their children, the male figures who may be-come more significant to daughters and grandsons when the daughters' family lacks teamwork and affection. In many families, a woman's father may compensate for shortcomings of her spouse in providing her son with a model of adequate manhood.

Table 7.27. Regression on Current Affective Closeness of G1 Grandparents and G3 Grandchildren, as Perceived by G2 Parents, by Gender and Type of Grandparent (G2 Sample)

	Grandparent Type [a]				
Predictor Variables	Maternal Grandmother	Maternal Grandfather	Paternal Grandmother	Paternal Grandfather
Affective Closeness of Parent–Child Dyads				
G1–G2	.34***	.35***	.35***	.52***
G2–G3	.31***	.30***	.33***	.29***
Family Cohesion of				
G2's Family of Origin	.15***	.13**	.08	.07
G2's Family of Procreation	.01	−.12**	.12*	.25***
Age of G3 Grandchild	−.07	−.08⁺	−.07	−.13***
Geographic Distance between G1 and G2	−.09*	−.09*	−.03	−.05
R^2	.31***	.28***	.35***	.47***
N	(326)	(326)	(340)	(240)

[a] Closeness ratings for G3 relationships to maternal grandparents by G2 women and to paternal grandparents by G2 men.

*** p < .001
** p < .01
* p < .05
⁺ p < .10

As expected, the younger the grandchild, the closer the relations between grandparents and grandchildren, but this is significant or verges on statistical significance only for the grandfather–grandchild relationship, suggesting relations to grandmothers may retain greater closeness as grandchildren mature than is the case for grandfathers (Eisenberg, 1988). Lastly, geographic distance is also negatively related to intimacy between the alternate generations, but significantly so only for maternal grandparents. Women interact with their parents on a more intimate and continuing basis in adulthood than men do, with shared activities and exchanges of help between the generations. This means proximity of residence will also provide grandchildren with more occasions for informal, intimate contact with their maternal than paternal grandparents, even if the latter live just as close by.

One general finding across the discrete lines of analysis we pursued in tracing the impact of marital discord or happiness is the close interdependencies across family relationships. Not only does the past have continuing effects on current family relations, but what happens to one relationship has ripple out effects on many other family relationships. A second theme is the consistency with which we find greater resilience and stability in female bonds between the generations: Mothers and daughters, and grandmothers and granddaughters share special bonds that persist through time and across personal crises.

Conclusion

If there is any one general comment to make in summarizing the numerous threads of analysis reported in this chapter, it is that early family life has significant effects that extend over long stretches of time. In both persistence effects and in cross-generational transmission, we have reported evidence of the continuing direct effects of early family on current relations between parents and adult children, and the transmission from one generation of similar characteristics to the next generation. By way of summarizing the chapter, we shall discuss four general patterns that run through the analysis we have presented.

Cross-Generational Transmission

We have reported that the quality of G1 parents' marriage was echoed in the marital happiness of G2 adult children. Similarly, we have found a significant tendency for parents to transmit the same skills their own parents had taught them to their own children. Although there is evidence of a long-term trend toward greater parental emphasis on ensuring that sons acquire some domestic competencies, and for children of both sexes to acquire some skills in handling tools and machinery, there continues to be a very marked traditional differentiation in the rearing of daughters compared to sons. It strikes us that this encourages precisely what has been noted in recent sociological research: Although increasing numbers of women work on a steady basis while rearing young children, and more women are entering demanding occupations once considered the exclusive domains of men, the household division of labor has remained remarkably unchanged, with even full time employed women carrying the major burdens of home maintenance and child care (Beer, 1983; Berk & Berk, 1979; Hill & Stafford, 1980; Hochschild, 1989).

We also found a cross-generational transmission of a more global quality of family life, as measured by the index of Family Cohesion. Those who grew up in happy, cooperative, interesting families tend to create families of their own with similar characteristics. This was only significantly the pattern for women, however, no doubt because it has traditionally been women who set the emotional tone of a home, who decide on styles and routines of home maintenance, and who serve as social managers and affective monitors for social contact with kin, neighbors, and friends. It was also of interest to find that family cohesion has a sleeper effect, an impact that is not apparent until children are adults with independent lives of their own. Developmental issues dominate adolescence, crowding out, at least temporarily, any influence of the cohesive or fragmented quality of early family life until children marry and have children of their own.

Children's vs. Parents' Perspectives

The great bulk of research on family relationships has relied on data from one informant, typically a married women reporting on her marital and maternal roles. Had our data on the influence of early family life been confined to what adult women reported about the early phases of childrearing, we might have concluded that the past matters little for the quality of the current relationships between parents and adult children. The major systematic finding in a variety of analysis topics reported in this chapter is how different the world looks from the perspective of adult children. For them, the past colors the present. Parents may forgive and forget, and renegotiate a new style of relating to their adult children, but grown children are still significantly influenced in their relationship to their parents by what transpired many years earlier. This will come as no surprise to family therapists, but it is a point family sociologists have not been sensitive to.

We also noted that fathers seem to be more affected than mothers by past events: The intimacy level between fathers and adult sons still shows the mark of the sons' adolescent years. The beginning of value clashes between fathers and sons may also take place in adolescence, and persist in subsequent years. Men relate to each other in different ways than women do, and the content of their interaction is more apt to focus on nonfamilial domains of life. Hence, the conversations between fathers and sons are more likely to involve controversy than is the case between mothers and sons, and even more so than between mothers and daughters. We believe, though we cannot cite any supportive evidence, that parents tend to feel more comfortable and "at home" literally and figuratively with their daughters and their daughters' spouses than with their sons and daughters-in-law, precisely because women largely determine the cuisine, childrearing values, and social activities of a household. Little wonder, then, that fathers and sons often find a new and safe common ground when the son has children of his own. In families in which the paternal line matters in some special way, there may also be a new and meaningful bond between father, son, and grandson, but these relationships are disturbed by marital tension in the middle generation in a way that does not occur in relations among women as mothers, daughters, and grandmothers.

Gender as a Subjective Axis in Family Life

As implied in the summary comments above, gender remains a highly significant axis of family life, not only in the organization of household activities and in childrearing, but in the emotional climate of the family, and in the impact of the past on current relations. There is a general sense of greater flexibility, more willingness to let the past be forgotten, perhaps more ease in working through unresolved issues left over from childhood, in the relations between the women in the two generations of the family. Even when we have entered the gender-linked personal trait of Expressivity into a multivariate analysis, gender per se often retains its statistical significance, and does so in the direction of greater subjective closeness, and, as we shall see, more social interaction and help exchange between women in the family.

It was also striking to note the many ways in which men have a more precarious or contingent bond with members of the family. Men who married at a very young age have less happy marriages and less cohesive families today than men who married at a more mature age, but age at marriage had no such effects in the case of women. A man's age showed a reverse effect on intimacy with adolescent children: The greater the age difference between fathers and children, the more intimate the relationship with daughters, but the less intimate the relationship with sons. Stress in the parental marriage showed effects on men's relations with sons, with whom they are less close, whereas stress in the parental marriage has little effect on the affective closeness of mothers and their adult children. Even grandfathers move to the periphery of the affective grid of family life if there is tension in a child's marital relationship, whereas grandmothers, particularly maternal grandmothers, have relations with grandchildren that are by comparison more stable and enduring, regardless of the quality of the marriage in the middle generation.

Impact of Value Consensus on the Affective Tone of Parent–Child Relations

The source of most surprise to us was the finding that the extent to which parents and children report sharing similar or different values played so significant a role in affective closeness between the generations. We were prepared, from the long history of clinical psychology, to find early family life affecting current relations, and, from accumulated research in sociology, to find some significant transmission from one generation to the next, but we were not prepared to find that dissensus in core values (religion, politics, general outlook on life) would depress the emotional closeness of parents and adult children. We shall explore this issue from quite another perspective in the following chapters, when we turn from sentiment to behavior, and analyze the determinants of social interaction and help exchange. An important question we shall bring to that analysis is whether social behavior, visible to both partners to a relationship in a way that sentiment is not, is also affected by Value Consensus, or whether normative obligations and the social rituals attached to such obligations override disagreements on value issues or mask the private feelings of affection or strain that are in the background of social interaction and help patterns.

Finally, we trust the analysis reported in this chapter demonstrates that there is much a social researcher can learn about past events and their influence on current relationships even in a cross-sectional survey. Few of us will ever embark on a long-term prospective study that follows families from early childrearing to beyond child launching. Hence, most family researchers must rely on biographic data to provide any depth to an understanding of why people do what they do and with what affect in the here and now. Sampling, data collection, and analysis techniques have all undergone dramatic technological change in the past few decades, but the goals of the social sciences remain the pursuit of knowledge and "verstehen," and, as Kierkegard reminds us, we have to live life forward, but can only understand it "backward." Adult development may be an ongoing process that involves more change than constancy, but change does not preclude the continuing influence of personal traits, norms, and behavior rooted in early experiences as a child and an adolescent. Knowing the history of a nation helps us understand the parameters within which a society changes under varying socioeconomic and cultural conditions. Knowing the biography of individuals does no less, for it enriches our understanding of the parameters within which choice and change take place.

Notes

1.   This is a fair inference from Miriam Johnson's persuasive argument concerning a far sharper difference between the wife and the mother role than between the husband and the father role in American families (Johnson, 1988), and Francesca Cancian's analysis of gender differences in the expression of love (Cancian, 1987).

2.   Thirty percent of the G2 women have fathers less than 25 years older than themselves, and 33% have fathers from 33 to 50 years older than themselves.

3.   This replication of the regression analysis reported in the text is not presented here, but we might note that essentially the same profile of significant predictors of Affective Closeness was found for the G2–G3 dyad as we reported in the text for the G1–G2 dyad. Men who are much older than their daughters also report more intimacy with daughters than men with a smaller age difference between themselves and their daughters. Interestingly, there was a significant difference in the father–son relationship: as noted in the text, sons report greater intimacy with fathers closer to themselves in age, but from the fathers' perspective, this does not hold. Men report more intimacy with sons the greater the age difference between them, much as they did where daughters are concerned. Clearly there is a mismatch here between fathers and sons' views of the effect of age on their relationship.

4.   Furthermore, parents do not speak in mathematical symbols but words; consequently a critical test of the effect of diluted parental investment was to show, as Blake does, that the larger the family, the lower the verbal test scores of children (net of measures of social status and cognitive ability), whereas family size has no relation to children's mathematical test scores (Blake, 1989).

5.   The parental Affection and Authority scores are summated from the separate indices on Maternal and Paternal Affection and Authority indices that appeared in earlier regression analyses.

6.   Other analysis (data not shown) found that sons of Catholic women are less apt to divorce, and more apt to share their mothers' views on controversial issues such as abortion than sons of non-Catholic women, while religious affiliation of mothers had no relation to whether daughters had ever been divorced or to the daughters' views on women's rights. All told, preliminary analysis of our dataset showed so few differences by religious affiliation that this variable was deemed of little substantive significance in the final analysis reported in this volume. Where religious affiliation did show significant effects, we have reported them.

7.   We will report, in Chapter 9, that low-income children in fact provide more varied help to their parents than high-income children, partly because the former are more apt to remain in their hometowns and hence available to provide hands-on assistance, and partly because their social lives are more embedded in family and kin than is the case for better educated, high-income adult children.

8.   Note that we did not directly measure and compare the values subscribed to by children and their parents. Our measures are judgment calls by respondents on whether they and each of their parents share "very similar" to "very different" views on religion, politics, and general outlook on life.

9.   It is also possible that with increasing years of marriage, women's views are more influenced by those of their husbands than men's views are changed by their wives, which would have the effect of a greater gap in values between adult daughters and their parents over time than in the case of sons. But we have no independent evidence to support this interpretation.

10.   That this profile has become more common among women in recent years is suggested by the fact that age shows the strongest coefficient of all the predictor variables in the equation on Dominance among women ($-.27$***), twice the size of the standardized beta coefficient on age in the equation on Dominance in men ($-.14$**).

11.   Preliminary analysis showed no relation between a parent being widowed or not and current Affective Closeness; hence marital status of parent was not included in this analysis.

12.   Note, however, that Dominance shows a positive and significant coefficient in equations A2 and C2 in Table 7.11 (father–son Closeness based on ratings by the adult child). Adult children who are high in both Expressivity and Dominance, net of each measure, report being closer to their fathers than those low on these personal trait measures. But though positive, we did not find any significant effect of Dominance in the larger G2 sample regression analysis reported earlier in Table 7.9 for either sons or daughters. Hence, we should probably not make much of this particular finding.

13.   The same general profile was found in comparable correlation coefficients between past Family Cohesion and current dimensions of solidarity for the G2–G3 parent–child dyads, with absolute means across the solidarity measures of .14* with ratings by G2 fathers (vs .17* for G1 fathers), .21*** with ratings by G3 adult children (vs. .26*** for G2 adult children).

14.   See Table 3.10.

15.   Further analysis of the consequences of religious intermarriages is not reported in this book. But we might summarize one important finding from a special analysis of young (under 45) married respondents currently rearing children: Our data show that religious intermarriage reduced both marital happiness and family of procreation cohesion, net of family size, income, education, family troubles, and health measures.

16.   Tabular material reported in the text is limited to G2 respondents as parents and G3 adult children. A replicated analysis of the G1–G2 dyad found essentially the same pattern as that reported in the text for the G2–G3 parent–child dyad.

17.   The children in these equations are on average 32 years of age, with a standard deviation of 10 years; the mothers are on average 58 years of age, with a standard deviation of 12 years. Most of the "children," then, are mature young adults under 40, not late adolescents or very young adults as in most previous studies of intergenerational influence.

18.   There were too few cases of separated or divorced G2 parents in the small spinoff sample of G3 children to provide useful information from the children to compare with the ratings provided by separated and divorced parents themselves in the main survey.

Social Interaction
between the Generations _____ 8

Conversation overheard on a Manhattan subway between two women in their 60s:

"So tell me, Sadie, what's with your daughter Millie?"
"Millie? Much better today. Now she thinks she'll stay on her job. Yesterday she was ready to quit."
"And your son Sam?"
"Sammy? Who knows what's with him? You'd have to ask his wife's mother. She knows more than I ever do."

Introduction

In this chapter and the two chapters to follow, we shift from how parents and adult children *feel* about each other to the manifestation of those feelings in social *behavior*. We begin with social interaction between parents and children, a necessary basis for the analysis of the extent and type of help that is exchanged between the generations, the subject of Chapter 9. Many kinds of help that close kin provide to each other require accessibility for social interaction: Help with childcare, domestic chores, or caregiving during an illness assumes some face-to-face contact. Other types of help could theoretically be given in the absence of face-to-face contact: Providing money or a loan, giving advice, or providing comfort could be done across great distances, through phone conversations, or by mail. However, it seems likely that even these latter types of help would be offered more frequently to those who live nearby than to those who live at a great distance, because social interaction provides the opportunity to learn about the problems and

365

needs of a parent or child, and to reciprocate with information about one's own problems and needs. More detailed information in turn may stimulate the exchange of help. In view of these considerations, attention to geographic distance separating parents from adult children and the frequency with which they are in touch with each other is a prerequisite to an understanding of the help exchange pattern.

How often parents and adult children see each other is not exclusively a function of the geographic distance between them. Some parents rarely hear from or see children who live in the same city, while other parents and adult children travel across the continent several times a year to visit each other, or engage in long telephone conversations once a week. Social interaction, like help exchange itself, is influenced by social norms and idiosyncratic biographic factors as well. Consequently, we shall analyze what *determines* frequency of social interaction, net of the sheer geographic distance separating parents and adult children. In doing so, we shall try to identify the current characteristics of parent and child that trigger more or less social interaction, and test the extent to which subjective closeness of the relationship (that occupied our attention in Chapter 7), and normative obligations to primary kin (the focus of Chapters 4 and 5) contribute to frequency of intergenerational contact, net of geographic distance and the sociodemographic characteristics of parent and child.

Geographic Distance and Social Interaction

Geographic Distance between Parents and Adult Children

Table 8.1 brings together the distribution on geographic distance between parents and adult children from our four primary data sets: the geographic distance between G2 respondents and their G1 parents, for the total G2 sample and for the smaller G1 sample; G2 respondents and all their G3 adult children (childset file); and the smaller G3 sample of adult children. The fact that we conducted telephone interviews with parents and children of the G2 respondents regardless of where they lived has ensured a similarity between the distance distribution of the G1 sample of parents and that of the total G2 sample of respondents reporting on the distance between themselves and their parents. As the cumulative percentage columns in the table show, 58% of the total G2 sample of 890 respondents with at least one living parent reside within 35 miles of each other, the same percentage found for the smaller G1 spinoff sample of the 322 parents we interviewed. A similar pattern is shown for G3 children, with 70% of the 1632 adult children and their G2

Table 8.1. Geographic Distance between G2 Respondents and Their Parents and Adult Children (All Data Sources) [a]

Geographic Distance	All G1 Parents Now Alive		G1 Parents in Spinoff Sample		All G3 Adult Children		G3 Children in Spinoff Sample	
	%	Cum. %	%	Cum. %	%	Cum. %	%	Cum. %
Live Together	7.6	7.6	10.2	10.2	24.2	24.2	21.5	21.5
Less than 10 miles	35.6	43.2	34.2	44.4	30.2	54.4	32.0	53.5
11–35 miles	14.6	57.8	13.4	57.8	15.9	70.3	18.9	72.4
36–100 miles	8.3	66.1	9.0	66.8	8.8	79.1	8.7	81.1
101–500 miles	14.2	80.3	18.6	85.4	7.9	87.0	9.5	90.6
501+ miles	19.7	100.0	14.5	100.0	13.0	100.0	9.4	100.0
N	(890)		(322)		(1632)		(275)	

[a] Percentage distribution of mileage distance between G2 respondents and their parents, and their children.

parents living within a 35 mile radius of each other, very close to the 72% of the 275 G3 children we interviewed.[1]

The reason a rather high proportion of G3 adult children is still living with their parents (24%) is their youth: Many of them are still attending post secondary schools and colleges; others are employed on their first post schooling jobs; most are unmarried; and more young sons reside at their parents' home than daughters because women marry at a younger age than men. Table 8.2 shows the residential pattern of G3 adult children by gender and age. Slightly more than half of the sons under 25 years of age are living at home (53%), to 41% of the daughters. Up to the age of 30, more sons than daughters reside with their parents, whereas over the age of 30, the balance tips to the daughters (9% of daughters over 40 years of age, to 6% of sons), a faint echo in our data of the lower marriage and remarriage rates of women than of men over the age of 40.

But young adult sons are *also* more apt to live far from their parents than young daughters; among children under 25 years of age, almost twice as many sons as daughters live more than 500 miles from the Boston area (25 vs. 14%). In many G2 families, young adult daughters have married and settled in the Boston area, while many sons live a considerable distance from Boston, either attending colleges and universities, or holding down first post schooling jobs. Many of these young adult sons may return to the Boston area in the future, as suggested by the much lower proportion of sons in their late 20s who live more than 500 miles away than is the case for sons in their early 20s.

With a diverse and booming economy, world-renown universities, museums, and orchestras, and easy access to Cape Cod bays and open

Table 8.2. Geographic Distance between G2 Parents and All Their G3 Adult Children by Age and Gender of Child (G2 Sample, Childset File) (in Percent)

	Age of G3 Adult Children							
	18–25		26–30		31–40		41 or Older	
Geographic Distance	Son	Daughter	Son	Daughter	Son	Daughter	Son	Daughter
Live with Parent(s) (%)	53.2	41.2	19.6	13.5	8.3	8.7	5.6	9.2
N	(295)	(308)	(168)	(171)	(216)	(196)	(144)	(131)
Children Living Apart from Parents								
Under 35 miles	44.1	58.6	65.9	74.4	52.9	64.2	69.1	58.0
36–100 miles	16.7	11.0	5.9	7.4	15.6	14.5	8.9	11.8
101–500 miles	13.8	16.6	11.1	6.1	13.3	5.0	6.6	12.6
501+ miles	25.4	13.8	17.0	12.2	20.2	16.2	15.4	17.6
N	(138)	(181)	(135)	(148)	(198)	(179)	(136)	(119)

ocean, the Boston area can remain a highly desirable location for young adults, and hence there are fewer wrenching separations between parents and young adult children in this New England metropolitan center than in many parts of the country. Middle-aged Bostonians may be just as likely to see older parents take off for warmer climes in Florida as they are to have a young son or daughter take off for jobs in the midwest or on the west coast![2] *From half to two-thirds of our G2 respondents live within an hour's drive (less than 35 miles) of their parents and of their adult children.* This high degree of geographic proximity sets the stage for high levels of social interaction and of help exchange.

Social Interaction between Parents and Adult Children

Measurement of Interaction. To make most efficient use of interview time in a study designed to explore many dimensions of the parent–child relationship, we framed questions concerning contact that embraced initiative from either side of the relationship. Typical contact questions ask respondents how often they visit a parent or a parent visits them (2 items), and assume the "visit" takes place at one or the other home, thus excluding face-to-face contact elsewhere, e.g., at church or at a relative's home. We chose instead to phrase the question in terms of how often respondents "see" a parent or child, bypassing location of and initiative for the social contact. So, too, the question on telephone contact was put in terms of "speak by phone" rather than asking respondents the two questions of how often they phoned their parent and how often they received a call from a parent.

Frequency of Social Interaction. Table 8.3 provides a profile of four aspects of social interaction by gender of parent and adult child: Panels A and B directly concern the frequency of interaction (Panel A on seeing and Panel B on phoning), while Panel C shows the satisfaction dimension and Panel D the felt obligation for more contact than at present. Three-quarters of the G2 respondents report having phone conversations with a parent at least once a month, and more than half report face-to-face contact at least once a month. There is less frequent contact with fathers than with mothers, particularly between sons and their fathers. Indeed, 1 in 5 daughters reports *daily* phone conversations with their mothers compared to only 1 in 20 sons and their fathers!

Most respondents report satisfaction with their current pattern of contact. If they would prefer anything other than their present contact level, it is overwhelmingly for seeing each other more often (Panel C). Note that the desire for more contact is more prevalent concerning fathers than mothers, suggesting the less frequent contact with fathers

Table 8.3. Profile of Social Interaction between G2 Adult Children and Their G1 Parents by Gender of Parent and Child (G2 Sample) (in Percent)

	Gender of G2 Child and G1 Parent			
Interaction Variables	Mother–Daughter	Mother–Son	Father–Daughter	Father–Son
A. Frequency of Face-to-Face Contact				
Daily	17.1	11.1	12.9	13.2
Several times to once a week	28.4	28.7	26.8	22.7
Several times to once a month	19.1	26.7	20.4	26.4
Several times to once a year	32.2	30.6	34.2	44.0
Never	3.2	2.8	5.8	3.7
	100.0	99.9	100.1	100.0
B. Frequency of Phone Contact				
Daily	22.8	8.7	6.9	5.2
Several times to once a week	43.6	43.3	37.0	34.7
Several times to once a month	19.3	31.0	30.8	45.8
Several times to once a year	5.2	10.3	14.3	15.1
Never	9.1	6.7	10.9	9.2
	100.0	100.0	99.9	100.0
C. Satisfaction with Contact Frequency [a]				
Same as now	59.2	60.1	52.0	52.4
Prefer more often	37.2	37.4	45.2	45.8
Prefer less often	3.6	2.4	2.8	1.8
	100.0	99.9	100.0	100.0
D. Obligation to be in Touch More Often [b]				
Percent Yes	38.2	42.6	42.3	49.3
N	(473)	(358)	(325)	(273)

[a] Question asked was: "If you could do so, would you *like* to be in touch with your mother [father] more often, less often, or about the same as now?"

[b] Question asked was: "Do you feel you *should be* in touch with your mother [father] more often than you are these days?"

than mothers is not a function of stress in the relationship, but the press of other obligations and job demands on time and energy. Beneath the preference for more contact may be a feeling of obligation as well, as suggested by the high proportion of respondents who say they feel they "should be" in touch with a parent more often than they are (a range from 38 to 49% in Panel D of Table 8.3).

The data in Table 8.3 are all from G2 respondents in their roles as adult children. Data from the G1 sample of parents suggest the child feels greater obligation than the parent to have more contact. This can be seen below, in the proportion of G1 and G2 respondents who said they should be in touch "more often" than they are:

	G1 Mother	G1 Father
G1 parent says	25.4%	32.8%
G2 adult child says	35.8%	42.7%

There seems to be a greater touch of "guilt" on the part of fathers and of adult children concerning contact than is the case for G1 mothers, who report the lowest (25%) incidence of falling short of felt obligations.[3] It may also be the case that both mothers and fathers feel less obligation than the sons and daughters we interviewed, for the reason that most of the parents have more than one child. Visiting and phoning take time; hence parents of four or five children may feel less obligation to see more of any *one* child than each of their children feels about having more contact with their parents. It will be of special interest to explore the effect of family size in either generation for frequency of social interaction and of help exchange. Should large families reduce contact and help exchange, it suggests the reduced parental investment as a function of number of children is not restricted to the years of childrearing, but persists as a structural constraint on relations between the generations when the children are fully grown and independent as well.

Distance and Social Interaction

Table 8.4 confirms what one would expect, i.e., that geographic distance imposes serious limitations on the frequency of social contact between parents and adult children, with correlations in the range of

Table 8.4. Pearson Correlation Coefficients between Geographic Distance and Frequency of Social Interaction between G2 Adult Children and Their G1 Parents by Gender of Parent and Child (G2 Sample)

	Gender of G2 Child and G1 Parent			
Interaction Variables	Mother–Daughter	Mother–Son	Father–Daughter	Father–Son
Frequency of Face-to-Face Contact	− .83***	− .83***	− .75***	− .78***
Frequency of Phone Contact	− .33***	− .15**	− .16**	− .12*

*** p < .001
** p < .01
* p < .05

−.75 and −.83 in the case of face-to-face contact, and much lower correlations in the case of telephone contact, with a range from −.12 to −.33. Note that phone contact does not compensate for restraint on visiting that distance imposes; both contact measures are negatively correlated with geographic distance. Phone contact may bridge hundreds of miles separating parents and children, but long distance calls cost money, and hence the greater the mileage, the lower the frequency of phone contact.[4]

It is of interest to note the variation among the gender-specified parent–child dyads in the strength of the negative correlation between geographic distance and frequency of telephone contact: The correlation is barely significant statistically in the case of fathers and sons ($-.12^*$), but highly significant in the case of mothers and daughters ($-.33^{***}$). We infer two things from this finding: When parents and adult children live only short distances from each other, contact is more frequent with mothers than with fathers, because more mothers are available for daytime contact than are fathers. Mothers and daughters may have an implicit understanding that evenings are for spouses or shared telephone conversations with both parents; daytime phone conversations, if work schedules permit, can more readily be confined to dyadic exchange between the women. Hence, living at a distance is more strongly correlated with contact frequency for mothers than for fathers, not because women do more long distance phoning than men but more local phoning. Second, men earn more than women and pay family bills more frequently than women do, with the result that distance is less a curb on frequency of telephoning if at least one partner to the relationship is a man. Seen from this perspective, it is only mothers and daughters who may feel impelled to curb the impulse and desire for phone contact when a long distance separates them, while sons and fathers may feel freer to phone each other and their mothers or daughters.

Determinants of Frequency of Interaction

We turn now to the question of what determines variation in the frequency of social interaction between parents and children, over and above the pragmatic fact of geographic distance separating them. Not all children living a few miles from their parents phone their mothers every day; some do so rarely, while other parents and adult children visit several times a month and phone each other on a routine basis despite the fact of living quite far apart. We remember a neighbor in Chicago who had a routinized schedule of telephone calls every day: 8:30 in the morning, when the children had all left for school, was set aside for her "mother's call," and 9:00 A.M. was her time to call her mother-in-law.

Both the mother and the mother-in-law lived about 40 miles west of Chicago. Every other morning our neighbor called her sister in Milwaukee at 9:30. Whenever she had to leave home before 8:30 in the morning, she gave advance warning to her three women relatives to avoid their worrying that something had happened to her.[5]

Our analysis procedure will consist of a series of regression analyses on the frequency with which parents or children see and phone each other. All equations will contain the control variable of mileage distance between the partners to the relationship. Since distance correlates $-.79$ with "seeing" each other, and $-.34$ with "phoning" each other, distance will obviously show very significant beta coefficients and play a major role in elevating the size of the R^2 values, especially so in equations dealing with face-to-face visiting. Our discussion of findings will center on variables that show a significant contribution to frequency of interaction between parents and children independent of this distance variable.

The predictor variables embrace an array of characteristics of both the parent and the adult child and the quality of the relationship between them: the child's age,[6] marital and employment status, gender, and family size, and the parent's health condition, marital status, and family size. The relationship variable is the rating of the current Affective Closeness between the parent and child, which we have seen to be strongly influenced by earlier experiences in the family.

As mentioned above, the two family size variables have special structural interest. Our analysis is necessarily at the dyadic level of one parent and one adult child, but while all children have only one mother and one father, the parents themselves may have any number of children. As mentioned above, social interaction takes time and energy, and there may be limits to the frequency of interaction for parents with several adult children, much as parental investment per child is reduced in large families compared to small ones during the earlier years of childrearing. It is doubtful that our Chicago neighbor would have had long daily phone conversations with her mother-in-law were it not the case that her husband was an only child. Our neighbor was a substitute for the daughter her mother-in-law never had. So too, adult children who are rearing several children of their own have much less time for social visits and telephone contact with their parents than their unmarried or childless siblings have. The presence of grandchildren may increase the *interest* of the grandparents in visiting with their children and grandchildren, at the same time it reduces the frequency of such visits. Full time employment on the part of adult children may play a similar role, particularly in the frequency of contact between older women and their married daughters.

G2 Adult Children and G1 Parents. We begin with the data set that provides the largest case bases of parent–child dyads: the full G2 sample of Bostonians with a living parent. With this data set, two additional variables were added to the regression equations that were predicted to be significant in explaining variance in social interaction: The Value Consensus index, on the assumption that sharing similar values, like subjective intimacy, will predispose to both the desire for contact and to socially pleasurable encounters that reinforce the desire for repeated contact.

The second variable comes from the vignette data on normative obligations: a rating on the level of obligation respondents felt toward the primary kin of parents and children. Many social occasions, and indeed the frequency of contact itself among closely related kin, carry an element of obligation; many of us are expected to attend, and feel an obligation to attend a family Thanksgiving dinner, Christmas brunch, or even weekly Friday or Sunday night dinners with parents or an adult child. There may be subjective footdragging when we comply with these norms, as we reluctantly take off for the ritual visits, but take off we do. Even in the primary parent–child relationship, normative obligations may dictate frequent visits and phone calls independent of the subjective quality of the relationship. We predicted that sheer obligation would contribute to contact with fathers, but not necessarily to mothers.

In Chapter 6 we saw that there is a high degree of agreement in the contact frequency reported by G2 respondents and their parents: for example, a correlation of .89 between the frequency of seeing each other reported by G1 mothers and their G2 adult children, with somewhat lower correlations where phone contact is concerned (e.g., .62 for G1 mothers and their G2 adult children). It does not follow, however, that the same set of predictor variables will be significant determinants when data are gathered from the older generation as from the younger generation. It could be, for example, that having five other children lowers the reported contact by G1 parents, while being employed or not feeling particularly close to the parent lowers the contact frequency reported by G2 children. Furthermore, despite being a presumably "hard" behavioral variable, contact frequency may also carry subjective elements: For example, a widowed father may underreport frequency of contact simply because he is lonely, while the adult child may overestimate the frequency with which the widowed father is seen because, in the absence of the mother, such visits are more obligatory than personally gratifying.

We begin with data obtained from G2 respondents concerning the frequency with which they visit and phone their parents, following which we shall explore whether any differences emerge in the profile of determinants when the data come from the parent compared to the child. At this first step in the analysis, we compare what determines contact with mothers versus fathers, with gender of the adult child as a dummy variable in the equations. Later in the analysis, with the increased case bases provided by the Childset file, we will replicate the analysis separately for the four parent–child dyads.

Table 8.5 shows the results of the regression analysis on seeing and phoning mothers and fathers from the perspective of G2 respondents as adult children. Increasing geographic distance reduces, and Affective Closeness significantly increases, contact with both mothers and fathers. Sharing similar values also increases contact with both parents, but significantly so only in the case of face-to-face visiting. It is much easier to engage in conversation by phone without confronting basic disagreements on values and life-styles than it is in face-to-face contacts,

Table 8.5. Regressions on Contact Frequency [a] between G2 Adult Children and G1 Parents by Gender of Parent (G2 Sample) (Standardized Beta Coefficients)

Predictor Variables	A. Contact with G1 Mother		B. Contact with G1 Father	
	Visit	Phone	Visit	Phone
Relationship Characteristics				
Geographic Distance	−.79***	−.34***	−.71***	−.20***
Affective Closeness	.15***	.23***	.27***	.33***
Value Consensus	.07***	.03	.09**	.08+
Characteristics of G2 Child				
Gender	.03	.16*	.02	−.01
Age	−.01	−.13**	.05	−.12**
Married (dummy variable)	.02	.00	−.01	−.01
Number of Children	−.09***	−.06+	.03	−.05
Fulltime Employed (dummy variable)	−.06*	−.17***	−.08*	−.05
Obligation to Primary Kin [b]	.03	.07+	.09**	.11**
Characteristic of G1 Parent				
Widowed (dummy variable)	.03	−.01	.01	.02
Number of Children	.02	−.13***	−.02	−.06
Health	−.00	−.01	.01	.05
R^2	.68***	.25***	.64***	.25***
N	(595)	(595)	(444)	(444)

[a] Excluding all G2 adult children living with their parents.
[b] Mean ratings derived from vignette data set. See Chapter 4 for description of the normative obligation ratings.
*** p < .001
** p < .01
* p < .05
+ p < .10

which last longer and involve exposure to all manner of indicators of life-style differences. On the phone only the familiar voice is heard; one does not see hair or clothing, or whether the home is neat or in disarray, and we are less likely to engage in potentially controversial discussions of politics or religion during a telephone conversation than in the course of a long evening or weekend visit.

Whether the child is married or not, or the parent widowed or not, has no effect on contact frequency in the G1–G2 dyad. We had expected more frequent contact with widowed parents, but our data do not support this. Nor is the parent's health a factor in frequency of contact. We expected to find more frequent contact with parents in poor health than with parents in good health, particularly phone contact, but again, this expectation was not met. Indeed, only one parent characteristic is a significant predictor of contact frequency in the four equations: a significantly lower frequency of phone contact with mothers the larger the size of the family (siblings from the perspective of the adult child, children from the perspective of the mothers). As suggested above, we suspect this is due to the fact that telephone contact is by definition dyadic, whereas face-to-face contact can involve several children visiting their parents on the same occasion. The average G1 mother is a woman in her 60s, most of whom are not employed; hence, these women have the time for daytime visits and daytime phone conversation. But if they have a number of children, they may contact any one child less often than women with only one or two children.

Note too, that gender of the child is a significant predictor only in phone contact frequency with mothers: Daughters are in phone contact with their mothers more than sons are, a statistical confirmation of the example cited above involving our Chicago neighbor's morning phone calls to her mother and mother-in-law, and of the marginal distribution on phone frequency in the mother–daughter dyad, reported in Table 8.3.

G2 adult children who are employed, and those with a number of young children, are in less frequent contact with their parents, particularly their mothers, than those who are not employed or who have no children or only one child. Young unmarried adults can travel to visit a parent more easily than a married child with several young children in tow. In addition, children have two sets of grandparents, with the result that visiting with any one set may be reduced if the young parents wish to be equitable in providing access to the grandchildren for the four grandparents. Where both sides of the family reside in the same city, as we suspect[7] is the case for many of our Boston respondents, a rotation system may be adopted, for example, the first Sunday afternoon (or Friday night) of a month with the wife's parents, and the third Sunday with the husband's parents.

The adult child's age shows a significantly negative coefficient on contact frequency; the older the children (and hence the older the parents), the less often they are in contact with their parents, particularly in phone contact. Young adult children in their early 20s are less hampered by job, home and child responsibilities, and their parents are typically still vigorous middle-aged adults, a combination conducive to more frequent social interaction between the generations. It may also be the case that during the transition period from living with parents to living independently, both parents and young adult children feel a need for frequent contact to ease the adjustment to separation from daily contact with each other. Many parents may share our memory of weekly phone conversations and letters when children were college freshmen and the gradual reduction to a monthly phone call and an occasional note when the children were college seniors.

By contrast, adult children in their late 30s and early 40s are at a peak of family, home, job, and community involvement, and their parents, in their lates 60s and 70s, may be less inclined to visit frequently because of declining health, or because grandchildren are no longer fascinating toddlers but teenagers who prefer a social life with friends rather than elderly grandparents.

One last finding shown in Table 8.5 concerns the normative obligation rating toward primary kin: G2 respondents who scored high on the obligation measure are more apt to have frequent contact with parents than those who scored low. Apart from all the other predisposing factors that increase or reduce interaction, felt obligation level exerts some independent effect on sheer frequency of contact.[8] Note, too, that the coefficients on normative obligation are statistically significant only where contact with fathers is concerned and more so for frequency of phone contact than face-to-face contact. The implication is that the relationship with fathers is more conditional than the relationship with mothers; contact with father is given some added nudge by a feeling of obligation, while obligation and desire are more in accord in the case of mothers.

In Table 8.6 the regression analysis replicates in large measure that shown in Table 8.5. This time, however, use is made of the G1 parents' reports on contact frequency with their adult children (shown in Panels A and B as the set "2" of equations) as well as the G2 adult children's reports on contact frequency (shown in the set "1" of equations in Panels A and B). Note, however, that the case bases are sharply reduced because we now limit the G2 data to those G2 respondents whose mother or father was interviewed.[9]

In view of the small base Ns, particularly of G1 fathers, we have dropped three variables from the equations: the Primary Kin obligation rating, Value Consensus, and the marital status of the child.[10] Our primary concern is with whether the profile of significant predictors of contact frequency differs when the G1 parent reported contract frequency compared to their G2 adult children. A prior question is whether the smaller subgroups of G2 respondents whose parents were interviewed show any different pattern from the larger group of G2 respondents with at least one living parent. Inspection of the regression equations in A(1) and B(1) in Table 8.6 with those shown in Table 8.5 shows no major differences in the results, although statistical significance is not always reached due to the reduced base Ns in Table 8.6.

There are only a few major differences between the determinants of contact frequency reported by G2 children and those determining the contact frequency reported by G1 parents. The two equations in the columns under (1) in Panel A refer to contact with their mothers as reported by G2 adult children and the two equations in the columns under (2) in Panel A refer to contact with children reported by G1 mothers. (The counterpart comparisons concerning G1 fathers and their children are shown in Panel B.) Adult children and G1 mothers show the same profile of determinants, although one of the two coefficients may not reach statistical significance. For example, adult children report less frequent visiting with their mothers if they have several children ($-.11^*$) and less frequent phoning if they are employed full time ($-.17^{**}$); both variables also show negative coefficients in the contact reports of mothers, although they do not reach statistical significance ($-.06$ and $-.11$). G1 mothers and G2 adult children therefore show the same profile: more face-to-face contact if they are emotionally close, live nearby, and have few or no children (or grandchildren), and more phoning if the adult child is young, female, not employed full time, and the mother does not have a large family (fewer siblings from child's perspective).

G1 fathers, by contrast, do show a few significant differences when the determinants of their contact frequency with adult children are compared with the determinants of contact with fathers reported by the children. The most striking of these differences concerns the father's marital status and the condition of his health: Married G1 fathers report more visiting and phone contact with their children than widowed or divorced fathers do, whereas their fathers' marital status, while positive, has no effect on the children's reports of contact frequency. Our contact measures do not specify who initiates contact, which may mask some significant differences in contact initiation between fathers and children. Since it is typically women who make social arrangements for get-togethers of family members, men may see far more of their children while their wives are alive than when they become widowers. Not being

Table 8.6. Regressions on Contact Frequency [a] between G2 Adult Children and G1 Parents by Gender of Parent: G2 vs. G1 as Respondents (G1 and G2 Samples) (Standardized Beta Coefficients)

	G2 Child as Respondent		G1 Parent as Respondent	
Predictor Variables	Visit	Phone	Visit	Phone
A. Mother–Child	**(1) Contact with G1 Mother**		**(2) Contact with G2 Child**	
Relationship				
Distance	−.82***	−.38***	−.82***	−.41***
Affective Closeness	.10*	.19**	.09*	.25***
Child Characteristics				
Gender (Female = 1)	.01	.13*	−.06	.10*
Age	−.02	−.13*	−.07	−.14*
Number of Children	−.11*	.09	−.06	−.08
Full Time Employed				
(dummy variable)	−.04	−.17**	−.05	−.11
Parent Characteristics				
Married (dummy				
variable)	−.02	.04	.07	.11
Number of Children	−.03	−.27***	−.04	−.13*
Health	−.03	.06	−.02	−.05
R^2	.69***	.30***	.67***	.28***
N	(164)	(164)	(164)	(164)
B. Father–Child	**(1) Contact with G1 Father**		**(2) Contact with G2 Child**	
Relationship				
Distance	−.76***	−.35***	−.74***	−.26***
Affective Closeness	.30***	.29***	.18***	.23***
Child Characteristics				
Gender (Female = 1)	.04	.11	.12	.11
Age	−.14*	−.07	.02	−.03
Number of Children	−.12	.03	−.00	−.04
Full Time Employed				
(dummy variable)	.07	−.03	.15**	−.01
Parent Characteristics				
Married (dummy				
variable)	.04	.00	.16***	.16*
Number of Children	−.13*	−.05	−.12*	.01
Health	.01	.03	.13**	−.02
R^2	.71***	.26***	.69***	.20***
N	(109)	(109)	(109)	(109)

[a] Excluding all G2 adult children living with their parents.
*** $p < .001$
** $p < .01$
* $p < .05$
+ $p < .10$

habituated to initiating contact, widowed men, however lonely, may simply not contact their children, whereas women continue to initiate social contacts when they become widows, much as they did while their husbands were alive.

G2 fathers also report more visiting with their children if they themselves are in excellent health than if they are in poor health, but the health condition of their fathers plays no role in the contact frequency reported by adult children. Again, a subjective element may be masked by our contact measures; perhaps men in poor health actually see their children and speak to them by phone as often as men in good health do, but the inactivity associated with poor health may make contact harder for men to initiate at the same time they feel greater need for contact with adult children. To show physical weakness and distress may also be more difficult for elderly men than women, because it affronts their sense of masculine pride.[11] Then too, when husbands are in poor health, wives provide whatever caregiving is necessary, and the women may restrict social get-togethers to spare themselves the work involved in preparing for them and to spare their husbands the excitement associated with social occasions, particularly if these occasions involve active and noisy young grandchildren. This interpretation is consistent with the finding that poor health of fathers is associated with reduced visiting (.14**) but not reduced phoning ($-.02$).

The third predictor variable that is unique to G1 fathers' report of contact frequency with adult children is the employment status of the child; men report more contact with children who are employed full time than they do with children who are at home or at school. This holds only for face-to-face contact, not for contact by phone. Except for the retired fathers among the G1 men, most men are employed full time. When a son or daughter is also employed full time, any visiting between the generations will take place in nonwork hours (evenings, weekends, and during vacations). Adult children who are not employed, i.e., housewife-daughters rearing young children, can see their mothers by day and may cut down on evening and weekend visits. As a result, fathers may in fact see more of their employed daughters than their homemaking daughters. As we will see below, this is consistent with the pattern that emerges when the employment status of parents is included in the regression equations: Full time employed women see and phone their adult children *less* often, while full time employed men have *more* contact with their adult children.

G2 Parents and G3 Adult Children.   We turn now to our second major dyad of parents and adult children, the G2 respondents as parents and their G3 children. One in four of these children is still living at home, so we exclude them from all the regression equations on contact frequency that follow. Since the G3 sample is our smallest data set, the base *N*s are unfortunately small, particularly for G2 men (93 cases). Table 8.7 replicates, with G2–G3 data, the analysis conducted with G1–G2 data (Table 8.6).

Our expectation that the same profile of contact determinants would emerge for the G2–G3 dyad as for the G1–G2 dyad was confirmed only in part: For both dyads, distance reduces and Affective Closeness increases the frequency of seeing and phoning each other. Daughters, whether G2 or G3, are in more frequent phone contact with their mothers. So too, the number of children the parent has reduces the contact frequency with the particular one child in our samples. Hence, the same impact of family size is found for G1 parents and G2 parents. Also, more times than not, parents who are married and living with their spouses have more frequent contact with adult children than widowed or divorced parents.

On the other hand, there are some differences between the G1–G2 dyads and the G2–G3 dyads, some of them particularly puzzling and for which we have no ready explanation. Married G2 mothers are in more frequent contact with their adult children than widowed or divorced mothers, significantly so where phone contact is concerned. By contrast, in the G1–G2 analysis, marital status of the G1 parents was significant only for fathers.

A second example of difference between the dyads concerns the effect of employment status of the adult child. In the G1–G2 analysis we reported that phone contact with mothers was reduced if the child was employed full time, and contact with fathers was increased if the child was employed. But employment status of the child shows no significant patterning in the G2–G3 dyad.

One last discrepancy between the G1–G2 and G2–G3 dyads is worth noting, because there is a significant reversal of the direction of effect. We noted earlier that G1 fathers report *less* contact with their adult children when their own health is poor than when it is excellent. Yet in Table 8.7 G2 fathers report *more* contact with their adult children if they are in poor health. Indeed, all eight coefficients on Health are negative in the G2–G3 dyad analysis, while in the G1–G2 dyad analysis five of the eight coefficients were positive. It remains very unclear, in view of these contradictory findings, whether and what effect poor health of fathers has on frequency of social contact with adult children.

Contact between G2 Parents and All Their G3 Adult Children. Our last venture into an analysis of the determinants of contact frequency between the generations uses data in the Childset file of all G3 children of

Table 8.7. Regressions on Contact Frequency [a] between G2 Parents and G3 Adult Children by Gender of Parent: G2 Parent vs. G3 Child as Respondent (G2 and G3 Samples) (Standardized Beta Coefficients)

	G3 Child as Respondent		G2 Parent as Respondent	
Predictor Variables	Visit	Phone	Visit	Phone
A. Mother–Child	**(1) Contact with G2 Mother**		**(2) Contact with G3 Child**	
Relationship				
Distance	−.73***	−.26***	−.76***	−.29***
Affective Closeness	.18***	.18***	.29***	.37***
Child Characteristics				
Gender (Female = 1)	.04	.20**	−.01	.22**
Age	.01	−.03	−.09	.01
Number of Children	.02	.06	.01	−.06
Fulltime Employed				
(dummy variable)	.02	.05	−.01	−.00
Parent Characteristics				
Married (dummy				
variable)	.07	.23**	.05	.24**
Number of Children	.05	−.01	.05	−.11
Health	−.04	−.02	−.03	−.01
R^2	**.59***	**.23***	**.66***	**.32***
N	(120)	(120)	(120)	(120)
B. Father–Child	**(1) Contact with G2 Father**		**(2) Contact with G3 Child**	
Relationship				
Distance	−.77***	−.13*	−.79***	−.24***
Affective Closeness	.19**	.25**	.27***	.57***
Child Characteristics				
Gender (Female = 1)	−.10	.07	.10	.11
Age	−.10	.07	−.15+	−.14
Number of Children	−.16**	.05	.02	−.09
Full Time Employed				
(dummy variable)	−.07	−.06	.03	.11
Parent Characteristics				
Married (dummy				
variable)	.08	.02	.11+	.18*
Number of Children	−.11+	−.21*	−.04	−.33***
Health	−.08	−.11	−.11*	−.19
R^2	**.65***	**.17***	**.69***	**.45***
N	(93)	(93)	(93)	(93)

[a] Excluding all G3 adult children living with their parents.
*** $p < .001$
** $p < .01$
* $p < .05$
+ $p < .10$

our G2 respondents. We cannot exactly replicate the equations in terms of predictor variables, but this data set has sufficient cases to permit a comparison of parent–child dyads with gender of both parent and child specified. The G2 personal interviews did not inquire about the employment status of each of the adult children; hence, we have used the employment status of the G2 parents for this analysis, a reasonable substitution considering that daytime contact between parents and adult children will be reduced if *either* member of the parent–child dyad is employed full time. With sufficient cases, we can also included the index on Value Consensus that had to be dropped from the G1 and G3 sample analysis because of the large number of missing values on this variable. Our prediction was that social interaction between fathers and sons would be especially sensitive to the extent of shared values between the men in the family, because the issues involved, such as politics, are more typically a focus of conversation between men in the family than between women or between men and women. We also include the overall rating of Family Cohesion in this analysis, as a direct test of whether past family experience shows any continuing impact on social interaction between the generations. The cohesion index refers to the family of procreation from the perspective of G2 parent-respondents, and the family of origin from the perspective of the G3 adult children.

Table 8.8 provides the results of this analysis, which we shall discuss first in terms of what is common across all four dyads, and then in terms of the factors that are unique to particular dyads. All four parent–child dyads show the following common determinants: geographic distance decreases, and Affective Closeness increases frequency of interaction. Family size in both generations reduces contact frequency in all eight equations, although the coefficients are significantly negative only in frequency of phone contact. The G3 child's family size shows a significantly negative impact on contact only with fathers: Fathers and daughters, and fathers and sons, see less of each other and phone less often, the more children the G3 generation is rearing. The extent to which parents and children share similar values has a positive effect on social interaction in all eight equations.

Mother–daughter interaction. The greatest contrast among the four dyads is that between the mother–daughter and the father–son relationship. The mother–daughter relationship emerges as relatively immune to the influence of changing life circumstances, implying greater stability and a much less conditional quality to the mother–daughter interaction pattern. Apart from distance and Affective Closeness, the only variable that affects interaction frequency between mothers and daughters is the number of children the mother has: G2 women who have

Table 8.8. Regressions on Contact Frequency [a] between G2 Parents and G3 Adult Children by Gender of Parent and Child (G2 Sample, Childset File) (Standardized Beta Coefficients)

	Type of G2 Parent–G3 Child Dyad			
Predictor Variables	Mother– Daughter	Mother– Son	Father– Daughter	Father– Son
A. Regression on Visiting				
Past Family Cohesion [b]	−.03	.07	.09*	.05
Relationship Characteristic				
Distance	−.71***	−.68***	−.74***	−.72***
Affective Closeness	.27***	.17***	.34***	.23***
Value Consensus	.08+	.02	.02	.12**
Child Characteristics				
Age	.06	−.06	.20***	.00
Number of Children	−.07	−.03	−.14**	−.16**
Married (dummy variable)	.01	.10*	.07	.15*
Parent Characteristics				
Married (dummy variable)	.08+	.08+	.07+	.11*
Number of Children	−.02	−.02	−.05	−.08
Health	.01	.04	.09*	−.13**
Fulltime employed (dummy variable)	−.02	−.11**	.07	.15**
R^2	**.64***	**.55***	**.73***	**.67***
N	(249)	(249)	(187)	(162)
B. Regression on Phoning				
Past Family Cohesion	.01	.16**	.12+	.03
Relationship Characteristic				
Distance	−.35***	−.22***	−.16**	−.18**
Affective Closeness	.37***	.26***	.43***	.39***
Value Consensus	.09	.03	.03	.11*
Child Characteristics				
Age	.03	.04	.34***	.02
Number of Children	−.08	−.09	−.14*	−.17*
Married (dummy variable)	.10	.05	−.08	.28***
Parent Characteristics				
Married (dummy variable)	.08	.19***	.09	.24***
Number of Children	−.12*	−.14**	−.18***	−.21***
Health	−.09	−.06	−.08	−.23***
Fulltime employed (dummy variable)	−.08	−.01	.12+	.22***
R^2	**.38***	**.24***	**.31***	**.44**
N	(249)	(249)	(187)	(162)

[a] Excluding all G3 adult children living with their parents.
[b] Family of procreation from perspective of G2 parents, and family of origin from perspective of G3 children.

*** $p < .001$ * $p < .05$
** $p < .01$ + $p < .10$

have several children report less frequent phone contact with any one adult child. Contact between mothers and daughters is not affected by the marital status of either mother or daughter, nor by the health or employment status of the mother, nor the age and family size of the daughter.

Father–son interaction. By contrast, the interaction profile of fathers and sons is highly responsive to a number of factors. The extent to which the two men share similar values has a significant impact on the frequency of interaction, implying some avoidance on the part of at least one of the men (probably the sons) when they are aware they hold different values. Marriage of the son significantly increases frequency of contact, in this instance not only between fathers and sons, but mothers and sons as well. Since sons' wives, like our G3 daughters, probably retain high involvement and interaction with their parents, this implies that for men, marriage is followed by a significant increase in contact with older relatives.

Fathers' own characteristics also play a significant role in father–son social interaction. Perhaps of greatest interest is the finding that married fathers who are employed full time, see more of their sons than widowed, divorced, or retired fathers do. Withdrawal from the workaday world following retirement may therefore remove an important ground for identification with each other and reduce interaction between men in the family. Note that by contrast, men's being employed full time shows no effect on the interaction profile of fathers and their daughters, and in the case of the employment status of mothers, there is a significant reversal: Contact frequency goes down significantly between mothers and sons when mothers are employed full time.

Contact between fathers and sons is also more frequent if the fathers' health is poor, perhaps because sons can substitute for or supplement their fathers' role in the parental household, for example, through help with home maintenance or advice on financial matters.

Father–daughter interaction. The most striking and unique characteristics of the profile of interaction between fathers and daughters is the significant increase in contact (both seeing and phoning each other) with increasing age. No other dyad shows so large a Beta coefficient as that on the effect of age on phone contact between fathers and daughters. In fact, apart from the two powerful variables of distance and Affective Closeness of the relationship, the Beta coefficient of .34*** on age of daughter in its effect on phoning frequency with fathers is the largest of the 32 coefficients in the equations on phoning frequency across the four dyads. This increase in contact frequency with age in the father–daughter relationship is consistent with the increase in intimacy over the adult years between fathers and daughters that we noted in a previous chapter.

Overall, the interaction analysis emphasizes, yet again, the much greater conditional quality to the relationships of men in the family: marital status, employment, health, family size, and value consensus affect the interaction of men as fathers and as sons, whereas there is greater stability across changes in life circumstances in the interaction profile of women as mothers and daughters. In anticipation of the analysis of help exchange between the generations in the following chapter, we are therefore alerted to the possibility that contact frequency may play a quite different role in the help exchange pattern depending on the gender composition of the parent–child dyad.

Conclusion

The predominant characteristic of our G2 respondents is the widespread access they have to both their own parents and to their adult children. Marriage may typically involve the establishment of separate households in American families, but the adult children do not move far away in the majority of cases. Close to half of the G3 children between 18 and 25 years of age still reside with their parents, and even 20% of G3 sons in their late 20s continue to do so. Sixty percent of the G2 respondents who have one or both parents alive live less than 35 miles apart, as do 70% of the adult children of our G2 respondents. For only a minority of the main sample would a visit with either a parent or an adult child require a drive of more than a few hours.

Contact between the generations mirrors this access profile: from a third to almost half of the G2 respondents see a parent at least once a week; one in five adult daughters has daily phone contact with her mother. The majority are satisfied with the frequency of their contact with parents, and among those who are not satisfied, the preference is overwhelmingly for "more" contact rather than less. Contact by visiting or phoning is more frequent with mothers than with fathers, largely because more women have daytime hours for such contact, especially with their daughters, than men do. But both men and women are even more likely to express a desire for more frequent contact with their fathers than with their mothers, no doubt because the press of jobs precludes as much contact with fathers as with mothers. Despite the high contact profile, close to half the G2 respondents feel they "should" be in touch with their parents more often than they are.

To bridge the distance separating the residences of parents and children takes both time and money, and distance represents *the* major factor affecting the frequency of interaction between mothers and adult children in all the parent–child dyads we analyzed. In contact with fathers, however, the quality of the relationship has even more of an influence than sheer opportunity as indexed by geographic distance: Affective Closeness of fathers and adult children is *the* most significant determinant of frequency of contact with fathers, especially for telephone contact, which may have a smaller obligatory element than social visiting does.

Of special interest was the general tendency for family size to reduce social interaction between the generations. This was not an invariant pattern, since we have noted positive signs on the Family Size Beta coefficients in some equations. This is an interesting and important variable; hence, we have brought together a profile of findings across the several regression tables reported above in a summary table.

Table 8.9 provides this profile, showing the direction and statistical significance of the Beta coefficients on Family Size as a factor in intergenerational contact frequency from the 28 regression equations in which it appeared. Since we used the family size of both generations, there were 56 Beta coefficients in all: of these, 42 (75%) were negative, and 14 were positive. More important, *none* of the positive coefficients was statistically significant, whereas *half* of the negative coefficients

Table 8.9. Summary of Direction and Statistical Significance of Family Size Effects on Frequency [a] of Contact Between Parents and Adult Children (All Samples)

	Family Size Has			
	Negative Effect	Positive Effect	N	Negative (%)
A. All Beta Coefficients	42	14	(56)	75
Number Statistically Significant	20	0	(20)	100
B. Family Size in				
Parental Generation	24	4	(28)	86
Child's Generation	18	10	(28)	64
C. Gender of Parent				
Mother	20	8	(28)	71
Father	24	4	(28)	86
D. Type of Contact				
Visit	21	7	(28)	75
Phone	21	7	(28)	75

[a] Based on beta coefficients on parent's family size (either G1 or G2 as parent) or child's family size (either G2 or G3) that were shown in Tables 8.5 through 8.8, a total of 28 equations, each of which contained the two family size variables.

were. Panel B of the table suggests that family size of the parental generation poses more of a constraint on intergenerational contact than it does on the younger generation: 24 of the 28 coefficients (86%) on the number of children the parents had are negative, compared to 18 of the 28 (64%) on the number of children the younger generation is rearing. From Panel C it can be seen that the restraint on contact associated with having a large family is slightly more typical of contact with fathers than with mothers, while Panel D shows no difference by type of contact in the prevalence of negative or positive coefficients.

Putting together the results of Panels B and C suggests that mothers may initiate more contact with, and perhaps provide domestic help and childcare to married children rearing a number of children. The "children" of G3 parents are typically quite young; where proximity permits, G2 parents (especially mothers) may lend assistance to G3 children and the G4 grandchildren they are rearing. This must remain a speculative inference, however, in view of the fact that our contact measures do not permit us to specify who initiates the contact. We shall return to this issue in the chapter to follow on help exchange, where our data are very explicit on the direction of help flows between the generations.

The overall effect of family size in reducing social contact between the generations has very general significance as a life course phenomenon. Diluted parental investment as a function of family size does not end when the child leaves home, but persists across the life course and perhaps beyond the death of the parents, because the money, goods, and property that remain when parents die will be spread more thinly the larger the size of the family.

Notes

1.   Note that had we limited interviews with parents and children to those living within even a wide 100 mile radius of the Boston SMSA, we would have excluded one-third of the parents and one-fifth of the children.

2.   Indeed, apart from neighboring states in New England, Florida telephone exchanges were the most prevalent source of contact for the interviews with G1 parents of our Boston respondents.

3.   There is additional evidence of general normative obligations to kin involved in these responses. Analysis showed significant correlations between the General Kin Obligation score from the vignette data and responses to this item concerning feeling obliged to have more contact with parents than is the current pattern. Interestingly, the correlation is only significant where fathers are concerned, not mothers (.15** for fathers and .01 for mothers).

4.   We suspect, but do not have empirical data to confirm, that parents and children who reside in the same community have more frequent but shorter telephone conversations, while those who are separated by long distances make fewer but longer telephone calls.

5. Indeed, we learned of this family pattern on one occasion when our neighbor forgot to tell her mother of an early dental appointment. Her mother phoned us to request that we go next door to be sure her daughter had not passed out or had a heart attack.

6. Age of parent and child is too highly correlated (.86) to permit inclusion of both variables in a regression equation.

7. We do not know this for a fact, because we did not ask respondents how far away their parents-in-law lived.

8. In preliminary analysis, we used the Mean Obligation scores toward *all* kin (as measured with the vignette data), rather than the Mean Obligation score to *primary* kin (parents and children). The Primary Kin obligation measure increased the size of the Beta coefficients: for example, the equation on phone contact with Father had a Beta coefficient of .09** with the general Kin Obligation Score, while, as seen in Table 8.5, the Beta coefficient increased to .11** when the norm measure was the more narrowly defined and relevant Primary Kin Obligation Score.

9. This is a reduction from 595 G2 respondents reporting on contact with mother in Table 8.5 to 164 G2 respondents whose mothers were interviewed, the case base in Table 8.6, with a comparable reduction for fathers from 444 G2 respondents in Table 8.5 to 109 G2 respondents in Table 8.6.

10. Both the Kin Obligation and Value Consensus ratings have a larger number of missing values than most variables in the study, and marital status of the child showed no effects in any equations in Table 8.5.

11. Robert Rubenstein gives several portraits of elderly widowed men, who felt great psychic pain and social loss when their wives died, but who were not able to reach out to others for the comfort and sociability they clearly needed (Rubenstein, 1986).

Help Exchange between the Generations _____ 9

Observation of a mother upon the birth of a granddaughter, her daughter's second child (first child was a son):
"You will only understand what I mean years from now, but Kris's birth is very special to me. Now we have three generations of women in the family, and you and I have become more alike. I have you, and you have Kris. We women understand each other better, and we do more things for each other."

Introduction

The analysis of geographic distance and social interaction in the previous chapter has set the stage for one of the most important topics in this study: the extent and type of help exchanged between parents and adult children. We will explore the types of help given to and received by parents and adult children, with special attention to variation by gender, phase of the life course, and relative income level of parent and child. Following the descriptive analysis of the help pattern, we present the results of a regression analysis that draws on variables we have explored in depth in previous chapters and tests their predictive power in explaining variation in the extent to which the generations help each other.

To the extent the data permit, we will replicate the analysis of the help exchange pattern shown by G2 respondents in their roles as adult children in relationship to their G1 parents, with an analysis of the help exchange pattern shown by G2 respondents in their roles as parents in relationship to their G3 children. In the course of the regression analysis, we shall explore the contribution of earlier family characteristics, and a wide array of current characteristics of the parents and of the adult children (e.g., health, personal traits, marital and employment status, family size, income) and qualitative measures on the relationship between them (affective closeness and value consensus). Throughout the analysis, we shall control for the major "opportunity" factors that contribute to the exchange of help between the generations—a measure of interaction frequency and geographic proximity.

Measurement of Help

We begin with a brief reminder of the rationale for our selection of items to measure the help exchanged between parents and adult children (see Chapter 1 for details). Because we wished to specify gender of parent and child wherever possible and to obtain identical information concerning each adult child of our respondents, it was necessary to devise a simple, easily administered series of questions about the help given to and received from each parent and each adult child of the respondents. We opted for a list of nine types of help, and asked respondents to simply respond "yes" or "no" to whether they had given (or received) each kind of help "over the past year or so." No attempt could be made to gauge the amount of time or the frequency with which each type of help was given or received during the preceding year.

Our concern in designing the help items was to have a great variety of types of help that were as relevant and appropriate to parental giving and receiving as to child giving and receiving. This would permit the construction of identical indices for both parents and children and for both directions of help between them. We selected some types of help that were *expressive*, such as being comforted during a personal crisis, and others that were more *instrumental*, such as job prospects or contacts. We were also concerned to avoid reliance only on types of help that depend on residential proximity. Thus, although we asked about help with domestic chores and care during an illness, which rely directly on proximity, we also asked about other types of help, such as advice, comfort, special gifts, or money, that do not necessarily depend on proximity because they could be handled by phone or mail.

A third concern was to devise types of help relevant to men as well as women. Special gifts can be exchanged by either sex, just as advice, comfort, job leads, or money can be. For types of help that might be linked to gender, such as domestic chores, we gave examples of "yardwork" to counter the linkage of women to childcare and cleaning. The item on making or fixing something cited examples appropriate to men as well as women: painting a room or repairing an appliance, the kinds of things traditionally associated with male domestic activity, along with sewing something, traditionally linked with female domestic activity.

The nine help items are listed below; the labels to be used as abbreviated indicators in subsequent tables are italicized, with the full phrasing of each item as read to respondents following the label. These are the items and exact phrasing in the questions concerning help *received* by children from their mothers and fathers. The references to babysitting or taking care of children were dropped from the questions on help *given to* parents; otherwise the items were identical.

Advice: Advice on a decision you had to make.

Comfort: Comforting you in a personal crisis of some kind that upset you.

Illness: Helping out during an illness you had, or someone in your family had.

Chores: Helping you with your regular chores, such as shopping, yardwork, cleaning, or baby sitting.

Fix: Fixing or making something for you, like painting a room, repairing an appliance, or sewing something.

Home: Taking care of your child(ren), pets, plants, or home while you were away.

Gift: Giving you a special gift of some sort.

Job: Help in connection with a job, such as telling you about a job prospect, or contacts that helped you in your job.

Money: Financial help with money or a loan.

We will begin by describing the extent to which help of these various types varies by gender of parent or child, marital status, age, and income level of parent and child. When we attempt to explain variation in the help pattern, in a later section of the chapter, we will place greater reliance on three summated indices constructed from the nine items. Those of most general utility are measures of the Extent of Help given or received, a summation of the number of types of help respondents gave or received, indices that therefore range from 0 to 9, which we have converted to the more familiar metric of 0 to 100 as we have done with other indices. For each respondent, then, there is a score on the extent of help given and the help received from each living parent and each child of theirs over 18 years of age. In addition, we constructed a Reciprocity Index, which is a count of the number of types of help that were both given and received within each parent–child dyad.

Types of Help Exchanged by Gender of Parent and Child

Incidence Level of Types of Help

Table 9.1 provides the full detail on the incidence level of the nine types of help exchanged between G1 parents and G2 adult children, by

Table 9.1. Incidence Level of Types of Help Exchanged between G1 Parents and G2 Adult Children by Gender of Parent and Child (G2 Sample) (in Percent)

Type of Help	Type of Parent–Child Dyad			
	Mother–Daughter	Mother–Son	Father–Daughter	Father–Son
A. Help Given by G2 Child to G1 Parent				
Personal Care/Support				
Advice	76.7	72.1	44.9	55.9
Comfort	79.1	67.2	47.1	45.4
Illness	48.8	35.5	33.6	32.7
Domestic				
Fix/Make Things	50.4	61.2	39.8	53.7
Home	41.1	39.5	37.0	37.4
Chores	59.4	47.5	48.1	36.4
Instrumental				
Special Gift	89.2	75.7	76.2	59.6
Job Leads	14.3	13.8	11.4	17.8
Money	19.2	20.7	9.0	12.6
B. Help Received by G2 Child from G1 Parent				
Personal Care/Support				
Advice	69.0	57.0	59.6	64.1
Comfort	62.4	44.8	46.4	33.0
Illness	35.3	25.7	31.9	20.4
Domestic				
Fix/Make Things	45.7	38.5	40.7	32.6
Home	41.7	33.3	34.3	26.4
Chores	42.5	43.8	36.4	23.0
Instrumental				
Special Gift	81.2	65.4	61.7	48.1
Job Leads	21.9	19.6	18.3	29.6
Money	41.6	34.1	43.2	38.9
N	(472)	(358)	(324)	(270)

gender of the parent and of the child. These data permit us to describe the types of help that are structured by gender, and the direction of flow between the older and younger generations. That is to say, we ask to what extent and on what types of help mothers give (or receive) more help than fathers, to what extent and on what types of help daughters give (or receive) more help than sons, and are there types of help that tend to flow from parent to child, and other types of help that tend to flow from child to parent.

With nine types of help, four parent–child dyads, and two directions of intergenerational flow, there are 72 percentages in the detailed incidence levels shown in Table 9.1. The flow of help from child to parent is shown in Panel A, and that from parent to child is shown in Panel B. Even a casual inspection of these data shows a very wide range in the incidence of help exchange, from a low of 9% of the G2 women who report that they gave money to their fathers during the past year, to a high of 89% of the women who report that they gave a special gift to their mothers during the preceding year. The general impression projected by the data in Table 9.1 is of pervasive flows of help between the generations in both directions; on many types of help, there is just as high an incidence of help given to a parent as there is of help given to a child.

To facilitate summarizing these detailed incidence figures, we shall reorganize the results to highlight the major differences that emerge in three comparisons on the symmetry or assymetry of the help pattern: by generation, by gender of the parent, and by gender of the child.

Generational Symmetry

We begin with the symmetry of help levels by generation. Take, for example, the incidence level for giving or receiving "advice" in the father–son relationship: 56% of the G2 sons report having given their fathers advice during the past year, while a somewhat larger proportion, 64%, report having received advice from their fathers in the preceding year, suggesting the flow of advice is slightly greater from fathers to sons than from sons to fathers. To depict the extent of symmetry or asymmetry in the intergenerational help flow, each of the nine types of help for each of the parent–child dyads was therefore classified by the percentage difference between giving and getting help, with the results shown in Table 9.2.

Inspection of the top rows compared to the bottom rows of Table 9.2 identifies the kinds of help that tend to be asymmetrical in the flow between the generations: For example, from 20 to 25% more G2 sons report providing comfort to their mothers than report they received comfort from their mothers. By contrast, the balance tips to the opposite direction in the case of giving money or a loan; a far larger proportion of G2 adult children report receiving money from their parents than report giving money to their parents.

Symmetry of exchange on this aggregate level of analysis is shown by the types of help items that appear *between* the broken horizontal lines in the table. Symmetry is apparent only between daughters and their parents, involving similar levels of help on home-centered matters such

Table 9.2. Extent of Asymmetry in Type of Help Exchanged between G1
Parents and G2 Adult Children by Gender of Parent and Child (G2
Sample)

	Type of Parent–Child Dyad			
Give:Get Balance	Mother– Daughter	Mother– Son	Father– Daughter	Father– Son
Adult Child Gives More Than Gets by (%)				
20–25	—	Comfort	—	—
15–19	Comfort Chores	Chores Advice	—	—
10–14	Illness	Gift Illness	Gift Illness	Illness Comfort Gift Home Chores
5–9	Advice Gift	Home	Chores	—
Reciprocal (%)				
0±4	Fix Home	—	Home Comfort Fix	—
Adult Child Gets More Than Gives by (%)				
5–9	Job Leads	Job Leads	Job Leads	Advice
10–14	—	Money	—	Job Leads
15–19	—	—	Advice	—
20–25	Money	—	—	Fix
26 or more	—	—	Money	Money

as fixing or making something, watching a home during the absence of
the other, or providing comfort during a personal crisis.

Overall, the table shows the nature of the asymmetry in the types of
help that flow between the generations: *Adult children report giving more
help of a personal supportive variety* (e.g., comfort or care during an illness)
*to their parents than they receive in kind, whereas parents give their children
more instrumental help* (e.g., money or a loan, job leads, or advice about a
decision confronting the person) *than they receive from their children.* The
implication is that this is a life course phenomenon, in which parents
help children in their transition to adulthood with money and advice or
information helpful to securing or advancing in a job, and children help
parents in more personal traumas centered on illness and loss that
increase in the later years of life. We will explore life course patterns in
help exchange in some detail in a later section.

Symmetry in Types of Help by Gender of Parent

Table 9.3 shifts attention to the second of our three questions about symmetry of help incidence levels: the extent to which G1 mothers and fathers differ in the level of help given to and received from their children. Several points are strikingly illustrated in this table. For one, more G1 mothers both give and receive help than is the case for G1 fathers; more of the women give help of a domestic and personal, supportive variety, and their children reciprocate in a similar manner

Table 9.3. Extent of Asymmetry in Type of Help Exchanged with G1 Mothers and G1 Fathers by Gender of G2 Adult Child (G2 Sample)

Mother:Father Difference	*G2 Daughters*	*G2 Sons*
A. Help G2 Child Gets from G1 Parent		
Mother Gives More Than		
Father by (%)		
15–20	Comfort, Gift	Gift
10–14	Illness	Comfort
5–9	Advice, Home, Fix, Chores	Illness, Home, Chores, Fix
Similar or Minimal (%)		
0±4	Money, Job Leads	—
Father Gives More Than		
Mother by (%)		
5–9	—	Advice, Money
10–14	—	Job Leads
15–20	—	—
B. Help G2 Child Gives to G1 Parent		
Mother Gets More Than		
Father by (%)		
30 or more	Advice, Comfort	—
20-29	—	Comfort
15–19	Illness, Chores	Advice, Gift
10–14	Fix, Gift, Money	—
5–9	—	Fix, Money
Similar or Minimal (%)		
0±4	Home, Job Leads	Illness, Home, Job Leads, Chores
Father Gets More Than		
Mother by (%)		
5 or more	—	—

with comfort, help with chores, and gifts. The areas in which fathers loom larger than mothers is help in the form of job leads, money or a loan, and advice, but this is the case only where sons are concerned. More significantly, in the flow of help from adult children to their parents, *none of the nine types of help is given more often to fathers than to mothers*, as highlighted by the lack of a single entry in the bottom row of Panel B in Table 9.3. Greater maternal than paternal investment of time, affect, and energy in early childrearing may pave the way for this gender-differentiated channeling of help to older parents from mature adult children.

Symmetry of Types of Help by Gender of Child

This same gender linkage holds when attention shifts to the contrasts between G2 sons and G2 daughters (shown in Table 9.4). Just as more fathers than mothers give advice, money, and job leads, so too more sons specialize in these types of help than do daughters. Women's family specialization in personal support, kinkeeping, ritual occasions, and domestic maintenance are apparent in all three summary tables. Whether as mothers or as daughters, women are more involved in giving comfort, exchanging special gifts, helping out during illnesses, and lending a hand with daily chores, child care, or watching over plants, pets, and mail if they reside close enough to provide such home-watch during the absence of the parent or child.

Reciprocity and Types of Help Exchanged

Aggregate level analysis, which suggests a symmetrical pattern of help, does not necessarily mean reciprocal exchange on an individual level. Different individuals may be involved in giving, say, advice to a mother than are involved in receiving advice from a mother, even though, as a group, as many mothers as adult children give and receive advice. A more direct test of the extent of reciprocity within the types of help we have examined is shown in Table 9.5, in the form of correlation coefficients between giving and receiving the same type of help. The most prevalent form of reciprocal exchange is, not surprisingly, giving special gifts; as many of us have experienced, those who receive a special gift from someone tend to feel obligated to give a gift in turn. Special gifts head the list of types of help that tend to be reciprocated.

Many other types of help may operate not on the grounds of social obligation, but as reflections of habit and the ease of the relationship: If you are intimate enough to share a personal crisis with someone and to

Table 9.4. Extent of Asymmetry between G2 Sons and G2 Daughters in Help Exchanged with G1 Parents by Gender of Parent (G2 Sample)

Daughter:Son Difference	*G1 Mothers*	*G1 Fathers*
A. Help G2 Child Gets from G1 Parent		
Daughter Gets More Than		
Son (%)		
15–20	Comfort, Gift	—
10–14	Advice, Chores	Comfort, Chores, Gift
5–9	Illness, Home, Fix, Money	Home, Fix
Similar or Minimal (%)		
0±4	Job Leads	Illness, Money
Son Gets More Than		
Daughter (%)		
5–9	—	Advice
10–14	—	Job Leads
15–20	—	—
B. Help G2 Child Gives to G1 Parent		
Daughter Gives More Than		
Son (%)		
15–20	—	Gift
10–14	Comfort, Gift, Illness, Chores	Chores
5–9	Advice	—
Similar or Minimal (%)		
0±4	Home, Job Leads, Money	Comfort, Illness, Home, Money
Son Gives More Than		
Daughter (%)		
5–9	—	Job Leads
10–14	Fix	Advice, Fix
15–20	—	—

be comforted by them, it is probable that the partner's personal crisis will also be shared and you will comfort them in turn. Comfort, advice, and domestic help of various kinds are clearly exchanged by many parents and adult children, as suggested by the significant correlations on these types of help shown in Table 9.5. On the other hand, being at very different phases of the life course, an illness serious enough to involve caregiving from someone in the family is more apt to strike an elderly parent than a young adult child. In the reverse direction, finan-

Table 9.5. Extent of Reciprocity within Types of Help
Given and Received by G1 Parents and G2 Adult
Children (G2 Sample)
(Pearson correlation coefficients between giving and
receiving the same type of help)

Type of Help	G2 Child– G1 Mother	G2 Child– G1 Father
Special Gift	.47***	.52***
Comfort	.33***	.37***
Chores	.31***	.35***
Fix/Make Things	.29***	.23***
Home-watch	.27***	.40***
Advice	.27***	.33***
Job Leads	.24***	.26***
Illness	.22***	.15*
Money or Loan	− .07	.08

*** $p < .001$
* $p < .05$

cial need or hearing about job prospects is more likely to apply to young adult children than to middle-aged or elderly parents. Hence, the correlations on such help items are quite low.

The type of help that is the *least* likely to be reciprocated is providing and receiving money or a loan. The general pattern is clearly for money to flow *down* the generational hierarchy, particularly from fathers to sons. We will investigate this more closely at a later point by introducing income level of the parent and child as an indicator of need or resource capacity in relation to the types of help exchanged.

Effect of Marital Status of Parents and Adult Children on Help Exchange

In most of our analysis, the parent–adult child dyad has been viewed in isolation, as though the primary social bond in the lives of parents and adult children was the relationship between them. We have qualified this emphasis when we considered the competing demands represented by family size in the two generations, as in the regression analysis of social interaction reported in Chapter 8. But, of course, life for most adults in American society does not center on their parents, but on their spouses and dependent age children. The marital relationship, fraught with risk though it is in a high-divorce society, is a stable emotional anchor in the adult lives of most of us, persisting long after our parents are dead and our children have left home.

Many types of help that are provided to an older parent or to a young adult child may rebound to the benefit not just of the individual parent or child we gave it to, but to their spouses as well. When a daughter helps her mother with domestic chores, the father may also benefit, for example, by enjoying a clean home or a good meal. Even a special gift, if it is something like a household appliance rather than personal apparel, may be enjoyed by both parents, not just the one we addressed on a gift card. Analogously, many types of help that parents give to grown children are extended to children-in-law as well, such as contributing to the down payment on a married daughter's house or a gift of an air conditioner to a married son.

But if the larger kindred, and, in particular, the ongoing relationship between parents and adult children, serves as a latent matrix of potential support in times of need or crisis, we would expect an uneven flow of help between parents and adult children as a function of their marital status. To explore the implications of this general function of the family, we have analyzed the incidence level of the nine types of help by the marital status of the parent and of the child. Concern here is with the "solo" parent or child, typically a widowed parent in the first instance, and an unmarried or divorced child in the second instance. The results of this intensive analysis are not reported in detail here. Rather, we provide a summary table of the statistically significant differences in the reported incidence of the nine types of help from or to widowed parents compared to married parents, and to unattached adult children compared to married children.

Table 9.6 shows the results, in Panel A by the marital status of the parent and in Panel B by the marital status of the child. Any type of help that does not appear in a particular column showed no difference in the incidence of help given or received during the preceding year between married and unattached children (or parents).

Take, for example, the data pertaining to the mother–daughter relationship in Panel A: The results indicate that significantly more children report giving money or helping out during an illness when the mother is widowed than when she is married, an expectable outcome since married mothers have a spouse to help out if they are ill, and they generally enjoy much higher incomes than widowed women do. Analogously, the general profile is for more adult children to report receiving help from married than from widowed mothers in many types of help, including getting advice, money, help with chores, a gift, or job leads. Marital status of the mother made a difference for only two of the nine types of help daughters gave their mothers, but six of the nine types of help daughters received from their mothers. The absence of a particular type of help in a column of Table 9.6 means there were no significant differ-

Table 9.6. Significant Differences by Marital Status of G1 Parents and G2 Adult Children, in Types of Help Exchanged, by Gender of Parent and Child (G2 Sample)

Direction of Help and Dyad	G1 Parent–G2 Adult Child Dyad			
	Mother–Daughter	Mother–Son	Father–Daughter	Father–Son
A. Marital Status of Parent [a]				
1. G2 Child to G1 Parent				
More Help to Widowed Parent Than to Married Parent	Money*** Illness*	Illness*** Money*** Advice*	Advice*** Illness* Money* Fix/Make* Chores+	Advice+ Comfort+
More Help to Married Parent Than to Widowed Parent	—	—	Home+	Home+ Chores+
2. G1 Parent to G2 Child				
More Help from Married Parent Than from Widowed Parent	Chores*** Money*** Advice** Home** Gift* Job*	Advice*** Money*** Fix/Make*	Fix/Make* Home+ Illness+	Money+ Gift+ Advice+
More Help from Widowed Parent Than from Married Parent	—	—	—	—
B. Marital Status of G2 Child [b]				
1. G2 Child to Parent				
More Help from Unattached Child Than Married Child	Chores**	Chores*** Home***	Fix/Make* Chores* Comfort+	Home+
More Help from Married Child Than Unattached Child	—	—	—	Advice*
2. G1 Parent to G2 Child				
More Help to Unattached Child Than Married Child	Advice*** Money*** Job*** Comfort**	Advice*** Money*** Job*** Comfort***	Advice*** Money*** Job*** Illness**	Advice*** Money*** Job* Comfort*
More Help to Married Child Than Unattached Child	—	Home*	—	Home*

[a] Marital Status of Parent: Widowed parents vs. parents married and living together.
[b] Marital Status of Child: Unattached children are never married, separated, or divorced vs. currently married.

*** p < .001   ** p < .01   * p < .05   + p < .10

ences by marital status of the parent or of the child. For example, providing comfort to a parent or receiving it from a parent is not affected by the marital status of the parent; widowed mothers are comforted by their daughters as often as married mothers are, and just as large a proportion of daughters report having been comforted by widowed mothers as by married mothers.

An interesting general pattern that emerges from this analysis is the following: *widowed parents give less but get more varied help from adult children than married parents do, whereas unattached children both give and get more varied help from parents than married children do.* There is also a hint in these data that gender of the child takes on special significance when a parent is widowed, as suggested by the finding that significantly more daughters help widowed fathers than married fathers with domestic chores, fixing or making something, and significantly more sons help widowed mothers than married mothers with money and advice. *Daughters provide traditional female help to widowed fathers, and sons provide traditional male help to their widowed mothers.*

It is of course the case that marital status is strongly related to the age of both parents and children. On average, widowed parents are older than married parents, and unattached children are younger than married children. We shall test whether marital status retains its significance with a control on age in the regression analysis later in the chapter. We turn now to an explicit focus on the changes that occur in the help exchange between the generations along the life course trajectory.

Life Course Trajectory in Help Exchange

To provide an introductory overview of the life course trajectory in the help exchanged between the generations, Figure 9.1 shows graphically the mean rating on the general Extent of Help Given by parents to adult children, and by adult children to their parents. We use a fine, 5-year age break on parental age, to capture changes that occur in the elderly years, when parents are over 60 years of age. To ensure adequate case bases, we rely on the childset file of the G2 sample; hence, the dyad is the G2 parent and the G3 adult child. (The same life course pattern, though with less age detail, is found in the G1–G2 dyad; data not shown.) Two trends are readily seen in this figure: One is the steep decline in the extent of help that parents give to children as the parents age, most dramatically when parents enter their 70s. There is a similar, but more gradual decline in the extent of help children give to their parents over the life course, with a modest upturn when parents are over 80 years of age.

The help ratings shown here are those made by G2 respondents as

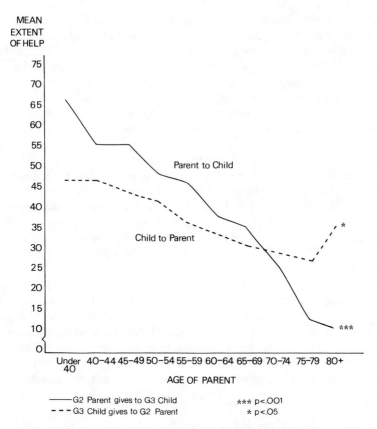

Figure 9.1. Life course trajectory in help exchange between G2 parents and G3 adult children (G2 sample, childset file). (Mean ratings on help indices, 0–100 metric.)

parents, which contributes to the second pattern shown in the graph, i.e., the extent of help for most of the life course shows higher means in the flow from parent to child than from child to parent. Parental help to children continues well into the adult years of the children, with the balance reversing only when parents are over 70 years of age.[1] As the population over 85 years of age increases in the decades ahead, the profile of help by children to parents may become more curvilinear, with increasingly more extensive help provided by adult middle-aged children to very old parents.

The extent of help exchanged is strongly affected by the gender of the parents and of the adult children. Figure 9.2 illustrates this graphically: The average extent of help given by mothers compared to fathers is shown in Panel A, and the help children gave to mothers compared to fathers is shown in Panel B.

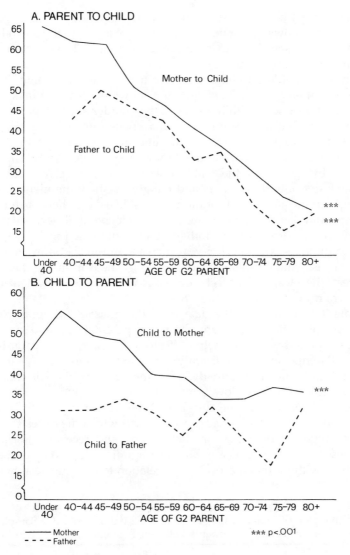

Figure 9.2. Life course trajectory in help exchange between G2 parents and G3 children by gender of parent (G2 sample, childset file). (Mean ratings on help indices, 0–100 metric.)

Two things are in sharp focus in these graphs. First, more extensive help flows in both directions between mothers and children than between fathers and children at all points of the life course. Second, both mothers and fathers show significant declines in the extent of help given to children as they get older, but in the help received from children, the decline with parental age is significant only for mothers. This does not mean older mothers get less extensive help than older fathers, because, as the graph shows, the statistical significance is due to the much higher levels of extensive help to mothers in their middle years when the children are young adults.

Gender of the adult children is also a factor in the profile of inter-generational help exchange. Figure 9.3 shows the mean ratings of help given and received within each of the gender-specific parent–child dyads. (Note that we are here using data concerning the G1 parents and G2 adult children.) A significant decline in parental help to children across the life course is found in all four parent–child dyads. The major contrast by gender of the child concerns the help profile involving mothers; not only do mothers and daughters show the highest means throughout the 40s and 50s of the mothers' lives, but there is an upturn in help from daughters to mothers that is steeper and begins earlier in the life course of the older mothers than is the case for the help from sons to mothers. With each 5-year increase in the age of mothers over 65, there is a higher mean on the extent of help from the daughters, whereas the mean help level from sons to mothers shows an upturn only when mothers are in their 80s.

Table 9.7 summarizes the data from these last three figures, in the form of correlation coefficients between parental age and the mean ratings on the three major help indicators, for each of the parent–child dyads. Parental age is significantly correlated with extent of help given to adult children in all four dyads, while none of the correlations is significant for the help flow from children to parents.

Table 9.7 also shows the correlations between parental age and the mean scores on the Help Reciprocity index, which measures the num-bers of types of help that are both given and received. Reciprocity declines the older parents are, but very significantly so only in the help exchange with mothers, especially in relation to daughters.[2] When chil-

Table 9.7. Effect of Parental Age on Extent and Reciprocity of Help Exchange by Gender of G1 Parent and G2 Adult Child (G2 Sample) (Pearson correlation coefficients between Parental Age and Help indices)

| | *Extent of Help* | | | |
| | *Parent to Child* | *Child to Parent* | *Extent of Reciprocity* | *N* |
G1 Parent–G2 Child Dyad				
Mother–Daughter	−.36***	−.05	−.31***	(462)
Mother–Son	−.39***	−.06	−.28***	(357)
Father–Daughter	−.20***	−.03	−.11*	(360)
Father–Son	−.23***	−.05	−.16*	(266)

*** $p < .001$ * $p < .05$

dren are in their 20s and 30s, and their parents in their 40s and 50s, there is a good deal of help between the generations that is similar in type (e.g., mother and daughter doing domestic chores for each other), but as the parents get older and the children are mature middle aged adults, a complementary exchange pattern replaces the reciprocal pattern, e.g., money to mother, who in turn makes something for a daughter or provides advice drawn from her experience in life.

There appears to be more complementarity in the help exchange between fathers and their adult children, as suggested by the much lower correlations between parental age and the extent of reciprocity in types of help, e.g., fathers providing advice or money while sons and daughters help with chores, fix an appliance, or take care of a home in the father's absence.

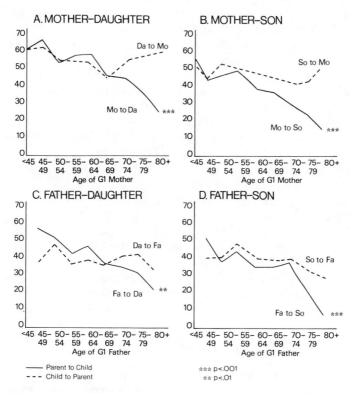

Figure 9.3. Life course trajectory in extent of help exchange between G1 parent and G2 child by gender of parent and child and age of parent (G2 sample). (Mean ratings on help indices, 0–100 metric.)

It is of interest to examine some of the specific types of help given and received, because the mean extent measures hide some important differences in the relation of parental age to types and direction of help flows between the generations. We selected six of the nine types of help for this closer inspection to illustrate three patterns: One in which both directions of help decline with age, a second in which only parental help to children declines, and a third in which help from children increases while help from parents decreases across the life course.

Life Course Changes in Job Leads

Providing information about job prospects or client/customer contacts relevant to an occupation is the type of help that declines over the life course of both parents and adult children. It is when adult children are getting started in life that job prospects and contacts matter most, something middle-aged parents, at their prime of engagement in the world of work, are best able to provide. Once the parents have retired, they have lost such connections and their adult children are well established on their own and need less help on job-related matters. Figure 9.4 shows that decline in job-relevant help with increasing parental age, a life course change that is significant within all four parent–child dyads and both up and down the generational hierarchy.

Parents in their early middle years show particularly high proportions who gave their sons job leads; many of their daughters, by contrast, will have temporarily withdrawn from the labor force and need less help of this type than their brothers, and, if married, their husbands may be helped in this way by their own parents. There is also a significant minority of adult children who provide assistance in this domain of life to their parents. Increased experience in the labor force involves more extensive network connections of the kind that may assist the older parents. Daughters also show an increase in advice concerning jobs to their mothers as the latter move into their 50s. For some mothers this may be the point of their reentry into the labor force; other mothers may benefit from referrals by their children to customers or clients, e.g., women who manage retail shops or work as real estate agents.

Life Course Changes in Advice and Comfort

Giving advice on a personal decision or providing comfort during a personal crisis are types of help that show a sharp decline in the flow from parent to child, and stability across the life course in the help from child to parent. The "command" peak of the life course in mature

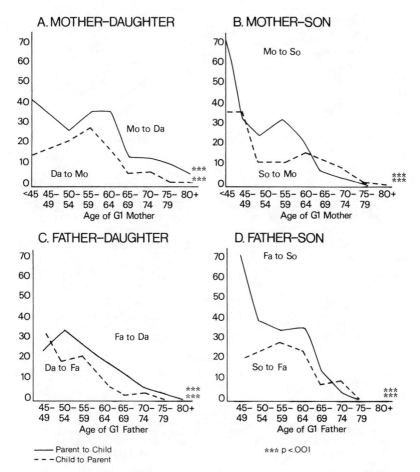

Figure 9.4. Life course trajectory in exchange of *job leads* between G1 parents and G2 adult children by gender of parent and child and age of parent (G2 sample). (Percentage report *giving* or *receiving* help with job prospects or contacts during the past year.)

middle age—when accumulated experience, extensive network connections, income, and knowledge of many institutional sectors of a community are at their peak—is reflected in the data shown in Figure 9.5, on the flow of advice from parents to children.

A large proportion of parents in their late 40s and early 50s gave advice to an adult child, but this level declines rapidly once parents are over 65 years of age. It is interesting that both sons and daughters also show a high level of advice giving to their mothers when the latter are in

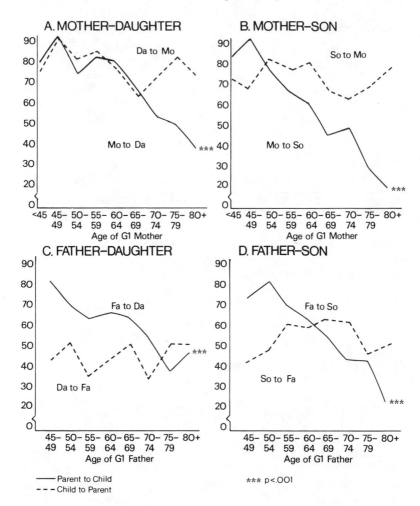

Figure 9.5.   Life course trajectory in the exchange of *advice* between G1 parents and G2 adult children by gender of parent and child and age of G1 parents (G2 sample). (Percentage report *giving* or *receiving* advice on a decision made during the past year.)

their 40s and 50s; in fact, almost twice as many sons and daughters have advised their mothers as have advised their fathers. We suspect this is due to two factors: More women undergo changes in life pattern in their 40s than is true for men—returning to school, becoming involved with politics or community organizations, entering the labor force—changes on which their children's recent experiences may be relevant and helpful.

Second, the somewhat greater superordinate position of men as presumed (if not actual) heads of their households may dampen advice giving by young adult children to their fathers, even when the children believe they could help their fathers. There is even a hint that when the superordinate and subordinate positions on the age-gender axis meet, as they do in the father–daughter relationship, the balance is most strongly tipped to advice flowing from parent to child, i.e., from father to daughter. That balance is retained until the father's very elderly years; only when fathers are over 75 years of age do more daughters give advice to their fathers than fathers to daughters.

Providing comfort during a personal crisis also shows a decline with parental age in the incidence level of help from parents to children, and relative stability in the incidence level of children providing comfort to parents (Figure 9.6). The general pattern at all ages is for more children to comfort their parents than parents comfort their children. This may reflect the reality of the lives of those from middle age on. Middle-aged parents may be seeing their own parents through terminal illnesses and death, with their children providing comfort during the process; by their 50s, many women cope with illness and often the death of their husbands; and by their 60s and 70s surviving men and women begin to cope with issues centered on their own health, retirement, and prospective death, while their children have settled into mature middle age with fewer personal crises than marked ‹their youthful transition to jobs, marriage, and childbearing, and by midlife most adult children have spouses who provide comfort and support.

Life Course Changes in Help with Domestic Chores

Help with domestic chores shows a life course pattern rather like that of providing comfort: More children help parents with such chores than parents help their adult children (Figure 9.7). The parent-to-child profile declines rapidly with the age of the parent while child-to-parent help with domestic chores remains relatively stable as the parents age. The one striking exception is the help daughters give to their mothers as the mother grows older: There is a sharp increase in the proportion of daughters who report having helped their mothers with domestic chores with each older age group of mothers above 65 years of age. Hence, the life course profile approaches a curvilinear pattern in the mother–daughter relationship: A large proportion of young adult daughters in their 20s still reside at home and many help their mothers with domestic chores. Following a decline during their own childrearing years, an increasing proportion of daughters once more provide assistance with domestic chores when their mothers are older, and many are widowed.

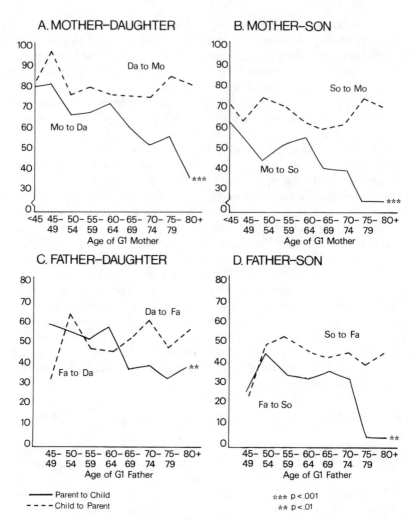

Figure 9.6. Life course trajectory in *providing comfort during personal crises* by gender of parent and child and age of G1 parent (G2 sample). (Percentage report *giving* or *receiving* comfort during a personal crisis during the past year.)

Life Course Changes in Help with Money
or Personal Caregiving during an Illness

Our last examples of help exchanged between the generations—that of giving or receiving money or a loan, or caregiving during an illness—have a unique life course profile, as seen in Figures 9.8 and 9.9. The direction that money moves between the two generations is very strong-

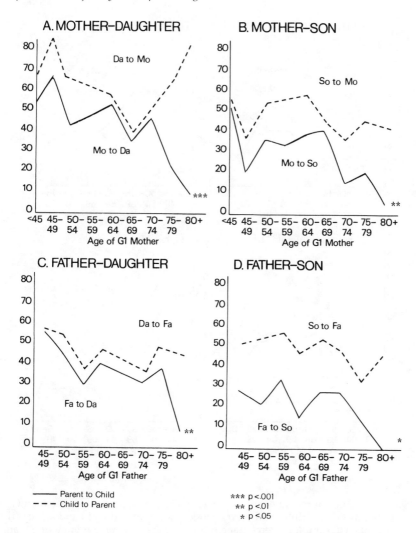

Figure 9.7. Life course trajectory in exchange of *help with regular domestic chores* between G1 parents and G2 adult children by gender of parent and child and age of G1 parents (G2 sample). (Percentage report *giving* or *receiving* help with domestic chores during the past year.)

ly influenced by parental age. As with most other types of help, financial aid from parents to children drops rapidly across the life course, but unlike other types of help, an increasing proportion of children provide some financial help to their parents as the parents age. The only exception is financial help from sons to fathers which does not increase with the age of the father. An increasingly larger proportion of sons and

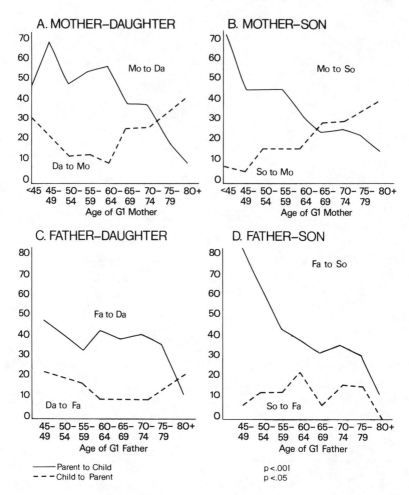

Figure 9.8. Life course trajectory in the exchange of *money or loans* between G1 parents and G2 adult children by gender of parent and child and age of G1 parents (G2 sample). (Percentage report *giving* or *receiving* money or a loan during the past year.)

daughters give money to their mothers as the mothers age, the need for which is rooted in the fact that the lowest income level of all gender-marital status subgroups in the society is found among elderly widowed women, as we saw in Chapter 3.

Help during an illness (of their own or someone in the family) shares some characteristics with the pattern shown on financial aid; there is a declining proportion of parents who help children during an illness as the parents get older, while there is a significant increase in the propor-

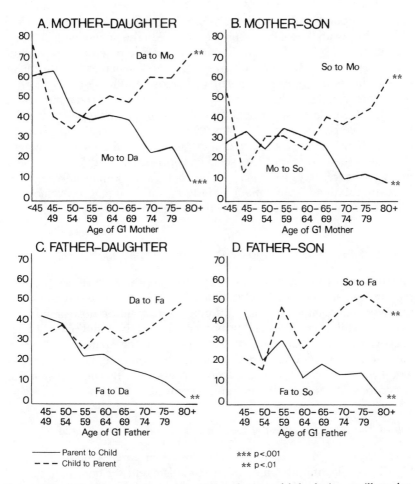

Figure 9.9. Life course trajectory in the exchange of *help during an illness* between G1 parents and G2 adult children by gender of parent and child and age of G1 parents (G2 sample). (Percentage report *giving* or *receiving* help during an illness during the past year.)

tion of adult children who report having helped a parent during a personal illness. The relationship to parental age is much stronger in the help flow to mothers than to fathers, no doubt reflecting the fact that women, being younger on average than their spouses, take care of their husbands during illnesses more often than men care for their younger wives in old age. Hence there is a greater need for children to provide help when mothers are themselves old and ill than is true in the case of elderly fathers.

The one point of difference between financial aid and personal care-giving during an illness concerns the balance in the flow of help between the generations; in the case of financial aid, more parents help children than the reverse—children aiding their parents—whereas care during an illness shows the reverse pattern, with more adult children reporting having provided such help to parents than parents report having helped their children. This is a particularly strong contrast in the case of fathers. Gender role patterns are in strong evidence: It is socially appropriate, and economically feasible, for fathers to assist children with money, especially their sons, but less socially appropriate, and less often eco-nomically necessary, for sons to help their fathers financially. By con-trast, financial aid from sons to elderly mothers is more prevalent and often economically necessary when mothers are widowed.

Effect of Geographic Distance on Help Exchange

We turn now to the question of how the geographic distance between parents and adult children affects the help exchange between them, and whether this distance has any different impact on the flow of aid from parent to child than from child to parent. We begin with the early adult years when some children remain at home with their parents and others have gone on to independent households of their own; we shall investi-gate how shared versus nearby residence affects the flow of help be-tween parents and adult children in their 20s.

Shared Households vs. Nearby Residence of Young Adult Children

The move of young adult children from their parents' home is often a highly significant and sometimes traumatic event for both parents and children. Pride, relief, and separation anxiety may be experienced simul-taneously. Many mothers worry about what their children will eat, and some adult children are surprised to experience "homesickness." Clear-ly there are changes in many daily habits and routines for both genera-tions immediately following the move of young adult children to places of their own. We can investigate a few aspects of this early adult transition by comparing the help exchange between young adult chil-dren and their parents under two conditions: when the adult child remains at home, and when the adult child lives independently but still close enough for some continuation of help exchange with the parent. Hence, we restrict the comparison to adult children who reside less than 10 miles from their parents' homes. Since there are many developmental and social changes taking place as children make the transition from adolescence to adulthood, we further subdivide each residential group by the age of the child: those 18–24 years of age vs. those 25–30 years of age. The data set used in this analysis is the Childset file of all the children of the G2 respondents.

Tables 9.8 through 9.10 provide the major results of this analysis. Table 9.8 shows the mean score on the Extent of Help exchanged between parents and children as a function of residence and age of the child. Here we can see the beginning of the attenuation of parental help to adult children that was so dramatically indicated in the life course trajectory described above: There is a significant drop in the extent of help from parents to children as the child matures from an 18-year-old late adolescent to a mature 30-year-old; so too, parental help is reduced as children move out of the parental household to a nearby place of their own. Both variables show approximately equal strength in this reduction of help extent level, and together there is a drop by half in these average ratings, from a mean score of 60.2 when the adult child is under 25 and living with the parent to 28.9 when the child is in his or her late 20s but living less than 10 miles away.

The flow of help from child to parent is also affected by the transition

Table 9.8. Extent of Help Exchange between G2 Parents and G3 Adult Children by Age of Child and Residential Proximity [a] (G2 Sample, Childset File) (Mean Rating on Extent of Help Indices, 0–100 Metric)

Direction of Help	Residence	Age of Adult Child		Significance of Age
		18–24	25–30	
A. G2 Parent to G3 Child				
	Live Together	60.2	46.3	**
		(253)	(66)	
	Live less than 10 miles apart	45.8	28.9	**
		(84)	(166)	
	Significance of Residence	**	**	
B. G3 Child to G2 Parent				
	Live Together	52.3	50.6	
		(264)	(68)	
	Live less than 10 miles apart	37.1	37.2	
		(85)	(164)	
	Significance of Residence	**	**	

[a] Table restricted to children between 18 and 30 years of age who live with parents or 10 or fewer miles apart.
** $p < .01$

from living at home to living nearby, but here further maturation of the child has no effect on the help flow. Whether under or over 25 years of age, the help profile is the same, but it drops from just over 50 among children living with their parents to 37 if the adult children live nearby. Clearly residential pattern and a child's age have more impact on the help flow from parent to child than from child to parent.

The picture can also be examined at closer range, by observing the incidence level for specific types of help rather than the overall extent of help. One would assume that helping with domestic chores would be affected when children take even a nearby apartment compared to living in the same home with parents, but other types of help, such as advice, comfort, gifts, or job leads, could be given just as readily when parents and children live close to each other as when they share a home.

Table 9.9 suggests this is not the case, however, especially in the help exchange between parents and the younger of the two age groups, children under 25 years of age. Of the 18 comparisons between the first and second columns in this table, only one (home care in the absence of the other) departs from the general pattern of more help from and to parents among those who reside in the same household than among those separated by a few miles. The exception of home-watch may reflect a tendency for young adult children still living with their parents to go along with parents when they take vacations, while the adult children who live apart are more independent, probably working rather than studying, and some may have married and center their social life and personal needs on the spouse, not the parents.

Table 9.10 summarizes the effects of age and residential proximity by classifying the types of help that showed major or minor relationships to proximity within the two age groups. Work-relevant help from parents heads the list among the young adults, with more help to children at home than away from home, no doubt reflecting the transition the children are still undergoing in finishing training and getting a foothold in the occupational world. But sharing a residence increases by 10–20% the help from parents on advice, comfort, doing chores, and making things for younger adult children at home. Cooking and taking care of personal laundry may be services many mothers continue to perform for young adult children, much as they did while they were in high school, but each personal service declines by the time the children are in their late 20s. Children, in contrast, continue to provide services of a domestic nature if they remain at home in their late 20s. In the transition to adulthood, parents may withhold the provision of personal services and guidance as their children take on more responsibility for themselves and contribute to household maintenance rather than benefit from their parents' efforts.

Note, too, that money flows both ways more often when children

Table 9.9. Incidence of Types of Help Exchanged between G2 Parents and G3 Adult Children by Age of Child and Residential Proximity (G2 Sample, Childset File) (in Percent)

		Age of Adult Child			
		18–24		25–30	
Direction of Help	Type of Help	Live with Parents	Live Nearby [a]	Live with Parents	Live Nearby
A. G2 Parent to G3 Child					
	Domestic				
	Fix/Make	63.4	51.8	45.6	48.8
	Chores	53.2	40.0	36.8	44.0
	Home Care	29.5	33.3	22.7	35.5
	Personal Care/Support				
	Advice	87.9	72.9	72.1	60.2
	Comfort	64.2	51.8	57.4	50.6
	Illness	41.4	29.4	42.6	25.9
	Instrumental				
	Special Gift	77.4	68.2	60.3	65.1
	Job Leads	50.9	28.2	30.9	18.7
	Money/Loan	71.3	38.8	48.5	44.6
B. G3 Child to G2 Parent					
	Domestic				
	Fix/Make	57.4	36.5	60.3	46.4
	Chores	83.4	61.4	83.8	47.0
	Home Care	70.9	41.2	61.8	38.0
	Personal Care/Support				
	Advice	47.5	35.3	50.0	42.8
	Comfort	57.4	50.6	52.9	48.8
	Illness	42.3	28.2	42.6	33.7
	Instrumental				
	Special Gift	78.9	65.9	70.6	67.5
	Job Leads	9.8	9.4	7.4	8.5
	Money/Loan	24.5	5.9	26.5	7.2
	N	(265)	(85)	(68)	(166)

[a] Adult child lives less than 10 miles from parents' residence.

share a household. For those attending college, parents typically provide a major part of the funds needed for tuition and living expenses; but among those who are employed yet remain living with their parents, many children contribute to household upkeep by giving parents a portion of their salary to cover room and board.[3]

Overall Impact of Distance on Extent and Reciprocity of Help

The overall degree of correlation between geographic distance and the extent and reciprocity of help exchange is shown in Tables 9.11 and 9.12. Data in this instance come from G2 respondents concerning the mileage

Table 9.10. Summary of Effects of Age of Child and Residential Proximity for Type of Help Exchanged between G2 Parents and G3 Adult Children (G2 Sample, Childset File)

Direction of Help / Effect of Residential Proximity	Age of Adult Child	
	18–24	25–30
A. G2 Parent to G3 Child		
Living Together *adds* to Help Incidence		
More than 20%	Money/Loan	—
	Job Leads	
10–20%	Advice	Advice
	Illness	Illness
	Comfort	Job Leads
	Chores	
	Fix/Make	
Less than 10%	Special Gift	Comfort
	Home Care	Money/Loan
Living Together *reduces* Help Incidence		
Less than 10%	—	Chores
		Fix/Make
		Special Gift
10–20%	—	Home Care
B. G3 Child to G2 Parent		
Living Together *adds* to Help Incidence		
More than 20%	Fix/Make	Chores
	Chores	Home Care
	Home Care	
10–20%	Advice	Fix/Make
	Illness	Money/Loan
	Special Gift	
	Money/Loan	
Less than 10%	Comfort	Advice
	Job Leads	Comfort
		Illness
		Special Gift
Living Together *reduces* Help Incidence		
Less than 10%	—	Job Leads

distance and help they give to and receive from their G1 parents, with no restriction on age or shared households. Hence, the case base underlying these correlations include adult children in their mid-40s living a thousand miles away as well as children in their 20s who live a few blocks from their parents.

All the correlations in Table 9.11 are negative and significant: The

Table 9.11.   Effect of Geographic Distance on Extent and Reciprocity of Help
    Exchange by Gender of G1 Parent and G2 Adult Child (G2 Sample)
    (Pearson Correlation Coefficients between Mileage Distance and Help
    Indices)

G1 Parent– G1 Child Dyad	Extent of Help			
	Parent to Child	Child to Parent	Extent of Reciprocity	N
Mother–Daughter	−.27***	−.41***	−.30***	(472)
Mother–Son	−.24***	−.23***	−.25***	(357)
Father–Daughter	−.18***	−.27***	−.17**	(323)
Father–Son	−.20***	−.28***	−.21***	(271)

*** $p < .001$
** $p < .01$

further away from each other parents and children live, the less extensive is the help exchange between them and the less reciprocity is
involved (i.e., doing the same types of things for each other). The size of
the correlation coefficients shows considerable variation, however, as
seen in the range represented here: Geographic distance has the greatest
impact on the help daughters give to their mothers (−.41***), and the
least on the extent of help from fathers to their daughters (−.18***). In
three of the four comparisons, distance reduces help from children to
parents more than it does the reverse flow of help from parents to
children. There is also a suggestion that reciprocity level is particularly

Table 9.12.   Effect of Geographic Distance on Types of Help Exchanged
    between G2 Adult Children and G1 Parents (G2 Sample) (Pearson
    Correlation Coefficients between Mileage Distance and Help Measures)

Type of Help	G1 Mother		G1 Father	
	Child Gives	Mother Gives	Child Gives	Father Gives
Home-watch	−.37***	−.30***	−.35***	−.23***
Chores	−.25***	−.26***	−.19**	−.23***
Illness	−.23***	−.21***	−.18**	−.16**
Fix/Make Things	−.21***	−.12**	−.20***	−.19**
Job Leads	−.13**	−.07*	−.16**	−.10*
Advice	−.10**	−.10**	−.15**	−.07
Money or Loan	−.09**	−.10**	−.06	−.08
Special Gift	−.07	−.07	−.04	−.02
Comfort	−.05	−.11*	−.04	.02

*** $p < .001$
** $p < .01$
* $p < .05$

responsive to geographic distance in same-sex relations; distance reduces reciprocity between mothers and daughters more than mothers and sons ($-.30$ vs. $-.25$), and between fathers and sons more than fathers and daughters ($-.21$ vs. $-.17$).

It is also clear, from the evidence in Table 9.12, that no type of help shows a compensatory increase as a consequence of great distance between parents and children; that is to say, neither parents nor children report more gift giving or advice giving when they live far apart and can not help with more mundane daily tasks such as domestic chores or personal caregiving. The data on the help between G1 parents and G2 children show a consistent negative relationship with geographic distance: All 26 statistically significant correlations are negative, as are 9 of the 10 correlations that are not significant. *Across all types of help, then, geographic distance reduces frequency of social interaction, and, hence, the opportunity to inform or learn about needs and problems; consequently geographic distance reduces the actual incidence of all types of help flows between the generations.*

Parents' vs. Children's Reports on Help Exchange

Data previously shown that compares the help given to or received from a parent or child have all been reported by the same individuals, G2 respondents telling us about help exchange with their parents, or with their adult children. A next step in the analysis is to assess how closely parents and adult children report the same level of help, by comparing, for example, the extent of help G1 mothers report giving to adult children with the extent of help their G2 children report they received from their mothers.

Table 9.13 is based on the G1 parents' reports of help given and received, together with the help reported by those of their G2 children we interviewed. The mean ratings are grouped in a way to facilitate comparing the levels reported by parent and child, together with the correlation coefficients between the two separately obtained Help Extent measures.

There is a tendency for donors to claim giving more help than recipients acknowledge receiving: Both mothers and fathers report receiving fewer types of help from children than children report giving to their mothers and fathers. This same tendency holds for the flow of help from fathers to children: Fathers claim giving more help than children acknowledge receiving. The single exception is the flow of help from mothers to children: Mothers report giving less help than children say they have received from their mothers. These are not very strong differ-

Table 9.13.   Mean Ratings and Pearson Correlation Coefficients between G1 Parents' and G2 Children's Reports on Level of Help Exchange (G1 and G2 Samples)

Direction of Help Exchange	Mean Help Rating (0–100 Metric)		Pearson Correlation Coefficient	
A. G1 Parent to G2 Child				
G1 Mothers to Children				
Mothers report they GAVE Child	42.4			
		(193)	.55***	
Children report they GOT from Mother	46.6			(193)
		(306)		
G1 Fathers to Children				
Fathers report they GAVE Child	46.7			
		(127)	.54***	
Children report they GOT from Father	40.2			(127)
		(219)		
B. G2 Child to G1 Parent				
G2 Children to Mothers				
Mothers report they GOT from Child	43.2			
		(190)	.51***	
Children report they GAVE Mother	50.9			(190)
		(304)		
G2 Children to Fathers				
Fathers report they GOT from Child	36.5			
		(127)	.37***	
Children report they GAVE Father	40.8			(127)
		(218)		

*** p < .001

ences, but they are consistent across the two dyads, G1–G2 reported here, and G2–G3 (data not shown). We have no direct empirical evidence to support an interpretation of this result, but suspect there is what might be called *frustrated altruism* among many mothers of grown children, i.e., holding back on the desire to be of help out of awareness of the child's need or preference for independence, which may contribute to a tendency for women to underestimate the amount of help they actually provide to their children.

The second major result in Table 9.13 concerns the size of the correlation coefficients between the parents' and the adult children's reports of help. All the correlation coefficients are significant, but the pattern on help from children to fathers is less strongly correlated than the other three dyads: .37 between fathers' reports of help received from children and children's reports on help given to fathers, whereas the correlations are at the .5 level for the other three dyads. Although the magnitude and statistical significance of these correlations indicate a strong general pattern of agreement between parents and adult children concerning the help flow between them, there is obviously still much room for generational differences as well.

We turn now to a major source of variation in the direction of help flows between the generations, the resource base of the partners, as indexed by their total annual income for the year before they were interviewed (1984).

Effect of Relative Income Levels on Help Exchange

We noted in Chapter 3 that income level varies across the life course; it is not a stable cohort characteristic, such as educational attainment. This difference between education and income is reflected in the fact that the correlation between the educational attainment of parents and children is statistically significant while income is not. In our data, the correlation between the income of G2 children and their G1 parents is practically zero ($-.02$). From the life course curve of earnings reviewed in Chapter 3, with its steady rise from the early 20s to a peak in the late 40s, and its gradual decline over the late middle years and old age, it is clear that the relative income of parents and children is highly dependent on where on the life course parents and children are located. A young person just starting out will on average earn very much less than a middle-aged parent, whereas the income of a middle-aged child will on average be considerably higher than that of an elderly parent.

This pattern is shown empirically with data from the G1 parents and G2 adult children: Figure 9.10 graphs the mean total annual income of the parents and adult children by gender and the age of the parent (or child). The income of G2 sons and daughters goes up rapidly between their 20s and 40s, while the income of G1 fathers and mothers declines from the 40s to their 70s. Top earnings are enjoyed by sons and fathers in their 40s and early 50s; women show lower income levels than men at all points on the life course; and the lowest average income of all is that of elderly mothers in their 70s.

Average statistics obscure individual variation. Even among similar-aged dyads of adult children and parents, one would find a great deal of variation in the incomes they enjoy; some young adults quickly move up the social class hierarchy and reach higher income levels than their parents enjoyed at any stage of their lives, while other adult children show marked status slippage and never attain the income level enjoyed by their parents in their prime. It is this issue of relative income levels of

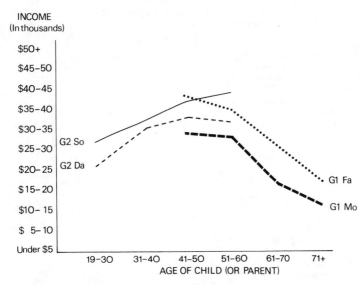

Figure 9.10. Mean annual total income in 1984 of G1 parents and G2 adult children by gender and age of parent and child (G1 and G2 samples).

parents and children that we now explore; this analysis will contribute to the major task of the chapter, to ascertain what complex of determinants explains the extent and direction of the help exchange between parents and children.

The analysis plan is to examine the extent of help as a function of either parents' or adult children's income, and to determine whether the extent of help is equally responsive to parents' and adult children's income levels. We will do this first separately for parents' income and children's income, and then examine the joint effect of parents' and children's income on the help levels reported, with a view to which types of help are most and which least responsive to discrepancies between the incomes of parents and children. Because of the importance of age as a factor in both earnings and extent of help, we will summarize the main results with a regression analysis of help flows as a function of income of parent and of child, with age and geographic distance as control variables.[4]

Table 9.14 provides the data relevant to the first two questions: the impact of parents' income on extent and direction of help exchange (Panel A), the impact of children's income (Panel B), and the average ratings as given by the G1 parent and by the G2 adult child for each direction of help exchanged at each income level (shown in proximate pairs of rows within each panel). Also shown in the right-hand column

Table 9.14. Extent of Help Exchange between G1 Parents and G2 Children by Gender of Parent and Total Annual Income of Parent and Total Annual Income of Child (G1 and G2 Samples) [a] (Mean Help Ratings, 0–100 Metric)

Direction of Help G1 Parent–G2 Child	Total Annual Income [b]			Correlation between Help and Income
	Low	Medium	High	
A. Help Extent and Parents' Income				
G1 Mother to G2 Child				
Mothers report they GAVE Child	37.1	42.3	55.2	.25***
	(77)	(64)	(36)	
Children report they GOT from Mother	40.2	44.2	56.3	.23***
	(95)	(111)	(84)	
G1 Father to G2 Child				
Fathers report they GAVE Child	37.2	48.3	50.7	.15*
	(23)	(57)	(46)	
Children report they GOT from Father	26.2	37.2	49.8	.35***
	(39)	(90)	(81)	
G2 Child to G1 Mother				
Mothers report they GOT from Child	41.5	43.0	47.8	.06
Children report they GAVE Mother	52.2	47.4	52.1	.01
G2 Child to G1 Father				
Fathers report they GOT from Child	41.4	34.6	37.4	.04
Children report they GAVE Father	40.4	38.5	43.8	.08
B. Help Extent and Children's Income				
G1 Mother to G2 Child				
Mothers report they GAVE Child	52.1	37.1	38.4	− .21***
	(58)	(61)	(67)	
Children report they GOT from Mother	56.6	40.9	43.1	− .22***
	(92)	(102)	(101)	
G1 Father to G2 Child				
Fathers report they GAVE Child	55.5	41.9	41.4	− .26***
	(37)	(49)	(37)	
Children report they GOT from Father	45.1	31.5	42.5	− .12+
	(64)	(75)	(72)	
G2 Child to G1 Mother				
Mothers report they GOT from Child	49.4	38.4	43.4	− .07
Children report they GAVE Mother	57.2	47.4	50.1	− .13*
G2 Child to G1 Father				
Fathers report they GOT from Child	40.1	33.6	33.3	− .08
Children report they GAVE Father	46.2	35.6	40.4	− .09

[a] Parental giving and getting help and parents' income as reported by G1 parents in telephone interviews; child giving and getting help and children's income as reported by G2 respondents in personal interviews. All G2 respondents whose parents were interviewed are used in this table; Child base Ns differ from Parent bases Ns because all children reported on help to each living parent, while only one parent was interviewed.
[b] Parents' total income is, on average, lower than children's income. Hence, income classification differs slightly in the 3-way income codes used for parents and children. For Parents: Low = under $15,000, Medium = $15,000–$35,000, High = over $35,000. For adult children: Low = under $25,000, Medium = $25,000–$40,000, High = over $40,000.
*** p < .001   * p < .05   + p < .10

of Table 9.14 are the correlation coefficients between extent of help and income level.

The general pattern shown in this complex set of data can be seen most readily in the correlation coefficients, and in a graphic way in Figure 9.11, which shows the results just for the mother–child relationship.[5] Both G1 mothers' and G1 fathers' income are strongly and significantly related to the level of help given to children (as reported by both parent and adult child): The higher the parents' income, the more extensive the help given to adult children. Parental income, however, is

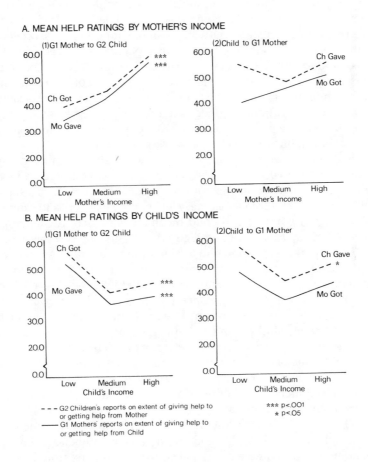

Figure 9.11. Help exchange between G1 *mothers* and G2 adult children by (A) total annual income of mothers and (B) total annual income of children (G1 and G2 samples). (Mean rating on help indices, 0–100 metric.)

not related to the amount of help children gave to their parents. (None of the four correlations on parental income and children's help to parents, shown in Panel A, is significant).

Children's income is also strongly and significantly related to the level of help received from parents, but in the opposite direction: The higher the child's income, the less extensive is the help provided by parents. By and large, the flow of help from children to parents is very weakly related to either parents' or children's income levels. Note, however (as seen most readily in graphic form in Figure 9.11), that the correlation coefficients are very low for the child-to-parent help levels because of a tendency to curvilinearity: Low- and high-income children give more help to parents than medium-income children do, a pattern that holds for six of the eight possible comparisons in Table 9.14. The implication is strong that the greater knowledge and connections associated with higher income among the more mature parents are invested in help of various kinds to adult children, particularly low-income children with the greatest need for such assistance. But the kind of help that children, even of high income, can give to older parents, is far less associated with social and occupational connections than with the personal caregiving and domestic help that takes time and physical and emotional energy rather than money or useful network connections.

This interpretation remains a weak one thus far, because there is no relationship between income level of parents and children, and we have only shown the relationship between income and help levels separately for parents' or children's income. Hence, the next step is to examine the joint effect of parental and child income on the help exchange profile. This is done in Table 9.15 and Figure 9.12. The help responses reported by the G1 parents are shown to the left of the table and figure, and those reported by the G2 children to the right. The profile shown is very similar, whether it is the parent or the child reporting on the help pattern. The major finding concerns the interactive impact of income when parents' and children's income are brought together in relation to help exchange. Mothers and fathers agree, as do parents and children, that *the most extensive pattern of help given by parents to children is found between high-income parents and low-income children, and the least extensive pattern of help is from low-income parents to high-income children.* Both parental resources and children's likely needs mesh. As seen in the data to the left in Panel A of Table 9.15, the range is from a low of 27.5 on the 0–100 scale in help from low-income mothers to high-income children, to a high of 62.2 in help from high-income mothers to low-income children. (A comparable pattern is shown for fathers, from 26.6 to 59.9, respectively.)

Table 9.15. Mean Help Ratings Reported by G1 Parents and G2 Children by Income of G1 Parents and G2 Children and Gender of Parent (G1 and G2 Samples) (Help Indices, 0–100 Metric)

Direction of Help	Child's Income	Parent's Income			Child's Income	Parent's Income		
		Lo	Med	Hi		Lo	Med	Hi
A. G1 Parent to G2 Child								
Mother GIVES Child					Child GETS from Mother			
	Lo	48.5	56.9	62.2	Lo	56.3	54.8	61.5
	Med	32.9	40.8	52.2	Med	38.0	38.9	45.4
	Hi	27.5	41.1	52.3	Hi	28.1	38.2	58.5
Father GIVES Child					Child GETS from Father			
	Lo	42.2	58.9	59.9	Lo	42.0	45.6	50.4
	Med	36.9	41.2	46.5	Med	18.6	29.8	42.8
	Hi	26.6	41.8	45.8	Hi	23.3	34.5	53.2
B. G2 Child to G2 Parent								
Mother GETS from Child					Child GIVES Mother			
	Lo	53.5	43.7	49.9	Lo	58.8	52.5	60.6
	Med	35.6	38.0	43.2	Med	50.8	43.9	42.8
	Hi	35.5	49.9	48.3	Hi	48.5	46.7	53.5
Father GETS from Child					Child GIVES Father			
	Lo	37.7	38.8	44.4	Lo	46.8	43.5	49.7
	Med	40.7	29.6	32.5	Med	33.3	35.4	36.3
	Hi	35.5	24.4	34.7	Hi	46.6	35.7	40.7

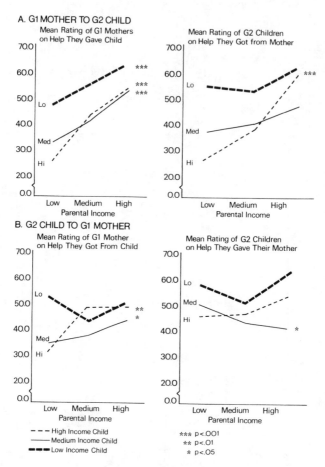

Figure 9.12.   Mean ratings on help exchange between G1 mothers and G2 adult
children by income of mother and child (G1 and G2 samples) (help indices,
0–100 metric).

Note, too, that children's income level has much less effect on parental giving when parents' income is high than when it is low: *Well-off*
parents provide help to well-off children as well as to children who are poorly
off financially, while low-income parents concentrate their help on less well-off
children.

The reverse profile, however, is not found in our data; the reciprocal
in the case of help flows from children to parents would be high-income
children giving the most extensive help to low-income parents, and low-

income children giving the least extensive help to high-income parents. But *whether rated by parent or child, it is low-income children who give the most extensive help to parents.* G2 low-income adult children even report giving more help to high-income parents than high-income children do; for example, a mean help score of 44.4 among low-income children vs. 34.7 among high-income children giving to high-income fathers.

Of course, we must keep in mind the nature of the help measures; they tell us nothing about the *amount* of money flowing between the generations: A high score on the help index means only that a more diverse array of types of help are given or received. Hence, a high-income daughter could be largely supporting an elderly parent with a monthly check but no other services, in which case her score would be only 11, while a low-income son may have a score of 89 because he provides help of every sort *except* money.

It is therefore of special interest to explore the impact of differential income of parents and children on the *types* of help exchanged between the generations. To simplify this step in the analysis, we restrict the data to the reports by G1 parents. The full data are shown in Table 9.16, from which we selected for graphic illustration in Figure 9.13 only the extreme four cells in the 9-cell cross-tabulation of parent and child income. To facilitate the discussion, we will label these four cells as follows:

Down (Downwardly mobile children): high-income parents and low-income children.

Equally High (Stable upper status children): high-income parents and high-income children.

Equally Low (Stable lower status children): low-income parents and low-income children.

Up (Upwardly mobile children): low-income parents and high-income children.

We do not assume any permanency to these relative status positions of parents and children. Income discrepancies, as we saw earlier, may be as much a function of where on the life course the parent and child are located as they are of any long-standing social class position. But help exchange is in the here and now, and it is the *current* resources of the parents and children that are most relevant to our analysis, not their past or future earnings and social positions.

Table 9.16 shows the incidence level of nine types of help by income level of parent and child and the direction of flow. The first three columns in Panel A of the table refer to the flow of help from G1 parents to adult children, and the last three columns in Panel B refer to the flow of help from G2 children to their parents. The types of help are roughly

Table 9.16. Types of Help Exchanged between G1 Parents and G2 Adult
Children, as Reported by G1 Parents, by Income Levels of Parent and
Child (G1 and G2 Samples) (in Percent)

Type of Help	Child's Income	A. G1 Parent to G2 Child Parent's Income			Child's Income	B. G2 Child to G1 Parent Parent's Income		
		Lo	Med	Hi		Lo	Med	Hi
Money	Lo	43.8	65.6	96.2***	Lo	28.1	3.1	0.0***
	Med	36.1	33.3	52.2	Med	5.6	6.5	0.0
	Hi	36.1	37.8	52.9*	Hi	13.3	10.8	9.1
Job Leads	Lo	28.1	31.3	53.8*	Lo	25.5	21.9	23.1
	Med	8.3	15.2	36.4**	Med	5.6	8.7	4.3
	Hi	6.7	24.3	20.6	Hi	0.0	8.1	18.8*
Advice	Lo	51.6	81.3	88.5***	Lo	62.5	40.0	60.0
	Med	44.4	54.6	82.6**	Med	40.6	50.0	54.1
	Hi	20.0	56.8	72.7***	Hi	42.3	39.1	45.5
Comfort	Lo	75.0	78.1	76.9	Lo	62.5	65.6	42.3
	Med	47.2	45.7	65.2	Med	40.6	50.0	54.1*
	Hi	43.3	54.1	73.5*	Hi	63.3	54.1	62.5
Illness	Lo	28.1	50.0	52.2	Lo	50.0	37.5	38.5
	Med	25.7	34.8	30.4	Med	38.9	35.6	39.0
	Hi	16.7	24.3	44.1*	Hi	50.0	54.1	48.5
Fix/Make	Lo	46.9	62.5	53.8	Lo	43.8	40.6	73.1**
	Med	33.3	32.6	43.5	Med	47.2	41.3	34.8
	Hi	26.7	45.9	52.9+	Hi	30.0	43.2	36.4
Home Care	Lo	40.0	32.3	28.0	Lo	40.6	37.5	53.8
	Med	30.6	32.6	34.8	Med	22.2	28.3	39.1
	Hi	26.7	27.0	24.2	Hi	6.7	24.3	53.1***
Chores	Lo	34.4	40.6	23.1	Lo	59.4	43.8	65.4
	Med	22.2	23.9	26.1	Med	47.2	32.6	43.5
	Hi	13.3	32.4	21.9	Hi	20.0	51.4	33.3
Special Gift	Lo	81.3	81.3	76.0	Lo	87.5	81.3	80.8
	Med	61.1	65.2	65.2	Med	77.8	60.9	72.7
	Hi	73.3	72.2	79.4	Hi	76.7	73.0	72.7

*** p < .001
** p < .01
* p < .05
+ p < .10

ranked by the impact that parental income has on that help type. A
graphic mode is used in Figure 9.13 for six of the nine types of help. The
bars to the left of the vertical line show the extent of help from parent to
child, and the bars to the right show the help level from child to parent.
A comparison of the relative length of the bar to the right and left of the
vertical line gives a quick impression of the balance between giving and
getting help of various types, and the impact of different mobility
profiles in such a balance can be seen by the four proximate bars within
each type of help shown.

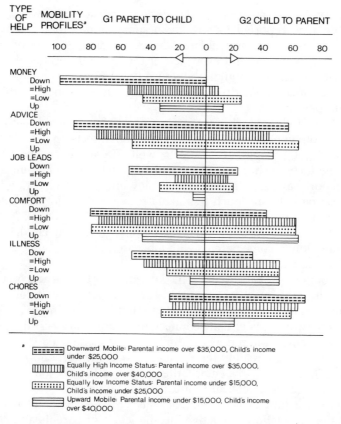

Figure 9.13. Incidence and balance of help exchange between G1 parents and G2 adult children by selected types of help and intergenerational mobility profile (G1 and G2 samples) (in percent).

It can be seen immediately, in both table and figure, that money is not only more apt to flow from parent to child than the reverse, but, in particular, from better-off parents to their less well-off children, i.e., the downwardly mobile children in Figure 9.13. Indeed, helping out with money or a loan shows the sharpest contrast of all in flow direction as a function of relative income level of parent and child: 96% of high-income parents gave some financial aid to low-income children in the preceding year; by contrast not a single low-income child gave any financial aid to a high-income parent.

Note, too, that the child *most* likely to give a parent financial aid is not the upwardly mobile child but the low-income child with comparably low-income parents: 28% of low-income children gave some money to a low-income parent, which is double the proportion of upwardly mobile children who reported having given some money to a parent (13%). Thus, almost all of the well-off older generation help the poor in the younger generation, and even half of the well-off parents also helped high-income children, but in the return flow, more low-income children than high-income children report having given money to their low-income parents.

Job leads follow much the same pattern as financial aid, with income level of both generations showing significant effects on the incidence of help with job prospects or contacts; well-off parents are most likely to help low-income children (54%), and even 28% of the low-income parents report having helped a similarly low-income child with job leads, whereas parents are much less likely to have given job leads to high-income children (21% by high-income parents and only 7% by low-income parents). Also like financial help, high-income children do not help their low-income parents with job leads at all (0%) while 25% of the low-income children had done so.

This pattern probably reflects the very different social and occupational worlds encountered by parents and children who differ in socio-economic status; socially mobile adult children may simply not have as many relevant kinds of daily connections that could assist their parents as low-income children with similarly low-income parents have. A plumber-son may readily refer someone needing carpentry work done in their home to a carpenter-father, while a lawyer-son may be less inclined to make a referral to a carpenter-father.[6]

There is a hint of class-related skills in a few types of help when examined in relation to relative income levels of parents and children. Making or fixing something, for example, was most prevalent among low-income children who helped their high-income parents, projecting the image of a skilled craftsman son doing things in his well-off parents' home, or a low income daughter making a quilt for her well-off mother. A full 73% of low-income children report such help to their high-income parents, compared to 44% to low-income parents, while among high-income children, the fix/make type of help is much less frequently reported (30%), just about the same low level as reported by low-income parents doing things for high-income children (27%).

A similar pattern is shown for help with domestic chores, where income level of the adult children is more strongly related to help incidence than parental income. At all income levels of the parents, in fact, low-income children provide more hands-on help than high-income children do, i.e., doing chores, fixing and making things, or watching a home in the absence of the parents. Low-income parents may take pride in the success of socially mobile children, but the children they can count on to devote time and physical energy to their daily maintenance are less successful, low-income children. Overall, *upwardly mobile children and their parents engage in the least exchange of help, whereas downwardly mobile children and their parents engage in the most help exchange.* Hence, our data show the most extensive intergenerational help and greater interdependency when both parents and children have low incomes. Socially mobile adult children in business and professional occupations are often under a social obligation to participate in community affairs, and their leisure hours are often reduced by other more directly work-related activities as well. As a result, successful children provide less help to their parents than their less well-off siblings do.

The analysis of the impact of income on help exchange up to this point has been a static portrait of the relationship between income and type or extent of help during the year prior to our interviews. But we have seen that the extent of help changes over the life course just as income does. Indeed, our data on G1 and G2 respondents show that parental income goes down with the age of the parent and child income goes up with the age of the parent. In the case of G1 fathers, for example, the correlation of father's age with his own total income is $-.37$, while the correlation of father's age and his adult children's income is $+.21.$[7]

Because both age and income have significant impacts on the help exchange pattern, we resort to a regression analysis on the extent of help with the predictor variables of parent's income, child's income, parent's age, and geographic distance. We also compare the results of the regression analysis when the dependent variable is the rating given by the parent with the results when the rating was given by the adult child.

The results of this analysis are shown in Table 9.17. The equations on help between G1 mothers and G2 adult children are shown in Panel A, and those on help between G1 fathers and their children are shown in Panel B. Within each panel, the equations dealing with help from parent to child are shown in (1) and those dealing with help from child to parent in (2). The two proximate columns within (1) and (2) contain the equations with ratings from the parent (the first of the two columns) and those with ratings from the adult child (the second of the two columns).

Two major results are shown in these data. The first is that the contribution of parental and children's income to help exchange remains essentially the same with a control on parental age. This is most consistently the case in the parent-to-child help pattern: For both fathers and mothers, the extent of help given to children goes up with increasing parental income, and down with increasing income levels of the adult children. *Independent of the life course dynamic of changing income levels, then, the relative income of parent and child influences the extent of the help given by parents to adult children.*

Table 9.17.   Regressions on Help Exchange between G1 Parents and G2
Adult Children, of Annual Income of Parent and of Child, Parental Age,
and Geographic Distance: Parent vs Child Reports on Extent of Help
Given and Received (G1 and G2 Samples) (Standardized Beta
Coefficients)

A. G1 Mother and G2 Adult Child

	1. Mother to Child		2. Child to Mother	
Predictor Variables	Mother re GAVE to Child	Child re GOT from Mother	Mother re GOT from Child	Child re GAVE to Mother
Parent's Income	.12	.14*	−.01	−.00
Child's Income	−.13*	−.17**	−.03	−.12*
Mother's Age	−.30***	−.20**	−.19**	−.04
Geographic Distance	−.26***	−.26***	−.40***	−.31***
R^2	.25***	.20***	.21***	.12***
N	(174)	(174)	(174)	(174)

B. G1 Father and G2 Adult Child

	1. Father to Child		2. Child to Father	
Predictor Variables	Father re GAVE to Child	Child re GOT from Father	Father re GOT from Child	Child re GAVE to Father
Parent's Income	.11	.31***	−.03	−.09
Child's Income	−.24***	−.08	−.08	−.10
Father's Age	−.10	−.15+	−.01	−.00
Geographic Distance	−.27***	−.21**	−.21**	−.30***
R^2	.17***	.21***	.05	.11**
N	(122)	(122)	(122)	(122)

*** $p < .001$
** $p < .01$
* $p < .05$
+ $p < .10$

Note, however, that age remains a significant negative factor, net of
income levels of parent and child, suggesting there are many other
aspects of the aging process besides the decline of income that are
relevant to the help exchange between the generations. It is only the age
of the mother that is significant statistically, not the age of the father.
This is consistent with the findings reported earlier on the overall life
course trajectory in extent of help, e.g., in Figure 9.2, which showed
much stronger declines with parental age in the parent-to-child flow of
help from mothers to adult children than from fathers to adult children.[8]

The equations in set (2) of Panels A and B show a consistent profile,
though not a strong one as judged by statistical significance: In help
from adult children to parents, both parents' and children's income

levels have negative coefficients, i.e., help from children is more extensive the lower the income of both parent and child, independent of
where on the life course the parents and children are located.

One last finding suggested by the results in Table 9.17 concerns the
different perspective of the parent and the child in the help ratings they
gave. Judging from the size of the standardized Beta coefficients, parents seem more influenced by their children's income level and children
by their parents' income level in reporting the types of help given (in the
case of parents) or received (in the case of children). There is a hint here
of some individual differences in help ratings when parents and children differ: Parents seem particularly aware of the potential *needs* of
their children as a function of the child's income, while children are
more aware of the potential *resources* of the parents as a function of
parental income. This interpretation is consistent with the fact that the
pattern is strongest in the case of fathers, whose earnings account for
most of the total annual income of parents, and whose parental role is
most sensitive to monetary matters. When G1 fathers rated the help
they gave their children, the coefficient on child's income is very strongly negative ($-.24***$), whereas when the child rated the help received
from their fathers, their own income, while negative, was not statistically significant ($-.08$). Reciprocally, G1 fathers with higher income
report giving more to adult children than low income fathers, but the
coefficient on parental income is much lower in the fathers' ratings (.11)
than in the child's ratings on help received from fathers ($.31***$). The
question of generational responsivity to different circumstances in the
lives of children or of parents will be seen below, as we place income
level into a larger set of predictors of the help exchanged between
parents and children.

Determinants of Extent of Help Exchange Between the Generations

Premises Underlying the Analysis

We turn now to a broader array of factors that influence the level of
help exchanged between parents and adult children. In doing so, we
draw on findings of previous chapters, and posit a predictive model that
includes characteristics of the parent–child relationship, such as affective closeness and extent of shared values; measures of what the family
of origin was like early on; accessibility as measured by interaction
frequency and geographic distance; and a variety of current characteristics of both partners to the relationship. An elaboration of the four

premises underlying this analysis of determinants of help exchange is as follows.

First, apart from the marital bond, the parent–child relationship is the most important kinship relationship in most peoples' lives. A number of factors press for high levels of help between parents and children when the circumstances of their lives require help: internalized social norms rooted in kinship and religious values; personal indebtedness to one's progenitors; past experience that emphasizes the latent function of kin as the people with both the desire and the obligation to celebrate achievements, to commiserate failures, and to apply balm when pains are experienced in life.

A second premise underlying the analysis concerns the transition from adolescence to adulthood. There are numerous social markers along the adult life course that index the growing independence of children from their parents: completion of school, first real job relevant to a career trajectory, independent residence, marriage, and the transition to parenthood. The events such markers refer to rarely occur in any close synchronization; they occur over a number of years. Nor is 20 years of childrearing responsibility extinguished in one fell swoop; parents have internalized the habit of helping their children that may persist for some time even when the children are employed adults residing in apartments of their own. As suggested above, we believe many parents experience some frustration of their desire to continue to provide such help out of concern for encouraging the independence they know to be important to their adult children. The great increase in the number of years of schooling considered desirable and necessary in a technological society extends the period of time during which children are not fully emancipated from dependence on parents. By 22 years of age, young adults may have been sexually mature for a decade, but many are not yet economically self-supporting. Independent of the child's chronological age, this predicts that children who are unemployed, attending school, or unattached in terms of marital status (either because they have not yet married or because they suffered a failure in marriage) will continue to receive help from their parents.

The third premise of the analysis concerns the responsivity of parents and adult children to each other's circumstantial needs. Sensitivity to the current circumstances in the lives of close intimates suggests that adult children will provide help to their parents as a function of the parents' needs, just as parents give help to children in need. Being widowed or in poor health represent two common circumstances of need in the older years that trigger elevated levels of help from adult children.

The fourth and last premise underlying the analysis concerns the influence of past family events on the contemporary help exchanged between the generations. Normative obligation and circumstantial need aside, the quality of the parent–child relationship established over the earlier years will show a continuing effect on the level of help exchanged between the generations. We have seen that growing up in a happy cohesive family paves the way for adult children to feel close to their parents, whereas factors in the past have less influence on parents' current feelings of intimacy toward their children. If the help pattern shows the same structure, children's help to parents may be more affected by experiences in the earlier phases of life in the family than parents' help to children.

Predictor Variables Tailored to the Premises of the Analysis

The analysis was designed to test these propositions by including several categories of predictor variables in the regression equations. They are as follows.

Early Family Life.   Two variables will be used as indices of the quality of earlier years of family life: the global rating of Family Cohesion, and Extent of Family Troubles during the years respondents were growing up or rearing children. The question we pose is whether past family experience makes any contribution to current help exchange, independent of current relationship characteristics, accessibility, or characteristics of the partners to the relationship.

Current Relationship.   Because opportunity and accessibility are important proximate determinants, we include geographic distance between parent and child in all regression analyses. Our focus is therefore on what determines help levels, net of accessibility as indexed by the mileage distance between the residences of parent and child. As a measure of social interaction, we will rely on the frequency of telephone contact between parent and child. As seen earlier, visiting frequency is far more dependent than phoning frequency on the sheer pragmatics of mileage distance, e.g., a correlation of $-.83$ between distance and frequency of face-to-face contact compared to only $-.15$ between distance and frequency of phone contact (in this example, between mothers and sons). Both geographic distance and phoning frequency serve as control variables in what follows.

Of greater interest is the quality of the relationship between parents and children, as measured by current Affective Closeness. We have seen that the current ratings of intimacy have deep roots in earlier family life characteristics (Chapter 7), and are significant determinants of the frequency of social interaction between the generations (Chapter 8). Drawing on previous analysis, we predict that children's help to parents will be significantly enhanced by the affective closeness of the relationship, but parental help to children only modestly so, if at all.

Another variable in the current relationship category is the mean rating scores from the normative obligation vignettes dealing with parents and children, identified as Primary Kin Obligation.[9] We shall test whether a general normative obligation to primary kin exerts any direct effect on the help pattern when a wide variety of other individual characteristics of parent and child and the quality of their relationship are in the same regression equations.

The last predictor variable concerning the current relationship is Value Consensus, the extent to which respondents perceive similar or dissimilar values between themselves and their parents (or their children). We have seen that Value Consensus affected both subjective closeness and social interaction. In the analysis before us, we wish to test whether parents and adult children exchange more help if they sense a high degree of shared values than if they are aware of basic differences in their views.

Characteristics of Parent and Child.   The third major set of variables to be explored as potential determinants of help exchange consists of individual characteristics of the respondents. From the descriptive analysis of the individual help items in previous sections of this chapter, we carry forward the marital status and income level of both parent and child. The condition of health of parents is another critical predictor variable, particularly for the older parent–child dyads, since physical limitations and chronic illnesses of the parent may precipitate increases in help provided by adult children and decreases in the help parents give to their children.

Age is of course a necessary control throughout the analysis, because we have already established how strongly help exchange is affected by phase of the life course. Age of parent and child is so highly correlated (.86), that we can use only one age measure in any particular equation. Apart from serving as a necessary control variable, we also wish to test whether there are any residual effects of age when a number of age-related variables are in an equation.

A predictor variable of special interest is the number of children in the two generations, because children represent competing demands on the time and energy available to parents and adult children. In Chapter 8 we reported that parents of large families interacted less frequency with any one child than parents of only one or two children. Here we explore whether a similar pattern holds in the exchange of help between the generations. It is less clear whether having few or many siblings will affect the extent to which children help their parents. If it does, then parents of large families receive more overall help from children later in life than do parents of small families.

Family size of the adult children may also play a role in the extent of help exchanged between the generations. Young adults who are rearing several children have less time and energy to provide help to their older parents than a young adult with only one child, but what of the reverse? Will older parents extend more help to adult married children when there are a number of grandchildren than when there is none or only one? We know that parents, typically mothers, often become more closely involved with their adult children following the birth of a grandchild (e.g., Fischer, 1986), but it is not clear whether this increased involvement is a short-run matter surrounding the birth of a child or a more long-standing attribute of grandparenthood. And what happens when the middle generation is employed on a full time basis, as so many adult women are nowadays even when children are of preschool age? Are grandmothers in closer touch, and do they provide more help when a daughter is employed despite having several young children? Because employment is largely a daytime activity, it may be that mothers and daughters provide more help to each other when daughters are housewives than when they are employed, whether or not the daughter is also rearing young children.

The last set of characteristics of parents and children to be included in the equations is the personal traits of Expressivity, Dominance, and Drive. As we saw in an earlier chapter, Drive is our closest approximation to an age-related physiological variable. Help of most varieties involves not just emotional and social commitment to another person, but physical energy and time. Hence our prediction was that parents with high Drive may give more varied help to their children than less energetic and hardworking parents do. Furthermore, if parents tend to help children in need, as we predict they do when children are still not economically self-supporting or when children have undergone a divorce, will they also provide more help to children who depart from the mode of vigorous healthy early adulthood, i.e., children with low Drive? Our prediction is that High Drive parents give more help to children, particularly Low Drive children.

Gender of parent and child is of course a major concern in the projected analysis. We have already established that women both give to and receive more help from adult children than men do, and we have reported some striking differences between mother–daughter and father–son dyads. We wish to explain at least some part of the reason for these gender differences in the regression analysis to follow.

There are data limitations, however, to the analysis we can attempt. With a wide array of predictor variables, we need to rely on as large a case base as possible. This means the analysis centers on the G2 main sample, first in the role of G2 respondents as adult children, and later in the role of parents of adult children. Because the largest array of variables relevant to the analysis consists of characteristics of the G2 respondents themselves, the help exchange analysis of the G1–G2 dyads uses many child characteristics, but few parent characteristics, while the reverse situation applies in the analysis of the G2–G3 dyads, i.e., many parent characteristics but few child characteristics.

Help Exchange Between G2 Adult Children and G1 Parents

Tables 9.18 and 9.19 present the results of the regression analysis of help exchange between G1 parents and G2 adult children, as reported by G2 respondents: Table 9.18 on the flow of help from parent to child and Table 9.19 on the help from child to parent. As even a casual glance at the number of significant asterisks suggests, a great many predictor variables contribute to the variance in the help exchange pattern in all four dyads. In discussing the results, we first examine the variables with significant effects in at least three parent–child dyad equations, and then the variables with special significance only for a particular dyad and any contrast by the direction of help, i.e., parent to child vs. child to parent.

The opportunity factor variables of geographic distance and phoning frequency show significant effects on the extent of help in all dyads and both directions of help extent. Since we have already noted that sheer proximity affects frequency of social interaction, it is of particular interest to note that the frequency of phone contact, net of geographic distance, provides a significant impetus to the extent of help exchanged; many types of help can obviously be provided in the course of such phone conversations, such as advice, job leads, and comfort.

The quality of the current relationship between parents and adult children also shows consistent effects in all dyads and both directions of flow. Note, however, that these are all ratings by the adult child, because we shall see below that the effect of closeness of the relationship is less strong and often not statistically significant when data are provided by the parent. Whether G2 respondents report similar or dissimilar values from their parents shows no effect on the extent of help exchanged, again in either direction. Here too, there will be a significant qualification when we rely on data from parents as opposed to children.

Despite the presence of many predisposing or enhancing predictive

Table 9.18. Regressions on Help from G1 Parents to G2 Adult Children by Gender of Parent and Child as Rated by G2 Child (G2 Sample) (Standardized Beta Coefficients)

Predictor Variables	G1 Parent–G2 Child Dyad			
	Mother–Daughter	Mother–Son	Father–Daughter	Father–Son
Past Family				
Family Cohesion	.17***	.07	.14***	.13*
Family Troubles	.03	.03	.03	.03
Current Relationship				
Phone Frequency	.10**	.18***	.34***	.15**
Affective Closeness	.18***	.13**	.13**	.21***
Value Consensus	.06	.03	.07	.02
Primary Kin Obligation	.06	.03	.14**	.09*
Geographic Distance	−.22***	−.26***	−.11**	−.20***
Characteristics of Parent				
Solo (dummy variable)	−.19***	−.12***	−.12**	−.08
Number of Children	−.06+	−.06+	−.05	−.07
Health	−.02	.02	−.00	.06
Characteristics of Child				
Age	−.56***	−.54***	−.43***	−.47***
Solo (dummy variable)	.19***	.02	.24***	.00
Total Income	−.12***	−.17***	−.03	−.16***
Full Time Employed (dummy variable)	−.15***	−.23***	−.05	−.22***
Number of Children	.03	.05	.05	.09
Expressivity	.08*	.07	.08	.12*
Dominance	.07	−.04	−.04	−.03
Drive	−.13**	.05	−.22***	.03
Health	−.03	−.03	.01	−.02
R^2	**.56***	**.50***	**.52***	**.48***
N	(365)	(279)	(250)	(218)

*** $p < .001$
** $p < .01$
* $p < .05$
+ $p < .10$

variables in the eight equations, our measure of Primary Kin Obligation shows a consistent pattern of adding a positive increment to the help levels given or received from parents. Significant effects, however, are restricted to the help exchange with fathers. It may "take" a generalized norm of obligation to heighten the exchange of help between fathers and adult children, whereas help between mothers and their children is either given more spontaneously or with greater sensitivity to the needs of either partner. This latter point is also given some support by the fact

Table 9.19. Regression on Help from G2 Adult Children to G1 Parents by Gender of Parent and Child as Rated by G2 Child (G2 Sample) (Standardized Beta Coefficients)

	G1 Parent–G2 Child Dyad			
Predictor Variables	Mother–Daughter	Mother–Son	Father–Daughter	Father–Son
Past Family				
Family Cohesion	.15**	.07	.03	.08
Family Troubles	.02	.08+	.11*	.01
Current Relationship				
Phone Frequency	.08+	.21***	.25***	.14*
Affective Closeness	.19***	.19***	.31***	.19**
Value Consensus	.01	.05	−.02	−.05
Primary Kin Obligation	.06	.09+	.08+	.09+
Geographic Distance	−.34***	−.20***	−.24***	−.28***
Characteristics of Parent				
Solo (dummy variable)	.04	.17***	.12*	−.01
Number of Children	.07+	−.00	.07	−.03
Health	−.17***	−.18***	−.23***	−.20***
Characteristics of Child				
Age	−.19***	−.14***	−.15*	−.16*
Solo (dummy variable)	.06	.05	.14***	−.13*
Total Income	−.05	−.07	−.06	−.13*
Full Time Employed (dummy variable)	−.06	−.14*	−.03	−.20**
Number of Children	−.06	−.08	−.04	−.03
Expressivity	.15***	.15**	.00	.02
Dominance	.04	.12*	.06	.02
Drive	−.09	−.08	−.07	.14*
Health	−.02	.05	.10	.12*
R^2	**.37***	**.29***	**.39***	**.32***
N	(365)	(279)	(250)	(218)

*** $p < .001$
** $p < .01$
* $p < .05$
+ $p < .10$

that in almost all the analysis we have done on help from parents, with many child characteristics as predictor variables, those with the largest R^2 values concern help from mothers rather than from fathers.

Independent of such current relationship characteristics, the regression analysis shows direct effects of variables concerning the earlier years when G2 respondents were growing up, more so in the help G2 adult children report receiving from their parents than in help they have given recently to their parents: Over and above the influence of current relationship characteristics and current circumstances in the lives of both partners to the dyads, those who grew up in families that were experienced as happy and cooperative units (high Family Cohesion) report more extensive help exchanged between the generations over the past year. In a surprising effect, earlier Family Troubles do not depress but enhance the extensiveness of help exchange between parents and children though this is significantly the case only in the help adult women report having given to their fathers.

When we investigated the type of troubles involved, it was reports of early sickness and a death in the family that were most related to elevated current help exchange. Though we cannot pinpoint this exactly, it may be that a history of parental ill health established an early caregiving pattern by children that persists into the child's adulthood. Note too (in Table 9.19) that it is cross-sex dyad equations in which Family Troubles is either significant (father–daughter) or verges on significance (mother–son), suggesting the possibility that sons from troubled families continue to give more help to their mothers, and daughters to their fathers. We have noted such gender role complementarity before, and we see it again in what follows, with more help by sons to widowed mothers, and daughters to widowed fathers.

The marital status of both parent and child has special significance for the help exchange profile: Divorced or widowed parents give *less* extensive help to adult children than married parents do, but at least in the cross-sex dyads such solo parents are the recipients of *more* help than married parents. Consistent with our comments on family troubles and the earlier analysis of parental marital status on specific types of help in the previous section of this chapter, more varied help flows from daughters to widowed fathers and from sons to widowed mothers.

Marital status of the adult child has a rather different profile of effects on help exchange. Women respondents who are either unmarried or divorced report receiving more help from their parents than married women do, but whether a son is married or not shows little relationship to the help received from parents. In the help given to parents, gender of child in fact shows a reverse effect: Unmarried or divorced daughters report giving more help to their fathers than married daughters (just as they receive more help from their fathers) but, in the case of sons, being married is associated with more, not less, help to fathers.

Parental concern for the vulnerability and needs of unattached daughters is also suggested by the findings on the Drive levels of the adult children: It is Low Drive daughters who receive more help from both their mothers and fathers, while Drive level of sons shows no effect on parental help. It may be that parents can compensate for Low Drive daughters falling short in their primary sphere of responsibility, i.e., in home maintenance and child care, more readily than they can for Low Drive sons, whose primary area of adult responsibility in the workplace would be more difficult for parents to compensate for.

Another instance of current circumstantial need is represented by parental Health, and the results show that adult children provide more varied help to parents in poor health than to those in good health. But parental health shows no significant or consistent pattern of effects on the help parents provided to children. The latter finding may be linked to the fact that parental help is less hands-on physical help with daily needs than is the case for the help provided by children to their parents; hence, health and stamina are less relevant to parental help to children. The health status of the adult children shows little or no effect on help exchange, with only one in eight equations showing a significant effect: Sons in good health provide more help to their fathers than do sons in poor health.[10]

Personal traits of the G2 adult children show significant effects in several equations. Adult children high in Expressivity provide more help and get more help than those low in Expressivity (i.e., all eight equations show positive signs on the coefficients). But these are significant effects only in certain dyads and directions of help flow: High expressive children report giving more help to their mothers than low expressive children, but the children's Expressivity level shows no effect on the level of help extended to their fathers. Expressivity of the adult children has less effect on the help given to them by their parents except in the two same-sex dyads of mother–daughter and father–son. Dominance level of the adult children shows only one significant effect, in the interesting instance of sons providing help to their mothers: High Dominant sons give more varied help to their mothers than Low Dominant sons, suggesting that sons willing and able to "take charge" are more inclined to be help providers to older mothers, many of whom are widowed and in need of help, though the presence in the equation of a control on marital status of the parent shows the dominance-help pattern is not restricted to widowed mothers, but independent of their marital status.

Family size in either generation has only weak effects on the help pattern, but it is a consistent one: Parents of large families provide less help to adult children but get somewhat more help from their adult children (i.e., all signs are negative in Table 9.18 on help from parents, and all are positive in Table 9.19 on help from adult children). Exactly the reverse profile is shown for family size of the children: Those with several children get more help from parents, while adult children with heavy family responsibilities give less varied help to their parents than do those who are childless or have only a small size family. Hence, the effect of family size shows a common pattern in both generations: Large families restrict level of help given and enhance level of help received.

We have left the discussion of economic status variables for last, because we wish to extend the analysis with special consideration of the employment and family responsibilities of daughters and their effects on the help exchanged with mothers. Table 9.18 shows that low-income children receive more extensive help from parents than high-income children (highly significantly so in all but the father–daughter equation); and Table 9.19 shows a similar profile of low-income children giving more varied help to their parents than high-income children do (though significantly so only in help from sons to their fathers). Indeed, looking down the column of significant coefficients in the help from sons to fathers suggests a coherent profile: Fathers get most help from sons who are married, low-income men in excellent health who have High Drive, a profile that projects the image of a sturdy young adult son carrying his own family responsibilities yet providing active help to his father that entails skill, energy, and time. By contrast, high levels of help from sons to mothers involves sons high on both Expressivity and Dominance: men with empathic concern combined with a willingness to "take charge" by providing assistance to elderly widowed mothers.

The full time employment of the G2 adult child has a consistent depressing effect on the level of help exchanged between the generations: Full time employed sons and daughters give less help and receive less help from both mothers and fathers than children who are not employed full time. Since age of child is a control variable in these equations, this finding is not restricted to young children still attending school, but applies as well to older married sons and daughters. We had expected that employed daughters, in particular those who had children, might report more, not less help from their parents, especially their mothers. This result prompted more concentrated attention to the circumstances of the daughters in the analysis of the help indices. The effect of women's employment on intergenerational relations has been of concern in numerous quarters in recent years; in social gerontology, researchers have asked if this increased set of responsibilities carried by the "middle" generation cuts into their availability as personal caregivers to elderly parents (Brody, 1981, 1982). Most elderly adults, however, do not require such caregiving until very late in life, by which time the children reared by the middle generation are no longer of dependent age. The impact of younger adult women's employment on relations with and possible help from their mothers is also important. We can explore this issue by putting a more narrowly focused empirical question to our data on help exchange, i.e., how does employment status and family size of G2 daughters relate to interaction and help exchange with their G1 mothers?

To answer this question, we confine attention to G2 married daughters under 40 years of age who live less than 35 miles from their mothers and who vary in terms of the degree of childrearing responsibilities they carry (as indexed by the number of children they have) and their employment status (full time or part time employment vs. being housewives). Table 9.20 shows the mean ratings on social interaction (in Panel A) and the help exchange and reciprocity between such mothers and daughters (in Panel B) by family size and employment status of the daughters.

A consistent profile emerges from the data in Table 9.20: Visiting and telephone contact are most frequent when daughters are at home rearing three or more children. So too, the level of help exchanged between mothers and daughters is most extensive when daughters are at home rearing a number of children. The daughters carrying the greatest double set of responsibilities (full time employment and rearing three or more children) see and speak to their mothers by phone *least* often, give their mothers the least help, and receive the least in return compared to any combination of employment and family size shown in the table. These data emphasize the importance of daytime availability for high levels of contact and help reciprocity between mothers and their married daughters; whether the daughter has one or five children matters less than the fact of her not being employed at all as the basis for high levels of contact and help that flows in both directions between mothers and daughters. As one can note in almost any shopping mall in the country, older women and their daughters, often with a youngster or two in tow, frequently engage in joint shopping trips, and we may assume that in the privacy of their homes they help each other with cooking, cleaning, mending, or other domestic chores, accompanied by a steady flow of conversation concerning family relations or childrearing that involves the exchange of advice and provision of comfort under conditions of stress.

Hence, employment of either the mother or the daughter may restrict the exchange of help between them. The regression results in Tables 9.18 and 9.19 do not include a measure of the employment status of G1 mothers, but only of the G2 adult children. It is striking that in an equation with so wide an array of predictor variables, that the adult child's employment status nonetheless shows significant effects on the help level and does so significantly where mothers are concerned, in both directions: The child's full time employment reduces not only the level of help the child gives to the mother, but also the help such mothers give to their adult children.[11]

Table 9.20. Mean Ratings on Interaction and Help Exchange between G1 Mothers and G2 Married Daughters by Family Size and Employment Status of Daughters[a] (G2 Sample) (Interaction and Help Indices Converted to 0–100 Metric)

Dependent Variable	Employment Status of Daughter	Family Size of Daughter			Significance of Family Size
		None	One or Two	Three or More	
A. Social Interaction					
1. Frequency of Visiting					
	Full Time Employed	75.8	74.4	63.3	**
	Part Time Employed	74.4	80.1	61.5	**
	At Home	—	88.9	90.1	
	Significance of Employment		*	**	
2. Frequency of Phoning					
	Full Time employed	71.5	78.7	62.9	*
	Part Time Employed	81.5	81.5	70.1	*
	At Home	—	90.1	87.1	
	Significance of Employment		*	**	
B. Help Exchange					
1. Help FROM Mother					
	Full Time Employed	58.8	53.3	46.6	*
	Part Time Employed	63.3	58.8	44.4	**
	At Home	—	73.3	81.0	
	Significance of Employment		**	***	
2. Help TO Mother					
	Full Time Employed	64.4	58.8	46.6	+
	Part Time Employed	67.7	59.9	50.0	*
	At Home	—	66.6	65.5	
	Significance of Employment		*	***	
3. Extent of Reciprocity					
	Full Time Employed	45.5	38.9	30.0	**
	Part Time Employed	46.6	42.2	32.2	**
	At Home	—	55.5	58.8	
	Significance of Employment		**	***	

[a] Base: Married daughters under 40 years of age who live less than 35 miles from their mothers.
*** $p < .001$
** $p < .01$
* $p < .05$
+ $p < .10$

Help Exchange Between G2 Parents and G3 Adult Children

All the data in the regression analyses above were provided by G2 respondents in their roles as adult children, but with a far less varied array of parent characteristics than of their own as the adult children. Most of the G2 respondents with a living parent are adults under 45 years of age, with an average age of 32. We can now supplement the analysis reported above by shifting to the roles of G2 respondents as parents of adult children. In this shift, the data are largely from G2 respondents over 45 years of age, with an average age of 61, whose adult children are on average 30 years of age. This time, however, the same interesting array of characteristics that appeared earlier as "child characteristics" now becomes "parent characteristics."

One change was necessary in the set of predictor variables used in the analysis of G2–G3 help exchange. The main survey did not ask for the income of respondents' adult children, because we did not think parents could reliably report such information. Hence, we substitute the child's educational attainment for the income variable used in the G1–G2 analysis. This is a poor substitute, at best, since there is much less variance in educational attainment of children than of income, and for young adults such as the G3 children of respondents, education and income do not correlate very significantly, yet income no doubt is a better predictor of help from parents to children than educational attainment per se.

Tables 9.21 and 9.22 report the results of the regression analysis of determinants of help exchange between G2 parents and all their G3 adult children, separately for the four parent–child dyads. The four equations on help from parents to adult children are shown in Table 9.21, and those on help from children to parents in Table 9.22.

In discussing the results of the regression analysis, we will highlight the significant predictor variables that hold for all four parent–child dyads, then those unique to gender of parent, child, or a particular parent–child dyad. We will also note the respects in which results are similar or different in this shift from G2 respondents as adult children to G2 respondents as parents.

As in all previous analysis, geographic distance and age show significantly negative coefficients in both directions of the help exchange between parents and children. Contact frequency and Affective Closeness show positive signs in all eight equations, though not uniformly at a statistically significant level in the G2–G3 analysis as they were in the G1–G2 analysis.[12]

So, too, the more children G2 parents reared, the less help they report having given to any individual adult child, though this is a far stronger pattern for help from mothers than from fathers. In fact, the standardized Beta coefficient on family size is second only to age of the adult child in the equations on help given by G2 mothers to their daughters ($-.24***$) and their sons ($-.24***$). These are much larger Beta coefficients than we reported in the G1–G2 analysis ($-.06^+$ for both daughters and sons). Whether this reflects greater awareness when it is women reporting in their roles as mothers than when they reported as adult children is not clear.[13]

Table 9.21. Regressions on Extent of Help *from G2 Parents to G3 Adult Children* by Gender of Parent and Child as Rated by G2 Parent (G2 Sample, Childset File) (Standardized Beta Coefficients)

Predictor Variables	G2 Parent–G3 Child Dyad			
	Mother–Daughter	Mother–Son	Father–Daughter	Father–Son
Past Family				
Family Cohesion	.08	.01	.02	.09
Family Troubles	.11*	.02	.14*	.12*
Current Relationship				
Phone Frequency	.11*	.08	.25***	.31***
Affective Closeness	.13**	.07	.11	.13*
Value Consensus	−.00	.06	.01	.18***
Geographic Distance	−.12**	−.13**	−.28***	−.21***
Characteristics of Parent				
Solo (dummy variable)	−.02	.05	−.05	−.05
Total Income	.12*	.14*	.04	.21***
Full Time Employed (dummy variable)	.08	.04	−.11	−.02
Number of Children	−.24***	−.24***	−.10	−.14*
Expressivity	.07	.01	.03	.17**
Dominance	.00	.06	.02	−.13*
Drive	.16**	.12+	.05	.03
Health	−.07	.02	−.04	.11+
Characteristics of Child				
Age	−.26***	−.35***	−.33***	−.39***
Solo (dummy variable)	.19***	.12*	.09	.00
Education	.03	.09	.04	−.16**
Number of Children	.13*	.14*	.09	.11
R^2	**.39***	**.36***	**.33***	**.50***
N	(278)	(294)	(188)	(207)

*** $p < .001$
** $p < .01$
* $p < .05$
+ $p < .10$

Family size in the younger generation, which showed a modest or no effect on help exchange in the G1–G2 analysis, is positively related to help from G2 parents; G2 parents report giving more help to their adult children, the more grandchildren there are, significantly so in the help G2 mothers report giving to both sons and daughters.

Income of parents exerts a strong positive effect on help to adult children in the G2–G3 dyad: The higher the income enjoyed by G2 parents, the more extensive the help they report giving to their adult children, while in three of the four equations on help from G3 children

Table 9.22. Regressions on Help *from G3 Adult Children to G2 Parents* by Gender of Parent and Child as Rated by G2 Parent (G2 Sample, Childset File) (Standardized Beta Coefficients)

Predictor Variables	G2 Parent–G3 Child Dyad			
	Mother– Daughter	Mother– Son	Father– Daughter	Father– Son
Past Family				
Family Cohesion	.04	−.02	.01	.15*
Family Troubles	.04	−.05	.05	.07
Current Relationship				
Phone Frequency	.13**	.08	.26***	.24***
Affective Closeness	.23***	.18***	.11	.18**
Value Consensus	.05	−.01	.02	.11⁺
Geographic Distance	−.20***	−.28***	−.31***	−.27***
Characteristics of Parent				
Solo (dummy variable)	.09	.17**	−.07	−.05
Total Income	−.04	.05	−.08	−.01
Full Time Employed				
(dummy variable)	.07	.01	−.05	.10
Number of Children	−.03	−.05	.04	−.04
Expressivity	.02	.02	.05	.11⁺
Dominance	.00	.13*	.03	−.01
Drive	.10	−.00	−.03	−.06
Health	−.12	−.04	−.05	−.05
Characteristics of Child				
Age	−.14**	−.22***	−.12	−.24**
Solo (dummy variable)	.26***	.03	−.01	.03
Education	.04	.11⁺	.06	−.11⁺
Number of Children	.01	−.00	−.07	.07
R^2	**.28***	**.25***	**.28***	**.38***
N	(278)	(294)	(188)	(207)

*** $p < .001$
** $p < .01$
* $p < .05$
⁺ $p < .10$

to their parents, the signs are negative, i.e., a slight tendency for children to give more help to low-income than to high-income parents. Note, also, that it is only the father–son relationship that shows a significant negative coefficient on the child's education; G3 sons with less education both receive and give more help to their fathers than very well-educated sons.

Of very special interest is the finding on Drive level. It will be recalled from the G1–G2 analysis that parents gave Low Drive daughters more help than High Drive daughters. Here, in the G2–G3 analysis, Drive is a parent characteristic, and Table 9.21 shows that mothers with High

Drive ratings gave more help to their sons and daughters than Low Drive mothers did, a pattern that seems consistent with the kinds of hands-on domestic and child care help that is typical of maternal help to adult children and grandchildren. Note that since Drive is very highly age-related, as shown in Chapter 2, the two figures who emerge as significant in the regression analysis represent departures from their age group: Low Drive young women in their 20s and 30s and High Drive older women in their 50s and 60s.

Another dyad-specific profile that holds in both the G2–G3 and G1–G2 regression analysis concerns the mother–son help exchange: In both dyads, sons gave significantly more help to mothers if they are widowed or divorced, and if the son is High on Dominance.

A special profile involving the personal trait measures is shown in the regression equations on the father–son dyad. Although Expressivity as a characteristic of the parent shows positive signs in all eight equations, it is statistically significant only in the father–son relationship: G2 men with High Expressivity gave significantly more help to their sons and receive more help in turn than fathers low in Expressivity. Note, too, that it is G2 fathers low on Dominance who give more help to sons. Looking across the profile of significant predictors of help exchange in the father–son equations projects a very special image of high levels of help from nurturant fathers who share similar values with not especially well-educated sons from whom they in turn receive a variety of help.

One last pattern worth noting for the contrast between G1–G2 and G2–G3 dyads concerns the two variables on early family life. Both Family Cohesion and Family Troubles show positive Beta coefficients in almost all the equations. In the G1–G2 analysis, more significance was found on Family Cohesion, whereas in the G2–G3 analysis, it is Family Troubles that shows more significant coefficients in help from parents to children. In Table 9.21, three of the four equations show that the more troubles reported from earlier years in the family, the greater the contemporary help from parents to adult children. Note that the early family differs between the two dyads: In the G1–G2 dyad, respondents as adult children were telling us of troubles in their families of origin; in the G2–G3 dyad, respondents as parents are telling us about troubles in their families of procreation. We suspect this makes a difference of an interesting sort. Looking back as adult children, G2 respondents may be particularly sensitive to problems involving the adults in their families, such as prolonged illness and death. Indeed, it was the subscores on Health Troubles that was most related to continuing elevated help levels from G2 children to G1 parents.

In looking back as parents to the early years in their families of procreation, G2 respondents may be more inclined to think of troubles created by children. This was suggested by the finding (data not shown) that elevated help levels relate to the Deviance subscore (based on rebellious child, trouble with law or school authorities) and the Emotional Problems subscore (based on drug or alcohol abuse, or serious emotional problems); Deviance in particular relates to problems more apt to involve the children in the family than the adults. It could therefore be the case that some G2 parents are continuing to provide advice, comfort, and perhaps even financial assistance in connection with professional therapy for some of their young adult children, half of whom are now in their 20s.

One final note on the comparison of the analysis of help exchange in the G1–G2 dyad and the G2–G3 dyad: Despite the fact that G2 respondents were reporting as adult children in the G1–G2 analysis, and as parents in the G2–G3 analysis, and despite the fact that more variables concerned the parent in the G2–G3 analysis whereas more variables concerned the child in the G1–G2 analysis, both sets of equations show the same pattern in the total amount of explained variance: In all eight comparisons of the R^2 values, the explained variance in help levels is much higher in the Parent-to-Child help flow than in the Child-to-Parent flow, and in three of four comparisons, more variance is explained in same-sex parent–child dyads than in cross-sex dyads. The R^2 values are brought together from the four relevant tables, below:

	Mother–Daughter	Mother–Son	Father–Daughter	Father–Son
Variance explained				
G1–G2: Parent to Child	.56	.50	.52	.48
Child to Parent	.37	.29	.39	.32
G2–G3: Parent to Child	.39	.36	.33	.50
Child to Parent	.28	.25	.28	.38

We suspect a major reason for this pattern relates to the very different positions parents and adult children occupy on the life course trajectory. Parental help to children has a long prehistory, going back many years, and with a deeply held sense of obligation to provide help to children of any age when they are in need. The nature of the child's need will differ in adulthood, but the grooves of parental habit are in place: personal crises, job shifts, marital formation or disruption, low incomes, heavy child care responsibilities, low energy, and so forth. Adult children, by contrast, most of whom are in their 20s and 30s, are still engaged in renegotiating their relationship with their parents, and, for many of them, it is still a novel experience to provide advice or comfort, job leads, or money to a parent rather than to be the recipients of such help as they were for 18 or more years of their young lives. In much the same way, it is a novel experience going against the grain of decades of habit for much older parents to be the recipients of help from middle-aged children. We suspect, too, that the transformation of the parent–child relationship when the child becomes an independent adult is more difficult for cross-sex than for same-sex dyads, which may be why we could explain less variance in the help exchange between mothers and sons or fathers and daughters than we could for mother–daughter and father–son dyads.

Conclusion

In stepping back from the detailed analysis of social interaction and help exchange between the generations that has been reported in this and the preceding chapter, we shall summarize and discuss some of the most significant patterns shown in our data. The most important of the findings concerns changes in interaction and help exchange patterns over the life course, and the stability with which gender of parent and child structures the frequency and nature of the social interaction and help exchanged between the generations.

Accessibility of the generations to each other is the foundation for any significant interaction and exchange of help. As in all previous research on intergenerational relations, our Boston sample shows very high proportions of respondents who live within reasonably close distance of their parents and adult children.[14] Close to 60% of our main respondents who have living parents live less than 35 miles apart, and 70% who have adult children over 18 years of age also live less than 35 miles from each other. That degree of close proximity takes on added significance in view of two major findings of the study: Great geographic distance between parents and adult children reduces not only the frequency of visiting but even of telephone contact, and it reduces not only help that by definition requires easy access—i.e., hands-on help with domestic chores, home-watching, or personal care during illness—but also help that could be provided across the miles by mail or phone such as providing comfort, or giving advice, money, or a loan.[15]

Knowledge of each other's daily activities and the sharing of the problems and pleasures they entail are difficult to gain when long distances separate family members. It was clear from our data that such knowledge is more prevalent between mothers and daughters than any other parent–child dyad, for we have seen that one in five women respondents reports daily telephone conversations with her mother. Two-thirds of the women speak to their mothers by phone at least once a week, compared to 40% of the men who have phone contact with their fathers this frequently. Almost half of the women see their mothers at least once a week, compared to a third of the men. The majority of the respondents are satisfied with the frequency with which they are in touch with their parents, and, if they are not, their preference is overwhelmingly for more rather than less contact.

In a close parallel to the gender differences in frequency of contact, we have found a comparable profile in help exchanged between parents and adult children: None of the nine types of help we inquired about was given more often to fathers than to mothers; and as mothers, women gave more varied help to their children than did men. A similar profile was shown for the adult children, with the result that the help exchanged between the generations was most extensive in the mother–daughter relationship.

Both social interaction and help exchange vary markedly across the life course. Upon completion of schooling and entry into the workforce, most young adults establish independent residences, but they do not typically move very far away, and contact and help exchange remain remarkably high. Status transitions may be dramatic and frequent events in early adulthood, with graduation from school, setting up an apartment, weddings, and first births often occurring in swift succession, but none of these events involves a very abrupt change in the relations between the generations, particularly between parents and their daughters. Indeed, the marriage of a son is associated with a resumption of more contact and help exchange with his parents. The grooves of long-standing habit are in place that no doubt motivate many parents to continue to provide a variety of assistance to young adult children, as we have seen in the provision of advice, money, or loans that parents report giving young adult sons and daughters.

Our data have also provided clues to the ways in which the generations respond to the special needs of their significant others, all of them illustrating Matilda Riley's point that extended family relations represent a "latent matrix," which may be activated under circumstances of crisis or celebration (Riley, 1983). These events may be of short duration, surrounding an illness, a job loss, or a marital disruption, or they may be of much longer duration, such as remaining unmarried throughout one's 20s, or becoming a widow in one's 60s. Thus, we found that parents give more varied help to unattached daughters than to married daughters, and sons show elevated levels of help to widowed mothers, patterns that hold independent of the age of the child or the parent. The analysis of help behavior therefore matches the normative obligations reported in Chapters 4 and 5, which showed that unattached daughters and widowed mothers evoked the highest level of felt obligation of all the kin and nonkin we investigated. In this chapter, we also reported that the ratings on normative obligations to primary kin (parents and children) contributed a significant increment to the help adult children gave their fathers and reported receiving in turn.

We have also seen that help between the generations is very responsive to income differences between parents and children: The higher the income of parents, the more extensive is the help they give to adult children, especially low-income children. So too, we found a tendency for parents to give more varied help to daughters who rated themselves low on Drive, as though to compensate for the daughters' departure from youthful energy and bounce; interestingly, it was parents who were themselves high on energy and stamina who provided the more extensive help to adult children.

As young adult children become increasingly established in work and family responsibility in the transition from early to middle adulthood, parental help declines, whereas the children's help to parents continues at about the same level. As the parents enter old age, there is an upturn of help to parents, from daughters when their mothers are in their mid-60s, and from sons somewhat later, when parents are in their mid-70s. Hence, there is a gradual reduction in the gap between parental help over child help from early in the adult years to later in the life course.

Reciprocity in the help exchange between the generations also declines across the life course trajectory, a finding of very special interest. If we view the whole 50-odd span of years from the birth of a child to the death of the parent, we can place our findings in a larger life course perspective on the direction and nature of the bonds between the generations. During the childrearing years, parental investment is high and children are recipients who may reciprocate with affection but with little by way of actual help to their parents. In adolescence, children may begin to share some domestic responsibilities, but it is not until they reach their 20s that parents and children reciprocate in any meaningful way in the help they provide to each other. Providing advice, comfort in a personal crisis, significant gifts, care during an illness, or money all presuppose such maturity. There may then be two or more decades during which the parent–child relationship becomes more peer-like and reciprocal, as the two generations renegotiate their relationship and relate to each other as fully mature adults. As we have seen, the balance may shift yet again in the parents' last years of life, as complementarity replaces reciprocity in the help exchange between the generations. As a daughter of 10, a mother may feed, clean, and protect her; as a young adult with a family of her own, the daughter and her mother may share shopping, food preparation, advice, and marital or social problems; as a middle-aged daughter whose children are off on their own, the daughter may become the provider of help to her mother by shopping, food preparation, caregiving during illness, or providing comfort and advice. For only a very small proportion of adult children is there any need to provide the kind of total caring for an elderly parent that they experienced from the parent in their own childhood.

Our findings suggest that the more intensive investment women make in early childcare and training may pave the way for reciprocity in the help exchange between themselves and their daughters a decade later, with a "payoff" even later in the life course, when the mothers have become widows, often with social, personal, and financial problems.

We have also noted some tendency for types of help to be differentiated along gender lines when parents are widowed, with more help from daughters to their fathers and from sons to their mothers, each providing help on tasks or roles previously performed by the deceased parent: Sons provide money and advice to widowed mothers, while daughters provide personal care and comfort to widowed fathers.

The help parents give children tends to be more instrumental (advice, job leads, money), while the help children give parents tends to be personal, hands-on, caregiving. Higher income and social status of the middle-aged parent may therefore redound to the benefit of young adult children getting established in life. But by the time the parents are in their elderly years, it is hands-on personal caregiving that is more at issue, and this involves the kinds of tasks low-income children have the ability and the time to provide for their parents. There may be great pride in seeing a child earn an advanced degree and take an important position several hundred miles away, but it will be the child who left school earlier, took a local job, and remained in the parents' community who will be the primary source of comfort and assistance in the parents' declining years.

The analysis of the determinants of the extent of help exchanged between the generations has shown a remarkable robustness on many measures rooted in early family life. The cohesiveness of the early family and the quality of the emotional bond between parent and child earlier on show continuing direct effects on the frequency of contact and extensiveness of the help exchanged between the generations. Although both parents and adult children may rise to occasions of great need in each other's lives, they do so with more or less grace and frequency, as a function in part of the quality of the early years of life when their lives were intimately intertwined. Each generation, then, carries its personal family history forward in time, and our understanding of the relationship between them is enriched by the knowledge of their shared past.

Notes

1. To what extent this pattern has been modified historically, as the elderly in American society have improved in health and financial status, is an interesting issue but one our data do not permit us to answer. Despite the improved health care, the existence of Medicare, and Social Security benefits, today's elderly receive more extensive help from children than they give to their children. Of course in the more affluent sectors of society, children may be "compensated" for the help they give very elderly parents when they become beneficiaries of the goods, property, and funds under their parents' wills, an issue we address in Chapter 10.

2. Note that the data in Table 9.7 concern G1 parents and G2 adult children, as did Figure 9.3, whereas Figures 9.1 and 9.2 involve G2 parents and G3 adult children. Hence, the same life course and gender pattern are shown for both the G1–G2 and the G2–G3 dyads.

3. This latter is an inference, not grounded in empirical observation. We know little about the extent to which adult employed children contribute financially when they remain in the parental home. We suspect norms are in flux in this domain, with some children contributing heavily to the household budget, and others nothing at all.

4. The analysis is restricted to the G1–G2 dyad. Similar results were obtained with data from the merged G2–G3 interviews.

5. The results for fathers mirror those for mothers in most respects where the impact of income on help is concerned. The major difference is that men report higher levels of giving help to children than children report having received from fathers, while the reverse holds in the mother–child relationship, i.e., as shown in Figure 9.11, at all income levels, children report they got more help from mothers than the mothers themselves claim they gave to their children.

6. The lawyer-son may also feel some social hesitation to refer his friends to a carpenter-father, whereas a lawyer-son might well refer his friends to a physician-father.

7. The counterpart correlations of income with the age of G1 mothers are slightly higher, $-.45$ with the mothers' total annual income, $+.26$ with their children's income, reflecting the larger proportion of very elderly among the women and the marked reduction in women's income when they become widows.

8. The earlier data concerned the G2–G3 dyad, while the regression results shown in Table 9.17 concern the G1–G2 dyad; hence, there is a consistency in the effect of age on help pattern in our two parent–child dyad data sets.

9. This variable is available only for G2 respondents. Since a significant minority of G2 respondents did not complete the vignette booklets after their long personal interviews, case base reduction because of missing values on this measure precludes our making any consistent use of the kin norm obligation ratings in the analysis of help exchange, particularly when gender of parent and child is to be specified.

10. It is also the case that parental health ratings show much greater variance, i.e., a much larger proportion in really poor health, than is the case for health ratings of the adult children, with much less "effect" of health of child than of parent in the help exchange analysis as a consequence.

11. We should emphasize the point that our help measures concern only the *variety* of help exchanged between the generations. It is possible that many G1 mothers provide a great deal of help to employed adult children, especially their married daughters, in the form of regular day care of children, rather than a diversity of types of help. On the other hand, daily care of children is highly likely to be combined with other home-based types of help.

12. Affective Closeness is not significant in the help level from G2 fathers to their

daughters, or G2 mothers to their sons; nor is contact frequency significant for either direction of help in the mother–son relationship.

13.   It is also possible that in using data from the Childset file, which duplicated data on parents as many times as there were adult children to match, the Beta coefficients on family size become exaggerated as a consequence of overrepresentation of parents with large families.

14.   We were particularly careful to obtain as exact a measure of the mileage distance between respondents and their parents and adult children as possible. Whenever a respondent could not readily tell us how many miles away a parent or child lived, we obtained the name of the town or city and coders then calculated the mileage distance between the residences.

15.   We included an item on letter-writing as a third possible contact measure in the pretest interviews, but so large a proportion of respondents reported no letter-writing to parents or children at all that we dropped the item from the final version of the questionnaire. Birthday cards and holiday greetings may continue to be exchanged, but telephone contact seems to have largely replaced letter-writing.

Help beyond Death:
Legators and Beneficiaries
of Insurance Policies
and Written Wills _____ 10

"All of my estate, real and personal, tangible and intangible, of every nature and description and wherever located, not intending hereby to exercise any power of appointment that I may have at the time of my death, I give to my spouse, _____, if my spouse survives me by thirty (30) days; otherwise, I give the same to my issue who so survive me, per stirpes."

> Typical language in a personal will under
> Commonwealth of Massachusetts law

Introduction

In many families across the country, the summer months are the time when the generations come together for leisurely visits. These are occasions for catching up with new developments in each other's lives, for reminiscing, and for indulging in the pleasures of picnics, ballgames, and picture-taking. In the summer of 1984 when this study was being designed, we enjoyed visits from our own G3 children and one surviving G1 parent, Alice's mother. We were struck, during these visits, by discussions of passing on favorite objects in the family to another generation. Our two daughters discussed who would get the familiar, battered 40-year-old soup pot and a food-spattered old cookbook. Their 84-year-old maternal grandmother asked who would like to have her silver cream pitcher and her sapphire ring, and she announced that she was making a set of doll's clothes identical to those she made for her daughter 60 years earlier, clothes we were to hold in reserve until our granddaughter (G4), then 2 years of age, was old enough to enjoy and appreciate them!

461

These conversations made us realize how little is known in family sociology about the transmission of goods and property from one generation to the next. We could not remember any major publication in family sociology on inheritance since the 1970 study by Marvin Sussman, Judith Gates, and David Smith. In recent years, the question of inheritance has taken on new salience in research by economists on intergenerational transfers.[1] Yet to judge by our experience and observations, family members show considerable interest and engage in much discussion about these intergenerational transfers. In our part of the country, in western Massachusetts, an observer sees a good deal of evidence of the "throw away" society, or its next approximation in the dozens of weekend "tag" and "yard" sales at which a few coins can forestall the movement of used objects to the town dump. Less visible but more important may be the informal giving from one generation to the next, of valued, if not necessarily valuable, objects with great sentimental meaning.

The deeper significance of discussions about who in the younger generation should inherit objects that older kin treasured during their lifetimes is the respect for and pleasure taken in the continuity of a family line. Parental concern for children does not end with death: It persists every time a parent identifies a child as a beneficiary of a life insurance policy or a written will, and every time a parent passes along some valued object to a child or grandchild. Descendants provide us with some continuity of self, through the reassuring sense that beyond our death our genes persist in the persons of our children and grandchildren, and our social personality persists through memories of us, through family stories about us, and through the property, goods, or money we transfer to our descendants. The silver cream pitcher acquired at her wedding in 1920 has passed to a G3 grandchild who may use it for pancake syrup while a G4 child inspects her image in its shiny surface much as her G2 grandmother did as a child.

The fruit of our summertime discussions in 1984 was the inclusion in the design of the personal interviews of several questions on the informal transmission of goods, the incidence of insurance polices or of written wills, and who the beneficiaries were. We asked our respondents if they or their spouses had ever inherited any of a variety of goods; whether they were the beneficiaries of anyone's insurance policy or will, and, if so, who the legators were; whether they themselves had insurance policies or had written a will, and, if so, who their beneficiaries are. Anticipating that many of our respondents would not yet have written a will, we also asked a hypothetical question on who their beneficiaries would be were they to draw up a will. It is to these data that we turn in this chapter, a fitting last topic in a study of parent–child relations, since it illustrates parental concern of a very poignant kind, to provide for people in advance of one's death.

The topic is also a good one on which to explore an issue that has long been of interest: What do people do who have no descendants, either because they never married, or because they never had children? Having grown up in a family with a number of unmarried aunts and uncles, we knew personally how important we were as child-surrogates in the lives of unmarried and childless kin, just as we treasured our relationship to such childless relatives because our parents were overworked and too poor to provide us with the treats those unmarried aunts and uncles brought to us. But what happens when childless adults write a will? Do they make nieces and nephews their beneficiaries, or do they move out of the family sphere to friends, institutions, and charity, or bypass writing a will all told? These are not idle questions. In an era with a lowering marriage and remarriage rate, and an increase in voluntary childlessness, one wonders what emotional and social ties will replace the primary bonds to descendants for this growing segment of the population. Our analysis of beneficiaries of insurance policies and wills will therefore give special attention to the childless adults in our Boston sample, not just to those who have been on center stage throughout the previous chapters—those who have themselves experienced parenthood.

Respondents as Beneficiaries

Our data suggest a remarkably high level of transfer of goods between households and families. Clearly not everything is discarded through tag sales in the suburbs of Boston! Respondents were asked if they (or their spouses) had ever received each of nine types of things from someone before or after they died. The most common goods to be transferred in this way were photographs: As seen in Table 10.1, three in four respondents report having received these reminders of times past. From experience we know such photos and albums are likely to record the early growth and development of children, their siblings, and perhaps go back in time to when the parents were themselves children and grandparents were young adults. From somewhat more than a third to approximately half of the respondents possess things such as books, painting, jewelry, dishes or silverware, furniture, and a family Bible or family history, things that had been passed on to them by members of their families. Least often cited (by fewer than one in five respondents) were vehicles of some kind, stocks or bonds, land, or other property.[2]

Panel B of Table 10.1 shows that roughly half of the respondents had

Table 10.1. Inheritance of Material Goods *ᵃ* by Type
and Number of Goods and Gender (G2 Sample)
(in Percent)

Material Goods Inherited	Women	Men
A. Type of Goods		
Photographs	76.5	71.5
Books or paintings	51.4	48.3
Jewelry	56.0	48.0
Dishes, silverware	55.7	45.7
Furniture	46.9	42.2
Family Bible or history	43.5	37.6
Land or property	18.9	15.8
Stocks or bonds	16.7	14.7
Cars, trucks, etc.	14.7	13.1
N	(773)	(564)
B. Number of Types of Goods Inherited		
None	15.9	19.7
1–3	31.4	34.7
4–5	26.2	22.4
6–9	26.6	22.9
N	(805)	(588)

ᵃ Question read: "Were any of the following things ever passed on to you [IF
EVER MARRIED: or your (husband)(wife)] from someone before or after they
died?"

received *four or more* such types of material goods from someone in the
past, with little difference between men and women in either the overall
extent of such inheritance, or the specific types of material goods involved. One reason men are almost as likely to report inheriting jewelry
or dishes and silverware as women is because the question asked if
either the respondent *or* a spouse had received such material goods.
Another reason may be the absence of a sister to whom parents might
otherwise have transferred such goods. And, of course, in some families
with particular concern for the paternal line, the transfer of certain
goods to sons may be customary.[3]

Table 10.2 shows the variation in the extent of material goods inheritance by age, gender, and marital status. In both age groups, never-
married women report a much higher average number of things they
received from someone than never-married men do, projecting the
image of the "traveling light" bachelor while the older unmarried
daughter is the recipient of numerous hand-me-downs and family heirlooms.

Age makes much less difference among the married than the unmarried adults, perhaps because parents tend to pass along things to young

Table 10.2. Mean Number of Things Inherited by
Age, Marital Status, and Gender (G2 Sample)
(Score Range: 0–9)

Marital Status	Gender	Under 40	Over 40
Never Married	Women	3.2	4.6
		(99)	(38)
	Men	2.1	3.2
		(110)	(15)
Ever Married	Women	3.6	3.7
		(277)	(389)
	Men	3.4	3.6
		(193)	(269)

married children when they first establish a household and the parents themselves wish to replace child-worn household goods once the children have grown and left home.

Our question was not specific enough to differentiate between formal transmission of goods through a legal will and informal arrangements. Nor did we ask who the donors were from whom the respondents obtained these kinds of material goods. It is clear that in making formal arrangements for such transfers, the transmission is predominantly from parent to adult child. Table 10.3 shows the prevalence level reported by respondents when they were asked if they or their spouses were beneficiaries of wills or insurance policies and who the legators were. Approximately half the respondents report that their parents or parents-in-law were the legators. A small minority (between 7 and 14%) report having been beneficiaries of their grandparents or their spouses' grandparents. A slightly larger proportion (between 11 and 20%) specified some "other relative." Only a very small proportion reported a nonkin legator: 3% of the men and 6% of the women.

Table 10.4 examines more closely the age, gender, and marital status of those who are or were beneficiaries in their *parents'* insurance policies or wills. Once again, there are no significant gender differences, but a striking difference by marital status: Unattached adult children are much more likely to be beneficiaries of their parents than married adult children. This pattern is consistent with the findings reported in Chapter 9 on the help exchange between the generations, where we found a persistent tendency for parents to extend more varied help to unattached children than to married children. Such differential concern seems to carry over to the provisions parents make for their children following their own death. The contrast by marital status is particularly strong among those over 40 years of age, by which time unmarried children are far less likely to marry. Thus, 40% of married sons over 40

Table 10.3.   Percentage Who Report They (and/or Their
Spouses) Are or Were Beneficiaries [a] of Specified
Persons by Gender (G2 Sample)

Legator	Women (%)	Men (%)
Own Kin		
Parents	56.7	53.4
	(728)	(526)
Grandparents	13.2	13.9
	(743)	(548)
Other Relatives	20.4	14.8
	(744)	(540)
Spouse's Kin (among ever-married respondents)		
Parents	39.8	40.8
	(588)	(404)
Grandparents	7.4	8.4
	(583)	(412)
Other Relatives	11.3	11.4
	(603)	(413)
Nonrelative	5.6	2.9
	(746)	(544)

[a] Question read: "To the best of your knowledge, are you or were you [IF EVER
MARRIED: or your (husband)(wife)] a beneficiary in any of the following
persons' wills or insurance policies?"

years of age report they were or are beneficiaries of their parents,
considerably below the 60% of older never-married sons, a pattern
found among older daughters as well.

Respondents as Legators

Age, Gender, and Marital Status

Taking out life insurance is a more customary practice among American adults than drawing up a written will. Many young adults take over
insurance polices on their own lives from their parents, and once they
begin their own families, the chances are strong that they will increase
coverage to provide some economic cushion in the event of their death
while children are still very young. Indeed, a full 79% of our Boston
respondents report carrying life insurance. As seen in Figure 10.1, the
peak of carrying insurance is in the middle years (at 86%), when many
children still require support, and their parents, especially their fathers,
are at some actuarial risk of premature death. But insurance coverage is
high at all stages of the life course.

Table 10.4. Percentage Who Are or Were Beneficiaries
in Their *Parents'* Insurance Policies or Wills by Age,
Marital Status, and Gender (G2 Sample)

Gender	Marital Status	Under 40 (%)	Over 40 (%)
Women	Never Married	73.5	55.6
		(83)	(36)
	Ever Married	66.9	46.6
		(239)	(369)
Men	Never Married	66.3	60.0
		(92)	(15)
	Ever Married	65.1	40.4
		(169)	(250)

Writing a will, by contrast, is very strongly related to phase of life: it is rare among young adults (less than 10%), increases rapidly as adults enter their 40s and 50s, and peaks at two in three adults in their 60s.

The impact of marriage and family responsibility on the motivation of adults to protect dependents can be seen by contrasting the prevalence of insurance and written wills between single and married adults. The pattern is shown in Figure 10.2. At all stages of life, ever-married adults are more apt to carry life insurance and to have a written will than never-

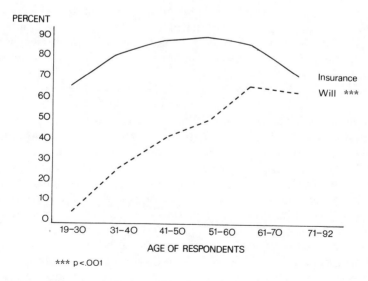

Figure 10.1. Percentage who carry life insurance and have a written will by age (G2 sample).

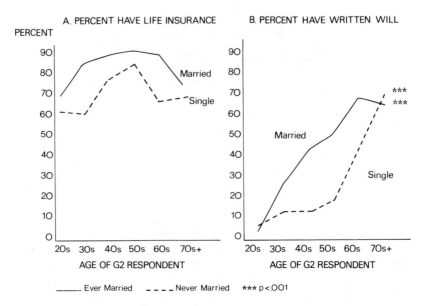

Figure 10.2. Percentage who have (A) life insurance coverage, and (B) written will by age and marital status (G2 sample).

married adults. The contrast is particularly sharp for the years from 30 to 50 when married adults carry the heaviest responsibility for dependent children. For adults who never married, the stimulus to writing a will seems more narrowly related to aging and impending death, for there is a sharp upturn in writing wills among single adults only when they reach their 60s.

Both Figures 10.1 and 10.2 show a fall-off in the proportion carrying life insurance in the elderly years. But in Panel A of Figure 10.2, it can be seen that never-married elderly do not show such a drop-off; only married adults do. This suggests that the age–insurance pattern is not showing a cohort difference (i.e., that today's elderly were less socialized to the importance of insurance than more recent cohorts). We suspect the decline is related to two factors. The first is a change in the nature of the policies people carry at one stage of life compared to another: The amount of term insurance carried may be lowered once family responsibilities have been fulfilled, paid-up annuities may be converted to other types of savings, and death benefits and income for surviving spouses under retirement and pension plans may lower the necessity for carrying special life insurance policies among the elderly.

The second reason for the decline in proportion carrying life insurance and having a written will among those over 70 years of age is that there are fewer men in the oldest age group. Panel A in Figure 10.3 shows the life course trend in the prevalence of having written wills among ever-married men and women; the data indicate that the proportion of men who have a will continues to climb after they pass their seventieth birthday, but it drops sharply among ever-married women over 70. Married couples tend to have wills jointly drawn, while many widows, themselves beneficiaries in their husbands' wills, do not draw up their own wills to cover the disposal of money, possessions, and property in the event of their death. If deceased husbands' wills had made provision for the death of both husband and wife, one would expect the elderly women to report just as high a prevalence of having a written will as men, but this is clearly not the case. By contrast, among the minority in our sample who have never married, women exceed men in providing for the disposal of their goods, money, and property through a written will, even more so among the older adults than the younger.[4]

Table 10.5 permits a closer inspection of what is going on in the older years—i.e., among those over 40 years of age—by specifying marital status more exactly and showing the proportion of men and women who have a written will in the four marital statuses. A written will is reported by the majority of both married men (55%) and married women (54%). This figure remains about the same among widows (57%), but there is a sharp increase among widowers (72%) compared to married

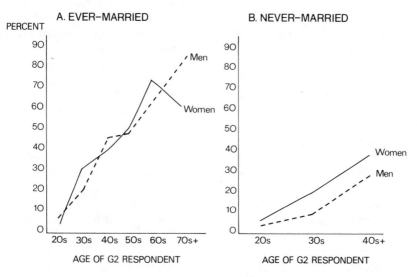

Figure 10.3. Percentage who have a written will by age, gender, and marital status (G2 sample).

Table 10.5. Percentage Who Have a Written Will
by Gender and Marital Status, Among Those
40 Years of Age or Older

Marital Status	Women (%)	Men (%)
Never Married	36.8	26.7
	(38)	(15)
Separated/Divorced	27.6	30.8
	(58)	(26)
Married	53.7	55.2
	(246)	(221)
Widowed	57.1	72.2
	(91)	(18)

men (55%). It is likely that widowed men have more goods, money, and property to dispose of in the event of their death than is true for widowed women. We do not know if widowers have more such resources than married men, but clearly they have lower annual incomes than married men, as we saw in Chapter 3. Becoming a widower, then, seems to be associated with an even greater tendency for men to "tidy" up their affairs, while widows are less apt to do so. This gender difference may blur in future cohorts of the elderly, as a consequence of greater economic independence on the part of women and more interchangeability between husbands and wives in money management.

One other point of interest in Table 10.5 is the difference between married adults and separated or divorced adults: Married men and women are far more apt to have a written will than are separated and divorced men and women. Among men, 55% of the married but only 31% of the separated and divorced report having a written will, with an equally marked contrast among women (54% among married, compared to 28% among separated or divorced women). We did not ask for the date of the divorce or the date a will was drawn up, but legal colleagues inform us that following a divorce, adults who had wills during their marriage may revise them, but they do not abandon having a will. This suggests that the absence of a written will among separated and divorced adults may reflect a long-standing lesser commitment to provide for marital partners and dependent children than that felt and shown by adults who remain in intact marriages. Some indirect support for this interpretation is provided by the analyses reported in Chapter 5, which showed that respondents who had ever been divorced had much lower obligations to all categories of kin than married or never-married respondents had. In any event, the formerly married are more like those who never married than they are like married or widowed adults over 40.

Determinants of Having Insurance and a Will

Age and gender are so closely related to marital status that we can not draw firm inferences on the basis of data shown thus far. We shift now to a regression analysis on the determinants of carrying life insurance or not, and having a written will or not, to provide a firmer explanation.

In addition to age, gender, and a dummy variable on marital status (never-married = 1, all other marital statuses = 0), we add several potential determinants of the two dependent variables of insurance and wills. The impact of family responsibility is tapped by two measures: a dummy variable on being childless (childless = 1, one or more children = 0), and the number of children among those who have at least one child. Those who have inherited material goods from someone in the past may be alert to the importance of providing for loved ones in the event of one's death, and, hence, more predisposed to carry insurance and to draw up wills. We therefore added the number of things adults inherited in the past to the array of predictor variables.

Normative obligations to kin may also predispose people to carry through on internalized norms by taking out insurance and writing a will. Hence, we enter the mean rating on felt obligation to Primary Kin (parents and children) from the vignette data into the equation. Though with less assurance of its contribution, we also enter Kin Embeddedness, on the expectation that those whose lives are heavily focused on the world of family and relatives may make greater provision for loved ones than those oriented to a larger social world of friends and work colleagues. The reason for the lack of assurance on the contribution of this measure stems from hints in preliminary analysis that adults high on Kin Embeddedness tend to be low-income, highly religious people, who score low on the self-rating of Dominance, which projects an image of some tendency to dependency on others that may depress rather than enhance providing for loved ones through insurance and wills.

Lastly, we enter both educational attainment and total family income into the equations, with quite different expectations for their contribution to explaining the dependent variables. The insurance industry has succeeded in persuading people in all walks of life of the desirability of carrying life insurance, and many employers automatically include some minimal insurance policy among employee benefits. But the legal profession has not yet done any comparable job of educating the public on the desirability of having a will that specifies who is to be one's executor, who will have the power of attorney in gaining access to one's money, and what should be done in disposing of one's possessions. To die intestate runs the risk of adding hardship, confusion, and complexity to the grief of loved ones in the difficult months following a death. Our prediction was that educational attainment predisposes to having a will, but plays no role in whether adults carry life insurance or not. Since legal fees are incurred in writing a will and insurance premiums come due with regularity, income level should be a significant determinant of both wills and insurance.

Table 10.6 shows the results of the two regression analyses. Social norms have long prompted the view that responsible adult behavior should include carrying life insurance to cover the costs associated with one's death and burial, regardless of the amount of family responsibility one carries. This was implicit in the high prevalence of insurance carried at all stages of the life course, and it is also reflected in the results of the regression analysis shown in Panel B. The only significant predictors of whether respondents had a life insurance policy or not are gender, marital status, and income: Married men with sufficient income to do so carry insurance, but even these three variables together explain very little of the variance in insurance coverage, as indexed by the modest R^2 of .08. In this domain of social life, the norms involved are widely accepted in all sectors of society: It is particularly incumbent on men when they marry, but more generally for adults at all stages of the life course, to carry life insurance.

Table 10.6. Regressions on Having a Written Will and Carrying Life Insurance (G2 Sample) (Standardized Beta Coefficients)

Predictor Variables	A Written Will	B Insurance Policy
Family Characteristics		
Never Married (dummy variable)	.03	−.11***
Childless (dummy variable)	−.21***	−.02
Number of Children	−.11***	.03
Number of Things Inherited in Past	.06*	.03
Mean Rating on Primary Kin Obligations	.04	.00
Kin Embeddedness	−.05+	.05+
Social/Demographic Characteristics		
Age	.49***	.06
Gender	.03	−.13***
Total Family Income	.19***	.12***
Education	.11***	.02
R^2	.30***	.08***
N	(1112)	(1112)

*** p < .001
* p < .05
+ p < .10

The profile of significant predictors of having a written will or not is quite different. The social and legal desirability of having a written will is a less widely held view. In addition, wills cover a much wider array of life circumstances than insurance policies: Taking out insurance involves specifying how much or what proportion of the insurance money goes to each of one's beneficiaries. In drawing up a will, most people are also concerned about who will hold executor authority in disposing of one's worldly possessions as well as one's money, who will sell (or get) one's house, cars, jewelry, etc., and, even more importantly, who will have responsibility for one's children, in the event that both parents die before the children reach maturity. The authors witnessed a rash of discussion and actual drawing up of wills while living in a housing development with mostly other young couples, like ourselves, rearing children under 10 years of age; this epidemic of will writing was in the aftermath of an automobile accident involving a neighbor, in which both husband and wife were killed, leaving three young children unprovided for. However low the probability of such dual deaths of young parents, empathy for the children and identification with the deceased parents were powerful motivators to minimizing the tragic dilemma of one's own children becoming orphans by drawing up wills that specified who was to carry responsibility for rearing the children and to provide them with money to assist in that childrearing.

Hence it is that being a parent of even one child is a critical motivator for writing a will: The dummy variable on Childless is the second strongest coefficient in equation A. But this does not imply writing a will takes place when the child was first born. As we saw in Figure 10.1, will drafting is highly age related, which is also shown in the regression analysis in that age shows the highest standardized coefficient in the equation (.49***). Writing a will protects one's adult children from some degree of conflict among them, to the extent that the legator specifies to whom and in what proportion moneys and worldly possessions should go, and who shall carry executor authority in implementing the bequests and disposing of goods and property.

The predictions concerning income and education are also confirmed, with written wills more prevalent among those with higher educational attainment and higher income, whereas insurance coverage is related to income but not to educational attainment. Even young poorly educated adults are socialized to the desirability of life insurance coverage. The background experience of having inherited material goods in the past contributes an additional, modest increment to will writing. Although it shows a positive coefficient, the Primary Kin Obligation rating does not contribute any significant increment to the writing of wills, and Kin Embeddedness verges on statistical significance, but with a negative sign, meaning those highly embedded in their kin world are less, not more, apt to have a written will. This adds further to our sense that Kin Embeddedness includes some tendency to psychological dependency *on* others rather than responsibility *for* others.

The extent of family responsibility, as measured by the number of children respondents have had, is also a highly significant predictor of written wills, but in an opposite direction from prediction: Those with few children, not those with large families, are more apt to have a written will. This is no spurious finding, on the grounds that family size masks socioeconomic status factors, since it holds, net of educational attainment and income level. The inference we draw from this finding is that both factors—a large family and not having a will—may be the consequence of a lower level of responsibility to take charge of one's life and perhaps less ability to avoid more responsibility than can be comfortably carried.

Beneficiaries of Respondent-Legators

Our Boston respondents were asked who the beneficiaries are in their written wills. Anticipating that only a rather small proportion of a sample would have a written will, we also asked the hypothetical question of who they would make their beneficiaries for "either money or things you own" were they to draw up a will. In the analysis to follow, we shall refer to the first instance as "actual" wills and the hypothetical second instance as "probable" wills. In either case, respondents were not asked an open-ended question on who the beneficiaries are (or would be), but specifically whether or not certain people or institutions were or would be provided for. Thus, respondents were asked if they have provided for, or would provide for children, spouse, parents, siblings, nieces or nephews, friends, institutions (examples offered were church, museum, or library), and a charity of some kind.

It is to these actual or probable beneficiaries that we now turn. Table 10.7 provides the incidence of the numerous beneficiaries by gender of respondent and whether the beneficiaries are actually provided for in a written will, or merely potential beneficiaries were the respondents to draw up a will. The primacy of immediate family responsibilities shows clearly in the incidence levels: Children and spouses head the list, with no differences between men and women, or between those who have already drawn up a will and those who have not.[5]

Beyond this inner core of spouse and children, smaller proportions of respondents have provided for other close kin; members of their families of origin (parents and siblings) have already been provided for in approximately 1 in 4 or 5 cases of actual wills, trailed by nieces and

Table 10.7. Actual vs Probable Beneficiaries of Wills by Gender (G2 Sample) (in Percent)

Actual or Probable	Women		Men	
Beneficiaries	Have Will	Have No Will [a]	Have Will	Have No Will
Kin				
Children	99.6	97.4	95.0	94.4
	(232)	(342)	(159)	(234)
Spouse	90.5	84.6	96.1	92.6
	(189)	(338)	(154)	(258)
Parent(s)	27.2	61.8***	21.4	59.2***
	(125)	(387)	(84)	(304)
Sibling(s)	23.8	54.0***	16.4	52.1***
	(235)	(476)	(165)	(368)
Nieces/	12.0	32.5***	11.8	28.5
nephews	(250)	(474)	(170)	(347)
Nonkin				
Friends	10.3	29.9***	4.5	25.6***
	(261)	(495)	(177)	(382)
Institutions	11.7	26.3***	8.4	23.6***
	(265)	(502)	(178)	(382)
Charity	10.2	31.3***	7.3	29.6***
	(265)	(501)	(178)	(382)

[a] Hypothetical question to those who do not have a written will: "If you were to draw up a will, would you make any of the following beneficiaries for either money or things you own?"
*** p < .001

nephews in 1 in 10 actual wills. Nonkin are cited at about the same frequency as siblings' children. There is also a consistent tendency for more women than men to include other kin and nonkin in a will. The gender difference is particularly marked in the case of friends, where twice as many women as men report having included a friend in an actual written will (10 vs. 5%).

There is also a decided contrast between actually including many types of beneficiaries in a written will, and expressing one's probable intentions. Hypothetical questions are always an invitation to put forward the good, moral side of the self. Both women and men refer to parents, siblings, nieces and nephews, and the three types of nonkin beneficiaries two to three times more frequently in response to the hypothetical will questions than they report on the provisions of actual wills. In one instance, involving men providing for a friend, the friend is cited five times more often by men who have no will now than by men who do have a will (26 vs. 5%). Once confronted with the actual value of one's worldly goods in savings, property, and personal possessions, and one assesses their adequacy to meet the probable needs of a surviving spouse and children over a number of years, realistic assessment may dampen good intentions and contract the circle of beneficiaries cited in the will that is finally drawn up.

The contrast between actual and only probable beneficiaries may mask a major difference between those with and those without a written will: Wills are written in the later stages of life, not in early adulthood. Hence, it may simply be the case that it is younger people, without wills, who cite parents, siblings, and friends, whereas older people, who have actually written a will, no longer have living parents, and do not expect siblings or friends to outlive them. On the other hand, one would expect intentions of older persons to embrace charities and religious institutions to a greater extent than young adults just starting out in life, yet the same pattern is shown on both close kin and these categories of nonkin.

Clearly an interpretation of the results shown in Table 10.7 requires a further step of analysis. What circumstances in life predispose adults to include siblings, nieces, and nephews in a will? And who makes provision for formal organizations such as a church, a museum, or a charitable agency? Is it the case that the strong relationship of age to writing a will explains the difference discussed above? To answer these questions, we selected siblings, nieces, and nephews from the category of kin, and institutions and charities from the category of nonkin, for a more detailed analysis.

Siblings and Siblings' Children as Beneficiaries. We include the same set of variables in the analysis that was used in the preceding regression analysis. In this instance, however, we are predicting whether or not siblings are beneficiaries in actual or probable wills (Panel A in Table 10.8) and whether or not nieces or nephews are beneficiaries in actual or probable wills (Panel B of Table 10.8). We predicted that childless, never-married adults, or adults with few children of their own, would, all else equal, be more inclined to include siblings and siblings' children in their wills. This assumes siblings are age-peer substitutes for spouses, and nieces and nephews for one's own children. It also implies that by making such lateral moves from the direct line of descent, adults are in a sense keeping things "in the family." One could imagine some social circumstances, in which adults have been very alienated from their families and have avoided taking on family responsibilities of their own, having the effect of bypassing kin all told when it came to drawing up their wills, leaving money and possessions to charity, the church, a political movement, or friends rather than to close kin.

But there is no evidence in our Boston data of such deep alienation or bypassing of family members. Childless adults are not turning away from the world of family; they merely move laterally and have provided

Table 10.8. Regressions on Specific Beneficiaries of Actual or Probable Written Wills: Siblings and Nieces or Nephews (G2 Sample) (Standardized Beta Coefficients)

Predictor Variables	A. Siblings as Beneficiaries		B. Nieces/Nephews as Beneficiaries	
	Actual Will	Probable Will	Actual Will	Probable Will
Family Characteristics				
Never Married (dummy variable)	.11*	.08*	.07	.04
Childless (dummy variable)	.25***	.20***	.35***	.31***
Number of Children	−.13**	−.17***	−.06	−.08
Number of Things Inherited	.02	.03	.08	.10**
Mean Rating on Primary Kin Obligation	−.02	.09**	−.06	.07*
Kin Embeddedness	.01	.04	.04	.05
Social/Demographic Characteristics				
Age	−.22***	−.19***	−.08	.01
Gender (Female = 1)	.10*	.05	−.02	.05
Total Family Income	.02	−.03	−.05	−.07+
Education	.11+	.01	.01	−.03
R^2	**.30***	**.26***	**.22***	**.15***
N^a	(350)	(702)	(350)	(702)

[a] Base N for all regression equations restricted to G2 respondents who have at least one sibling.
*** $p < .001$
** $p < .01$
* $p < .05$
+ $p < .10$

for, or plan to provide for siblings, nieces, and nephews instead of children and spouses. It is family characteristics, not socioeconomic status factors, that determine the inclusion of siblings in written wills: Young adults, especially women, those who never married or remained childless, or had very few children of their own tend to provide for siblings. If they have yet to draw up a will, these same factors play a critical role, and, in addition, there is an extra increment to providing for siblings and their children if the respondents scored high on normative obligations to primary kin.[6]

The determinants of citing nieces and nephews as beneficiaries (Panel B of Table 10.8) are more limited in number; the primary determinant is being childless in both the actual and probable will equations. Age is not significant here, as it was for siblings. Siblings are most salient when writing a will takes place in early adulthood, a stage of life when ties to brothers and sisters retain the intensity they had while one was growing up. Older adults, facing the reality of their own mortality, would be less likely to cite siblings, since the odds are great that many will not outlive the legators. Like one's own children, nieces and nephews will be alive when bequests are made under the terms of a will.

If our reasoning is correct, that nieces and nephews may be viewed as child substitutes for childless adults and become more salient in the older years when concern for the transmission of goods and money increases, it should follow that being childless is a particularly salient predictor in the intentions to provide for nieces and nephews among older respondents. When age is only one of many predictor variables, the coefficient on Childless in the probable will equation was .31*** and the R^2 was .15***. When the same equation was replicated with a restriction to respondents over 40 years of age, the coefficient on Childless increased to .54*** (from .31) and the R^2 increased to .35*** (from .15). For older adults, twice as much variance in the provision for nieces and nephews in a hypothetical will is explained than we reported in Table 10.8, and all the increase is attributable to the one predictor variable of being childless. As childless adults get older, then, their motivation to provide for nieces and nephews seems to get stronger and more narrowly focused on the fact of having no direct descendants of their own.

There is a similar hint in the array of predictor variables on providing for nieces and nephews (as there was for siblings) that past experience of inheritance and normative obligation levels are more relevant to and drawn on in stating one's intentions than in actual will drafting: Both variables—having inherited a number of things in the past and higher than average felt obligation to primary kin—are significant predictors of "probable" wills with bequests to nieces and nephews. Lastly, while income and educational attainment were relevant to whether or not adults had a written will, they play no significant role in the choice of beneficiaries. Status factors affect taking the legal steps to cover transfer of money and possessions, whereas family characteristics affect to whom the money and possessions are to go.

Nonkin as Beneficiaries.   Providing for lateral kin is not the only option open to childless adults. Nor are children the only beneficiaries of those who have had children. We saw earlier that a sizable minority of our respondents either has or would consider making provision in their wills for charities or institutions such as a museum, library, or a church. What predisposes adults to making such provisions outside the family realm?

To answer this question empirically, we devised a single three-category index from the responses to the two questions on "charity" and "institutions" (0 = neither charity nor institutions cited; 1 = either charity or institutions cited; and 2 = both cited) and regressed the same set of predictor variables used in the above analysis of siblings and siblings' children as beneficiaries on the combined index of providing for charities and/or institutions. We also include a measure of Religiosity in the equation (as tapped by church attendance frequency) on the premise that there are ethical and moral components common to both making a charity a beneficiary and participation in religious life.[7] We also included the number of siblings respondents had, on the assumption that larger extended families may reduce the impulse to provide for nonkin institutions when adults draw up a will or contemplate doing so.

The results of the regression analysis suggest a very different profile of factors played a role for respondents who have actually provided for nonkin institutions in their wills compared to those who responded to the hypothetical question. The primary predictors in the actual will equation (Panel A in Table 10.9) are marital status, age, education, past experience of having inherited things, and religiosity: Older, well-

Table 10.9. Regressions on *Charities and Institutions* as Actual or Probable Beneficiaries in Written Wills (G2 Sample) (Standardized Beta Coefficients)

Predictor Variables	A. Actual Written Will	B. Probable Written Will
Family Characteristics		
Never Married (dummy variable)	.21***	.02
Childless (dummy variable)	.02	.19***
Number of Children	.02	.02
Number of Siblings	−.09	.07*
Number of Things Inherited	.14**	.06+
Kin Embeddedness	−.04	.03
Social/Demographic Characteristics		
Age	.12*	−.04
Gender (Female = 1)	.03	.02
Total Family Income	−.04	−.06+
Education	.12*	.04
Religiosity	.09*	.13***
R^2	.14***	.07***
N	(394)	(807)

*** p < .001 * p < .05
** p < .01 + p < .10

educated adults who never married and who have been frequent church-attenders provide the profile of those who have already made provision for charities and institutions in their wills.

It is also the case that the standardized coefficient on past inheritance is larger here than in equations on kin as beneficiaries (.14** in Table 10.9 vs. a range of .02 to .10 in previous equations on kin as beneficiaries). The material goods we asked about in the interview included, almost by definition, "old" things: books, family histories, photographs, paintings, a family Bible, jewelry, silverware. Both family donors and the recipients of such objects may be reflecting the same kind of predilection for tradition, and taste preferences for heirlooms and antiques, that motivates the desire to contribute to the preservation of the past to which museums, libraries, and many churches are dedicated.

The profile of determinants of contributions to charities and institutions in response to the hypothetical will question is quite different: religiosity plays a greater role and past inheritance a lesser role; low income rather than high education is associated with contemplated contributions to charities. Neither age nor marital status matters, while childlessness has the largest standardized coefficient in the equation. And against expectation, it is adults from larger families (i.e., with more siblings) who show the greater predisposition to cite charities and institutions as beneficiaries.

But all told, less than half as much variance is explained in the probable will equation as in the actual will equation, though neither is very large compared to regression analyses of kin as beneficiaries (.14 in the actual will equation, and only .07 in the probable will equation). With age not a relevant predictor, this suggests many younger people, many years away from actually drafting a will of their own, are responding in terms of moral and religious values. But those with a large kindred may eventually prefer secondary kin as beneficiaries. It seems unlikely that many such adults will ever in fact draw up a will that transfers goods or money to nonkin charities and institutions, with the exception of the childless among them.

Conclusion

For most of our Boston respondents, the transfer of money, property, and goods takes place within the circles of very close kin, children and spouses above all others. Special circumstances in personal life, such as remaining unmarried or not having children of one's own, predispose adults to move laterally within their kindred and to make bequests to siblings, nieces, and nephews. For others, high religiosity, past experience in inheriting from others or high scores on normative obligations to kin predispose toward making bequests to charities and institutions.

But with a fertility rate now stabilizing at very small families and with an increased proportion of young adults expressing their intention and desire to remain childless, there will be fewer siblings and fewer nieces and nephews to become beneficiaries in the absence of children in the future, with the result that childless adults may show an increasing tendency to transfer their money and property from the family sphere to charitable agencies and public and private institutions.

Perhaps the most interesting implication of this analysis of wills is the evidence it provides of parental concern for children that extends beyond the life of the parents. We have noted an attenuation of help exchange from parents to children in the elderly years (in Chapter 9), coupled with a strong retention of positive affection and intimacy between the generations as they move through the life course. But parental concern for the well-being of their children is clearly apparent in the priority shown to children when adults contemplate or plan the transfer of their remaining money, property, and material goods after their death. Those adults who never had children of their own are not alienated, selfish individuals adrift in an anomic, secular society; they are closely tied to their parents, who in turn continue to show concern for their unattached children, to interact with them socially even more often than with the married children now rearing the G4 generation. And childless adults who retain relationships with their siblings, if they have them, often look to nieces and nephews as surrogate-children, and remember them when they write their wills. Not having had a family of their own, they provide for those familiar to them from their families of origin and siblings' descendants.

Overall, there is no hint in these data of family breakdown, of anomic individuals out for private gain; there is, instead, much evidence of a fundamental stability to family structure, and of deep and abiding ties between the generations across the entire life course. The human bond of parenthood is not latent, but clearly manifest in all the dimensions of the intergenerational solidarity we have investigated, and it is a bond that begins before the birth of a child and persists beyond the death of the parent.

Notes

1. The economics model is clearly apparent in the titles of many such articles, for example, the "Capital Accumulation and the Characteristics of Private Intergenerational Transfers" (Kurz, 1984) or "The Family as an Incomplete Annuities Market" (Kotlikoff &

Spivak, 1981). Other examples of recent work by economists are Bernheim et al. (1985) and Blinder et al. (1983). A recent call for more research by a sociologist is that by Marvin Sussman (Sussman, 1983).

2. Incredibly, we neglected to include "cash" on our list, an omission we very much regret.

3. In teaching a course on family and kinship over many years, it was almost always the case that the family histories students brought in to share with us were histories of their fathers' family line.

4. There were not sufficient cases of never-married among older respondents to permit any finer age classification. Hence, the oldest group shown in Figure 10.3 among the never-married men and women combines all adults over the age of 40.

5. Although all the incidence levels involving spouses and children are above 85%, there is a slight tendency for women but not men to show higher incidence levels in providing for children than for spouses, perhaps because husbands have lesser economic need than wives do, and are more likely to die before their wives.

6. Other regression analyses included the general rating score (across all categories of kin) and the subscore on Secondary Kin obligations rather than the Primary Kin ratings, but no differences emerged from that analysis compared to the coefficients on Primary Kin obligations shown in the text.

7. In addition, "church" was one of the three institutions interviewers mentioned to illustrate what was meant by "institutions," which may have had particular salience for deeply religious respondents.

Summary _____ Part V

Overview and Looking Ahead _____ 11

Introduction

By the time a research project nears completion, almost all social researchers are aware of things they wish they had done differently in study design or variable specification. It is often difficult to tell whether such belated realization of gaps or errors in design and measurement could have been anticipated, or whether one perceived them only as a consequence of data analysis. Hindsight is much easier to come by than foresight.

Fortunately, regrets concerning design omissions and inadequate measurement are balanced against accomplishments and the hope that one's findings will point the way to new investigations in the future. The intellectual pleasure of data analysis and delight in empirical discoveries provided countless peak experiences over the 5 years during which this study was a major commitment, indeed obsession. Intrinsic rewards and confirmations of expectations far outweighed the frustrations and disappointments inherent in the research process.

In this concluding chapter, we are particularly concerned with looking ahead to "next steps" in studies of intergenerational relationships, gender, parenthood, and the life course. Consequently, we provide a rather special and limited summary of findings, and give more attention to sharing our regrets and suggesting fruitful directions that future research could profitably take.

Overview of Findings

Our emphasis in this overview of findings will be on broad themes that cut across two or more lines of analysis reported in the preceding chapters. It is appropriate, however, to first facilitate access to the more specific findings in the study. These can be found in the concluding sections of most substantive chapters, especially so for the two chapters on normative obligations to kin (Chapters 4 and 5), on the direct and indirect effects of early family life on the quality of contemporary parent-child relationships (Chapter 7), and on a wide array of early family and current characteristics as determinants of social interaction and help exchange between the generations (Chapters 8 and 9).

For readers with special interest in particular constructs used in the analysis, we provide a very special guide to the empirical findings: Table 11.1 lists all the major variables used in the analysis, and the specific tables or figures in which major findings on each variable were reported. The variables are organized in five categories: Panel A, measures of the major dimensions of the current parent-child relationship (both G1–G2 and G2–G3); Panel B, measures concerned with the family of origin of G2 respondents; Panel C, measures referring to the family of procreation of G2 respondents; Panel D, social–demographic characteristics; and Panel E, personal/attitudinal characteristics of respondents. Within each of these five categories, variables are listed in alphabetical order, with tables and figures cited in column 1 if the variable was treated as a dependent variable, or in column 2 if the variable was used as an independent variable.

By combining the information shown in Table 11.1 with information provided in Chapter 1 on construct measurement and sample location, readers can trace any particular variable from definition to empirical findings. For example, readers with special interest in the personal trait of Expressivity will find its operational definition in Panel B of Table 1.8 in Chapter 1, and will learn that the measure was used in all three surveys in the study (from Panel B of Table 1.9). Panel E of Table 11.1 permits easy location of the major tables and figures that included the Expressivity measure, i.e., the determinants of Expressivity (in column 1) in Table 7.8 in Chapter 7, and the 11 figures and tables in which Expressivity was used as an independent variable in an analysis of some dimension of the parent–child relationship (in column 2).

Parent–Child Relations in the Larger Kindred Context

Comparative analysis is an essential tool in social science inquiry. Two comparisons helped to highlight the specific nature of the parent–child relationship: the position of this relationship in the broader context of the total life course in comparison with other direct-line kin, and the ways in which obligations toward parents and children differ from obligations to other kin.

Our findings on the extent of multigenerational lineages and change in lineage composition over the life course provided a corrective to the

Table 11.1. Tabular Sources of Findings on Major Variables in the Study [a]

Variable	(1) As Dependent Variable [b]	(2) As Independent Variable
A. Current Parent–Child Relationship (G1–G2 or G2–G3 Dyads)		
Affective Closeness	1.4, 1.7, 6.1–6.4, 7.10–7.13, 7.23, 7.24, F6.1, F7.1–F7.5	8.5–8.8, 9.18, 9.19, 9.21, 9.22, F6.1, F7.4
Help Exchange	1.4, 1.7, 6.1–6.14, 7.13, 9.1–9.22, F6.1, F9.1–F9.13	F6.1
Interaction	1.4, 1.7, 6.1–6.4, 7.13, 8.3–8.8, 9.20, F6.1	9.18, 9.19, 9.21, 9.22, F6.1
Normative Obligations (Parent and Child)	4.1–4.11, 4.15–4.18, 5.1–5.5, 5.11–5.15, F4.1, F4.2	4.5, 4.12–4.14, 4.18, 5.6, 5.7, 8.5, 9.18, 9.19, 10.6, 10.8
Value Consensus	1.4, 1.7, 6.1–6.4, 7.7, 7.11, F6.1	7.10–7.12, 8.5, 8.7, 8.8, 9.18, 9.19, 9.21, 9.22
B. Family of Origin		
Affection (Maternal or Paternal)	1.5, 1.7	5.10, 5.11, 5.15, 7.2, 7.4, 7.6, 7.8–7.12, F6.1, F7.4
Affective Closeness (At 10, 16, 25 years)	1.7, 7.5, F3.4, F6.1	7.6, 7.10–7.12, F6.1, F7.4
Authority (Maternal or Paternal)	1.5, 1.7	7.2, 7.4, 7.5, 7.8–7.12, F7.4
Cohesion	1.5, 1.7, 7.4, 7.13, F7.4	5.10, 5.11, 5.15, 7.5, 7.10–7.12, 9.18, 9.19, 9.21, 9.22
Family Size	3.9	7.1, 7.2, 7.4, 7.5, 7.6, 8.5, 8.6, 8.9, 9.18, 9.19, 9.21, 9.22, F6.1, F7.4
Financial Well-being	1.5, 7.1, F7.4	7.4, 7.5, F7.4
Gender Role Socialization (Skill Transmission)	1.5, 3.7, 7.19, F3.5, F3.6	7.6, 7.8, 7.9, 7.18
Intact Family	3.3	5.10, 5.15, 7.3, 7.4, 7.6, F6.1, F7.4
Parents' Education		7.1, 7.2, 7.4–7.9, F6.1, F7.4
Parents' Marital Happiness	1.5, 7.2, 7.15, F7.4	7.4, 7.8
Qualities Important in Childrearing	1.5, 3.6	
Religious Affiliation		7.6, 7.7, 7.11, 7.12
Religious Intermarriage	3.10	7.14
Troubles	1.5, 3.4, 3.5, F7.4	5.11, 5.15, 7.1, 7.4, 7.5, 7.7, 7.10–7.12, 9.18, 9.19, 9.21, 9.22, F7.4

Table 11.1. (continued)

Variable	(1) As Dependent Variable [b]	(2) As Independent Variable
C. Family of Procreation		
Affective Closeness (10, 16 years)		7.2
Affection		7.3, 7.16
Authority		7.2, 7.3, 7.16
Cohesion	7.3, 7.16	
Family Size	3.9	2.5, 5.14, 7.3, 7.8–7.12, 7.20, 7.21, 8.5, 8.6, 8.9, 9.18–9.22, 10.6, 10.8, 10.9
Gender Role Socialization	3.7, 7.17–7.19	7.16
Marital Happiness	7.2, 7.15	7.3, 7.23, 7.25, 7.26, F7.5
Qualities Important in Childrearing	3.6	7.16
Troubles	3.5	7.3, 7.16
D. Social–Demographic Characteristics		
Educational Attainment	1.8, 3.11, 7.6, F6.1	3.12, 5.7–5.9, 5.11–5.15, 7.2, 7.6–7.9, 7.16–7.18, 7.20, 7.21, 9.21, 10.6, 10.8, 10.9, F3.11, F3.12, F6.1
Employment Status	1.2, 1.3, 1.8	2.3, 2.5, 8.5–8.8, 9.18– 9.21
Income	1.8, 3.11, 3.12, F3.9, F3.11, F3.12	2.3, 5.14, 5.15, 7.8, 7.9, 9.14–9.17, 9.21, 9.22, 10.6, 10.8, 10.9, F9.10– F9.13
Lineage Composition	3.13, 3.14, 3.15, F3.13	
Marital Status	1.2, 1.3, 3.9, F3.7	2.3, 2.5, 5.12, 5.14, 5.15, 8.5, 10.2, 10.4–10.6, 10.8, F2.8–F2.10, F2.13, F3.10, F10.2, F10.3
Race/Ethnicity	1.2, 1.8	5.13, 5.15
Religious Affiliation	1.2, 1.8	5.15, 7.11, 7.12, 7.17, 7.18
Religiosity	1.8	7.20, 7.21, 10.9
Religious Intermarriage	3.10, 7.14	
E. Personal/Attitudinal Characteristics		
Attitudes: Contemporary Issues	1.8, 7.20, 7.21, 7.22	7.7

Table 11.1. (continued)

Variable	(1) As Dependent Variable [b]	(2) As Independent Variable
Best/Worst Years	1.6, 1.8, 2.5, F2.12, F2.13	
Dominance	1.6, 1.8, 2.1, 2.4, 2.5, 7.8, F2.1, F2.2	7.10, 7.11, 7.12, 7.16– 7.18, 9.18, 9.19, 9.21
Drive	1.6, 1.8, 2.1, 2.4, F2.1, F2.2, F2.4–F2.6	2.3, 2.5, 9.18, 9.19, 9.21
Drive Reduction	1.6, 1.8, F2.3–F2.6	
Expressivity	1.6, 1.8, 2.1, 7.9, F2.1, F2.2, F6.1	5.14, 5.15, 7.10–7.12, 7.16, 7.17, 9.18, 9.19, 9.21, F6.1
Health	1.6, 1.8, 2.2, F2.12	2.1, 2.3–2.5, 7.10–7.12, 8.6–8.8, 9.18, 9.19, 9.21
Kin Embeddedness	1.6, 1.8, F2.8	2.3, 10.6, 10.8, 10.9
Kin Salience	1.6, 1.8, 4.16	5.10, 5.11, 5.15
Positive/Negative Affect	1.6, 1.8, 2.3, F2.7, F2.9, F2.10	2.1

[a] Reference is to tables, unless numbers are preceded by an F (figures). There are no entries for Age or Gender because these variables are present in almost all tables or figures.
[b] Also included in this category are marginal distributions of the variables or construct measurement.

widespread assumption that increased longevity in recent decades in western societies has had the effect of greatly increasing the prevalence of lineages of four and even five or more generations. At no point in the life course did we find more than a fraction of 1% of our respondents to be members of five or more generation lineages. The *modal* generational depth at any decade of the life course was *three generations*; fewer than one in four adults at any point in the life course belonged to *four* generation lineages.

With an average of 28 years between the generations, adults on the average would be 84 years of age when they could celebrate the birth of a fourth generation greatgrandchild, and this remains an uncommon event. More typically, births in one generation are accompanied by deaths in the alternate ascendant generation. Thus, the transition from their 20s to their 30s is associated with a doubling in the proportion with at least one child (from 28 to 68%), together with a sharp drop in the proportion with at least one living grandparent (from 62 to 27%). The transition from adults' 40s to their 50s involves a similar exchange of lineage members, with a decline in the proportion with even one living parent from 71 to 38%, and a dramatic increase in the proportion with at least one grandchild (from 16 to 51%).

In a larger historical framework, what is more significant as a modal profile of American families is the fact that the majority of adults between 30 and 50 have both a living parent and at least one child of their own. Under 30 years of age, the modal three-generation lineage consists of ego, parents, and grandparents; and over 50 years of age, ego moves into the oldest generational position, and the modal lineage therefore consists of ego, children, and grandchildren. Less than 20% of adults under 40 years of age belong to lineages of four or more generations. Indeed, there is almost as large a proportion of older adults over 70 years of age who have *no* direct line kin at all (19%), reflecting the high childless rate for their cohort.

Consequently, the great gift of increased longevity in terms of intergenerational relationships is not the prevalence of multigenerational lineages of great depth but the fact that the parent–child relationship persists for 50 years or more, and for more than half of those years the child is also a parent.

Our analysis of normative obligations to a wide array of kin also helped to highlight the very special quality of the parent–child relationship. Average obligation ratings are equally high toward both parents and adult children (8.3 on a 10-point scale), and relatively impervious to qualifications that matter in obligations to other types of kin: Neither gender, nor marital status, nor the nature of the crisis or celebratory circumstance showed any significant effect on the obligations respondents reported toward parents or toward children. By contrast, less closely related kin showed significant variation in the degree to which they were obligating as a function of these qualifying characteristics, with greater obligation shown to women and unmarried members of a kin type than to men and married members of a kin type. Although consanguineal kin generally evoked much greater obligation than affinal kin, the special nature of the parent–child relationship was also shown by the relatively high obligation ratings evoked by stepparents and stepchildren, suggesting it is the *position* of parent or child that was of major salience to our respondents, overriding the fact that these are affinal kin.

The normative obligation component of the study also emphasized the special significance of gender in kinship structure: Kin related to ego through women as connecting links evoked higher obligations than kin related through men, and women respondents showed higher obligations to secondary and distant kin than did men. Women also showed significantly greater obligations to descendent kin than to ascendant kin (e.g., more obligation to children than to parents, to grandchildren than to grandparents), whereas men showed less contrast in obligation level to descendent compared to ascendant kin. We also showed that to a large extent, this gender difference operates through the intermediary of gender-linked personal traits: It was Expressivity rather than gender per se that contributed significantly to an increment in felt obligations to kin as well as to nonkin such as friends and neighbors. High expressive adults of either sex feel greater obligations to help others than do adults low on Expressivity.

Perhaps the most striking finding in the kinship norm analysis was the systematic patterning of the normative structure: What mattered most for obligation level was not a specific *type* of kinperson, but the degree of relatedness of ego to the various kintypes. Grandparents, grandchildren, and siblings—all related to ego through *one* connecting link—evoked comparable levels of felt obligation (between 6 and 7 on the 10-point scale); aunts and uncles, nieces and nephews—related to ego through *two* connecting links—showed similar levels of obligation (between 4 and 5 on the scale); while the lowest obligation level was to cousins—related through a minimum of *three* connecting links (a mean of 3.2 on the scale).

Influence of Early Family Characteristics

In almost every analysis topic pursued in the course of the research, we found significant persistence effects of a variety of characteristics of the early family of origin on subsequent sentiment and behavior of adults in their current relationships to children, parents, or spouses. We were particularly impressed by such findings when the data concerning the early family were obtained from the parents and the current characteristics from the adult child, i.e., independent reports from G1 parents and G2 adult children, or from G2 parents and G3 adult children.

Cross-generational transmission was also apparent in the analysis, i.e., the replication in the family of procreation of characteristics of the family of origin. For example, we found that marital happiness of G1 parents was significantly related to the marital happiness of G2 adult children, and the same cross-generational pattern was shown between marital happiness of the G2 generation and that of the G3 children who had married. Frequency of religious intermarriage between G1 parents was also significantly related to intermarriage in the G2 generation.

When pressed back even further in time to the qualities G1 parents brought to their marriages, we reported a number of consequences of parental affection for the quality of relationships in the family of origin and characteristics of the G2 children as adults. Parental Affection and Family Cohesion translate into warm and cooperative, intact families of origin headed by happily married parents, and, years later, the adult children from such families tend to be high on Expressivity, happily married, with cohesive families of their own. The latter finding was especially true for women: Women who had close relations with openly affectionate mothers who established cooperative routines in the family, upheld high standards for children's behavior, and taught their daughters a variety of skills, tended to have similar households and families as adult married women. This was not nearly so strongly the case for men, in large measure because the tone of family life, and routines and standards established to run cooperative households, is more a function of the responsibilities traditionally carried by women than by men. This is why, incidentally, many older parents find the households established by their daughters to be more familiar than those established by their sons (whose wives set the tone, routines, cuisine, and so forth).

We were in fact surprised to find that even in so highly structured a domain as kinship normative obligations, we could demonstrate several significant effects of early family experiences: Those who grew up with affectionate parents, in cohesive, intact families, and who had particularly good relationships with relatives they loved or admired, tend to internalize high levels of commitment to civic duties and to higher levels of felt obligation to a variety of kin, and even to nonkin.

Few Americans acquire skills for parenting or learn how to run a household through formal education. This private aspect of life is therefore more subject to the influence of parents, who stand as models for parenting, and who provide training in skills useful to the management of a household. We found significant transmission from one generation of parents to the next, of the qualities adults considered important in rearing children, and in the array of skills they taught their children.

Several findings suggest both interesting antecedents and consequences of divorce in one generation for relations in the next generation. Marital unhappiness may or may not result in divorce, but most divorces are preceded by marital tension and distress. What showed clearly in our data was that marital unhappiness of the parents involves a realignment of the intimate bonds in a family, with sons and daughters far more apt to remain close to an unhappily married mother than to the unhappy father. These coalitions also extend to the grandparent–grandchild relationship, for we found lower ratings of intimacy of grandchildren with their paternal grandparents than with their maternal grandparents if their parents' marriage was not a happy one. It seems likely that unhappily married women share their marital problems with their parents to a greater extent than do men, and this may be coupled with some disengagement from or cooling out of women's relationship with their husbands' parents (children's paternal grandparents) as marital tension increased. Hence, even before a divorce occurs and children see less of their fathers and fathers' kin, a realignment of affect and behavior may have taken place, such that divorce has a less disruptive and dramatic impact on intergenerational ties of children than postdivorce studies tend to assume.

There were also hints in our data of kinship-related predispositions to divorce. The analysis of variation in kin obligations showed that adults who had been divorced had lower levels of obligation to all types of kin, and indeed toward nonkin as well. In particular, divorced men showed lower obligations to children, and divorced women showed lower obligations to parents. To some degree the nature of parental custody is implicated here; because child custody is overwhelmingly held by women, sole responsibility for children may crowd out strong obligations to parents. So too a divorced father who carries little financial or daily responsibility for rearing children may feel less obligation toward children.

But the fact that divorced men and women report lower obligation to *all* types of kin and nonkin suggests there may also be some preselection involved, such that those who divorce were less embedded in their kindred, less sensitive to the problems of other people, and more focused on their own personal needs and gratifications before divorce was even considered. The further finding that divorced adults were far less likely to have written wills than married adults strikes us as consistent with preselection along these lines, because drawing up a will is itself a manifestation of concern for the welfare of others and personal responsibility for others.

Not all transmission and influence between the generations is one-directional, from the older to the younger generation. The analysis of intergenerational influence on attitudes toward contemporary issues, reported in Chapter 7, showed as much influence of children on parents' attitudes as parental influence on children. What was also clear, however, is that the two-way influence pattern is more typical of the mother–adult child relation than of the father–adult child relation, at least in the more private domain of life tapped by our attitude scales (contraceptive access for teenagers, and abortion rights).

Family Size

One of the more interesting structural variables in the analysis was the sheer size of the family. Status attainment research has long reported that large families depress educational attainment and subsequent occupational status of the children (Blau & Duncan, 1967; Sewell & Hauser, 1975; Featherman, 1981). In our data set we reported that large sized families of origin depressed the adequacy of family financial well-being, which in turn restricted how far children went in their schooling.

We also found that large family size was related to lower parental investment, i.e., that parents with a number of children provided less training to individual children in the skill areas we measured than parents with few children. This is a hint of an additional factor that depresses the educational attainment of the individual child: less parental input and training means less drawing in of the child into the adult world and its pragmatic concern for managing the domestic economy, and less cognitive stretching of the child to understand the concerns of adults, including, no doubt, the nature of work and the demands of specific jobs held by the adults in the family. By implication, single parent-headed households, particularly when there are a number of children involved, will show even less parental investment of time and energy per child than two-parent households.

But the effects of growing up in a small vs. a large family do not end with the adult independence of the child. We also reported that parents with a number of adult children report less frequent social interaction and less extensive help to each of their adult children (although the total investment of time and effort across all children may be larger for parents who reared many as opposed to few children). If the adult child in turn has a large family, the flow of help to the older generation is similarly reduced compared to those with small families. In an analysis not reported in this book, when attention is narrowed to younger respondents who were currently rearing children (married respondents under 45 years of age who had at least one child), we found that large family size was related to less happy parental marriages for both men and women, and, for women, this was particularly the case if the average interval between births was very small.

There is an implicit contrast between the effect of family size when viewed from the perspective of the parent compared to the child. A number of pregnancies closely timed is difficult for the mother, presses on the financial resources of the family, places a strain on the parental marriage, and the parents invest less time and energy in each child. The result may be lowered educational attainment of the children who grew up in large families. But growing up in a large family may be experienced more positively by children. Indeed the retrospective assessment by children from large families in our study is that their families of origin were *more* cohesive than those of adults who grew up in small families. Perhaps children from large families develop closer ties to their siblings; certainly there is more choice involved for close sibling pairs to emerge who share similar interests and tastes in a large than in a small size family. Large households also put a premium on more cooperative teamwork in sheer household maintenance. Less status attainment and less economic success on the part of the adult children from large families also increase the probability that the children will remain in the area in which they grew up. Close ties to local siblings may be an additional magnet holding such adult children in communities familiar since childhood. Years later, these less "successful" but accessible adult children will carry the greater burden in providing care for elderly parents, but this responsibility can be shared among siblings rather than falling on the shoulders of one adult child if the family was a large one to begin with.

Gender as a Salient Dimension of Intergenerational Relations

Gender of parent and child is a highly salient axis of family life and intergenerational relations. On topic after topic, we have found that ties among women were stronger, more frequent, more reciprocal, and less contingent on circumstances than those of men. Women's ties to women, as mothers, daughters, sisters, or grandmothers, provide important social and emotional connecting links among members of a family and lineage. None of the nine types of help we specified was given more often to fathers than to mothers, and both mothers and daughters report more reciprocal exchange of varied types of help to each other than fathers and sons or cross-sex parent–child dyads did.

Types of help between the generations also tend to be channeled along traditional gender lines: Fathers are more apt to give advice, money, and job leads to children than mothers are, and, similarly, sons are more apt to give such instrumental types of help to their parents, whereas mothers and daughters more often provide comfort, help with domestic matters, special gifts, and care during illnesses. Help flows also reflect the marital status and gender of parents and children. Widowed parents of both sexes give less but receive more help from children than married parents do, and children seem to provide complementary help to widowed parents: sons by giving advice, money, and help with household repairs to widowed mothers, and daughters by providing their widowed fathers with care during illness and help with domestic chores; in both cases the help is more extensive to the widowed parents that to married parents, whose spouses can contribute such gender-linked types of help.

Unattached children are the recipients of more varied help from parents than married children (just as widowed parents get more help from their children than married parents do), but unlike widowed parents, unattached children also provide more help to their parents than married children do. Interestingly, parental concern for adult children who do not have a spouse is also shown in provisions they made in the event of their death: Respondents who have never married report being beneficiaries of their parents' insurance policies and written wills more often than married respondents do.

Gender-Linked Personal Traits. The personal trait measure of Expressivity played an interesting and important role in the analysis reported in this volume. We found that Expressivity explained to a great extent why women had higher obligations toward secondary and distant kin than men did: Expressivity was more significant than gender per se. High expressivity also contributed to the explanation of why mothers were more open to influence by their children on attitudes toward contemporary issues than fathers were: If you wish to please and to be helpful to others, you must listen to them and seek out ways of accommodating differences between yourself and a significant other. This open, relational quality, more typical of women than of men, has the same effect on parent–child relations for men as for women: High Expressive men not only have more intimate relations to their parents and extend more help to them, but are in turn the recipients of more help than Low Expressive men. High expressivity in sons was of particular importance in increasing social interaction with mothers.

The analysis of the determinants of Expressivity stressed the importance of affectionate mothers who invested time and energy in rearing their children, by incorporating the children in household routines and teaching them skills in domestic chores and household management. It is now an open question whether the roots of expressivity will remain the same in the future, in view of the rapid increase in employment of women with very young children. We know little about how women's employment affects the training they give to their children nor how much children contribute to household maintenance when their mothers are employed.

To date, little attention has been paid by family researchers to the contribution of children to household maintenance. Most researchers on household labor do not even inquire about the contribution of children; they merely assume housework is performed by the parents, possibly supplemented by paid help. Indeed, in one of the few studies that investigated the contributions of children to home maintenance, parents claimed they asked for children's help in the home not because they *needed* such help but because some modest work in the home was good for "character building" (White & Brinkerhoff, 1981). As Viviana Zelizer has argued, children in western societies have become defined by their sentimental, noneconomic value, with the consequence that child work can no longer remain "real" work; it is "only justifiable as a form of education or as a sort of game" (Zelizer, 1985, p. 97). Family sociologists have not noted that teaching children skills in the domestic setting brings them into closer and more frequent exposure to their mothers' mode of thought and sentiment, nor that in the process they might develop a helping orientation toward other people rather than being focused on their own ego gratification.

What is happening to the skill training of children as mothers of ever-younger children spend their days in the workplace rather than the home is an open question. A note from their mother listing chores for children to do when they return from school is no substitute for the social exchange that takes place when children share work in the home in partnership with their mothers or fathers. Nor is a 2-minute microwave meal eaten on the run a substitute for a leisurely talk while making pasta or lingering to chat over cups of hot chocolate. Pressure to get husbands more involved in household chores and childcare does not necessarily translate into the transmission of a high valuation of service to others and the open expression of feelings, core elements of Expressivity. In another line of analysis not reported in this book, our data showed that younger men stress Status and Conformity as important values in rearing children, while younger women give more emphasis to Autonomy. If this means that proper behavior subserving status gains is the message children get from their fathers, and self-sufficiency and independence the message children get from their mothers, the direction of value change in the coming decade may not be conducive to a greater prevalence of expressivity in the younger generation. There are clearly critical issues that need to be faced by parents and by family researchers, once the linkage between child training, parental investment, and gender role socialization within the family is appreciated for the contribution they make to the personal traits children will carry with them into adulthood.

Life Course Profile of Intergenerational Ties

Viviana Zelizer (1985) ably describes the remarkable transformation that took place in the value and role of children in American families between 1870 and 1930. In rural America and early industrial urban America, children made economic contributions to the household before they were in their teens, and often became major supporters of widowed mothers before they left adolescence. In the late nineteenth century families under financial stress relied on children's employment (Haines, 1985), whereas in the late twentieth century wives now replace children in supplementing family income. Zelizer traces the wrenching institutional changes that took place as children became economically "useless" but socially "priceless." In the decades since 1930, parents have supported their children for an increasing number of years, often extending well into the child's 20s, as skilled technical and professional training became the route to adult economic independence and security.

In the 1980s, we also witnessed a great polarization in the timing of marriage and of births. Among the poor urban population, births to unmarried teenagers have risen sharply in recent years, while among better educated families, sons and daughters often marry only in their late 20s and produce first grandchildren in their mid-30s. But parental support and help flows to children do not end with marriage and independent residence. As we have seen, there is a good deal of help exchange between the generations during the early adult years, particularly when the income level of the children is low and that of the parents relatively high.

As adult children become established in work and family responsibility, parental help declines, whereas the children's help to parents continues at about the same level. As parents enter old age, there is an upturn of help to parents, from daughters when their mothers are in their mid-60s, from sons somewhat later, when parents are in their mid-70s. Of very special interest is the fact that the help pattern tends to be reciprocal in nature for two or more decades, when children are in their mid-20s to mid-40s and parents in their mid-40s to mid-60s. It is only very late in the lives of the parents that complementarity replaces reciprocity in the help exchange between the generations. Full circle is reached only very late in the lives of parents, when personal caregiving is often required, though rarely at the level of total dependency that marked the caregiving all parents give to very young children.

What is remarkable is the further finding that intimacy between parents and adult children actually increases over the adult years, whether the quality of the relationship is rated by parents or by their children. At all points along the life course the mother–daughter relationship is a closer one than the father-son relationship. We also noted that the father–son relationship is more responsive to current characteristics of the son and the earlier quality of the relationship between the two men than is the case for other parent–child dyads. For example, stress during the sons' adolescent years continues to show a negative effect on the intimacy of the father–son relationship years later, whereas adult daughters' relationship to their parents is less affected by events during adolescence.

Furthermore, men's relationship to each other is more affected by status and value differences between them, perhaps because what men discuss with each other carries the mark of their nonfamilial activities at work and in the community to a greater extent than the interaction between women in the family does. This contrast between male and female relationships may also help explain why a son's becoming a father himself not only shows an increment in the young father's Expressivity, but in the Affective Closeness between the older father and his son. Whatever the differences in education, jobs, and politics between the two men, the birth of a grandchild provides a new common ground of family concern and pride they can share.

There is, all told, a steadier beat to the quality of the relationships between women in the family than between men or cross-sex pairs. At numerous points in our analysis, there was a far more precarious quality to men's ties to family members than women's: Men who married outside their faith or at very young ages were less happily married than women who intermarried or married when they were less than 20 years of age. We believe children of an intermarriage, more likely to be reared in the faith of their mothers, had a special shared connection with their mothers that excluded their fathers. Marital tension within intact marriages also showed no impact on intimacy of children with their mothers, but was related to stress in the relationship with their fathers and paternal grandparents. At younger ages than we could study, other research suggest more negative impact of divorce on sons than on daughters (Hetherington & Arasteh, 1988).

Strain in the relationship with parents during adolescence, particularly if children engaged in socially deviant behavior, showed trace effects in the affective closeness of the relationship years later: Troublesome behavior that depressed the intimacy in the relationship between fathers and sons had a continuing depressant effect on intimacy when the sons were mature adults, a pattern that was not shown in the other three parent–child dyads. In addition, differences in education, income, or general outlook on life were associated with less frequent social interaction and less help exchange between sons and their parents, but these difference measures had little or no effect on the ties between daughters and their parents. The cumulative effect of such gender differences was seen in almost all regression equations, with higher R^2 value$_{\smile}$ in equations dealing with men's relationship to parents or children than in equations dealing with women's relationship to parents or children, emphasizing in a dramatic way the more contingent quality of men's ties to the family than women's. Margaret Mead long ago caught this gender contrast in family roles in lectures at Columbia University when we were graduate students, by defining fathers as the "children's mother's spouse," effectively demoting the father from a primary to a secondary kin type!

To what extent findings such as ours are historically bound cannot be determined with any confidence. If long-term social trends in the direction of secularism and individualism are reflected in intergenerational relations and obligations, we would have expected young adults in 1985 to report lower levels of obligation to kin than older adults did. But, as we have seen, our results show a strong and opposite effect: Younger adults report higher levels of obligations to a wide array of kin than older adults do. In the absence of any prior research on kin normative obligations of the kind we have studied, we cannot tell whether today's young adults feel less obligated to kin than young adults did in the past. But it is possible that here too, the opposite would be found, i.e., that precisely because parental support now extends over so many more years of child dependency than in the past, today's "priceless" children take leave of the parental home with a higher level of felt obligations to parents than was the case in earlier periods of our history when children pulled their weight by contributing to family income at very tender ages. In sum, it is possible that today's better educated children discharge obligations to their parents in the years after they leave home, whereas in the past, children built up less obligation and discharged it while they were young and shared their parents' homes.

But any conclusive evidence awaits the passage of time and future research that builds on and extends our findings. What the directions of such future research can and ought to be, based on our experience and findings, is the question to which we now turn.

Suggestions for Future Research on Intergenerational Relations

In preparing to write this final section of the book, we reviewed all the early memoranda and drafts of instruments, to refresh our memory of the rationale for numerous decisions made during the first year of the project. Overall, and in view of the data analysis and writing that intervened, most of those earlier decisions seem in retrospect to have been good ones. But inevitably there are also several regrets, many of which imply directions that ought to be taken in future research that builds on our results. We turn now to a discussion of these issues.

Sampling

Our original expectation was that we would obtain a main sample of 1600 respondents and spinoff samples of 450 to 500 parents and a similar number of adult children. But the fielding of the main survey took longer and was more expensive than anticipated, largely because of the difficulty of maintaining an experienced team of interviewers during a time of high employment in the Boston area, and the large number of call-backs necessary to find respondents at home. This is now endemic to field surveys because of the high employment rate of married women. The direct impact on the study design, however, was the necessity to cut back on the size of the spinoff samples. Rather than 900 to 1000 parents and adult children, we had to be satisfied with 600 (323 parents and 278 adult children), to stay within our budgetary limits. But to sustain an analysis that called for a specification of the four parent–child dyads left fewer than 100 cases in several dyads. Although this was sufficient when using central tendency statistics, the base *N*s were much too small to sustain more rigorous multivariate analysis.

It also meant that we used a great deal of time in the main sample interviews obtaining names, addresses, and telephone numbers for all the parents and all the adult children of our G2 respondents, but in the telephone spinoff samples, we contacted only a small proportion of them (22% of the parents and 26% of the adult children). In retrospect, it would have been wiser and more efficient to have worked out a randomized selection procedure in advance of the personal interviews with the main sample. Since the interview forms listed all respondents' children by order of birth, it would have been a simple matter to develop procedures for the selection of one child per respondent for whom access information was requested. Such a procedure would have cut down the interviewing time for the main survey, and permitted the larger sized spinoff samples we had hoped for.

Because most of our measures were specifically designed for this study and national samples are at least four times more expensive than local samples of a comparable size, we have no regrets that we opted for a sample of the Boston metropolitan area. We are now in a far better position to design instruments for use in a more expensive national survey. This is particularly the case for the study of kinship obligations, for reasons to be discussed below.

Our biggest disappointment flowed from an erroneous assumption concerning lineage composition. In the absence of any prior survey that inquired about the prevalence of direct line kin in the ascendant and descendant generations from ego, we had assumed our sample would include several hundred people with both a living parent and an adult child. Based on that assumption, we expected to obtain spinoff cases of parents and living children of the same respondents, so that we would have a significant number of three-generation lineage cases. This was an ill-informed and naive expectation, as we now know from the analysis summarized above and detailed in Chapter 3. Were we to seek such three-generation lineages in view of our current knowledge, we would do so in a snowball fashion: i.e., to begin with a random sample of adults, gain access to and interview a living parent, and, if that parent's parent was still alive, gain access to and interview that person. The same two-step procedure could be followed for the two descendant generations of older respondents in the original sample, first with an interview with a child, and then with a child of that child. This procedure would still rely on proximate generations who are most likely to have the access information one needed, and most likely to cooperate in making a referral to the parent or child in question.

Even assuming one could develop a sizable set of three-generation lineages, it is no easy task to analyze such data. Even in a basically dyadic analysis, we found it difficult to keep in mind *which* dyad and from *which* partner the data we were analyzing came from. A three-generation lineage sample would provide *three* perspectives on the relationships involved. If a great number of relationship dimensions are covered and there is variance among them by these three perspectives, the data analysis becomes quite complex. Not having sufficient cases of G1, G2, and G3 respondents from the *same* lineages, our analysis was limited to using measures from two generations concerning three family relationships. A good example is in Chapter 7, where we analyzed grandchild–grandparent Affective Closeness (as rated by the G3 grandchildren) as a function of marital discord in the parental marriage (as rated by G2 parents). Perhaps it is the complexity of the data sets and data analysis that explains why there are no full-scale research monographs as yet from any of the major three-generation studies that have been under way in the United States.

We considered, but had to abandon, any effort to obtain information from or about the siblings of respondents in the main sample, and although we obtained identical information about each child of the respondents, no effort was made to include more than one child from the same family in the G3 spinoff sample. Nor did we seek to interview any spouses of our respondents. Consequently, although we had data about respondent's relationship to each of their parents, the sample of parents did not contain both parents of any respondents, and parents reported only on their relationship to our main sample respondents, not any other of their children. As a result, our comparisons of mothers with fathers, or sons with daughters, were necessarily of parents and children from different families rather than the same families. It would be desirable for some future research to conduct an intensive analysis of help exchange between the generations with detailed data on the help given and received between each parent and each adult child in a sample of families.

Parents-in-Law

In retrospect, we also think it was an error to limit, as severely as we did, information on the relationship between respondents and their parents-in-law. Just as it is difficult to gauge the total amount of help parents receive if you know only the extent of help between a parent and one child rather than all children, so too it is difficult to assess variation in help flows to parents without knowing what competing needs are being met in flows of help exchanged with spouses' parents (ego's in-laws). But our analysis of in-law relationships (both parents-in-law and children-in-law) was restricted to the one dimension of inter-generational solidarity, Affective Closeness.

There is an additional rationale for emphasizing the importance of having data on parents-in-law as well as parents. There has been much concern in social gerontology for the problems of the middle-generation child, particularly the daughter, if she is coping with the personal caregiving needs of an elderly parent while still rearing her own children (e.g., Norris, 1988). But the demographics of generational timing suggests this may be less widespread than is generally assumed. Help by a child to an elderly parent is most needed when the parent is widowed and that is increasingly a characteristic of those well into their 70s. This means the daughter is likely to be in her 50s, and very few women that age still have very young children; most are in their 20s and 30s, not teenagers.

Far more prevalent than coping simultaneously with help to elderly parents and children among middle-aged couples may be coping with crises in the lives of both sets of parents (wife's parents and husband's parents), or the widowed mothers of both the wife and the husband, or an elderly widowed mother while a husband undergoes unusually early traumatic illness. One woman of our acquaintance was deeply conflicted because she could not provide the assistance she wished surrounding her daughter's pregnancy and birth because of her husband's heart attack and the necessity to provide personal caregiving to her widowed mother-in-law. The mother-in-law was particularly dependent on her daughter-in-law for such help because she had only sons and no daughters.

A study design based on a selected sample of middle-aged couples is suggested by these observations, obtaining data from both husband and wife concerning the various dimensions of their relationship to each of their living parents and parents-in-law. If preliminary analysis identified cases of multiple problems requiring the investment of time, money, and personal caregiving to both a parent and a parent-in-law, a parent and a spouse, or a parent and a child, follow-up interviews could then be conducted to pursue, in depth, the impact of the role-bind these situations may impose on the middle generation and the strategies they use to deal with conflicting obligations.

Household Division of Labor

One last regret is that we did not obtain measures on how married respondents managed their households, in particular the extent to which there was sharing of responsibility, the extent of task allocation by gender, and time devoted to major family tasks by husband, wife, and children old enough to contribute significant assistance. This would have added a missing dimension to the analysis of skill transmission from parent to child because it would have given some behavioral content to the actual models parents displayed to their children. Extrapolating from the findings on long-term effects of skill training of children, it would be of special importance to build in measures of children's actual contribution to household management in terms of the types of tasks involved, the amount of time children contribute to household maintenance, and the extent to which such help involves shared participation with a parent or delegation of tasks fulfilled by the child alone.

Contemporary Attitudes

Our motivation in designing the attitude items on contemporary issues (contraception, abortion, women's rights, and religious instruction in the schools) was to locate our respondents in their time (1984–1985) and place (metropolitan Boston) by measuring where they stood on currently controversial moral, ethical, and political issues. We anticipated generational differences on such issues, and wished to explore something of the intergenerational dynamics of agreement or disagreement on such issues between parents and adult children. It was not part of our original intention to use these data for an analysis of intergenerational influence. Had this problem been at the center of our attention at the design stage, we would not have dropped from the pretest draft of the survey questionnaire a range of other issues it contained (attitudes toward racial integration of the public schools, maternal employment and its impact on children, civil rights, environmental problems). This was an unfortunate decision, for the reason that the analysis of intergenerational influence could not definitively conclude that mothers but not fathers were involved in the two-way influence process, because our indices all referred to personal topics that may be discussed far more often with mothers than with fathers. It is quite possible that on issues concerning race, the environment, or politics, significant intergenerational influences occur between fathers and adult children. But this remains only a possibility for some future research inquiry, not something we could confirm empirically in this study.

Kinship Normative Obligations

The factorial survey method had never been applied to the study of kinship obligation, and, in retrospect, we think our decisions concerning the dimensions built into the design of the vignettes were wise ones.

We assumed gender and marital status would be important qualifiers of kin obligations in the vignettes, just as we expected them to be important qualifiers on the major dimensions of solidarity between parents and adult children in the analysis based on the interview data. We expected, but did not find, much variation in obligations as a function of type of crisis or celebration or the duration of the crises. But one needed to explore these possibilities to demonstrate such results. Now that the vignette data have been analyzed, our suggestions center on next steps for future research on normative obligations. There are three specific suggestions we would urge from this perspective, as follows.

Reverse the Direction of Obligation.   One of the striking results of the norm analysis was the finding that obligation levels were significantly lower among older adults than younger adults. This finding is consistent with an overall life course interpretation, to the effect that young people bring to their transition to adulthood an accumulation of "indebtedness" to the kin who surrounded them during their dependent years, which is discharged in the course of adulthood. A logical next step would be to reverse the direction of obligation, and to investigate the degree of obligation adults feel is owed to them by various types of kin and of nonkin. It does not automatically follow that because obligation to others declines with age, that obligations to ego increase with age. The elderly may feel they have fulfilled their obligations to others, and the torch of obligation passes to the next generation, not that others are now indebted to them. It may also be the case that the elderly feel their own children have obligations to them, but other types of kin do not.

Expansion of Kintypes.   Just as we regret not having obtained more information in the survey instruments on parents-in-law and siblings, so too we think the array of kintypes should be expanded in any future study of kin obligations. In particular, more affinal kin should be investigated. This includes an array of siblings-in-law (spouses of ego's siblings, siblings of ego's spouse, and spouses of ego's spouse's siblings); spouses of grandchildren; and, to test the limits of the obligatory kindred structure, such figures as the parents of a child's spouse, who are normally not defined as kin (Schneider, 1980). In view of the relatively high obligation level to stepparents and stepchildren, we would also include full, half, and stepsiblings, together with children and grandchildren born out of wedlock.

We noted in Chapter 4 that we did not include spouses because we thought respondents would consider it foolish in the extreme to be asked how obligated they would feel to provide emotional or financial aid to a spouse who lost a job, or had undergone surgery. But we need to confirm this empirically rather than to simply assume that the marital bond involves the highest obligations of all. Nor should it be assumed that all respondents would give a top rating of "10" where a husband or wife was involved; those who never married, who are divorced, or who are living through a very unhappy marriage might, in fact, vary markedly in the level of obligation they feel is due to a spouse.

Our next suggestion is of particular relevance to the inclusion of spouses in any future research on normative obligations.

Enlargement of the Obligating Circumstances. It would be unwise to assume that because we found little variation in obligation level by the crisis and celebratory circumstances built into the design, that the life situations that stimulate obligations do not need further investigation. A logical next step would be to enlarge these circumstances to embrace quite different circumstances, in particular those that pose some ethical and legal conflict. How obligated would adults feel to help a kinperson who had a gambling debt to pay back? someone who had just returned from serving a prison sentence? who was fired from a job because of sexual harassment of a co-worker? And what of a kinperson who was a serious alcoholic, a drug addict, or a manic-depressive?

Running through these examples is the concept of individual culpability and the analytic question of how closely related a kinperson has to be before adults would feel obligated to help someone whose behavior was unethical or illegal rather than a victim of disease, a household fire, or a plant closedown. This is the potential vignette dimension on which, by expanding the levels involved to cover unethical or illegal triggering circumstances, one might find considerable variation in obligations to even very close kin—spouses, children, and parents.

Refinement of Construct Measurement

Our last suggestion, relevant to future research that builds on our study, concerns measurement of the constructs that were most significant in the analysis we have reported. We have often stressed the point that because of the large number of specified persons and the multidimensional measures required on intergenerational solidarity, each construct had to be operationalized in as parsimonious a fashion as possible. Although the great array of variables strengthened and enriched the multivariate analysis we conducted, it is nonetheless the case that many major constructs would benefit by improved measurement. We call attention to several that seem particularly important to refine in future research.

Help Exchange. It would be of considerable interest and importance to specify in much greater detail than we were able to do exactly how much time, money, and energy is invested in the major types of help that are exchanged between parents and children. Money flows are a natural and important focus here, and could be readily summed across all the adult children of an older parent. This would permit a next step in exploring the impact of family size on intergenerational help, providing an answer to questions such as: What is the total amount of money parents give to all their children and receive from all their children? How does this money flow vary by phase of the life course? How much is given and received per child and how does this vary by family size, controlling for total income of parent and child?

Biomedical Measures. Rather than relying on such proxy variables as our Drive measure and the one-item self-rating of general condition of Health, it would be desirable to incorporate behavioral measures of chronic illnesses and disabilities, number of days spent in bed per year, number and type of medications used, frequency of medical visits, restrictions on daily self-care and on home maintenance, health and life-style regimen, height and weight, and so forth.

Closely related to such behavioral measures and self-reports on health status is the subject of illness, and we feel it would also be useful to tap adults' reactions to the illnesses of parents, children, spouse, and self. It is our impression that adults vary significantly in their tolerance for the sights and odors of illnesses (e.g., blood, stool, urine, body odor, nudity), as well as their tolerance for senile fragility and dependency, perhaps particularly in parents who had been towers of strength to them in their childhood. These have obvious relevance to the willingness and capability of filling caregiving roles vis-à-vis elderly parents, parents-in-law, and spouses. It is often said that women have higher tolerances in these matters than men; if so, this may contribute to the far more significant role of daughters and wives in elder care than of sons and husbands.

Personal Traits. We have relied on crude measures of Expressivity and Dominance in the interpretation of inter- and intragender differences in intergenerational relations. We think it would be fruitful to explore these same personal traits in a more role-specific manner. It is quite possible that even self-ratings of such qualities would show differences between spouse, parental, and occupational roles. We all know people who are timid and shy at work but tyrants at home; women who are submissive as wives but domineering as mothers; or other women who strike us as steely and distant professionals in an office but soft and affectionate creatures at home. Our study has spoken to the active, concerned, and helpful side of women in their roles as mothers and daughters, but it is mute on the qualities of the same women as wives and workers, as it is on men as husbands and workers. It is of great importance to establish the extent to which personal traits are role specific, and what differentiates those who show the same qualities in all their major roles from those whose personal traits are highly structured by role domain and situation.

A Concluding Note

In the preface to this volume, we mentioned that the study has had a long history of gestation, going back many decades in our personal lives, a much shorter period of time in our professional lives. For Alice, the professional interest goes back to the mid-1960s and a collaboration with David Schneider on an American–English kinship study, a project that was prematurely aborted with very few publications flowing from it (A. S. Rossi, 1965, 1968; Schneider, 1980); for Peter, professional interest was vicarious (over the shoulder of his wife) for many years, and an active one only for the duration of this project.

These past 5 years have provided a wonderful experience of personal and professional collaboration, and it is with an anticipatory feeling of "separation anxiety" that we approach the last few words in the last chapter of a very long volume. We learned a lot in the course of this research, and we have tried our best to describe clearly what we have found while being true to the robust nature of a complex data set. We are hopeful that this offspring of ours will find a welcoming audience, and that we shall hear announcements before too long of a new generation of descendants.

Notes

1. No attempt was made to include every single table or figure in which a variable appeared in Table 11.1. A qualitative judgment was made, based in part on statistical significance, in part on substantive relevance of a given variable to the analysis focus of each table or figure. Age and gender do not appear in this reference table, because these major variables appear in almost all tables and figures in the book.

Sampling Design
and Fielding
Results _____ Appendix A

Sampling Design

The selection of respondents for the G2 main sample was based on an area probability sample of housing units in the Boston Standard Metropolitan Statistical Area (SMSA). Towns in the Boston SMSA were ordered in serpentine fashion, so that outer suburban towns, then inner suburban towns, then Boston City neighborhood areas with similar racial and ethnic compositions were contiguous. A list of census tracts within towns ordered in this manner was created that included estimates of the number of housing units in each census tract. Then a sample of blocks or groups of blocks was selected proportionate to size estimates based on the 1980 census. The design called for the selection of 228 clusters that were expected to average 11 housing units per cluster, based on census estimates, corrected by field listing of housing units by staff from the Center for Survey Research. The sample yielded 2537 households, which was representative of the households within the Boston SMSA within the limits of normal sampling variability.

The sampling design called for interviewing one designated adult per household. The process involved contacting a household and listing all adults living in the housing unit by their age from oldest to youngest. From this list, interviewers selected a specific adult within the household to be the respondent, following a randomized "Kish" selection table stamped in the coversheet of the interview form.

Two special modifications were made to the basic sampling design. In samples of housing units, each household has the same probability of falling into the sample, but since large households have the same probability as small households, persons living in one-person households have five times the chance of being in the sample as persons in five-person households. In Metropolitan Boston, approximately one-third of those interviewed in such a sample would reside in one-person households, while such adults constitute only 16% of the adult population. As a result, a procedure was followed to select persons in one-person households at one-half the rate of other adults in households with two or more adult members. This procedure ensured that the probability of selection of adults in one- and two-adult households would be the same.

The second modification concerned households in which there were both young unmarried adults under 25 years of age and older or married adults. In such households, the young unmarried adults were excluded from the listing of those eligible to be selected as respondents. The purpose of this was to exclude young adult children still living with their parents from being the specific designated respondents, a procedure we considered desirable because their parents were more salient to our study purposes and would provide a good deal of information about *each* of their children, not merely the young unmarried child still living at home.

Fielding: Process and Results

The basic interview schedule was pretested in the summer of 1984. Experienced interviewers conducted 50 interviews (half men, half women) from a sample of convenience in households in the greater Boston area. These data were intensively analyzed and the schedule revised to make the task of carrying out a standardized personal interview easier for both interviewers and respondents. The revision involved dropping a number of measures to shorten interview length, enlarging response categories to overcome highly skewed response distributions, and substituting items when interviewers reported difficulty in respondent comprehension.

The revised main sample questionaire was fielded between the fall of 1984 and the spring of 1985. The field operation was a difficult one, because the personal interview was lengthy, averaging an hour per respondent, though this varied greatly as a function of how many children the respondent had and whether the respondent's parents were still alive. In addition, a special feature of the design, a self-administered vignette booklet on kin obligations, was added at the conclusion of the personal interview, which respondents filled out while the interviewer answered questions concerning the rating task and checked over the personal interviews. This added an average of 15 minutes to the time spent with respondents. Another 5 to 10 minutes was added to obtain names, addresses, and phone numbers for each living parent and each adult child of the respondents. All told, then, the average interview length was an hour and a half, which interviewers felt added to the proportion who refused to be interviewed and the difficulty of arranging adequate time for the interview.

The years 1984 and 1985 were also years during which the economy of the Commonwealth of Massachusetts was on a sharp upturn. Unemployment rates were among the lowest in the nation. As shown in Chapter 1, the G2 main sample showed only a 2% unemployment rate. This made for difficulty in recruitment and retention of interviewers by the Center for Survey Research. Responses to local newspaper ads had yielded over 200 applicants in the early 1980s, but this dwindled during 1984 to fewer than 10. The result was considerable turnover of interviewing staff and a longer-than-expected number of weeks in the field. Some 51 interviewers conducted 5 or more interviews for the study, of whom 23 had experience on previous studies with the CSR, and 28 were newly recruited and trained for this project.

Toward the end of the field phase, to keep the refusal rate to a tolerably low level, a variety of special techniques was adopted: Difficult to reach respondents in several central city neighborhoods were sent letters offering a fee for interviews conducted at the Survey Center (14 interviews were obtained in this way); a shortened version of the questionaire was developed that could be conducted by telephone (49 interviews), and the number of call-backs was increased from a minimum of 6 to 10 or more calls to find respondents at home. Where the designated respondents did not speak English, interviewers translated if they could, arranged for another interviewer to do the interview, or relied on a household member who could speak English to serve as an interpretor. Despite these efforts, some 45 designated respondents could not be interviewed because of language difficulties.

The second phase of data collection involved telephone interviews with adult children or parents of the G2 respondents. When asked to provide names, addresses, and telephone numbers of their parents, 70% of the G2 respondents provided some information about their parents, but only 63% gave the detail needed to actually reach a parent by letter or phone. In the case of adult children, 79% of the G2 respondents gave some information, but again only 60% provided the addresses and telephone numbers at which we could reach them. Interviewers reported numerous comments by respondents when access to parents was refused, to the effect that a parent was very ill or convalescing, hard of hearing, understood English poorly, or was grieving in reaction to a recent death, a profile suggesting a protective stance on the part of many G2 respondents to spare their parents stress or embarrassment. In the

Table A.1.   Summary of Field Results

A. G2 Main Sample		
Total Sample of Housing Unit Addresses		2537
Nonsample		
Address not a dwelling	51	
Group quarters	1	
House vacant	108	
Noneligible one-person households [a]	364	
Total Eligible Sample		2013
Sample		
Interviews	69%	1393
Refusals	24%	480
Illness	2%	35
Language	2%	45
Not at home after repeated calls	2%	38
Other	1%	22
B. Spinoff G1 and G3 Samples		
Total Sample for which follow-up was attempted		689
Interviews	88%	603
Refusals	6%	43
Other (illness, language limits)	6%	43

[a] A systematic sample of half the households found to be occupied by only one adult was deleted from the sample. See text for detailed explanation.

telephone interviews with G1 parents, many of whom were very elderly, interviewers were careful to suggest that if the interview went on longer than the respondent wished, they would be glad to call back at some preferred time to complete the interview.

From the pool of G1 parents and G3 adult children, we selected cases for the spinoff samples following a procedure that ensured as equitable a distribution of same-sex and opposite-sex parent–child dyads as possible. In case selection, no restriction was placed on their geographic distance from Boston except that the parents and children had to reside in the continental United States or Canada.

Special letters were sent to the selected G1 parents and G3 children, alerting them to a pending telephone interview, and informing them that we had obtained their names, addresses, and telephone numbers from their parent or child, as the case may be. All letters were personally addressed, and referred to the parent or child by full name, e.g., "your daughter, Mary Smith," or "your mother, Jane Jones."

Fielding results for the three samples are shown in Table A.1. Of the 2013 persons in the total eligible G2 sample, 1393, or 69%, were personally interviewed. Refusals were 24% of the total, while in 7% of the cases, interviews could not be conducted because of illness, a language barrier, the potential respondent was not available despite 10 or more callbacks, or other miscellaneous reasons. As seen in panel B of Table A.1, a total of 689 parents and adult children were approached, and we had an excellent response to our call: 88% granted an interview, yielding spinoff samples of 323 G1 parents and 278 G3 adult children.

Respondents vs. Nonrespondents

A major advantage and unique characteristic of our design is the fact that respondents in the spinoff samples of parents and adult children can be compared with *nonrespondents* in the two generations, because we asked a wide array of questions concerning each parent and each child of the main G2 sample of respondents. Table A.2 shows the case distribution involved. Note that data on the major variables in the study were gathered *about* and *from* each child and each parent of the G2 respondents. For example, 835 respondents gave ratings of affective closeness to their mothers, and 194 of these mothers who were interviewed also rated their affective closeness to the child in our main sample. Hence, we were able to test whether there was any tendency to bias in the main spinoff sample by comparing *respondent* parents with *nonrespondent* parents on their personal characteristics and on the same measures of family relationships reported by their adult children in the G2 sample. (The comparisons involved are indicated by dashes enclosed by arrows in Table A.2.)

An analysis of the respondent parents compared to the nonrespondent parents showed a few consistent but nonproblematic differences. Respondent G1 parents were on average 2 years younger than non-

Table A.2. Case Distribution of Respondents in Three Samples and Non-respondents in G1 and G3 Generations

Generation	Number of Respondents	Number Reported by G2	Number of Respondents		Number of Non-respondents
G1 (Parents)	323	599 Living Fathers	129 Fathers	<---> [a]	470 Fathers
		835 Living Mothers	194 Mothers	<--->	641 Mothers
G2 (Main Sample Respondents)	1393		588 Men		
			805 Women		
G3 (Adult Children)	278	550 Sons	136 Sons	<--->	414 Sons
		531 Daughters	142 Daughters	<--->	389 Daughters

[a] <---> Comparison to test for selection bias.

respondent G1 parents; better educated, but with a mean difference of only 1 year of schooling; in slightly better health; seen somewhat less often, and involved in help exchange with their G2 children to a slightly lesser degree. No differences were found between the two groups of parents on affective closeness, degree to which they shared common values with their children, or level of family cohesion during their childrearing years. (The operational definitions of these constructs are given in Chapter 1.) This profile, combined with interviewer comments on some of the reasons respondents refused to give access to their parents (hearing defect, illness, language difficulty), suggests some protective stance on the part of the adult children toward their elderly parents, but no evidence that respondents refused access because the parent–child relationship was tense and strained. A comparison of respondent G3 adult children with nonrespondent G3 children also showed minimal differences, and none was health and age-related as in the case of the G1 parents.

References

Adams, B. N. (1968a). The middle class adult and his widowed or still married mother. *Social Problems, 16*, 50–59.

Adams, B. N. (1968b). *Kinship in an urban setting*. Chicago: Markham.

Adams, B. N. (1970). Isolation, function and beyond: American kinship in the 1960s. *Journal of Marriage and the Family, 32*, 575–597.

Allen, K. R. & Pickett, R. S. (1987). Forgotten streams in the family life course: Utilization of qualitative retrospective interviews in the analysis of lifelong single women's family careers. *Journal of Marriage and the Family, 49*, 517–526.

Almanac Atlas and Yearbook. (1987). Boston: Houghton Mifflin.

Alwin, D. F. (1984). Trends in parental socialization values: Detroit, 1958–1983. *American Journal of Sociology, 90*, 359–382.

Alwin, D. F. (1988). From obedience to autonomy: Changes in traits desired in children, 1924-1978. *Public Opinion Quarterly, 52*, 33–52.

Alwin, D. R. (Forthcoming). *From obedience to autonomy: Changing orientations to children in the twentieth century*.

Angres, S. (1975). *Intergenerational relations and value congruence between adults and their mothers*. Unpublished Ph.D. dissertation, University of Chicago.

Aries, P. (1978). The family and the city. In A. S. Rossi, J. Kagan, & T. K. Haraven (Eds.), *The Family*. New York: W. W. Norton.

Barranti, C. C. (1985). The grandparent/grandchild relationship: Family resources in an era of voluntary bonds. *Family Relations, 34*, 343–352.

Beckman, L. J., & Houser, B. B. (1986). The consequences of childlessness on the social-psychological well being of older women. In L. E. Troll (Ed.), *Family issues in current gerontology* (pp. 333–349). New York: Springer.

Beer, W. R. (1983). *Househusbands: Men and housework in American families*. New York: Praeger.

515

Bengtson, V. L. (1985). Diversity and symbolism in grandparental roles. In V. L. Bengtson & J. Robertson (Eds.), *Grandparenthood* (pp. 11–26). Beverly Hills, CA: Sage Publications.

Bengtson, V. L., & Black, K. D. (1973). Intergenerational relations and continuities in socialization. In P. B. Baltes & W. K. Schaie (Eds.), *Life span developmental psychology: Personality and socialization* (pp. 207–234). New York: Academic Press.

Bengtson, V. L., & Cutler, N. E. (1976). Generations and intergenerational relations: Perspectives on age groups and social change. In R. H. Binstock & E. Shanas (Eds.), *Handbook on aging and the social sciences* (pp. 130–159). New York: Van Nostrand Reinhold.

Bengtson, V. L., Mangen, D. J., & Landry, P. H. (1984). The multi-generational family: Concepts and findings. In V. Garms-Homolova, E. M. Hoerning, & D. Schaeffer (Eds.), *Intergenerational relationships* (pp. 63–79). New York: C. J. Hogrefe.

Bengtson, V. L., & Robertson, J. (Eds.), (1985). *Grandparenthood*. Beverly Hills, CA: Sage Publications.

Bengtson, V. L., Rosenthal, C. J., & Burton, L. M. (1990). Families and aging: Diversity and heterogeneity. In R. H. Binstock & L. George (Eds.), *Handbook on aging and the social sciences*. New York: Academic Press, 3rd edition.

Bengtson, V. L., & Schrader, S. S. (1982). Parent-child relations. In D. J. Mangen & W. A. Peterson, (Eds.), *Research instruments in social gerontology* (vol.2, pp. 115–128). Minneapolis, MN: University of Minnesota Press.

Bengtson, V. L., & Troll, L. (1978). Youth and their parents: Feedback and intergenerational influences in socialization. In R. M. Lerner & G. B. Spanier, (Eds.), *Child influences on marital and family interaction: A life-span perspective* (pp. 215–240). New York: Academic Press.

Benson-von der Ohe, E. (1987). *First and second marriages*. New York: Praeger.

Berk, R. & Berk, S. F. (1979). *Labor and leisure at home*. Beverly Hills, CA: Sage Publications.

Berk, S. F. (1980). *Women and household labor*. Beverly Hills, CA: Sage Publications.

Bernard, J. (1972). *The future of marriage*. New Haven, CT: Yale University Press.

Bernheim, B. D., Shleifer, A., & Summers, L. H. (1985). The strategic bequest motive. *Journal of Political Economy, 93*, 1045–1076.

Blake, J. (1987). Differential parental investment: Its effects on child quality and status attainment. In J. Lancaster, J. Altmann, A. S. Rossi, & L. Sherrod (Eds.), *Parenting across the life span: Biosocial dimensions* (pp. 361–376). New York: Aldine de Gruyter.

Blake, J. (1989). *Family size and achievement*. Berkeley, CA: University of California Press.

Blake, J., & Davis, K. (1964). Norms, values and sanctions. In R. E. L. Faris (Ed.), *Handbook of sociology*. Chicago, IL: Rand McNally.

Blau, P., & Duncan, O. D. (1967). *The American occupational structure*. New York: John Wiley.

Blinder, A. S., Gordon, R. H., & Wise, D. E. (1983). Social security, bequests and the life cycle theory of saving: Cross-sectional tests. In F. Modigliani & R. Hemming (Eds.), *The determinants of national saving and wealth* (pp. 89–122), New York: St. Martin's Press.

Bradburn, N. M. (1969). *Structure of psychological well-being*. Chicago, IL: Aldine.

Brim, O. G. Jr. (1968). Adult socialization. In J. Clausen (Ed.), *Socialization and society*. Boston, MA: Little, Brown.

Brim, O. G. Jr., & Kagan, J. (Eds.). (1980). *Constancy and change in human development*. Cambridge, MA: Harvard University Press.

Brim, O. G. Jr., & Wheeler, S. (1966). *Socialization after childhood*. New York: John Wiley.

Brody, E. M. (1981). Women in the middle and family help to older people. *The Gerontologist, 21,* 471–480.

Brody, E. M., Johnson, P. T., Fulcomer, M. C., & Lang, A. M. (1983). Women's changing roles and help to elderly parents: Attitudes of three generations of women. *Journal of Gerontology, 38,* 597–607.

Brody, E. M., & Lang, A. (1982). They can't do it all: Aging daughters with aged mothers. *Generations,* (Winter), 18–20.

Brody, J. A., Brock, D. B., & Williams, T. F. (1987). Trends in the health of the elderly population. *Annual Review of Public Health, 8,* 211–234.

Burton, L. M. (1985). *Early and on-time grandmotherhood in multigeneration black families*. Unpublished doctoral dissertation, University of Southern California.

Butler, R. N. (1963). The life review: An interpretation of reminiscence in the aged. *Psychiatry, 26,* 65–76.

Cain, M. (1985). Fertility as an adjustment to risk. In A. S. Rossi (Ed.), *Gender and the life course* (pp. 145–160). New York: Aldine.

Cancian, F. (1987). *Love in America*. Berkeley, CA: University of California Press.

Caplow, T. (1982). Christmas gifts and kin networks. *American Sociological Review, 47,* 383–392.

Caplow, T., Bahr, H. M., Chadwick, B. A., Hill, R., & Williamson, M. H. (1982). *Middletown families: Fifty years of change and continuity*. Minneapolis, MN: University of Minnesota Press.

Cherlin, A. (1981). *Marriage, Divorce, Remarriage*. Cambridge, MA: Harvard University Press.

Cherlin, A., & Furstenberg, F. (1986). *The new American grandparent*. New York: Basic Books.

Chodorow, N. (1978). *The reproduction of mothering*. Berkeley, CA: University of California Press.

Collins, R. A. (1986). *A micro-macro theory of creativity in intellectual careers*. Paper presented to a thematic session on Social Structures and Human Lives, at the American Sociological Association, New York, September 1.

Daniels, P. & Weingarten, K. (1982). *Sooner or later: The timing of parenthood in adult lives*. New York: W. W. Norton.

Dannefer, D. (1984). Adult development and social theory. *American Sociological Review, 49,* 100–116.

D'Antonio, W. V. (1985). The American Catholic family: Signs of cohesion and polarization. *Journal of Marriage and the Family, 47,* 395–406.

Davis, K. (1984). Wives and work: Consequences of the sex role revolution. *Population and Development Review, 10*(3), 397–418.

Davis, K., & van den Oever, P. (1982). Demographic foundations of new sex roles. *Population and Development Review, 8,* 495–511.

Easterlin, R. (1987). The new age structure of poverty in America. *Population and Development Review, 13*(2), 195–208.

Eisenberg, A. R. (1988). Grandchildren's perspectives on relationships with grandparents: The influence of gender across generations. *Sex Roles, 19,* 205–217.

Elder, G. H. Jr. (1974). *Children of the great depression.* Chicago, IL: University of Chicago Press.

Elder, G. H. Jr. (1982). Historical Experience in the later years. In T. K. Hareven (Ed.), *Patterns of aging* (pp. 75–107). New York: Guilford.

Elder, G. H. Jr., & Liker, J. K. (1982). Hard times in women's lives: Historical influences across forty years. *American Journal of Sociology, 88*(2), 241–269.

Elder, G. H. Jr., Liker, J. K., & Cross, C. E. (1984). Parent-child behavior in the great depression: Life course and intergenerational influences. In P. B. Baltes & O. G. Brim Jr. (Eds.), *Life-span development and behavior* (vol. 6, pp. 111–158). New York: Academic Press.

Elder, G. H. Jr., & Rockwell, R. C. (1978). Economic depression and postwar opportunity: A study of life patterns and health. In R. A. Simmons (Ed.), *Research on community and mental health* (pp. 249–301). Greenwich, CT: JAI Press.

Elder, G. H. Jr., & Rockwell, R. C. (1976). Marital timing in women's lives. *Journal of Family History, 1,* 34–53.

Espenshade, T. J. (1984). *Investing in children.* Washington, DC: The Urban Institute.

Faris, R. E. L. (Ed.) (1964). *Handbook of sociology.* Chicago, IL: Rand McNally.

Featherman, D. L. (1981). The life-span perspective. In *National Science Foundation's five-year outlook on science and technology* (vol. 2, pp. 621–648). Washington, DC: U.S. Government Printing Office.

Featherman, D. L. (1986). Biography, society, and history: Individual development as a population process. In A. B. Sørensen, F. E. Weinert, & L. R. Sherrod (Eds.), *Human development and the life course: Multidisciplinary perspectives* (pp. 99–152). Hillsdale, NJ: Lawrence Erlbaum.

Fischer, L. R. (1979). *When daughters become mothers.* Unpublished Ph.D. dissertation, University of Massachusetts (Amherst).

Fischer, L. R. (1981). Transitions in the mother-daughter relationship. *Journal of Marriage and the Family, 43,* 613–622.

Fischer, L. R. (1983). Mothers and mothers-in-law. *Journal of Marriage and the Family, 45,* 187–193.

Fischer, L. R. (1986). *Linked lives: Adult daughters and their mothers.* New York: Harper & Row.

Flacks, R. (1967). The liberated generation: An exploration of the roots of student protest. *Journal of Social Issues, 23,* 52–75.

Freeman, D. (1974). Kinship, attachment behavior and the primary bond. In J. Goody (Ed.), *Character of kinship.* London: Cambridge University Press.

Friedan, B. (1981). *The second stage*. New York: Summit.

Furstenberg, F. (1981). Remarriages and intergenerational relations. In R. Fogel, E. Hatfield, S. Kiesler, & E. Shanas (Eds.). *Aging, stability and change in the family* (pp. 115–142). New York: Basic.

Garfinkel, I., & McLanahan, S. S. (1986). *Single mothers and their children: A new American dilemma*. Washington, DC: The Urban Institute.

Gerstel, N. (1988). Divorce and kin ties: The importance of gender. *Journal of Marriage and the Family, 50*(1), 209–219.

Goldthorpe, J. H., & Hope, K. (1980). *The social grading of occupations*. Oxford: The Clarendon Press.

Gutmann, D. (1968). An exploration of ego configurations in middle and late life. In B. L. Neugarten (Ed.), *Middle age and aging* (pp. 58–71). Chicago, IL: University of Chicago Press.

Gutmann, D. (1975). Parenthood: A key to the comparative study of the life cycle. In N. Datan & L. H. Ginsberg (Eds.), *Life span development and psychology: Normative life crises* (pp. 169–174). New York: Academic Press.

Hagestad, G. O. (1977). Role change in adulthood: The transition to the empty nest. Unpublished manuscript, Committee on Human Development, University of Chicago.

Hagestad, G. O. (1982a). Divorce: The family ripple effect. *Generations*, (Winter), 24–31.

Hagestad, G. O. (1982b). Parent and child: Generations in the family. In T. M. Field, A. Huston, H. C. Quay, & G. E. Finley (Eds.), *Review of human development* (pp. 485–499). New York: John Wiley.

Hagestad, G. O. (1984). The continuous bond: A dynamic multigenerational perspective on parent-child relations between adults. In M. Perlmutter (Ed.), *Parent-child relations in child development, The Minnesota Symposium on Child Psychology*, vol. 17, 129–158.

Hagestad, G. O. (1985). Continuity and connectedness. In V. Bengtson & J. Robertson, (Eds.), *Grandparenthood* (pp. 31–48). Beverly Hills, CA: Sage Publications.

Hagestad, G. O. (1987). Parent-child relations in later life: Trends and gaps in past research. In J. B. Lancaster, J. Altmann, A. S. Rossi, & L. R. Sherrod (Eds.), *Parenting across the life-span: Biosocial dimensions* (pp. 405–434). New York: Aldine de Gruyter.

Hagestad, G. O. (1988). Demographic change and the life course: Some emerging trends in the family realm. *Family Relations, 37*, 405–410.

Hagestad, G. O. & Burton, L. M. (1985). Grandparenthood, life context, and family development. *American Behavioral Scientist, 29*, 471–484.

Haines, M. R. (1985). The life cycle, savings, and demographic adaptation: Some historical evidence for the United States and Europe. In A. S. Rossi (Ed.), *Gender and the life course* (pp. 43–64). New York: Aldine.

Hess, B. B., & Waring, J. M. (1978). Parent and child in later life: Rethinking the relationship. In R. M. Lerner & G. B. Spanier (Eds.), *Child influences on marital and family interaction* (pp. 445–529). New York: Academic Press.

Hetherington, E. M., & Arasteh, J. D. (Eds.) (1988). *Impact of divorce, single parenting and stepparenting on children*. Hillsdale, NJ: Lawrence Erlbaum.

Hill, C. R. & Stafford, F. P. (1980). Parental care of children: Time diary estimates of quantity, predictability, and variety. *Journal of Human Resources, 15,* 219–239.

Hill, R., Foote, N., Aldous, J., Carlson, R., & MacDonald, R. (1970). *Family development in three generations.* Cambridge, MA: Schenkman.

Hodge, R. W., Siegel, P. M., & Rossi, P. H. (1964). Occupational prestige in the United States, 1925–1963, *American Journal of Sociology, 70,* 268–292.

Hoffman, S. D., & Duncan, G. J. (1988). What are the economic consequences of divorce? *Demography, 25,* 641–645.

Homans, G. C. (1950). *The human group.* New York: Harcourt, Brace.

Howard, J. (1978). The influence of children's developmental dysfunctions on marital quality and family interaction. In R. M. Lerner & G. B. Spanier (Eds.), *Child influences on marital and family interaction: A life-span perspective* (pp. 275–298). New York: Academic Press.

Inglehart, R. (1977). *The silent revolution: Changing values and political styles among western publics.* Princeton, NJ: Princeton University Press.

Jackson, J. S. (1979). *National survey of black Americans.* Ann Arbor, Michigan: Institute for Social Research.

Jackson, J. S., & Hatchett, S. J. (1986). International research: Methodological considerations. In N. Datan, A. L. Greene, & H. W. Reese (Eds.), *Life-span developmental psychology: Intergenerational relations* (pp. 51–76). Hillsdale, NJ: Lawrence Erlbaum.

Jewett, S. O. (1982). *The country of the pointed firs.* New York: W. W. Norton.

Johnson, C. L. (1983). A cultural analysis of the grandmother. *Research on aging, 5,* 547–567.

Johnson, C. L. (1985). Grandparenting options in divorcing families. In V. L. Bengtson & J. Robertson (Eds.), *Grandparenthood* (pp. 81–96), Beverly Hills: Sage Publications.

Johnson, C. L. (1988). Postdivorce reorganization of relationships between divorcing children and their parents. *Journal of Marriage and the Family, 50*(1), 221–231.

Johnson, C. L., & Catalano, D. H. (1981). Childless elderly and their family supports. *The Gerontologist, 21,* 610–618.

Johnson, M. M. (1988). *Strong mothers, weak wives: The search for gender equality.* Berkeley, CA: University of California Press.

Keith, P. M. (1986). The social context and resources of the unmarried in old age. *International Journal of Aging and Human Development, 23,* 81–96.

Kennedy, L., & Stokes, D. (1982). Extended family support and the high cost of housing. *Journal of Marriage and the Family, 44,* 311–318.

Keniston, K. (1968). *Young radicals: Notes on committed youth.* New York: Harcourt, Brace.

Kimball, G. (1988). *50/50 parenting: Sharing family rewards and responsibilities.* Lexington, MA: Lexington Books.

Kohli, M. (1985). The world we forgot: An historical review of the life course. In V. W. Marshall, (Ed.), *Later life: The social psychology of aging.* Beverly Hills, CA: Sage Publications.

Kohn, M. L. (1959). Social class and parental values. *American Journal of Sociology, 64,* 337–366.

Kohn, M. L. (1969). *Classes and conformity: A study in values.* Homewood, IL: Dorsey Press.

Kohn, M. L., Schooler, C., Miller, J., Miller, K. A., Schoenbach, C., & Schoenberg, R. (1983). *Work and personality: An inquiry into the impact of social stratification.* Norwood, NJ: Ablex.

Korn, S. J., Chess, S., & Fernandez, P. (1978). The impact of children's physical handicaps on marital quality and family interaction. In R. M. Lerner & G. B. Spanier (Eds.), *Child influences on marital and family interaction: A life-span perspective* (pp. 299–326). New York: Academic Press.

Kornblatt, J. R. (1985). *White water.* New York: Dell Publishing.

Kotlikoff, L. J., & Spivak, A. (1981). The family as an incomplete annuities market. *Journal of Political Economy, 89,* 372–381.

Kurz, M. (1984). Capital accumulation and the characteristics of private intergenerational transfers. *Economica, 51,* 1–22.

Lancaster, J. B., Altmann, J., Rossi, A. S., & Sherrod, L. R. (Eds.), (1987). *Parenting across the life span: Biosocial dimensions.* New York: Aldine de Gruyter.

LaRossa, R., & LaRossa, M. (1981). *Transition to parenthood: How infants change families.* Beverly Hills, CA: Sage Publications.

Lawson, A. (1988). *Adultery: An analysis of love and betrayal.* New York: Basic Books.

Leavitt, D. (1989). *Equal affections.* New York: Weidenfeld & Nicolson.

Lenski, G. (1961). *The religious factor: A sociological study of religion's impact on politics, economics, and family life.* Garden City, NY: Doubleday.

Lerner, R. M. (1984). *On the nature of human plasticity.* New York: Cambridge University Press.

Lerner, R. M., & Spanier, G. B. (Eds.) (1978). *Child influences on marital and family interaction: A life-span perspective.* New York: Academic Press.

Leslie, L. A., & Grady, K. (1985). Changes in mothers' social networks and social support following divorce. *Journal of Marriage and the Family, 47,* 663–674.

Lesthaeghe, R. (1980). On the social control of human reproduction. *Population and Development Review, 4,* 527–548.

Lesthaeghe, R. (1983). A century of demographic and cultural change in western Europe: An exploration of underlying dimensions. *Population and Development Review, 9,* 411–435.

Lesthaeghe, R., & Surkyn, J. (1988). Cultural dynamics and economic theories of fertility change. *Population and Development Review, 14,* 1–46.

LeVine, S., & LeVine, R. A. (1985). Age, gender, and the demographic transition: The life course in agrarian societies. In A. S. Rossi (Ed.), *Gender and the life course* (pp. 29–42). New York: Aldine.

Lewis, M., & Rosenblum, L. A. (Eds.), (1974). *The effect of the infant on its caregiver.* New York: John Wiley.

Litwak, E. (1960a). Occupational mobility and extended family cohesion. *American Sociological Review, 25,* 9–21.

Litwak, E. (1960b). Geographical mobility and extended family cohesion. *American Sociological Review, 25*, 385–394.

Litwak, E. (1969). Primary group structures and their functions: Kin, neighbors and friends. *American Sociological Review, 34*, 465–481.

Lynd, R., & Lynd, H. (1929). *Middletown: A study in contemporary American culture*. New York: Harcourt, Brace.

Mangen, D. J., Bengtson, V. L., & Landry, P. H. Jr. (1988). *Measurement of intergenerational relations*. Beverly Hills, CA: Sage Publications.

Markides, K. S., Bolt, J. S., & Ray, L. A. (1986). Sources of helping and intergenerational solidarity: A three generation study of Mexican Americans. *Journal of Gerontology, 41*, 506–511.

McLanahan, S. S., Wedemeyer, N. V., & Adelberg, T. (1981). Network structure, social support, and psychological well-being in the single-parent family. *Journal of Marriage and the Family, 43*, 601–612.

McLaughlin, S. D., Melber, B. D., Billy, J. O. G., Zimmerle, D. M., Winges, L. D., & Johnson, T. R. (1988). *The changing lives of American women*. Chapel Hill, NC: University of North Carolina Press.

Meyer, J. W. (1986). The self and the life course: Institutionalization and its effects. In A. B. Sørensen, F. E. Weinert, and L. R. Sherrod (Eds.), *Human development and the life course: Multidisciplinary perspectives* (pp. 199–216). Hillsdale, NJ: Lawrence Erlbaum.

Mindel, C. H. (1979). Multigenerational family households: Recent trends and implications for the future. *The Gerontologist, 5*, 456–463.

Mortimer, J., & Simmons, R. (1978). Adult socialization. *Annual Review of Sociology, 4*, 421–454.

Neugarten, B. L. (1973). Personality changes in adult life: A developmental perspective. In C. Eisdorfer & P. Lawton (Eds), *The psychology of adult development and aging* (pp. 311–335). Washington, DC: American Psychological Association.

Neugarten, B. L., & Daton, N. (1973). Sociological perspectives on the life cycle. In P. Baltes & W. K. Schaie (Eds.), *Life span development psychology: Personality and socialization* (pp. 53–71). New York: Academic Press.

Neugarten, B. L., & Gutmann, D. (1968). Age-sex roles and personality in middle age: A thematic apperception study. In B. L. Neugarten (Ed.), *Middle age and aging* (pp. 58–71). Chicago: University of Chicago Press.

Newton, M. (1973). Interrelationships between sexual responsiveness, birth, and breast feeding. In J. Zubin & J. Money (Eds.), *Contemporary sexual behavior: Critical issues of the 1970s*. Baltimore, MD: Johns Hopkins University Press.

Norris, J. (Ed.) (1988). *Daughters of the elderly: Building partnerships in caregiving*. Bloomington, IN: Indiana University Press.

Oppenheimer, V. K. (1974). The life cycle squeeze: The interaction of men's occupational and family life cycles. *Demography, 11*, 227–245.

Oppenheimer, V. K. (1982). *Work and the family: A study in social demography*. New York: Academic Press.

Paley, V. G. (1984). *Boys and girls: Superheroes in the doll corner*. Chicago, IL: University of Chicago Press.

Parke, R. (1988). Families in lifespan perspective: A multilevel developmental approach. In E. M. Hetherington, R. M. Lerner, & M. Perlmutter (Eds.), *Child development in the life span perspective*. Hillsdale, NJ: Lawrence Erlbaum.

Popenoe, D. (1988). *Disturbing the nest: Family change and decline in modern societies*. New York: Aldine de Gruyter.

Reiss, A. J. & Hatt, P. (1961). *Occupations and Social Status*. Glencoe, IL: The Free Press.

Reiss, I. L. (1986). A sociological journey into sexuality. *Journal of Marriage and the Family, 48*, 233–242.

Riley, M. W. (1983). The family in an aging society: A matrix of latent relationships. *Journal of Family Issues, 4*, 439–454.

Riley, M. W. (1987). Aging, health, and social change. In M. W. Riley, J. D. Matarazzo, & A. Baum (Eds.), *Perspectives in behavioral medicine: The aging dimension* (pp. 1–14). Hillsdale, NJ: Lawrence Erlbaum.

Rindfuss, R. R., Morgan, S. P., & Swicegood, G. (1988). *First births in America: Changes in the timing of parenthood*. Berkeley, CA: University of California Press.

Rossi, A. S. (1965). Naming children in middle class families. *American Sociological Review, 30*, 499–513.

Rossi, A. S. (1968). Transition to parenthood. *Journal of Marriage and the Family, 30*, 26–39.

Rossi, A. S. (Ed.) (1970). *Essays on sex equality by John Stuart Mill and Harriet Taylor Mill*. Chicago, IL: University of Chicago Press.

Rossi, A. S. (1973). *The feminist papers: From Adams to de Beauvoir*. New York: Columbia University Press.

Rossi, A. S. (1977). A biosocial perspective on parenting. *Daedalus, 106*(2), 1–31.

Rossi, A. S. (1980). Aging and parenthood in the middle years. In P. B. Baltes & O. G. Brim, Jr. (Eds.), *Life span development and behavior* (vol. 3, pp. 138–207). New York: Academic Press.

Rossi, A. S. (1982). *Feminists in politics: A panel analysis of the first national women's conference*. New York: Academic Press.

Rossi, A. S. (1984). Gender and parenthood. *American Sociological Review, 49*(1), 1–18.

Rossi, A. S. (1987). Parenthood in transition: From lineage to child to self-orientation. In J. Lancaster, J. Altmann, A. S. Rossi, & L. Sherrod (Eds.), *Parenting across the life span: Biosocial dimensions* (pp. 31–84). New York: Aldine de Gruyter.

Rossi, A. S. (1989). A life course approach to gender, aging, and intergeneratinal relations. In K. W. Schaie & C. Schooler (Eds.), *Social structure and aging: Psychological processes* (pp. 207–236). Hillsdale, NJ: Lawrence Erlbaum.

Rossi, A. S., & Rossi, P. E. (1977). Body time and social time: Mood patterns by menstrual cycle phase and day of the week. *Social Science Research, 6*, 273–308.

Rossi, P. H. (1989). *Down and out in America: Extreme poverty and homelessness*. Chicago, IL: University of Chicago Press.

Rossi, P. H., & Berk, R. A. (1985). Varieties of normative consensus. *American Sociological Review, 50*(3), 333–346.

Rossi, P. H., & Nock, S. L. (Eds.) (1982). *Measuring social judgments: The factorial survey approach.* Beverly Hills, CA: Sage Publications.

Rossi, P. H., Simpson, J., & Miller, J. (1985). Beyond crime seriousness: Fitting the punishment to the crime, *Journal of Quantitative Criminology*, 1(1), 59–90.

Rossi, P. H., Waite, E., Bose, C., & Berk, R. (1974). The seriousness of crimes: Normative structure and individual differences, *American Sociological Review*, *39*, 224–237.

Rubenstein, R. L. (1986). *Singular paths: Old men living alone.* New York: Columbia University Press.

Rubin, L. B. (1985). *Just friends: The role of friendship in our lives.* New York: Harper Row.

Schneider, D. M. (1980). *American kinship: A cultural account.* Chicago, IL: University of Chicago Press.

Sewell, W. H., & Hauser, R. H. (1975). *Education, occupation, and earnings.* New York: Academic Press.

Schoen, R., Urton, W. L., Woodrow, K., & Baj, J. (1985). Marriage and divorce and in 20th century American cohorts, *Demography*, *22*, 101–114.

Shanas, E. (1980). Older people and their families: The new pioneers. *Journal of Marriage and the Family*, *42*, 9–15.

Shanas, E., Townsend, P., Wedderburn, D., Friis, H., Milhoj, P., & Stehouwer, J. (1968). *Old people in three industrial societies.* New York & London: Atherton and Routledge Kegan Paul.

Shapiro, E. R. (1978). *Transition to parenthood in adult and family development.* Unpublished Ph.D. Dissertation, University of Massachusetts (Amherst).

Sherrod, L. R., & Brim Jr., O. J. (1986). Epilogue: Retrospective and prospective views of life-course research on human development. In A. B. Sørensen, F. E. Weinert & L. R. Sherrod (Eds.), *Human development and the life course: Multidisciplinary perspectives* (pp. 557–580). Hillsdale, NJ: Lawrence Erlbaum.

Simon, B. V. (1987). *Never married women.* Philadelphia: Temple University Press.

Simons, J. (1980). Reproductive behavior as religious practice. In C. Hohn & R. Mackensen (Eds.), *Determinants of fertility trends: Theories Reexamined* (pp. 133–145). Liege: Ordina Editions.

Smelser, N. (Ed.) (1988). *Handbook of sociology.* Newbury Park, CA: Sage Publications.

Spanier, G. H., & Thompson, L. (1984). *Parting.* Beverly Hills, CA: Sage Publications.

Spence, J. T., & Helmreich, R. L. (1978). *Masculinity and femininity: Their psychological dimensions, correlates, and antecedents.* Austin, TX: University of Texas Press.

Sussman, M. B. (1983). 1981 Burgess Address: Law and legal systems: The family connection. *Journal of Marriage and the Family*, *45*, 9–22.

Sussman, M. B. & Burchinal, L. (1962). Kin family network: Unheralded structure in current conceptualizations of family functioning. *Marriage and Family Living*, *24*, 231–240.

Sussman, M. B., Cates, J. N., & Smith, D. T. (1970). *The family and inheritance.* New York: Russell Sage Foundation.

Sweet, J. A., & Bumpass, L. L. (1987). *American families and households.* New York: Russell Sage Foundation.

Taylor, R. J. (1986). *The extended family as a source of support to elderly blacks.* Ann Arbor, MI: Institute for Social Research (unpublished manuscript).

Thornton, A., & Rodgers, W. L. (1987). The influence of individual and historical time on marital dissolution, *Demography, 24*(1), 1–22.

Treas, J. & VanHilst, A. (1976). Marriage and remarriage rates among older Americans. *The Gerontologist, 16,* 136–143.

Treiman, D. (1977). *Occupational prestige in comparative perspective.* New York: Academic Press.

Troll, L. & Bengtson, V. L. (1979). Generations in the family. In W. R. Burr, R. Hill, F. I. Nye, & I. L. Reiss (Eds.), *Contemporary theories about the family* (vol. 1, pp. 127–161). *Research-based theories.* New York: Free Press.

Uhlenberg, P. (1980). Death and the family. *Journal of Family History, 5,* 313–320.

U.S. Department of Justice. (1984). *National Survey of Crime Seriousness.* Washington, DC: Bureau of Justice Statistics.

U.S. General Accounting Office. (1977). *Report to Congress: The well being of older people in Cleveland, Ohio.* Washington, DC: HRD-77-70.

Vinovskis, M. A. (1981). An epidemic of adolescent pregnancy? Some historical considerations. *Journal of Family History, 6,* 205–230.

Weitzman, L. J. (1985). *The divorce revolution.* New York: Free Press.

White, L. K., & Brinkerhoff, D. B. (1981). Children's work in the family: Its significance and meaning. *Journal of Marriage and the Family, 43,* 789–798.

Whyte, W. F. (1943). *Street corner society.* Chicago: IL: University of Chicago Press.

Zelizer, V. A. (1985). *Pricing the priceless child: The changing social value of children.* New York: Basic Books.

Author Index

Subject Index _____

Note: An additional aide to locating findings of special interest is Table 11.1 in Chapter 11 (pp.486–489) which lists all the tables and figures in which the major variables in the study were used as dependent or independent variables.

A

Abortion, *see* Attitudes on contemporary issues
Adult child sample, 23–24
Affect Balance
  by gender and age, 67–68
  operational definition, 38
  sample location, 43
Affect, Negative
  determinants of, within age groups, 71–73
Affect, Positive
  determinants of, within age groups, 71–73
Affectional Solidarity, *see* Affective closeness
Affective closeness, 6, 47
  correlation with other solidarity measures, parents vs. children, 260–263
  effect on intergenerational influences, 342–344
  effect of parental marital happiness on, 344–348
  by geographic distance, 254–256

of grandparent-grandchild as function of parental marital happiness, 351–358
life course trajectory in, 276–281
operational definition, 30
parent vs. child reports on, 255-259
to parent vs. parent-in-law as function of marital happiness, 349–351
sample location, 41
Affinal kin
  obligations to vs. other kin types, 172–173, 193, 205–206
  obligation strength by obligation type, 214–215
Age as life course marker, 52–53
Age as a research variable, 10–13
  and aging, 11, 14
  and cohort, 11, 53, 87–89
  and historical period, 11, 86–89
Age differences between parent and child, 12–13, 94–96
  effect on parent-child closeness in adolescence, 290–296
  effect on value consensus, 300–305

531

F

G